THE
REBEL

THE
REBEL

A Biography of
RAM JETHMALANI

SUSAN ADELMAN

Sdé

PENGUIN

SHOBHAA DÉ BOOKS
Published by the Penguin Group
Penguin Books India Pvt. Ltd, 7th Floor, Infinity Tower C, DLF Cyber City,
Gurgaon 122 002, Haryana, India
Penguin Group (USA) Inc., 375 Hudson Street, New York, New York 10014, USA
Penguin Group (Canada), 90 Eglinton Avenue East, Suite 700, Toronto, Ontario,
M4P 2Y3, Canada
Penguin Books Ltd, 80 Strand, London WC2R 0RL, England
Penguin Ireland, 25 St Stephen's Green, Dublin 2, Ireland (a division of
Penguin Books Ltd)
Penguin Group (Australia), 707 Collins Street, Melbourne, Victoria 3008, Australia
Penguin Group (NZ), 67 Apollo Drive, Rosedale, Auckland 0632, New Zealand
Penguin Books (South Africa) (Pty) Ltd, Block D, Rosebank Office Park, 181 Jan
Smuts Avenue, Parktown North, Johannesburg 2193, South Africa

Penguin Books Ltd, Registered Offices: 80 Strand, London WC2R 0RL, England

First published in Shobhaa Dé Books by Penguin Books India 2014

10 9 8 7 6 5 4 3 2 1

ISBN 9780670087921

Typeset in Sabon by R. Ajith Kumar, New Delhi
Printed at Replika Press Pvt. Ltd, India

A PENGUIN RANDOM HOUSE COMPANY

This book is dedicated to my husband, Martin Adelman, who encouraged me to undertake this project from the beginning and throughout the months of work that ensued. Professor of law and provocateur in the same spirit as Ram, whenever I ran up against a difficult legal question he routinely said, 'You can read. Law is not that difficult to figure out.'

Contents

Foreword

Of the sternly majestic and eloquent advocates the Indian Bar has had in the last six decades, Ram Jethmalani has acquired a unique stature. Ram has great stamina to argue and deliver performances with captivating skill, law-logic, astute activeness and innovative interpretations. Watching Ram in action in a court is a treat for court-watchers and an enlightening lesson for youngsters. Ram's life, as he himself says, has been inextricably woven with the law and the courts of justice.

This biography, following *Maverick Unchanged, Unrepentant*, delves into the private side of the life of Ram, captioning a wide range of relations among family and friends, drawing largely on first-hand accounts and some from a wide sweep of sources. While the intricacies and details given in the book reflect the propinquity of the author with Ram and his family, she has not attempted to boost Ram's greatness. The book tells us what Ram actually is with his family, in his social life, his professional life and in his political life.

The book, written by a person who lives thousands of miles away, serves as a wonderful guide for the general reader, law students, budding lawyers, and all those who are keen on understanding the intricacies of law and justice as it extensively deals with pro bono causes fought and argued by Ram and his incisive art of cross-examination. It contains a fascinating account of some of the leading contentious legal issues of the day in which Ram's role is singular and significant.

Ram has rushed towards major flashpoints in Indian political history. The author has succinctly marked down all the important events of Indian political and legal history linked to the life of Jethmalini. The reading of the book is the journey through the political controversies in India after Independence. The milestones of Indian politics and history have shaped Ram's career and many of the milestones of Ram's career have left their imprint on the history of India.

There is no mystery about Ram's individual actions. He is a man who has stood up against corruption in public life and communal violence. He has always tried to reconcile conflict and bring peace among the community and for that he has been conferred with the Human Rights Award and World Peace through Law Award.

Ram at the age of ninety-two has retained a boyish charm and a sense of fun. He does not hide his youth as 'he still does things he used to do when he was nineteen'. With lawyering in his blood, teaching in his heart and politics his passion, Ram is a truly extraordinary and multifaceted personality. This book is an inspiration to the present and future generation of lawyers.

R.M. Lodha
Former Chief Justice of India

Introduction

Ram Jethmalani has been called many things—a legal legend, a wizard of the law, and the greatest lawyer in India. He has also been described by epithets that are considerably less flattering. What is beyond doubt is that, at 90 years of age, his legal career started before the partition that created modern India and Pakistan, and it has spanned the entire history of post-colonial India.

Few figures in India have dominated the headlines, been a magnet for controversy, commanded respect, evoked anger, and earned reverence in such great measure. As a young immigrant lawyer, he started out defending his refugee community's right to write their own language in their own script, and as a venerable senior lawyer he has become known for defending the most notorious figures of India. He also has become one of the most senior Members of Parliament, serving for more than 35 years.

Over the last 70 years, several themes have emerged in his life.

Ram served both as the Union Minister of Urban Affairs and Employment and as the Union Minister of Law, Justice and Company Affairs. Immediately thereafter, he formed the Ram Jethmalani Kashmir Committee, to mediate between India, Pakistan and the rebels of Kashmir. He commands enough respect on both sides of the border to be able to travel freely between Pakistan and India on missions of peace.

A lifelong legal educator, he played a major role in initiating the National Law Schools of India, itself an accomplishment that would merit him a place of great honour in the legal profession, but in the fullness of his life, this achievement has almost been forgotten.

Ram may be the most pro-Israel politician in Asia, another role that is not widely known. He was a strong champion of Israel even when the Indian government would not allow an Israeli embassy, and it is a story that has not been told before. But Ram has never been sectarian. He lectures widely about the peaceful beginnings of Islam, when great early leaders emphasized learning and education. He has argued a landmark case in which he contrasted Hindutva with Hinduism, and he had to analyse whether Hinduism is a religion. He believes in astrology, and he remembers wistfully the gentle Sufis of his childhood in Sindh.

Sindhis are a minority community in India, and perhaps that is why Ram has vigorously defended the rights of all minorities, from lower caste Hindus to Christian Dalits, to Tibetans who fled from the Chinese into the Indian Himalaya. In one famous case, and in parliamentary debates for years later, he fought against great odds to establish reservations to help backward classes, some consequently calling him the Father of Social Justice in India.

Ram burst into public prominence during the state of Emergency in the late 1970s, when he was the chairman of the Bar Council of India and a powerful opponent of the Indira Gandhi regime. In Washington, DC, he spoke eloquently against this Emergency before a Congressional committee. Soon after his presentation, Jimmy Carter was elected President of the United States, and he vigorously condemned dictatorial governments. When President Carter was inaugurated, Pakistan called for elections and so did India. Ram was first elected a Member of Parliament on his return to India, immediately after the Emergency was lifted and elections called.

Ram, helped in earlier years by his daughter Rani and later by his son Mahesh, both lawyers, has fought for years against the abuses of the Nehru–Gandhi dynasty. Whether it was Indira's assumption of dictatorial powers, the acceptance of kickbacks to buy arms, or the deposit of vast amounts of illegally gotten gains in European banks, Ram and his family never stopped fighting to expose it all.

Critics complain that Ram fights institutional corruption, but he defends the rights of criminals. That is true—he believes just as much in individual rights of everyone as he does in his cherished ideal of the heroic lawyer who stands up against oppression, fights injustice and is a guardian of freedom. Despite being in personal peril, Ram waded in with 50 lawyers to intercept a bloody pogrom against Sikhs in Delhi after Prime Minister Indira Gandhi's assassination.

Ram, above all, is the quintessential lawyer, the grand master of the rules of evidence and of cross-examination. His creative questions and original arguments are a matter of legend, often offered to the great amusement of the court.

Married to two women at the same time, he had children with both, and he has always maintained other close female friendships. He recently told a large audience of students that he still does things he used to do when he was 19, but that he would not give any details. This author will not give any either.

He argues enough cases for rich clients to maintain an enviable lifestyle, but 90 per cent of his cases are still pro bono. In a country where corruption is endemic, he has served as a minister without becoming any richer from that work. Probably he became poorer because he had to forgo his legal practice during that time. In the Ministry of Urban Affairs, he initiated a policy of transparency that caused at least one law professor to call him the Father of the Indian Freedom of Information Act. He has waged a lifelong campaign for judicial accountability, and he is still pushing for his National Judicial Commission Bill to be enacted.

Ram has written articles for the *Indian Express*, the *Asian Age* and many other publications. In the late 1980s, he posed 10 questions a day for 30 days to Rajiv Gandhi during the investigation of the Bofors scandal. These articles read like a legal mystery novel, and they played an important role in bringing down the Gandhi government. In his late eighties, he founded a new newspaper, the *Sunday Guardian*.

Generous to a fault, Ram supports his extended family, an army of family retainers, pro bono clients and various hangers-on. Ram says that his philosophy of life is to make as many people as possible happy.

This book arose out of a 40-year friendship with Ram and his daughter Shobha. Dr Shobha Gehani was a resident in paediatrics at the Children's Hospital of Michigan when I was a fellow in paediatric surgery. In 1973 my husband was acting dean of Wayne State University Law School, and when we left on a trip to India, Shobha urged us to call her father, the chairman of the Bar Council of India. We had no idea what to expect. Ram picked up the telephone himself and said he would send a car immediately. Since then we have been to India many times, Ram to the United States many times, and our friendship has broadened to include most of the family. We have learned how truly amazing Ram is, and we have learned about times when he is not.

My hope is that, by presenting both sides of the many controversies that have swirled around him, this book will introduce readers to the Ram we know. For accuracy, and for a sense of what the public has read about him over the years, I have quoted liberally from the press, not all of it necessarily complimentary. The press truly has been a rich source of information, even when it was wrong, so I have endeavoured to tread carefully around questionable quotes or else to flag them for the reader. I have been scrupulous about following the journalistic stricture of requiring at least two sources for every fact that could be questioned, even if only one source appears in this text. Over the years many of Ram's words and actions have been denounced by the press; lengthy quotes from these articles are reproduced to allow the reader to imagine the impact that they must have had both on Ram and on the public. Where possible, I also have quoted verbatim the court's recitation of the facts in a legal case as well as selected portions of verdicts, in order to minimize errors that might otherwise creep into my legal discussion. This author is a surgeon, after all.

People have asked why a surgeon in America would write a biography of a lawyer in India. My answer is that Ram Jethmalani is by far the most interesting, most extraordinary person that my husband and I have ever met, to say nothing of being proud to call him a friend. Who else could compare?

1

The Exile

On the night of April 28, 1976, the police escorted Ram Jethmalani, chairman of the Bar Council of India, to the airport, to fly into exile for the second time in his life. Indira Gandhi, the Prime Minister of India, had proclaimed a State of Emergency, and Ram faced arrest.

As he passed the familiar landscape of barely discernible huts and unlit shops in the night, watched the autorickshaws and smelled the cow dung–fires, he had no idea if he could ever return. For all he knew, the Emergency might never end.

Ram's actions, both in going to America and in testifying there before Congress, would play a role in terminating Mrs Gandhi's Emergency, but he did not know that yet.

On June 25, 1975, Mrs Gandhi had arrested leaders of the Opposition: J.P. Narayan, Atal Bihari Vajpayee, L.K. Advani, and Morarji Desai. Between 1975 and 1976, 140,000 Indians were detained without trial. According to the American Bar Association,[1] 'In one state, Maharashtra, a detailed survey found 2,013 detained persons still in prison.' 'Incidentally,' the journal reported, '5.8 per cent were lawyers.'

What caused this calamity? What was the big emergency? Why did Ram have to escape? The headlines will give the reader the flavour of the time. Indira Gandhi was the daughter of the first Prime Minister of India, Jawaharlal Nehru. After her mother died in 1936, she became her father's hostess, confidante and surrogate. Her name came from her husband, Feroze Gandhi, no relation of

1

Mahatma Gandhi. Nehru and many of his fellow freedom fighters had been lawyers. After Nehru died, despite her desultory education and no legal background, Indira Gandhi became Prime Minister of India in 1966.

She faced staggering problems. The monsoons failed in 1965 and in 1966, causing famine, rising prices, and civil unrest. Indira came to power in the midst of a 'palace intrigue' within the Congress party and within her cabinet.[2] The Punjab was boiling with demands for a separate Sikh state. Congress party activists were pushing to nationalize the banks. The Communists were staging worker demonstrations. Indira's Congress party divided into two factions.

Immediately after Indira Gandhi's re-election in March 1971, East Pakistan tore violently away from West Pakistan. In five weeks, more than 10,000[3] refugees flooded from East Pakistan into India, mostly to West Bengal. India had to clothe them, feed them, and house them in camps. Up to 3 million people were killed. Henry Kissinger warned India that it could not count on American help if China became involved. Prime Minister Indira Gandhi promptly signed a 20-year friendship agreement with the Soviet Union.

On December 3, 1971, Pakistan attacked India. On December 6, India recognized independent Bangladesh, and on December 16 the 93,000-man Pakistani army surrendered. The refugees went home and Indira Gandhi became a heroine—until she signed a peace treaty with Zulfiqar Ali Bhutto of Pakistan at Shimla, and Bhutto tricked her into an unwritten side-agreement that hobbled India–Pakistan relations for years.

Now the monsoon failed again, and 180 million people suffered a drought. The Organization of the Petroleum Exporting Countries (OPEC) raised oil prices, which raised the costs of imports and caused inflation, especially of food prices. Food hoarding and corruption ran rampant. Prime Minister Gandhi asked the World Bank and the International Monetary Fund for emergency help, and they pressured her to devalue the rupee.

No economist, Indira Gandhi responded by nationalizing food sales, which led to shortages and countrywide food riots, especially in Gujarat. A firebrand politician, Jayaprakash Narayan, began agitating in Bihar, and later he combined forces with students protesting in Gujarat. The socialist George Fernandes organized a countrywide railway strike, which Prime Minister Gandhi brutally quashed in 20 days. Sikkim went into its own patriotic crisis, culminating with India annexing Sikkim.

In the midst of all this chaos, another socialist, Raj Narain, filed a petition in the Allahabad High Court to challenge Indira Gandhi's 1971 election. On June 12, 1975, the court held that Indira was guilty of election malpractice and the misuse of government machinery. Even more stunning was a ruling that she must leave Parliament for six years. On June 25, Prime Minister Gandhi went to the President of India to request a State of Emergency. This is the Emergency that Ram described in his speeches as an emergency for Indira, not an Emergency for India.

On September 26, Parliament passed an amendment to the Constitution that put the elections of the Prime Minister, Speaker of the lower house of Parliament, President, and Vice President of India beyond judicial scrutiny. This and subsequent amendments gave Indira Gandhi dictatorial powers.

A landmark case went to the Supreme Court in 1976 to challenge these amendments, and the court ruled that Parliament could not alter fundamental constitutional rights. The Prime Minister retaliated by skipping over the judges who had voted against the government's position, choosing a new Chief Judge who lacked seniority but who had supported her amendments, a 'committed judge'. The legal profession was outraged. Ram was the chairman of the Bar Council of India at that time, and he wrote scathingly about the idea of 'committed judges'. He called it 'an era of judiciary made to measure'.

The government now started jailing opponents under both the Maintenance of Security Act (MISA) and the Smugglers and Foreign Exchange Manipulators Act, which allegedly had been passed to catch smugglers. Mrs Gandhi imposed censorship on the press, and her son Sanjay sent a virtual army of thugs to mow down Muslim slums and to force vasectomies on the poor.

It was in this environment in early 1976 that Ram was invited

down south to Palghat (now Palakkad) to address the Third Kerala
State Lawyers Conference as chairman of the Bar Council of India.
He had warned them that he planned to speak his mind, but they
did not revoke the invitation. Ram is a man who would not look
very large in stature on the podium, but he has a powerful voice.
At a time when people were being jailed for saying much less, he
said of Mrs Gandhi's son Sanjay, 'Your next Prime Minister is going
to be a failed motor mechanic.'

Ram delivered a blistering indictment of what he called the
phoney Emergency. He called Mrs Gandhi and her son criminals.
He said, 'There is no Emergency; this is a phoney Emergency!
The Emergency exists either in their brains or because they think
they have lost the confidence of the people. But I think that the
primary objective of this Emergency is to conceal the criminality
of Sanjay Gandhi. The mother wants to protect her son. Stories of
his corruption are now coming forth. Questions have been asked
in Parliament. I have no doubt that these are the reasons.'

Many of the attendees who were members of the bar, the
judiciary, and even the press quietly slipped away lest they be
identified in the audience. The speech was published.

The district magistrate of Palghat issued a warrant for
Ram's arrest. His mistake was in not arresting Ram on the spot.
Intimidated by Ram, he called the commissioner of police in
Bombay and asked him to do so. As it happened, the police liked
Ram. The commissioner of police stalled, asking, 'How do I know
you are indeed the district magistrate? I must see the warrant,
particularly when you want me to arrest the chairman of the
Indian Bar.'

Ram returned to Bombay three days later, and the famed Nani
Palkhivala, 'instructed by 300 lawyers' who rallied around Ram,
went to the Bombay High Court to obtain an injunction that would
restrain execution of the warrant. This could keep him out of jail
only as long as the Bombay High Court had the power to do so.
This legal power was about to be challenged.

In the interim, as long as he was free, Ram bitterly denounced
the Emergency to every audience he could reach. Ram has often

quoted Sanjay Gandhi as saying, 'Bring Ram Jethmalani to me, dead or alive.'

Ram would find out whether the Bombay High Court's restraining order could keep him out of prison only when the Supreme Court of India decided the case of *ADM Jabalpur vs. S.S. Shukla*.[4] This case involved many detenus and multiple lawyers, and Ram represented one of the detenus. The detenus argued that the rights to life and liberty in Article 21 of the Indian Constitution could not be suspended, even if a national emergency is proclaimed.

In his opening speech, Ram told the judges he was appearing for the thousands of detenus rotting in India's jails. Then he continued, 'Milords you will not be impressed by the fact that I am only appearing for one detenu . . . now I am going to tell you that I am appearing for all five of you. There are 102 lawyers in the Nasik jails . . .'

He went on to warn the justices that the Chief Justice of Ghana helped draft the country's preventative detention law. When the law came into effect, the Chief Justice was the first one to be picked up. For two years nothing was heard. Then a cryptic notice appeared announcing that he had died a natural death.

On April 28, 1976, a majority of the Supreme Court bench ruled, 'In view of the Presidential Order dated 27th June 1975 no person has any locus to move any writ petition under Art. 226 before a High Court for habeas corpus or any other writ or order or direction to challenge the legality of an order of detention . . .'

This case became a symbol of the Emergency, an Emergency which abrogated the ability of a judge to grant a writ of habeas corpus. When we come back to discuss the period of the Emergency in detail, we will analyse its significance.

For this introduction, the importance of the case was that Ram's injunction was lifted. Either he must go to prison or leave India. His colleagues urged him to leave.

That night he had one social function to attend, the marriage of young Gulam Vahanvati, who became the Attorney General many years later, and whose father was a friend. Ram says, 'At the party, I whispered to him that I would not see him for a while, and I went directly to the airport, escorted to the airplane by the commissioner of police.'

Ram went to stay with his daughter Shobha in America. There he obtained a teaching position at Wayne State University Law School in Detroit, Michigan. My husband, Professor Martin Adelman, arranged his appointment.

Ram was the first Indian to receive political asylum in America during the Emergency. Soon after, Prime Minister Gandhi withdrew her ambassador from Washington. These were the first moves in what became a multi-decade Jethmalani family battle with the Nehru–Gandhi dynasty.

Later we will learn that Ram returned to India to run for Parliament against H.R. Gokhale, the Law Minister of India, who, according to Ram, carried a warrant for Ram's arrest in his pocket.

2

Sindh

Ram Jethmalani came from Sindh. Sindh is now a state in Pakistan, but its territory was the ancient cradle of the Indian civilization. Before Sindh ever existed as a state, long before the Mughals, there was an Indus Valley civilization of Mohenjodaro and Harappa that has been dated as existing between 3300 BC and 1300 BC, one of the oldest civilizations in the world, but its cities already had stone houses, baths, brick streets, and underground drainage systems. The residents domesticated animals, used bronze tools, and had their own writing system. Nobody knows why or how, but that world vanished.

Civilizations came and went. The Romans named the great river running through this land the Indus river, but it was known to the Assyrians as the Sinda, to the Greeks as the Indos, and to the Arabs as Al-Sind. From this, Sindh took its name, and from Sindh came the name India.

Legend has it that Sindbad the sailor comes from Sindh, Alexander the Great sent out a fleet from the Indus river and Darius I of Persia extended his rule to the Indus. The Government of Sindh webpage proudly writes that the Mughal Emperor Akbar the Great was born in Sindh in 1542.

The Sindh of Ram's childhood had a rich tradition of handicrafts, and produced fine cotton and silk textiles, pottery, metal work and leather. Sindhi merchants sold their wares in bazaars from Istanbul to Persia, Samarkand, Sumatra, and Burma.

The returning merchants had a tradition of benevolence, with one acclaimed hospital furnishing all care free of charge. The Sindhi language comes from Sanskrit, with words added from Persian, Arabic, Turkish, and even English. The script is closely related to the Perso-Arabic script. This linguistic synthesis with its vast vocabulary inspired a rich tradition of writers, poets, and philosophers. It is the language of some of the most haunting love songs known as ghazals.

Ram holds that the religions of Sindh blended in a rich fabric of Hinduism, Sikhism, Islam, and Sufism. Sufism originated there in the ninth–tenth centuries, a mystical, ascetic religion similar to Islam but famous for its music and dance. Shikarpur itself was famed for its love of classical music.

In his speeches and writings, Ram always emphasizes that he was born in Shikarpur in the north of Sindh, now in Pakistan. Though it had a Muslim majority, 'it had the distinction of a gentle culture born out of the synthesis of the two cultures, Hindu and Muslim, in which on the Hindu festival of Diwali, Muslim children got new clothes and Hindu children got them only when Id was being celebrated'. The Sindh that Ram knew was 'the land of the Sufis where Hindus worshipped at Muslim Khankas and shrines and Muslims worshipped at the Asthans and Deras of Hindu saints'.

He writes, 'Sindh, where I was born, was the cradle of Sufism. Our greatest poet, Shah Abdul Latif, was a disciple of Hindu mendicants, who preached the gospel of love and charity and the annihilation of the ego. A breathtaking and magnificent synthesis of the two faiths, Hinduism and Islam, had been achieved in Sindhi society.'[1]

Into this gentle land, the British clomped roughshod. Sindhi historians report that the British marched into a port city, Thatta, that they realized was as big as London. General Charles James Napier conquered Sindh at the Battle of Miani in 1843, sending back a storied message in Latin, *pecavi*, I have sinned. Until April 1, 1936, Sindh was part of the Bombay Presidency, a broad region extending down the western coast of India and as far west as Aden.

After the British dammed the Indus river in 1935, Sindh became rich agricultural land, with the Hindus accumulating huge plots of land, usually farmed by Muslim agricultural workers.

On February 17, 1947, a newly independent Sindh opened its first state assembly, but Sindh's separate existence ended with Partition. The new state of Pakistan swallowed Sindh on August 15, 1947.

In his battle to conquer Sindh, General Napier's most valiant opponent was Diwan Jethmal, the Governor of Shikarpur. This author visualizes a dashing figure of a man, wearing a turban, dressed in the flowing robes of the day, riding across the desert, a legend in his time and beyond. After the battle, he fled to Afghanistan, where he became a minister. The name Jethmalani means son of Jethmal, Ram's great-great-grandfather.

Jethmal's son Notandas came back to Shikarpur. A sybarite with four wives who was entranced by dancing women, he became the first district magistrate in Shikarpur after the British took over. His son was Gurmuhkdas, a highly respected, successful lawyer, and Ram's grandfather. The son of Gurmuhkdas was Boolchand, a less successful lawyer, and Ram's father.

In 1922, Boolchand married Sita. She took the married name of Parvati, and they lived under the watchful eye of Boolchand's formidable parents, overlooking the courtyard in the commodious Jethmalani haveli. In her house, Tejiba, her mother-in-law, was boss.

Shikarpur was a special city in Sindh. Sindhi businessmen from most cities along the Indus river engaged in trade as far away as Bukhara and Samarkand, and at home they built palatial havelis (carved wooden mansions). The speciality of Shikarpur was banking, and they did well. They invested in beautifying the city, built a large hospital and a medical college, and contributed generously to charity.

Shikarpuris would enjoy leisurely evenings of music and dance. Famous dancers would be invited from Lahore, Bombay (now Mumbai), and Calcutta (now Kolkata), and there was a grand annual musical competition for artists from all over India. The winners would be showered with rewards. The local men meanwhile would loll comfortably in swinging 'peenghas' or cots, dhotis wrapped around their waists, and offer golden guineas to singing courtesans.

When Ram became a Member of Parliament, his house in Delhi had such a swing in the garden, and if dancing girls had appeared, we can imagine him throwing golden guineas at them too.

Despite all this indulgence, even the peaceful town of Shikarpur had to submit to the realities of the British Raj. Ram's politically aware grandfather would have followed the fortunes of the Raj with great interest, mindful of Jethmal's history. The first Anglo-Afghan War ended in a notorious battle in 1842 in which the Afghans massacred an entire British army of 16,500 soldiers, sending one British doctor out to walk away and tell the tale. Jethmal would have been a heroic figure to succeed in such an environment and to send a son safely back to Shikarpur under the British.

When Ram was born on September 14, 1923, the priest told his parents, 'Jethmal has come back.' Ram's mother was 14. Ram has described how his mother was more like an older sister. Ram was the only child until his sister Sarla, who he adored, was born eight years later.

As a child Ram was especially close to his grandfather. His grandfather would take him to the train station to put a coin on the tracks, and after the train passed, they would peel the flattened coin off the tracks with delight. Ram has loved trains ever since. When he was very small, Ram would pretend to be asleep in the evening, so his grandfather would carry him upstairs to bed. When he was barely a bit older, his grandfather would ask him to massage his painful muscles. Ram would ask where the pain was. His grandfather would tell him to massage in one place, and he would say that yes, that was the site of his pain. Again in the next place his grandfather would say yes, that too was the site of his pain. As his grandfather directed him from spot to spot, little Ram the future lawyer would stop and cross-examine his grandfather as to where exactly this pain was.

Ram first went to a local school, Tekchand Pathshala, for which his father paid Rs 4 a month. The rest of his education was in English, and Ram made the language his own. In fact, some have called Ram the greatest English-speaking lawyer in the world. That may or may not be, but few would question his mastery of the language.

Certainly, his teachers were impressed. He entered school as usual in the first standard. Within three months he had been promoted into the third standard, and not long after that, into the fifth standard. This made him the youngest and smallest boy in the class. One day a tall bully picked up Ram and lifted him into the air with a taunt about how Ram thought he was so smart. With the courage he would show often in later life, little Ram jumped up and struck him as hard as he could. Ram not only surprised the bully, but he also surprised himself.

Another surprise came a bit later. When asked as an adult whether he believes in God, he normally answers diffidently, 'I give him the benefit of the doubt.' When he was nine years old, and his sister Sarla an infant, they went down one day to play in the river. Suddenly, they found themselves with water over their heads and in danger of drowning. He saw that Sarla was going down, and he managed to grab her by the hair. He then felt himself drowning. What happened next was not clear, but somehow both of them found themselves on the shore, coughing up water. He swears he is no believer, but he could find no explanation for their survival other than divine intervention.

At his next school, the New Era School, he was a star pupil, and he won a debating prize, which attracted the attention of the principal of the Sindh Model School, located 38 kilometres away in Sukkar. As a result, he was sent away from his warm maternal home to a harsh boarding school. Even worse, he had to stay in the Spartan conditions of the adjacent Bramhacharya Ashram. The boys would have to get out of bed for lathi practice and yoga at 4 a.m., even in the winter. Ram recalls that time as one which gave him discipline, but it also instilled in him a fear of physical privation.

At Sukkar, Ram became a champion debater. His fame only grew when he won one debate, turned around in a show of brio to argue the opposing side, and won again. Coming from the little town of Shikarpur to the big city of Sukkar, he felt himself to be a small-town boy and, to boot, he was smaller than the other children because of all the grades he had skipped. With all these feelings, one day he had a moment of inspiration when he reached into the hat only to pick the peculiar topic 'I'm sorry'. 'It came to me in a flash that I should talk about things I am sorry for.' One example he used was 'We had once assaulted a teacher, and on that day I was not sorry, although I am sorry now.' Able to express his thoughts perfectly, he won the debate. In the interscholastic debates, at eleven years old, Ram's performances were so spectacular that the audience would throw gold guineas at him. He collected these with pride and brought them home to his mother. He liked to say that this was the first money he ever earned.

In Ram's adult years, he was to become a favourite guest on TV, and the give and take between Ram and the other guests, Ram and the anchor, or Ram and the hostile interviewer would become some of India's favourite theatre. Watching these programmes, it is easy to see that the boy debater grew into a formidable grandmaster of debate, taking enormous pleasure in demolishing the other side.

Ram demonstrated many of his lifelong interests as a boy. When he was six or seven, he was mad about Dolly, a girl two years his senior. He often talked about how he used to look at her all the time. Nothing came of it, but they remained friends forever. He last saw her just before she died, at age 80.

At 11 or 12, he was watching a train come in and through the window he spotted a woman who was an extraordinary beauty. His mouth agape, he stared, transfixed. This did not escape the attention of the woman's husband. Once the train stopped, the husband called him into the train. Pointing to his wife, the husband said, 'This thing is to be seen, but nothing further.'

He managed to make some trouble in school too. One day when he was 14, the principal called all the students to come to the schoolyard at 1 p.m. When they asked why, he said, 'I am going to thrash Ram Jethmalani for ruining the morals of the school.' It seems that Ram had asked the boys in his class what they did at night to amuse themselves in their rooms. They said they usually would read or study, and he said he would teach them something they could do by themselves that would be much more fun.

Ram had often tagged after his grandfather into court, and he was intent on following him into the law. His father, however, had found little reason to love the law. After his two promotions, Ram graduated at age 13, and Boolchand insisted on enrolling him at Chellaram Siraldas College to study science. The next year, a rather miserable young Ram was forced to transfer into an engineering programme at DJ Sind College in Karachi. A stellar pupil became a desultory, disaffected engineering student. He remembers going to a lovers' bridge in Karachi every evening to curse his father.

Ram was so unhappy that he prayed constantly that God would rescue him. He was saved when Bombay University opened up a two-year law course in Karachi. Even better, the school only required a two-year intermediate degree, called interscience, prior to enrolment. Ram talked himself into getting the required degree when he presented for his two-year examination. The only questions the examiner asked were about a certain technical device: 'I think it was a torsion magnetometer, or something like that. I told him that look I do not know anything about this machine. I only need to pass my intermediate degree and then I will go to law school.'

This was the first important argument in Ram's career, and he won it. He entered the SC Shahani Law College in 1939, staying at the Shewa Kunj hostel in Karachi that many Sindhi students favoured at that time. Ram remembers his professors and the quality of their instruction as excellent. No doubt it seemed that way after he had been suffering through calculus and chemistry at a dull science college for two long years. On the other hand, this was not Harvard, not Oxford, not even a three- or four-year LLB course. It was a provincial school in Karachi, which was hardly the centre of the world, and no observer could possibly have predicted that a student from this school would become one of the most celebrated lawyers of India. Ram's career is a tribute to raw talent, hard work, and a certain creative genius. He was and is a self-made man.

Ram sprinted up to the top of the law school class, graduating on April 24, 1941 at age 17. Now his problem was that the rules of the Sindh Bar Council prevented him from practising law until age 21. Ram already had the self-confidence to take the matter up with the Chief Justice of the Sindh High Court, the formidable Sir Godfrey Davis. Ram argued that the 21-year rule was passed after he had entered law school. It would be unfair, he said, to apply this retrospectively to a student who had entered law school with every expectation of practising law and supporting a family as soon as he finished school. Sir Godfrey Davis bought the argument. It helped that Ram had achieved a first class first in law school, the highest possible grade.

Ram won his first case as a lawyer. Sir Godfrey Davis recommended a special exemption for those who had been in law school while the 21-year rule was passed. Ram was the first to be granted the exception, which was how he began his law practice at age 18.

3

The First Important Relationships

Now it was time for a young man to marry. At the age of 18, on May 4, 1941, Ram married Durga Ahuja. From the start he did not like the business of an arranged marriage. When his grandfather took him to meet his prospective bride he remembers that the two young people never made eye contact. The families thought the marriage would be quite suitable, since the bride's father was a wealthy businessman who owned a department store in Bombay, the family lived in an elegant haveli, and it seemed an excellent match for such a prominent family as the Jethmalanis. Ram was appalled when he discovered the financial wrangling behind arranging the marriage, and despite his initial lack of interest in the girl he ultimately decided that he would marry her no matter what the outcome of their negotiations.

The marriage was a grand affair, with Ram riding in on a white horse, dressed in his finest, according to custom. Durga was 16, a beauty, resplendent in glittering gold and silk, and she would adore Ram for the rest of her life.

Ram's feelings were more complicated. By now he was an attractive young man, with a bronze complexion, an intelligent face, and a sparkling wit. He had already noticed other girls, and he was aware of how to use his charms. His sisters remember more than one schoolboy crush. Marriage to a young girl from Shikarpur with no education and nothing in common with him was not going to put blinders on an incipient roving eye. Nevertheless,

Durga had a radiant smile that could compete with anyone's, and it would not take long before they started a family, beginning with three daughters in a row. At almost the same time, his second sister, Sundri, was born. A family of girls was beginning to take shape.

In 1942 Ram moved to Karachi with Durga, and also with his sister Sarla, who was 11 or 12 years old. Sarla lived with Ram and Durga until she fell in love with Tulsi Wadhwa and married him in 1947. Ram started in practice with a senior lawyer, Hira Kundanmal, who unfortunately died shortly afterwards. He then joined Hashmatrai Chainani, but by that time he was already pursuing a more eminent partner, Allahbaksh Karimbaksh Brohi. Brohi was a philosophy professor at a madrasa, but Ram knew he had graduated from law school. As only he could, Ram used all his arts of persuasion until he convinced Brohi to join him. Their firm became Brohi and Co., and it still exists today.

A.K. Brohi was a highly respected Muslim philosopher and intellectual seven years older than Ram who also came from the Shikarpur region. His brother, Ali Ahmed Brohi, was an eminent scholar, newspaper editor, military man, political figure, and military rebel, famous for his role in the Royal Indian Navy Mutiny of 1946.

His obituary[1] told the tale: 'He served in the Royal Indian Navy (before Partition), and travelled all over the world. He was among the Royal Indian Navy officials who initiated the mutiny against the British Raj from February 18 to 23 in 1946 and was among those who were given capital punishment by the British administration but escaped due to partition of the subcontinent.'

The obituary continues:

In [an] interview, Mr Brohi had said that unrest among the naval ratings had been brewing for some time. One of the Indian captains had been held in solitary confinement for 17 days in Bombay Naval base on the suspicion of having scribbled, 'Quit India' on the deck of HMIS *Talwar* where the commander-in-chief was to take the salute. On Feb 18 came the open defiance in Bombay. A large number of ratings refused breakfast and declined to fall in line for parade. The entire establishment was in a state of open mutiny. Added to that was the insulting behaviour of the British commander who was accused of having called the ratings: 'sons of bitches, coolies and junglees'.

The sailors marched on the streets of Bombay and anti-British defiance reached a feverish pitch. By sunset that day the strike involved about 20,000 ratings from all the ships in Bombay harbour and eleven shore establishments. The Union Jack was hauled down. Soon the strike spread to 74 ships, four flotillas and 20 naval bases . . .

[A] naval central strike committee was formed. They demanded food and equal pay for British and Indian sailors, release of political prisoners and the withdrawal of Indian troops sent by the British government to Indonesia. They renamed the Royal Indian Navy the Indian National Navy. On their ships the mutineers flew the flags of the Congress, Muslim League and Communist Party.

On Feb 21, fighting broke out in Castle Barracks. Next day the strike spread to naval bases in other parts of the country, and even some ships on the high seas were affected. About 300,000 workers participated in the general strike on that day. There were moving scenes of fraternization by the common people of Bombay in support of the striking sailors . . . 230 people were killed and more than a thousand wounded . . .

The mutiny, however, could not be sustained. On Feb 23 came the surrender. The central strike committee sent out the last message to the nation before dissolving itself. 'Our strike has been a historic event in the life of our nation . . .'

Ram has often described this event, known as the Royal Navy Revolt, as one of the three principal reasons why the British left India. The second was that the British were exhausted by World War II. The third was that the Labour leaders in London were bothered by their consciences after talking about freedom throughout the war.

A.K. Brohi became Ram's teacher, philosophy professor, and family friend. Ram's daughter Rani wrote[2] that Brohi was 'also a philosopher. He later became the Pakistan High Commissioner to

India. He was the lawyer who prosecuted President Bhutto, leading
to Bhutto's ultimate conviction and death sentence . . . He was a
very popular teacher . . . [and] wrote a book . . . in 1950 on Private
International Law on the subject.'

Rani also wrote, 'I remember very fondly Brohi uncle's visits
to India and ours to Pakistan after partition to meet his family. He
introduced me to philosophy and his own thoughts in his book. He
was a great letter writer and author of *Adventure in Consciousness*.
I looked forward to his mail. His three daughters—Masooma,
Tahira and Hafiza—were close friends. They were about my age.
Of all my father's friends, I loved him the most. In fact when he was
High Commissioner in Delhi we would be invited to his gatherings.'

Ram's partnership with Brohi was started on a handshake, and
that never changed. In their practice, Brohi attracted the work, and
Ram did it. Within six years of opening their practice, 20 out of
20 cases admitted each Monday in Karachi would be Brohi and
Co. cases. If Ram needed money he went to the firm's clerk, and
the clerk gave it to him. When Ram left for India he had no bank
account of his own and only Rs 10 in his pocket. Brohi wrote him
when he reached Bombay, 'Whatever you want, let me know.' Ram
refused, 'I am trying my manhood here.'

Brohi became Law Minister of Pakistan in 1953; Ram would
become Law Minister of India several decades later. On March
23, 1956 Pakistan unveiled its first Constitution. While it was
being drafted, Ram was on the telephone almost daily with Brohi,
consulting on points of law in the Indian Constitution. Ram says,
'My fingerprints were all over that Constitution.' Unfortunately,
it only lasted for two years.

In 1956, while Brohi was Law Minister, he had a case before
the Supreme Court of East Pakistan. Taking advantage of the
circumstances, he insisted that Ram come to Dhaka to act just one
more time as his junior. That was the one time the government of
Pakistan ever paid Ram.

One gift from Brohi that Ram remembers fondly was a Morgan
sports car. Ram bought it in Bombay, but the seller was about to go
to Pakistan, so Brohi offered to pay him Rs 3000–4000, the price

of the car, when he arrived in Karachi. Ram's family remembers seeing him tool around in the cute little three-wheeled car. It came to a sad end in a fit of sectarian violence when migrants who had moved to Bombay from Pakistan burned it.

Ram benefited one more time from Brohi's generosity when he made a trip to Damascus in 1957, and he wrote Brohi that his plane would stop in Karachi. Brohi knew very well that Ram was always impeccably dressed, and when Ram landed, a tailor was waiting for him with a new suit that Brohi had ordered for him. All Ram had to do was try it on, then the tailor quickly left and brought back the finished suit before Ram left for Damascus.

There was more to the Damascus story, quite apart from the extremely charming young lady he met there on several evenings. Ram claims that he was unaware that this was a leftist delegation. When the head of the delegation was delayed, Ram became the head of the delegation, and he was invited to give the keynote speech on the first day. The speech he delivered was a thunderous anti-Communist speech. The problem was that the sponsors of the trip were Communists. The next leg of the trip, to Moscow, was promptly cancelled.

In 1965, Brohi was appointed Pakistan's High Commissioner to India, and Ram would stay with him at the Pakistan House when he came to Delhi. He tells the story of a party he once gave in Delhi. On this festive occasion, in the presence of diplomats and members of Delhi society, Brohi said that he would like to stay in India and represent Nehru's government. In the background, the German ambassador was heard to observe that he would be fired if he said such a thing. Brohi was recalled forthwith.

In 1967, Ram and his old friend Satram Rajani went one last time to Pakistan to visit Brohi. After Brohi died, Ram sent money to his wife. When his heirs squabbled over his estate, they called Ram to Karachi to mediate the settlement.

Ram feels indebted to Brohi for many things. Not only did Brohi help Ram complete the undergraduate liberal education that he never had, but Brohi also gave him a virtual postgraduate degree in philosophy, a subject he remains interested in today. Anyone who looks at Ram's library will be amazed to see how many volumes of philosophy, history, and religion are in it, many of them heavily annotated in Ram's cramped writing.

Brohi introduced Ram to many friends and associates who later became major figures in the Pakistani bar, judiciary, and government. This became important when Ram assumed the role of an intermediary between India and Pakistan in the Kashmir conflict. Because of his contacts, he had exceptional access to principal figures in Pakistan; he enjoyed their trust to an unprecedented degree, and he was able to travel to Pakistan with impunity.

Ram recalls three times when he saw Muhammad Ali Jinnah argue cases in court, and he was impressed, even though Jinnah lost the cases. Brohi called Jinnah 'a good advocate but a poor lawyer'. Ram recounts that after Jinnah graduated from law school he went to Karachi to interview for a position with a Hindu lawyer. The lawyer told him his qualifications were excellent; then they began to talk salary. Jinnah insisted on Rs 100 a month, but the Hindu refused to go over Rs 75, so Jinnah returned to Bombay, which obviously provided him with a wider platform. Ram says: 'If that Hindu hadn't been a miser, there would not have been a Pakistan.'

4

Early Career

Ram began his legal career in Karachi. The capital of Sindh, Karachi, was graced by beautiful landmark buildings, the classical Italianate Sind Arts College, the spacious British-built Empress Market, and the wide Elphinstone Street. Karachi was just developing into a seaport. The natural deep-water port, Keamari, was protected by a breakwater, and wharves were built throughout the early 20th century. The port area was where Ram's second wife-to-be, Ratna, was born in 1922, since her father served there as a health officer. Of some interest, Ratna's father, Dr Shahani, had studied medicine at GMC College in Bombay, the same medical school that Ram's daughter Shobha attended many years later. In the 1920s, a little airport, Drigh Road, arose near the port. This was the airport Ram left from when he went to Bombay as a refugee.

Right after law school, Ram's first criminal case showed a creative flash.[1] The father of an exceptionally pretty girl demanded a dowry from an eligible suitor, even though normally a boy's family would demand dowry from the bride's family. The father then pocketed the money and called off the engagement. The suitor and his family discovered that the girl's father had pulled the same con game numerous times in the past, and they needed a lawyer. Luckily, they found Ram.

Usually this would be argued as a breach of contract. Ram's argument was different. He said a breach of contract only occurs when a party enters into a contract and subsequently changes his mind. In this case, the accused had had no intention of honouring the contract. The intent was to commit fraud. From the beginning they intended to cheat the suitor out of money. This was a criminal offence. Ram's unexpected argument prevailed.

Another case concerned a contractor who had built a school which collapsed. Ram's defence was based on language in the Local Boards' Act, which said that any person acting under the orders of the local board is prima facie protected, i.e., there can be no prosecution. The other side argued that this man was an independent contractor, and that he did not act 'under the orders of' anyone. Ram analysed the phrase 'under the orders of', showing the court the dictionary definition of the word 'order', which included a section saying that it also could mean 'a request'. Ram said that under this definition even he could be said to be acting under orders, if orders also could mean requests. Ram won the case, greatly enhancing his reputation.

Eventually, Ram decided he needed a master's degree in law. In March 1944 he went to the Government Law College Library in Bombay to prepare for the exam. In June, on his first try, he became one of only three to pass the LLM exam, out of 16 who took it, a major achievement.

From then up to the time of Partition, Brohi and Co. was the dominant firm in Karachi. Ram handled most of the cases, working up to 16 hours a day. Somehow though, three girls were born at that time, Mohini in 1944, Rani in 1945 and Shobha in 1947. Unfortunately, in 1947, Mohini, the firstborn girl who he adored, died suddenly of pneumonia at age three, during a trip to Shikarpur, leaving Ram devastated.

None of this workload was good for Ram's marriage. He went to Bombay alone to study while Durga was pregnant with Mohini, and this was only one of many prolonged absences. At home in Karachi, Ram's work took up all his time. Then came three girls in a row in a world where a wife was supposed to produce boys for her husband. One girl, Rani, was sent off to the house of a childless aunt. The aunt cared for her lovingly, but Rani never forgot that she had been sent away. Worst of all, his beloved Mohini died on

Durga's watch. At the time of Partition, Ram sent Durga and her daughters to stay with Durga's father in Bombay while he tried to hold on to his practice in Karachi.

5

Partition

The world was moving from crisis to crisis while Ram began his life as a young lawyer.

The Government of India Act of 1935 was Britain's ill-fated attempt to restructure India. Instead, it activated the Muslim League, and it transformed the Congress into a political party. From then on, Mohandas (Mahatma) Gandhi, a Gujarat-born lawyer, led an escalating Indian independence movement.

While the independence movement was building momentum, on September 3, 1939, a war began in Europe. The next day, Lord Linlithgow, the Viceroy of India, proclaimed that India had entered the war along with Britain, even though he had never consulted the Indian authorities. Nevertheless, the Indian army that fought in World War II was the largest volunteer army in history, more than 2.5 million men strong. The war cost the lives of more than 36,000 Indians; 34,354 were wounded and 67,340 were taken prisoners of war.[1] A reaction against the British was inevitable.

Muhammad Ali Jinnah, the Father of Pakistan, was a lawyer from a Gujarati family too, but his family had moved to Karachi before he was born. The towering figures of Gandhi and Jinnah, along with the other lawyers who led the freedom fight in India, deeply impressed Ram with the power—and the responsibility—of the bar to address injustice and to take action against it, regardless of personal consequences. Many of his boldest and rashest actions were inspired by the desire to reach the heights of nobility that his legal forbearers achieved in that struggle.

In 1940, Jinnah persuaded the Muslim League to adopt the Lahore Resolution, which demanded that India be divided into two separate states, one Muslim, the other Hindu. The Muslim country was to be called Pakistan. In August 1942 the Congress party started the Quit India movement.

Mayhem broke out. The violence started with factory workers in Bombay, and soon it spread to peasants and students all over India.[2] The British ruthlessly attempted to suppress the movement. During all this, the Japanese invaded Assam, and Bengal suffered a great famine.

The 1945–46 elections swept in the Congress party, which captured 90 per cent of the votes. Jinnah's agitation for an independent Pakistan led to the Great Calcutta Killings of August 1946. This left an estimated 4000 dead, arousing Hindus to kill some 7000 Muslims in Bihar, which caused riots in the Punjab. Finally on August 15, 1947, India was partitioned into two states, India and Pakistan.

Partition was announced at midnight on August 15, 1947. The states of Punjab and Bengal were divided into Indian and Pakistani portions. Sindh went entirely to Pakistan. Since it was not divided, the impact on Sindh was not as immediate as it was on the Punjab. Punjab had been roiling with unrest since an infamous British massacre of Sikhs in 1919, near their Golden Temple in Amritsar. Sindh was comparatively peaceful, with no more than low-grade grumbling from Muslim borrowers who resented rich Hindu moneylenders.

The carnage started in west Punjab in March 1947, when the Muslims attacked Hindus and Sikhs. The hail of counterattacks from both sides, train ambushes, arson, rapes, and general mayhem caused a loss of life beyond anyone's ability to guess, maybe several hundred thousand, maybe a million lives lost. Fear and danger caused mass migrations. Over the course of the last few months of 1947, some 5 million Hindus and Sikhs fled West Pakistan for India, and perhaps 5.5 million Muslims flooded from India into West Pakistan. Including the population exchange between East and West Bengal, probably 12.5 million people were uprooted from their ancestral homes.

The consequences were immense. Ironically, the leaders of both sides only lived long enough to see their beginning. On January 30, 1948, Mahatma Gandhi would be assassinated, and on September 11, 1948, Muhammad Ali Jinnah would die of tuberculosis. Some say that if the British knew that Jinnah was dying of tuberculosis they could have waited, and avoided the tragedy of Pakistan.

In early 1947, Karachi was quiet. The problems only started when Muslims crowding in from India filled up the available housing. Coming as they did on a religious quest, they were called muhajirs, a name that came from hejira, Mohammad's trip with his followers from Mecca to Medina. They believed that they deserved houses of their own, but for that they had to displace an equal number of Hindus and Sikhs from their homes. While many Hindus and Sikhs left Karachi soon after Partition, voluntary migration alone could not free up enough houses for the thousands who flooded in. Problems were inevitable.

This was tragic. Before Partition, Karachi had been composed of a rich blend of Parsis, Hindus, Muslims, British, and Goan Christians.[3] Hindus always dominated business, banking, and the law. With the exodus of so many important Hindu citizens, courts and offices were closed for hours or even days each week. People also believed that India had encouraged 'low-caste' sanitation workers, the harijans, to leave Karachi to create a crisis of public health.

Then the rumours started. Muslims would slaughter Hindus instead of goats and sheep on Id-ul-Zuha. Hindus would be poisoned. Hindu and Sikh shops would be looted and burned. In fact, some were looted, and next came stabbings and robberies, followed by a citywide curfew. New refugees began to forcibly seize Hindu homes even if the residents had just locked them to go out for a walk.

Ram decided to go to Bombay to see what the circumstances would be if the family moved there, then he returned to Karachi.

In September 1947, Ram saw his family off on a refugee ship

to Bombay, cared for by Satram Rajani, Ram's old cricket partner from Shikarpur. This was the pattern in those months. The head of a household would send or take the family to India for safety, then stay in Karachi to safeguard the house and business, hoping that the family either could return later or at least could sell their property properly. Crowds of Sindhi refugees, among them Ram's parents, grandparents, sisters Sarla and Sundri, were assigned lodgings in deserted World War II army barracks in refugee camps.

Many Sindhis were sent to camps in Kalyan, more than 80 kilometres north-east of Bombay. An estimated 100,000 Sindhis went through these refugee camps. Each barrack had a large central hall, rooms at each end, and bleak sanitary facilities. The Jethmalani family remembers being assigned to a refugee camp in Pune. Ram remembers that the family first stayed briefly in Koliwada, a fishing village outside of Bombay that had one of the many camps for refugees from Punjab and Sindh. The family remembers living in buildings with four families in a row, each with a hole in the floor for sanitary use.

Durga, Shobha, and Rani did not live in a refugee camp. They went directly to stay with Durga's parents in Bombay.

After he sent his family to India, Ram tried to continue his booming law practice in Karachi until the worst problems would pass. He also stayed in his Karachi house to take care of Sarla's husband, who was dangerously ill with pleurisy.

Ram continued his law practice under the shield of Brohi until the day that everything changed in Karachi. The history books record that the first riots in Karachi began on January 6, 1948. Ram, Sri Jaisinghani, Ram's associate in Bombay, and Ram's brother-in-law Mohan Shahani were there at the time; speaking independently, they are all quite clear that it was on February 6, 1948, following Mahatma Gandhi's assassination on January 30, that the real riots took place. Mohan remembers it vividly, since his father was the local health officer, and it fell to him to deal with the injured and the dead.

Sindhis and Sikhs had streamed down from all over Sindh to the seaport of Karachi in order to ship out to India.[4] While the

Sikhs massed in the safety of a gurdwara, they were surrounded and hacked to death by mobs of refugees armed with knives. The death total was 206 people,[5] with many more butchered, legs or arms cut off. The attackers were not Sindhi Muslims, but Muslim refugees from India. Rioting mobs spread across the city. They looted, seized, and burned houses and businesses. Muslims and Sikhs murdered each other on sight.

Not surprisingly, Muslim and Hindu accounts of these three days are at variance. Muslim accounts claim that no more than 30–50 Hindus were killed and that prompt intervention of officials contained the violence. Hindus remember pillaging and personal danger. Ram found out about the riots when he was in his office, and he only made it safely home through the mad streets because he had grabbed a Jinnah-style hat off the head of the office clerk and put it on. Between the hat and his Pathan driver, he passed in cognito when he drove from his office to the house.

Ram hid in his house on Artillery Maidan Road with his brother-in-law for three days, expecting a mob to break down the door and kill them at any minute.

At first Brohi thought 'the madness of Partition was temporary'. Finally, with sadness, Brohi told Ram that he could no longer guarantee his security. On February 18, 1948, Ram Jethmalani flew in a Dakota airplane, a converted 21-seat, two-engine military plane, to Bombay, using a ticket that a client had given him as a fee. Ram was born in India, grew up in India, and started his career in India, but now he arrived in India as a refugee from Pakistan.

He landed on the single airstrip of the airport at Santa Cruz and made his way through crowds of porters, beggars, and oddities towards his luggage. Bombay was less crowded then than it is now, but he drove into town through narrow roads choked with people, cars, bullock carts, and cattle.

When Ram arrived in Bombay, he was horrified to find his family in a squalid refugee camp. The family has heard Ram say many times that at that very moment he resolved that he never again would be poor.

The hundi banking system comes from Shikarpur, and Ram

soon located a hundai from Shikarpur who could finance the family's move out of the camp to a house. They moved to a town on the main road between Bombay and Pune, sharing the house with another Sindhi family. The location was good, and it attracted many of the Sindhis who could get out of the camps.

Ram's third sister, Maya, was born on December 29, 1947, in David Sassoon Hospital in Pune. The very next day, the family had left the hospital, because they did not have the money to pay the bill. Sarla was pregnant at the same time, and she delivered her son in January. Even worse, Ram was embarrassed that his mother had a child at the same time that he was having children. Ram's mother, 14 when Ram was born, was 42 when Maya was born. When his mother became pregnant again, Ram insisted she have an abortion.

It is interesting to note that it was Ram who moved his family out of the refugee camp, gave the orders, and took responsibility for the family. Ram explains that his grandparents were old, and his father was depressed. At age 25, Ram was the head of the family.

And what was that family? All girls. Granted, Ram had a father and grandparents, but beyond that he had a mother who was like a sister, three actual sisters, and soon there were three daughters. He would eventually have two wives, and in the end two sons would come along. Throughout his life Ram sought out women as his confidantes and closest companions. Perhaps that pattern became established early.

Ram always says that his family lived in a refugee camp, but for less than six months. His very first act in India was to get them out of the camp. In his view, there is no excuse for anyone to remain in a refugee camp forever. This colours his view of the Middle East. In the 1970s, when he became vice president of the World Peace through Law Centre, he once had to listen to a Palestinian lawyer bemoan how his people languished in refugee camps because of the evil Israelis. Ram answered impatiently, 'Tell me, how many refugees have you? One million? Two million? Why don't you just send them to us in India? We will take care of them. We know how to take care of refugees. We have the experience.'

6

Bombay

Ram Jethmalani began his Indian law practice in 1948, one year after the modern country of India was born. The story of Ram's career is also the story of India. The milestones of India's politics and history have shaped Ram's career, and many of the milestones of Ram's career have left their imprint on the history of India.

The Jethmalani family moved to a Bombay that was still young. Today's megacity of 20 million people began as a collection of fishing villages on seven islands: Mahim, Worli, and Parel in the north, Mazagaon and Bombay Island in the middle, Colaba and Old Woman's Island (Little Colaba) in the south. Land reclamation joined them together in the middle of the 1800s. Only when the Suez Canal opened in 1869 did Bombay make the transition from an Arabian Sea port to a world port. Under the British Raj, Bombay was the capital of the Bombay Presidency, which extended from Aden through what is now Pakistan, down to the state of Mysore in south India.

It was only in 1946 that the Bombay airport moved out of the little airstrip at Juhu Beach that used to flood during the monsoons. Its first home consisted of two abandoned hangars in a small Royal Air Force airport in Santa Cruz. Tata Airlines only became Air India in 1946, and Air India flew its first Lockheed Constellation in March 1948.

The Bombay of those days was not the Bombay of flyways and shopping malls. It was a vast, sprawling town, with slums along the road from the airport, and with endless rows of small shops the colour of the earth. Commercial Bombay was at the tip of what we now know as South Bombay, called the Fort area in those days. Churchgate was one of the Fort's gates, and from there the Western Railway Line went north to the airport at Santa Cruz. The elaborate marble Flora Fountain was in the centre of town; the Town Hall and Victoria Station were landmarks. Ambassador cars, taxis, autorickshaws, bullock carts, cows, beggars, and schoolgirls all shared the same streets, amid the deafening noise of continual honking.

In front of the Gateway of India was the Taj Mahal Palace, and next to it was Green's Hotel, with an interesting story. Jamsetji Tata, already a rich industrialist, reputedly built the Taj in 1903 because he was angered by a sign in front of Green's that said 'No dogs or Indians allowed'. His Taj was so lavish and became so popular that it drove Green's out of business. In 1973, Green's was levelled, and the Taj built a new wing, the Taj Mahal Tower, on its site.

Next to the Taj in a wide open space were snake charmers, trainers with dancing bears, showmen staging fights between a snake and a mongoose, flute sellers playing their attractive tunes, the occasional naked fakir, and an infinite number of dirty children prepared to follow a visitor all day until they got their baksheesh. At night, crowds of prostitutes swarmed towards any man leaving the Taj.

On the roads were cars, wooden bullock carts, cows, porters pulling all manner of conveyance overflowing with merchandise, rickshaws, and pedestrians. Next to the roads one could see barbers squatting on the ground, or even dentists. Even doctors in little booths plied their trade, their walls advertising that they would cure earaches, sore throats, or 'left-sided headaches'. Chinese or Parsi bonesetters offered anyone suffering with a backache their standard cure—a sharp kick in the back. For a dislocation, they would quickly wrench an elbow or a shoulder back into place.

After Partition, new states were created from the old British provinces, and in 1960 the Indian remnant of the Bombay Presidency was split into two states, Gujarat and Maharashtra.

Bombay emerged as the capital of Maharashtra, changing its British name to the Marathi name, Mumbai, in 1995. For the sake of historical accuracy, we will not use the name Mumbai until we reach 1995, although denizens of old Bombay and old India hands still tend to forget, speaking of Bombay even today.

Ram's family remembers living for a year in Pune before moving back to a house in Ulhasnagar, a new township built from the old military camps of Kalyan. A large Sindhi community remains in the area to this day, and some call the township Sindhunagar. The house that Ram bought was valued at Rs 8000, the exact amount that the Indian government was willing to authorize for Hindu refugee homes.

Shobha thought the government home was cute. The homes were attached bungalows, each with a veranda, called a thalla, where they could sleep outside in hot weather. Ram's parents lived in this house until Maya finished high school; then they moved to Panchshila, on C Road in Bombay. Ram's grandmother was not with them; she died in Karachi before they left. Ram's grandfather always lived in the house at Ulhasnagar, except for a brief stay in the Panchshila house, until he died. But we are getting ahead of ourselves.

Ram found an office for his father in Kalyan. At first Boolchand was very depressed, and it was difficult for him to start back in practice. A great believer in numerology, Ram urged his father to change the spelling of his name from Bulchand to Boolchand. After that Boolchand did well, eventually becoming president of the Kalyan Bar Association. Boolchand practised law well into the 1980s, even while he lived at Panchshila and commuted to his office in Kalyan by train. His daughters remember him carrying bananas every day for his lunch. His wife always handled the family finances, but she died early, leaving him with unfamiliar responsibilities. One day the laundryman came, and he turned his eyes upward, telling the dhobi to look above to his wife for the money.

For good reason, this period in the life of the Jethmalani family calls to mind a description[1] of the world in which Ram grew up: 'In the 17th and 18th centuries Shikarpur in upper Sind became the most important banking and trading centre, not only of Sind but of west Asia and northern India.'

Hindu businessmen spread all over the world. 'They lived in far flung places of the world, leaving their wives and families home in Sind and visiting them rarely or as frequently as distance and work would allow.' Older Sindhis agree that these travelling businessmen had a girl in every port. Another tradition that Sindhi men seem to have brought from their predominantly Muslim environment was that of multiple wives. Many of the Sindhi men of Ram's generation had at least two wives, to say nothing of girlfriends and mistresses. They considered it normal. In Ram's early life in India and his later years in Delhi, he has been true to his origins.

Thus, leaving his family in their house, Ram and Vishin Meghani, another refugee Sindhi lawyer, moved into a seedy Bombay residence, Carvalho's Guest House, run by a Guyanese man, for Rs 105 a month. The food was scanty and sometimes rotten. Breakfast consisted of a thin slice of bread, one egg, and a cup of tea. Lunch was supposed to be delivered to his office, but it left the rooming house before they did, arriving in the form of little more than one or two slices of bread, gravy without meat, and a banana. Ram would save the banana, buy a carton of Milkmaid milk, and slice the banana into it for a treat. When Ram complained to the proprietor, he said, 'No, no, Ram. You are intellectual workers. You should not eat too much.'

'Every week there was suicide in that place. My companion and childhood friend suggested we get out or one day we will have to commit suicide.' They fled as soon as Ram acquired a flat in Byculla, called Star Mansion, from a Muslim moving to Karachi. He gave Ram the key to his flat, and Ram gave him the keys to his house in Karachi. Ram subsequently obtained an allotment order from the Bombay land requisition authorities, but the landlord in Byculla was not happy. He filed a suit, and Ram had to defend himself. The matter dragged on at length until it was finally resolved.

Byculla was an area in South Bombay built in part on landfill that extended from one of the seven islands of Bombay. While South Bombay was still enclosed by the Fort and a moat, Byculla was outside the moat and healthier, and it had a population of both Muslims and Baghdadi Jews. When the railway station was completed in 1857, textile mills moved in, many of them established by the Sassoon family of merchants from Baghdad. The Sassoons had built a grand synagogue there—the Magan David Synagogue—several charitable institutions, and a free medical clinic. In 1936–37, a sectarian dispute had caused fierce riots, but it was quiet when the Jethmalanis moved in. While they lived there, what they remember were the many little Muslim shops in the neighbourhood, the synagogue, and a fine Jain temple.

In 1948, Ram, Durga, Rani, Shobha, Ram's parents, Sundri, and Maya moved into a second-floor flat in the Star Mansion. Even Vishin Meghani stayed there briefly.

In 1950, Ram moved Durga, Rani, Shobha, and his sister Sundri to Panchgani, a hill town near Pune. Ram had gone to fetch Sundri from his parents' house in Ulhasnagar in the middle of the night, to take her to Panchgani too for a good education, but his parents begged him to please leave Maya with them.

Panchgani sits in the picturesque Western Ghats. The girls remember a charming house, a garden, and lovely wooded hills. They remember how quiet it was: 'there was nothing there'. Panchgani was especially renowned for its fine private schools. Shobha was a day scholar for one to two years. Rani and Sundri went to a boarding school run by the Sisters of the Cross, where they made many friends. The film star Nargis, Sanjay Dutt's mother, was a frequent visitor.

The girls remember their maid, Manju, who had lost her nose from smallpox. They also remember the day Durga went out for a walk, and a porcupine followed her home. Late on another night, a tiger stalked Durga. One night Shobha was the last child to leave a school event, because Durga had expected someone else to take her home. She began walking down the hill in the dark, and suddenly right above her an eagle swooped down. She ran as quickly as she could, only stopping for a quick prayer at a little Mother Mary's grotto, then scampering down the path so fast she dropped her favourite—and only—doll.

Durga was stalked by more worries than tigers—worries about her marriage. Ram came often for festive weekend visits with the family, but Shobha remembers that when she used to sleep with her mother as a small child, her mother would cry herself to sleep. Her mother would tell her that her feet hurt.

Once he settled his family, Ram concentrated on building his law practice. At first, with no work at all, he almost took a job as a magistrate. At the last moment, while on the bus going to take the job, Ram thought 'What am I doing?' and he turned back to try his luck in building a practice. A man Ram calls 'a briefless barrister' had let out half of his office to a cotton merchant, and he agreed to give Ram 'table space' in the other half. While Ram worked at his desk, shreds of cotton would fall on his head from the cotton bales overhead.

The first month he earned Rs 30 for writing three notices, and he spent Rs 60 on rent—at Rs 4.8 to the dollar in those days. Vishin started out in practice with him, but once he looked at the economics of their practice, he left. Maybe that was premature. In his second month of practice Ram made Rs 1300.

Bombay was filled with Sindhi refugees, some old clients, and many who remembered Ram from Karachi. Everyone seemed to have legal problems, either over personal property or their businesses. This meant a steady stream of disputes over titles, property rights, rents, hundis, deeds, partnership contracts, petty criminal matters, and dealings with the municipality. Ram's practice started in the lowest court of Bombay, the small claims, or small causes, court. He even handled his own rent control dispute over the Star Mansion.

Fortunately, one lawyer had turned over three pro bono cases to him, which gave Ram a chance to make a real impression on the community. Ram claims he was the only refugee who paid income tax in his first year. Perhaps he was the only one who reported his income.

One day, a banker came to Ram for help in getting out of a partnership he had entered into with a foreign national.[2] Once the banker completed a lengthy explanation of his problem, Ram looked up calmly and told him that any such partnership was illegal under the Foreign Exchange Regulation Act. All Ram had to do was dictate a letter to that effect. After that, all the Sindhi bankers came to Ram.

In 1957, Sarla and her husband, Tulsi Wadhwa, moved to the city of Zehedhan in Iran. Her husband's father had a dried-fruit factory there, but her husband was an exceptionally unlucky businessman. After a series of financial problems, the last straw came when her eldest son somehow burned down the factory. Ram had to drop everything, run to Iran, and pay their debts. After that they moved to Tehran, where Tulsi worked in a bank by day and gambled by night in a fashionable nightclub. The club had elegant patrons, and it was filled with plenty of gorgeous women dressed in their finest, catnip to Ram when he came to Tehran. Rani visited Sarla there; so did Ram's sons Janak and Tony, and Shobha, who came back home sporting the latest in Tehran finery, cosmetics, and fashionably streaked hair. Finally the club closed when the Shah of Iran fell in 1979.

Sarla and her family returned to Bombay in 1979, even though Tulsi had no real prospects for work. Ever since the factory fire, Ram has supported the Wadhwa family, especially after Tulsi died in 2004. Sarla had three sons, two of whom have problems that require continued medical support, and Sarla developed her own medical problems as she aged. Her son in Australia does his best to help, but Australia is far away. Other than what that son contributes, Ram takes care of everything. That is his nature.

Although Ram's father did establish a small legal practice in Kalyan, it has been Ram—since his twenties—who has taken responsibility for the whole family, for his sisters when they were in need, for his own children's medical bills, and for the grandchildren's apartments or tuition. The Jethmalani family truly is a patriarchy, and Ram grew from a young prodigy to become a traditional patriarch.

7

Early Practice in Bombay

Ram gained early notoriety by defending the dacoits in the famous Bruce Street Dacoity on January 10, 1949. This was a brazen heist right next to the Central Bank of India, near Flora Fountain square in downtown Bombay.[1] The dacoits had studied the day and time when Tata textile workers normally were paid and when the cash was transported by truck to the Tata Mills. At 7 a.m., while bags of money were being loaded into a Tata van, four dacoits pulled up in a black car, grabbed the bags of money at gunpoint and sped off through the middle of downtown Bombay. The news story created a sensation.

According to Ram, the first defence lawyer on the case took his money, spent it, and promptly retired from the law to an administrative position. Ram agreed to take the case pro bono. By some legal sleight of hand, he somehow convinced the jury to let off some of the accused. The Bombay Sessions Court was impressed, so much so that after that they sent him their free legal aid cases, called dock briefs, which helped build his reputation as a criminal lawyer.

This has been the pattern of Ram's career. By now most of his cases are pro bono, legal language for free of charge. If the client is innocent but cannot pay, Ram tells him not to worry about it. If the client is a pious religious figure, a member of a minority that is suffering discrimination, or an impecunious personal friend, Ram takes the case, and he works just as hard on it as he would for a paying client. If he is trying to raise funds for a charity or maybe a law school, he asks rich clients to donate their fee to the cause. If a rich person jolly well can and should pay up, these fees alone will reimburse Ram enough to make up for all the pro bono cases that year.

Ram's generosity has generated many tales. He always carries packets of biscuits for children who rap on his car window when his car stops at a light. He believes it is a sin to pass a beggar on the street without handing him something. His family tells many tales of the leeches and hangers-on that he has acquired over the years, giving them money generously without a care in the world.

A variety of characters have stayed in Ram's house in Bombay, later in Delhi and Pune, happily eating and sleeping for free. Whenever one of them has turned up, the family has held their breath to see how long they will stay—sometimes it has been for weeks on end—or what they might appropriate when they leave. Some say Ram is naïve, and that he can be taken in by any sob story. That is not likely. He feels that he gains merit by helping those in need. It does not cost much, and it gives him pleasure.

Speaking of pleasure, Ram's story is one of contrasts. His family first found out that Ratna Shahani had entered his life in 1952. The daughter of the former Assistant Health Officer of Karachi, Dr Hotchand Shahani, she was one of the first female graduates of SC Shahani Law College in Karachi and the first female lawyer that Ram had ever met. When they came to Bombay her father became a doctor in Colaba, and they lived nearby in Amarchand Mansion, a lovely home opposite the Cooperage football ground and close enough to the Bombay High Court for Ratna to walk to court. The flat was on the first floor, convenient for Ratna when she wanted to disappear for some social life.

Ratna's persona contrasted sharply with that of Durga. Ratna was slim and well turned out in spotless white saris, wore a fashionable hairstyle, and applied her make-up expertly. She had been one of the first among her Sindhi circle in Karachi to learn how to apply make-up. She was educated, and she was Ram's colleague, practising in the same courts.

In many interviews Ram has said that they had first met in Karachi in 1947, and they married secretly, on the fly, in 1947, realizing that Partition could separate them for an indefinite amount of time. His official Parliament biography says they married in 1951. In a previous biography[2] he is described as marrying her first in 1947, then again on October 24, 1952 in Delhi, choosing Delhi because bigamy was illegal in Bombay at that time. The Hindu Marriage Act was passed in 1955, outlawing polygamy from that time forward in the rest of the country, but pre-existing marriages were grandfathered in.

We can only say that, knowing Ram, you would think that five years between 1947 and 1952 was a long wait before he could consummate the marriage.

The family relates some of the more dramatic events of their courtship. Ratna's three siblings were all within two to three years of her age and very close to her. Along with their parents, they begged her not to elope. Ratna's family banished her to her aunt's home when they realized she was serious, but, madly in love with Ram, she ran away from her aunt's house and eloped. They all remember that after Ratna had already gone off with Ram, Dr Shahani, his wife, an uncle, and a friend drove the six hours from Bombay to Panchgani, where they burst into the home, demanding to see Ram. Ram came out to meet him while he was in the middle of shaving, half of his face covered with shaving cream. While Durga, the girls, and Ratna cowered in the background, Dr Shahani placed himself between Ratna and Ram, and demanded that Ram send Ratna back to Bombay, while Ratna's mother begged her daughter to come back home. Ram stood his ground.

They returned to Bombay from Panchgani soon afterwards, and Durga decided to make one last attempt to save her marriage. She grabbed Shobha and went to Dr Shahani's house in Colaba to prove that Ram was a married man with children. Shobha remembers entering a very grand house with huge rooms, tall windows of Venetian glass, and ornate 16-foot ceilings. Ratna's parents and sister were all inside. Once Dr Shahani understood the situation, he took Shobha to the swing in the veranda and held her kindly, but it was too late for him to do anything about his own daughter. Embarrassed in front of their community, the parents did not talk to Ratna until she became pregnant with her son.

After that they reconciled, and Durga's children established a very warm relationship with Ratna's parents and family. Her brother Mohan was a great favourite, and Shobha used to tease him that he was her boyfriend. Ratna's younger sister's son, Harish, was very close to Durga's son Tony, possibly even closer than to her own son Janak. When Ram contracted a near-fatal case of typhoid and was writing his will, it was Dr Shahani who came over to tend to him.

Ram has often spoken of how well his wives got along and how well his daughters adapted to the presence of Ratna in their lives. He believed that by regularly 'fulfilling his conjugal duty' to Durga, he was a good husband. He once famously told an interviewer that his second wife was happier than the interviewer's only wife. Still, now that both wives are dead, only the picture of Ratna has a fresh garland in Ram's house.

Durga had little choice but to accept reality. With two little girls, she did not want a divorce, and Ratna was not going to disappear. Their lives were inextricably tied together. They had even more in common once they both realized that Ram was entertaining other women. At the time of the Emergency, when Indira Gandhi arrested so many prominent Indian leaders, even some of his supporters said that Ram should have stayed in India and gone to jail like the rest. Durga said with a wicked smile, 'He should have gone to jail. It would have been better for everyone, and we would have saved a lot of money.'

8

Refugee Cases

A refugee himself, Ram handled several high-profile refugee cases that were important to his early career.

India became a republic on January 26, 1950, now Republic Day. One of the first challenges for the fledging country was the great flood of refugees from Pakistan. To handle them, India passed the Bombay Refugees Act on March 29, 1948. The preamble begins with the intention that 'it is expedient . . . to regulate the movement of refugees with a view to facilitating their relief and rehabilitation and to securing public health, sanitation and safety . . .'

Using this act, the state of Bombay mistreated, restricted, and evicted many Sindhi refugees. Soon after it was passed, Ram filed a public interest case, a PIL, in the Bombay High Court to challenge the act. Khatu Cooper and Ratna both worked with him. Ram told the court that, in Akola, Muslim shops and Sindhi shops sat side by side, but the Akola Municipal Corporation had only decided to demolish Sindhi shops. Focusing on Article 14 of the act, Ram argued that it was not within the competence of a state legislature to control the movements of humans. This falls within the list of central government legislative powers, under the last category—residual powers. Prof. G.N. Joshi, a well-known constitutional expert, representing the government, defined a refugee as one who came from a different country, but these refugees had travelled from what was then India to India. The stunning result was that Chief Justice Chagla and Judge Tendulkar declared the Bombay

41

Refugees Act of 1948 ultra vires. This means that the act that the Bombay Legislature passed was beyond its purview, and the act was void.

Ram tells the story in his speech at the Bombay Bar Association memorial meeting held for Khatu Cooper.[1] 'Soon enough, we refugees had a grievance against the Government of Bombay. They had passed a legislation that enabled them to treat refugees almost like animals. They couldn't afford lawyers. They came to me and I went to Khatu. We both sat together and ultimately decided that . . . the act will have to be challenged. But Khatu spotted a weakness in our argument. We wasted days and days to find an answer. Neither of us succeeded. Ultimately, I told Khatu that we should just make the argument and rely on the opposition. We were opposed by someone whose book on constitutional law was our textbook. Lo and behold, the act was declared ultra vires and the most unanswerable argument was never made.'

In fact, there were several cases on this matter at that time. One Sindhi refugee in Chembur Colony, Sanwaldas Gobindram, was given three days to leave his house in a refugee camp.[2] This case started with a writ of mandamus directing the state of Bombay 'from enforcing an order made under Section 7, Bombay Refugees Act, 1948, against the petitioner. The order requires that the petitioner shall leave the Chembur colony with all his belongings within a period of 3 days from the date of the service of the order and shall not re-enter the said colony.'

Prof. Joshi gave his definition of a refugee, which would be one who moved from one country to another, not the situation in this case, when the refugees moved from what was India to what now is India.

In its verdict, the Bombay High Court gives examples of the ways the act humiliated refugees—or even just law-abiding people who were evacuated because of Partition—evicting them to 'maintain public order, public health, or sanitation'.

Specifically, the court held that Section 7 of the act was ultra vires. That was the important point for Ram and his refugee community. The court also accepted his argument that Section 7 of the act, which empowers the 'Provincial Government to order refugees to reside in particular camps, places or areas' cannot fall within the scope of the entry 'public health'. As Ram argued, just because someone had to evacuate the new country of Pakistan does not mean he is dirty, unhygienic, and destitute.

Ram continued to defend refugees. In 1955,[3] a land dispute arose. The land was vacant when a Mr Tyaballi first purchased it and subsequently built on it. In August 1951, the Bombay Municipality filed a suit in the Bombay High Court to eject Tyaballi. A consent decree ordered him to deliver the plot vacant and clear of all structures. If he failed to remove the structures he was to give up possession of the plot, together with the structures standing on it, to a Mr Bhagwandas. Tyaballi did not remove the structures.

One of Ram's arguments was that under the consent decree, Tyaballi had agreed that if he did not remove the structures by a particular date, the structures would belong to the municipality. Thus Ram's client Bhagwandas would become a tenant of the municipality, who could not be ejected by a decree against Tyaballi. Ram's novel argument was that 'his clients were the tenants only of the structures and not of the land and . . . as far as the structures were concerned there was clearly a transfer to the municipality'.

The court said, 'We find it rather difficult to conceive how a structure can be transferred divorced from the land on which it stands.'

Nevertheless it held '. . . it is clear that on the facts of this case where the municipality has become entitled to claim possession of the land . . . and where the municipality is not interested in the structures put up on this land it is no answer by the appellants that [Tyaballi] put up structures and let them out to tenants'. Ram's creative argument carried, and the refugee community now had a new way to defend their homes and businesses from illegal demolition.

These refugee cases profoundly influenced Ram's future career by attracting the attention of the leaders of the Bombay Bar. Queen Victoria had granted a charter to the High Courts of Bombay, Calcutta, and Madras allowing them to take original cases in addition to appeals. There used to be a rigorous exam—the Original Side (OS) exam—for lawyers to argue these cases. Until 1976, OS advocates had to be briefed by a solicitor. Those who passed the OS exam, so-called OS lawyers, were the legal elite in Bombay, many of them Parsis. Among the Parsi lawyers who dominated the Bombay Bar, both before and after the exam was discontinued, were Nani Palkhiwala, Soli Sorabji, and Fali Nariman. Khatu Cooper was one of these and one of the few who had passed the O.S. exam in one sitting.

Ram's arguments in the decision that declared the Bombay Refugee Act ultra vires impressed Khatu mightily. People were so happy that day they practically carried Ram on their shoulders. Ram's picture was in the *Times of India*. Ram says this was the case that made his career. Khatu told his peers that Ram deserved to join their ranks at the pinnacle of the Bombay bar. Khatu's wife Mani—also a lawyer and a close friend—says Khatu was Ram's first friend in the Bombay bar and his best friend.

Another refugee case that Ram took concerned the Sindhi language itself. Since the land of Sindh now is entirely within Pakistan, Sindhis in India, like the Jews for many centuries, became a people without a land. That made them vulnerable.

Article 343 of the Indian Constitution says, 'The official language of the Union shall be Hindi in Devanagari script.' Devanagari is the script of Sanskrit and Hindi, easy to recognize because of a characteristic line on top of each word. Sindhi was traditionally written in the Sindhi–Arabic script, which was adapted from Persian and Arabic. Arabic has 29 characters however, and Sindhi has 52, in order to capture its unique sounds. While Sindhi can also be written in the Devanagari script, Devanagari lacks some of the letters needed for the particular music of Sindhi.

When the former Bombay Presidency was dismantled, the language wars began. Marathi and Gujarati speakers fought for their own separate states. Gandhi wrote and spoke widely of the

need to have one script, Devanagari, for all languages in India.[4]
The Constituent Assembly of India sat in Delhi in December
1948 and debated whether the medium of instruction in school
should be in only one script or whether it should allow regional
languages and scripts.[5] In this setting, the government of Bombay
passed a resolution requiring that Sindhi must be taught using the
Devanagari script. Probably another important underlying reason
was that, since the Sindhi script looks like Arabic, it aroused their
still fresh resentment of Muslims. That script made them suspicious
that the Sindhis carried over an affinity for Muslims from Pakistan.
This resolution was a clear rejection of anything Muslim.

Although some of the new Sindhi immigrants supported the
change to Devanagari, Sindhi poets and writers were appalled
at the prospect of losing their script. Without it they could not
capture in writing the special lyricism of the Sindhi language.
On behalf of the Sindhi community, Ram filed a PIL in the High
Court of Bombay. Ram argued this as a matter of constitutional
law, and his explanations convinced the court. As a result of the
court ruling, the Ministry of Education issued an order on March
9, 1950 requiring that both the Perso-Arabic and the Devanagari
scripts be allowed for teaching the Sindhi language in schools. Ram
became known as the man who saved the Sindhi language from
extinction in India. Ram was 27.

The Jethmalani family now moved 16 miles north of Colaba
to Andheri. Today it is one of Bombay's wealthiest suburbs, but
that was yet to come. Durga, Shobha, Ram, Ratna, and Ram's
grandfather moved there as guests of Ram's old friend Satram
Rajani and his family. Ram even built a badminton court for his
old cricket partner. Rani and Sundri were still in boarding school,
but Shobha and Satram's daughter Shaku became fast friends.

Ram and Ratna soon decamped to South Bombay, complaining
that the commute was too long from Andheri, but Durga and
Shobha stayed on for a year. Shobha remembers playing with
Shaku. 'There was a hen farm in our backyard. The cook and we
girls chased them to catch them for dinner! One day we hid two
chicks from the cook in a basket. Unfortunately we closed the lid

only to find them dead the next morning! We were quite devastated.'

Shaku remained a friend of the family even after her father died, and years later Ram asked his long-time friend Shaku to supervise his apartment at Advent.

Ram and Ratna moved into an apartment on the first floor of Morrison's Hotel, which is in South Bombay on Marine Drive, cozied up next to the art deco Regal Cinema. They lived there and Ram maintained his office there for two years. This was one of the cinemas that the Sindhis loved to patronize, along with the Strand and the Eros Cinema. In those days they would go to the cinema at night and attend Sunday morning jam sessions in the Ritz or the Airline Hotel, dancing for hours. In addition, many of the popular Bombay clubs had their own dance nights. It was a time of friendship, drinking, and socializing.

Many of the Jethmalani apartments were right by Marine Drive, still new at that time, since it was only built between 1935 and 1940.[6] This wide boulevard now curves majestically along a natural bay of the Arabian Sea, extending from Nariman Point to Malabar Hill, today some of the best addresses in Bombay, though in those days Nariman Point was still sand. At night, the streetlights look like a curving string of pearls, the Queen's Necklace. Pictures from the 1940s show elegant cars and uncrowded sidewalks, the people dressed splendidly. A row of turn-of-the-century buildings look out across the boulevard to the sea, one of the longest rows of art deco buildings in the world.

Sindhis from all over the city used to congregate there on Saturdays to promenade and catch up on their gossip. The taxis were all imported Buicks and Chevrolets, charging 6 annas a mile. Ram used to tool around in his Singer car, one of the few Sindhis to have a car at all, although he often could not use it because he had loaned it out to a friend who wanted to impress his girlfriend.

In 1952, Shobha and Durga returned to Bombay, and Shobha went to Walsingham School on Malabar Hill. A grand Mughal-style castle with broad lawns and a commanding view of the sea, it originally was built in 1940 by the Maharaja of Kutch. Later, Mrs Adcock, an American, bought it and made it into a private

American-style girls' school, at the time the best in Bombay. Now it is hemmed in by humdrum new wings; tall buildings impede the view of the sea and the lawn in front has become a wide driveway. While Shobha studied there, she was impressed by the marble floors and stairs. Rani continued as a boarder at St Joseph's Convent.

Ram's two families now criss-crossed South Bombay. When Ratna became pregnant, her parents finally reconciled with her, and she stayed with them through her pregnancy and delivery. On November 19, 1955, her son Janak was born prematurely, weighing less than five pounds. Durga became pregnant just as Janak was born, and the relationships between the two wives suddenly became stormy. Ram actually fought with Durga, trying to convince her not to deliver another child. The family remembers those days as pure chaos.

A priest told Durga that she was going to deliver a boy, and she dug in her heels, refusing to abort the child. This caused a rift between Ratna and Durga, and it extended to Durga's daughters. At first Ratna had taken care to develop a warm relationship with Durga, Shobha, and Rani, but once Durga became pregnant, Durga and her daughters were packed off to an apartment in a building called Bharat Mahal for the duration of her pregnancy. Durga did attend Janak's naming ceremony, the chhati, also held at Bharat Mahal.

Durga delivered Mahesh on August 9, 1956, exactly nine months after Janak was born. Mahesh means great ruler, and it is another name for the god Shiva. Mahesh was so robust and ruddy his sisters called him Tony, for Tony Curtis, the handsomest movie star of the day. Nobody precisely remembers Tony's naming ceremony.

Janak would grow up to study at McGill University and go on to a career in financial management. Tony is the son who would study at Oxford, follow his father into law, and become his presumptive successor in politics.

While Ram and Ratna made their life with their new baby, Durga and her children embarked upon an odyssey of moves up and down Marine Drive and Colaba. There were two flats in Colaba, the first one tiny and cramped, the second in a better building, fittingly called Bela Court. Later there would be Shalimar, and Hemprabha, both close to Marine Drive. Sometimes the buildings were named for their street or, in a venerable Bombay tradition, the building itself had a name.

One of these moves took them so far away from Walsingham that Shobha had to take a bus to school one and a half hours each way, alone, at eight to nine years old. Her other classmates came by car, but Shobha only could if a car was available, not an important matter perhaps, unless you were a status-conscious young girl.

By the time Rani returned from boarding school, Durga, Rani, Shobha, and Tony were in a flat in a building called Shalimar. Shobha and Rani now attended Queen Mary School in Bombay, also an excellent school, with girls who were less spoiled than the girls of Walsingham.

Durga's apartments had good enough addresses, not the houses Ram and Ratna stayed in, but respectable. Durga's family knew their place, but they knew how to laugh about it all too. In many ways these were some of the happiest days the family can remember.

Ram and Ratna threw grand parties for the glitterati of Bombay. The girls were often invited to these, but they always returned to Durga to spend the night. They were children of the first wife, and they knew it. Rani was the one who resented her mother's situation the most. The two half-brothers were less bothered. They inherited generous personalities from their father, and they have always gotten along well since they were 10-year-olds at the Jesuit Campion School. Janak came to Campion school in a car and with a maid. Tony came by bus, but he made up for it with more friends and better marks.

As teenagers, both boys went to boarding school at St Paul's in Darjeeling, and the family would come to visit them twice a year. Sometimes Ram would take Ratna, other times Durga, rarely both. The mothers always visited the principal, a prim Englishman. Once when Durga came to his office, after Ratna had visited six months before, he looked at Durga quizzically and said, 'Mrs Jethmalani, how you have changed!'

After Janak's birth, Ram and Ratna moved to Hughes Road, near the posh Altamount Road, and Ram moved his offices from Morrison's Hotel to the downtown area by Flora Fountain. Shobha says Ratna and Janak had more stability in their lives than she and Tony did. Even Rani and Sundri, in Panchgani at boarding school, had more stability than she did.

Eventually, Ram bought a flat in a building called Panchshila, which he paid for with a Rs 5000 loan that his grandfather gave him, on condition that he could stay there too. Ram's grandfather stayed there briefly, but he soon realized he preferred Ulhasnagar.

The whole family remembers that Ram obtained the flat through pugri. This is a system to avoid rent control that started at the time of the Raj. An interest-free security deposit is paid upfront to prevent a tenant from being evicted, and it is refundable when the tenant leaves. The tenant still pays rent. Ram eventually paid the necessary money to get the apartment out of pugri.

At first Ram, Ratna, and Janak lived on the first floor, while Ram's office was still in Flora Fountain. Then they moved briefly to a larger flat on the third floor, the first-floor flat remaining Ram's office.

In the early 1960s, Ram and Ratna moved out to a fine new building, called Advent, on Foreshore Road, a very glamorous building in those days, the first to be built there on reclaimed land. The apartment has gone through intermittent spasms of remodelling ever since. A Russian decorated it at first. Since at that time they could see and hear the sea from the windows, he extended the dining room, put in a glass enclosure paved with multicoloured stones, and installed turtles. In time, the turtles were strolling all over the apartment. In one phase of decorating, Ram bought a piece of art at an exhibit for very little money to make the artist happy. In time, this appreciated in value, but Ram had no idea. One day he casually threw it into the dustbin.

In the early 1970s when we first saw the apartment, it was decorated in bordello red. It reached its most unforgettable state when the building management stripped it down to a shell while they repaired the decaying infrastructure. That year not only was the living room peeled back to the studs in the wall, but the floor also was completely gone, replaced by a huge hole. Visitors had to step gingerly around the chasm to avoid falling through. In the apartment below was an older couple, the Peerbhoy family. Looking down the hole in the floor, Ram was surprisingly unperturbed. All he would say was, 'I only dread that I fall into the arms of Mrs Peerbhoy.'

Following that, it all was put to rights and properly decorated in sedate tones of beige, until recently that is, when the ceiling fell down in Janak's room, exposing a nest of termites. When the termites were found in a succession of ceilings, at one point the furniture sat piled in the middle of the living room, where the dog happily chewed it while the workmen made their repairs. When the family suggests they get a better place, both Ram and Janak refuse, saying, 'This is our lucky house.'

When Ram moved to Advent, Durga and her children moved to the third-floor flat at Panchshila. This is where Shobha lived when she went to college. Rani later moved in with Ram and Ratna while she went to law school. When she graduated, Ratna, Rani, and Ram would go to court together. After Ram's grandfather died, his parents moved to the first floor of Panchshila while Maya went to Jai Hind College and on to GS Medical College. Sundri was there briefly too when she came back from school, but then she married Bihari Lulla almost immediately.

Once Shobha had married, Ram's parents had died, and Maya had moved away, Ram sold the third-floor flat to buy an apartment for Rani in Delhi. Now Durga moved back to the first-floor flat where Ram's office was. Ram worked there daily as did his associate Sri Jaisinghani, and people constantly paraded in and out. It was a beehive of activity, and Durga was right in the middle of it all. Ram's clients often went from his office to take a cup of tea with Durga. These were Durga's happiest days.

Durga lived out the rest of her life in the first-floor flat. That was where she was living when her two sisters died of heart attacks, and when her brothers committed suicide, first one, then the other. That was where she lived when she lost her parents and when one brother died of acute pancreatitis, all within a few years. And that was where she died in 1997, one of the last three survivors of a family that had 13 children.

While this litany of moves may seem gratuitous and perhaps confusing, there is a reason to go through it all. Most Indians assume that all of the Jethmalani children were brought up like Indian royalty, and in many ways the boys were. In the case of Shobha and Rani, many professional colleagues regarded them as queens even though they had serious careers, but the truth was more complicated. The girls and their mother did not exactly run from apartment to apartment ahead of the bill collector, or at least that was not how they remembered it, but theirs was not a regal childhood.

The earliest apartment they lived in with their mother was very humble indeed, and some of the later ones were quite pedestrian. With all that, the Jethmalani family had an endless ability to get together and laugh about their adventures, never taking themselves seriously. Perhaps it will not be a surprise that Shobha spent her career as a paediatrician in an inner city Detroit Medicaid clinic, taking care of underprivileged minorities. Similarly, Rani devoted virtually all of her legal practice to marital law, settling dowry debts and defending downtrodden, battered, or burned wives.

Still, when Ram entered Parliament and lived in Delhi, it was Rani who stayed with him and acted as the lady of the house. Her friends say that nobody loved Ram more than Rani did.

In truth, both girls always idolized their father, as did both boys. In return, Ram lavished on them the best education money could buy, and as much love and attention as he could. Whenever he had time he would pack them all up for a jaunt somewhere enjoyable. If he only had a day, they would be off for the pleasures of Juhu Beach or rural Alibaug, neither one far from Bombay. If he had a few days, it would be a family trip for everyone to a hill station, to Shimla, Kashmir, Ooty, Coimbatore, Goa, or Mysore. If he had a big case in Delhi, he might book the whole lot of them at the Taj Mahal Hotel or the Oberoi, for a luxurious holiday. Many years later, Ram took the entire family on a cruise, but the time when he could afford that was yet to come.

9

Smugglers and Lovers

While the Jethmalanis trekked all over South Bombay, the country was becoming fertile ground for smugglers. This could only serve to enrich Ram, who many called the 'smugglers' lawyer'.

After independence, India became obsessed with strict licensing regimes and five-year plans modelled after the Soviet Union. Nehru nationalized the largest enterprises in 17 industries. In order to start any company, produce a product, or expand production capacity, a private company had to satisfy up to 80 government agencies, and, once the licences were granted, the government regulated production. The government imposed high tariffs and low quotas on all imported consumer goods, particularly luxuries, and it banned some items altogether. The state not only required a licence to produce anything, it also decided what could be produced, how much, at what price, and what sources of capital it would permit. Businesses required bureaucratic approval to lay off workers or even to shut down. Thus was born the Licence Raj.

Smuggling was nothing new in India. Karachi and Bombay are on the Arabian Sea, and traditionally a robust boat traffic has shuttled between them. As early as 1878, the Raj tried to control smuggling by passing the Sea Customs Act, followed by the Indian Tariff Act, the Air Customs Act, the Land Customs Act, the Customs Acts of 1934 and 1962 and the Maintenance of Internal Security Act of 1971. All this legislation failed of course, because the economic incentives to smuggle were overwhelming. India virtually shut off imports through high tariffs, low quotas, and outright banning, slowing the economy to a crawl. India finally passed the Conservation of Foreign Exchange and Prevention of Smuggling Activities Act (COFEPOSA) in 1974. All of this legislation made Ram rich.

Critics disparage Ram as 'simply' a smugglers' lawyer. An economist would explain that in the restrictive trade environment of the Licence Raj, one of the few ways to keep the economy alive was by smuggling goods into the country. At any rate, during the 1950s and 1960s, enterprising traders, many of them Sindhi, did their best to keep the economy lubricated.

Not an economist, Ram simply told people, 'When I see a man come into my office with his pockets bulging with smuggling money, I consider it my duty to relieve him of this wealth.'

By the late 1950s, Ram had plenty of work, and his life had established the pattern that continues today. He does his best thinking early in the morning, alone. He studies some cases for weeks, working out his arguments, the counterarguments, the traps that await him, and the traps he will set. In Mumbai, he goes to the Bombay Gymkhana Club to play badminton, before he returns home for a hearty breakfast. The Gymkhana is an old British club where, as recently as the 1970s, you could close your eyes, and imagine you were listening to old British soldiers from Sandhurst talking about honour and glory. Ram recently was feted as the oldest member who plays badminton at the club.

After breakfast Ram goes either to the office or to court. He eats little at lunch and dinner.

Ram prefers to avoid team conferences with other lawyers, though he is happy to talk over cases with young associates. In these meetings, Ram the law teacher emerges, expounding upon a fine legal point or an arcane rule of evidence. He remembers the details of relevant cases from decades before. His voice gathers power; he pounds the table, he grins and frowns, and he refuses to take telephone calls. His face, normally a light bronze, flushes with emotion. This is Ram in his glory.

In contrast to many lawyers, and certainly most senior

advocates, Ram is content to have briefing lawyers and clients drop in any time, day or night. He often works in the office until late at night, and he still can find them waiting to see him when he returns home from a party. Indeed, Ram and Ratna always enjoyed their social life, both of them filled with an endless supply of bawdy jokes. They entertained at home, at clubs, and at restaurants. Any night of the week they might attend a mammoth wedding party, a reception, or some other glamorous event, but Ram always got up early the next day to tend to business. These parties, of course, required Ratna to wear suitably elegant saris and jewellery. As fast as Ram made money, she spent it. Fortunately, he has always been able to make more.

The court in which Ram made his name as a senior advocate was the Bombay High Court. This is a magnificent castle of justice that the British built in 1878 to symbolize the power and glory of the Raj.[1] Reminiscent of the Royal Courts of Justice in London, it is on the Esplanade, a grand oval maidan, once adjacent to the Fort walls of Bombay. Next to it are the neo-Gothic buildings of the High Court, Secretariat, University Library, and Convocation Hall, the Public Works Department Offices, and the Post and Telegraph Office. Originally designed to look grandly out at the Arabian Sea, the complex is unique in India. The court building was based on sketches of castles on the Rhine.

The careful observer will see blue basalt and red sandstone exterior walls, circular stairways in the turreted towers, gargoyles, and rows of pointed arches. The interior has a profusion of stone sculptures and richly carved teak wood. The Criminal Court is a 40-foot-high octagon positioned in the centre of the building, the floor paved with Italian mosaic.

In the early days, British-trained barristers such as Mahatma Gandhi, Muhammad Ali Jinnah, and B.R. Ambedkar, the author of the Indian Constitution, practised here, as did the great freedom fighters for Indian independence.

Apart from the Bombay courts, Ram has argued more than 250 cases in the Supreme Court of India alone. The count of all the published opinions of his High Court and Supreme Court cases runs to 500–600, maybe more, and the criminal cases are not even published, because they are heard by the sessions court. It would be safe to say that no attorney in the United States has ever had such a career.

The first Ram Jethmalani case listed in the Supreme Court records was in 1957, less than 10 years from his arrival in Bombay. This was a refugee matter that tested the constitutionality of the Bombay Land Requisition Act. Many of the next cases involved smugglers apprehended under various customs acts, particularly the Customs Act of 1962.

According to Sri Jaisinghani, Ram's former junior, smugglers once constituted 90 per cent of Ram's practice. Sri says Ram could not win these cases because under the Sea Customs Act a signed admission of guilt from the smuggler was admissible in court, and it became part of the record. As opposed to that, rules that dated back to the British Raj prevented the police from presenting a statement from the accused to the court, for fear of police coercion.

In one Supreme Court case, Ram contended that a customs officer is just like a police officer; he has the right to arrest and interrogate a suspect, and he should operate under the same rules. The court answered that, in contrast with the police, the customs officer does not have a 'lock-up'.

That may be true, but the customs officer managed to produce a signed statement virtually all of the time. Customs officers often arrested smugglers on one day, and the signed confessions appeared a day or so later, by which time the smuggler had a crop of fresh bruises. Even so, the record does show some successful appeals under the Sea Customs Act, in one of which, *Manharlal Bhogilal Shah* in 1971, Jaisinghani actually represented the client along with Ram.

Some of India's laws are real antiques, such as this charming one under which a client of Ram's was arrested: The Tamil Nadu Prevention of Dangerous Activities of Bootleggers, Drug-Offenders, Forest-Offenders, Goondas, Immoral Traffic Offenders and Slum Grabbers Act, 1982.

India has always strictly limited the importation of gold, and many smugglers made their entire fortunes importing it. In 1962, India passed the Gold Control Act, barring private citizens from owning pure gold and only allowing licensed dealers to deal in pure gold or coins. None of that diminished India's insatiable appetite for gold. With millions of dowries and bridal gifts each year, India is a huge gold market, possibly the largest in the world. Indian divorce laws vary according to religion, but few give divorced women very much. Indian mothers teach their daughters that gold is their only security.

After 1962, smuggling soared and with it a massive black market. India was rife with schemes to convert black money to white. It seemed that everyone knew how the rich spent their black money, and where to get the best exchange rates. In 1971 the official rate was about Rs 7 to the dollar. The black money rate could be as high as Rs 15 to the dollar if you knew the right person. The streets were filled with touts who accosted tourists with the refrain, 'Change money? Good rate.' My husband went off once with a man on the street to meet the big boss, to get a better rate. There they laughed and chatted while the boss showed my husband how they hustled nervous tourists on the street with scams like handing them rolls of newspaper wrapped in rupees. I waited in a panic for my husband to come back, fully believing he had been kidnapped.

The Jethmalani family remembers the *Choraria* case because one of the accused smugglers had his teeth replaced with gold teeth—purportedly so he could no longer be identified by a certain witness. They also remember that Ram took the family to stay in the Taj Mahal Hotel in Delhi while he argued one case. In all, the Choraria family was prosecuted multiple times from 1960 on under the Sea Customs Act, none with a great result from their point of view. In *Laxmipat Choraria vs. State of Maharashtra, 1964*,[2] the court opinion tells a story that could have come from a novel. A Chinese intermediary approached Sophia Wong, a Chinese air hostess from Hong Kong, asking her to carry a suitcase of gold and semi-precious stones from Hong Kong to a certain person in Calcutta. Unfortunately for him, Sophia Wong was engaged to a police sub-inspector, and she went straight to the Hong Kong police to give them a signed statement revealing the plot. As the Supreme Court wrote, now the trap was laid. The Chinese intermediary met her to demonstrate the use of a special suitcase that was cleverly designed to hide the gold. According to a signal prearranged with the police, Miss Wong slammed the door of the room. The police were hiding right in the house, and they sprang out to arrest the intermediary. Calcutta police investigations revealed highly incriminating evidence against Global Agencies, which was owned by the Choraria brothers. Hong Kong police found and photographed more evidence against the intermediary in Hong Kong. Bombay police found additional evidence at the Bombay address of B.L. Choraria and Co. To complicate matters, discrepancies and inconsistencies began to appear in Miss Wong's story.

Miss Wong was arraigned as an accused. Now Ram and his co-counsel argued that her evidence no longer was admissible. The court did not buy it, since the customs officer never put her up for trial.

Ram next argued that photocopies submitted by the Hong Kong police were copies of illegally detained documents, thus inadmissible in evidence. The prosecution refuted that argument, and the court ruled against Ram's client.

Ram argued to the Supreme Court 'that Ethyl Wong (sic) could not be examined as a witness because (a) no oath could be administered to her as she was an accused person . . . and (b) it was the duty of the prosecution and/or the Magistrate to have tried Ethyl Wong (sic) jointly with the appellants'. Ram continued 'the Magistrate should have promptly put her in the dock because of her incriminating answers'. The court ruled Choraria guilty.

Just incidentally, Mr Choraria's family also stayed at the Taj. One day his wife took off her diamond solitaires, wrapped them in tissue paper, and left it on a counter. The maid assumed it was waste paper, and she flushed it down the toilet. Both the Jethmalani and the Choraria family waited in suspense for two days until the hotel authorities reported that the diamonds had come out in the hotel sewage.

The Supreme Court ruled against the Choraria brothers and their accomplices of course, because they were guilty as a mouse in a wedge of cheese. What was interesting, besides the gold teeth, was how relentlessly Ram approached the defence of these smugglers, how he approached the evidence, and how he challenged the competency of the chief witness. Ram systematically picks away at apparently open and shut cases, whittles down apparently solid evidence, and bears down on how the evidence was gathered, by whom, whether it was obtained legally, and whether the arresting officer deliberately altered the evidence. Ram may personally investigate the scene of an event to see if it passes muster.

Many people have asked how Ram approaches a case. The answer lies in the details. He has often argued that detaining authorities were unreasonably slow to turn over copies of documents, statements, or other materials, or that a detenu was not furnished documents in his own language. Perhaps he will chide the court that the detenu had not been allowed his legal right to examine witnesses. In one case he objected that the detaining authority knew that a previous detenu had been released for the same offence.

Ram has often argued that the maximum total amount of time for which a detenu can be held is fixed, so time served on a previous order of detention should be taken into account, making his client eligible for bail. When authorities prolong proceedings beyond statutory timelines, Ram contends that it vitiates the detention. One detenu had retracted a previous statement, but the information was withheld from the authorities; Ram caught it. Every departure from legal procedure or from the rules of evidence, no matter how small, is an opening to get his client off, or at least out on bail.

Ram questions whether a witness was indicted, as with Miss Wong. He looks at how a confession was obtained and whether documents were secure from tampering. As in the *Choraria* case, he questions whether photocopies were altered, why they were submitted instead of originals, and whether a handwriting expert had authenticated a letter.

Ram does not just focus on the credibility of the witness or inconsistencies in the story, he also asks whether an explanation is plausible, often providing an astute psychological analysis of what a person normally would or would not do under comparable circumstances. For instance, he might ask whether a witness had altered her testimony in fear of self-incrimination or repercussions. He thinks creatively, and he exploits every mistake the authorities make.

Even a signed confession is no barrier to a successful appeal when Ram uses his arts of rhetoric, cross-examination, and sly innuendo. There is no secret to his techniques, beyond their cleverness, clarity, and originality.

Above all, he has an encyclopaedic knowledge of the law, which never fails to impress clients. Even judges are in awe. More than one star-struck young lawyer has reported hearing a judge ask Ram to give him the exact language of a statute.

When criticized for defending smugglers, Ram teaches his students that 'The great milestones of the law have not been laid in cases of respectable people, but with people who are disreputable.'

The case of a Sindhi lover catapulted Ram's name into the press. In 1959, an affair developed between Sylvia, the wife of a decorated Parsi naval officer, Commander Kawas Nanavati, and a 34-year-old Sindhi playboy, Prem Ahuja. As Ram tells the story, Prem was carrying on at the same time with two other women, an army wife and an air force wife. Sylvia was 'a fantastic beauty', and the susceptible Prem fell for her. When Nanavati found out about the affair, he went to confront Prem at his house. Prem was clad in nothing but a towel. Whatever transpired would become a subject of cross-examination in court, but at the conclusion, Nanavati shot him. He then went promptly to the police station to turn himself in. Ram quotes a Supreme Court justice, 'Nanavati was an honest man until he met his lawyers.'

Ram did not represent either side. He had no right of audience nor did the court officially recognize his presence in the courtroom. He did have what is called a 'watching brief' from Prem's sister, Mamie Ahuja, who knew him by his reputation. Ram's role was 'to protect the interests of the deceased', and to assist C.M. Trivedi, the public prosecutor in the trial court. Later his job was to assist Y.V. Chandrachud, the public pleader in the High Court. This is the same Chandrachud who later became the Chief Justice of India, and to whom Ram wrote during the Emergency, chiding him for his decision in the habeas corpus case.

Ram was seen in the courtroom, recognized, and watched closely by the press, especially the *Blitz*, a newspaper started in 1941 by a Parsi editor, Rustom Karanjia. Not surprisingly, the *Blitz* strongly supported the Parsi Commander Nanavati in its lurid weekly articles from December 2, 1961 to January 13, 1962. The press was fascinated by the story of Ram the puppeteer pulling the strings. Everyone in Bombay bought the *Blitz*, and they all read about Ram, the Sindhi lawyer behind the scenes. Ram calls this 'the most important milestone of my career'.

The case started at the Greater Bombay Sessions Court. Ram prepped Trivedi carefully before the trial, but to his shock, in his opening statement Trivedi pulled back, suggested that it was not a murder but culpable homicide with sudden provocation, which had a maximum penalty of 10 years, as contrasted with premeditated murder, which is punishable by death or life imprisonment. Observers believed that bribes had exchanged hands.

Ram wanted out of the case, but a repentant Trivedi crawled back to him for help. Now Trivedi followed the line of cross-examination that Ram had prepared for him. Notably, he asked the surgeon on the stand why Prem would start the alleged fight without his glasses on and how the two protagonists could have gotten into such a scuffle that the gun could go off accidentally while a towel remained wrapped around Prem's waist, undisturbed. In the newspapers, Ram was credited with developing the theatrical cross-examination.

Public sympathy, whipped up by the *Blitz*, was on the side of Nanavati, the brave naval officer, the wronged husband, a handsome figure in court, resplendent in full uniform and decorations. Rumour had it that one female juror winked at him. Another story was that Parsi girls wrote messages to jurors in lipstick. He was acquitted eight to one. Even the judge thought the verdict was perverse and that the jury had shown bias. The judge himself referred the case to the High Court.

Ram had crafted the arguments that enabled the judge to send the case up to the High Court. Now the High Court had to agree that the verdict was perverse, and in this case the High Court itself questioned how it could void a jury verdict. Using Ram's arguments, the government, represented by Y.V. Chandrachud, explained that the lower court judge had given misleading instructions to the jury and hence it was not necessary to show perversity. The argument was that a judge can defer from a jury verdict and send a case to a High Court only if a jury verdict was perverse, but the test of perversity only applies to a jury verdict if the jury was properly charged. As to the charge in this case, however, Ram identified eight instances of misdirection, and these arguments were presented very ably by Chandrachud.

The High Court held Nanavati guilty. The Supreme Court dismissed the appeal and upheld the verdict of life imprisonment.

This case inspired two books,[3] and a movie.[4] It also was fictionalized in *Midnight's Children*, by Salman Rushdie

The history of jury trials in India was quite limited at it was confined to a handful of cities in the country and that, too, in serious criminal cases only. As a result of this case, however, legislation was passed ensuring that there were no more jury trials in India.

After serving several years in prison, Nanavati still had strong supporters, and Ram became involved again. Bhai Pratap, an old Sindhi freedom fighter from the time of Independence, now a wealthy businessman, was in prison for alleged smuggling. Thanks to his political connections and the efforts of one Sindhi leader who wanted him released, his record was re-examined. The conclusion was that the prosecution had made a mistake, and he was innocent. The government hoped to pardon Pratap and Nanavati together, but they needed the Sindhi community to agree. It helped that Pratap also was a friend of Ram's.

An attorney, Rajni Patel, a friend of Krishna Menon, walked into Ram's Bombay apartment one day with the beauteous Sylvia to tell him the circumstances and to say that two Parsi secretaries in the government wanted to pardon Nanavati. To do so though, they needed a letter of assent from Prem's sister, Mamie Ahuja. They asked Ram to convince her to accept the pardon. Ram went to Mamie and she agreed. After it all, Kawas Nanavati and Sylvia reconciled and moved to Canada.

The first high-profile case that Ram and Sri Jaisinghani did together was of another lover, a sadhu who seduced and abducted 29-year-old Indira Nagpal. Indira was the daughter-in-law of a wealthy, pious family who owned a building that housed a temple on the ground floor. A long-haired 22-year-old sadhu used to hold regular religious meetings in the temple, attracting the notice of the daughter-in-law, as well as numerous other women and even men, all of whom apparently found him fascinating. One night the sadhu came up to Indira's sixth-floor room and seduced her. After that, Indira disappeared, and the family reported a missing person to the Azad Police Station. Normally this would not impress the police, since Bombay has many missing persons, but fortunately, one of the family's drivers volunteered that he had seen Indira go into a car driven by the sadhu.

The police and Sri waited all night at the sadhu's house, and they arrested him as soon as he appeared. On first questioning, the sadhu denied any knowledge of Indira's whereabouts. After 'extreme third degree' he remembered more and he led them to her. She was staying with an elderly woman, the sadhu's accomplice, in Ghatkopar, and she pretended to be in a trance, not even recognizing her husband or father-in-law, and not aware of where she was. On the way to the police station, Sri told her to continue her act[5] and to tell the police that she did not know what she was doing in that house. An accomplished liar and actress, according to Sri, she recited her story perfectly.

The case went to court with the charge of abduction. Sri and Ram were appointed public prosecutors. One important witness was a newspaper editor from Pune, who testified that the sadhu had claimed to have supernatural powers—he could drive from Bombay to Pune in three minutes. Another was a man who testified that his 70-year-old mother was so taken by the sadhu that she insisted he give the sadhu Rs one lakh. The sadhu clearly was a con man who seduced for sex or money. The sadhu now feigned a breakdown, and court had to be adjourned.

In a side conversation during the court procedures, the sadhu revealed to his lawyers that he had taken Indira to the Apollo Hotel next to the Regal Cinema many times, and she had performed a certain service on him, believing she was servicing a 'Shiva lingum'. This is the organ that belongs to Lord Shiva. When the police went to the hotel, the frightened staff confirmed that they had given the sadhu a room numerous times without registering it on the hotel registry. The Nagpal family drivers also confirmed they had driven Indira there and waited for her many times. The sadhu crowed that this proved it was an elopement, not an abduction.

The magistrate first agreed to let the sadhu out on Rs 20,000 bail for the rest of the trial, but when he asked him where he lived, the sadhu answered vaguely, 'I live in the Himalayas.' Bail was cancelled.

The sessions court sentenced the sadhu to 18 months on top of the 18 months he had already served. An appeal to the High Court failed, as did an appeal to the Supreme Court when the husband and father-in-law threatened to commit suicide out of shame if the Supreme Court ruled it was a case of elopement.

The case went on for two years. Crowds of observers had to be turned away from the courtroom every day. People came from as far as 800 kilometres away to watch. The press revelled in the daily details. In the end, his honour salvaged by the opinion that it was an abduction, Indira's husband took her back.

Ram was learning early lessons about the power of the press. Over the years Ram has been accused repeatedly of being a publicity hound, of playing to the press. In these two high-profile cases, Ram simply did his job, and the press used Ram's cases to build their circulation. In time, Ram learned to use the press. From the point of view of an editor or a television interviewer, Ram is a superb interviewee, never dull, always unpredictable, often outrageous. For this reason, the press courts him. According to a Harvard Law School study,[6] by 2009–12, Ram's name was referenced in 499 articles in the *Times of India*, only topped by Prashant Bhushan, at 638 times, and G.E. Vahanvati, at 568 times. In one interview that went viral, Ram engaged in a shouting match with a belligerent interviewer. After the taping, a grinning Ram invited him to stay and share a drink.

Srichand (Sri) Bhagwandas Jaisinghani began to work with Ram almost by chance. Sri remembers meeting a man at a bus stop, who asked him if he knew Ram. Sri did not, although he had seen him in court. The man asked if Sri could read his legal papers, call Ram, and brief him. He called Ram that night. They talked for a while, amazed that they came from the same community in Pakistan but had never worked together. Shortly after that, Sri became Ram's junior.

Sri's father actually had decided not to leave Karachi. One day when Sri was a little boy playing in the street, a Muslim boy tapped him on the shoulder, saying he had heard they were planning to stay. When Sri said that was true, the boy asked to be taken to his father. The boy's family had come from Bombay, and they needed a place to accommodate their extended family, which always squabbled over use of the kitchen and bathroom. Sri's family had a flat with two bathrooms, two toilets, and two kitchens.[7]

The boy's father offered to switch homes with them. They had a home on an attractive beach in Bombay, in Shivaji Park. Sri had an uncle who was a Bombay lawyer; he visited the beach house, verified what the boy had said, and assisted them in obtaining two letters from the authorities declaring them to be the caretakers of the place. With this assurance, the two families traded houses, and Sri's family moved to a house on a beach.

Sri's association with Ram lasted 38 years, until Ram became Law Minister and Sri became Additional Solicitor General of India. In some ways it was an odd couple. Both are Sindhis, both methodical advocates, but that is where the similarities end. Ram is flamboyant, profligate, with an eye for women. Sri might have a bit of a roving eye, but he has stayed out of trouble, watches his money like a hawk, and every rupee he ever made is well invested. One night his family and the Jethmalani family went to dinner at the Taj, with Ram expecting to pay. Instead, Sri surprised everyone by taking out a big wad of rupees. The family asked why he had so much money in his pocket. He said it was in case he had a heart attack and might have to go to the hospital. They expressed the hope that paying the bill would not give him that heart attack.

When Sri Jaisinghani was appointed Additional Solicitor General, he would stay at Ram's house. One night he fell asleep calmly in his usual bed on the guest room floor, only to wake up in the middle of the night to loud snoring next to him on the bed. He jumped up in fright, first thinking there was a wild animal in the room. When he realized it was a man, he ran out of the room, waking up the whole house. It turns out it was a cousin of Deepchand, Ram's seldom sober personal aide. The man, in search of a place to stay, had sneaked into the guest room and crawled into Sri's bed.

Another day a fellow politician, later to become chief minister, imbibed too much at dinner. They tucked him off to sleep in Sri's bed, and Sri slept elsewhere. In the morning, Sri got up and started dressing for his court appearance, but his shoes were missing. The politician had gotten up early in the morning, still tipsy, put on Sri's shoes, and gone home. Someone had to drive to his home and back to fetch Sri's shoes before he went to court.

10

The 1960s and China

The events of the 1960s set the stage for the momentous 1970s in India. The headlines were dramatic. The Chinese swarmed across the Indian border in 1962, leading to the Sino-Indian war. Nehru, crushed by China's perfidy, died on May 27, 1964. Lal Bahadur Shastri succeeded him. The monsoons failed again, causing a devastating famine. The Sikhs became restive in the Punjab. Tensions over Kashmir led to the second Kashmir war and an Indo-Pakistan war. Accusations of Chinese meddling in the affairs of Kashmir were rampant. The Tashkent Agreement created a ceasefire line in Kashmir, but Shastri died that night. Indira Gandhi came to power and began a stream of anti-American rhetoric. Sanjay Gandhi began his rise to power with a licence to set up a Maruti automobile factory.

At home, life went on, and so did death. Ram's mother died unexpectedly on a trip to Calcutta at age 60. The younger Jethmalanis proceeded with their education. Shobha went to Jai Hind College, then Grant Medical College. After finishing at St Xavier's, Rani took an LLB and an LLM at the Government Law College. Maya went to Bombay University, then to K.E.M. College in Bombay to study physiotherapy. In their separate apartments in Bombay, Ratna and Durga kept themselves busy with friends and family; Ratna lunched and played cards with friends at her clubs, and they doted on their respective sons.

Ram began his engagement with politics. He raged in speeches and in writing about the Chinese invasion and the pusillanimous Indian reaction. He wrote, 'Nehru had forgotten Indian geography under the Bandung Panchsheel hypnosis.' This referred to a 1955 conference of 29 non-aligned African and Asian states that was held in Bandung, Indonesia, where China played a conciliatory role which Ram believed was frankly deceptive. In 1954, Nehru signed a treaty with China, outlining five principles of coexistence, most of which were honoured in the breach.[1]

The border conflict began when India discovered Chinese maps depicting large portions of India as part of China. It deteriorated further when the Chinese built a high mountain road through this region, of which, according to Ram, Nehru feigned ignorance. It only became worse when the Dalai Lama fled Tibet for India. In October 1962[2] China invaded, capturing about 36,000 square miles in the Arunachal Pradesh region and about 14,500 in the Aksai Chin. Nehru had never believed that China would invade, and he was strongly criticized for his incredulity. Ram has insisted for years that this invasion and subsequent treaties violated India's honour.

'Non-alignment proved to be a lofty pretension that became a cruel joke. No non-aligned country came to our help in 1962. The only two countries that promptly provided substantial aid were the US and Israel, both well outside the non-aligned fold.' Ram curtly says that this was while India still refused to grant Israel an embassy.

Ram calls this Chinese invasion a national humiliation. Ram has written: 'Chou En Lai continued to make a fool of the gullible Jawaharlal Nehru. After swallowing Tibet, he assured India that there was no territorial dispute or controversy between India and China. Nehru continued to rely on the McMahon Line, knowing full well that China had not accepted it, except during the settlement with Burma. In April 1954, surprisingly, Nehru formally recognized Tibet as a part of China without even insisting on the Chinese acceptance of the McMahon Line as the border between India and China.'[3]

Ram goes on to say: 'Pandit Nehru saw no way to resolve it and he died a broken man, his credulity badly exposed; his Chinese policy and Panchsheel in shambles and his life's work ending in smoke.'

Later when Ram was in Parliament, he would rail against India's inaction, saying they had passed a resolution vowing that India will not rest until every inch of the territory has been regained but India has done nothing to regain its lost territory. Ram wrote: 'Smt. Indira Gandhi without any quid pro quo restored full diplomatic relations at the Ambassadorial level with China in 1976.' There have been high-level diplomatic visits between China and India, even treaties of economic cooperation, but these have only reinforced the status quo. Ram even claimed that Rajiv Gandhi made a deal with the Chinese that allowed them to invade.

Ram quotes Chinese military scholars who turn the tables on the standard Indian history, claiming that India had first taken 90,000 square miles by force, then another 33,000 square miles from China. He warns that China accuses India of illegally occupying Sikkim, and China continues to supply military equipment to Pakistan. With the greatest contempt, he has written: 'Our leaders then kept lying to the nation that everything was well with India–China relations.'[4]

The border with China is adjacent to Kashmir, and many in India believe that China has meddled in this long-running border dispute, especially during the second Kashmir war that ended with the Tashkent declaration of 1966. Years later when he established the Ram Jethmalani Kashmir Committee, Ram made it a personal commitment to mediate the Kashmir dispute, with all its international ramifications.

11

The Bar and the Bar Council

Parliament created the Bar Council of India in 1961. Ram was elected a member of the Maharashtra Bar Council in 1964, and he was elected chairman of the Bar Council of India in 1970. This put him at the very top of India's Bar, no small achievement.

In an article[1] about what they call India's 'Grand Advocates', Marc Galanter and Nick Robinson describe 'a stratum of legal superstars in India . . . who are very much in demand and widely known'. They identify them as 'the most visible and renowned legal professionals' in the country. The authors know of no parallels to this position outside of Southeast Asia.

They explain that these grand advocates have a 'nuanced knowledge of both formal and informal judicial procedure' and reputations that are hard to share with juniors. They usually practise by themselves, assisted by a few clerks and juniors. They spend most of their time in the Supreme Court or High Court, typically meeting their clients at home or on their veranda—a perfect description of Ram's practice.

Critically, 'the performance of the lawyer is overwhelmingly oral rather than written', which means the lawyer focuses on 'courtroom advocacy rather than advising, negotiating or planning'. Their arguments may not be fully developed or even appear in the written submissions, and judges will cite them in their opinions. Since they only appear after being briefed by lawyers who act in the capacity of solicitors, these advocates function as barristers, paid by the appearance, not by the hour. Generally they appear in a wide range of legal areas, few specializing in only one area of law. Ram's practice has been at the pinnacle of this tradition.

Still, why did the Bar Council of India elect Ram? After all, his many critics loudly accused him of defending smugglers, of keeping scoundrels out of jail, of being willing to do anything for publicity, and of setting aside his scruples for cash. On the other hand, since Ram began teaching at the Government Law College in 1953, he had acquired a reputation as a captivating law teacher, a formidable practitioner of the great art of cross-examination, and a peerless expert in the field of evidence.

One of Ram's former juniors is Bhagwan Keswani, who worked with Ram from 1966 to 1982. As far as he is concerned, Ram is the finest lawyer in the world:[2] 'Not the finest in India as some people say, but the finest in the world. He is a genius. No one can come close to him in intellect and knowledge of the law. Such a man is born once in 500 years. And he has a tremendous sense of humour.'

Fali Nariman, one of the senior leaders of the Bar in India, says that Ram's reading is wide-ranging, and it goes far beyond the requirements of the case. He is always well prepared and so persuasive that the court has to accept what he says. That is Ram on the law. As far as politics is concerned, 'He is a stand-alone chap. He doesn't give a damn' for what others think. That difference in his behaviour—in the courtroom versus in politics—has been remarkable throughout his life.

In his autobiography,[3] Nariman describes Ram as 'a lawyer cast in a heroic mould (you could wake him up in the dead of night and he would be ready for legal battle) . . .'

Keswani says Ram's legal abilities encompass criminal law, civil, and even labour law. He says Ram had never taken a labour law case until the lovely Maria Bijlani came along. Because he so appreciated her charms, he agreed to represent her when she was fired. Now, he had to start learning the relevant labour law. 'In the labour court he got a thumping judgement in her favour,' says Keswani. 'The judge said he had been on the bench for many years, but he never heard anyone give a better explanation of the labour law. Her boss literally collapsed in the witness box. The judge asked him, "Do you have a bladder problem? You are leaving the witness box every few minutes to go to the bathroom."'

That story is reminiscent of my husband's story of Ram when asked to inaugurate a conference on patent law, hardly his field. To my husband's amazement, Ram launched into one of the finest discussions of patent law he had ever heard. He would not have been surprised if the unsuspecting audience was left thinking that patent law was Ram's area of expertise.

One of Ram's clients was a man who was charged for smuggling in whisky under the Bombay Prohibition Act. Caught with 12 bottles of Scotch, he was arrested and sent to jail for six months. Knowing that Ram was fond of his Scotch, he asked to have Ram take his appeal. It was such an open and shut case that people asked why, but he insisted. Judge Patel, a complete teetotaler himself, looked down from the bench and asked Ram if he could come up with even one point in his client's favour. If he could, he would let him off. Ram simply said, 'He supplies the best Scotch. Not just any Scotch. The best.' The judge let him out on bail.

One lawyer used to boast that he could put as many lawyers as he wanted in his pocket. He would say he could put this one in his pocket, also that one, yet another one. Ram finally said, 'With so many lawyers in your jacket, you have more law in your pockets than you have in your head.'

Ram had a certain amount of sympathy for a man accused of rape. One day he was defending an engineer charged with statutory rape. No matter how busy Ram was, he never would miss a hearing on this case. When asked why, he answered, 'Basically the man is a lover. I can't let him down.' 'But,' the questioner insisted, 'he is charged with rape!' 'Yes,' Ram answered. 'But, that is the culmination of love.'

One of Ram's former juniors claims that once Ram's clerk gave him the wrong brief, and he still argued the case brilliantly by memory. Ram says that the story is apocryphal, but the story would illustrate how he wins so many cases. He knows the facts, and he knows the law. First, he studies a complicated case alone, often getting up at 4 a.m., to be sure he is not disturbed. This is critical. He reads the written documents slowly and with great concentration. He compiles thick books of notes, not a common thing for an Indian lawyer to do. He reads far beyond what is necessary for the case itself. Later in the office, on a hunch, he may send his junior to research an arcane point of law that has little likelihood of coming up during the trial. He focuses laser-like on what is important, and he quickly disposes of weaker arguments. When briefed about a case he often will close his eyes and seem to be asleep, then he will open them with a sharply worded query. He cross-examines the client at length.

Keswani, Jaisinghani, and Mani Cooper all worked in his chambers for years, and all say he works prodigiously, harder than anyone else they have ever met. The article describing India's 'Grand Advocates'[4] warns that many of these lawyers consider their preparation to be adequate even when it is not: 'When you reach 85% you are good to go . . . It's not worth putting in the extra 15%, which takes 50% of the time. It's not that the lawyers couldn't perform, but there is no incentive.' Here is where Ram differs completely from that description. Ram gives 125 per cent.

The author remembers once seeing Ram appear by invitation to argue a moot court case. Normally, established lawyers, with no actual client in a moot court, put very little into their arguments. Ram arrived with two juniors and a thick packet of briefing papers that had numerous yellow markers affixed to key pages.

Having never seen Ram in court when he was young, this author did see him at one month short of his 90th birthday, and we will try to give some insight into his unique style. Now shorter and slenderer than he used to be, with thinning white hair, he walks confidently into court, with his juniors trailing behind, through a gauntlet of well-wishers. People stop him at every step to shake his hand or bend to touch his feet. As soon as he is spotted entering a courtroom, people throng in, filling the seats, then the aisles, then the spaces between the rows of seats. Flanked by his briefing lawyers, when he rises to argue, he starts out with a slow, clear recitation of the facts, engages in some jocular repartee with the judge, perhaps tells a joke. As he presents his case, he argues in a slow cadence, using his powerful voice as a bass instrument. He articulates one phrase at a time, allowing the judge to make notes, but, most important, letting the phrases drop with full effect before he goes on. Only when he gets into the substance of his argument does he pick up the pace, and when he comes to the peroration, his voice thunders.

He prefaces his recitation of applicable statutes by telling the court that he spends as much time teaching law students as he does practising law, and then he delivers a law lecture to the court. After all, to Ram everyone seems like a student today. Judges in India have to retire at age 65. Every sitting judge in India today is at least 25 years younger than Ram.

Clerks come in and out of the courtroom thumping down two-foot-high stacks of documents and files, and junior lawyers scurry about shoving exhibits and statute books in front of him. His instructing lawyers prompt him with dates and names; Ram is unruffled. The courtroom door opens, admitting a blast of noise from the corridor outside, and Ram continues calmly. The judge treats him with great deference. At the time of the lunch break the judge says that they will reconvene after lunch, to which Ram says that he no longer eats lunch. The judge smiles and says he knows that, but at his age, he still needs lunch. Ram stands upright, only holding the podium lightly, for two hours before lunch and two hours after, and he will stand all morning too if the case starts before noon—at an age of almost 90. He never drinks water during his appearance, saying he is a Sindhi camel. If Ram tells the court he wants to stop at 4 p.m., the judge says, 'Mr Jethmalani, if you wish to break at 4 p.m., we will break at 4 p.m.' When he walks out, people touch his feet.

Appearing for the defence, as he usually does, on the day this author observed, he began by describing the standard of evidence that the prosecution needs to prove, creating an impression that nobody could comply with such a strict standard. He also reminded the judge that if he cannot accept any one element of the prosecution's case, the whole case must fall—if one card is false, the whole deck must be discarded. He described the requirements to be fulfilled in filing a charge, and he warned that if the prosecution does not comply with every jot and tittle of the standard for each charge, the charge must be thrown out.

He goes back to the statute to read the language, point by point. Then he reads the definition of critical words, word by word. Are they alleging forgery? Then what is the definition of forgery? Does it apply to this case? Lawyers concede that this is what all lawyers do, but the trick is in the way he does it. With his rhythmic phrasing, his perfectly timed pregnant pauses, and his resonant voice, he conveys an authority beyond just his words. At Ram's age, his words now sound as though they come from an oracle, until he cracks a bawdy joke.

The next week after we saw him in court, Ram walked in with the wrong glasses on, and he argued his case from memory. Similarly, his brother-in-law recalls that Ram spoke several times to his Rotary Club while only referring to a card in his palm that had key words on it, able to stay focused on his main argument and come back to it even after digressing into stories and jokes. Now Ram, at almost 90, is still able to repeat the performance, even in court.

When asked how he argues a case, Ram says that normally he knows from the first day what his defence will be, based upon weak links he has spotted in the prosecution's case. He asks himself to imagine how vulnerable the crucial witness is. 'How much can I demolish him?' He focuses on what is important. 'I accept part of the prosecution if I can.'

Of course, some of what Ram does could be classified under tricks of the trade. Fali Nariman says that lawyers routinely have their ruses, like holding a paper and occasionally consulting it during a cross-examination. All the while the nervous witness assumes that the paper has a damaging statement of his, and he feels constrained to tell the truth lest he get caught contradicting what is on the paper, which of course, is blank.

Yet Ram says he has learned from American lawyers to 'do something of an investigation. Hardly any lawyer does that in

India.' In one example, the accused killer led the police to a well in which he allegedly had thrown a murder weapon. Police divers found a knife at the bottom of the well. Ram went to the scene and found a guard. He asked him if he was always posted there and whether he had seen the events of a certain date. The guard answered both questions in the affirmative. He asked next whether the guard remembered seeing the police come to that location at any other time or if he had seen the police for the first time on the day that the accused was supposed to have led them there. The guard answered yes, he had seen them come two days before. Ram asked how they had come, and he answered, 'In a jeep, sir.'

On further questioning, the guard told Ram that the police had arrived and gone over to the well. 'He almost told me that they did something.' Ram went to the police station, requested the log books for every police jeep, and he found that a jeep had gone to the scene two days before. When he put on the case in court, it was perfectly obvious that the police had planted the evidence.

Ram teaches his law students to ask: What are the possible answers? For each answer, what are the questions?

One story about Ram concerned a Mr Dutt, the general manager of Metal Box Limited. He had been accused of molesting an attractive female employee, and the case was tried in an industrial court. During Ram's cross-examination, Mr Dutt said, 'Sir, I believe that I know what your next question will be.' Ram answered, 'Yes, and I know what your answer is going to be.'

The judge peered down from the bench and asked Mr Dutt to write on a piece of paper what he thought Ram's next question would be. He also requested Ram to write on another piece of paper what Mr Dutt's answer would be to his next question. The judge put the two pieces of paper in his pocket, and he directed Ram to continue his cross-examination. In fact, Ram's next question was as Mr Dutt had predicted, and Mr Dutt's answer was what Ram had written down.[5]

Arun Jaitley has been quoted in an article as saying that he is a master of cross-examination, 'almost prophetic'.[6]

In the same article, Ram says, 'Cross-examination is a dying art.

You have to be able to sniff out the guilt. Lawyers forget the most important thing is not law, it is facts.' An outstanding reporter, Shoma Chaudhury, says she watched Ram work on a case for 10–12 hours one day, surrounded by lawyers who all needed to get up at one time or another for breaks or food, but, completely focused, Ram only drank one glass of water.

Ram says it is a matter of basic logic to project what circumstances will occur if what the witness says is true. Police once claimed to have seen a terrorist get out of a car and hand a bag of money to terrorists in another car. The police also described their location while they observed this action. Ram knew it was at least a half hour walk from the scene because he had gone there to inspect both locations himself before the trial.

In cross-examination he asked, 'Did you see them pass the bag of money while you were pursuing them or were you parked at the time?' The police answered that they had been sitting in the police car, parked at the location they identified. Ram asked, 'Then how did you see them?'

All he had to do now was describe to the court the distance between the parked police car and the site of the alleged hand-off. 'All possible routes of escape have to be blocked first.'

Ram cautions about accepting assumptions. He quotes the story of the American lawyer Clarence Darrow in his famous 'monkey case' on validity of evolution. The other lawyer pointed grandly to show that the snake was punished by being made to slither on his stomach forever after, until Darrow asked, 'But sir, do you know how the serpent walked before he was cursed?'

Ram gives as an example his cross-examination of two Parsi brothers from the movie industry, Cavas and Eruch Irani. Ram's client was Seth Vishnandas,[7] a Bombay moneylender. Vishnandas would loan money, take a post-dated cheque for the sum plus interest and deposit the cheque on the due date. The Iranis had married two sisters, and the third sister was married to the Bombay commissioner of police. They borrowed Rs 3 lakh from Vishnandas, but when he presented their cheque to the bank, he found insufficient funds.

The Iranis had a scheme that could have come from the movies. They wrote a letter to the commissioner of police alleging that while on a trip to the Central Bank a bag containing their chequebook had disappeared, and they sent their accountant to Vishnandas with a cheque representing the original debt plus added interest. That cheque turned out to have a false signature. Later that day the accountant returned, apologizing because that cheque was not covered. He asked Vishnandas not to deposit it, but to wait for his boss to come over and sign a new, blank cheque. As the wait stretched into the afternoon, Vishnandas agreed to hold the blank cheque for the time being.

The police came to Vishnandas a few days later, requesting him to write a letter affirming he was paid in full. They also searched the premises, found the two cheques the accountant had left, and said they came from the chequebook that supposedly had been stolen.

Ram believed that even though the banker charged 24 per cent interest, which was not illegal, he was not guilty of this crime. In court, Ram questioned the Irani brothers about why they had not reported the supposedly stolen bag right away at the nearest police station. After that he asked, 'Why did the concerned brother write a letter to the commissioner? Also, the bag must have contained other valuable documents and, perhaps, even money. Why was the chequebook the only item mentioned as lost? If a person visited the Central Bank, it must have been to transact some business. What was that business?'

The police had taken Vishnandas's ledger book, so Ram hired an accountant to reconstruct details of the Irani loan from their business chequebook. Obtaining a search warrant, he seized the Irani business account books, and the entries correctly showed the amount due, to be paid back in instalments. So far, there had been one payment of Rs 65,000. On questioning, the Iranis claimed they had borrowed the money from a total of 13 different bankers. Ram suspected that they had obtained the money through a crooked hawala racket that he knew about in Bombay. In this racket, dishonest bankers did not actually lend the money; they just wrote out a receipt that affirmed 'I have received the amount', which they gave to the supposed debtor. The objective is to create a false record. Ram sent a friend to obtain hundis (receipts) from the 13 bankers, in the name of the judge! At his request, the court now issued a summons to each. Most absconded, but those who remained had to admit to giving fraudulent receipts.

Ram found another payment of Rs 1 lakh, and he cross-examined the Iranis to find out where this money came from. They claimed it had been lent to them by their gatekeeper. Ram asked the gatekeeper where he had gotten the money from. His father. When? When he died. When? 25 years ago. Ram asked where he had kept the money. In his house. What was the house like? A hut. Why not put it in a bank? The gatekeeper said he did not trust banks. Did he have a guard at his house? No. The case was over. The only remaining issue was settled by a handwriting expert who testified that the forged cheque would never have been cashed at a bank. Ram won, but as might be expected, 'the judge was not at all amused about the hundis made out in his name'. When Ram tried a similar stunt with another judge, that judge almost threw him in jail.

The 1967 elections brought George Fernandes into Ram's sights. According to the Supreme Court: 'The corrupt practice alleged was that the first respondent made some speeches, and that the first respondent and two others, with the consent and for the benefit of the first respondent, made false statements, casting aspersions on the character and conduct of the second respondent, and that those and other false statements were published as news items in the daily newspaper *Maratha*.' The real accusation was that Mr Fernandes had said his opponent, Mr Patil, was against Muslims and Christians.

Ram argued in the Bombay High Court 'that there was knowledge and acquiescence on the part of Mr Fernandes and as there was no repudiation of what the *Maratha* published against Mr Patil, Mr Fernandes must be held responsible'. Ram always says that if an accused does not publicly deny the accusation or sue the accuser, he must be guilty.

At one point in the trial, Ram asked Fernandes whether he

remembered a certain girl, Shoshana Padhye, who had been spotted handing out his handbills at a rally, this being an unfair election practice. Since the girl was one who he preferred not to discuss in public for his own reasons, Fernandes was temporarily flummoxed until he could recover his composure and answer.

Meanwhile, both Ram and his daughter Rani became involved in a matter of international importance, the relationship between India and Israel.

12

Israel

Ram may very well be the most pro-Israel political figure in Asia. Others have surely been active on behalf of Israel, but Ram's involvement is heartfelt to an extraordinary degree.

Ram has written: 'The partition of India has been very much akin to the Jewish Diaspora 2000 years ago. The Sindhi Hindu has almost been relegated to the position of the wandering Jew. One must however recognize a major difference between the two situations. Though the Sindhi Hindu has encountered hostility, he has not suffered the indignity and persecution of the Jews. But the emotional trauma of a people left without a land to call their own is just about the same.'[1]

Ram has always explained that the Sindhis are the Jews of India. For years my husband and I did not understand why, but now we do. The reader will too, after reading this chapter.

Ram always was highly critical of India's official posture toward Israel, especially during the Indira Gandhi government. Even though India extended formal recognition to Israel in 1950, Israel was not allowed to open an embassy in Delhi until 1992. The Jewish agency did establish an immigration office in Bombay, and that was converted to a trade office, later a consulate, not an embassy. Ram has long said that when the Chinese invaded India in 1962, the Israelis sent arms, but that Nehru denied it, claiming India just bought arms from a company in Israel.

This attitude did reflect India's participation in the Non-

Aligned Movement, a group of nations in support of anti-colonial movements in the Arab world, but most observers would say that the main reason for the Congress party's hostility to Israel was their need to court Muslim votes. Most important, once India took the Kashmir dispute to the UN, Nehru needed the support of Arab states, and he feared jeopardizing these chances by permitting Israel to have a diplomatic representation in India.[2]

India had several Jewish population centres: the Cochin Jews in southern India, the Bene Israel in the north, and the Baghdadi Jews in Surat, Bombay, and Calcutta. By the 1950s and 1960s, 25,000 to 30,000 Indian Jews may have migrated to Israel, including 20,000 Bene Israel from Maharashtra, 3500 from Cochin (now Kochi), and most of the Jews who had come to India from Baghdad. In Israel, they formed colourful communities which carried on many traditions of Indian food and clothing into the next generation, though these traditions are now disappearing.[3]

It is of some interest that when Ram moved his family to Byculla, it was the centre of Jewish life in Bombay, with the Magan David Synagogue, the Sir Jacob Sassoon Free High School, a building in front of the Sassoon United Fabrics Shop called the Sassoon Trusts, where the Judean Club held forth, and several cafés patronized by Jews chatting and playing backgammon.[4] Later when Ram and Ratna moved next door to the Regal Cinema, they moved right into the centre of the South Bombay Jewish community, which was served by the Keneseth Eliyahoo Synagogue. Nearby was the magnificent David Sassoon Library and Reading Room, located on the Esplanade, across from the Jehangir Art Gallery. Ram may not even have realized it, but he was exposed to Jewish culture, Jewish learning, and Jewish philanthropic efforts both in Byculla and in South Bombay. One wonders how important that may have been in impressing him with the values of the community.

In 1973, Ram took us to the island of the 'white Jews of Cochin', where a few remained after the others had migrated to Israel. In front of a shop we saw a nameplate with the name Cohen, and we asked the man in the window if he was Mr Cohen. He said yes. We asked if he owned the shop. He said no, but he would be happy to call Mr Cohen.

Ram told us the story that when the Jews arrived at the Malabar Coast they went to the maharaja to ask for his protection. He listened with interest to their enthusiastic description of their God and said graciously, 'Your God sounds very powerful. Please, put him up on this shelf with our Gods.' The first Jewish dwellings huddled up against the palace wall, and the Jews lived there in perfect peace. Problems came only when the Portuguese brought the Inquisition to Goa, but that, too, passed.

Ram has always said that his house was the de facto Israeli embassy in India, and this was all because of Ya'akov Morris, the head of the Israeli consulate in Bombay from 1969 to 1971. Ya'akov is also the father of the eminent Israeli historian Benny Morris. Benny Morris remembers very little of his father's time in India, but he does remember how lovely Rani looked in her saris. The Morris family and the Jethmalani family became very close.

We are doubly fortunate that Ya'akov Morris left an unpublished biography and that his son has allowed this author to share portions of it. Morris described his trip to Cochin, four years before our visit:

> In Cochin were the remnants of a Jewish community that traced its origins back to the 11th or 12th Centuries. It had been given a Royal Charter by the local Rajah of the area which permitted them to settle and create a colony of their own named 'Jewtown'. About seventy families remained, the majority having migrated to Israel with the original copper plates on which the Charter had been inscribed. The street of the colony outside the Rajah's palace had wrought iron Shields of David amid the bare protecting ground floor windows. Most of the houses were deserted. The clock tower of the palace had two faces, one toward the courtyard with ordinary numerals, the second, facing Jewtown, with Hebrew lettering.[5]

In those days, India not only confined the consul's accreditation to the state of Maharashtra, but it also prohibited him from travelling out of the state, especially not to Delhi, in his official capacity.[6] Officially, he could only travel within India as a foreign national, but for practical purposes, there was no real restriction until the early

1970s. Until then the consul could easily access India's Minister of External Affairs or even the Prime Minister. Israel and India even exchanged trade and scientific visits over the years, and diplomats made both official and unofficial contacts in both countries until the 1970s. When Indira Gandhi came to power, all that changed. It became difficult for Israelis to even obtain an Indian passport.

Before he began his trip to India, Ya'akov Morris knew he would need more than luck. Sixteen years after Nehru promised full and unrestricted diplomatic relations, Israel still had just a consulate in Bombay. He says that Israel had tried to improve its diplomatic relations with India, and it even supported India at the UN in its disputes with Pakistan. Unfortunately, Krishna Menon represented India at the UN, and the Israelis found him to be anti-Semitic, anti-Zionist, and anti-Israel. They believed his attitude dated back to when he ran for the British Parliament in a heavily Jewish neighbourhood, and lost.

Morris ascribes the hostile Indian attitude towards Israel to their dependence on the USSR to shield them against Communist China's 'territorial claims to large stretches of northern India', a fear of Arab states siding with Pakistan at the UN, a hope that Arab states would become trade partners, and the government's need of the Muslim vote.

He says that Nehru and Gandhi also came from Britain bearing 'the anti-Zionist legacy of the British Fabians who had looked upon Arab nationalism as a revolutionary and anti-imperialism phenomenon, and upon the Zionist movement as a British "tool"'. This is why the Non-Aligned Movement mattered.

Morris was appointed for his communications skills. He says that since the Indian government was unfriendly he was urged to go straight to the people, but, in an obvious contradiction, he was warned to use extreme caution. As it was, he 'achieved so much success in the information and propaganda field that my situation became diplomatically tenuous. Arab and Communist diplomats constantly pressurized Indira Gandhi to make me persona non grata . . . towards the end of my posting in Bombay, I had begun to wonder if I would first be expelled or recalled. By this time the Ministry in Jerusalem was nearing the conclusion that a low-profile diplomat would be better in Bombay than a high-powered information man.'

So what did Ya'akov Morris do that so shook up Delhi?

The Morris family enjoyed living in a lovely furnished apartment overlooking the sea, although this was India. Just across the street were huge Parsi mansions, and below their apartment window squatted a small colony of villagers in cardboard or tin shacks, washing and defecating among the rocks.

The consulate was on Peddar Road, in an old apartment house owned by a rajah. Soon Morris received a visit from a Miss Sophy Kelley, principal of the Hill Grange High School and College. She was general secretary of the Bombay Indo-Israel Friendship Association, an organization founded after the 1967 war in Israel at the behest of 30 Members of Parliament.[7] She invited him to a reception in his honour, but the group was unimpressive. The attendees were undistinguished, and they only represented one political party.

At another event he met Khushwant Singh,[8] and the two bonded immediately. Singh had started a Friendship Society in Delhi, and among the members were prominent persons of the press who were unable to work with the Friendship Association in Bombay. Morris met with the Bombay Association to suggest some changes, but they complained immediately to Jerusalem that he was interfering with their work. Ram was the vice president of the association, and, disregarding their complaints, he invited Morris to come over to talk about starting out fresh with new branches.

Morris met Ram at his house, and he also met Rani, describing her as 'a very attractive young woman who had graduated in law and was lecturing, as an Assistant Professor, at Bombay University. She volunteered to help her father get new branches started, beginning with young professionals of her own peer group whom she could call together in Bombay . . . Out of that meeting a second Bombay Friendship group came into being which decided to request affiliation with the Bombay Association. Ram agreed to be its Chairman; Rani its ad hoc convener.'

The Bombay Association rejected the idea. Thus was born a new organization, the Indo-Israel Friendship Federation, with Ram the chair and Rani the convener. Maya remembers attending meetings at Ram's home at Advent.

The Morris family hosted rounds of buffets and dinners, and they met the cream of Bombay's political, professional, and cultural society. They found the Governor of Maharashtra, a Muslim, and his wife to be gracious, charming, and fascinated with biblical archaeology. The mayor of Bombay invited them to the wedding of his son, a 'mammoth outdoor affair with almost 2,000 guests. The groom entered the proceedings, according to custom, on an adorned elephant. Sadie [Morris] had never seen such an array of magnificent fabrics as those of the saris worn by the guests.'

Ya'akov Morris and his family immersed themselves in a Bombay that was pulsating with culture. Members of the wealthy Parsi community had built a concert hall where they could enjoy western music played by world-class celebrities. The Morrises often attended Indian dance performances and marathon premiers of new Indian films, of which 'few were of less than four hours long, crowded with local celebrities, film stars, and theatre people'.

They loved the Bombay Flea Market. 'It was said that if the wheel discs of your car were stolen in the morning, you would find them on sale at the Flea Market the same afternoon.'

The Jethmalanis' second Friendship group in Bombay:

[C]onsisted primarily of people from the world of culture and the arts. Khushwant Singh, who spent most of his time in Bombay, was one of its most active members . . . Another celebrity of the group, a prominent ceramicist, was Indira Gandhi's niece, Mrs Pandit . . . Neila de Souza, the group's secretary, wrote intriguing children's stories.

One evening Khushwant brought along to the group an astrologer who wrote a weekly column in his journal. He did astounding things at the meeting. Although he had never met any of the people present, nor did he know anything of their lives, he singled persons out and told them things about their past that were so accurate he left everyone gasping. Some of things were most intimate, such as past operations, the exact nature of the illness, and where. Others were about people's love lives, family happenings, difficulties professionally. It was an astounding performance. After it, I ceased to be disbelieving and cynical about the claims of astrology. I had even less reason not long afterwards to doubt the extra-sensory and the esoteric, for I witnessed a Yogi stop his heart beat and pulse for more than two minutes, under medical supervision, and restart them at will. The Indian Minister of Health told me during this demonstration that he knew of a Yogi who had been buried in a coffin under heaps of earth for 36 hours and had emerged alive.

Ram, too, believes in these occult arts, and he often consults his stars before a consequential decision. When a numerologist told him that the numerical value of the name Shoba was inauspicious, he added an 'h', making it Shobha, just as he had changed his father's name. When he decided to run for president, many years later, an astrologer told him to wear several rings on his fingers, each with a specific gemstone, in order to give him luck. He has worn them ever since.

On Sundays, Morris and his family would drive to Juhu Beach, 'where friends had a seaside villa, and where all manner of wonders were to behold, ranging from snake-charmers, with their cobras swaying out of wicker baskets, to magicians, jugglers and dancers of every kind. Out of modesty, women would go into the sea there fully clothed. Coconut milk from the stalls was the favorite refreshment.'

The trouble began when the Israeli Foreign Ministry sent Morris a Syrian map of India that Israeli soldiers found in the Golan Heights. The map showed two-thirds of India shaded in and marked as Muslim territory. The legend said, 'And in every country shall arise an Islamic State.' Morris, ever the publicist, called a press conference. The map became front-page news. The Syrian ambassador called his own press conference, and 'All hell broke loose.'

Morris wrote, 'The Soviet Embassy, as well as the Arab representatives had been circulating propaganda of the most vituperative kind against Israel.' The *Blitz* 'carried as a headline, "Kick Israel Consul Out".'

Morris was called on the carpet by the Director General of India. Dressed down for misdeeds as the representative of a friendly country, Morris produced a sheaf of vicious anti-Israel propaganda from the Indian press, and he asked if this was the way a friendly country would behave. The meeting ended up in a draw.

Meanwhile Morris describes the 'mushrooming of new branches of the Indo-Israel Friendship Federation'. The association put out a bulletin, by subscription only. It was read widely, and the consulate received so many letters from people volunteering to join the Israeli armed forces that it had to develop a polite form letter to decline them.

'We were therefore particularly happy when news came from Kashmir that a group of young Muslim intellectuals had established a Kashmir–Israel Friendship Association, and, with the letter, an invitation to the Consul to visit it.' The Morris family first took a vacation in the gorgeous state of Kashmir and its capital, Srinagar. There were 'about 60 young people at the meeting, most of them university graduates and unemployed'. Afterwards, the Morris family went to enjoy the rivers and mountains.

Upon their return, the Director General confronted Morris with a Pakistani newspaper trumpeting 'that the Israel Consul in Bombay had been to Kashmir and, in connivance with the Indian Government, had made the visit in order to study the possibilities of setting up military border villages such as those Israel had established "for aggression against its Arab neighbors".' Morris managed to laugh it off.

A reporter set a trap at a press conference when Morris visited an Indo-Israel Friendship group in the Punjab. He read out an extract from a book entitled *India's China War*, which documented Israel's assistance to India. Since he knew it was true and he was unaware that it was classified information, Morris did not deny the story, giving all the main papers a scoop. Morris wrote, 'The Israeli Consul had "confirmed" the story, apparently by not denying it. A blistering cable came from Jerusalem soon after my return to

Bombay saying "Don't you know the arms incident is classified—deny it." The fact is that no one had thought of briefing me about it before my departure from Jerusalem and I wondered, after the information had been leaked by the Indian Ministry and after it had been published in a book, whether it still was classified.'

'The Indo-Israel Friendship Federation had by now become so widespread, having reached a total of more than 90 branches throughout the country that the Jethmalanis reached the conclusion that it needed a central headquarters to maintain contact with them and sponsor nationwide projects.' This meant they needed to establish a house in Delhi.

> The Jethmalani's found one, a fully detached, two-storey modern villa, which Ram rented in his own name. Rani volunteered to act as the National Secretary and get the offices going, a sacrifice that impressed me greatly as it meant she was prepared not only to take leave from the Jethmalani law firm in Bombay of which she was one of the partners, but also from her family home there. The budget of the office and house was provided by donations from wealthy Jewish families in Calcutta and elsewhere as well as from some branches whose members were able to afford the extra levy . . . One thing that the Assoc. took pride in was that it did not take any money from the Israeli Consulate.
>
> The Head of the Asian Division of my Foreign Ministry was my next visitor soon afterwards. He met a large number of the Federation's Friendship groups, including those of a new student wing in New Delhi already comprising thousands from many of the Capital's colleges. We travelled to a number of branches in various towns and he was greatly impressed with the Federation's growth and its New Delhi Centre.

To celebrate Israel's Independence Day, Morris planned two huge functions. The official party at a Bombay hotel hosted 'officials of Maharashtra and Bombay, members of political parties and cultural organizations, and people from various Friendship groups, including the original Bombay Association whose leaders were

astonished at the caliber of those present from the Federation . . .
The second party was at the Federation house in New Delhi, and
it caused quite a stir in the Capital. Almost the entire diplomatic
corps, led by Ambassador Keating of the U.S., attended.'

In their enthusiasm, Morris and the Jethmalanis were pushing
their luck, and there were to be consequences. 'The various branches
of the Friendship Federation had concluded that the time had come
to hold a national conference. The Bombay Association . . . was also
preparing for a National Conference.' This would not be pretty.
The Bombay Association's complaints reached Jerusalem and the
Prime Minister while the Indian government was still smarting
from the big bash on Independence Day.

Jerusalem instructed Morris to cancel the Federation conference,
even if they did have 91 branches across the country. 'Before long,
I received a private letter . . . informing me that the Ministry had
decided to appoint a successor to me as Consul in Bombay . . . The
Jethmalani's were infuriated. "If Israel," they said, "looks with as
little importance at our activities on its behalf, why should we be
more concerned than they?" In a matter of months, the Centre
was closed down.'

The Jethmalani family recovered from the affront to their friends
with their love for Israel still intact. They met the Morris family
once again when they came to India after being posted to New
York, and the Morrises confided in them how much better things
had been in Bombay.

Ram has written and spoken about Israel in every possible venue
ever since, especially in Parliament, never missing an opportunity
to express his admiration for the accomplishments of the Jewish
people. He says his sympathy is based on his revulsion for Hitler's
atrocities, but many Hindu refugees from Muslim Pakistan also
have a tradition of solidarity with Israel.

Ram's first trip to Israel was memorable—remembered by the
family as a speech to the Knesset! Ya'akov Morris had arranged it,
telling them that Ram was the greatest friend of Israel in India, and
Ram soon received an invitation to come and speak. In actuality it
was a speech to a Knesset committee. In it, he told the members,

'Though you claim to be a Jewish state and India claims to be a Hindu state, in fact we both are secular democracies and we must join hands and fight the enemies of secular democracy together.' All the same, Rani was thrilled, and she talked for years about how her father addressed the Knesset during the time of Golda Meir.

Ram's sister Maya and Rani went to Israel in 1971 with a group of 15 college students, on a trip organized and arranged by Ya'akov Morris's wife, Sadie. Maya remembers that they attended a student conference on the challenges of development at Hebrew University in Jerusalem. They stayed on campus, met wonderful people, and had a great time. After the conference they travelled all over Israel, from north to south and east to west, for 10 days. The country in which Maya dreamed of looking for a job after college was Israel.

The ramifications of Ram's high regard for Israel have reached far. Ram was the one who talked Mother Teresa into writing a letter of recommendation to the Nobel Prize Committee, urging them to award the Nobel Prize to Elie Wiesel.

Ram has written, 'No one, however hard-hearted, can deny that the story of the Jews between the Diaspora and the creation of Israel is a tragic epic of world history. Add to this moving account the horrendous story of Hitler's Final Solution, the gas chambers, the killing fields of Nazi Germany and the murder in cold blood of six million of this unfortunate race . . . Yet the PLO's charter, in its Arabic version, even today proclaims as its prime political objective "to wipe Israel off the world's map". This so, despite Arafat having generously declared that he will, after all, allow Israel to exist, but on his own terms.'[9]

The first Israeli ambassador to India was Ephraim Dubek, who served from 1992 to 1995. He remembers Ram as a good friend.[10] As soon as he arrived in India, Ram had greeted him warmly and offered him any assistance he might need. He says that Ram definitely put pressure on Prime Minister Rao to establish an Israeli embassy in India, although nobody could say that the embassy was established because of any one person. In fact, Rao told him, 'If I was not an old man I would not have taken the risk to change our relationship with Israel.'

Dubek says that Ram also defended Israeli citizens who needed his legal help. Dubek says, 'Israel was Ram's baby. He had a lot of babies, but Israel certainly was one of them.'

In 2004, Ram was an invited speaker at the Jerusalem Summit, a Judeo-Christian think tank founded in 2003 with a pro-Israel agenda.[11] Until recently, it still held yearly conferences to which it invited pro-Israel speakers from around the world.

Ram is proud to say that when Mark Sofer retired as Israeli ambassador in 2012, he singled out Ram for an accolade at his retirement party in Mumbai. There he called Ram 'one of the stalwarts who pushed incessantly for the establishment of relations between Israel and India'. Sofer also remembers warmly how devoted to that cause Ram and his family were.[12]

In 2010, President Harper of Canada called an Anti-Semitism World Conference in Ottawa,[13] inviting speakers from all over the world to participate in the sessions, most of which were closed to the public. Irwin Cotler, a Canadian Member of Parliament, wrote an article saying that by far the best speech was made by an Indian. That speaker was Ram. He ended his speech with the following:

How you managed to preserve your racial and cultural integrity, guarded with jealous love your oldest rituals and traditions, patiently and resolutely awaited the day of your deliverance, have evoked the admiration and earned you the sympathy and reverence of all the good people of the world. But the wicked, wallowing in religious fanaticism, have been burning with malice and hatred. Like the pusillanimous child that tries to crush the insect it dare not look at they spawned a Hitler who planned your genocide but ended in his own shameful suicide.

After more than 2000 years of wandering your friends have watched with profound admiration your restoration to your ancient but never forgotten home. What Drama could rival the grandeur of your sufferings and the justice and glory of its end. 'What fiction could match the romance of this reality', wrote Will Durant, the historian.

The Christian world has owned its wrongs of the past and is

even busy making recompense and providing protection against those who are still encompassing your extinction as a free people. Those who genuinely follow the pristine and peaceful Islam of the Prophet are not amongst them. It is the followers of a counterfeit version known as the Wahabbi faith generated from Saudi Arabia in the late 18th Century by an evil non-human being—Ibn Wahabb. The core of that faith is that all Mushrikun have forfeited their right to live. According to his teaching the Mushrikun include Jews, Christians, Hindus, all non believers and Muslim Shias too. Jihad against these and their destruction is a religious duty.

Osama Bin Laden is a Wahabbi and his quarrel with the Saudi regime is that it is not sufficiently Wahabbi.

All the secular democracies of the world—and Canada is one of them—must come together and master this menace to all civilization—not merely Israel or the Jews of the world.

No Government that spawns terrorists and terrorist organizations is fit to be a member of the United Nations. To prevent such Governments from acquiring access to nuclear weapons is a categorical imperative of our survival.

Diplomacy, dialogue and delay are only steps towards suicide. Prevention is much easier than cure. Anti-Semitism has to be wiped out before it destroys its victims and their friends too. That means practically the whole civilized world.

You need foolproof insurance against the trauma of another holocaust. I know you have powerful friends. But friends can become fickle depending on the sacrifice friendship needs and the kaleidoscope of conflicting interests when the critical time arrives.

Your faith in your Prophets, your will, your valour, your nukes and nuclear submarines are more reliable policies of insurance.

May God Bless you.

13

1970s

The Green Revolution may have made headlines in India in the 1970s, but in fact, it was a time of drought, famine, an oil crisis, inflation, shortages, corruption, nationalization, strikes, dictatorship, detention without trial, and press censorship. At the end, it was a time of new political beginnings, of committees to investigate the past regime, and a backlash that would bring Indira Gandhi back.

By now the Jethmalani children were all adults. Rani lived in Delhi and received a blood transfusion that would ruin her life. Shobha married and moved to Detroit in 1971 to do a residency in paediatrics. Janak went to McGill University in Canada and started a career in America. Maya left for Canada in 1973, and Pratap Gidvani pursued her until they married. Sarla Wadhwa and her husband returned to Bombay in 1979 when the Shah of Iran fell.

With strong urging from Rani, Mahesh went to Oxford to study philosophy, politics, and economics (PPE) at the venerable Merton College, dating back to the 13th century, one of the oldest colleges in Oxford. One of his Dons was Vijay Joshi, a friend of Rani's, Manmohan Singh's economic adviser in 1991 when, with Singh as the Finance Minister, Prime Minister Rao embarked upon an ambitious programme to abolish the Licence Raj. When Mahesh applied, it was Joshi who the college called to verify that Mahesh could speak good English. In his days at Merton, Mahesh was known as a good student with a quick mind, also as the 'King of the Quad'. That related, among other things, to the girlfriend who stayed in his room for a period of time, even though girls were not permitted to stay overnight in the quad. An acorn does not fall far from the tree.

After Oxford, Mahesh did the standard conversion course for the study of law, and then he went to London to qualify as a barrister with a coveted six-month pupilage under John Wilmer QC of Grey's Inn. In all, it took five years. When he returned to begin his practice in Bombay, at first he was adamant about wanting to make his mark independent of his famous father. Once he became established, the two of them often worked on major cases together, a formidable father–son tag team. In recent years they also have been allied in many of their political activities, Mahesh the cool strategist, Ram the impulsive one who follows his inner promptings.

By now Ram's cases came to reflect his lively interest in politics, but occasionally we find a vignette that was less serious. In 1978, the Delhi High Court wrote: 'The learned counsel for the appellants, Mr Ram Jethmalani and Mr R.K. Garg in particular, urged that the identification of persons not previously known to the witnesses was the weakest type of evidence. Mr Ram Jethmalani drew our attention to certain observations made by Glanville Williams in the course of his Hamlyn Lectures on The Proof of Guilt (3rd Ed., pages 106–124). Glanville Williams refers to various writers on the subject including some well-known trials.' The court then quotes one example that Ram cited to them—the case of a man named Adolf Bech, who was wrongly identified in a line-up by no fewer than 12 women. Remarkably, these not only were women he had defrauded, but they also included ones to whom he had made love.

Ram's interest in politics started when he campaigned for Krishna Menon in a 1967 by-election, apparently unaware of how leftist Menon's beliefs were, but charmed by his use of language. Once when asked why he did not self-identify as a Communist, Menon responded by asking if a prostitute labels herself a prostitute. Menon also once said, 'The Englishman's search for condiments was the reason for India's loss of independence.'

Ram first wanted to run for Parliament on the Congress party ticket in Mumbai, but, since he was not a member of the party, they turned him down. After he was elected chairman of the Bar Council of India, he decided in February 1971 to run for Parliament from the territory of Ulhasnagar and Kalyan, the heart of the Sindhi community, as an independent. He counted on support from the Bharatiya Jan Sangh party (BJS), a predecessor of the Bharatiya Janata Party (BJP), and he planned to call in chits from the Shiv Sena party for past legal work. That was to avoid running as a candidate of the Shiv Sena party, a controversial Hindu nationalist party.

What Ram had not realized was that his territory extended up through the Western Ghats almost to Pune. Shobha campaigned with him, also going out alone, canvassing in a jeep up and down the mountains to Pune, in the dark, five to six hours from Bombay, less than a year after her marriage. As a newly-wed, Suresh was less than thrilled about her absences.

After spending large sums of his own money for the campaign, Ram was amazed when he lost. He had assumed he would get a good show of votes from the large Sindhi populations in Ulhasnagar and in the towns on the outskirts of Pune. To his surprise, there was a lot more to Maharashtra than Sindhis.

There also was more to life than politics and law. Ram and Ratna continued their active social life, and Ram continued his own personal social life. One day Ratna found out that Ram was going to London and that a certain lady friend would be on the same plane. Not one to miss a beat, Ratna called the airline office and booked herself a flight on the same plane. Ram had to change his friend's ticket, if he did not want turbulence inside as well as outside of the plane.

There were laughs in the office too. One visiting German lady kept talking about how much she loved hot curry. Bhagwan Keswani, Ram's junior, made the hottest curry in town, so Ram told him to make some for her. She was thrilled. Sweat pouring down her face during the dinner, she could not stop raving about the curry. The next morning she woke up and had to run to the bathroom, then again, and once again. 'It was like fire,' she reported, 'just like fire.'

'Now you know,' Ram said brightly, 'why Indians use water instead of toilet paper.'

Not funny at all were India's preventative detention laws. In 1971, Parliament passed the Maintenance of Internal Security Act (MISA), and this gave the government an important tool for terrorizing political opponents. The original purpose of MISA may have been to catch smugglers, but the government soon took advantage of it through a series of amendments, slamming its enemies into jail without trial, seizing property without a warrant, and wire-tapping in the name of threats to national security. Ram's experience with refining the rules of evidence in his smuggler cases would prove to be invaluable when he defended the victims of these abuses.

In the early 1970s, citizens who were subjected to preventative detention had little recourse but the courts; later even that door would close. One rather stunning case[1] shows the extent to which detenus had lost their civil liberties.

Ram's client was first detained under MISA of 1974, subsequently under the Conservation of Foreign Exchange and Prevention of Smuggling Activities Act, 1974. The poor man did not even try to appeal his detention. He appealed to the Bombay High Court because his jailers would not allow him to get money from his family to buy extra food, clothing, bedding, toothpaste, toothbrush, or toilet soap. They would not let him see his family, write, or receive letters regularly and they would not let him play chess or cards, claiming they were just following the dictates of MISA. Ram and his co-counsel brought this tale of mistreatment to the court, and Judge Shah Vimadalal wrote a scathing judgement which said in part:

> The first of the impugned provisions . . . prohibits a detenu from supplementing his diet even at his own expense.
>
> The next Clause . . . a detenu is allowed to receive from his own relatives or friends every month not more than Rs. 30 which can be utilised by him on such objects and in such manner as might be permissible under the Rules. There is absolutely no reason, and no relation with the objects of the Act, which

should compel the imposition of such a drastic restriction . . . The learned Government Pleader contended that if more money is made available to a detenu in jail, it might be 'misused' thereby, according to us, faintly suggesting that it might be used for the purpose of bribing the jail staff . . .

The next . . . is Clause 15 under which a detenu is ordinarily permitted to write two letters per week and to receive four letters per week which, of course, are subject to being censored . . .

The [next] restriction . . . is, in our opinion, purely punitive in nature. There is no reason whatsoever, and no relation with the objects of the Act, which would demand that a detenu should not be permitted to use normal toilet requisites like tooth-paste, tooth brush, tooth-powder, or toilet soap of his own choice at his own cost.

. . . Clauses 23 and 24, under which a detenu is not permitted to smoke a cigarette or use tobacco of his own choice, or to play any indoor games like cards, chess, draughts, or carom. It passes our comprehension how such prohibitions can have any nexus with the object of the Act or could be considered to be necessary in the interest of jail discipline. There can be no doubt whatsoever that these restrictions have been imposed with a punitive intent and are entirely uncalled for.

The judge held:

1. That a detenu is not a convict, that the power to detain is not a power to punish . . .
2. That the power of preventive detention is qualitatively different from that of punitive detention, that the purposes of preventive detention and of punitive detention are different

Finally he directed that the petitioner should be permitted 'such funds, not exceeding the sum of Rs. 200 per month . . . from any of his relatives or friends, and to purchase or receive from private sources at proper hours food, clothing, bedding, and other necessaries, including toilet requisites, toilet soap, cigarettes and tobacco . . . as well as to meet persons with whom he may desire to communicate at proper times and under proper restrictions'.

The judge's indignation was clear, but this was only one case heard by a compassionate judge and defended by two excellent lawyers. Many more detentions lay ahead.

Ram's former juniors recall a double murder case, in which a Mr Parvati, in a fit of jealousy, murdered the mother and child of a former friend and associate who had upstaged him in educational and professional achievements, and who had married a more attractive wife. Ascribing the man's success to his mother, Mr Parvati went to the house of his rival, drank a cup of tea with the mother and stabbed her 39 times. Seeing that a five-year-old had witnessed the murder, he stabbed the child 18 times. A servant spotted him, but turned away to run off quickly. As the case began, Mr Parvati came to see Keswani with a bag, which he did not accept, and then went to the house of another lawyer in the chamber, Mani Cooper, with the bag, but she refused to open her door.

Ram's defence was insanity, not helped by Mr Parvati's repeated pedantic corrections of his written statement—interrupting to correct a comma here and a period there. Ram reminded the court that immediately after the murder, Mr Parvati was seen calmly sitting on a swing at home, eating an orange. Ram blamed his action on an amphetamine psychosis. The sessions court ruled that he was not a lunatic, but he was not exactly sane either.

Mr Parvati received a death sentence, later reduced to life, but he was a perfect prisoner, earning the admiration of his jailers for good conduct. An amateur astrologer, he claimed he knew he would be released early. Indeed, he was let out of jail after seven and a half years.

Starting in 1971, the government began passing a series of amendments to the Indian Constitution, unprecedented in their number and reach. Ram excoriated them both in private and in public. As chairman of the Bar Council of India, he wrote a 'Chairman's Page' in the *Journal of the Bar Council of India*, a perfect forum for addressing the entire legal profession. In this journal, he called the last week of April 1973, 'the darkest in the history of this free nation' because of the following legal case:

Though it was not one of Ram's cases, *Keshavanand Bharati vs. the State of Kerala & Anr.* on April 24, 1973 had repercussions that went far beyond 1973. This was one of the few times in history that the Supreme Court sat as a special bench of 13 judges, and it held hearings for over 76 days. The question was whether Parliament had the right to pass amendments to the Constitution even if they altered the fundamental rights it guaranteed. At issue were two particularly alarming amendments. The 24th Amendment, passed in November 1971, which gave Parliament the right to alter, change, or repeal fundamental rights that are in the Constitution. The other was the 25th Amendment, passed on April 20, 1972, which restricted property rights, allowing the government to take over private property and to decide how much to pay.

On April 24, 1973, the Supreme Court, by a vote of seven to six, ruled that Parliament could not change fundamental rights in the Constitution. Justice Khanna received the credit for swinging the other judges to the majority.

Chief Judge Sikri was scheduled to retire the next day, and Indira Gandhi disregarded all precedent by passing over the next three judges who were in line because they had voted against the government. Instead, she reached down to appoint Justice A.N. Ray as the next Chief Justice, because Ray had supported the government. The three judges resigned in protest, leaving the court even more pro-government.

Ram and the entire legal profession loudly proclaimed that by passing over the judges who voted against her, she had encaged and emasculated the judiciary. The government answered that it wanted judges who were 'forward looking' and who understood 'the winds of change'. As chairman of the Bar Council, Ram protested this attack on the independence of the court in many meetings, and he wrote a strongly worded article in the Bar journal, saying, 'It is tragic enough to have a government which pretends to abolish poverty but which has not the faintest notion of how to produce wealth. It is still more tragic to have a court which wants the people to be free but which has no clear notion of what is necessary to secure political freedom.'[2]

The Bar Council of India, the Supreme Court Bar Association, and local bar associations observed May 3, 1976 as a Bar Solidarity Day, on which lawyers abstained from work. The Supreme Court Bar association passed two resolutions against 'the attack on democracy, rule of law and independence of Judiciary'.

Nani Palkhivala was the lawyer who had argued so successfully against the government on this case. His unique contribution in this case was the doctrine that Parliament had no authority to amend 'the basic structure of the Constitution'.[3]

In November 1975, there was a call to reconsider this judgement, and Nani Palkhivala appeared before a bench of five judges to argue that there was no need to call another bench of 13 judges for reconsideration. His arguments were so eloquent that the court dissolved the bench and dropped the idea. Justice Khanna wrote: 'The height of eloquence to which Palkhivala rose on that day had seldom been equalled and never surpassed in the history of the Supreme Court.'

Born and educated in Bombay, Nani Palkhivala was only four years Ram's senior, but he already was established when Ram arrived from Karachi. Ram recognized him as a prodigy, and he was the one lawyer in India with whom Ram was proud to be compared.

When Palkhivala died, Ram wrote a fond tribute to him,[4] calling him a brilliant lawyer and economist. Quoting from Herbert Spencer in favour of capitalism and against socialism, Ram could have been describing himself. Both also shared a broad interest in religion and philosophy, and both shared an interest in creating a National Judicial Commission to reform the process for judicial selection.

One sentence that Ram wrote to describe Palkhivala also describes him: 'He regularly took a header into deep water and the splash usually shocked envious spectators.'

Ram always says that Palkhivala was his lawyer. When the district magistrate of Palghat in Kerala issued a warrant for Ram's arrest, his friend Khatu Cooper was the first lawyer to be notified. Soli Sorabjee met him at the Bombay airport. Sorabjee and Ram's son Mahesh drafted the petition for a stay of the warrant, and the

Cooper home was where the petition was typed, the typewriters clattering all night. Since Ram was the chairman of the Bar Council, 300 hundred lawyers signed the petition.

It was Palkhivala who led over 300 lawyers to the house of the judge to deliver the petition, and the judge granted a crucial interim stay of the order of detention, giving Ram breathing time.

To request a permanent injunction, Khatu Cooper represented Ram, but Judge Aggarwal of the Bombay High Court dissolved the interim injunction, saying 'to leave Ram Jethmalani at large was endangering the safety and security of the country'. In the end, it was Khatu Cooper who went to the appeals court to obtain an injunction that gave Ram until June 11 to argue the case that would determine his fate. In Ram's mind though, Nani was his lawyer.

In the middle of all these serious matters, my husband and I innocently planned a sight-seeing trip to India, our second trip. We had enjoyed the first one so much that we returned, with telephone numbers for the families of various friends. Our first call to another friend's family netted a servant who did not speak English. Our second call turned out to go right through to Shobha's father, who said, 'Oh, I will send the car immediately.' And that is how we met Ram.

We had no idea who he was, nor did we know anything of the political situation in India, but we learned fast. We met Ram and Ratna in the Advent apartment, which was decorated in one of its more festive styles. Durga joined us on several occasions. We met a charming lady who seemed to be a special friend of Ram's. Ram took us to parties and to dinner at fancy restaurants. We talked about India and its politics. Ram and Ratna entertained us with a stream of jokes, and they wanted to hear new ones from us, the more risqué the better.

At one party a Sindhi businessman laughed that he was about to take a trip to America and he could not take anyone but his wife and mistress. 'And look at them,' he said. The party had to laugh, because the two of them were almost identical, rotund, smiling, hardly young.

Ram took charge of our travel schedule. In the first city, he instructed us to stay with his clients. These turned out to be rich Marwaris who laughed one evening that their stomachs were too big for them to use an Indian toilet. For our trip to Aurangabad, he sent us to a colleague who turned out to be the dean of the untouchables' law school. He was bright, aggressive, and he needed a keynote speaker for a ceremony the next day to break ground for a new building. My husband the law professor dropped down on him from the heavens. The next day a freshly painted sign advertised the featured speaker, 'Professor Martin J. Adelman, Wayne State University, Eminent Personality.'

Ram saw that Cochin was on our schedule, and he arranged to meet us there, which is when he showed us the white Jews of Cochin. In Delhi, he sent us to have lunch at the Gymkhana Club with the wife of a military attaché. She and her family had lived in Moscow and Paris, and in a Swiss boarding school her daughter had met a friend from Keego Harbor, Michigan. She visited the friend there once, staying in her little summer home by the lake. Now, the mother asked us for help getting her daughter into a Michigan college, because—after living in the great capitals of the world—her daughter wanted to live in Keego Harbor.

Ram sent us to meet the family of Ramnath Goenka, the founder and managing editor of the *Indian Express*. Their compound once had been the British Madras Club, which had a sign in front: 'No dogs or Indians allowed.' When the British left, the Goenkas bought it for their headquarters. Their private home was in the mammoth former clubhouse, all built of white marble, with Chola bronzes mounted on pedestals throughout the main floor.

Ram often comes to Michigan to see Shobha. We have travelled often to India, where we visit Ram, and where my husband has been invited to lecture. Forty years after we first met, it seems like the time to write this biography.

14

The Emergency and Its Aftermath

The Emergency was a decisive event in Ram's life, just as it was a defining event in the history of India. First, the disasters that caused the state of Emergency demand some elaboration. Many books have been written on the subject, but we will rely especially on two accounts written by authors who actually participated in the events they describe.

P.N. Dhar, the former head of Indira Gandhi's secretariat and close adviser, writes that from April 14 to May 21, 1971, the war over East Pakistan created 3.5 million refugees, and by December the number reached 10 million, 'the largest number of refugees ever to cross an international boundary in so short a period'.[1] Inder Malhotra, a personal friend of the Gandhi family,[2] agrees that Indira Gandhi acquitted herself well during this deluge and in the two-week war that gave birth to Bangladesh. Malhotra calls it her finest hour.

Maybe, but it was her reason for proclaiming a state of External Emergency, which she conveniently never lifted. It may even have given her the idea of calling a state of Internal Emergency when she faced her next crisis. Ram would later point out that an Emergency could have been invoked many times in the past, but that in the past, the government was committed to democracy.

In Dhar's account, the chain of events leading to the Emergency started with the 1974 railway strike and a mass movement that Jayaprakash Narayan led that same year. The Indian railway system is the country's largest public sector employer, and it is the backbone of the economy, employing over 1.4 million people in 1974. When several unions went on strike, George Fernandes centralized them into a nationwide strike. His intention was to bring down Indira Gandhi's government by bringing railway transport to a dead stop. Fernandes was a formidable demagogue, but Indira Gandhi's government crushed the strike in 20 days. According to Malhotra, more than 20,000 railway men were arrested under the Maintenance of Internal Security Act (MISA), some of them badly beaten. He calls this episode a dress rehearsal for the strikes to come.

The 1972 drought caused a sharp increase in food prices, and that caused students in Ahmedabad, the capital of Gujarat, to initiate a series of strikes that became increasingly violent. Examinations had to be cancelled, universities closed, the economy disrupted. The students wanted the state assembly to be brought down because of corruption.

Jayaprakash Narayan, a Gandhian socialist and revolutionary, came out of retirement to unite all this anti-government sentiment. Calling for a comprehensive revolution—social, economic, political, and ideological—he recruited farm workers and other labourers to participate in boycotts, work stoppages, and no-tax campaigns. The Communist Naxalites got into the act, with an estimated 500 casualties and 70 deaths, including one government minister.

In the midst of all this disorder, on April 2, Morarji Desai announced a fast unto the death, or until the Gujarat assembly held new elections. The government gave in and called a nationwide election.

On June 12, when the results were counted, Indira Gandhi learned she had lost to a coalition headed by Desai, and the Allahabad High Court handed down a momentous decision. Ruling on an election dispute that had started four years earlier, the court ruled that Indira Gandhi could remain Prime Minister, but it debarred her from elective office for six years. This encouraged Narayan and others to call for a police and army mutiny, to force her resignation. By now, Dhar believed, this deluge of malice had rendered Mrs Gandhi impervious to all charges of corruption, and she came to believe that all attacks on her party were really attacks on her.

Though the most serious charges had been dropped, just leaving charges of minor election fraud, the title of Prashant Bhushan's book was correct, *The Case That Shook India*. What shook India the most was what happened next. After Nani Palkhivala argued her appeal in the Supreme Court, Mrs Gandhi obtained a temporary stay on June 24 that allowed her to attend the Lok Sabha, but she was unable to vote, speak, or draw a salary. Despite all the pressures on her, according to Malhotra, it was her son Sanjay who insisted she not resign, since he had the most to lose in the long run. On the fateful day of June 25, 1975, Mrs Gandhi informed President Ahmed that her government would impose a state of Internal Emergency.

Ram could not have been completely surprised. He had been highly critical of the Nehru government, and he became even more critical of the daughter after she rose to power. He had a long list of grievances. Ever since Chou En Lai annexed Tibet, Ram thought he had made a fool of a gullible Nehru, luring him into complacency until China invaded India in 1962. Ram considered that war a humiliating defeat, compounded by India's passivity and cowardice in the aftermath. Ram believes that Nehru died a broken man, his credibility badly exposed and his non-alignment in a shambles.

Another sin that Ram could never forgive was Nehru's socialism. He believed that the Licence Raj had killed Indian entrepreneurship for decades. He also could not forgive Nehru for his treatment of Israel, and he totally rejected his anti-Americanism.

Ram's strongest indictment was that Nehru had foisted his daughter on the country. Ram wrote that even before she came to power, 'She persuaded her reluctant father to topple the Communist government in Kerala and impose President's Rule.[3] This was the first time since Independence that India had so grossly misused Article 356. Indira had accused the Kerala Communists of complicity with China, outraging her husband Feroze, who died a year later of a heart attack.'

Ram has described Indira Gandhi as a poorly educated woman,

a dropout from Oxford thoroughly unprepared for office. He has also accused her of letting Pakistan Prime Minister Bhutto hoodwink her at Shimla after the 1972 war with Pakistan.[4]

As Prime Minister Indira Gandhi revealed her anti-democratic tendencies, Ram often quoted US Senator Dirksen's parable of the frog. If you put a frog right into boiling water, he will jump out. If you put a frog into cold water and bring it slowly to a boil, he will be boiled before he realizes he needs to jump out. Ram believed that the greatest danger to democracy and to the rule of law would occur when the heat was turned up gradually under the nation's civil rights.

The word 'outspoken' hardly conveys a sense of Ram Jethmalani when he gets fired up. His oratory builds upon itself in volume, the devil take the consequences. His daughter says sometimes she is afraid he will break his hand, the way he pounds it on the table. His face goes from the colour of a summer suntan to red, and his thick eyebrows knit together. In these dire times, Ram was charged up, loaded, and took direct aim at the government. His speeches, writings, and private comments expressed his opinions with crystal clarity, frightening his friends and delighting his enemies.

Soon after June 25, 1975, Parliament passed a string of edicts, acts and constitutional amendments. Parliament suspended Article 14 of the Constitution, which gives the right to request the court to enforce equality before the law; Article 21, which protects life and property; Article 22, which protects against arrest or detention without being informed of the reason; and Article 19, which guarantees the right of a judge to grant a writ of habeas corpus. In January 1976, it suspended the rights of freedom of expression and peaceful assembly.

On August 4, the Lok Sabha passed a bill that enabled Mrs Gandhi to appeal against the Allahabad verdict. August 5 saw MISA broadened. In August, the 38th Amendment was passed, barring the courts from reviewing the President's declaration of an Emergency. On August 10, Parliament enacted a 39th Amendment to specifically negate the Allahabad High Court judgement, and to put the election of the Prime Minister, Speaker of the Lok

Sabha, President, and Vice President beyond judicial scrutiny. Parliament also postponed the March 1976 elections to March 1977. A presidential ordinance imposed censorship of the press on December 8, and on January 28, 1976 the Lok Sabha made government censorship permanent.

Under Ram's chairmanship, the *Journal of the Bar Council of India* published articles with conspicuous gaps where the censor had deleted passages. In Madras, the government tried in every way possible to harass the *Indian Express*, one of the principal opposition papers in the country. They even taxed newsprint, as the Goenkas told us in Madras.

The Goenkas described many ways in which the government tried to shut their newspaper down, and how Ram countered them. The close working relationship that Ram developed with the Goenka family would come back to haunt the Gandhis when the Bofors scandal broke in the 1980s.

After his speech in Kerala, now that a warrant for his arrest was hanging over his head, Ram travelled all over to speak wherever he had an opportunity, like an avenging angel. Defiantly refusing to be shut up, he talked about the abuses of the Emergency, while his family waited, terrified, for the moment when he would be sent to jail. Even his friends were afraid to be caught associating with him or his family. After all, this was a time when thousands of detenus were thrown into jail without trial. The Amnesty International Report of 1975–76 even documented a large number of cases of governmental murder and torture, both in and out of the jails.

Also during that time Ram's house was raided, and so was Khatu Cooper's. At the Cooper house the police seemed intent on making sure the silver was not smuggled. Fortunately, they had sales certificates for everything. According to one story, Ram was playing badminton when the police arrived, and he told them he would join them when he was done. Meanwhile in his house, the police were going on and on looking for Ram's speeches. Ram calmly asked, 'Would you like to hear my speech?' He then proceeded to turn on the tape and sit cool as a cucumber for an hour and a half while the police listened. After that, they left.

Khatu's wife, Mani Cooper, was a young lawyer in Ram's chambers at the time, and both of them were in the midst of defending a Yugoslavian man who had thrown a prostitute out of a balcony window one morning. They both were scheduled to appear in court on that case on the day their houses were raided, so they had to send Sri Jaisinghani. And the Yugoslavian? Ram's defence was that the prostitute was drunk and fell off the balcony. The man went free.

The court decision that would determine whether Ram went to jail was the seminal case of the Emergency, the *Additional District Magistrate vs. Shivakant Shukla* of April 28, 1976,[5] popularly known as the habeas corpus case. It tested whether a political prisoner or anyone else detained in jail under MISA during the Emergency still had the right to appeal this detention by obtaining a writ of habeas corpus.

Up to 140,000 detenus were thrown into India's jails without trial. Nine courts, including the Madhya Pradesh High Court, Allahabad High Court, Karnataka High Court, Delhi High Court, the Nagpur Bench of the Bombay High Court and the Rajasthan High Court, had ruled that detenus had the right to appear before a magistrate to seek a release through a writ of habeas corpus. The government appealed all 43 of these cases, including those of four Members of Parliament, to the Supreme Court.

Chief Justice A.N. Ray, the 'compliant' judge who Indira Gandhi chose in 1973 after the *Keshavananda Bharati* (Fundamental Rights) case, headed a bench of five. Incidentally, the *Keshavananda Bharati* case was tried before a bench of 13, and for a case of this importance, it is interesting to see that they chose a bench no bigger than the required minimum of five. Mrs Gandhi had bypassed three judges to appoint Justice Ray to the court; the joke in Delhi was that he 'called her every day for his instructions', and, as Chief Justice, he was the one who selected the size of the bench and the judges. Of course, bench selection cannot be challenged in India without a risk of being jailed for contempt, so this question could never come up. This bench included Justices A.N. Ray, M.H. Beg, Y.V. Chandrachud, P.N. Bhagwati, and H.R. Khanna.

A stellar team of 12 advocates argued the case, including the eminent Shanti Bhushan, Ram Jethmalani, Anil Divan, and Soli Sorabjee. The night before the case, they chose Shanti Bhushan as the lead counsel. At the conference, the lawyers discussed their strategy, laughed, and joked. Ram said, 'The Supreme Court of Timbuktu has decided that a prostitute can be a virgin with retrospective effect.'

Every leading counsel in the country but Nani Palkhivala appeared for the detenus.[6] He reportedly explained, 'I was asked to appear in Habeas Corpus cases. I had a strong feeling that no purpose would have been served. Except for Justice H.R. Khanna, we had a bench of hopelessly weak judges who would have done anything to gain the favours of the then government.' There may have been another reason. Palkhivala was the vice-chairman of Tata Sons Ltd by then, and the Tata enterprises wanted to conduct their business without governmental interference.

Some have opined that if he had been involved, the result may have been different.

The first arguments were presented on December 14, 1975, and four months later, on April 28, 1976, the 236-page decision came out, four to one in favour of the government. Ram's injunction would no longer keep him out of jail.

This decision marked the nadir of the Supreme Court in India. While other cases also have been severely attacked, this is the blackest in legal history, but why?

In brief, the question before the court was whether a person who was detained in jail still had the right to petition for habeas corpus while the Emergency laws were in effect, or whether the new laws passed during the Emergency had taken away the right of a detenu to question his detention.[7]

Despite its final opinion, the court says of the writ of habeas corpus: 'It is perhaps the most important writ known to the constitutional law of England, affording as it does a swift and imperative remedy in all cases of illegal restraint or confinement. It is of immemorial antiquity, an instance of its use occurring in the thirty-third year of Edward I. It has through the ages been jealously maintained by courts of law as a check upon the illegal usurpation of power by the executive at the cost of the liege.'

Niren De, the Attorney General, arguing for the government, said the rights to life and liberty that are guaranteed by Article 21 of the Constitution could no longer be enforced or even recognized by the court, including the Supreme Court. The detenus have no locus standi, and their writ petitions would have to be dismissed.[8]

The next day Justice Khanna asked Niren De: 'Life is also mentioned in Article 21 and would Government argument extend to it also?' De's answer became famous: 'Even if life is taken away illegally, courts are helpless.'

As the arguments came to an end, Ram addressed the court:

Never has this court dealt with a case so momentous as this one—a case on which the survival of the freedom of all except the ignorant and the sycophant depends. It is almost right to say that democracy is already in the coffin. The government wants the court to slam shut its lid—something so dirty that it would rather want to do it for them.[9] You will be locking up the door of your own sepulchre for all time to come. The free world is watching to see how a great court reacts and conducts itself in the face of supreme tragedy. You may afford to be contemptuous of contemporary opinion but long after your identity as judges is forgotten, posterity will read your judgment and draw its own conclusions. Will you bequeath to it an image of glory or of contempt, is the choice before you. Do remember that the Emergency can be made permanent by those who are determined to make themselves permanent.

Ram continued:

We do not speak merely for our formal clients on record but the hundreds of thousands of innocent men and women who are cut off from their dear ones and condemned to a life of maddening loneliness and impotence, while they hear through Samachar [the government news agency] of the servile self-seekers celebrating the rise of a new dynasty to power. We speak for all of us because each one of us is a potential detenu. It may sound a little bizarre, but I speak even for the members of this court. Once the restraints are gone and free institutions buried, there is no knowing on whom the Frankenstein of naked power will turn. It will not spare even those who shun the race for power. It may even turn on its erstwhile friends and admirers.

In conclusion, Ram told the court, 'It is not your job as judges to assist a phoney Emergency. You must err on the side of liberty today even as Lord Atkin did during a real emergency.'

Ram's full argument reached the detenus in jail in a secretly circulated paper, *Evening View*.

A.N. Ray delivered the majority decision on behalf of himself, Justices Beg, Chandrachud, and Bhagwati. In later years, both Chandrachud and Bhagwati would recant, repent, explain, and apologize. The key portion of the decision read:

1) In view of the Presidential Order dated 27 June 1975 no person has any locus standi to move any writ petition under Art 226 before the High Court for habeas corpus or any other writ or order or direction to challenge the legality of an order . . . of detention on the ground that the order is not under or in compliance with the Act or is illegal or is vitiated by mala fides factual or legal or is based on extraneous considerations.

2) Section 16A (9) of the Maintenance of Internal Security Act, 1971 is constitutionally valid . . .

4) Article 21 of the Constitution is the sole repository of rights to life and personal liberty against State.

The last point still amazes Sri Jaisinghani. He says that all the judges but Justice Khanna, the sole dissent, were spineless. Not only did the judges deprive India's detenus of the right to challenge their detention, but they also ruled that the fundamental rights to life and liberty only exist because of Article 21 of the Indian Constitution. He asks, 'How can that be? Does a person only have the rights to life and liberty because of Article 21 of the Constitution? What if there were no Constitution? You still have a human right.'

Within the judgement itself there are stunning statements: The court says that the new Emergency provisions must be regarded as the basic structure of the Constitution. It also says that the concept of the rule of law does not apply to Emergency provisions, since the Emergency provisions themselves contain the rule of law for such situations.

What this meant, to the everlasting shame of the Gandhi government and for the first time in the history of India, was that the government can eliminate the rule of law!

In his opinion, Justice Beg explains that once there is a prima facie valid detention order, it is a complete answer to a petition for a writ of habeas corpus. The High Court cannot inquire into its validity.

Ironically, the judge who became most famous in this case was Justice Khanna, the lone dissenter. In his dissent he wrote: 'What is at stake is the rule of law . . . the question is whether the law speaking through the authority of the Court shall be absolutely silenced and rendered mute . . .'

Khanna concluded his dissent with an oft-quoted paragraph:

Before I part with the case, I may observe that the consciousness that the view expressed by me is at variance with that of the majority of my learned brethren has not stood in the way of my expressing the same. I am aware of the desirability of unanimity, if possible. Unanimity obtained without sacrifice of conviction commends the decision to public confidence. Unanimity which is merely formal and which is recorded at the expense of strong conflicting views is not desirable in a court of last resort. As observed by Chief Justice Hughes . . . judges are not there simply to decide cases, but to decide them as they think they should be decided, and while it may be regrettable that they cannot always agree, it is better that their independence should be maintained and recognized than that unanimity should be secured through its sacrifice. A dissent in a court of last resort to use his words, is an appeal to the brooding spirit of the law . . . when a later decision may possibly correct the error into which the dissenting judge believes the court to have been betrayed.

Justice Chandrachud claimed later that he had shifted his stand at the last minute because he would have been in the minority anyhow, but his opinion still shows the naïvety of the majority: 'Counsel after counsel expressed the fear that during the emergency, the executive may whip and strip and starve the detenu and if this be our judgment, even shoot him down. Such misdeeds have not tarnished the record of Free India and I have a diamond-bright, diamond-hard hope that such things will never come to pass.'

Chandrachud may very well have tried to hold his diamond-bright hope during the Emergency, but any knowledge of 'realpolitik' would have forewarned him of its futility.

Khanna knew better. He wrote in his dissent that: 'there was no remedy against illegal detentions, unauthorized demolitions, official tyranny, torture, murder, and mayhem'.

Justice Khanna was next in line to become Chief Justice of India until he wrote this dissent. When his junior, Justice M.H. Beg, superseded him in January 1977, he resigned. Justice Khanna wrote in his autobiography that he had asked Mr De, the Attorney General: 'In view of his submissions would there be any remedy if a police officer because of personal enmity killed another man?' The answer of Mr De was unequivocal: 'Consistently with my argument,' he said, 'there would be no judicial remedy in such a case as long as the Emergency lasts.'

A famous *New York Times* editorial lauded Justice Khanna on April 30, 1976:

If India ever finds its way back to the freedom and democracy that were proud hallmarks of its first eighteen years as an independent nation, someone will surely erect a monument to Justice H.R. Khanna of the Supreme Court. It was Justice Khanna who spoke out fearlessly and eloquently for freedom this week in dissenting from the Court's decision upholding the right of Prime Minister Indira Gandhi's Government to imprison political opponents at will and without court hearings . . . The submission of an independent judiciary to absolutist government is virtually the last step in the destruction of a democratic society; and the Indian Supreme Court's decision appears close to utter surrender.

Justice Khanna became a hero after this case, and he is also regarded as the influential vote in the *Keshavananda Bharati* case. A man of great integrity, he was appointed Law Minister in the Charan Singh government in July 1979, but he resigned three days later. He was asked to run for President, but he did not. It has been said that in a room full of angels, Justice Khanna would make the angels look dirty. There is no monument to him, but his portrait hangs in the Supreme Court.

Justices Beg, Chandrachud, and Bhagwati, in that order, were all rewarded by becoming Chief Justices.

Incidentally, Fali Nariman wrote after Chandrachud died[10] that it was Chandrachud's outstanding argument for the state in the *Nanavati* case that propelled him to the front rank of Bombay lawyers. This argument was the one that Ram Jethmalani had written behind the scenes.

Justice Chandrachud later apologized for his decision in the habeas corpus case.

Justice Bhagwati was the next to apologize: 'I was there—I plead guilty. I don't know why I yielded to my colleagues. In the beginning, I was not in favour of the view that the majority took. But ultimately, I don't know why, I was persuaded to agree with them. I still feel that the whole judgment was against my conscience. I have always been for freedom, freedom of speech and freedom of expression; I have always believed and always stood by these principles. It was an act of weakness on my part.'[11]

Justice Bhagwati claimed that, out of contrition, he later worked to change several offensive clauses of the Constitution: 'I realized that I had made a big error and so I started developing Articles 14, 19, 21, 32, as no one else has done. I practically re-wrote these articles.' Commentators have observed tartly that is not the job of a judge to rewrite the Constitution.

Shortly before he died, the Attorney General who argued the case, Niren De,[12] sought out Judge Iyer at a social event to make his confession:

What was the agony in my soul, which gave me sleepless nights?

It was about my defence of the Emergency. I did not want a ghastly law which would banish judicial jurisdiction in the face of subjective executive violence. I thought of the strategy of shocking the judges into sanity, into rousing their revulsion, into reading down the deadly law, into claiming space for judicial invigilation as haven of human rights. So I urged the damned extreme position hoping that humanist jurisprudence would be the indignant robed reaction. So I pressed, against my heart but with the expectation of awakening the aghast protest of the Bench.

If the police abused power the court would not sit and watch with cauterised conscience but would act in fiat justicia spirit—so, I thought, would be their response. I wanted the robes to rage against that violent view I propounded and come down on such Emergency inhumanity. But, to my surprise, barring Khanna, the other justices heard but did not furiously resist. I felt sad as a jurist but found success as Counsel.

In other words, he claimed he was arguing the case on behalf of the government, and at the same time he hoped to demonstrate to the judges that his proposed result would be a disaster? Not likely.

In 1978, Parliament passed the 44th Amendment, largely nullifying the vilified habeas corpus decision and taking away the power of the President to suspend Article 21.

The Supreme Court never actually reversed their decision. In January 2011, the papers reported that a two-man bench of the Supreme Court[13] admitted in another case that the decision in the habeas corpus case was erroneous. While setting aside another judgement in 2009, Justice Ganguly wrote: 'There is no doubt that the majority judgment of this court in the A.D.M. Jabalpur case violated the fundamental rights of a large number of people in this country.' Perhaps so, but that was not a formal reversal.

So finally even the court itself apologized, but none of this helped Ram in 1976.

On the afternoon of the day the decision was handed down, Ram knew he would be arrested unless he left the country immediately. Meeting with a selected group of lawyers at the home of Nani

Palkhivala, he told them that with 102 lawyers in jail in Nasik alone, 'I am prepared to be the 103rd but I want to leave India to tell the world about the phoney Emergency.' He assured them, 'Please do not suspect that I am afraid to go to jail.'

His colleagues told him to go, but they asked, 'How will you go?' He replied that they must remember he was a criminal lawyer, 'Leave it up to me.'

Later in the afternoon Ram argued one last case before a magistrate. As 5 o'clock approached, the time the court normally rises, Ram asked the magistrate if he would stay overtime to allow him to complete his client's case, since he planned to leave India that day. In an unprecedented move, the magistrate gave his permission, and they continued until 6 p.m., by which time Ram had finished his work in India for the time being.

15

America

It is impossible to know how important Ram's contributions were to ending the infamous Emergency, yet one could trace a direct line from his receiving political asylum to his testimony before Congress, to statements by Daniel Patrick Moynihan, to dire threats by President Carter giving a warning to dictatorial governments, to the sudden announcement by Mrs Gandhi that India would hold elections.

Ram had his suitcase packed, his passport in hand, and his airline tickets ready when the habeas corpus decision was handed down. He went to the airport escorted by his long-time partner, Sri Jaisinghani, and by the Bombay deputy commissioner of police. He flew first to his sister Maya, in Toronto, Canada, and next to Detroit, where Shobha lived and Durga was visiting. Now he needed a job. My husband, Professor Martin Adelman, introduced him to Dean Donald Gordon of the Wayne State University Law School, who offered him a position as a visiting professor, teaching comparative constitutional law in the fall semester.

One of the first things Ram wrote in the US was an impassioned letter to Mrs Gandhi:[1]

'Dear Prime Minister,

I thought you would not personally read a letter from me but I have been persuaded by your Ambassador that I am wrong. I must therefore bring to your attention a state of affairs which is regrettable if not tragic.

You have declared on numerous occasions that you are using emergency powers only against those who are preaching violence and fomenting chaos and that you have no intention of suppressing legitimate criticism of your measures actual or contemplated.

I belong to no political party. I went out of the Congress Party some years ago when it failed to fulfill its pledge to the nation and one to me personally. In 1971, I contested the parliamentary election as an independent from a Maharashtra constituency despite pressure from opposition parties to join one or the other. I have publicly pleaded for compulsory sterilization, demonetisation of currency, strengthening the country's agricultural base, wages linked to output, attracting foreign capital for industrial growth, getting rid of an expensive federal structure, and above all replacing the men who have run the country for so long with such disastrous consequences.

I am a criminal lawyer. My clients confide to me and I have access to sources of information which even you with the RAW and CMI don't. I know the corrupt acts of your colleagues and some whom you have installed as party bosses throughout the country. You cannot possibly find fault with the anguished and strong utterances of one who sees those very persons masquerading as the saviours of the poor people of India . . .

One must concede however that you command a parliamentary majority. Your right to remain in office is unquestioned. When the Allahabad High Court unseated you, your friends asked me to write to the press my views on the constitutional problem of your resignation. I wrote a long article in the *Illustrated Weekly* supporting your right to remain in office. It was the honest lawyer in me that compelled me thus to write though I have otherwise been a critic of your domestic and foreign policies.

But this I did when you had not yet destroyed the democratic process. I honestly feel:

1. That India's Constitution interferes with none of your economic policies. Every item of your twenty point programme can be vigorously pursued with the framework of the existing Constitution.

2. That suppression of people's liberty of free speech and criticism is wicked and immoral. All honest advice becomes heresy and only self-serving sycophants thrive. The dishonest rich have nothing decent to say. They are not affected in any way.

I have aired these convictions in public. I have done so vigorously and fearlessly. But I have never preached violence. I am not a demagogue and I have addressed only highly educated audiences composed principally of lawyers.

I have publicly endorsed your twenty point programme as well as your claim that democracy also imposes restraints on the opposition.

Instead of respecting an opponent possessed of courage and integrity, your government's response has been an order of detention, ostensibly made by the District Magistrate of Palghat in Kerala. I stepped into that place for the first and last time to inaugurate the Third Kerala State Lawyers Conference in my capacity as the Chairman of the India Bar Council. In legal proceedings before the High Court, your government is a party and it has supported the order of detention.

My petition in the High Court may fail as a result of the latest Supreme Court pronouncement, but that is beside the point. The crucial issue is—Do you wish to suppress all dissent? If such is not your intention, you must undo the wrong done to me by your subordinates.

Currently, I am in the United States of America grappling with a possible second migration of my life; the first took place when your party partitioned India. I will survive but in bitterness against you. And in this free country people will draw their own inferences from the plain facts of my case. Of course you can afford to say you don't care.

I want to return to my country in dignity and freedom and I write this only to put your democratic protestations to the test.'

There was no answer. Ram applied for political asylum in America on July 7. On August 24, 1976, Ram became the first person from India to receive political asylum during the Emergency. Subsequently, there were Subramanian Swamy, Makarand Desai, and possibly two more. Ram credits pressure on his behalf from 'a highly placed Jewish member of the Vice Presidential staff', as well as from Mr Charles Rhyne, president of the World Peace through Law Centre in Washington, Mr Sigmund Timberg, the ex-vice-president of the American Bar Association, Mr Steven Cohen, Mr William Butler of the International Commission of Jurists, and many others.

Mrs Gandhi correctly viewed Ram's political asylum as American recognition that she persecuted political opponents. Two months later, in September 1976, she abruptly recalled the Indian ambassador to the United States, Ambassador Triloki Nath Kaul. Perhaps it would be a stretch to say that she recalled him because of the way he mishandled Ram's political asylum, but the replacement, Ambassador Kewal Singh, did specifically mention to the *New York Times* that the Indian government was displeased with the US decision to grant Ram political asylum.

Nominally, Ram lived with Shobha and Suresh in their Grosse Pointe house, but he was constantly out and about on the road, taking his case to the American people. Though his office was right next to my husband's, Ram was too busy for us to be able to describe all of his activities. We rarely saw him socially the whole time.

In the middle of his activities, writing and speaking to teach America about the Emergency, Ram even defended two clients in London, the Narang brothers, accused of smuggling antiquities. He would lecture to his law students, jump on a plane, and fly to London repeatedly. His junior Mani Cooper assisted him, because most Indian lawyers were intimidated during the Emergency, afraid to openly go to London to help Ram. Mani, a part-time professor of criminal law in two law colleges, played an important role in the last week of the trial, since Ram needed an Indian lawyer to testify about the relevant Indian law. With that assistance, Ram got the brothers off.

Even in exile in America, Ram relished teaching, as he always does. While teaching along with the scholarly Professor Edward Wise, Ram taught his students about the fight to return democracy to India. One piece that Ram wrote for his students was priceless, Ram Jethmalani at his most biting. At the time India faced a proposal for a commission to rewrite the Constitution, and Ram offered a 'proposed' preamble for a 42nd Amendment to the Constitution of India.

This 'proposed preamble' and 'proposed amendment' were published in the *Wayne Law Review* and later Ram reprinted them in the *Journal of the Bar Council of India*:[2]

'Whereas my late father, Pundit Jawaharlal Nehru, and his father, the late Pundit Motilal Nehru, ended British Colonial Rule in India despite severe obstruction from reactionaries like Mahatma Gandhi, Sardar Patel, Jaya Prakash Narayan, Vir Sararkar and others too numerous to be mentioned;

Whereas the Indian People gratefully installed and continued till his death Jawaharlal Nehru as their Prime Minister overlooking his living in a world of illusions leading to a Chinese attack and occupation of twenty-five thousand square miles of Indian territory;

And, whereas the late Jawaharlal Nehru was a soft brained democrat given to such suicidal impulses as the rule of law and inalienable rights of the common man;

And, whereas judges representing vested interests had a field day during his time by gunning at government's actions and setting at naught the projects of its ministers;

And, whereas continuous criticism of ministers and exposure of their corruption and misdeeds made possible by a foolish Constitution containing an outdated Bill of Rights were proving a serious obstacle in the people's path to progress;

And, whereas the promises of the Freedom Movement have turned into nightmares and the disgruntled leaders of the opposition permanently kept out of the sinews of power and equal opportunities of amassing illegitimate wealth have of late lost their patience and are crying themselves hoarse, the noise making it impossible for the Prime Minister to concentrate on her affairs;

And, whereas the Press has become too big for its boots and not able to read the signs of the time has stubbornly rejected the self evident proposition that I, Indira Gandhi, was and am Gandhi's India;

And whereas our faithful friends and allies the Russians and their local agents the Communist Party of India have rightly diagnosed that all the ills that ail the nation flow from the deadly virus called the Constitution of India;

And, whereas the illiterate masses of India neither understand democracy nor the deep and still undischarged debt they owe to the Nehru family;

I, Indira Feroze Nehru Gandhi, the godsent protector of the Nation's interests, do hereby ordain and declare: The Constitution which the people of India gave to themselves on the 26th of November, 1949, is permanently exorcised and outlawed;

Having sucked into myself the powers of the People of India and recognizing no other sharer in the sovereignty thus assumed save and except my son, Sanjay, born out of a singularly unfortunate wedlock with the late Feroze Gandhi, do hereby further ordain and declare that the future constitution of India shall be what the President of India wants it to be: Provided that he shall be bound to want only that which I order him to want.'

A new 42nd Amendment did pass in India on April 1, 1977, which did curtail fundamental rights and impose changes to the structure of the constitution, making India a 'Socialist Secular' Republic.

Before the proposed 44th Amendment passed, Ram also wrote a long letter to the President of India pleading for him, as a fellow lawyer, to oppose an amendment that would 'institutionalize dictatorship and facilitate dynastic rule'. He warned, 'It makes you totally superfluous.' Ram reminded him of his oath to uphold the Constitution and asked, 'Will you sign the death warrant of India's democracy?'

Ram made sure to get word of the Emergency to 'every major Radio and Television and every leading newspaper'. Ram met journalists from the *American Bar Association Journal*, *Newsweek*, the *Detroit Free Press*, and the *Washington Post*, resulting in numerous published articles. He met executives of the International League for the Rights of Man, World Habeas Corpus, Ad Hoc Committee for Human Rights in India, Committee for Freedom in India, numerous other American figures, and other prominent Indians who were in America at that time.

In September 1976 the *American Bar Association Journal* published an editorial, starting with the premise:[3]

'The President of the United States declares an "emergency" and suspends a series of constitutional rights, including the right to a writ of habeas corpus. The president of the American Bar Association speaks out publicly against this action at a state bar association meeting and becomes the target of a government warrant. The Supreme Court finds the government's actions valid. The president of the ABA flees the country rather than being arrested, leaving behind his wife and daughter, both lawyers, and a prelaw college-age son. Although he is an establishment citizen of his country, yet he is a refugee from it. He takes up residence in India and secures a semester's employment at a law school, while the government prepares to confiscate his property and to displace him with an ex officio president who also will be a law officer of the federal government.

It can't happen here? Let us fervently hope so, but it has happened in India—a post World War II democracy—in fact, the world's most populous until the events of the last months have crumbled those hopes under the heel of autocracy.

Ram Jethmalani, chairman of the Bar Council of India, a bar association of more than 150,000 members, fled India this summer to escape arrest for his outspoken opposition to the repressive measures instituted by the Indian government in 1975. The rights of Mr Jethmalani and other Indian lawyers, as well as the public in general, to speak out against this action and to criticize the government have been suppressed. Indeed, as Mr Jethmalani told a congressional committee in June, in 'a single jail in Bombay state there are nearly one hundred lawyers detained without any charges.' India's four independent news agencies have been forced into a new single agency controlled by the government, which also operates radio and television. Before he left India, Mr Jethmalani said, even his chairman's page in the *Journal of the Bar Council of India* was censored by deletions, an action he defied. Now he is in Detroit and will lecture this fall at Wayne State University.

While India's constitution contains a provision permitting a declaration of emergency, Mr Jethmalani's testimony before the congressional committee clearly casts doubt on the "emergency" engendered by Prime Minister Gandhi, which he branded as "fraudulent." "The claims made for the benefits of the emergency," he declared, "are as phony as the emergency itself. That trains run on time is a notorious justification for totalitarianism."

Had the events that have taken place in India and threatened its legal profession occurred in a more remote or obscure nation, we might excuse our lack of attention to and concern for fellow lawyers. But India is not a two-by-four state. It was a vast democracy of the East, with an advanced constitutional statement of rights, and it boasts the second largest legal profession in the world, one sharing with us the heritage of Anglo-American law. Perhaps it would be well for us to contemplate not only what we can do to support our Indian colleague of the law, but also what lessons we should heed to protect our own democracy and professional independence.'

In February 1977, the *ABA Journal* published a long article from a Delhi barrister and advocate of the Supreme Court, Shyamla Pappu. Titled 'Rebuttal from India', it says in part:[4]

'The comment captioned "A Lawyer under Fire" appearing in the September, 1976, issue of your journal (page 1181) gives one an idea of the abysmal ignorance and phenomenal prejudice with which you look upon the developments in India during the past one year and a half. It may impress as a piece written with a pen dipped in vituperative vitriolic, but not as a fair objective comment. You betray a pathological eagerness to presume that democracy in India is dead and then to shed your tears. Pray, hold back your tears.

Democracy in India is as vigorous as ever. Indeed, the masses of the people of India participate in the process of shaping their own destiny more actively today than ever in the past . . .

For the information of your readers, let me put the record straight about Mr Jethmalani's displacement from the chairmanship of the Bar Council of India. The resolution unanimously passed by a full meeting of the Bar Council of India on 12th September 1976 reads as follows: 'Since Shri RB Jethmalani has left India and has obtained political asylum in USA and he is not likely to attend council meetings to carry out functions of the chairman, it is hereby resolved that Shri RB Jethmalani ceases to be chairman of this council from this date.' The government had nothing to do with this resolution. The Bar Council of India is a statutory body functioning independently of the government. If the members of such a body unanimously decided that their chairman, by his seeking political asylum in another country, had ceased to hold the post, how could that be a charge against the government of India?

Just because the chairman of the Bar Council of India chose to seek political asylum in the USA and a few lawyers are under detention due to their involvement in subversive activities, you cannot jump to the conclusion that the legal profession is under duress. In fact the members of the bar are absolutely free to carry on their professional work and to express their views publicly . . .

The emergency was proclaimed because there was an organized attempt to derail democracy and to halt socioeconomic changes. Far from being fraudulent, it is a healthy manifestation of India's resolve to protect democracy.'

This article was a joke. The Bar Council voted out Ram as chairman for one simple reason. Ram was in the United States and obviously could not preside over meetings or perform his duties as chairman in absentia. The resolution explicitly refrained from criticizing anything Ram had said or done. The cavalier statement that 'a few lawyers were under detention due to their involvement in subversive activities' was in flagrant disregard of the truth; the cream of the bar and the principled opposition were in jail. Anyone who read her article would recognize political double-speak worthy of George Orwell's satire of political thought-control, *1984*.

Of interest, Mrs Pappu acted as an envoy of Mrs Gandhi in the United States for three months, seeking to present the government's case wherever possible. In every instance she was denied a forum unless she would agree to have Ram speak from the same platform. She refused, and, according to Ram, eventually she returned to India without ever delivering a speech.

There were two more articles in the *ABA Journal*. In January 1977 an advertisement announced that Ram was available to address bar associations, groups of lawyers, or law students. Interested persons were to contact the Committee for Freedom in India, headed by S.R. Hiremath of Chicago, but by now, it was too late. Ram had already gone home. But we will come back to that.

The next entry in the *ABA Journal* was in November 1977, a short article:

'We rejoice that Ram Jethmalani, the former chairman of the Bar Council of India who had to flee his country during the eclipse of democracy there, received the human rights award at this year's meeting in Manila of the World Peace through Law Conference.

'Mr Jethmalani was the shining head and symbol of the free legal profession of India when Mrs Gandhi's government imposed its autocratic rules, and he came to the United States under threat of imminent arrest in 1976. Here he became one of the rallying points of public and professional interest and concern with conditions in India . . .'

Mr Shrikumar Poddar, staying in Okemos, Michigan during that time, had met Ram shortly after he arrived in Michigan. At an Indian dance recital, Ram asked a woman where he might find a Mr Poddar. The woman was Mrs Poddar, and she invited Ram to stay with them for several days. Mr Poddar did his best to find speaking engagements for Ram, specifically in New York and New Jersey. In New Jersey, Ram was shocked to find out that the group of Indians he was speaking to were pro-Naxalite. For a while Ram believed that all the Indians living in the United States were Communists.

Mr Poddar, too, had been very active in his work against the Emergency. His group, Indians for Democracy, held a big rally in Washington on June 29, soon after the Emergency was proclaimed, with huge press coverage. On August 15, the Indian Independence

Day, they held a demonstration in Washington that was twice as big, but press coverage was minimal, with the exception of the *Washington Post*. When they inquired around, they heard that Henry Kissinger had told the papers not to cover the protest because it was against American interests.[5]

Indian activists in America believed the Russians had encouraged the declaration of Emergency, and that within a month America had moved to counter this Russian influence by providing several million dollars in aid to India, both through the World Bank and directly. After that, America became a supporter of the Emergency, i.e., it became an American Emergency.

The American people universally supported democracy, opposed the Emergency, and exerted pressure on Congress. Congress was highly critical of the Emergency, holding hearings on the subject in June and in September 1976.

As Mr Poddar describes it, other Indian figures contributed to the drumbeat against the Emergency in America. Rajni Kothari came at about the same time as Ram. He also received political asylum and lectured widely, as an academic from Mrs Gandhi's brain trust. He wrote one article, 'End of An Era', that filled the whole issue of *Seminar*. A thousand copies were photocopied and widely disseminated despite censorship in India. Nayantara Sahgal, Nehru's sister's daughter and a very prominent Indian writer, also wrote and spoke against the Emergency. Makarand Desai, a BJP minister from Gujarat, also spoke out. Subramanian Swamy not only made speeches in America, he even returned to India to denounce the Emergency right on the floor of Parliament, slipping out before the startled authorities had the wits to arrest him.

Mrs Gandhi cancelled the passports of four prominent Indian critics of the Emergency while they were in America. Two of these were Mr Poddar and Mr Rajni Kothari, but neither of them actually turned in their passports. Of the Indians who denounced the Emergency in America, Poddar says that Ram and Kothari had the greatest stature in India, but Ram's position as chairman of the Bar Council of India made him the most prominent.

The cancelled passports were part of a pattern. Just before Ram left Bombay he was defending a group of Indian nationals living in the Gulf states whose passports had been taken away. When he left, the cases went to Mani Cooper.

Mr Poddar's suspicions about the suspicious attitude of the United States towards India are borne out by the correspondence between the Embassy of India and the Department of State in 1976:

January 8:[6] 'Ambassador Saxbe recommended that the United States withhold, limit, and delay joint cooperative projects, including foreign aid as a means of demonstrating official U.S. displeasure at occasional vociferous public criticism of the United States in India. Saxbe also indicated that he would ask United States Senator George McGovern to request from Prime Minister Gandhi specific citations of U.S. interference in Indian affairs during his upcoming meeting with her.'

January 17:[7] 'The Embassy reported the DCM's conversation with Indian Joint Secretary of the Americas Teja in which he informed the Indian Government that the U.S. would not proceed with its program of bilateral development assistance to India for fiscal year 1976 because of "insufficient mutual trust" between the U.S. and India.'

February 5,[8] from the Department of State to the Embassy of India: 'Secretary of State Kissinger assured Ambassador Saxbe of his "full support" in expressing U.S. displeasure with recent official criticisms of the United States from the Indian Government. He also gave notice of recent decisions to withdraw the U.S. offer for developmental assistance for fiscal year 1976, to delay negotiations for . . . food assistance, and to deny an extension for satellite instructional television programming for India.'

October 12, 1976,[9] Memorandum of Conversation on the subject of the Secretary's Meeting with the Indian Foreign Minister Chavan and under-secretary for Ambassador-designate Kewal Singh:

'Foreign Minister: There are also some irritants on our side. There are the Fraser hearings on human rights in India. It was an exercise to keep the Indian Parliament quiet.

Secretary: As I have said publicly, I am in total disagreement with Fraser. He would make us the world's policeman. There are certain human rights which are important.

Foreign Minister: One of the people who appeared, Jethmalani is now boasting he has gotten asylum in the U.S. for criticizing us.

Secretary: It is inevitable that the Fraser Committee hears witnesses who are violently opposed to the government in power. You are not the only case. Every time I see a Foreign Minister, he has some complaint. We certainly would not take kindly to India's holding hearings on civil rights in the U.S. These hearings are superficial. It is an outrageous procedure.'

In fact, by far the most important presentation that Ram made in America was before this very Congressional Sub-Committee,[10] dubbed the Fraser Committee after its chairman, Donald M. Fraser of Minnesota. The hearings were held in two sessions, June 23, 28, and 29, then September 16 and 23, 1976.

On June 28 and 29, the committee heard testimony from Ram as well as Dr Homer A. Jack, Secretary General, World Conference of Religion for Peace; Revd James K. Mathews, Bishop of the Washington Area United Methodist Church; Charles Reynolds, International Secretary of the Ludhiana Christian Medical College; Leila Kabir Fernandes, wife of George Fernandes, chairman of the Socialist Party of India and president of the All-India Railway Men's Federation; and Shrikumar Poddar, founding member of the Indians for Democracy.

Revd Mathews launched into a bland, smoothly argued defence of the Emergency. He first described the dire circumstances that made the Emergency necessary, saying that the coalition opposing Prime Minister Gandhi had nothing positive to offer as an alternative but only sought to create chaos; the offences for which she was tried at Allahabad were trivial, and the Emergency was 'not extra-constitutional'. The President of India is authorized to proclaim a state of Emergency when necessary to protect the nation from external or internal threat. The vast majority of the prisoners were economic offenders: black marketers, hoarders, moneylenders, and profiteers. Meanwhile by all accounts, conditions have improved economically in India.

Mr Jagjit Singh Chohan, President of the International Council of Sikhs, testified next. A medical doctor, he had served as Minister of Finance of the Government of Punjab. Now he was in America, his passport revoked. He testified that 14,000 Sikhs in the Punjab and more than 100,000 people in all of India were in prison without trial.

Ram Jethmalani followed. He specified that though the record showed him to be chairman of the Bar Council of India, his latest information was that the Bar Council planned to substitute an ex-officio chairman in his place. He related the circumstances that led to his seeking asylum in the America. Referring to the *ADM Jabalpur* decision, he said that as a result in this Emergency 'the executive has the power to detain a person indefinitely in any cruel or subhuman conditions. The government, if it so chooses, can starve a prisoner to death and yet there is no right [for] a citizen to approach the courts for any judicial review.'

Ram said:

> In a situation like this, I suppose there are only three choices which are open to those who do not wish to surrender to sullen silence, and are determined to carry on some kind of active struggle for the restoration of Indian democracy.
>
> The three choices are that you should either get arrested and remain indefinitely in jail or go underground and resort to violence, and the third choice is to leave the country and work from without . . . I may sound a bit of a coward, but I have made the third choice, and that is why I am here in this country today testifying and burning my bridges behind.
>
> The first result of my testifying before you is going to be that my passport will be cancelled, perhaps tomorrow, and I will have no means of getting back home—perhaps if I get back home I will get into jail . . .

Ram submitted an article that he had written for the *Journal of the Bar Council of India*, saying, 'The theme of this article is that the government's claim that an emergency is essential for executing its economic policy is a complete and total fraud.'

He described elements of the Constitution, continuing:

Now, therefore you see that the only surviving rights in the Indian Constitution were the rights of personal liberty, expression of thought, the right of assembly, the right of practising your religion and the right of equality. To my mind it is absurd for anyone to suggest that these require curtailment in the interest of any social, political, or economic reform. If these rights have to be curtailed, they have to be curtailed because you want to destroy democratic dissent, because you want to put yourself above all criticism, and because you do not wish to hear things which are unfavourable.

Ram simply described Revd Mathews as a clergyman who had fallen victim to Mrs Gandhi's propaganda, sent to speak for the government.

In Ram's testimony, he recounted three telling tales: One was when a thief imitated Mrs Gandhi's voice on the telephone to a bank, requested money, and was able to walk away with $80,000. Ram said that this clearly demonstrated that Mrs Gandhi had access to bank money on demand. The man was discovered, jailed, and found dead in prison. The government called it heart failure. An investigating police officer begged to differ. He then died of heart failure. An associate sobbed at the funeral that he knew the truth. Later he died, run over by a car.

The next example was Sanjay Gandhi, who went from playboy to head of a $10 million car manufacturing complex on a 300-acre parcel of land that he obtained at bargain prices.

The third was the bombing and murder of a Mr Misra, the former railway minister who helped Mrs Gandhi suppress the railway strike. The actual suspects were arrested and released. They were replaced by a new set of 'suspects', who conveniently were members of a sect that had accused Mrs Gandhi's administration of corruption.

Ram produced an article from the *Journal of the Bar Council* with dots replacing certain words. On the top of the page was a clear statement that 'the dotted portions had been removed by the censor'. He also submitted a *New York Times* article about the Emergency titled 'Fading Hope in India'.

Ram then came back to the subject of Revd Mathews, asking the rhetorical questions when and how long he actually had lived in India, snorting, 'On the second page of his testimony he makes the point that some have gone so far as to liken Indira Gandhi's India to Adolph Hitler's Germany.' Ram even says he was wrong in believing there was hope for democracy in India.

Ram described an episode in which a lady member of a state legislature was arrested and 'put into a cell which was infested with rats and roaches. On her left was lodged a lunatic and on her right was a leper.'

Ram reports that the government denied 300 lawyers the right to assemble in a meeting. He says, 'This is the state of so-called human liberties in the country, and I am surprised that Reverend Mathews is prepared to say that conditions are not as bad as in Hitler's Germany.'

Ram continues, 'Reverend Mathews says he is very sorry that there is censorship of the press in India. But he says in attempted justification that many of the Indian newspapers have been discriminating and often irresponsible in what they publish as news.'

Charles Reynolds, International Secretary of the Ludhiana Christian Medical College, testified next, as a frequent traveller to India who was acquainted with the Prime Minister. After describing the state of extreme disorder that led to the proclamation of emergency, he said, 'Obviously strong action was needed, but has it been justified in the ensuing year? The answer can only be strongly in the affirmative.' He then went on to extol the salutary economic effects of government actions during the Emergency.

After that, Chairman Fraser engaged Mr Reynolds in a very pointed exchange, repeatedly asking why it was necessary to put Members of Parliament in jail in order to carry out economic and agricultural reforms.

Another committee member, Mr Derwinski, asked Ram whether printed matter, including foreign periodicals, was censored, 'It includes censorship of foreign press coming into India?'

Ram answered, 'Undoubtedly. I am a regular subscriber to the *Times*, *Newsweek*, and *The Economist* in London. I only get those issues in which there is no reference to Mrs Gandhi. If there is any reference to Mrs Gandhi which is capable of being remotely critical of her, that issue never reaches me.'

Mr Reynolds responded, '. . . essentially press censorship as press censorship no longer exists. There is a self-disciplining by the Press Council who have accepted certain rules for themselves . . .'

Mr Fraser asked, 'Do you expect the statement Mr Jethmalani has given today will be honestly and reasonably accurately reported in the Indian press?'

Mr Reynolds: 'It may not be reported, because in a sense it might be considered as an inflammatory statement. But we must never feel that the ears of India are completely blocked, or the eyes.'

Mr Fraser: 'There is some censorship then?'

Mr Reynolds: 'Yes sir.'

Mr Fraser: 'Your defence of the emergency decree has a familiar ring to it. It tends to run along essentially the lines that I have heard in defence of the military junta in Chile or the abrogation of political rights in South Korea, to name just two, or martial law in the Philippines.'

Mr Fraser invited Ram to rebut the testimony of Mr Reynolds.

Ram said, 'In the first place, it should be a very strange kind of a truth which requires censorship to support it.'

Ram submitted a report written by Senator George McGovern upon returning from India: 'A number of news organizations have been harassed and foreign correspondents have been expelled.' Ram also pointed out that the supposedly self-censoring Press Council actually had been abolished and that the four independent news agencies in India had been liquidated. He went on to say that the laws against smuggling had antedated the Emergency, and recent economic improvements were the fruit of a good monsoon. Ram proceeded, point by point, to refute his testimony. After that, he asked for the United States to intervene, pulling out a pamphlet from the US State Department that read: 'Where the age-old antagonism between freedom and tyranny is concerned, we are not neutral. We shall never tolerate the suppression of fundamental liberties. We shall urge human rights and use our influence to promote justice.'

Mr Derwinski asked Ram whether the United States should ask the UN to look at the situation.

Ram: 'My own gut reaction to this kind of thing is that the United Nations will not be able to render any assistance because the majority of the members of the United Nations themselves are totalitarian powers and not democracies.' In answer to a follow-up question, Ram said, 'Let us not get involved with other members of the United Nations at all. Let this country assert its moral leadership and call a spade a spade.'

In the last interchange, Mr Reynolds continued to defend the Emergency, but Mr Derwinski asked, 'Can you honestly say that a Government which has 85 elected members of the legislative body, the Parliament, in jail is a truly functioning democratic government?'

The next day, Leila Kabir Fernandes submitted a statement on behalf of her husband, George Fernandes, chairman of the Socialist Party of India and President of the All-India Railway Men's Federation. Her husband had been in jail since June 10, 1976, and he was about to go on trial. She saw this as ominous since most detenus never went to trial. He was not allowed to write to her, and she did not know where he was. Her telephone was tapped, her letters opened, the newspaper that she ran shut down, and the police had come unannounced for her husband. Her brother-in-law had been cruelly tortured to extract information about her husband's whereabouts. Her testimony was compelling and tragic.

Mr Poddar testified, naming members of the Indian community now in America whose passports had been impounded.

Ram has been criticized harshly for his decision to leave the country. Why did he leave instead of going to prison like other leading opponents of the government? Some said it was because he was fond of the good life, of his women and of his Scotch in the evening. Others remember his disgust at dirty prison toilets. Supporters say it was a political mistake; he would have become Prime Minister or President if he had gone to jail. Others said that he chose to enjoy the comfort of friends and family in America instead. Shobha says that in fact while he was in America he was in great distress, striving to carry his message to the right ears, as urgently as possible.

After reading his testimony before the US Congress, it would be difficult to underestimate the power and effectiveness of these words in Washington, words that would never have been heard from any prison.

The World Bank gave India financial support, but during his re-election campaign for Senate, Daniel Patrick Moynihan, a former ambassador to the UN and to India, deplored Mrs Gandhi's request for arms, denouncing the World Bank's 'support of a dictatorial regime'. The newspapers quoted him widely as saying, 'Not one dollar to governments that deny human rights and subvert democracy.'

In November 1976, Jimmy Carter was elected President of the United States after an election campaign in which he emphasized human rights and expressed his clear disapproval of dictatorships that mistreat their own citizens.

Carter had 'pledged to make human rights the centrepiece of US foreign policy. Carter's thinking was not far from that of liberal Congressman Donald Fraser (D-Minnesota), who declared in hearings just after the inauguration, that the United States ought to avoid 'endorsing implicitly or otherwise India's suspension of civil rights'. The new President's emphasis on human rights threatened to collide head on with the Emergency.[11]

Fraser was the Congressman before whose committee Ram had testified.

On January 20, 1977, Carter took the oath of office, saying in his inaugural address, 'Because we are free we can never be indifferent to the fate of freedom elsewhere.'

On January 7, Prime Minister Bhutto of Pakistan called elections. On January 18,[12] just before Carter's inauguration, Prime Minister Gandhi of India unexpectedly called for elections. To be sure, neither Ram nor any member of her government claimed that her decision was due to pressure from America. She certainly had an escalating accumulation of problems at home, but she knew she would receive no help from the United States until she relieved herself of the burden of being considered a dictator. Also, he believes that 'her sycophants convinced her that she would get reelected'. All that being said, within two weeks of Carter's inauguration, at least two dictators of South Asia certainly figured out which way the wind was blowing in America.

As soon as Rani and Ram's brother-in-law Mohan Shahani found out that there were to be elections, they knew they had to get Ram a political ticket to run for Parliament. By this time the main Opposition parties were united in a common front, the Janata Party, to defeat Mrs Gandhi; George Fernandes, the head of the Socialist Party, was one of the leaders. He too was still in jail. Rani and Mohan went to the jail to talk to him, and he assured them that Ram would have a ticket, except he had to get back to India in time to file his candidacy for the election. They called Ram immediately.

Ram had rented an office on Fifth Avenue in New York, which he had inaugurated the very morning Prime Minister Gandhi announced the elections. Upon returning to Detroit, Ram walked next door from his office at the Law School to my husband's office to tell him that Mrs Gandhi had called elections for seven weeks from then, and his family wanted him to run for Parliament. How could he possibly mount a campaign for election in seven weeks?

My husband stills remembers answering, 'If she has given you seven weeks, then you have seven weeks.' All of Ram's confidantes agreed.

16

Return to India

Before Ram left for India in the morning, February 10, he went to the media. Both the Voice of America and the Canadian Broadcasting System took a particular interest in whether he would be arrested, and through the length of his over 17-hour flight home, they called Bombay every half hour to ask the government if they really were going to arrest Mr Jethmalani or if they might withdraw the warrant for his arrest.

Assuming he was not arrested, Ram's plan was to run for election to the Lok Sabha from the Bombay Northwest District, an area north of Bandra that includes Juhu Beach and the area around the Santa Cruz airport. He would be the candidate of the Janata Party, and he would run against the Minister for Law and Justice, H.R. Gokhale, who was widely blamed for the abusive Emergency legislation. For all Ram knew, he truly had the warrant for Ram's arrest in his pocket.

Ram knew he could be arrested on arrival, but he had to file his election papers in person within 24 hours. When he landed on the tarmac, he was met by a greatly relieved Ratna, Rani, and Sundri; a delegation of officials; and a wildly exuberant crowd throwing garlands at him. Until the police came rushing up to him to welcome him effusively, he did not know the official decision. As if in answer, one of the officers picked up a garland thrown by the crowd and garlanded him.

Ram asked what their intentions were. One officer answered,

'Sir we came to arrest you, but while you were on the plane we changed our mind and now we are coming to greet you.'

Notified of Ram's impending return by his family but also by word of mouth, the crowd of 5000 includes porters wrapped in sand-coloured shawls, women in bright saris, businessmen in long kurtas, beggars, and skeletons in rags, all massed in all directions. Right there, after some 20 stressful hours of travel, Ram gave his first campaign speech to joyously cheering fans.

That evening and for days to come, Ram told his voters, 'Mine is a unique election since my opponent is carrying around a warrant for my arrest.' This could have been literally true, because the sudden decision not to arrest him still had left the warrant enforceable whenever the government might wish. Until they finally withdrew the warrant, it remained hanging over Ram's head.

One thing Ram never did in this or any other campaign was to mention his opponent's name or position. He really was not running against him. In this campaign he was running against Prime Minister Gandhi.

His return plunged the Bombay family into a whirlpool of campaigning that was sudden and overwhelming, because the arrest warrant had not just hung over Ram's head alone.

While Ram was busy publicizing the Emergency in the United States, his family had lived in increasing isolation and under the threat of possible retaliation for Ram's defiance. About the few people they kept in touch with were Khatu and Mani Cooper, and even their telephone was tapped. Mahesh was in Oxford; Janak in Canada, Shobha and Durga in America. This left Rani living with Ratna, a somewhat fraught relationship. The phone was tapped of course. There were no parties at the Advent apartment, and their erstwhile friends stayed away. Sri says, 'It was very foolhardy to associate with the Jethmalanis.' Ram was using his salary from teaching in Detroit to support his US activities, and Ratna no longer practised law. Rani's small legal practice brought in very little. Ram had never cultivated the habit of saving his money. Sri Jaisinghani was left to carry on the law practice, and he donated half of his earnings to help Ram's family.

Ratna and Rani probably were more worried about Ram's possible arrest than he was, but the tension only escalated once they knew he was returning to the hornet's nest in Bombay. On the night that Ram returned, Rani fell deathly ill with gastrointestinal haemorrhage, was rushed to the hospital, and given blood transfusions. Twenty years later, she understood that these transfusions had given her hepatitis C, which finally destroyed her liver. Soon we will hear her story in her own words.

Ram campaigned with rising excitement, using Bhagwan Keswani's flat in North Bombay as his campaign office. Money and volunteers came from everywhere, especially law students and lawyers, angry at H.R. Gokhale for the worst abuses of the Emergency. Khatu Cooper was a faithful presence, speaking at any hour of the night, in Gujarati or Parsi, as needed.

Once it became clear in Delhi that the opposition would win, lawyers came to help Ram in Bombay in a great wave of support. It may not have been obvious to Ram, because he had been in the United States, but the rest of the country knew this election would unseat Prime Minister Gandhi and her entire government.

One evening at Ville Parle, Ram was flanked by Shatrughan Sinha, an actor and politician, other actors, Shobha, Rani, and Maya, all on a great podium. Ram gave a stem-winding speech to crowds stretching as far as the eye could see, and, in a fit of mass euphoria, the crowd surged towards the podium. Then the podium collapsed. The crowd went berserk and started pushing towards the three beautiful girls. Mohan Shahani ran in front of them immediately. All Shobha remembered was that someone picked her up, shoved her into a truck, and somehow she found herself safely left off in a hotel in Juhu Beach.

The night that the election results came in was a grand victory. In all there were six voting booths, each for 1000 voters. Mohan and Mani Cooper both monitored booths, to prevent cheating. At Mani's booth, one of the counters put a revolver on the table and turned his head intimidatingly towards her. By the end of two days of counting, 600,000 voters had voted overwhelmingly for Ram. A huge victory parade started at midnight.

On March 16, 1977, Ram celebrated with his colleagues with an exuberant speech at the High Court. Raj Narain, the man who had filed the fateful petition at the Allahabad court, beat Mrs Gandhi by a wide margin. Sanjay Gandhi was trounced by an unknown wrestler in his bid for Parliament. President Fakhruddin Ali Ahmed had died on February 11 of a heart attack, so the last act of Mrs Gandhi's Cabinet ministers was to ask the Acting President, B.D. Jatti, to lift the Emergency immediately. On March 22 after the last election result was tallied, Indira Gandhi tendered her resignation.

17

Member of Parliament

On March 23, 1977, Morarji Desai was sworn in as Prime Minister, and a new era began for India, also for Ram.

The biggest change in Ram's life was that he moved to Delhi, formally New Delhi, since today's city is just the latest in a series of cities built on the same site over thousands of years. Remnants of the older cities are still found in Old Delhi, where the market streets are clogged with unimaginable masses of people, and tourists take rickshaws through the markets to avoid being groped on the street. Shoppers have to find their way around goats, cows, chickens, and porters pulling carts full of merchandise. Far in the distance, a camel caravan might appear. New Delhi is another world, a British city of streets in formal patterns, landscaped roundabouts, and stately governmental buildings.

Driving through the governmental area today though, one still might pass six white cows grazing the grass along the sidewalk or perhaps spot a temple elephant ambling along the wide street. Nothing should be a great surprise, even the little monkeys running among the hedges.

As a Member of Parliament, Ram was entitled to a house on the Janpath, an iconic road running from the venerable British Claridges Hotel to Connaught Circle, seedy, but still the centre of British Delhi. Along its length are rows of shops with colourful merchandise from all the states in India, shoeshine boys, touts, pickpockets, beggars, and crowds of tourists. The house assigned to Ram was an old British mansion not far from Claridges, with a wide veranda, a large living room, and the always essential ceiling fans. On two acres of prime property with a wide lawn and a huge banyan tree in front, it became quite comfortable after Ram renovated it—at his own expense.

As a visitor drank tea on the shady veranda on a hot Delhi morning, the cook would inquire what he desired for breakfast; newspapers would arrive by bicycle and the laundryman would ask for the day's laundry. My husband said he now understood why the British never wanted to leave India. At night in the bedroom, little lizards chased each other up and down the walls. Ram said they kept him company in his office when he was working late. He liked to watch them copulate.

Ram lived in the Delhi house during the week, and he went home to Bombay on weekends, as he still does today. Of course he also travelled to the far corners of the country for cases, and to various law schools to teach. Ratna used to say that if Ram did not go to an airport for three days, he would go into withdrawal. Mind you, Ram did not go the way you and I do. In those days in Bombay, his car would drive out on the runway, right to the plane. Once this writer planned to ride with him to the airport in order to have the car for the rest of the day and realized that though it was getting close to departure time we were nowhere near the airport. 'Ram,' I remonstrated, 'you are going to miss your plane.' Unruffled, Ram's answer was, 'Don't worry, darling. They won't leave without me.' Everyone, as long as she is female, is darling to Ram.

Ratna never liked Delhi or politics. Her friends were all in Bombay. She loved to have lunch, trade jokes, and play cards at the Radio Club or the Bombay Gym. Durga, too, remained in Bombay or lived in Michigan helping Shobha take care of her sons, from the time of Sunil's birth in 1974 up until Girish reached the age of five in 1983. After obtaining her green card, she visited Michigan for several months every summer.

Ram used to stay with Rani when he came from Bombay to Delhi to appear before the Supreme Court. Now they both lived in the house on the Janpath, and Rani fitted up a little building on the premises as her office. Rani decorated the house tastefully with antique Indian art and proved to be a skilful hostess.

Whether they had soirees at the house or they went out to the elaborate social events of Delhi, many of their invitations came from Rani's huge coterie of friends. When they went out to big galas, they would make a grand entrance, sweeping in late of an evening, greeting their effusive admirers graciously.

It must be said that Ram found certain advantages in getting away—back to Bombay, maybe somewhere else entirely. Rani always noticed when an attractive woman had caught her father's eye at a party, or anywhere else. This put her in the unenviable position of either being an accomplice or a scold. That was one reason why she often blew up and left to stay with friends. Counting both wives, Ram now had three women to answer to for his predilections. Over time a sort of truce emerged, all of them recognizing that his love of women would never change.

Ram's life in Parliament combined politics with his law practice. It did not take long before many of his political colleagues came knocking on his door for legal services. One could even call the Indian Parliament a ready-made source of clients. He went to Parliament in what his family called his 'politician clothes', loose white cotton pants, a perfectly ironed flowing white kurta, and a crisp tan vest. Then he returned home and changed clothes to spend the rest of the day in legal work. He also wrote many newspaper articles for the *Indian Express*, and he found time to teach law students.

On court days, he left the house in an immaculate white shirt and bands. There were always clients, often crowds of clients, waiting to see Ram at home. If he tried to leave for a dinner engagement, anxious supplicants pushed forward: 'Sir, could I just have a word with you? Sir, would you please sign this paper? Sir, can I give you this document?' The scene brought to mind petitioners seeking an audience with an oriental potentate.

Absorbing as his life was, Ram still hoped to be Law Minister. It would have been poetic justice since he had defeated the previous Law Minister in his election, but instead Desai appointed Shanti

Bhushan, the lead counsel in the habeas corpus case. Even more important to Desai, Bhushan had been the lawyer for Raj Narain when he filed the petition against Prime Minister Gandhi in Allahabad. As is his wont, Ram did not ask for the position; he just waited to see if it would come to him purely on merit. When asked later why Desai did not appoint him, his answer was that Desai was a teetotaler, and he drank Scotch. Ram loved to jibe that even if Morarji Desai drank his own urine in the morning, he preferred Scotch at dinnertime. He also opined that the electorate probably would opt for his choice.

When Desai promoted prohibition, Ram teased him, 'Morarjibhai, I don't drink normally. I drink only occasionally, but now I will keep drinking to keep my right to drink alive.'[1]

On another occasion, Desai pleaded with Ram to behave, 'Mr Jethmalani I don't mind you drinking in private, but please do not praise your drink in public.' According to one story, Ram answered, 'You stick to your pissky and I'll stick to my whisky.'[2]

The day Desai resigned after a vote of no-confidence, Ram smiled sweetly, 'Morarjibhai, have you realized that all those who betrayed you were teetotalers? I hope some day you will have a good word for those who occasionally drink.'[3]

Some say that Subramanian Swamy told Desai that Ram liked his Scotch, but that hardly would have been necessary. All of Bombay knew Ram's lifestyle and that he had two wives. He made it no secret. The difference between the two men was one of temperament. Ram was flamboyant, Desai abstemious. Ram went to America; Desai sat in jail during the freedom struggle and the Emergency. Ram enjoyed a lively social life; Desai was famous for hunger strikes. Ram had a weakness for women; as Home Minister, Desai outlawed kissing scenes in movies. Ram was in the robust prime of his life; Desai was self-righteous, prudish, and over 80. Desai was the one who imposed prohibition on Gujarat.

Despite his insouciantly teasing Desai, Ram had discovered a serious new calling in Delhi. It might be called politics, but its pull was more powerful than that. It was public advocacy. The Desai regime was the first non-Congress party government in the history of

India, and it stepped into a morass of rampant corruption. This was when Ram found his voice as a reformer, at first of governmental abuses, later of the private sector too. Whatever Ram's personal indiscretions, he is incorruptible, and he is unforgiving of financial crimes. Ever since he first discovered his passion for political and social reform, it has come to consume him, often in what seemed reckless disregard for the personal consequences. The regime of Indira Gandhi had provided a target so broad that he could have shot in any direction and hit an injustice. Now he could define specific issues well enough to address them with his own fierce brand of logic. It was cream for the cat.

There was one minor side-show, a suit over Ram's election. There had been six contesting candidates. A sore loser, R.D. Paranijpe, disputed Ram's win, wanted Gokhale disqualified, and sought to be declared the winner. In this instance, even Gokhale supported Ram, and the petition was dismissed in November 1977.

Immediately after this election, there was very little time to start addressing the big issues, because the Janata Party, basically pasted together just to defeat Mrs Gandhi, was busy fighting over their choice of Prime Minister. Three men were in contention: Morarji Desai, Jagjivan Ram, and the wily Charan Singh. Desai emerged on top, but his coalition was shaky. The Cabinet never would hold both Charan Singh and Jagjivan Ram for long, and once Raj Narain joined them in plotting, Desai was outmanoeuvred. Desai lost a vote of no-confidence, and on July 28 Charan Singh became Prime Minister.

Desai did one thing—appoint the Shah Commission, chaired by J.C. Shah, a retired Chief Justice of the Supreme Court. Many believe this was one of his big accomplishments, but it 'turned into something of a cross between a U.S. Congressional inquiry and a Chinese people's court'.[4] Today we would call it a witch hunt. It was asked to investigate allegations of abuse of authority, excesses, malpractices, arrests, and atrocities committed during the Emergency, also to investigate Sanjay's forceful family planning programme and his indiscriminate and high-handed demolition of houses, huts, shops, and buildings in the name of slum clearance.

Susan Adelman

In addition, it was to investigate court appointments, misuse of the media, illegal search and seizures, and illegal detentions.[5]

Indira Gandhi refused to testify, and Sanjay appeared before the commission with a crowd of supporters in a 'free-for-all exchange of abuse and blows which culminated in the hurling of chairs'. [6] The report ran into three volumes, totalling over 500 pages, all castigating Indira and Sanjay Gandhi. This pleased her opponents, but it caused a public backlash of sympathy that paved the way towards Indira's later comeback. Later on, almost all copies of the Shah Commission Report vanished mysteriously. 'When Indira Gandhi came back to power in 1980, all the copies of the Shah Commission Report were withdrawn from all the libraries and buried without even an epitaph till now—it is reported that only one copy is available at the National Library of Australia.'[7]

It is amazing that she did return, but Malhotra explains her road back. After she had lost her election in 1977, she was assaulted by a series of committees and at first Mrs Gandhi was devastated. Gradually though she realized that the public were beginning to see her as a rejected woman under brutal attack. When the Harijans were beset by violence in Bihar, she visited them. Her enthusiastic reception encouraged her to make more speeches, the next one before a large audience in Delhi.

Still, her persecution continued. On October 3, 1977, Mrs Gandhi was arrested on corruption charges.[8] Probably the strongest advocate of arresting Indira was Home Minister Charan Singh; this was before he realized he would need her support to become Prime Minister. Malhotra described her arrest as a fiasco, because she immediately called out mobs of supporters to clamour for her release. The magistrate had to release her the next day because 'there was no charge against her'.

Indira Gandhi's return was foreshadowed on January 1, 1978, when the Congress party split into two: the supporters of Indira, called the Congress (Indira), and the portion that stood for socialism and secularism, called the Congress (S).

In the same year differences developed within the Janata

Party over the matter of dual membership with the Rashtriya Swayamsevak Sangh (RSS), and the Janata Party looked like it would break up. Ram bought some time by mediating a short-lived understanding, the Jethmalani Formula, but the Janata Party, fragmented after the 1980 elections, swept the Congress party back in. This was when Atal Bihari Vajpayee, L.K. Advani, and others spearheaded the formation of a new party, the Bharatiya Janata Party (BJP), and Ram emerged as the first all-India vice president of the BJP. This should have been an enviable launching pad for a major political position in the future, some even said for Prime Minister, but soon Ram would throw it away.

When he entered Parliament, Ram received a significant appointment—to the Privileges Committee, which had to determine whether Prime Minister Gandhi had committed a breach of privilege in 1974. This was when the Ministry of Commerce and Industry submitted a report to the Lok Sabha on alleged licence violations committed when Sanjay Gandhi's company, Maruti, had imported machinery. Indira Gandhi allegedly tried to stymie the report by charging the four responsible officials with corruption. She was asked to respond in writing to the committee's questions, but her lawyers provided her with multiple legal excuses. Those were easy for Ram to parry.

Next, Mrs Gandhi was requested to appear in person. After a long delay she did, but only to recite her constitutional protection against self-incrimination.[9] Ram's exchange with her was:

'Madam, you are not illiterate. You are supposed to be an educated and intelligent woman. Also, that provision applies to a prosecution in a criminal court. The Committee of Privileges is not a regular criminal court. It does not apply to us.'

Mrs Gandhi's response was still, 'My lawyers have advised me not to answer.'

Ram went on . . . 'Even when that provision applies, it is the court that decides which question you should answer and which you need not. Here we will allow you to decide. If you say the question will tend to incriminate you we will accept your view.'

Mrs Gandhi's response still remained, 'No, no, I will not answer.'

'Will you answer, "What is your name? What is your father's name?"' asked Ram.

Mrs Gandhi still refused to budge. Her next appearance before the committee did not go any better. The hearings went on for almost a year.

The committee chairman 'held her guilty of contempt of Parliament for obstructing four officials who were collecting information for a parliamentary question on Sanjay's Maruti car project', and Ram wrote a concurring opinion, which stated in part, 'Apart from fresh contumacy during our proceedings the original contempt is the grossest of its kind. The affront to the House is compounded by extreme callousness and malice against honest officers who have suffered tremendous harassment and humiliation at her hands. I would therefore recommend that the first respondent be committed for the duration of the session.' The committee requested an apology, nothing more, but Mrs Gandhi refused. Prime Minister Desai was clearly reluctant to prosecute her despite letters from Ram urging him to apply the law as impartially against her as they would against anyone else.

Ram actually met with Mrs Gandhi to discuss the apology. Through an intermediary, she asked to meet with him. Ram first notified the Prime Minister, and he met her at the house of A.R. Antulay in November 1978 at 11 p.m., in a bedroom. They sat together on a sofa, and they agreed to call each other by their first names. Ram began the conversation by proposing that they meet that evening as friends. All he wanted was for her to make a public apology for the Emergency and its excesses. He even offered to draft the apology. At one point she choked on a swallow of coffee and sneezed. Ram suggested she might be allergic to the coffee. Indira replied, 'No. I am allergic to you.' Said Ram, 'But I never got as close as the coffee cup did.'

In the course of their conversation, Indira asked, 'Supposing I decided not to sign the apology?'

Ram answered, 'We are only friends tonight. We will become political enemies again.'

At her request, Ram did draft the apology for her, but she never signed it. His enemies accused him of harassing Mrs Gandhi, but he responded that he had only asked for an apology.[10]

Parliament voted on December 19, 1978 to expel her from Parliament for the remainder of her term (until 1982), and to imprison her pending further consideration. Not surprisingly, once she came back to power, this sentence was roundly denounced by her party in a long parliamentary debate on May 7, 1981. Speaker after speaker accused the Janata Party and Ram of bias and of ramming through her sentence.[11] At any rate, the verdict did put her in Tihar Jail for a week. Now Charan Singh held a big rally for her, realizing he needed to curry favour with her in his machinations to replace Desai as Prime Minister. Ram warned him, 'After she has no further use for you she will spit you out like a sucked orange.' He was exactly right.

No sooner did Charan Singh enter office in July 1979 than did Indira Gandhi begin pressuring him to overturn an act of Parliament that Ram had originally initiated, the Special Courts Act of 1979. In the end, President Neelam Sanjiva Reddy dissolved Parliament. Singh never faced Parliament, and he became a caretaker Prime Minister until the January 1980[12] election. Ram says that Singh never enjoyed a minute of his prime ministership.

The bill that had upset Indira Gandhi so much was one that Ram had introduced as a Private Member Bill—the Special Courts Bill of 1978. The bill established special courts to expeditiously try those who acted in gross violation of justice or abused their positions during the Emergency. Sitting or retired judges of the High Court were to preside. In January of 1978, Ram's bill went to the Supreme Court for an advisory opinion.[13] A seven-member bench of the Supreme Court reviewed it, recommended several changes, and ruled that Parliament could consider the amended bill.

Parliament duly considered the court's recommendations, and it incorporated them into the Special Courts Act, passed in 1979. This was the act to which Indira Gandhi objected so much that she destroyed Charan Singh's prime ministership, after all his scheming.[14] Not the only Private Member Bill that Ram has introduced, it was just one of his attempts to remodel the court system.

The highest profile legal case of that time was known as the *Kissa Kursi Ka* case,[15] meaning 'the story of the chair'. The word 'chair' in this context symbolizes power. A Mr Amrit Nahata produced a movie by the name to caricature the Emergency, the dictatorship of Prime Minister Gandhi, and the thuggery of Sanjay, and it had been completely suppressed during the Indira Gandhi regime.

In 1978, Desai appointed Ram and Sri Jaisinghani as public prosecutors at the request of the Central Bureau of Investigation (CBI), since it badly needed prosecutors who would not accept bribes. Ram accepted Desai's offer with pleasure, as did Sri Jaisinghani. Ram said they should pay him only one rupee.

The problems had started when Indira's Board of Censors refused permission to screen the movie. The moviemaker filed for a court order, and the court ordered the Board of Censors to review the film.

Sanjay and V.C. Shukla, Indira Gandhi's Minister of Information and Broadcasting, decided to destroy all copies of this film. They loaded 13 steel trunks containing 150 spools of film on trucks, sending them under special escort from Bombay to Delhi. In Delhi, the spools were transferred to two Maruti vehicles, taken to Maruti Limited, Sanjay's auto company, and burned. After the Emergency was lifted, the police raided Maruti Limited, found incriminating evidence and arrested two security guards immediately. Both of them signed statements documenting how the spools had been burned. They then were pardoned and let go. The prosecution compiled a lengthy list of 138 witnesses.

The case started in the sessions court in 1978, went on appeal to the Delhi High Court on April 11, 1978, and it went to the Supreme Court on May 5, 1978. Early in the sessions court trial, Sanjay was accused of bribing the witnesses. The High Court ruled that Sanjay could remain out on bail. Ram and Sri appealed to the Supreme Court to cancel his bail, in order to prevent his access to the other witnesses. That became a critical argument.

The Supreme Court case came before Justice Y.V. Chandrachud, one of the judges who had voted for the government in the habeas corpus case. For this reason, when he came up for Chief Justice,

70 lawyers had petitioned Prime Minister Desai not to appoint him. One of those lawyers was Ram. The Law Minister, Shanti Bhushan, had requested opinions from the state chief justices, but virtually all agreed that to pass over him would be to commit the same offence Prime Minister Gandhi had committed. With his seniority, he must be appointed. Now Ram had to present his case before a Chief Justice Chandrachud.

The trial started in sessions court in February 1978, four days after the scheduled date, because Sanjay had managed to obtain a court-ordered delay. By the first day of the trial, the first security officer still supported the prosecution, but the second guard had flipped.

In Ram's cross-examination of the second guard, he responded to Ram:[16]

'What I said yesterday was false. Today I am telling the truth.'

'Why?' asked Ram.

'Because my mother told me to always tell the truth,' the man responded simply.

'When did she tell you this?' asked Ram.

'When I was a boy,' was the reply.

'For all these years you seem to have forgotten your mother's instructions,' commented Ram. 'So why remember it today?'

Some witnesses testified that Sanjay had offered them a bribe to testify in his favour. The court added a more serious charge—tampering with the evidence—the penalty for which is imprisonment.

After one security guard had turned hostile, so did 17 more witnesses. By the time the third witness testified, it was clear that the case was fixed. Ram, as special prosecutor, contended that Sanjay should no longer remain out of jail on bail since clearly he would tamper with witnesses if allowed at large, but the High Court allowed him out on bail.

On the question of bail, the Supreme Court began by saying,[17] 'Rejection of bail when bail is applied for is one thing; cancellation of bail already granted is quite another. It is easier to reject a bail application in a non-bailable case than to cancel a bail granted in such a case.' Nevertheless, after listening to Ram and Sri lay out the evidence that Sanjay had tampered with witnesses, the court said that, 'the evidence points in one direction only, leaving no manner of doubt that the respondent has misused the facility afforded to him by the High Court by granting anticipatory bail to him. The sequence of events is too striking to fail to catch the watchful eye.'

The court ruled 'we allow the appeal partly, set aside the judgment of the High Court dated April 11, cancel the respondent's bail for a period of one month from today and direct that he be taken into custody'. Ram and Sri had the satisfaction of sending Sanjay Gandhi to Tihar jail on May 5, 1978. His term actually stretched out longer, lasting until his mother stood for re-election.

After 10,000 pages of evidence and 140 witnesses, in a 500-page opinion, the sessions court convicted both Sanjay and V.C. Shukla on 14 counts, ordering sentences of two years of rigorous imprisonment on each count, to run concurrently. Both of them appealed immediately to the Supreme Court. They were in luck; by then Indira Gandhi had become Prime Minister again.

The aftermath of the Kissa Kursi Ka case became a three-ring circus.[18] Sanjay moved a petition against Ram on February 22, 1980 for using false evidence, and on cross-examination, Ram demonstrated that Sanjay had committed perjury. Sanjay dropped his case.

Maneka Gandhi, Sanjay's wife, alleged publicly that Rani had consorted with a police officer connected to the case, and Rani sued Maneka for defamation. The Bombay public was loudly in favour of Rani. Certain she could not have a fair trial in Bombay, Maneka petitioned the Supreme Court for permission to transfer the case to Delhi.[19]

In his verdict, Justice Krishna Iyer wrote:

'Assurance of a fair trial is the first imperative of the dispensation of justice, and the central criterion for the court to consider when a motion for transfer is made is not the hypersensitivity or relative convenience of a party or easy availability of legal services or like mini grievances.

One of the common circumstances alleged in applications for

transfer is the avoidance of substantial prejudice to a party or witnesses on account of logistics or like factors . . . In the present case the petitioner claims that both the parties reside in Delhi and some formal witnesses belong to Delhi; but the meat of the matter, in a case of defamation, is something different. The main witnesses are those who speak to having read the offending matter and other relevant circumstances flowing therefrom. They belong to Bombay in this case and the suggestion of the petitioner's counsel that Delhi readers may be substitute witnesses and the complainant may content herself with examining such persons is too presumptuous for serious consideration.'

Justice Iyer refused the transfer, writing, 'The magistrate is the master of the orderly conduct of court proceedings and his authority shall not hang limp if his business is stalled by brow-beating. It is his duty to clear the court of confusion, yelling and nerve-racking gestures which mar the serious tone of judicial hearing.' He said further, 'Every fleeting rumpus should not lead to a removal of the case as it may prove to be a . . . surrender of justice to commotion.'

Since then, the Indian courts have cited this case as precedent a whopping 55 times, because it establishes the grounds necessary for moving a trial from one location to another. Not only that, but Justice Iyer's opinion is so eloquent that it is tempting to quote whole paragraphs as literature. This is a perfect example of the elegant language for which the Indian courts at their best are known around the world. After the verdict, Maneka wrote a letter of apology to Rani, and they made up.

Rani actually defended Maneka when her husband Sanjay died without a will in June 1980, and Indira, now Prime Minister again, evicted her from the house.[20] Because of the convoluted laws that govern inheritance in India, Rani had to show that since Maneka is a Sikh, and Sanjay a Parsi like his father, theirs was a mixed marriage obligated to marry under the Special Marriages Act. This affected their son's inheritance. Under the Hindu Marriage Act, one-third would go to the mother, one-third to the son, and one-third to the widow. Under the Special Marriages Act, the son would receive two-thirds of the property, the widow one-third.

Indira asserted that she was Hindu and so was Sanjay, meaning that the Hindu Marriage Act would apply, and she should inherit a portion of the money that Maneka claimed for her son. And not only that, she was the Prime Minister. Not convinced that Sanjay was a Parsi, the court awarded the money to Indira. Anyhow Indira left the disputed money to her grandson in her will. By now Rani and Maneka were fast friends. When Maneka ran for election on the BJP ticket, Rani and Ram contributed to her campaign. Her son is an active Member of Parliament today and has been a spokesman for the BJP.

Ram's joy at sending Sanjay to jail in the *Kissa Kursi Ka* case only lasted until both Sanjay and Shukla were released on bail by order of the Delhi High Court, pending appeal. After that, elections on January 6, 1980 brought Indira back to power.

The final appeal on the *Kissa Kursi Ka* case came to the Supreme Court in 1980, but both Ram and Sri Jaisinghani resigned as public prosecutors on the grounds that Sanjay was the de facto Prime Minister. For this appeal, the new prosecutor, J.S. Vasu, the Advocate General of the Punjab, 'took 15 minutes to dispose of a record that ran into 6,500 pages,'[21] filling 20 volumes' and three Supreme Court judges wrote a 55-page order of acquittal.[22] Sri cites this case, along with *Antulay vs. Nayak and ADM Jabalpur* (the habeas corpus case) as one of three in which the highest court of the land failed its nation.

One last item of business was still pending at the end of Desai's tenure. In 1978, Desai appointed a commission to consider several aspects of affirmative action, the Mandal Commission, and it reported back in 1980. The final report recommended reservations and quotas for what India calls scheduled castes, tribes, and other backward classes (OBCs), altogether 52 per cent of the population. Many of the assumptions and recommendations proved to be deeply controversial, and we will see how dramatic the effect was when they finally were implemented 10 years later. That, too, was a matter in which Ram would become deeply involved.

18

Early 1980s

Indira Gandhi and the Congress party returned to power on January 6, 1980. It was less than two weeks after the Soviet Union invaded Afghanistan, and the United States was pouring money and arms into Pakistan to offset an expanding Russia. War was about to break out between Iraq and Iran. This was the year that Assam boiled over with anger against the 100,000 Bangladeshis living there, and thousands were killed. The Asian Games came to Delhi, and Sanjay built the infrastructure with conscripted labour. On June 23, 1980, Sanjay died in an airplane accident. Disaster struck a factory community of Bhopal in 1984. Another cycle of droughts and price increases caused communal violence in the north. A Sikh insurgency in the Punjab ended in a raid on the Sikh Golden Temple, and Prime Minister Indira Gandhi was assassinated. The government hit back.

Mahesh returned from Oxford, joined the Bombay Bar in 1981, and opened an office at Jolly Makers Chamber, on Nariman Point near the Oberoi Hotel, an excellent address. Later he bought a second office, and this is where Ram works today when he is in Mumbai. Rani was admitted to practise before the Supreme Court, took an office in Delhi, and began a career of avenging wronged women. Ram, fresh from a brand-new knee replacement from Detroit, was re-elected to Parliament in 1980. The three Jethmalani lawyers were poised to take on the world.

Despite the gathering international storm clouds, Mrs Gandhi and her son Sanjay returned to power, interested above all in settling scores. Corruption soon spread, especially in Parliament. Sanjay had picked a number of his own candidates for Parliament, many just opportunists who regarded a seat as a ticket to riches.

All this was beyond the ability of a Ram Jethmalani to intervene. Even as a Member of Parliament, he effectively could do nothing. That left him to concentrate on his legal work. Fortunately for a famous lawyer, India had no shortage of thieves, scoundrels, and crooked politicians.

Ram had several professional contacts with the Bombay underworld in the late 1960s, and he even represented Haji Mastan, a name on every list of his most notorious clients.

Mastan Mirza was another name on the list. Bombay's first celebrity gangster, his fame peaked during the 1970s and 1980s. He started as a poor boy from Tamil Nadu. After moving to Bombay he took to smuggling watches and gold. Government-imposed prohibition was a bonanza, enabling him to branch out into smuggling alcohol. He was jailed during the Emergency, got religion, and began calling himself Haji Mastan. He found his way into the film industry, adopted the conceit of white designer clothes, and travelled in a chauffeured Mercedes. Now a man of the people, he founded a political party, devoted time to the poor, and became the subject of Bollywood movies.[1]

In 1969 another Bombay gangster, Yusuf Patel, fell out with Haji Mastan. One day when he was sitting in a café, a bullet grazed past Patel's right ear, leaving a gaping hole. Ram was asked to defend Mastan, who allegedly had hired a hit man to kill Patel. When Ram met Mastan in jail he denied the crime so vehemently that Ram believed him. The amazing feat was that, despite Mastan's reputation and high visibility, Ram succeeded in getting him acquitted.[2]

In 1984 Haji Mastan faced smuggling charges,[3] was detained under MISA, released, detained under COFEPOSA, released during the Emergency, and served under Smugglers and Foreign Exchange Manipulators Act (SAFEMA). In other words, this appeal to the Supreme Court came after Haji Mastan had been arrested for illegal activities under at least three anti-smuggling laws. His good fortune through all this legal alphabet soup was that both Ram and Rani represented him. Even better, they were able to show that the authorities had never supplied Mastan with copies of the documents that were necessary for his defence, and the court ruled that this error had vitiated the order of detention. Ram won on the simple premise that the arresting authorities had not followed proper procedures. The question of Mastan's guilt for actual misdeeds was not at issue. Haji Mastan was acquitted again.

Another infamous member of the Bombay underworld, Dawood Ibrahim,[4] was one of the most feared leaders of organized crime in India. He started as a smuggler in Bombay, corrupted the hawala system of informal banking, spread his operations throughout India, and eventually allegedly linked up with Al Qaeda. After the 1993 bombings in Mumbai, he was declared a global terrorist and escaped to Dubai.

On September 6, 1983, the gangster Amirzada Nawab Khan was brought to the sessions court, standing accused of the murder of Dawood Ibrahim's older brother. Amirzada was the nephew of another gangster, Lala, who was deep into a gang war with Ibrahim. While the judges were taking their seats on the bench, a 20-year-old man slipped into court, headed towards the prisoner, and shot him point blank from five feet away. The police shot him in the leg as he was about to jump out of a window from the courtroom to the street. This assassin was David Pardeshi, hired by two men at the behest of Dawood Ibrahim to avenge the murder of his brother.

With Pardeshi in jail, Dawood Ibrahim asked Ram and Mahesh to meet him in Dubai to discuss the case. He greeted them in Dubai at the head of a parade of white limousines, and he was surprisingly accommodating. He was happy to have Pardeshi plead guilty, but he wanted them to keep Pardeshi from getting the death penalty. The inference was that he intended to spring him out of jail. So a life sentence would be perfectly satisfactory. Ibrahim would pay the lawyers well.[5]

The deal was too tempting. Their defence was that Pardeshi was an orphan who had been driven to a life of crime by a vicious older brother, and he only took the contract under threat of being killed himself. They succeeded in lowering his sentence to life in prison, but eventually Pardeshi himself was killed in a gangland hit similar to the one he had perpetrated. Thus began the great gang wars in Bombay.

One of the remarkable aspects of Ram's career is how he moves easily between cases of criminal law, family law, contract law, and constitutional law. Sri Jaisinghani says that Ram knows more law than any other lawyer in India.

One complicated 1981 case, *A.K. Roy etc. vs. Union of India*,[6] involved both criminal law and constitutional law. Several Indian lawyers have admitted privately to this author that they are not exactly sure what it is all about. Now imagine Ram, while handling a large number of cases at the same time, with his responsibilities in Parliament, and with everything else going on in his life, keeping all the elements of the case straight.

At issue were the National Security Act of 1980, and its predecessor, the National Security Ordinance.

The case began when A.K. Roy, a Marxist Member of the Parliament, was detained under the ordinance by an order passed by the district magistrate of Dhanbad, on the ground that he was indulging in activities which were prejudicial to public order.

Ram had spent years establishing the rights of detenus, but when the 44th Amendment was enacted in 1978 to correct the abuses of the Emergency, it lacked some of the protections that detenus had before the Emergency. The National Security Act that passed in 1980 also failed to protect some detenus' rights, but it was not consistent with the 44th Amendment. To make things even worse, the 44th Amendment was not fully implemented by 1980. Two questions before the court were whether the National Security Act was constitutional and when it should apply.

We will not discuss the constitutional points, but it is interesting to look at Ram's arguments in defence of the hapless detenus.

Ram was one of several lawyers on this case. His assignment was to explain 'the vagueness and unreasonableness of the provisions of the Act and the punitive conditions of detention'.

Ram said, 'A cardinal requirement of the rule of law is that citizens must know with certainty where lawful conduct ends and unlawful conduct begins; but more than that, the bureaucrats must know the limits of their power.'

The court quotes Ram as citing the following US precedent: 'Fundamental fairness requires that a person cannot be sent to jail for a crime he could not with reasonable certainty know he was committing: reasonable certainty in that respect is all the more essential when vagueness might induce individuals to forgo their rights of speech, press, and association for fear of violating an unclear law.'

'Shri Jethmalani attacked the constitutionality of the very National Security Act itself on the ground that it is a draconian piece of legislation which deprives people of their personal liberty excessively and unreasonably, confers vast and arbitrary powers of detention upon the executive and sanctions the use of those powers by following a procedure which is unfair and unjust.'

The court summarized the elements of natural justice with which Ram said an act must be consistent: '(i) the detenu must have the right to be represented by a lawyer of his choice; (ii) he must have the right to cross-examine persons on whose statements the order of detention is founded; and (iii) he must have the right to present evidence in rebuttal of the allegations made against him.'

In addition, the detenu should know the reasons for his detention, and the board's proceedings should be open to the public. Also, the Advisory Board must examine whether all the obligatory procedural steps were taken and the right to be heard will be of little help if the detenu did not comprehend the right to be assisted by a counsel or to be represented by a counsel.

Ram also raised concerns 'relating to the post-detention conditions applicable to detenus in the matter of their detention. The learned counsel made a grievance that the letters of detenus are censored, that they are not provided with reading or writing material according to their requirements and that the ordinary amenities of life are denied to them.'

On the constitutional questions,[7] the court said that an ordinance was law and could affect life and liberty. The court also ruled that preventative detention was recognized under the original Constitution.

The court bought many of Ram's arguments in its verdict, writing: 'Provisions of section 3 of the Act cannot be struck down on the ground of their vagueness and certainty.' However, the courts must 'strive to give to those concepts a narrower construction than what the literal words suggest'.

The court granted some rights and denied others: 'The members of his household . . . must be informed in writing of the passing of the order of detention and of the fact that the detenu has been taken in custody. Intimation must also be given as to the place of detention, including the place where the detenu is transferred from time to time.

'If the detaining authority or the Government takes the aid of a legal practitioner or a legal adviser before the Advisory Board, the detenu must be allowed the facility of appearing before the Board through a legal practitioner.'

The court waxed poetic: 'If justice is to be done he must at least have the help of a friend who can assist him to give coherence to his stray and wandering ideas.'

'In the proceedings before the Advisory Board, the detenu has no right to cross-examine either the persons on the basis of whose statement the order of detention is made or the detaining authority.'

The detenu could rebut allegations against him before the Advisory Board by his own evidence, but the proceedings of the Advisory Board do not have to be open to the public.

'The Government must afford the detenus all reasonable facilities for an existence consistent with human dignity. They should be permitted to wear their own clothes, eat their own food, have interviews with the members of their families at least once a week and, last but not the least, have reading and writing material according to their reasonable requirements . . . Persons who are detained under the National Security Act must be segregated from the convicts and kept in a separate part of the place of detention.' The court attached considerable importance to the last point and repeated it several times.

The court obviously did a certain amount of picking and

choosing in deciding which rights to allow detenus, but Ram and his colleagues succeeded in restoring many of the earlier protections that detenus used to enjoy. That made the case significant, both for its legal precedents and as part of Ram's personal fight for detenus' rights. Oh, and the court held the National Security Act constitutional.

The next case is a dramatic example of Ram's fight against corruption, and his perseverance. It also was an albatross hanging around Ram's neck for years. While not the only interminable case in his career, it certainly was close. Though it is the sort of ongoing catastrophe that might dominate the life of someone else, for Ram it was ongoing background noise. For a non-lawyer, even for a lawyer, this cascade of court cases cannot fail to astonish.

Abdul Rehman Antulay, the Chief Minister of Maharashtra and past general secretary of the Congress party, had set up various public trusts between August 1980 and September 1981, one of which he called the Indira Gandhi Trust. Claiming they were charities, he collected funds through public contributions and used them for pay-offs and kickbacks to benefit the Congress party as well as himself. This was named the Cement Scam, because any contractor who wanted permission to buy cement had to make a 'voluntary contribution' of Rs 40 per 100 kilo bag to one of Antulay's 'charities', after which they calmly received their cement in seven to eight days. The same scam applied to anyone who wanted a liquor licence, a land allotment for construction, or a 'no objection' from the government for transfer of certain categories of tenanted commercial premises.

In 1981, the *Indian Express* ran an exposé of the Cement Scam, prompting Ram to file a corruption criminal prosecution on behalf of R.S. Nayak, a Member of the Maharashtra Legislature (MLA) from the BJP. Ironically, Antulay had once assisted Ram to leave India during the Emergency, but now Ram, Sri Jaisinghani, and Mahesh pursued him relentlessly.

The court explains: 'The running thread through various allegations is that the accused by abusing or misusing his office of Chief Minister obtained or attempted to obtain gratification other than legal remunerations as a motive or reward for doing or forbearing to do any official act as Chief Minister.' In short, he was a crook.

Nayak first prosecuted Antulay in a court of Special Judges on September 11, 1981. By 1982, Antulay had resigned his position as Chief Minister but remained an MLA. Appeals and counter-appeals focused on the question of whether he still was a public servant if he only was an MLA, not a Chief Minister.

After a series of writs and petitions, a five-man bench of the Supreme Court held on February 16, 1984[8] that an MLA was not a public servant, and it directed the case to be tried by the High Court, on the theory that this court was less liable to corruption in the case of a former Chief Minister than the lower court. This was an interesting decision, because the case became the first criminal case to be heard by a High Court, albeit under the direction of the Supreme Court.

In an April 17, 1984 appeal, Antulay asked for a Special Judge. A bench of two judges refused to overrule the larger bench.

After a one-year trial, Special Judge D.N. Mehta of the High Court framed 21 charges against Antulay, but he exonerated him on 22 other charges. Since these were the more serious charges, Ram and Sri filed an appeal on the 22 charges to the Supreme Court. Supreme Court Judges Bhagwati and Mishra ruled that Antulay was prima facie guilty on all 43 counts, said he deserved to be convicted on all of them and sent the case back to the High Court to proceed under a new judge.

Judge Shah of the Bombay High Court held that Antulay was not only prima facie guilty on all 43 counts, but that he was also prima facie guilty of conspiracy on most of these counts. He now framed 79 charges against Antulay.

Antulay filed a petition to the Supreme Court in 1986,[9] questioning the jurisdiction of the High Court judge, and the Supreme Court stayed the proceedings of the High Court. He questioned whether the 1984 Supreme Court decision of five judges that had referred his case to the High Court was legal, arguing that it had deprived him of one level of appeal—to the High Court—

because if it is decided by the High Court it could only be appealed to the Supreme Court. That appeal went to a bench of seven judges. On April 29, 1988, by a decision of five to two, the court overruled the unanimous decision of the five-judge bench and held that the trial, which had been 90 per cent completed, was void. The order transferring the trial to the High Court was not authorized by law. It ruled that the trial should be stopped, sent back to the Special Court, and started all over again from the beginning. Furthermore, the court held that they must start all over again to accumulate the evidence, even though by that time 10 of the original witnesses had died. One of the two dissenting judges said 'this decision does not make good sense or good law.'

There was more, much more, but the reader will get the idea by now that the case ping-ponged on every possible issue. From the venue to the choice of judge, to a stay on the operation of Antulay's trusts, to alleging conflicts of interest on the part of a judge; the defence used every delaying tactic known to man. Meanwhile Antulay took to the press, accusing Ram of a fictional financial impropriety, and Ram responded. Another politician made a new accusation against Ram; Ram rebutted, and so forth.

The case returned to the Supreme Court for the last time on December 10, 1991.[10] Antulay appealed to the Supreme Court, arguing the importance of a speedy trial, and asking whether a time limit should 'be fixed for concluding all criminal proceedings.' Saying this 'raises a very important constitutional question', the division bench directed the appeal to a constitutional bench. By this time, the political environment had changed, and the BJP instructed Nayak to change lawyers. The dogged persistence of Ram and Sri had become a liability. Nayak's new lawyer, Mr More, had waited until 1990 to file a writ in the Bombay High Court asking to continue the trial, and in 1991, a Special Judge was appointed to try the case. Ram arranged to be there.

The court heard two long, drawn-out cases in the same trial that day, and Ram slickly managed to represent the state of Bihar in the other one, a murder case[11] that had started in 1975, that had almost countless interim appeals since then. The *Antulay* case had accumulated more than 10,000 pages of evidence and its own spectacular number of petitions to the courts since 1981.

The judges sagely observed about the right to speedy trial, 'Delay is usually welcomed by the accused. He postpones the delay of reckoning thereby. It may impair the prosecution's ability to prove the case against him. In the meantime, he remains free to indulge in crimes.' They did add: 'Of course, there may be cases where the prosecution, for whatever reason, also delays the proceedings.'

The Supreme Court continued:

A large volume of evidence was led by him (R.S. Nayak) in Bombay High Court during the years 1984–86. As many as 57 witnesses were examined and 963 documents exhibited. The Bombay High Court spent almost a year in recording the evidence on behalf of the complainant, running into more than 1200 pages. He had practically closed his side. It must have necessarily cost him great effort apart from expense. All this came to nought with the judgment of this Court rendered in April, 1988.

It is true that after the judgment of Seven-Judge Bench of this Court in April, 1988, the complainant did not himself move the Government of Maharashta to designate a Special Judge for the case but waited till another person, an advocate, did so.

The petitioner has never been incarcerated—not even for a day. It is also not clearly established how this delay has prejudiced his case . . . he merely stated that six persons whom he wanted to examine at the trial have expired.

In fact, by now one-third of the original witnesses had died.

The court dismissed Antulay's appeal as well as the appeal in the other case, 'On a consideration of all the facts and circumstances of the case balancing process . . . the proper direction to make is to direct the expeditious trial on a day-to-day basis. Accordingly, we dismiss petition N. 833 of 1990 and direct the Special Judge designated for this case to take up this case on a priority basis and proceed with it day-to-day until it is concluded.'

In the end, the case went before a Special Court within the sessions court, which acquitted Antulay of all charges, even though the Supreme Court had ruled him guilty of every one. By now, Sri and Ram had washed their hands of the whole case. Sri says he spent five years of his life on it.

What happened? The politics had changed. Antulay had resigned from the Congress party, formed a new party, lost his bid for re-election and had a cardiac arrest, from which he recovered. By now Indira Gandhi was dead, and the BJP had other objectives. When the BJP took Ram off the case, Ram wrote in protest to L.K. Advani, the head of the BJP.

Advani did not deny that the BJP essentially let Antulay off. Dropping Ram and Sri suited their current objectives. Ram had become the driving force in this case, not Nayak. Ram is the one who wanted to fight corruption, even if he had to spend large sums of his own money and years of his life on it. He was like a bulldog with a bone in his teeth—nobody could pull out the bone.

In the end, this case established an important legal principle— that any private citizen could file a private complaint on corruption charges, even against a Chief Minister. In time the law was amended to say that an MLA is a public servant, and he requires the sanction of the appropriate authority for his criminal prosecution.

Meanwhile, Ram's friend Ramakrishna Hegde, the Chief Minister of Karnataka, jollied him back into the BJP party, and in April 1988 Ram re-entered the Rajya Sabha, from the state of Karnataka, sponsored by R.K. Hegde and Ramnath Goenka, of the *Indian Express*.

Ram's relationship with Goenka began during the Emergency, and it became even closer during the Bofors scandal—which we will discuss in a later chapter. Ram had an important role in keeping the *Indian Express* alive during the Emergency, and he made it a sell-out during the Bofors scandal with his 10 questions a day to Rajiv. As a candidate from Karnataka, Ram declared that the Goenka's guesthouse was his residence in Bangalore. Candidates for the Rajya Sabha can choose their district, and the residence they identify need not be their only residence; still some complained that Ram did not live there. Ram's rejoinder was that he always stayed there when he came to the National Law School in Bangalore to teach, and he still does. As a professor at the law school, Ram never even charges for transportation when he teaches. He even first joined the Masonic Lodge in Bangalore. His declaration of residence was challenged, but the challenge failed, in a decision by Justice M. Rama Jois.

There was some additional awkwardness. When Indira Gandhi had first proposed running for a Rajya Sabha seat from Karnataka in a by-election in 1978, she had claimed an ashram as her residence, but she was forced to run for the Lok Sabha from another district, Chikmagalur,[12] because someone had filed a criminal lawsuit over her stated residence, and Ram had supported the suit.

Syed Modi was a National Badminton Champion for eight years, representing India in many international championships. On July 28, 1987,[13] Modi was murdered, and two people were accused. With Ram as their lawyer, they were acquitted by the High Court of Allahabad, but in 1994 the CBI appealed.

The first accused was Sanjay Singh, a minister in Uttar Pradesh from July 22, 1982 to August 8, 1987. The second was Amita Kulkarni Modi, Syed Modi's wife. Amita was a marketing manager in Lucknow Sports, a position that Singh had urged her to take. Both were champion badminton players. The two accused had met and fallen in love in Beijing during the Third International Asian Invitation Championship in 1978. Despite her affair with Singh, Syed Modi and Amita Modi married on May 14, 1984.

The prosecution alleged that Amita and Singh conspired to kill her husband, when Amita's husband had pressured her to give up her relationship with Singh. The prosecution further claimed that hired hands shot Syed Modi as he was emerging from the stadium at Lucknow. As it happened, Sanjay Singh was a nephew of the Prime Minister, V.P. Singh. The Prime Minister called Ram, who had just arrived in New York for a vacation with his son, his daughter-in-law, and Ratna. Ram returned to India immediately, chartered a flight to Lucknow, and got Sanjay out on bail. Then he flew back to New York, exhausted, to restart his vacation.

In the sessions court, Ram argued that Syed Modi had known about the affair all along—he once had even given a gift to her lover. Under those circumstances, Ram asked, what was the motive? The court ruled that the material on record did not establish a prima facie case against Amita or Singh and that mere association between the two was not enough to prove a conspiracy. Amazingly, it acquitted both of them, and the High Court affirmed the acquittal. That was when the state petitioned the Supreme Court.

Shanti Bhushan represented Amita and Ram represented Singh. The Additional Solicitor General admitted there was only circumstantial evidence of a conspiracy. The court wrote that the prosecution could only suggest what the motive might be and that the mere suspicion of a motive is not sufficient grounds for a charge. The petition was dismissed.

Whatever Ram and Bhushan said, it must have been blinding if the court was unable to see a motive for a wife and her lover to have the husband killed. Of course a sceptic might ask whether the court would have found a conspiracy if Sanjay Singh were not the nephew of the Prime Minister. When Singh and Amita married, Ram was a guest at the wedding.

19

The Younger Jethmalanis Marry

By the 1980s, while politics, law, and public advocacy preoccupied Ram, the thoughts of the younger Jethmalanis turned to love. Ram made sure the wedding galas were everything his children could want, and the guests included distinguished figures of society, politics, and law. Anyone who has been to a real Sindhi wedding will never forget the glitter. If it is outdoors, the groom rides in on a white horse, in traditional coat and turban, escorted by musicians and dancing celebrants. Whether outside or in a five-star hotel, lights and bright banners festoon every tree and pillar. Food stations offer cuisine from all over India, often the world. Gleaming silk saris shimmer with gold trim, and the diamond necklaces are blinding. We have seen diamonds sewn into a sari.

With elegant invitations for each night, the wedding week features a formal schedule of events. One night, Muslim women draw henna designs on the hands and feet of the bride, bridal party, friends and family, paisleys that take days to fade. At the sangeet the night before the wedding, the women dress in chic outfits of the latest design, and everyone dances to deafening music. That is the night to gasp at the women loaded down with diamonds as big as headlights, set in gold. Some families put on a family dance show for their guests, rehearsing the routines for weeks before. At Jethmalani weddings, Ram's greatest pleasure is in joyfully accepting congratulatory kisses from all the women. Sometimes the bride and groom have watched and reminded each other that even if they had accidentally invited a woman who once had an affair with one of their fathers, it could not be helped. Otherwise who could they invite?

Except most of the Jethmalani weddings were not like that at all. Sarla married very young and Sundri married right after college. They had perfectly proper weddings, but the family certainly was not wealthy. There were problems too. When the marriages of Sundri's children ended in divorce, Ram was always there for them, if ever it should become necessary, in his role as the patriarch of the family.

Shobha was a slim, fair-skinned girl with finely etched features and a dazzling smile. Her courtship was romantic. Suresh, from a good Sindhi family, had been a classmate of Shobha's in medical school, where they were a couple. His parents also came from Pakistan, where his grandfather had owned a huge property with many tenant farmers. His grandfather had five wives in a row, all of whom had children, and some of whom died in childbirth. After coming to Bombay with a family of 12 half-brothers and sisters, Suresh's parents moved into an apartment on Altamount Road, across from the Mafatlal House at the time, now down the street from the 29-storey Ambani House.

In those days the Mafatlal estate and its gardens commanded the top of Cumballa Hill, and Altamount Road led up to it with graceful Bombay bungalows on either side. Today the estate has been replaced with apartment buildings, but stately peepul trees and massive banyans still line the street. The Gehani apartment, now remodelled in western style, is the one that Shobha and Suresh still enjoy today. With front and back windows open, airy breezes blow through, bringing the aroma of two old gulmohur trees with their huge orange flowers in the summer.

Shobha and Suresh broke up after medical school. Upset, Shobha went with her brothers for a six-month visit to her aunt Sarla in Iran. Suresh was desperate to get in contact with her, but he did not have her telephone number. One day he met Rani at a gas station, and she told him Shobha was coming back soon. The day Shobha returned to Bombay, she went to Ram's Advent apartment, and there was Suresh, sitting on the couch. This was in March. They eloped on May 1, 1970.

The marriage, no secret as far as Shobha's parents were concerned, was at Ratna's parents' home, Amarchand Mansion, in Colaba. Perhaps not by coincidence, Maharaj Laxman officiated, as he had done for Ram and Ratna's secret wedding. Shobha's parents and family were there, but Suresh's opposed the union at first, so they were kept in the dark. Twenty or more close friends and family also just happened to stop by that morning. Everyone remembers the wedding as a fun event, and Shobha as a gorgeous bride.

They had planned an elegant wedding reception for 300 guests at the legendary Bombay Taj Mahal Palace in February 1971, but it ended up with maybe 1000, maybe more; nobody knows. Ram was campaigning for Parliament that winter, and he told his constituents that his daughter was going to get married at the Taj Mahal hotel. And he gave them the date. Worse, he invited them to come. And come they did, excited about a wedding at the famous Taj Mahal hotel and expecting the very best of food and drink. The Taj, however, had planned for 300. Shobha remembers looking out in terror at the enormous crowd, while the Taj management scrambled to feed them. The bills rolled in at the same that Ram was trying to pay for his election campaign.

Shortly afterwards, Shobha and Suresh left for Michigan, to start their residencies in the United States, Shobha in paediatrics, and Suresh in pathology. They built a house in suburban Grosse Pointe, and raised two sons, Sunil and Girish. Since Shobha can arrange appointments with all the best doctors in Michigan, Ram travels to Detroit for any special medical procedures, whether on his eyes, knees, or coronaries. Shobha, a natural-born caregiver, has become the medical support for her entire extended family in India. With her background in utilization review at her clinic, she is a fearsome critic of medical costs and practices. Whenever disaster has struck, Shobha has flown to India, shepherded her family member through all the steps of diagnosis and treatment, threatened, cajoled, scolded, double-checked records, and reassured until the ailing patient recovered. She has done her best to keep them well.

Shobha's sons, Sunil and Girish, have gone into real estate, with considerable success. Sunil graduated from law school, but he now is an astute real estate developer who appears to have inherited the Ram gene, whatever that is. He is generous to a fault, a big spender, well liked and hugely successful. Except for the fact that he has a good head for business, he is the adult grandchild who most closely resembles his grandfather.

In April 1972, Maya came to Windsor, Canada, across the river from Detroit. After she finished studying physiotherapy at G.S. Medical College, she worked for three years in Bombay and then wanted to try her fortunes abroad. She applied for jobs in several cities, but her first choice was Jaffa, Israel. Given the political situation at that time, the family would not allow her to go, so she chose Windsor, close to Shobha.

In Bombay she had dated Pratab Gidvani. He was a graduate of the Bombay Indian Institute of Engineering, and he took a master's degree in engineering at the University of Pittsburgh. As soon as Maya arrived in Canada, she called Pratab. He arrived immediately. Maya was tall, willowy, and stunning, and Pratab hovered around her like a bee around a flower. When the time came for Pratap and Maya to decide about their future, they took a trip to visit friends in Montreal. They loved Montreal, stayed on for two more months, made their decision, and married in December 1973.

There actually were two marriages, one civil and the other religious. Before the civil marriage Pratab called a government office to inquire what he needed to get married. The clerk answered, 'Young man, do you have a woman?'

The Indian marriage was held on December 22, 1973, during a tremendous snowstorm. Only eight couples came. Shobha and Suresh arrived cold and bedraggled from Detroit, but they remember it was great fun. Maya and Pratab lived in Montreal for years; their son Rohan and daughter Lara were born and received their first college degrees there, and they returned to Bombay in the 1990s. Both children went on to obtain advanced academic degrees.

Janak was a cheery young man who resembled his mother,

Ratna. He married Manya Patil in a lavish rural wedding on the property of her father, who managed a sugar plantation. The whole family rode to the wedding in a train, and they were met at the station by the whole panchayat, the village elders. Manya's sister Smita Patil, one of the most celebrated Bollywood actresses, hosted a party at the Oberoi, and there also was a reception at the Turf Club in 1984. Janak's professional career took him from Touche Ross in Montreal, to New York, then to Drexel, Burnham, and Lambert. When the Drexel firm disintegrated in February 1990, he returned to Bombay.

Janak and Manya divorced in 1999, and in 2001 Janak married Monica Bijlani, a dentist living in England. The wedding was a bit lower-key than the first, but still very elegant, at the Ambassador Hotel in Mumbai. They divorced in 2003, but they have remained so close that they might as well be married. Even Manya is still part of the family in a sense, since Ram, ever well-disposed towards a charming young woman in distress, offered to attend her wedding whenever she remarried and even to give her away as a father. He did it too, totally ignoring what she had said in an angry interview with a society magazine immediately after the divorce. Unforgiving as yet, she had told them, 'Ever since I entered the Jethmalani family . . . all them are horny, even the dog.' Calmed down now and remarried, Manya is supervising the building of Janak's new house in Pune.

Janak is not a person at whom someone could remain angry. Always smiling, he has a kind word for everyone, and he has been consistently cheerful in the face of severe medical problems that would defeat most men. Janak's medical problems started in 2003 with symptoms in one leg; a brain lesion was discovered, and he demonstrated the symptoms of a stroke.

With his stroke symptoms, and while Mahesh suffered with a hip problem, the Jethmalanis attracted medical quacks and snake-oil salesmen of all sorts. The most memorable was a Rasputin-like character, an unctuous, super-polite flatterer. He offered the same treatment to Janak for his stroke as he did Mahesh for his hip, using a complicated contraption of his own devising to relieve the pain, along with some proprietary medicine that he swore contained no conventional analgesics. A markedly unimpressed Shobha arrived from America, asked him his credentials, and he told her he had a special degree from Russia to treat pilots in space. She asked if he had qualifications to treat human beings on earth. Shobha thereupon sent his pain medicine to two laboratories for analysis, and they reported that it contained a banned chemical. At least he apparently had good results when he treated the mother of Ram's associate, Lataa, in Madras.

After extensive rehabilitation, Janak still travels back and forth between his homes in New York, London, and Mumbai, owns horses, and is a regular at the races. Out of all Ram's children, Janak is the one he has been most supportive of, his firstborn son.

Janak's son from his first marriage, Kail, has just graduated from the University of Michigan, and he is preparing to go into the Jethmalani family profession. He did a summer internship in a major US law firm, making such a good impression that he already has a job offer. This is an achievement considering the current job environment for law graduates.

In 1989 Rani married Prem Jha, a journalist and newspaper editor in a wedding on the lawn of his father's house, C.S. Jha. C.S. Jha was a legend in his own right, having been an ambassador to Japan, permanent representative of India to the UN, high commissioner of India to Canada, Commonwealth Secretary, Foreign Secretary and ambassador to France—a truly skilled diplomat. My husband remembers being captivated while talking to him on the night of Tony's engagement party. Jha asked him why he was wasting so much time with him when all of Bombay society was at the party. My husband answered that nobody else there could possibly be as interesting as him. Jha had served in the government of six Prime Ministers.

Prem also was excellent company, but he was not a natural diplomat. He felt it was his duty to straighten out his father-in-law whenever he was in error, which apparently was often, in Prem's opinion. Shortly after the marriage, Rani fell in love with an adorable little boy in a foster home, Ali. She wanted to adopt him formally, but since he was Muslim, legal problems ensued. In time, she effectively adopted him as her son. It is difficult to tell what broke up her marriage, but it ended in divorce in 1995.

Ram has treated Ali as a true grandson. When Ali was a teenager and would run away from school, it was Ram who would go to Shimla and bring him back. Ram's staff in his Delhi house has always rooted for Ali, captivated with the story of the poor Muslim boy from an orphanage who became a Jethmalani. Even before Rani became ill, Ram provided for Ali's schooling and college, and after Rani died, Ram made sure that he inherited one of Rani's apartments. After he finished law school, Ram bought him a flat and arranged for him to work as a junior to a lawyer who Ram knows professionally. Shobha fixed up his first apartment, and she takes care that he is included in family events. Ali has a warm personality, uses the adopted name Jethmalani and has begun his law practice in Delhi, inspired by the family business.

After Mahesh returned from his five years studying in England, he began his Bombay law practice in 1981. He, too, is a senior advocate of the Supreme Court. As he has gotten older, he has come to resemble his father in his facial expressions, his voice, his writing, and his political leanings, which are noticeably more consistent than his father's. Like his father, he has a bronze complexion, the appearance of a joke playing over his features, perhaps a glower if he is really serious. In 1993, he married Haseena Lalvani, a gamine-like girl from a wealthy Sindhi family. The wedding was at the Taj Mahal hotel, with a reception afterwards at the Turf Club. The wedding party dressed at the very height of glamour, except for the priest. The pictures show a spectacular wedding couple, and in front of them a rather homely priest in a drab white dhoti, who had droned on interminably until the guests became restless. Rani, the feminist, had insisted they have a female priest, who she brought especially from the south for the occasion.

Mahesh and Haseena settled on Walkeshwar Road in South Mumbai in a penthouse apartment that commands a panoramic view across the bay towards the Oberoi Hotel in the distance. They immediately put in marble floors, walls, and a circular stairway to the terrace above. At the time Ram complained that the purchase was ridiculously expensive. Considering its value today, we would have to say that real estate is not one of Ram's areas of expertise.

Haseena, still slim as a teenager, is a much-watched trend-setter on Mumbai's fashion scene. She has filled their apartment with both Indian and western art, wall paintings, sculpture, and classic artefacts. She also runs a dress business with a partner, and together they sell custom-designed fashion-forward clothing. It is almost impossible to open the society pages of a Mumbai newspaper without seeing a picture of Haseena on page three. Now that Ram's wives have died, Haseena is the only living Mrs Jethmalani, and she and Mahesh have taken up the glamorous social life that Ratna and Ram used to enjoy, only on a grander scale.

As their daughter Serena approaches college age, she has developed an uncanny resemblance to Haseena. Ram is pleased to act the fond grandfather to her and to her two little twin brothers, Amarthya and Agasthya, but it offends his self-image—he sees himself as many things, but certainly not a grandpa. He has never even liked the friends of his daughters to call him Ram Uncle. One of Tony's little boys was once asked about his grandfather's girlfriends. 'Oh, he has too many to count,' he answered.

20

Sikhs and the Punjab

Sikhs are a tall people, resplendent in their turbans, famed as fighters, and staunchly independent. When Sikh leaders churned up the dream of a homeland of their own in the Punjab, the consequences were shattering. Ram stood up for them in the depths of their despair even when much of the country turned against them, and he has felt the repercussions ever since.

While the Jethmalani family held weddings, the Gandhi family held funerals. On June 23, 1980, Sanjay died in an airplane accident. Rumours abounded: it was no accident; his mother-in-law wanted him killed; it was because he threatened her during an argument. The rumour mill continued: Dhirendra Brahmachari, a supposed holy man patronized by his mother, had procured the airplane for him; the plane was unsafe; Sanjay was not trained to fly that particular type of airplane. According to another story, an air marshal had tried to tell the Prime Minister that Sanjay would violate safety regulations if he flew that plane, and the marshal promptly was placed on compulsory leave. The one thing that was certain was that his mother was devastated.

A chain of events beginning in the Punjab then led to Prime Minister Gandhi's death. The Punjab had gone from being restive to revolution, starting with the Akali movement in the 1920s. The Akali movement's original goal was to reform practices at Sikh shrines, but disputes arose over control of specific Sikh temples, gurdwaras, and the Akali demands gradually escalated. Finally, they demanded the creation of a separate Sikh country, Khalistan, within the Punjab.

The Sikh religion, an outgrowth of Hinduism, is monotheistic, forbids idols, rejects any beliefs it regards as Hindu superstitions, and centres around a holy book, the Guru Granth Sahib, portions of which they read every day. Most Sikhs include the word Singh, meaning lion, as a part of their names. The British enlisted many Sikhs, and trained them to become a powerful military force.

Led by Sant Bhindranwale, the Sikhs became increasingly militant, culminating in a holy war in 1982. Jagat Narain, a newspaper owner and editor who opposed the idea of Khalistan, was assassinated in the Punjab on September 9, 1981. Suspicion fell on Bhindranwale, who promptly locked himself in a gurdwara and published a set of demands. When Prime Minister Gandhi made the mistake of letting him out, he moved to the main gurdwara of the Sikh religion, the great Golden Temple complex in Amritsar. The media swarmed around the Golden Temple, as, like a pharaoh, Mrs Gandhi hardened her heart. Even her Russian allies begged her to back off.

Over the next year, the Akali party held violent demonstrations, and Mrs Gandhi arrested thousands of Sikhs. She released several thousand before the November 1982 Asian Games in Delhi, but Sant Harchand Singh Longowal, the leader of the Akali movement, still announced a plan to hold daily demonstrations in Delhi during the games. That plan was suppressed; however, on April 23, 1983, Sikhs in the Golden Temple shot and killed the senior police officer of Amritsar. By May 1984, 18 more were dead in Amritsar.

By now Bhindranwale had moved into the Akal Takht, the second holiest structure in the complex, facing the Golden Temple itself. Murderers terrorized the surrounding countryside. As a confrontation became inevitable, Longowal called Prime Minister Gandhi with an offer to negotiate.

On his own, Ram decided to go to Amritsar in May 1984 to understand the demands of Bhindranwale, Longowal and their followers, truly hoping to talk them out of the central demand for the formation of Khalistan. He believed the Khalistan movement was instigated by Pakistan, which even had training camps for Khalistan Sikhs. Ram also wanted to hear more about their other demands, which turned out to concern states' rights for the Punjab, water rights, Chandigarh as the capital of Punjab, and the number of Sikhs enlisted in military service. Much as Ram may have wanted to play a role as an intermediary, and much as he dreamed of defusing the crisis with love and friendship, it was not to be.

Ram was vice president of the BJP at the time, and the BJP expressed a strong disapproval of his intercession. The stand-off with Indira Gandhi continued unalloyed.

Her response to Bhindranwale's provocation was to be siege, followed by sending in the army for a horrendous attack in June—the infamous Operation Blue Star—which destroyed the holy Akal Takht and caused at least 1000 deaths, including that of Bhindranwale himself.

Longowal was arrested. Ram moved a writ of habeas corpus to get him out, and he was requested to resign his BJP position. Ram immediately offered his resignation from Parliament, but the party refused to accept it. This is Ram's response to censure, an offer to resign immediately, which normally is disregarded—until the day comes when it is not. This exasperates those who love him and who despair that he risks great political harm the day his offer finally is accepted. Whether it is commendable or foolhardy, no one can doubt Ram's courage.

The habeas corpus petition first went to a single judge, Judge Venkataramiah of the Supreme Court, on June 19, because it was vacation time. In general a case only goes before a judge during this time if it is extremely urgent, and it only will be heard by a single judge, who normally will only issue an interim judgement, not a final judgement. Thus, the judge could duck this question: 'The questions involved are too large and complex for the shoulders of a Single Judge to bear. These and other cases of like nature should be heard by at least seven learned Judges of this Court whose unquestioned judicial authority, erudition and acumen would be of great assistance in the restoration of peace in one of the States known for valour, devotion, spirit of sacrifice and sense of duty towards the country of the people residing in it.'[1]

Ram went back to the Supreme Court.[2] As a formality, he had to ask to meet privately with Longowal in prison, to ask permission to file a petition for habeas corpus on his behalf. The court accepted the petition and ordered a hearing on July 24, 1984. On June 25,[3] Ram and Rani returned to court with another writ of habeas corpus because Longowal had been released and detained again. On the first day of the trial, Ram had an attack of angina. Proceedings were suspended, but he returned to argue the case later that week wearing a Holter monitor. Finally, the court revoked Longowal's order of detention.

Ram went to the United States, and on October 23, 1984, he underwent an endoscopic dilation of one coronary vessel. A young Dr Narsingh Gupta was present during Ram's angiogram in Detroit, and he recognized Ram. To this day he loves to tell of how he sent Ram to an expert cardiologist he had studied with before coming to Detroit, Dr Geoffrey Hartzler in Kansas. Dr Hartzler was one of the pioneers of percutaneous transluminal coronary angioplasty, and Gupta felt strongly that his approach would be best for Ram, even if his own hospital in Detroit would lose the business. Dr Hartzler's procedure went beautifully, and the family remembers him as a fine, compassionate doctor. Gupta has been Ram's cardiologist ever since, and when Ram comes to town for his yearly check-up he always reserves several hours for their chat. Gupta was the one who ordered a repeat dilation when the coronary occluded again, and Ram credits him for his excellent health ever since. Indira Gandhi's health was in far more jeopardy.

On October 31, 1984, Prime Minister Indira Gandhi was gunned down by two of her own guards, both Sikhs.

Even as Rajiv Gandhi took office as Prime Minister, there already were whispers of an impending retaliation. It was a veritable pogrom against the Sikhs in Delhi, starting on October 31, 1984, starting when a mob attacked the cavalcade of President Zail Singh, himself a Sikh.[4] The general population may have started the riots at first, but soon Congress party workers were involved. On the second day the mobs turned towards arson, and the next day to murder. According to the official estimate, 2733 Sikhs were killed over three days in Delhi. Mahesh estimates there were 3000 deaths in and around Delhi.

The police only intervened to arrest any Sikhs who had the nerve to resist the mobs. The lawyer Ashok Jaitly and the author Khushwant Singh reported that they saw rioters commit arson right under the noses of the police, but no complaints were registered.

When told of the mayhem, Rajiv Gandhi's response lives in infamy, 'But, when a mighty tree falls, it is only natural that the earth around it does shake a little.'

Officials talked of imposing a curfew, but there was no curfew until the riots had gone on for three days. Ram returned immediately from the United States, against medical advice, one week after his coronary artery surgery. On the night of his arrival Leila Fernandes, the wife of George Fernandes, gave him a briefing. They went together to meet Narasimha Rao, Minister of Home Affairs, to urge him to stop the carnage, to declare a curfew and to call in the army. Ram later testified before the Nanavati Commission that investigated the riots that he found Rao's response to be 'indifferent, listless and unenthusiastic'. Ram reported that Rao simply assured him that he would take adequate steps. Ram was with him for thirty minutes while fires burned all over Delhi, and he observed that the minister took no telephone calls, nor did he give instructions to anyone for the whole time.

Of all the Sikhs murdered in the first week of November 1984, 1234 of them—almost half—were killed in east Delhi, largely in Kalyanpuri. The only arrests the police made were of 25 Sikhs, for possession of weapons!

In one block of Kalyanpuri, a local massacre is estimated to have killed 610 Sikhs, nearly a quarter of all the Sikhs killed in Delhi.

Ram and the lawyers of the Supreme Court Bar Association resolved they had to do something. Ram led a group of 50 lawyers in their bands. With him were Shanti Bhushan, Fali Nariman, Soli Sorabjee, Mahesh, Rani, and Rani's junior Lataa. Together they marched through the streets of Shakarpur, Pandav Nagar, and the blood-filled colonies of East Delhi. They pulled Sikhs to safety, pushing them out of the way of Congress party attacks from buses, and they herded them to safety into the nearest gurdwara. Rani took one man in her car to a public hospital, but he was turned away. She and Ram then took him to a private hospital.

They passed dead bodies and bodies that still were burning. They saw police with their nameplates on their shirts, apparently doing nothing.[5] Throngs armed with rods seethed around them. Thugs taunted them, 'You are going on a peace march?'

Ram and Rani went in front of the march and appealed to the crowd to disperse. Ram said, 'Sikhs have historically been defenders of India. If Sikhs are enemies of India, Punjab is indefensible. If Punjab is indefensible, the whole of India is indefensible.' Finally, Ram pushed Rani and Lataa aside, sat down on the side of the road and said to the rioters, 'If you want to kill me, kill me.' And he said he would remain until they left. Miraculously, the crowd receded.

The scene can only be imagined. A raging crowd in India means thousands of ragged people carrying weapons, maybe firebrands, pushing from behind, the masses in front at risk of being trampled. Ram is not a large man, of slender build today, with an appearance that is soft in repose, but can be fierce when impassioned; Ram alone would not intimidate a crowd. Then again, the sight of him offering himself up as a sacrifice, almost with sadness, could arouse their noblest feelings, and that was what he counted on—correctly. Some believe this was Ram's finest hour.

In the next few days, Rani ran a makeshift hospital in their house, nursing injured Sikhs.

One might ask why Ram passionately defended the Sikhs. To start with, there is an affinity between Sikhs and Sindhis. Ram believes that Sindhis are Sikhs without the five Ks. The five Ks are the signs of a devout Sikh: kesh—uncut hair; kara—steel bracelet; kanga—a wooden comb; kaccha—cotton underwear; and kirpan—a special steel dagger. Furthermore, many Sindhis attend Sikh temples and read from the Sikh holy book, the Guru Granth Sahib, in the morning. Ram's wife Durga used to read the daily portion of the Granth every morning, although Ram does not.

Then there was simple proximity. Sindh and the Sikh Punjab

are adjacent provinces; Hindus from West Punjab and from Sindh all fled to India at the same time. Most important, as an immigrant himself, Ram has a powerful feeling of sympathy for the beleaguered underdog and a compelling need to defend him.

That may also explain part of Ram's fraternal feeling for the Jews. In fact, it is amazing how much the Sikh religion and the Jewish religion have in common. The Sikh religion was established to trim away the superstitions that encrusted Hinduism. Sikhs are monotheistic, and they reject idols, as do Jews. In their religious services, they read the daily selection from their holy book. This also describes Judaism. Sitting on the floor of the Golden Temple, listening to the priest read the daily portion, not assaulted by the sight of any graven images, a Jewish worshipper will see or hear nothing that is incompatible with his own practices.

Ramnath Goenka knew that Ram had represented Longowal, and he urged Ram to make an attempt to mediate an agreement between Longowal and Rajiv Gandhi, in order to pacify the Punjab. Ram drove to Longowal's village to meet with him, and he was able to negotiate the Rajiv–Longowal accord of August 1985. In it, the government conceded some major Akali demands and promised to review others. In particular, they agreed that Chandigarh would be transferred to the Punjab, a commission would determine which Hindi-speaking territories should be transferred from the Punjab to Haryana, and an independent tribunal would adjudicate the water dispute. Elections were scheduled for the State Assembly and Parliament for September 1985; Longowal announced that the Akalis would participate in the elections. On August 20, 1985, terrorists assassinated Longowal.

In 1985 Ram lost his re-election bid to the film actor Sunil Dutt. That was the year of a sympathy vote for the Gandhi family after the assassination, and Congress swept the elections. Ram's loss was part of the fallout, so it was not a great surprise. Still his children and his brother-in-law Mohan Shahani monitored the polling booths while the votes were being counted. Ram remained at home. When one-third of the votes had been counted, it was clear that Ram would lose. Though he had the same number of votes as in the last elections, new voters had appeared and it was not even close. The dispirited team went to a hotel to call Ram and tell him he had lost. 'Where are you?' Ram asked. When they told him they were at a hotel, he asked, 'Why are you there?' He told them to go right back and make sure nobody cheated to make the margin look even worse.

At midnight Mohan went home to go to sleep, dejected. At 1.30 in the morning he was awakened by a call from Ram, who said he must come over for a drink. Apparently he had summoned everyone who worked so hard for him on the campaign, and together they drank to his defeat.

Indeed after Sunil Dutt's victory Ram and Sunil remained friends. Who would know that when Sunil's son Sanjay was found to have assault weaponry in his apartment after the 1993 Mumbai bombings that Tony (Mahesh) would be the first one to defend him? Or that Sunil's daughter Priya Dutt would beat Tony in his own run for Parliament in 2009?

In fact, following his father's trajectory, in 2009 Mahesh would contest for the Lok Sabha polls on a BJP ticket from North-Central Mumbai, losing to Priya Dutt of the Congress party. He actually got a good vote count, just not good enough. Mahesh has his father's charm without his mercurial nature. This was just his first bid for a seat in Parliament; there is every reason to believe that he will succeed in the future.

While he was running against Sunil Dutt, Ram had new symptoms of angina, and he had to return to the United States for a second angioplasty, which fortunately has served him well to the present.

Ram believes in miracles, that all disputes can be mediated, and that everyone can become friends at the end, and he is the one person who often can bring off this kind of magic. He has rushed towards major flashpoints in Indian political history, be it the Punjab or Kashmir, supremely confident that he can be sufficiently conciliatory and broadminded, with animus toward none. He knows that he can smile engagingly at both parties, crack jokes, extend his generous hospitality, charm everyone, tease out the points of contention and wisely help the warring parties reconcile. None of this prepared him for the radical ideology that killed Longowal for signing an accord. Even so, Ram was undaunted, and he wanted once again to reach the Punjab with a loving gesture.

In 1986, Ram travelled with two buses of journalists, politicians, and other opinion-makers to one of the most restless and dangerous areas of the Punjab. His purpose was to demonstrate goodwill from India to the most violent supporters of Khalistan. On the buses were signs reminding the rebels that Hindus and Sikhs are brothers and saying, 'Kill us before you kill the next innocent man, woman or child.' Their message was 'History unites us; our enemies would divide us, do not let them.' He took no security personnel with him, and the buses drove where nobody else would dare to venture. His was a message of love, which in his heart he always believes will solve all problems, and the residents seemed to understand it. He encountered no hostility, and many local residents even promised to renounce violence.

The 'kill me first' approach was the very strategy Ram had used in his march through the violent streets of Delhi during the pograms against the Sikhs, and he would use it again. It was akin to his reflex offer to resign whenever he is pounded by exceptionally heavy criticism. An astute psychologist, he knows how to call a bluff, and he is usually, but not always, successful. He would argue that he has calculated the risks. Or perhaps he is just listening to his heart.

Only one of Prime Minister Gandhi's assassins made it to court. The first, Beant, was killed on the spot. The other, Satwant, was wounded, but recovered well enough to go on trial. Two other Sikhs, Kehar Singh, and Balbir Singh, were apprehended and accused of being co-conspirators. Ram explains how he came to take the case: 'According to law, a death sentence must be confirmed by the High Court, and the High Court has to ask the convicts whether they want a lawyer at the expense of the state, and if so who. Well, both Balbir Singh and Kehar Singh said that they wanted my services, and the High Court asked for my consent.'[6] Ram makes it quite clear that 'a request from the High Court is treated as a command, with no option but to accept.' In fact, when the Delhi

High Court asked Ram to defend Kehar and Balbir, he agreed with alacrity, a decision for which he is still vilified to this day.

He did not defend either of the actual assassins, but both the public and the press have continued to confuse his defence of two alleged co-conspirators with defence of the actual assassins. They cannot or will not see the difference, and they accuse him of acting out of self-serving political motives. Sikh revenge was malevolent revenge, and by defending them, Ram was seen to be on the wrong side, the public even signalling their displeasure with demonstrations against him.

So much for political motives. The BJP requested that Ram resign as vice president of the party, and he did. This time they accepted his resignation. Some have said that this was the most disastrous move in his political career. Otherwise eventually he would have become Prime Minister. Perhaps Ram knew better. Some would say he was headstrong, that he refused to plan ahead. Very likely he was pleased with the idea of sacrificing his own interests for a cause. It is hard to tell. Even his friends say that he often acts first on his gut feeling, and he uses his brilliance later to justify his actions.

Even today, Ram is known as the lawyer who defended Indira's assassins—even if it is not true.

Addressing the anger against him for defending Balbir and Kehar Singh, in 1986 Ram wrote an article, 'Defence of the Despised'.[7]

'The accusation against me is that two of the accused allegedly involved in the conspiracy to kill the late Shrimati Indira Gandhi are so vile and their crime so dastardly that they must not be allowed to demonstrate their innocence. A lawyer who assists them must be a bird of a feather. He has no place inside a party that exclusively practices "value based politics".'

Ram argues: 'In a society governed by the Rule of Law, a person's guilt is for the Courts alone to determine. No one is guilty until the judicial process has exhausted itself and there is no further avenue left for the condemned man to establish his innocence.' He says, 'Even to remotely insinuate that the accused, whom I represent, are guilty or that they deserve to be hanged is contempt. Illegalities apart it shows a total lack of respect for a fellow human.'

Ram says it is so important for the accused to avail himself of the services of a lawyer that 'The Constitution makers introduced it in the Fundamental Rights chapter so that no tyrannical regime could curtail or destroy it. Article 22 declares that no accused shall be denied the right to consult and to be defended by a legal practitioner of his choice.'

Ram then quotes the Standards of Professional Conduct and Etiquette adopted by the Bar Council of India, which begin: 'An advocate is bound to accept any brief in the Courts or Tribunals before any other authority in or before which he professes to practice . . .'

Another standard reads: 'He shall defend a person accused of a crime regardless of his personal opinion as to the guilt of the accused, bearing in mind that his loyalty is to the law which requires that no man should be convicted without adequate evidence.' Ram should know. He drafted these standards.

This gives his logical, cerebral arguments, but there were more. Ram gets his back up when he is told not to do something because it will hurt him; his idea of honour is to do what he believes is right even, perhaps especially, if it puts him in harm's way. His role models are the great lawyers who went before him, India's freedom fighters.

There was one more reason. Ram was deeply convinced that both Kehar and Balbir were innocent. In the 40 years that my husband and I have known Ram, we have never seen him defend the innocence of a client more passionately, nor have we ever seen him more devastated at a miscarriage of justice than when Kehar went to the gallows. It had to have been Rajiv Gandhi who recommended to the President not to commute his sentence, and Ram has held it against him ever since. Rajiv would regret it.

The Economist published an analysis of the case on October 29, 1988, and it came to the same conclusion, that in one case the government was making a terrible mistake. *The Economist* agreed that Satwant (not Ram's client) was one of the two identified assassins, and his sentence was a foregone conclusion. The mistake was Kehar Singh, Ram's client.

Ram took the case pro bono, but even that caused some to carp that later he would raise his rates.

Balbir Singh was a Delhi policeman and one of Mrs Gandhi's security guards. He and one of the assassins, Beant Singh, were on duty together a few days before the assassination, and they were observed watching a falcon in a tree. This was taken as a sign that they prayed together for Indira Gandhi's death. Kehar Singh was the uncle of the assassin Beant Singh, and he was arrested because of this relationship.

The case[8] came before a three-judge bench of the Supreme Court. The court wrote that Beant Singh (deceased), Balbir Singh (Ram's client), and Satwant Singh (the other actual assassin) had openly expressed their resentment for Operation Blue Star. The court also wrote that they had met frequently to listen to inflammatory speeches calling for retaliation against Indira Gandhi. To be clear, Beant and Satwant were the actual assassins.

The headnotes summarize the case:

The prosecution case against Kehar Singh was that he was a religious fanatic. He had intense hate against Smt. Indira Gandhi for causing damage to the Akal Takhat in Golden Temple, Amritsar by 'Operation Blue Star'. He was in a position to influence Beant Singh, being the uncle of Beant Singh's wife called as 'Poopha'. He converted Beant Singh and through him Satwant Singh to religious bigotry.

It is alleged that Balbir Singh, like other accused had expressed his resentment openly, holding Smt. Indira Gandhi responsible for the 'Operation Blue Star'. He was planning to commit her murder and had discussed his plans with Beant Singh (deceased), who had similar plans to commit the murder. He also shared his intention and prompted accused Satwant Singh to commit the murder of Smt. Indira Gandhi and finally discussed the matter with him on October 30, 1984. In the first week of September 1984, when a falcon (Bazz) happen to sit on a tree near the main Reception of the Prime Minister's House at about 1.30 P.M.

Balbir Singh spotted the falcon, called Beant Singh there and pointed out the falcon. Both of them agreed that it had brought a message of the Tenth Guru of the Sikhs and that they should do something by way of revenge of the 'Operation Blue Star'. Therefore both of them performed 'Ardas' then and there. [Ardas is a prayer ceremony.]

At the direction of the High Court, the sessions court held the first trial in the Central Jail, finding all the accused guilty as charged and sentencing Satwant Singh, Balbir Singh, and Kehar Singh to death. Appeals were filed in the High Court on behalf of Ram's clients Balbir and Kehar Singh. The High Court sustained the verdicts of the sessions court. In their appeal to the Supreme Court, the accused contended that a trial in a jail does not conform to the Constitution's guarantees of an open and public trial, and that the High Court had no power to direct the trial to take place in the jail.

Not surprisingly, the Supreme Court upheld the death sentence for Satwant, one of the two assassins.

Moving on to Balbir Singh, the court describes how he was searched and how no evidence was found in his home except for a holy book, how he was taken to Yamuna Velodrome for the questioning, let go, then arrested again at a bus stop. Much was made of whether he really was let go or he absconded, and Ram emphasized that there were no witnesses to either arrest. The court agreed: 'It was further contended on behalf of Balbir Singh: . . . that his arrest at Najafgarh bus-stand was a make believe [fabrication]. He was not arrested there and indeed he could not have been arrested, since he was all along under police custody right from the day when he was taken to Yamuna Velodrome on November 1, 1984. He was not absconding and the question of absconding did not arise.' The court concluded that there was no credible evidence against Balbir, and he was acquitted.

Now coming to Kehar, the court repeated Ram's contentions, 'that there is no evidence that Beant Singh and his wife were deliberately taken by Kehar Singh to expose them to provocative [devotional songs] at the time of celebration of the birthday of a child'; indeed, 'Kehar Singh being an elderly person and a devout religious Sikh was keeping company with Beant Singh to dissuade the latter from taking any drastic action against Smt. Gandhi.' This was Ram's refutation of charges made against Kehar during the trial that was held in jail.

Kehar's problem was that the aggrieved wife of Beant, the dead assassin, gave the key accusations against him. The court even admitted that she was a hostile witness. She testified that Kehar had met in secret with her husband, and her husband had kept his golden ring in Kehar's home for some reason that was kept secret from her. When Beant and Kehar took a trip to Amritsar with their families, she testified, they talked between themselves in a secret way that she interpreted as sinister. She said that Kehar had inspired the two assassins to take Amrit, a religious purification ceremony and that Kehar must have known something about her husband's mindset that made him urge Beant to undergo purification.

The most manipulative assertion of all was her testimony about the 'post-crime conduct of Kehar Singh immediately after the news of assassination . . . he mentioned to his office colleague that "whosoever would take confrontation with the Panth, he would meet the same fate". The wife claimed that this statement alone proved "that Kehar Singh was a co-conspirator to assassinate Mrs Gandhi".'

From this evidence, such as it was, the court adduced Kehar's guilt: 'The charge of conspiracy against Kehar Singh with the accused Satwant Singh and Beant Singh since deceased has been proved without any reasonable doubt.' His sentence was death.

Ram filed numerous petitions for a stay of execution and ultimately petitioned the President of India for a pardon on October 14. The President's decision, it should be understood, is made at the recommendation of the Cabinet, which of course, includes the Prime Minister. It is little wonder that the pardon was denied. The President wrote, 'The President is of the opinion that he cannot go into the merits of a case finally decided by the Highest Court of the Land.' Ram challenged that rejection in the Supreme Court on the basis that the President had refused an oral hearing, and the court granted another stay on December 11.

A group of lawyers appealed the President's decision together on December 16, 1988, including Ram Jethmalani, Shanti Bhushan, Rani Jethmalani, R.M. Tewari, P.K. Dey, Sanjay Karol, Lataa Krishnamurthy, Dr B.L. Wadhera, Ms Nandita Jain and Mahesh Jethmalani. They asked 'whether there is justification for the view that when exercising his powers . . . the President is precluded from entering into the merits of a case decided finally by the Supreme Court; (b) to what areas does the power of the President to scrutinize extend; and (c) whether the petitioner is entitled to an oral hearing from the President.'

The first petition filed had been dismissed by the President on the grounds that, so far as the guilt of the accused is concerned, he could not second-guess the court. Ram challenged this in December 16 petition, arguing that in exercising his powers of pardon the President is not bound by the previous court's finding of guilt. He can even review that finding. In a significant ruling, this was exactly what the court held. Of interest, since the President was obligated to follow the advice of his Cabinet in this matter, the decision meant that the government was not bound by the original court decision that determined guilt. In his autobiography, the President mentioned Ram's doggedness in pursuing this case.

Despite all that, after the court's final verdict, Kehar was hanged along with Satwant Singh on January 6, 1989, on the basis of remarkably little evidence.

That was one of the saddest days in Ram's life. When Kehar Singh's son Rajinder came to him for a job, Ram hired him, and Rajinder worked in Ram's office for 10 years.

Another opportunity to support the Sikh community came when the Speaker of the Punjab Assembly asked Ram to appear on behalf of his son, Simranjit Singh Mann, a loud proponent of Sikh secession. Ram promised to meet with him, even though he strongly opposed his cause; he never wanted to see another partition of India. When he visited Simranjit Singh Mann in jail, he found a shattered man, a victim of the most cruel possible torture. Ram agreed to defend him.

This case started when the security police apprehended five Sikhs in a jeep that was speeding towards the Nepal border. They took them in for questioning at the police station, and, according to the court, 'One of the officers on duty identified one of them as Sardar Simranjit Singh Mann . . . , who had been dismissed from the Indian Police Service. An order of preventive detention under the National Security Act had been made against him on 28th Aug. 1984, but the detention order could not be served as he had gone "underground". The Special Branch, Patna, had informed the officers posted at the Check-Post that the passport of aforesaid Sardar Simranjit Singh Mann . . . had been confiscated and his movement outside India had been banned.'

A police search of the Sikhs' possessions revealed incriminating pro-Sikh, anti-India materials, and one of the Sikhs tried to bribe an officer to let them go. The defence raised questions about the procedures that police had used in the arrest and whether the attempted bribe should be considered apart from the other charges. After Ram visited the jail, he expressed disgust at the prisoners' conditions. The court requested a separate submission on this matter, and it ordered a prompt trial.

Mann was found guilty, and he spent five years in jail. While still in jail he was elected to Parliament, representing the Punjab.

Mann had been in and out of jail after a number of additional arrests by the time Ram took another case for him.[9] This time Mann was prosecuted under the Terrorist and Disruptive Activities Act (TADA) of 1985, for 'advocating, propagating, abetting and advising disruptive activities by his speeches when he questioned the sovereignty and territorial integrity of India. He is alleged to be preaching cessation of a part of Indian Territory for carving out of an independent State of Khalistan.'

The court quoted such inflammatory speeches as this gem: 'We do not accept the Constitution. After forming Khalistan we will form our own constitution. Ready and oil your arms.' Or this: 'We will not let live any Hindu in Khalistan. We by forming our Khalistan Raj, will become separate from India. In case any individual of India or Army or any other force took any action against us then we will fight them with our full force.' And this is the man who Ram had to defend against the charge that he proposed violence!

Somehow after Ram's defence, the court concluded: 'We are also of the view that the allegations of mala-fide made by the petitioner in the instant case are vague and ambiguous.' In the end, the court let him out on bail. No court observer would ever have given that result a chance.

Unfortunately Mann was unstable, some would say delusional. Once after he had received bail, Ram sent a junior lawyer to collect his signature and Mann later said about the junior, 'He was good looking. When I become Prime Minister I will appoint him a judge.'[10]

At least Ram had tried to do his best for a Sikh leader, whether he deserved it or not, to soothe the raw feelings of the Sikh community and to bring them back into the embrace of India.

21

Late 1980s

Ram was left in the political wilderness in 1985 after losing his seat in Parliament, but his legal practice boomed. Meanwhile, Parliament was preoccupied with a series of governmental commissions appointed to investigate the pogrom against the Sikhs, and it had to deal with violence in Sri Lanka.

Ram found plenty to do before he returned to the Rajya Sabha from Karnataka in 1988. He started a political party and disbanded it. He defended a husband accused of killing his wife, an underworld gangster, and he even sued a British peer. He defended godmen who ranged from slightly to decidedly ungodly, and in April, 1987, the Bofors scandal would break.

Rani ran for Parliament in 1989, contesting as a member of the Janata Party for the Lok Sabha constituency of Daman and Diu. She lost, but she felt that, as a woman, she had made an important statement by running for office in that district. Ram paid the bills.

Rani described the experience:[1]

Contesting elections in India is a herculean task, as constituencies are large and sprawling. The Union Territory of Daman and Diu is small geographically, but since it is separated by the Gulf of Cambay, Daman falling in the state of Gujarat and Diu proximate to Rajasthan, travelling from one part to the other takes two days by road. There are no flights to Diu. One has to be in the fittest of health and qualify for the Olympics in stamina to fight elections in the heat and dust of India with primitive, unconstructed roads full of ditches and potholes.

Though Ram's political loss in 1985 theoretically left him free to concentrate on his law practice, it hit him hard. Ten different parliamentary committees met and reported on the Sikh pogrom and all he could do was testify before the last one. He could only watch the committees wistfully; he could not sit on them.

In April 1987, Ram started a political party, naming it the Bharat Mukti Morcha, meaning a movement for the salvation of India. Disappointed with existing political parties, Ram wanted to present his manifesto of what good government should be, and it was worth it to him to pay for it. He invited other political parties to join in his movement, but the response was poor. Ramakrishna Hegde from the Janata Party in Karnataka and N.T. Rama Rao, Chief Minister of Andhra Pradesh, did join, but they only indulged him because they were his clients. Nobody really seemed to understand what he had in mind. Theoretical, impractical, and too expensive, it eventually had to be disbanded. This was an early example of Ram, the public intellectual.

Before that came an example of Ram, the lawyer, at his most obdurate. In July, 1984, he had infuriated Bombay's women's groups with one case he argued before the Supreme Court.[2] It did not help that Ram's record on feminist issues was somewhat suspect.

The case was brought against three sons and an uncle of a Mr Birdhi Chand, the owner of a cloth business in Pune. One of the sons, Sharad, a chemical engineer, was accused of poisoning and strangling his new wife, Manju. The Supreme Court told the story as only the Indian courts can:

> This is rather an unfortunate case where a marriage arranged and brought about through the intervention of common friends of the families of the bride and bridegroom though made a good start but ran into rough weather soon thereafter. The bride, Manju, entertained high hopes and aspirations and was not only hoping

but was anxiously looking forward to a life full of mirth and merriment, mutual love and devotion between the two spouses. She appears to be an extremely emotional and sensitive girl at the very behest cherished ideal dreams to be achieved after her marriage, which was solemnised on February 11, 1982 between her and the appellant.

Soon after the marriage, Manju left for her new marital home and started residing with the appellant in Takshila apartments at Pune. Unfortunately, however, to her utter dismay and disappointment she found that the treatment of her husband and his parents towards her was cruel and harsh and her cherished dreams seem to have been shattered to pieces. Despite this shocking state of affairs she did not give in and kept hoping against hope and being of a very noble and magnanimous nature she was always willing to forgive and forget. As days passed by, despite her most laudable attitude she found that 'things were not what they seem' and to quote her own words 'she was treated in her husband's house as a labourer or as an unpaid maid-servant'. She was made to do all sorts of odd jobs and despite her protests to her husband nothing seems to have happened. Even so, Manju had such a soft and gentle frame of mind as never to complain to her parents-in-law, not even to her husband except sometimes. On finding things unbearable, she did protest, and expressed her feelings in clearest possible terms, in a fit of utter desperation and frustration, that he hated her.

Not only this, when she narrated her woeful tale to her sister Anju in the letters written to her [which are dealt with in a later part of the judgment], she took the abundant care and caution of requesting Anju not to reveal her sad plight to her parents lest they may get extremely upset, worried and distressed.

Ultimately, things came to such a pass that Manju was utterly disgusted and disheartened and she thought that a point of no-return had reached. At last, on the fateful morning of June 12, 1982, i.e., nearly four months after her marriage, she was found dead in her bed.

As to the cause of death, there appears to be a very serious divergence between the prosecution version and the defence case. The positive case of the prosecution was that as the appellant was not at all interested in her and had illicit intimacy with another girl, Ujvala, he practically discarded his wife and when he found things to be unbearable he murdered her between the night of June 11 and 12, 1982, and made a futile attempt to cremate the dead body. Ultimately, the matter was reported to the police. On the other hand, the plea of the defence was that while there was a strong possibility of Manju having been ill-treated and uncared for by her husband or her in-laws, being a highly sensitive and impressionate woman she committed suicide out of sheer depression and frustration arising from an emotional upsurge. This is the dominant issue which falls for decision by this Court.

Both the High Court and the trial court rejected the theory of suicide and found that Manju was murdered by her husband by administering her a strong dose of potassium cyanide and relied on the Medical evidence as also that of the chemical examiner to show that it was a case of pure and simple homicide rather than that of suicide as alleged by the defence.

The trial court had found all of the accused guilty, sentenced three of them to prison and sentenced Sharad to death. The division bench of the Bombay High Court confirmed the death penalty but acquitted two of the others. The Supreme Court verdict ruled that the High Court had erred, and it gave a short course on the rules for circumstantial evidence, excellent reading for any student of law.

Out of the breadth of his legal knowledge, Ram too gave a lecture on the law, in this case on the requirements for the court to admit a dying declaration as evidence. In this case the High Court had decided as it did because it wrongly assumed that Indian law followed English law, but Ram knew better. This was the basis for Ram's defence.

The High Court accepted the view that the husband had poisoned his new wife. Ram argued before the Supreme Court that it should rely on Manju's letters to her family, which showed that

Manju had become increasingly desperate.

According to the court, 'Mr Jethmalani, learned counsel for the appellant, has vehemently argued that there was a very strong possibility of the deceased having committed suicide due to the circumstances mentioned in her own letters.'

Ram's argument was taken from the Indian Evidence Act, 1872. Section 32(1) reads:

(1) When the statement is made by a person as to the cause of his death, or as to any of the circumstances of the transaction which resulted in his death, in cases in which the cause of that person's death comes into question. Such statements are relevant whether the person who made them was or was not, at the time when they were made, under expectation of death, and whatever may be the nature of the proceeding in which the cause of his death comes into question. or is made in course of business.

Ram read the following sentence from the act to the court: 'statements, written or verbal, of relevant facts made by a person who is dead, are themselves relevant facts when the statement is made by a person as to the cause of his death.' A person who commits suicide is speaking of one of the circumstances which led to her death.

The distinction was that, 'In the English law the declaration should have been made *under the sense of impending death* whereas under the Indian law *it is not necessary for the admissibility of a dying declaration that the deceased at the time of making it should have been under the expectation of death.*'

In court, hearsay is not admissible in evidence unless an exception to the rule applies, and a dying declaration is an exception to the hearsay rule. In his lectures to students, Ram makes this point, but he describes three weaknesses of a dying declaration: 1) It is a statement, not an oath; 2) It is not subject to cross-examination; and 3) The deceased may have acquired information from the person who took the declaration. In one case, a dying declaration was given to someone who was also an eye-witness and who told the injured man just before he died who had committed the act. In this case, the deceased had made his declaration using testimony from someone else.

Taking all this into consideration, if the High Court wanted to know whether Manju was likely to have committed suicide, it should have read her letters, and it would have been perfectly legal under Indian law. Ram instructed the Supreme Court that this was critical to the case, and the court agreed.

Now the court reviewed the evidence that she had committed suicide:

> If there is anything inherent in the letters it is that because of her miserable existence and gross ill-treatment by her husband, Manju might have herself decided to end her life, rather than bother her parents . . . In the instant case, the evidence clearly shows that two views are possible—one pointing to the guilt of the accused and the other leading to his innocence. It may be very likely that the appellant may have administered the poison (potassium cyanide) to Manju but at the same time a fair possibility that she herself committed suicide cannot be safely excluded or eliminated. Hence, on this ground alone the appellant is entitled to the benefit of doubt resulting in his acquittal.

The court considered all the possible scenarios in which the husband might have forcibly administered the poison, and it dismissed them all as contrary to the medical evidence, concluding, 'The only other reasonable possibility that remains is that as the deceased was fed up with the maltreatment by her husband, in a combined spirit of revenge and hostility after entering the flat she herself took potassium cyanide and lay limp and lifeless.'

The three judges of the Supreme Court all delivered divergent judgements on the significance of the dying declaration, but all agreed on the acquittal of Sharad Sarda, Ram's client, ruling Manju's death a suicide. This became a rallying point for all the feminist groups in Bombay; they led protests against the judgement, and they even mounted a poster exhibition to illustrate that the court overlooked how Sharad had mistreated and betrayed his wife, then insulted Manju by portraying her as just an overly sensitive woman who demanded an unreasonable amount of attention from her husband.

Rani strongly disapproved of her father's defence, because Sharad was the very sort of cad she had been prosecuting for years in her own legal practice. As far as Rani was concerned, if he had driven his wife to suicide by his abusive treatment, the husband needed to be held responsible for Manju's death. Ram was unrepentant. He truly believed his client was innocent, and he was proud of his ability to successfully craft a defence based on a difference between English and Indian law that the High Court had overlooked. It took quite some time before the storm died down, both outside and inside of Ram's house.

One other element of the decision that has become a frequently cited precedent concerned admissibility of the evidence. Section 313 of the 1973 Code of Criminal Procedure, says:

'In every inquiry or trial, for the purpose of enabling the accused personally to explain any circumstances appearing in the evidence against him, the court:

1
(a)may at any stage, without previously warning the accused, put such questions to him as the Court considers necessary;
(b)shall, after the witnesses for the prosecution have been examined and before he is called on for his defence, question him generally on the case . . .

4
The answers given by the accused may be taken into consideration in such inquiry or trial, and put in evidence for or against him in any other inquiry into, or trial for, any other offence which such answers may tend to show he has committed.'

Ram argued that every piece of evidence against the accused must be put to him in his examination by the court, and that if this procedure is not followed, any circumstance that has not been put to the accused must be ignored. In its verdict, the court wrote that 'the High Court has mentioned as many as 17 circumstances in order to prove that the circumstantial evidence produced by the prosecution was complete and conclusive. Some of 13 [of] these circumstances overlap, some are irrelevant and some cannot be taken into consideration because they were not put to the appellant in his statement under s. 313 of the Code of Criminal Procedure.' Therefore, since these circumstances were not 'put to the appellant', the court ignored all of them in its final verdict.

After all this detail about what is required as evidence and what should be admissible, one cannot help but think back to poor Kehar Singh, who went to the gallows on the basis of accusations made up by a vindictive, bereaved wife who testified that her husband had killed Indira Gandhi because his uncle put him up to it. Her main 'proof' was that the two men were careful to talk where she could not hear them.

Abdul Latif Abdul Wahab Sheikh was another man accused of murder,[3] the type of client who needs a good criminal lawyer, but probably does not deserve one. Ram and Rani represented him. Abdul was accused, jailed, acquitted, but not released, because he was wanted for another offence. He was to be released on June 23, 1986, but then he was slapped with another order for his detention, this one under the Gujarat Prevention of Anti Social Activities Act, 1985. Under Article 22 of the Indian Constitution, no one can be detained longer than three months without an Advisory Board ruling that such a prolonged detention is justified. The Gujarat Prevention of Anti Social Activities Act required the Advisory Board to be constituted within three weeks, but that never happened. He still was not released. A fresh order of detention was issued on August 7, and an Advisory Board was constituted. It produced a report but only after three weeks.

Ram reminded the court that a person cannot be detained for longer than 12 months from the date of detention. The court asked, 'whether a law may be made providing for successive orders for detention in a manner as to render the protection of Article 22 (4) of the Constitution ineffective? For example, can a fresh order of detention be made every 89th day . . .?'

The court held that 'No law can be made providing for successive orders for detention in a manner so as to render the protection of Article 22(4) of the Constitution ineffective [and] if the report of the Advisory Board is not made within three months of the date of detention, the detention becomes illegal notwithstanding that it is within three months from the date of the second order of detention.' Abdul was allowed out on parole.

The greatest criticism of Ram has been that he defended reprehensible people. Ram answers that the punishment for being reprehensible is not necessarily a death sentence. Even the lowest of society have the same right to constitutional protection as those in the higher strata of society. Anyhow, the job of a criminal lawyer is to defend criminals. Where some may see a criminal lawyer without morals, others see a social reformer who is fighting for equal rights.

A lawyer like Ram juggles many balls in the air at the same time, but some cases never seem to go away, even as common cases come and go in an orderly fashion. Anyhow, an American lawyer would be shocked to know how many cases Ram handles almost single-handedly, simultaneously, with only one or two juniors to research particular points. While he handles an endless case, he takes on new cases, wages political battles, conducts a crusade against governmental corruption, writes newspaper articles, attends to two wives, samples what he calls other flavours of ice cream, starts a law school, teaches, and mediates the Kashmir dispute. Life for him is a bravo performance. A biographer can hardly keep up with him, much less present his activities in a logical order.

One case that went on from 1983 to 1993 was a battle of words with Lord Swraj Paul. Paul was born in the Punjab, moved to London, and became one of the richest men in Britain. Eventually, he became a British baron and a life peer in the House of Lords. It all started with a scandal that threatened to implicate the Gandhi family in 1975.

In 1975, the Indian State Trading Company (STC) signed a contract to buy sugar from a Swiss company, Compagnie Noga d'Exportation Importation.[4] Noga only supplied a sixth of the contracted amount, but, instead of suing, the STC renegotiated the contract to accept less sugar than had been agreed upon, at a lower price. In 1977, the Janata government tried to enforce the new contract, but now Noga supplied only a third of the new contracted amount. When the STC filed a claim in London, Noga claimed both parties always knew that the contract would never be enforced—obviously a fraudulent deal from the beginning. STC agents had deposited a $4.5 million commission in a Swiss bank,[5] and Swraj Paul was named as an intermediary.

When the government attempted to enforce the contract, Noga sent a letter reminding it of the money it had deposited in the Swiss bank. By this time Noga had sued Swraj Paul, and the scandal was widely reported.

Clearly this deal, if true, must have cost India dearly, and it opened Mrs Gandhi's government to corruption charges under the Prevention of Corruption Act. The CBI, under Prime Minister Desai, asked Ram to investigate. This delighted him; Mrs Gandhi would face major legal charges if she had been part of the scheme.

When Ram went to Switzerland, authorities stonewalled, quoting Swiss secrecy laws, but he learned that it was a 'federal crime to bribe foreign public servants on Swiss soil'. Based on that, Ram informed the Swiss that their police could investigate Swiss banks for crimes committed in Switzerland if the Indian government should so request. Cornered, the Swiss said they would need a new complaint.

Ram wrote a new complaint and sent it to New Delhi. Unfortunately, it arrived after the Desai government had fallen. With Mrs Gandhi back in power, the CBI obediently closed the case. Nevertheless, neither Ram nor Paul was willing to let it go.

On August 28, 1983, Paul claimed in an interview with the *Hindustan Times* that the Janata government and Ram had struck a deal with Mr Nissim Goan, the owner of Compagnie Noga, and that Mr Goan had agreed to the suit against Paul 'in exchange for STC dropping its claim and withdrawing its arbitration claim against him . . . a typical and sad case of how Mr Morarji Desai's

administration wasted government funds in sending people like
Mr Ram Jethmalani on jaunts abroad to malign people like me . . .'

Ram's response appeared in the *Indian Express*, 'Swraj is an
over-inflated balloon that needs to be deflated.' He concluded by
challenging Swraj to sue him.

On September 1, Swraj answered in the *Daily Mirror*, saying
in part:

> Corporate crooks cannot be protected by the machinations of
> legal hacks like Jethmalani . . . Jethmalani is lying . . . I have no
> time to waste on their petty hirelings. Defamation suits are not
> to be wasted on low-grade servitors like Jethmalani . . . It will be
> worthwhile for people to know that Jethmalani and his associates
> [sic] journeys through Europe to negotiate arms deals for
> clients like Israel are a matter of widespread talk in appropriate
> circles. Jethmalani proves himself a boring liar. Jethmalani is the
> contumacious lawyer from India's corporate dung-heap.[6]

Ahem. Ram sued Paul for libel in 1983, in London. Paul
countersued. By now Rajiv Gandhi was Prime Minister and the
CBI was unwilling to furnish the records Ram needed to defend
himself. He asked the Delhi High Court to direct the CBI to produce
the papers. The court so ordered, but the CBI continued to stall.
Ram knew that Paul's close connections with the Gandhi family
were protecting him.

In 1986, Ram went to the Delhi High Court to sue the CBI for
the records.[7] We can see from the very beginning how personal
the argument was:

> 2. The petitioner, a Senior Advocate of the Supreme Court of
> India, states that he is the plaintiff in a libel action instituted by
> him in the Queen's Bench Division of the High Court of Justice
> in England... the cause of action arises out of the statements
> made by Swaraj Paul in London to the correspondents of *The
> Hindustan Times* and *The Daily* which appeared on 28th August,
> 1983 and 1st September, 1983, respectively.

3. The petitioner also asserts that the defendant in that suit had made counter claim arising out of the petitioner's statement which appeared in *The Indian Express* dated 30th August, 1983.

The court quotes a letter that Ram wrote requesting the documents:

At a later stage during the investigation of the above case at the instance of the Government of India the CBI had asked my advice and for that purpose the files of the investigation were produced before me by the officers of the department. The investigation was, however, dropped sometime in 1981.

But on the 27th August, 1983 a vitriolic attack was made on my character and reputation by Mr Swaraj Paul and the libel statements appeared in the Indian press. Based on my knowledge and what I had learnt in the course of my professional duties I defended myself and repudiated the allegations made against me. In respect of these statements and counter-statements litigation is pending in the High Court of Justice, Queen's Bench Division, being Action 1983 J-6467.

While I remember the broad facts the Court has ordered some details to be furnished which I cannot state from memory. These can only be had from the statements and documents which are available in the files of that investigation.

For the purpose of defending my character and reputation I urgently require inspection and/or certified copies of the relevant papers and proceedings:

I have a legitimate substantial, urgent interest in securing these documents. These documents do not constitute official secrets nor do I seek any material covered by Ss. 123, 124 and 125, Evidence Act, I am fighting a litigation against a foreign national in a foreign Court and I conceive it as your duty to render me all possible assistance. It is not out of place to mention that in a democracy every citizen has a fundamental right to know subject to exceptions which have no application here.

Kindly treat this as urgent. I am willing to pay all the costs
and charges.

The CBI responded that 'there was no provision under the
Criminal Procedure Code to allow inspection or to furnish copies
of the same to any person when the case is not pending trial in
any court in India'.

The court ordered the CBI to produce the documents.

In 1988 the Delhi High Court[8] set aside the 1986 decision,
saying that 'Any dispute between the respondent and said
Mr Paul is not the subject matter of this writ petition, but the
subject matter of libel action pending in Courts at London. There is
no iota of public interest involved in allowing an individual access
to the correspondence or statements, if any, with the Director,
CBI.' From there it went on to the Supreme Court. By 1993 all
the parties had tired of it. Paul had been compelled to supply his
own business records, and these incriminated him. Paul finally
agreed to pay a settlement of 70,000 English pounds and to tender
an apology. According to Ram, he and Swraj have made up and
become friends. One wonders.

In fact, in 2010, following a parliamentary investigation into
another matter, Baron Paul was suspended from the House of Lords
and required to pay back £41,982 pounds. The investigation was of
three peers who claimed properties outside London as their primary
residences, so that Parliament would reimburse their home expenses
in London. As a result, Paul resigned from his party, and he was
ordered to step down from his position in Parliament.[9]

Continuing with tales from the edge, Ram once told us that
he had three godmen as clients. At the time they must have
been Chandraswami, Rajneesh—later called Osho—and Swami
Premananda, who was accused of rape. During the time of the
Bofors case, Ram represented Chandraswami in some matters,
believing that the cases had been brought for political reasons, as
he said in Parliament, 'In 1988, there is no doubt that not only I
was appearing for Chandraswami because I believed that at that
time he was being harassed but he also offered to help us in the

Bofors investigation which doubtless I was doing at that time along with some other colleague.'[10] We had already heard about Chandraswami's connections with the international arms dealer, Adnan Khashoggi, at that time, but there were more legal woes to come, fortunately not involving Ram.

Just to give a sense of the man: from 1990 to 2004, Chandraswami came under investigation for allegedly forging documents to show that former Prime Minister V.P. Singh's son had a secret bank account in the Caribbean island of St Kitts, an account that listed his father as beneficiary. He was acquitted of that charge in 2004.[11] In November 2001 he slid out of charges that he had received a large sum of money from Bangkok and transferred it out of the country in violation of the Foreign Exchange Regulation Act (FERA).

In 2003, Chandraswami and former Prime Minister Narasimha Rao were charged and acquitted of the allegation that they had cheated a businessman, Lakhubhai Pathak, during the Rajiv Gandhi administration in 1983. In 2004, Chandraswami convinced a trial court that this was a false accusation brought because he had been close to former Prime Minister Rao, and the court acquitted him. In November 2004, he was acquitted of 15-year-old forgery charges.

Also in 2004, the CBI told a Delhi court that Chandraswami may have financed Rajiv Gandhi's assassination. He also had been investigated for 15 years for violations of the foreign exchange laws, and on June 15, 2011 the *Indian Express* reported[12] that he paid a penalty of Rs 9 crores[13] for seven FERA cases. In none of these cases did Ram represent him.

Ram's current godman defendant is Asaram Bapu, also accused of rape. This case is ongoing.[14] What we know is that Asaram Bapu was born in Sindh and moved to Ahmedabad, Gujarat. In the late 1960s he began to style himself as Sant Sri Asaramji Bapu; he founded an ashram in the early 1970s, and now he has some 400 ashrams across northern India as well as all over the world, with thousands of devotees. In 2008 two boys disappeared from the Ahmedabad ashram, and when their bodies were found there were accusations that the ashram had engaged in black magic and

tantric practices. Subsequently two other boys disappeared under
unclear circumstances.

In August 2013, a 16-year-old girl accused Asaram of rape, and
he was arrested. When the press learned that Ram was representing
Asaram during the bail application proceedings, they were shrilly
critical of him. It only got worse when women activists heard that
Ram had cast aspersions on the victim. In one TV interview, Ram
angrily responded that they had completely misinterpreted the
police report that his instructing lawyers handed him to read, and
he left the interview.

He has submitted this history to the court: The girl filed a First
Information Report in Delhi five days after the event, which occurred
at the Swamy's ashram in Jodhpur. She claims that the attempted
rape was at midnight in the Swamy's room, and she says she cried.
In fact, her mother and three ashram employees were sitting just
outside the door, and they heard nothing. After the alleged rape,
she went out to her mother, and the two of them went 200 yards
away to join a group for dinner. The daughter said nothing to her
mother about any untoward event, and she enjoyed a good dinner.
She also slept well, still reporting nothing to her mother.

In the morning, the girl and her parents had to go to Delhi, and
the Swamy also planned to travel. The Swamy came in to bid the
girl and her parents goodbye. He recommended they go to stay and
pray in an ashram of his in Ahmedabad, since she was suffering
from an as-yet undiagnosed ailment. He provided them with a car
to go to the station. They had a good breakfast and drove to the
station. In the FIR she filed in Delhi, she reported that she was
suffering from an ailment for which she had been told to consult
with a doctor in a large city. The girl herself added to the FIR that
she was told to see the Swamy. A medical examination showed
her to have an intact hymen and not a single scratch. The sentence
saying that she had been told to see the Swamy is what so angered
the women's groups, who screamed at Ram that he must be mad.
She said she had a sexual illness for which the prescription was
to see the Swamy? Preposterous. The conclusion of the case has
yet to come.

My husband and I will never forget the night when Ram told us he would take us to a spiritual discourse by the godman Rajneesh, later called Osho. Rajneesh, a former philosophy professor, had started his religious teaching in India, gone to Oregon in the United States, came back to India in 1986 under a cloud, and established an ashram that attracted hordes of tourists to Pune. Some will remember Rajneesh—Osho—as the new age 'sex guru' who attracted a high-profile celebrity clientele from all over the world. Some will remember the stories of orgies in his Pune ashram. Others will remember the allegations of poisonings by his followers in Oregon. After he died in 1990, some remembered him as a great sage.

Ram had offered Osho legal assistance for years, and he wanted us to hear him speak. Upon our arrival, we saw what looked like several football fields worth of poor people squatting or sitting hip-to-hip on the ground with a huge Hollywood-size edifice in front of them, resembling an ornate several-storey-high billboard. It was decorated elaborately, and the godman was sitting high up, on a throne in a halo of luminous light, speaking in Hindi. We were led way down to the front of the field, where some sofas and carpets had been placed for Western guests. Seated next to me was a young American man, one of the godman's lawyers. As the godman spoke, the young man, eyes closed, swayed back and forth in rapture. Finally, unable to contain my curiosity, I asked if he understood Hindi. 'Yes,' he said, 'Well at least some, well maybe 10 per cent.'

Ram sat listening for a short while, then he began to fidget and said we had to go; the godman was so mesmerizing he was beginning to believe him. He may have been kidding, of course, but here are claims made by the adherents of Osho on their website:[15] 'Shri Ram Jethmalani recalled that he started as Osho's lawyer and ended up as his spiritual slave and that's what he remains to this day.' Recalling his association with Osho, he said in 1975 he was called to defend Osho. 'My problem was that Osho had an allergy to attend court and my brief was that he should not attend court for a single day. I succeeded.'

The same Osho website quoted Ram, 'I believe Osho was an intellectual giant,' declared the Law Minister. 'I believe his intellectual output is mind boggling and I believe that it would a great pity if the whole of India and indeed the whole world is not exposed to his great intellectual output as Osho is one of the greatest men this country has ever produced.'

22

Defending Politicians

Like Hindu godmen, Parliament and the world of politics proved to be a fertile field of clients for a criminal lawyer.

In 1988, Ram defended N.T. Rama Rao (NTR), a beloved film actor, director, and producer. Rao had played the gods Krishna and Ram in Telugu films, and he served three terms as Chief Minister of Andhra Pradesh. Some revered him as one of its greatest political leaders. This was typical. In India, many film stars have capitalized on their image by segueing right into politics. Indeed, Rao had often played opposite Jayalalithaa, an actress who also became the Chief Minister of Tamil Nadu. Rao's problems started in 1984.

The matter[1] came before the Andhra Pradesh High Court in Hyderabad. The judge began with this unusual statement: 'This is one of the extraordinary cases without any parallel, not a [case] of the mundane orthodox pattern, but a unique public interest litigation which seeks to explore the realm of accountability of the executive to the people through the judiciary, hence it assumes great significance and has naturally attracted considerable attention [sic] of the public.'

The petitioner, Sri Dronamraju Satyanarayana, was a former member of both the Lok Sabha and the Andhra Pradesh State Legislative Assembly. He was also the chairman of the Visakhapatnam Urban Development Authority. He had lost two elections, and he was on the warpath. He filed four petitions against N.T. Rama Rao, the Chief Minister, and the state government, claiming that NTR had usurped the office of Chief Minister and should be removed. He also requested a judicial commission to investigate NTR's alleged corruption and abuse of authority, and to impose penalties if he is found guilty. Even further, he wanted the court to determine whether the government should institute President's Rule in the state. That occurs when the central government disbands the elected state government and takes control of the state.

A full division bench of the court dismissed two of the petitions, leaving the other two to a bench of five judges. These were writs requesting a commission of inquiry and requesting punishment. An accompanying affidavit alleged fiscal crimes, corruption, dishonesty, political patronage, favouritism, misappropriation of public funds, breakdown of constitutional machinery, a resultant state of anarchy, extermination of extremists in fake encounters, deaths in police lockups, and related atrocities. This man was angry.

Ram questioned whether the petitioner was entitled to file these writs, because 'the two writ petitions are solely adversarial in nature and the motive is to settle political scores after the petitioner was defeated in the elections to the Andhra Pradesh State Legislative Assembly and the Office of Mayor of Visakhapatnam'.

Ram argued:

> The true public interest litigation is one in which a selfless citizen having no personal motive of any kind except either compassion . . . or deep concern [for] stopping serious public injury approaches the Court for either of the following purposes: (i)Enforcement of fundamental rights of those who genuinely do not have adequate means of access to the judicial system or statutory provisions incorporating the directive principles of State Policy for amelioration of their condition, (ii) Preventing or annulling executive acts and omissions violative of Constitution or law resulting in substantial injury to public interest.

The court asked Ram if it would be acceptable to his client if a bench of judges conducted an inquiry. His answer was:

It is the contention of [NTR] that the present petition discloses no cause of action, its pleadings and averments are vague, prolix, rolled up, scandalous and false. The petition is a perplexing misjoinder of desperate complaints, grievances and alleged causes of action. The reliefs and allegations cannot be correlated. It raises disputed' questions of fact which cannot be disposed of on the affidavits filed except to dismiss the petition. On the other hand [NTR] has nothing to hide or be ashamed of. He does not wish to avoid or shirk enquiry into any responsible allegations supported by prima facie evidence selected by the Attorney-General.

So, Rao would allow a panel of judges to conduct the investigation.

Shri Ramachandra Rao, the opposing counsel, claimed that his client had no self-interest involved and he should not be precluded from filing his case just because he is a politician.

Ram asserted that 'the doors of this Court should not be kept ajar for adjudication of adversarial issues brought in the garb of public interest litigation by politically motivated persons,' and that 'what could not be achieved by the Congress (I) party to which the petitioner belonged . . . unseating the ruling Telugu Desam Party in the elections, should not be permitted to be achieved indirectly through the instrumentality of this Court.'

Coming to specific charges, the court found that NTR had favoured a son-in-law in awarding a cordless telephone project, wrongly allowed a zoning change to benefit family members, given theatres owned by family members an exemption from entertainment taxes, and that NTR abused his position in setting up a steel plant. Another allegation was that he deliberately burned houses belonging to certain tribal people because they sheltered extremists. Thus, seven charges remained out of several hundred.

The court dismissed a writ petition for tax evasion as baseless, and it dismissed a request to appeal to the Supreme Court. In the end, one writ remained out of the original four. It remained to be seen whether an investigative commission would be set up. The case went to the Supreme Court, and the last writ was dismissed, a blow-out for the defence.

Another politician who came to Ram was Sharad Pawar, a member of the Congress party, Chief Minister of Maharashtra, and later the Minister of Agriculture. In 1991 he became involved in an election dispute that went to the Supreme Court after a March 30, 1993 decision of the Bombay High Court, Aurangabad Bench. After the assassination of Rajiv Gandhi, elections were moved from May 23 to June 12, 1991, and Gadakhyashwantrao Kankarrao was announced the winner of a Lok Sabha seat from Ahmednagar. The High Court set aside that election for corrupt practices and declared Balasaheb Vikhe Patil the winner.

Several appeals were filed in the Supreme Court, including one by Sharad Pawar, who was accused of corrupt practices along with Gadakh.[2]

Patil claimed that during the election campaign, Gadakh and Pawar had made the following false statements: Patil had a huge election budget of Rs 3 crores; he paid Rs 50 lakhs to the Janata Dal party; he paid Rs 20 lakhs to a Janata Dal candidate to shift to a different constituency, and he planned to distribute 5000 bicycles, saris, dhotis, as well as liquor, to voters in order to purchase votes. Thus these statements should render Gadakh's election void.

Sharad Pawar had a lawyer, but he panicked when the case reached the Supreme Court and called Ram. Ram, as usual, found a way to represent another respondent in the same case so he could support the Gadakh and Pawar legal team and show that no corrupt practice took place. First, he said the standard of proof must be that for a criminal charge, a higher standard than for a civil case. Also, 'the statements which were made by Gadakh and Sharad Pawar were only to caution the electorate against possible misuse of money power and to exhort them not to succumb to any such pressure or temptation.'

The court wrote, 'Shri Ram Jethmalani . . . submitted that political leaders have a duty to educate the electorate against possible malpractice . . . and making of such statements is desirable. Shri Ram Jethmalani also submitted that every allegation . . . is not moral turpitude.'

The court repeated the defence case: 'It is not every statement but only "a statement of fact" to which the provision applies . . . the statement of fact should be false . . . such statement should be made believing it to be false or at least not true . . . it should relate to the personal character or conduct etc. of any candidate; and it should be reasonably calculated to prejudice the prospects of that candidate's election. Unless all these requirements are satisfied, the statement does not constitute the corrupt practice . . .'

Analysing Sharad Pawar's statements, the court concluded that they all were statements of opinion, and none was a 'statement of fact' that would fulfil the required standard of proof. Elegant.

The court did scold Sharad Pawar: 'Judging by these standards, we are constrained to observe that some of the statements made by Sharad Pawar, the Chief Minister of Maharashtra, even though not amounting to corrupt practice under the enacted law, do not measure up to the desired level of electioneering at the top echelon of political leadership to set the trend for a healthy election campaign.' Yes, indeed.

It is fascinating to read this opinion, because once the judge was moved into a lawyerly discussion of the standard of proof, Pawar walked away a free man. Ram's handiwork is obvious. A standard part of Ram's modus operandi is to insist on a precise definition of the standard of proof. He literally picks apart the statute. This case highlights Ram's use of this technique.

23

Bofors

The sheer audacity of the 10 questions a day that Ram Jethmalani hurled at Rajiv Gandhi for 30 days kept the Bofors scandal on the front page of every Indian newspaper, and the Bofors scandal brought down the Gandhi government. That might be the headline. Of course, there were many people involved in this effort, particularly some tireless investigative journalists. Ram's most important roles were as a guiding spirit of the investigation and as a provocateur.

In April 19, 1987, the Swedish Radio company ran a story claiming that a Swedish armaments company, Bofors, had paid bribes for a contract to sell Howitzers to India. This began the Bofors scandal. The Indian government reacted as governments always do, with a denial. Reuters developed the story further, reporting that Bofors had secured a $1.3 billion contract by bribing senior Indian politicians and defence officials, and adding that four payments totalling 32 million Swedish kroner were transferred to secret Swiss bank accounts between November and December 1986.[1]

Now Bofors issued their denial, saying that it had paid no bribes, only 'winding up charges'.

The key official in the Swedish Department of Foreign Trade issued a statement saying that, in their negotiations, Swedish Prime Minister Olaf Palme and Indian Prime Minister Rajiv Gandhi had agreed on a precondition that there would be no middlemen.

Rajiv denied that any middlemen or non-governmental agencies had been involved.

Ramnath Goenka smelled a big story for the *Indian Express*, and he sent Ram to Sweden to investigate personally. Ram's chats with senior executives revealed—by the way—that after Bofors signed the contract with India, their chief executive, Martin Ardbo, threw a party to celebrate the solution of his company's financial problems.

Tehelka gave a detailed description of this party in a 2009 article,[2] an all-night city-wide bash to celebrate the contract, which they hoped would finally bring money and jobs.

Ram reacted to Rajiv's early denials as an experienced criminal lawyer and psychologist, 'My experience in handling circumstantial evidence has taught me that often false denials prove the truth of guilt more convincingly than positive evidence of it.'[3]

'I read with dismay this shocking and clumsy fabrication of the defence. Just as Lady Macbeth's first words on the discovery of King Duncan's slain body in her castle were a complete giveaway of her guilt, Rajiv Gandhi exposed his guilt by his government's strange and emphatic denial of the Bofors story broadcast by the Swedish radio.'[4]

The Indian Parliament debated the issue on April 20, but the Rajiv government rejected all demands for a parliamentary probe. As a result, the entire Opposition walked out, the first of several times in this affair. Soon the name Hinduja surfaced. This was a rich Indian business family who lived in London and had previously acted as agents for Bofors. Sindhis in origin, they once lived in Iran, and rumour had it that they were close to the Shah, that they even held money for the Shah's sister. The other name that the press unearthed was Win Chadha, a known broker for Bofors.

Now *The Hindu* became involved. The editor, N. Ram, assigned V.K. Ramachandran, an economist living in Sweden, to follow the story. When Rajiv Gandhi made a speech about his agreement with Olaf Palme, Ramachandran contacted the Swedish government to see if they would verify his claim. They denied any such conversation. On May 13, Swedish Radio reported that Bofors had paid 250 million Swedish kroner (Rs 50 crore) to middlemen in the deal, most of it already sitting in Swiss banks. This was too much for a commission. It had to be a bribe.

A Swedish government audit found evidence that illegal payments had been made, but the names of the agents were suppressed in the audit summary they released to India. Rajiv tried to explain everything. Arun Shourie, the editor of the *Indian Express*, wrote an editorial that detailed the many absurdities in his statements. Bofors offered to send a delegation to India to straighten things out, but Rajiv cancelled their trip. The *Indian Express* asked why.

On June 16, 'Ram Jethmalani openly accused Rajiv Gandhi of having received the Bofors kickbacks and dared the PM to prosecute him for libel if his accusation was false. He also petitioned the President for granting sanction under the Prevention of Corruption Act for prosecuting Rajiv Gandhi for having accepted bribes in the deal.'[5]

The next day Rajiv retorted, 'Should I reply to every dog that barks?'

Ram's answer appeared in the form of an open letter to Prime Minister Rajiv Gandhi in the *Indian Express*:[6]

The morning papers report that yesterday you called me a 'barking dog' not worthy of your notice in the presence of some of your colleagues and leaders of the Opposition.

I do not feel insulted in the least for dogs do not speak lies and they bark when they see a thief. I am proud to be a watchdog of democracy. You must thank your stars that I am not a Blood Hound. Over the years, your late mother and brother had both developed a healthy respect for me and had not ventured to use language resembling yours. I am sure you too will learn some day.

You are accountable to the people of India and the nation must institute an inquisition of its own, since you have crippled all legal processes.

Every day I propose to ask you 10 questions. This will continue for 30 days or until you are removed from office whichever is earlier. The people will draw their own conclusions from your answers or your refusal to answer them as the case may be. Here is the bunch for today:

(1) Has your wife informed you of the total estate left by her father who died early last month?

(2) Did he die testate or intestate?

(3) Does the estate include an expensive villa and a bank balance of more than 60 million dollars?

(4) What was his financial condition and the approximate worth of his total estate only about five years ago?

(5) What were the sources of livelihood of your father-in-law during the last five years (To the best of your knowledge of course)?

(6) What part of the estate has your wife inherited whether under a testamentary document or an intestacy?

(7) What has happened to her share of the estate?

(8) Have you or has your wife reported the inheritance to the Reserve Bank of India? If so, when?

(9) When you attended the funeral of Mr Olaf Palme in Stockholm were you accompanied by Ajitabh Bachchan and Mr Ardbo of Bofors?

(10) Did you insist on a meeting with Bofors, and was one held?

The newspapers say that my dear friend Shiv Shanker was present when you called me a dog and he boasted that he knew how to deal with me. Short of having me 'liquidated' you have no other method of silencing my bark.

The letter was a sensation. Readers asked who would dare to ask a sitting Prime Minister such outrageous personal questions in a public newspaper. They ate it up.

The next day's article asked:

(1) When the Swedish Radio's allegations of kickbacks to key politicians and defence officials broke upon this unsuspecting nation on the morning of 16th April did it cross your mind or

that of your advisers that Win Chadha of Anatronic General Corporation should be called and questioned?

(2) Were any inquiries of any sort made before your Government rushed to issue a public denial and attacked the Radio reports as malicious, motivated and baseless?

(3) Is it true that next day you presided over the Political Affairs Committee of the Cabinet? How long were the Bofors kickbacks discussed and on what investigation or inquiry did the committee endorse the earlier statement? Did the committee not act solely on information supplied by you?

(4) When did you or your Government take a decision to register a case against Win Chadha or is the case registered against some others and Win Chadha called only as a witness?

(5) Are you aware that there is no machinery by which the summons said to have been issued can be served in a foreign country? To what address is the summons directed? Does anyone know his present whereabouts? Have any inquiries been made about his present location? Is it true that Chadha has absconded without leaving any clue of where he is going or hiding?

(6) You have publicly claimed the other day that there was a middleman who had been working on the deal since 1977 and at your express intervention he was excluded from the contract. How did you bring about this result, by oral or written instructions? If so, to whom?

(7) Did you know the identity of the middleman you succeeded in excluding? I presume it was Win Chadha.

(8) Did he ever agree to walk out and did he tell you that he had received between 170 and 250 million Swedish kroners as compensation for winding up his middleman role?

(9) Did you as a child hear the story of the man in charge of a stable blamed for not running after a thief who stole his master's horse explaining that he was sure the thief would return to steal the saddle?

(10) Is this not precisely what had happened in the case of Win Chadha?

Ram's 10 questions a day were published on the front page of the *Indian Express*, and the newspaper's circulation soared. Soon papers all across the country were running the articles and readers were agog, eager to read each new instalment. Anyone familiar with the art of cross-examination would recognize that these questions were an artful legal cross-examination that made the case for the prosecution. The scandal's profile shot up.

Ram's associates claim that after a while Ram tired of writing the questions, and 'everybody' wrote some, Sri Jaisinghani, Mahesh, even Arun Jaitley. Ram claims that even though he was out of the country the latter part of the month, he faxed his articles to India. Any of that may be true, but the idea was Ram's. All agree that he wrote the earlier articles at least, and they read like a novel, a highly entertaining one at that. Bhushan writes that 'from that time onwards the choicest epithets of Rajiv Gandhi were reserved for Jethmalani.'

Chadha meanwhile had seen fit to relocate to America, and he began disposing of his Indian properties. He need not have worried. The Swedes would claim when they testified before an Indian parliamentary investigation that he had received no payments as an agent. He only received a 'winding up charge' when the contract was completed.

On June 30, the *Indian Express* revealed that Ram had changed the thrust of some of his questions to Rajiv. He 'sought to know about the present of a Rolls Royce and a Mercedes car to him by the King of Jordan, even as a contract was being negotiated by the Jordanian Airlines for executing the landing and traffic lights for several airports in India. Mr Jethmalani has said that receiving gifts by the Prime Minister from any person who is having business with Government violated the provisions of the Indian Penal Code.' His last questions that day were:

(9) Did your embassy in Sweden receive from 'Bofors' a letter dated April 24, 1987, in which the latter confessed that payments alleged by Swedish Radio had in fact been made, that they were made in a company in Switzerland,

and that they did relate to the contract of sale of guns to India?

(10) With this confession of 'Bofors', how did you state to a meeting of assembled Army commanders on April 26 that the Swedish Government had informed you that there were no kickbacks nor middle men?

(11) On or about the April 27, 1987, there was a debate in Parliament. Did you disclose to the House this important letter? If not, why not?

While Parliament argued about beginning an official inquiry, Arun Shourie wrote that the Indian public should get involved. They did, and they sent a flood of letters to the Swedish government asking for the names of the persons who received funds. The *Indian Express* and *The Hindu* continued to push the story, *The Hindu* relying on reporters V.K. Ramachandran in Sweden and Chitra Subramaniam in Geneva. The *Indian Express* effort was directed by a committee of four: Arun Shourie, Ram Jethmalani, S. Gurumurthy, and Ramnath Goenka. Together they formulated the strategy, and planned the articles. Some called the group of four masterminds at the *Indian Express* 'The Caucus'.

In August, the chief prosecutor of Sweden announced the beginning of a Swedish investigation, and shortly after that, the Rajya Sabha finally formed an investigative committee, the Joint Parliamentary Committee (JPC), under the chairmanship of P. Shankaranand. The Opposition refused to participate, leaving the committee solely composed of Congress party members. When the president of Bofors came to India to testify before them, they gave him unprecedented deference.

Three of Ram's June 22 questions titillated the public by suggesting the possible involvement of the premier film star of India, Amitabh Bachchan:

(1) The Amitabh-Ajitabh involvement has been in the news for quite some time and I believe that even you would not deny that these [sic] have come to your notice. You must be

aware that Ajitabh had refused to disclose to the press the exact source of his livelihood, the identity of the landlord who owns the property in which he lives and the nature of the business he carries on. Have you till today written to your friend or advised him in any manner whatsoever that he should supply all information to the public to dispel the thick cloud of suspicion that necessarily surrounds his sphinx like silence?

(2) Have you at any time instructed your agencies to report on these facts? (On the assumption that you could not secure this information privately even if you were so minded).

(3) The other brother Amitabh is a Member of Parliament and he could very easily answer these questions. Have you asked anyone to interrogate him? (This is very important because if there is no credible explanation of Ajitabh's stay in Switzerland, it is the legitimate inference that he is busy in something clandestine which, in the current 'situation,' can only be laundering of illegal funds for which the Swiss Bank system is known).

Now a 'godman', Chandraswami arrived in Madras, rumoured to be returning from a fact-finding mission in Europe. Enjoying the attention, he claimed to have the goods on Bofors.

The swami already had a colourful past, and he has become even more controversial since the days of Bofors. We have already seen Chandraswami was investigated and acquitted for charges of forgery, charged and acquitted—along with former Prime Minister Rao—of cheating a businessman, and investigated for years for possible FERA violations. So this is who they were dealing with.

When the names of Adnan Khashoggi, a world-class arms dealer from Saudi Arabia, and of Chandraswami, the slippery swami, surfaced in the Bofors scandal, Shourie and Ram tried to squeeze them for information. In an excellent article written later, Arun Shourie told the story.[7] In September 1987 Chandraswami called from Europe claiming, 'I am bringing the atom bomb.' He requested that representatives of the *Indian Express* meet him at the airport, and they did. So did the police, and he was arrested. The *Indian Express* wanted him out of jail and the government wanted him in jail, in both cases because he claimed to have the evidence on Bofors.

Chandraswami kept Shourie, Ram, and the whole *Indian Express* group at his beck and call for months, always holding out the promise of more information. As various charges of illegal activities piled up against him, Ram willingly defended him free of charge, certain that the charges had been trumped up by the Gandhi administration to silence Chandraswami.

At one point Chandraswami showed Shourie a tape that he said was a recording of Martin Ardbo, the president of Bofors, claiming he had received it from Adnan Khashoggi, a disciple of his. He also had photographs of the meeting and copies of letters from Ardbo to another disciple, the Sultan of Brunei. Ardbo reportedly was anxious to be the Sultan's security adviser, for a vast yearly salary. Most exciting, Chandraswami also claimed to have a piece of paper handwritten by Ardbo, giving the numbers of two bank accounts in the names of Rajiv and Sonia. In all, he knew how to adeptly string them along without ever handing over any evidence.

One evening Ram called Shourie to say Chandraswami was in a private hospital, and the CBI had him surrounded. A Dr Jain, another disciple, was sheltering him, creating the impression that he was ill. Shourie went over with a reporter and photographer, and he found Chandraswami shaking in fear of being arrested. His assistant, Mamaji, said that a briefcase containing the tape and the Ardbo papers was in Chandraswami's Mercedes. While they debated how to get it safely, a relative of Mamaji walked in, and they sent him to get the briefcase. Suddenly Shourie's father, who happened to be in the hospital, walked in wearing his dressing gown, and they handed him the briefcase, which he safely carried away.

When Shourie inspected his treasure, he found a letter in the briefcase denouncing Ram and Shourie to Rajiv. Furious, Shourie gave the letter to Ram the next day. Ram smiled and said the letter was a brilliantly written blackmail letter to Rajiv. In effect it said, 1) That Chandraswami knew a lot, 2) What he knew would cause an explosion, and 3) He was willing to tell what he knew if Rajiv would meet with him personally. This was a prelude to a deal with Rajiv.

When Shourie confronted Chandraswami, he asked what they were worried about. He just could open a bank account in Rajiv's name and have Khashoggi deposit $6 million in it. Then they could say that the money came from Bofors. Shourie took that to mean that Chandraswami did not have any hard evidence on Rajiv after all. The rest of the loot in the briefcase turned out to be flim-flam. The tapes were inconclusive. The supposed account numbers were telephone numbers. Only the photographs were real.

Once he had made a deal with Rajiv, Chandraswami planned to embarrass Ram. In the *Hindustan Times*, using a common name for the ruling clique of the *Indian Express* investigation of Bofors scandal, Chandraswami alleged that 'The Caucus representative Jethmalani followed me to Europe in May–June 1987 and had several meetings with me in Milano, Vienna and Paris.' He claimed that Ram had been trying to get him to use his connections with Khashoggi in order to obtain material to incriminate Rajiv and bring down the government, but he had foiled the plot.

That was not Chandraswami's only attempt to create trouble for Ram. He invited Ram to celebrate his 65th birthday with a grand bash on Khashoggi's yacht, named Nabila. It was docked in the Mediterranean, off the French Riviera. First they went to Monaco, to the villa of Sese Seko Mobutu, the President of the Congo, later Zaire. There, Chandraswami announced with much fanfair that he would conduct a ceremony, called a yagna. When they arrived, Mobutu was seated splendidly in a huge ceremonial chair, and they had to remove their shoes and sit on the floor while Chandraswami chanted impressive Indian chants.[8] At least Mobutu was impressed. He sat nearly in a trance. Ram knew Chandraswami had made up the words.

The next event was held on the yacht, where Ram, Mahesh, Rani, and a friend of Rani's, Sheila Mahboobhani, a flamenco dancer, luxuriated in the fabulous party that Khashoggi, his wife, and his daughter Nabila hosted. The wife turned out to be an enthusiastic follower of Chandraswami. Food and drink overflowed. The evening was heavenly. One lovely young French model appeared to be assigned to Mahesh and another to Ram, what Mahesh calls a 'honey trap'. Ram's offspring kept their wayward father safe. Whenever the photographer took a picture of Ram with a girl, or girls, Rani jumped into the picture. When Ram began looking too vulnerable to temptation, Mahesh made sure his behaviour remained respectable. The conspirators never got a single incriminating picture to use against Ram.

When *India Today* revealed the findings of an official technical evaluation of several guns, it turned out that the Bofors gun had rated a poor third to the ones made in Austria and France, as Ram reveals in his questions on June 23:

1) What are the requirements and specifications stipulated in the contract of March, 1986, about the guns to be supplied and their continuing serviceability after they are put in use in Indian conditions?

2) Are you aware that earlier when the gun was put through trials it had exploded because in achieving the required range so much heat and pressure were developed which the body of the gun could not bear?

3) Is it true that in November–December, 1986, the guns were tested at the Devlali School of Artillery and the following defects were discovered during the test: Compute switch on the display unit was defective; Barrel indicator did not function; Elevating cylinders were found to be leaking and the packings had become loose; The electrical firing circuits were defective and guns could be fired only manually and new circuits were demanded from Sweden; The control cables were snapped where it passed under the yoke of the castor wheel; The electric supply to the hydraulic system consequently did not work; The ammunition cranes were out of order since pipes leading into the hyd. motor were leaking; Engine oil filters were not supplied as spares and

due to this the replacement schedule which is due to change after100 hrs of operating time was increased to 150 hrs.

4) Were these defects brought to the notice of superior officers . . .?

5) Was the representative of Bofors present at these tests and were these defects brought to the notice of Bofors by any official communication?

6) Does it shock your conscience that Rs 50 crore went into Swiss accounts almost simultaneously with the tests that were being done . . .?

In his June 27, 1987 article, Ram raised critical questions to Rajiv about Ottavio Quattrochhi, a friend of the Gandhi family:

1) Have you heard the name of one Mr Octavio Quattrochhi,[9] an Italian gentleman?

2) Is it true that as a matter of fact, you and your wife are on socially intimate terms with him and that, as a matter of fact, it has become almost routine for you and your wife to visit his residence socially every Sunday?

Then came questions about the connections between Quattrocchi, a Mr Lalit Thapar, and Snam Proggetti, actually an Italian oil and gas industry contractor, even though Ram's questions create the impression it may be a person. He asked, 'Is it correct that Mr Quattrocchi commenced residing in India almost immediately after your marriage to the then Sonia Maino?' Question 11 asked, 'The growing activity of Snam Proggetti has raised several eyebrows particularly in political and bureaucratic circles.' He then raised the question 'does it not behoove you to allay the suspicions and misgivings . . . and offer a forth-right explanation regarding the excessive indulgence towards Snam Proggetti?

'I wish to alert you to the fact that the activities of Snam Proggetti and the Italian connection at large is a veritable Pandora's box . . .'

Sometime later, with the clarity of hindsight, Ram returned to the role of Quattrocchi,[10] starting with the questions he had asked Rajiv:

> I asked him 300 questions, not one of which was answered by him. Strangely enough, neither has anyone from the Gandhi family refuted Subramanian Swamy's statement that since 1984 Sonia's Gandhi's mother Paola Predebon Maino and friend Ottavio Quattrocchi, maintained regular contact with the Tamil Tigers. The mother used the LTTE for money laundering and Quattrocchi for selling weapons to earn commissions. To the best of my knowledge, this information remains unrefuted till today.

The LTTE refers to the Tamil Tigers from Sri Lanka.

> . . .The evidence available and the behaviour of the Congress party, whether it was in power or not, to stall and derail any effective investigation into the Bofors case lead to a clear inference that Quattrocchi was the face of Sonia Gandhi, and that this was her share of the deal. In July 1993, the Swiss courts had permitted official naming of the account operators, including Quattrocchi. Yet, before the CBI could question Quattrocchi and detain him, he bolted from Delhi on the night of July 29–30 1993. It is common knowledge that this was made possible through the direct intervention of Sonia Gandhi and the Congress government.
>
> The spurious and slapstick efforts made thereafter to secure Quattrocchi's extradition, the de-freezing of his accounts, the deliberate errors and gaps in documentation by the CBI that had the least intention of trying to extradite the accused Quattrocchi, only establish the misuse of the entire government machinery and tools to subvert legal processes and fool the people of our country. One must then read the proceedings of the Parliamentary Committee called the Shankaranand Committee, which tried to provide a bare fig leaf cover to an otherwise unclothed Rajiv.

Ram says he could have given the Quattrocchi family advice.

Just say, 'I am family. I came to know that the army sanctioned this purchase. I used insider information, and made money.'

He says they were so clumsy that 'They didn't even know how to lie intelligently.'

In the course of its own investigation, the Joint Parliamentary Committee (JPC) eventually announced that they had the names of persons who had received money. Since this money had found its way into Swiss bank accounts, the Swiss promptly denied that any criminal conduct had taken place on Swiss soil.

Atal Bihari Vajpayee led the Opposition attack on the JPC report. A bill was introduced to amend the criminal procedures for executing any summons from foreign courts. Ram opposed it, explaining the legal basis for his objection, and saying that it would compel magistrates to execute a summons from any banana republic. The Rajya Sabha wanted action, and it passed the bill.

The Swedish investigation into the Bofors transaction was forced to close for lack of government cooperation, but Arun Shourie, in Sweden at the time, obtained information they had collected in their files. The Swedish Audit Bureau did finally report out on June 1, 1987. This report consisted of a part which was released publicly and a part which was withheld. The secret portion confirmed that the principal beneficiary of bribes in the deal was 'an Indian who has been an agent for Bofors for 10–15 years', considered by *The Hindu* as 'a clear reference to Mr Win Chadha'.[11]

Ram tried to bring a legal action against Rajiv. He went to President Zail Singh in mid-June 1987 to ask for his sanction to proceed with a prosecution, but Singh consulted with the Attorney General, who either discouraged him or did not encourage him. The case that Ram built in his letter to the President was similar to the one in his 10 questions a day. Ram wrote:[12]

1. The Bofors deal was negotiated and finalized by Rajiv Gandhi himself.
2. Kickbacks are paid only to influence the person in whose power it is to conclude the deal. This was Rajiv Gandhi and none else.

3. When kickbacks were first disclosed . . . Rajiv Gandhi instead of verifying their veracity promptly dismissed their allegations as totally false . . .

4. When the Swedish radio persisted in their allegations and claimed that they had complete documentary evidence to back them up, Bofors . . . immediately admitted to the Indian ambassador that the allegations were true . . .

5. In spite of this confession being made by a co-conspirator . . . Rajiv Gandhi concealed this fact and lied to army commanders and Parliament within the next three days.

6. The factum and contents of the Bofors confession was not disclosed to Parliament . . .

7. He promised . . . a full probe by the Swedish government but instigated Bofors not to cooperate with the Swedish Audit Board and prevented the identity of the recipient being disclosed.

8. The Bofors President has publicly made two statements. Earlier he said the disclosure was being refused because the Government of India as customer was insisting on confidentiality. Now he has said that the recipient of the kickbacks is insisting on that confidentiality. Both these statements have not been denied by Rajiv Gandhi or his government . . .

9. Swiss law permits full disclosure in the situation presented in the Bofors case. Rajiv Gandhi refuses to make the appropriate requisition and instead dispatches a team of handpicked officials who have no capacity to secure evidence but a strong motive to obliterate it.

10. The second source of information is the Bank of Sweden as the paying bank. No approach has been made to it . . . no request strong or mild has been made to the Swedish government in appropriate form to secure this information from the Swedish bank . . .

11. The third source of information is Bofors. Cancel the contract until full information is yielded. Rajiv Gandhi dare not do this not because the army cannot do without guns

but because Rajiv Gandhi cannot survive the disclosure.

12. Ajitabh Bachchan acquires a million Swiss francs property in a fashionable locality in Montreux, on 3 April 1986, within less than ten days after the signing of the Bofors contract. Knowing that this cannot be accounted for, both he and his MP brother Amitabh Bachchan publicly lie and attempt to make the nation believe that this is a small apartment provided by Ajitabh's Swiss employers. Both brothers refuse to disclose the identity of the Swiss employers . . .

13. The last source of information would be Win Chadha . . . He was available at all relevant times in this country and he was quietly allowed to escape leaving the law enforcement agencies publicly mourning their impotence.

14. An honest minister who was keen on investigation has been unceremoniously hounded out of office . . .

Singh never granted the sanction.

On February 1, 1988, Arun Shourie published the details of 16 payments totalling over 200 million kroner that were deposited between February and December, 1986 in the Swiss bank account of Svenska Inc. That was $1,180,000, at 5.9 kroner to the dollar. He also documented 80 million more ($472 million) deposited in another Swiss bank by a number of corporations. Shourie also implicated Arun Nehru, a cousin of Rajiv Gandhi.

The report of the Indian investigation was submitted to Parliament on April 26, 1988, concluding: 'There is no evidence to show that any middleman was involved in the process of the acquisition of the Bofors gun. There is also no evidence to substantiate the allegation of commissions or bribes having been paid to anyone. Therefore, the question of payments to any Indian or Indian company whether resident in India or not, does not arise, especially as no evidence to the contrary is forthcoming from any quarter.' A whitewash.

The public was outraged, so was the press, even the papers which had supported the government thus far. Even so, the Congress continued to support the Gandhis. In the Lok Sabha debate in May, a Congress MP, K.K. Tiwari, went after Jaipal Reddy, Ram, and George Fernandes. He claimed that when Jethmalani and Fernandes went to Sweden, 'The truth they discovered was a red light area! They landed up in a red light area!'

Near the end of 1988, Ram thought he had found a link between the payoffs and the Gandhis. An employee who worked for an Indian company of which Sonia Gandhi was managing director told Ram that his company once collaborated with a US company that employed a Virginia Rodrigues. This was of interest because a Virginia Rodrigues was the treasurer and vice-president of Swenska Inc. The employee gave Ram a sample of her signature on a letter from the US company. Ram went back to Sweden to find out if the two Virginias were the same. Ram could not obtain a sample of her signature in Sweden, but he was told that she now was in Panama.

Ram sent Mahesh to Kansas[13] to follow up a lead, and he engaged a detective who had once worked for the Mossad, but the detective told Mahesh that no sooner had he arrived asking questions than the Noriega government went after him for snooping. He had been beaten to within an inch of his life. He said they were apparently dealing with the mafia, and no way would he stay down there any longer. Ram went to the press to report the coincidence that both these ladies were named Virginia Rodrigues, but in the end the American company denied ever employing any Rodrigues. The trail dried up, and Ram never could prove his case.[14]

The one who could prove her case was the ever-patient reporter for *The Hindu*, Chitra Subramanian. In mid-April 1988, she called her editor to tell him the Swedish government had given her photocopies of documents seized from Bofors. These documents demolished the claim that no Indian had received money, and they implicated G.P. Hinduja, who had been under suspicion all along. The Hindujas had managed to be as helpful as possible to *The Hindu* throughout the evolution of this story, so *The Hindu* showed them the photocopies before they published them.

The Hinduja brothers had lived in Europe since they left Iran. Their most lucrative business was in arms, and they had a long-standing link to Bofors. They had done many favours for *The*

Hindu, including arranging interviews for them with key figures, and they had done everything possible to ingratiate themselves with the press in general. Eager to distance themselves from the parties to the scandal, they even offered to finance part of the investigation.

They certainly were anxious to help, perhaps a bit too anxious; however, when Chitra Subramanian produced photocopies of documents that shed suspicion on them, the Hindujas claimed possible forgery. Ram was a friend of their father, and he had done some legal work for them in the past. Ram announced that he needed to see the originals to be sure, but if the originals appeared real he would denounce the Hindujas himself. Ram never saw any originals. In 2002 and 2005, Ram represented the Hindujas in court, to a chorus of criticism that after he had fought against corruption in the Bofors case, he turned around and represented one of the culprits.

Bhushan believes that the Hindujas' only real service to Bofors was influence peddling.[15] He believes that their service to the Indian government was to be a conduit for payoff money. Bhushan was convinced that the one who received commissions was Chadha. The Svenska payoffs went into his Swiss bank account, and the evidence that he received them was overwhelming.

Patience finally paid off. Chitra Subramanian fell into a goldmine of new documents from the Swedes, who were impressed by her diligence. *The Hindu* held publication until after the June 1988 election. When V.P. Singh beat a Congress party candidate in Allahabad, it did not bode well for Rajiv's next election, because V.P. Singh was the Finance Minister, later Defence Minister, who Mrs Gandhi had sacked from her cabinet for his bad habit of investigating her cronies for corruption.

After the election, *The Hindu* published everything, and S. Gurumurthy analysed the documents in a series of three articles for the *Indian Express*. After these, the Opposition called for a new parliamentary probe. In fact, after the debate in Parliament, one version circulating in Delhi was that a member had laughed at the government: 'It started by saying no payments had been made, and nothing had been paid into the Swiss banks. When it was established that actually payments had been made into the Swiss banks, the line that was taken by the government was "no commissions have been paid". When it was established that actually commissions have been paid and the documents established categorically that these were commissions that were paid, the government now says that "no bribes have been paid".'

In his press interviews, Rajiv was still denying that any commissions were paid on the Bofors deal. In November 1988, Parliament held a particularly acrimonious dispute. *The Hindu* now published more documents that advanced the story. Shanti and Prashant Bhushan, father and son, drafted a letter to the President calling for an investigation. This call was rejected.

Meanwhile, Rajiv, in a fit of desperation over the unfavourable media coverage, sent a bill to the Lok Sabha to suppress the press, the Defamation Act of 1988. This would make it easier to prosecute journalists for defamation, negate the presumption of innocence, and impose two- to five-year sentences for offenders. After 1000 journalists marched in protest, calling it 'the Black Law', fascist censorship of the most draconian kind, Rajiv withdrew the bill from the Rajya Sabha. 'In a front-page editorial Monday in the anti-government *Indian Express*, noted lawyer and Parliament member Ram Jethmalani wrote, "The bill makes a mockery of our justice system and lays the foundation for imminent tyranny."'[16] Ram actually went further than that, calling for non-violent protest, charging the Prime Minister with corruption, calling for his removal from office, and daring Rajiv to take him to court. Rajiv knew enough not to take him up on that dare.

In May 1989, the government heavily opposed the Comptroller and Auditor General Report to Parliament. The Opposition mobilized and attacked the government and the Congress rebutted. The Opposition demanded the Prime Minister resign, and in July they called a press conference, threatening that all Opposition members would resign from Parliament. The government dug in their heels. The debate in Parliament continued into October, until Rajiv announced there would be elections in November.

N. Ram, the editor of *The Hindu*, went to Sweden, and he was able to obtain the diary of Martin Ardbo, the chairman of Bofors. This demonstrated deep involvement on the part of Chadha, the Hindujas, Arun Nehru, and Ottavio Quattrocchi. Palme's personal involvement was exposed, and the whole cover-up appeared in detail. The Congress party claimed it was a forgery. Both *The Hindu* and the *Indian Express* ran with the story.

The Aftermath

When the November elections came around, the Congress party lost its majority. This really was the end of the Gandhi regime. But unaccustomed to being in power, the Opposition had to struggle to form a government. Two men contended for Prime Minister, V.P. Singh and Chandrashekhar, and a third name, Devi Lal, was raised as a stalking horse.

V.P. Singh was thrown out of Mrs Gandhi's cabinet because he enforced the smuggling laws too assiduously against her supporters. He had left the Congress party, formed a new party, the Jan Morcha, and became the president of a National Front that combined four Opposition parties. Chandrashekhar had started out as a socialist, become general secretary of the Congress party, left the Congress party, and become the president of the Janata Party.

Because of V.P. Singh's history, Ram supported him for Prime Minister. On November 30, 1989, he commenced a peaceful protest fast, a dharna, on the lawn of Chandrashekhar's bungalow to convince him to give up his bid for Prime Minister. He sat down under a shamiana, a type of open tent, and started his fast. The Janata chief's supporters immediately surrounded him and pummelled him viciously. The papers referred to it as a thrashing.

The police came, and so did Ram's supporters from his Bharat Mukti Morcha; horrified, they covered up his torn clothes with a shawl and escorted him to safety. Ram wanted to sit on a chair outside until he was assured that his protest had been registered, but his party members talked him into leaving. Chandrashekhar said later that he had known nothing of the attack. After he had time to think about it, he came up with an excuse, and apologized.

It is hard to know why Ram did that. Obviously he did not expect a thrashing. Whether he even expected his fast to change Chandrashekhar's mind is doubtful. Some thought Ram just wanted to curry favour with V.P. Singh in order to get into a position of power. If that is true, V.P. Singh comes out as an ingrate. Others believed that Singh would never appoint Ram to a high position because he did not trust him. He could never know when Ram might strike out on his own on an issue dear to him, whether or not his statements conformed to the party line. Ram refers to the whole episode as political theatre.

Immediately after the December 1989 election, V.P. Singh became the new Prime Minister. Eleven months later, Singh was replaced by Chandrashekhar.

After all the time and effort that he had expended on the whole Bofors episode, Ram ended up claiming perversely that no evidence rising to the necessary legal standard for criminal conviction— *beyond a reasonable doubt*—ever was produced against Rajiv. Even so, Ram says, 'I could convict a man on this evidence alone.'

When the Swedish radio had first broken the story, the government responded, 'This is an attempt to destabilize my government.' Ram calls this an answer that shows guilt.

'At hearing the nature of denial of the Rajiv government, I felt fairly convinced that the Swedish radio broadcast rang with a tangible veracity that all the denials of Rajiv and his conspirators could not demolish. If a jury were trying the case, I'm quite certain that the hollowness of the denial and its complete unsustainability would have been enough evidence for conviction.'[17]

He says that on cross-examination he easily could have created sufficient doubt in the mind of a courtroom, but it would not have been beyond all doubt. 'People have been convicted for a false alibi,' he says, citing the case of an assertion that a suspect was 1000 miles away from the site of the crime, when it turned out that he was not. Ram cites some examples: Why did the government not participate in the investigation that the audit bureau carried out in Sweden? Why did they refuse a copy of the report? Why did they refuse to meet with the Swedish chief prosecutor? Ram says there were at least 10 pieces of bad conduct, 'Enough to convict him in the court of the people. At least the evidence raises a strong suspicion.'

Ram fought the Bofors battle through the power of the media. He had written for the *Indian Express* before, but the 10 questions were his high point. His readers hung on his every word. The government quivered at every word. The *Indian Express* sold every word. Newspapers across the country published the questions, and people read all these papers. Granted, professional, full-time journalists made huge contributions, but none had the personal stature and prestige of a former chairman of the Bar Council of India, a Member of Parliament, a flamboyant lawyer, and the wielder of a needle-sharp pen. No one person can take credit for bringing down a government. Many people gave months of their time to this investigation. What we can say is that if any prominent person was the face of the story, if any one person reached all the readers in India, if any one person embarrassed the government the most, it must have been Ram.

Representing the Hindujas

Tehelka captured the paradox of Ram representing the Hinduja family in 2003: 'When the Bofors scandal broke out in the late 1980s, veteran lawyer Ram Jethmalani played a huge role in investigating the trail of corruption. Jethmalani famously put out "10 questions" every day . . . Stunningly, in 2003, Jethmalani agreed to represent the Hinduja brothers and succeeded in getting them off the hook from the courts.'[18]

The case against the Hindujas was not over until 2005,[19] by which time the government had changed, and the new government feared that a Hinduja conviction would implicate Rajiv. Ram's basic defence was that the Hinduja family had acted as agents for Bofors for years before the actual Bofors scandal. Any fee they took had nothing to do with this episode. The Hindujas were brokers, and Bofors used to borrow money for a brokerage fee. The court put it, 'I am informed that up to April, 1985, having agents was legitimate as the Government itself used to pay them commissions.'

Ram argues that taking a commission is not illegal. 'It becomes a punishable offense only when it is part of a conspiracy to bribe a public servant.'

Moreover, photocopied documents were initially presented as evidence against the Hindujas, but no one could ever produce any original documents. The court said 'That the relevant and material documents are not available in original and no copies duly authenticated in accordance with the Indian Evidence Act are available. It seems to me that if these documents are not proved by satisfactory secondary evidence and will not be ever proved at the trial, it will be a cruel joke on the accused to expose them to a long and arduous trial and waste public time and money which will be totally out of proportion to the results to be achieved. In fact, nothing will be achieved.'

The court ruled: 'From what has been noted and discussed above and on the basis of the statements made by the prosecution, no case can be proceeded with in respect of the Hinduja Brothers or the Bofors Company.'

Finally, the judge admonished, 'Before parting, I must express my disapproval at the investigation that went on for 14 years and I was given to understand that it cost the Exchequer nearly rupees 250 crores. During the investigation a huge bubble was created with the aid of the media which, however, when tested by court, burst leaving behind a disastrous trail of suffering. The accused suffered emotionally. Careers—both political and professional—were ruined besides causing huge economic loss. Many an accused lived and died with a stigma. It is hoped that this elite Investigating Agency will be more responsible in future.'

But the investigation did bring down the Gandhi government.

24

The End of Rajiv Gandhi

Rajiv had worse problems than Bofors, one of which was fatal. And Ram would become involved in every issue.

After Rajiv's mother was assassinated, the December 1984 elections had swept him into Parliament in a huge vote of sympathy for his family and party. In the largest electoral victory in the history of the party, the Congress won an 80 per cent majority in the Lok Sabha.[1] Rajiv immediately began to undo some of his mother's policies, loosen quotas and reduce tariffs. Most significant, Rajiv wanted to dismantle some of the Licence Raj, in order to start a transition to capitalism.

Flying in the face of that optimism, the worst industrial disaster of all time occurred in Bhopal, 1984. An American plant operated by Union Carbide suddenly began leaking poisonous gas, which spread insidiously throughout a workers' neighbourhood. An estimated 7000 died instantly from inhalation, and thousands more died later. The final out-of-court settlement was $470 million, an amount which Ram has criticized roundly. Many of the workers received little or nothing, and he says the government sold them out.

Ram has written[2] that Union Carbide knew its facilities were in poor shape two years before the event. After the disaster, he says, 'The Union of India, while posturing to be the guardian of the victims whom it double crossed completely, divested the victims of their right to sue, appropriating this right to itself through legislation. The legislation made it a statutory trustee of the compensation due to the victims, individually and collectively. Thus the government of India also appropriated to itself the victims' right to sue Union Carbide and those who in law were the effective and proximate cause of the tragedy.' Thus, the government settlement with Union Carbide deprived the victims of their rights.

The reason is that, when it first filed suit, India claimed losses of $3.3 billion, but in the settlement it agreed to accept $470 million, one-seventh of the amount claimed in the first place. Ram wrote that, 'The victims of Bhopal could not have been betrayed more inhumanly and cruelly.' He also proposed some reasons why elements in the government might have accepted money under the table as an inducement to accept a reduced settlement, and he asked for a full disclosure of the relevant records.

A propos, Ram has claimed[3] 'that a settlement took place at the Ritz Hotel in Paris and that it was worked out by Warren Anderson and a personal friend and representative of the then prime minister of India. Under this unofficial settlement, the government wanted to be paid secretly, under the table. When Union Carbide officers raised serious doubts regarding the Supreme Court's acceptance of this unfair and corrupt settlement, they were assured that the Supreme Court was not their worry. The negotiators would manage everything.'

When the case came up in January 2012, Ram appeared as an intervener to instruct the court on the right of victims to sue the Union of India and the state of Madhya Pradesh for fair compensation. The court acknowledged that the settlement with Union Carbide did not abrogate the victims' rights to sue the two governments or their ministers.

Rajiv's death did not come because of the Punjab, not because of Bofors, and not because of Union Carbide. It was a result of a sectarian dispute in Sri Lanka. Sri Lanka, formerly Ceylon, is divided between a Buddhist–Sinhalese majority and a Hindu–Tamil minority. India inevitably became involved in their dispute because the Tamils have strong ties to the adjacent Indian state of Tamil Nadu. In 1983 the Sinhalese tried to purge the island of Tamils. The Tamils fought back by forming the Liberation Tigers of Tamil

Eelam (LTTE), commonly known as the Tamil Tigers. Tamil Nadu and its chief minister, M.G. Ramachandran, supported the Tamils.

During Indira's time, President Jayewardene of Sri Lanka requested help from the United States, United Kingdom and other countries. Indira had opposed the presence of foreign troops in Sri Lanka. When Rajiv became Prime Minister, he wanted to work with the LTTE to achieve a peace accord.

In 1987, the army of Sri Lanka attacked Jaffna, a stronghold of the LTTE, and held it under siege. India started a humanitarian airdrop on June 4, 1987, and it subsequently sent in a peace-keeping force to disarm the Tamil Tigers. The plan was to clear the way for elections. Instead, the Tamil Tigers attacked the Indian army, which had to withdraw in 1990.

While the fighting was still at full force, Rajiv airlifted the leader of the LTTE, Velupillai Prabhakaran, to New Delhi to discuss the possibility of India's signing a peace accord with President Jayewardene of Sri Lanka. The discussions were cordial, ending with a gentleman's agreement that, among other things, included an understanding that Prabhakaran would not oppose the agreement in public and that the Tamil Tigers would have to make only a token surrender of arms.

Rajiv signed the Indo-Sri Lanka Agreement on July 30, 1987, but the LTTE considered Rajiv a traitor. There were many reasons. They believed the accord did not provide for an independent Tamil Eelam, the most important LTTE objective. They were angry that Indian intelligence agencies were arming their opponents and 'rounding up the LTTE militants for elimination'. The Indian army had not intervened when the Sri Lankan navy apprehended a group of LTTE leaders in a boat headed to Tamil Nadu. The encounter turned dramatic when, knowing they were to be brought back to Colombo, they all took cyanide capsules. One day after signing the accord, Rajiv was assaulted by a navy soldier with his rifle butt in Colombo, but he survived.[4]

What he did not survive, politically, was the November 1989 election, because of the Bofors scandal.

Nevertheless, Rajiv was still president of the Congress party.

On May 21, 1991 Rajiv was actively campaigning for a Lok Sabha seat in the next election when he stopped to make a speech in Sriperumbudur, near Chennai (formerly Madras) in Tamil Nadu. That was where he was assassinated by a female member of the LTTE, an early example of a weapon that was invented, not in the Middle East, but by the Tamil Tigers—the suicide bomber. In the culmination of an elaborately planned conspiracy, a woman named Dhanu Thenmozhi Rajaratnam bent down to touch his feet in an apparent show of respect and detonated a bomb belt that was strapped around her body. The bomb killed her, Rajiv, and 14 more people.[5]

Early speculation went from the LTTE, to Sikh militants, even the KGB, CIA, or Mossad. The *New York Times* cited the high tensions between upper caste and lower caste Hindus in India at the time, and the BBC gave examples of sectarian violence between Hindus and Muslims during the election campaign. The CBI chief investigating officer, K. Ragothaman, debunks all these alternate hypotheses in his book, *Conspiracy to Kill Rajiv Gandhi*. In it, he gives all the details of an LTTE conspiracy, complicated by the number of members who committed suicide with cyanide pills, rather than cooperate with a police investigation.

The Supreme Court blamed the chief of the LTTE, Prabhakaran, and it wrote that he had hatched the plot because, in an interview in August 1990, Rajiv had threatened he would send the army to disarm the LTTE as soon as he came back to power. Others said the Indian Army had forced Prabhakaran to hide in the jungle for two years, still others that the Indian Army had handed over a group of LTTE militants to Sri Lankan forces.

The Supreme Court trial was an appeal by 26 accused who the trial court in Madras had sentenced to death. Ultimately, 21 were acquitted,[6] the court writing that there was almost no evidence against them. In the end, only four were sentenced to death. The Supreme Court gave the only surviving member of the original five-member squad, Nalini, a death sentence, commuted to life imprisonment after she delivered a baby in prison. The other accused co-conspirators tried multiple manoeuvres to delay their execution,[7] including a request to the Designated Court for Ram, Shanti Bhushan, or another eminent lawyer to represent them. Reportedly, these lawyers all refused. The sentence was handed down on May 5, 1999.

In 1991, the Rao government appointed a commission to investigate the assassination. Under the chairmanship of Justice Milap Chand Jain, the Jain Commission report ran to nine volumes, named people, and devoted one whole volume to allegations against Chandraswami— the swami of Bofors fame—including the charge that he financed the assassination, though in the end the Commission did not regard the evidence as conclusive. The Commission also suspiciously investigated the associations between Chandrashekhar, Chandraswami and his friend Subramanian Swamy, also from Tamil Nadu. Saying of him, 'Dr Swamy cannot be believed when he changes his versions and when he is indefinite and when he does not support his version by any corroboratory evidence.'[8]

Also, on Subramanian Swamy, the report states: 'It would appear that a consistent and persistent effort is there on his part not to answer the questions which are most relevant in order to find out the truth.'[9]

J. Jayalalithaa, the leader of the All India Anna Dravida Munnetra Kazhagam (AIADMK) party, retained Ram to represent her against Subramanian Swamy, who had implicated her in Rajiv's assassination. The interchange between Ram and Subramanian Swamy escalated during the hearing until it resulted in a libel suit. This started with a Special Leave Petition dismissed by the Supreme Court in 1999. It went to the Delhi High Court first in 2000, and then in December of 2001,[10] finally ending with a case in the same court in 2006.[11] More of that shortly.

Subramanian Swamy, smarting from his exchange with Ram before the Jain Commission, attacked Ram in Parliament during a debate of the Commission Report,[12] coming up with multiple disparate allegations: Ram was pro-LTTE; a TADA court had once refused to allow Ram to enter the court; there was a photograph portraying Ram in incriminating circumstances.

Ram rebutted Swamy's accusations:

Shri Ram Jethmalani: It was said that some TADA Court in Mumbai had prohibited my entry into the court room because I had got something to do with Dawood Ibrahim. I have never heard more monstrous and irresponsible falsehood that was uttered. The TADA Court, which sits in Mumbai, is the highest security court. A list of every person who enters that Court, every advocate who appears in that court, is given to the security staff and only those persons whose list is given to the entrance door security are allowed to enter the court. I was appearing for two accused before the TADA Court. One was the famous actor, Sanjay Dutt, about whom everybody knows.

The other was a gentleman by the name Mr Azami. As a lawyer, I am entitled to believe that Shri Azami was totally innocent. We argued his case threadbare but the judge was, according to me, so perverse and wrong that he refused to admit him even to bail. We decided that we would not appear any longer in that court and I told my junior that hereafter I would not be appearing before this unreasonable judge. The judge asked my junior, 'Is this the final decision of Shri Jethmalani that he is not coming to my court?' My junior told him that, 'No, he will not.' Thereafter the intimation was given to the security at the gate that Shri Jethmalani is no longer one of the Counsels who would be appearing in the case. This is all that has happened. I cannot understand how any responsible person, a person who should be a responsible person, has been judicially determined to be a [*phrase removed by the Speaker of the Parliament] by the Commission. At least I have not been judicially determined so. Something has been alleged against me by a person who himself has been judicially determined as a . . .

Let us now talk about the photograph because that seems to be a little more interesting. In 1988, there is no doubt that not only I was appearing for Chandra Swami because I believed that at that time he was being harassed but he also offered to help us in the Bofors investigation which doubtless I was doing at that

time along with some other colleague. September 14 is my date
of birth. On 13th of September, I was on way to the United States
because my children stay in the United States and they decided
to celebrate my birthday in the United States. I was on my way
through Europe when Shri Chandra Swami said, 'If you come
to Monte Carlo, Mr Adnan Khashog[g]i is in possession of a
document concerning Mr Martin Ardbo.'

At that time he was trying to get a job for Mr Martin Ardbo.
He had been dismissed from Bofors. He was trying to get him a job
with Sultan of Brunei. He said, 'If you pass through Monte Carlo,
we will give you that document.' I badly needed that document,
I, my daughter and my son passed through Monte Carlo on the
13th of September. On the night of 13th September they did have
a big party in my honour. I was very happy that I was there. I was
enjoying myself fully. I was with my daughter. A photograph was
taken with Mr and Mrs Khashog[g]i in which I was a somewhat
westernised type. That was the photograph which my daughter
had kept in her drawing room. Somebody has stolen it.

Mr Chairman, Sir, Shri Swami claims that Justice Jain has been
very unfair to him. Whether he has been unfair to him or not, I
cannot decide. He may be right that Justice Jain has been unfair
to him. But, today, so far as we are concerned, there is a finding
recorded that he had not helped the Commission; that he had
spoken [*phrase removed by the Chair of Parliament] and that
he had kept truth back from the court which was determining
the cause of Rajiv Gandhi's death. This at least requires to be
investigated further by somebody . . . People whom the whole
world acknowledges to be persons of impeccable integrity are
being maligned by this kind of a man . . .

The interchange before the Jain Commission was of the same
intensity. In 2006, the case came back to the Delhi High Court
on its last appeal.[13] The court gave the history of the statements
Subramanian Swamy made to the press after Rajiv's assassination,
his allegations about Jayalalithaa, and his statements to the Jain
Commission.

Before the Jain Commission, Ram had accused Swamy of a political agenda, and Swamy accused Ram of everything in the book. The record reports that, 'The witness was asked to apologise for his remarks against Mr Jethmalani to the effect that he has two wives which was not at all relevant. The witness did not apologise and said that it was not derogatory and it is fact.'

The court gave the history. On June 2, 1993, 'press reports quoted the defendant [Swamy] as having stated that the then Chief Minister of Tamil Nadu, Ms J. Jayalalitha had been tipped off by the Liberation Tigers of Tamil Eelam [sic] (LTTE) on the assassination of late Shri Rajiv Gandhi, former Prime Minister of India. Defendant was stated to have informed the press that information of the assassination bid was passed on to Ms J. Jayalalitha around April 17, 1991 in Madras.'

The court writes that when Ram represented Jayalalithaa before the Jain Commission, he grilled Subramanian Swamy on the activities of the LTTE, the politics of the state of Tamil Nadu, and on other statements he had made.

The court goes on: 'Cross examination became gruelling and by 11.9.1995 took shape of an attempt to corner the defendant by trying to bring home the point that since the party to which the defendant belonged, namely, Janta Dal(S) lost all seats it had contested at the election, defendant was unnecessarily trying to malign Ms J. Jayalalitha. Probably, plaintiff wanted to establish political rivalry between the defendant and his client, Ms J. Jayalalitha.'

Swamy's written submission to the Jain Commission claimed the following: 'Mr Jethmalani's demand that he be told the sources [of Swamy's information] is illegitimate because he has been the counsel for those with close connection with LTTE, such as Ms Sasikala's relatives, Swami Permananda (a Sri Lankan Tamil in jail), and in fact he would have been the LTTE counsel itself, but for his heart by-pass surgery. Hence, his obsession with my sources is at the LTTE's behest. According to my information, Mr Jethmalani has been receiving money from the LTTE being deposited in his son's account in Citibank in New York. That such deposits take place has been admitted by Mr Jethmalani.' That was his most significant accusation against Ram. Oh, and Ram never had heart by-pass surgery.

The court writes that Ram had grilled Swamy because: 'It is pleaded that the plaintiff was bound, in the discharge of his professional duty to Ms J. Jayalalitha to expose the falsehood of the defendant. Since defendant had claimed before the commission that his allegations against Ms J. Jayalalitha were based not on his personal knowledge but on source, plaintiff was duty bound to cross-examine the defendant about the alleged source.'

Swamy claimed Ram had said: 'I asked the LTTE to assassinate Mr Rajiv Gandhi because Mr Gandhi was four years younger than me and because of my ambition to become the Prime Minister. If this standard of argument is permissible, then every politician is suspect we can conclude that since Mr Jethmalani has a declared ambition to become the President of India, therefore he being older than Dr Shankar Dayal Sharma, he should be plotting his murder with his Dawood Ibrahim connection.' Declared ambition to become President of India?

Dawood Ibrahim? That was the deliberate association of a notorious criminal with Ram, to prejudice the court. Swamy also claimed that Ram accused him of *not denying* that he had asked the LTTE to assassinate Rajiv. While this sounds circular, remember that Ram always says that a *failure to deny* or to sue for libel when faced with scurrilous charges is a sign of guilt.

The court writes, 'It is asserted by the plaintiff that the statement, apart from being false and reckless was inspired by malice and vicious animosity. It is asserted that the object of the defendant was to damage the personal, political and professional reputation of the plaintiff. Damages in sum of Rs 50 lacs [sic] have been prayed for.'

The Delhi High Court bought Ram's case, concluding that 'the defendant exceeded the limits of qualified privilege as his statement was quite unconnected with and irrelevant to the situation and suffers from redundancy of the expression.' The court further said, 'Considering the professional standing of the plaintiff and his stature in social life I award damages in sum of Rs 5 lacs [sic] in favour of the plaintiff and against the defendant.'

So Ram, one of the most famous and highly paid lawyers in the country, had invested all this time to defend his honour after being libelled while defending Jayalalithaa, a woman who only hindered him on his way to being Law Minister! Incidentally, by 2006 Ram and Swamy had become allies in a campaign to repatriate black money to India, so Ram genially said he would give the five lakhs to Swamy's children.

Some have said the public was suspicious of Ram because of his long history of defending perpetrators of notorious crimes. Others pointed to the precedent that he defended Kehar and Balbir Singh after the assassination of Indira Gandhi. Still others pointed out Ram's longstanding opposition to Rajiv. At the time of the assassination, as Ram has said repeatedly, it was completely untrue that he was defending the co-conspirators of Rajiv's assassins, but years later, he would do exactly that.

At the time, Ram had found himself threatened by a mob after Rajiv's assassination. Going out to talk to them, he asked them to choose two interlocutors to come inside, sit down, and tell him their complaint. When they said that they had heard he was going to defend the assassins, Ram answered, 'They have not asked me, but if they did, I cannot promise that I would not. But if Sonia Gandhi would ask me to prosecute them, I would be glad to do it, and I would ask only two rupees.'

Twenty years later, Ram was convinced that these men were falsely accused. Arguing that keeping the men in prison that long had already condemned them to 1000 deaths, Ram obtained a stay of execution in August 2011.

Addressing the judges, he said, 'You must start with the assumption that more than two years' delay is prima facie wrong. An undue delay violated Article 21 of the Constitution (Protection of life and personal liberty),' he added. He said that after Rajiv Gandhi's assassination in 1991, the judicial process was over by May 1999, with the Supreme Court confirming the death sentence pronounced by the lower court. A mercy plea presented to the

Governor of Tamil Nadu was disposed of in 10 days in October 1999. Jethmalani said the mercy pleas submitted for the second time were rejected by the Governor on April 25, 2000. A day later, they sent a mercy petition to the President. The petitions were rejected by the President after a gap of 11 years and four months in August this year.[14]

'The delay unless properly explained and justified makes death penalty immoral, illegal and according to me unconstitutional. The underlying legal argument is by delay in disposing of case, you are guilty for suffering of these convicts. The submission is that whether delay is justified,' he added.[15]

The Madras High Court agreed. As a result, 10 days before their scheduled hanging on September 9, 2011, 'three Rajiv Gandhi killers today got a reprieve from the Madras High Court which stayed their execution for eight weeks.'

'The High Court is doing justice. Be sure. They have stayed the execution,' Ram Jethmalani, who pleaded their case, told reporters after the court's interim order.[16]

' . . .The delay of 11 years in deciding their mercy plea was "mental torture" for the convicts, said Jethmalani. 'You make them suffer a thousand times. Is this justice?' Jethmalani asked.

Also, just before the court decision, the Tamil Nadu Assembly 'unanimously adopted the resolution moved by Jayalalitha requesting President Pratibha Patil to reconsider the mercy petitions rejected early this month.'

In November 2011, accompanied by the general secretary of the Marumalarchi Dravida Munnetra Kazhagam (MDMK) party, Vaiko, Ram spent about 15 minutes in the prison talking to the three men in the high-security central prison of Vellore. Needless to say, when the word got out, the city was abuzz. Ram told reporters, 'I wanted to hear it from them. They say they are innocent. I can't share what my clients have told me and what my convictions are,' he told reporters after the meeting. He was in Vellore to deliver a lecture. 'It was on the invitation from Vaiko that I have come here to meet them (convicts),' he said.[17]

The Supreme Court[18] allowed the petition for mercy of

V. Sriharan (aka Murugan), A.G. Perarivalan (aka Arivu), and T. Suthendraraja (aka Santhan) to be transferred from the Madras High Court to the Supreme Court, because a fair trial 'may not be possible in congenial atmosphere because of the agitation launched by different political outfits, extremist groups and lawyers and also because thousands of people gathered in the High Court premises and raised slogans outside and inside the Court premises'.

The matter was appealed to the Supreme Court, but the fate of the three accused was imperiled by a verdict in a subsequent case. This is the case of Khalistan Liberation Force (KLF) terrorist Devinder Pal Singh Bhullar, in which the Supreme Court said that a 'Long delay by the President or the Governor in disposing of mercy petitions of persons convicted under anti-terror laws . . .cannot be a ground for commutation of the death sentence.'[19]

The article explains that this decision 'paves the way for his execution and may have a bearing on the fate of over 20 convicts facing execution'.

'Among those whose execution has been stayed are three in the Rajiv Gandhi assassination case, though the Supreme Court had finally ruled that the killing of Rajiv Gandhi was not a terrorist act and taken the case out of the purview of the TADA.' In fact, Ram's clients said exactly that. The decision does not apply to them, because they were not terrorists. They performed a single act, aimed at one individual. As the court wrote, it was not an action against India, but a personal grudge that caused them to act.

Ram appeared as amicus in the Bhullar case. Afterwards, in a press interview on another case, he said,'Until the judgment was pronounced in the Bhullar case, all executions must be stayed.'[20]

Murugan, Perarivalan and Santhan had to wait until after January 21, 2014, when the Supreme Court handed down a verdict[21] on 13 writs, representing 15 defendants, some of whom had been in jail for over 20 years, some for more than 12 years since their first mercy petitions were filed. The judges made it clear that the petitions under consideration did not challenge the original death sentences. In all cases if the defendants had been executed promptly there would have been no cause of action. It was the lengthy imprisonment and delayed execution that formed the basis of the petitions.

As for the Bhullar case, Ram argued it was per incuriam, meaning a decision arrived at without a basis in statutes or relevant earlier judgements. Under these circumstances, it cannot serve as a precedent for other cases.

The court wrote that 'There is no good reason to disqualify all TADA [terrorist] cases as a class from relief on account of delay in execution of death sentence. Each case requires consideration on its own facts.'

Fifteen lawyers argued before the court, but Ram's arguments were the only ones which the judges quoted: 'We are of the view that unexplained delay is one of the grounds for commutation of sentence of death into life imprisonment and the said supervening circumstance is applicable to all types of cases including offences under TADA. The only aspect the courts have to satisfy is that the delay must be unreasonable and unexplained or inordinate at the hands of the executive,' the bench had said, agreeing with the arguments of senior advocate Ram Jethmalani, who assisted the court as amicus curiae in the 15 cases.'[22]

In all 15 instances the death sentences were commuted to life imprisonment, despite their being convicted terrorists.

One week later, Ram argued the cases of Rajiv's killers before a three-judge panel of the Supreme Court, even though the government was scrambling to get an adjournment. In fact, it was reported[23] that 'senior advocate Ram Jethmalani spilled the beans . . . Jethmalani said, "I know the Centre's gameplan. My suspicion is that they are seeking adjournments to buy time to draft a petition to seek review of the Supreme Court's January 21 judgment."'

At this writing, the verdict on the Gandhi assassins was still pending, but Ram was confident that his arguments would prevail. He also projects that by the time this book reaches the readers they will find that his prediction is fully justified.

25

The National Law School

One of Ram's fondest dreams came to fruition in Bangalore—the creation of a National Law School.

In the fullness of Ram's career, its many cases and its multiple political activities, his role in establishing the National Law Schools in India has been one of his least recognized. His former associate, Sri Jaisinghani, says this was Ram's greatest achievement.

The management guru Peter Drucker encapsulated Ram's devotion to teaching:[1] 'We are not aware whether anyone has asked the bold, stout-hearted Ram Jethmalani what he wants to be remembered for: a brilliant lawyer?, an able and forthright Minister?, a noted, though controversial public figure? I don't know. But we like to believe that Ram would love to be remembered as a person who made a difference in the lives of younger people—for he has been frequently lecturing and teaching at the Ambedkar Institute in Pune and at the National Law School in Bangalore. That he found the time to do this amidst his innumerable pre-occupations and his roaring practice shows an amazing commitment to the cause of higher education—the effort he put into teaching students of law makes me believe that he is a man who wants to be remembered as having been the teacher who converted some (even a few) brilliant students into first-rate lawyers.'

'If education is the technique of transmitting Civilisation (as Will Durant reminds us), we would like to salute our good and dear friend Ram Jethmalani for having so successfully transmitted, to a succession of law-students, the benefits of civilization.'

Some have said that Ram has made his greatest contributions to society as a law teacher. Certainly, teaching is one of the joys of his life. When he lectures, his voice bellows in passion; his face flushes; his eyes flash. He explains how to read a statute, and how not to miss subtleties. He illustrates points with off-colour anecdotes. He delights in showing off a defence that nobody else would have considered. He gives the details of cases from a half century ago. He glories in jokes another professor would never dare to tell.

No wonder his students reciprocate. During the break in one law school programme we remember, Ram walked out to the lawn to chat with a political colleague, and he was mobbed by students. They came up to him and touched his feet. They shyly asked if a friend could take a picture with him. They asked for his autograph. They stood around and just basked in his aura.

One year, my husband and I arranged for Ram to meet us at the end of a programme that was held in a law school. As soon as Ram appeared at the door of the lecture room, I innocently ran up the stairs to greet him, only to realize that throughout his descent down the steep stairs towards the stage, the entire audience of students and faculty had stood up and was applauding him excitedly.

Atal Bihari Vajpayee once asked Ram why he teaches. Ram answered, 'You are a great public speaker, but you know nothing of world history. Have you heard of King Solomon—he said the older you get, the younger should be your company.' Presumably, Ram was only talking about law students.

In case the reader wonders why Ram Jethmalani could be called a law teacher, we should look at the record. Ram was honoured by an appointment in 1953 as a part-time professor at the Government Law College in Bombay, where he taught criminal law, evidence, and conflict of laws. Some of his lectures were published in *Conflict of Laws*, a legal textbook, in 1956. He taught conflicts of law at the New Law College, 1956–58. He lectured to officers of the Indian navy on criminal law in 1968–70. He has taught evidence at Symbiosis in Pune since the university was established in 1977, and he still makes a special point of flying to Mumbai in order to drive to Pune almost every weekend to lecture, usually on Saturdays. Amazingly, he frequently gives them very short notice of his availability, but even so the whole college turns out for each lecture. He has taught at the K.C. Law College, Jai Hind Law College and Bandra National College, three colleges started by Sindhis. He has taught legal language, among other subjects, at the National Law School in Bangalore, and he taught comparative constitutional law at Wayne State University Law School in 1976. He is also an honorary professor at the Jawaharlal Nehru University in Delhi.

Once he asked my husband and me to join him on a trip. We were sitting in his apartment in Mumbai, and he told us he had chartered a private plane for Saturday in order to fly to Chandigarh, lecture to law students that Saturday night, then fly to Delhi on Sunday, all at his own expense. We thought it sounded too hectic, and we demurred. Ram, in his late 80s, went ahead. It turns out that was not the only time he has chartered a plane just to give one law lecture.

Ram funds a Ram Jethmalani Prize at Symbiosis University for excellence in evidence. The winner receives tuition for one year. He also lectures on medical ethics twice a year to healthcare professionals at Symbiosis. Traditionally, he is the yearly graduation speaker for the two-year MBA programme in hospital and healthcare management at Symbiosis, and he signs every one of the 1000 diplomas himself. He says that the school absolutely will not let him out of the obligation to sign every one. In 2013, his graduation speech was on professional malpractice, another subject on which he has taken cases, even though the average person would not think it.

One year, a Muslim boy from Kashmir who had failed the all-India examination for entrance to law school somehow found his way to Ram. Ram went to the National Law School at Bangalore and helped to get him admitted. At the end of the five-year programme, the young man was at the top of the class. Berkeley University invited him to California to study. They were willing to waive the tuition, but the other expenses were too much for him to afford, so the young man came back to Ram. Ram paid the $2000 necessary for him to take the offer from Berkley, and he went. Today the man is in practice in Kashmir, and he has played an important role to promote good relations between Kashmir and the rest of India.

Ram was elected vice-chairman of the Bar Council of India in 1968 and chairman in 1970. He served four years as chairman before he came to the United States in 1976. When he returned in 1977, he served four more years, four two-year terms in all. During the time he was chairman and also after his term ended, he worked on his vision of a National Law School. Before it got off the ground, we remember hearing him talk at length about how it should be structured and what his Legal Education Committee needed to do.

The Bar Council in India is far more powerful and has broader powers than the American Bar Association (ABA), because in India the Bar Council is in charge of all legal education. As contrasted with the ABA, the Advocates Act of 1961 gives the Bar Council statutory functions that explicitly authorize it 'To promote legal education and to lay down standards of legal education' and 'To recognise Universities whose degree in law shall be a qualification for enrolment as an advocate. The Bar Council of India visits and inspects Universities, or directs the State Bar Councils to visit and inspect Universities for this purpose.'

Ram was chairman of the Legal Education Committee of the Bar Council from 1970 through 1975, when the concept of a new National Law School was being explored.

The important difference between the new National Law School model and the older law schools in India is that the National Law Schools provide an integrated five-year course following high school. Before this, students studied for four years in college, followed by two years of law school. The five-year programme is a copy of the English system, integrating three years of undergraduate legal education with two years of professional postgraduate legal education, which include apprenticeship. Now the five-year programme is the most popular course in India, and the 12 National Law Schools are organized on this model.

The original design for the integrated five-year programme came from an article by Dr G.S. Sharma, published in the *Jaipur Law*

Journal in 1968. He argued that the Advocates Act made the Bar Council responsible for legal education, and they should adopt this British system. Prof. Upendra Baxi took up the idea, and he brought it to the Bar Council at the same time that Ram became chairman. The five-year model was formally introduced and approved by the Bar Council in 1985 when Ram was chairman of both the Bar Council and the Legal Education Committee.

Sri Jaisinghani remembers that Ram worked for years to establish this school, that he spent a considerable amount of his own money on it, and that his friendship with Ramakrishna Hegde was invaluable.

Hegde served as Chief Minister of Karnataka for three terms. Later, he served as a Cabinet minister in the BJP government of 1998, and he was a Member of the Rajya Sabha from 1996 to 2002. Ram represented his son Bharat in 1985 when he was accused of taking bribe money in the alleged 'MD seat scam'.[2]

This began when a man allegedly paid Hegde's son for help in getting his daughter into a postgraduate medical programme in Belgium. The son could not get her in, but he was accused of not returning all the money. The case went to a commission of enquiry, and the press reported all the details. In the middle of the two-and-a-half year investigation, the judge suddenly was nominated for a higher office. The press screamed that he had been taken off the enquiry for political reasons. The new judge did rule against Hegde's son, but Ram was able to establish that it was on the basis of faulty evidence. At any rate, the commission had not been authorized to impose a punishment, and the episode blew over, though it did cement the friendship between Ram and Hegde.

Certainly the National Law School began in Karnataka because of Ram's personal and political friendship with R.K. Hegde, which dated back to when they both worked together in the Janata Party. As Chief Minister, Hegde wanted the school as a feather in the state's cap as much as he wanted to help Ram. He also had a dream that Bangalore would become the artistic and intellectual capital of India. At the same time that he induced the National Law School to open in Bangalore, he also enticed the Indian Institute of Technology to start there. Karnataka was not the only state interested in the school either. The states of Uttar Pradesh and West Bengal were also early contenders, but Hegde had more to offer.

Hegde directed Bangalore University to allocate 14 acres of land just outside of Bangalore for the law school, and he also obtained a temporary accommodation from Central College—the oldest college of Bangalore—so the law school could start functioning immediately. Hegde ensured that the state of Karnataka provided a grant of Rs 50 lakhs—about $200,000 US dollars—to be paid over five years, and it immediately gave the school a start-up sum of Rs 10 lakhs, about $40,000.[3] The first students started in July 1988. The school moved into its permanent campus in 1990, and in 1991 it became a fully residential university.

According to Ram's former junior, Jaisinghani, some money also may have come from some of Ram's rich clients as a donation in lieu of legal fees, but university sources do not remember such a gift.

Hegde's most important contribution to forming the university was an act of the Karnataka State Legislature. Initially, Ram and Prof. Baxi thought their new creation would have to be a Deemed University. This means it is established by the Government of India without being affiliated with any pre-existing institution, an autonomous college that works like a university for the purposes of designing a curriculum, running courses, and awarding a degree. The problem was that when Prof. N.L. Mitra, Prof. Baxi and Ram met with Mr V.R. Reddy, the chairman of the Bar Council in 1986, they realized that this school's affiliation with Central College precluded it from being a Deemed University. Certainly Ram and the others did not want the law school to apply for Deemed status only to find out they could not get it. That meant they would need an act of the legislature to found an actual university. So, as it turned out, since the school could not become a college, it had to become a university.

Karnataka had to pass a statute. Prof. Baxi drafted the proposed bill overnight with Ram, and at the instance of Hegde, it was passed as an ordinance the next day by the Karnataka government, even though the legislature was not in session. The legislature formally passed the National Law School of India University Act of 1986[4] in its next session, within six months of passing the ordinance. Thus the National Law School started out as a full university founded by a central or state government.

In 1992, my husband taught with Ram at the National Law School in Bangalore for a week. I remember a campus with big trees and red earth paths. On the spur of the moment, Ram let it be known that he would give a lecture late in the afternoon the next day. The lecture fell on New Year's Eve, and the room was full to overflowing.

The first director-designate of the new law school was Prof. Upendra Baxi, but he declined, worried about who would pay the start-up and running expenses. The next professor approached was Prof. N.R. Madhava Menon, the secretary of the Bar Council Foundation at the time and a friend of Ram's. Ram and Reddy approached Menon, and he accepted the appointment as director of the pilot project.

Though it is ironic, Ram was never present at the inauguration ceremony for the National Law School. Some say it was just because he no longer was an official of the Bar Council. The school's foundation stone was inscribed with the names of Mr Reddy, the chairman of the Bar Council at the time, and Prof. Menon. Ram was not mentioned.

Menon told the Ford Foundation[5] that he was the one who came back from a trip to America in 1984 with the idea of a five-year model, and that he was the one who had lobbied various constituencies for support until the Bar Council decided to back his plan in 1985.

He also told the Ford Foundation that when the position as director was first offered to Prof. Baxi, India's top legal scholar, Baxi had a number of concerns. He had been working on behalf of the Bhopal victims, and he was disgusted with the way the government was handling the matter. He found it troubling to be working directly under the auspices of the Chief Justice of the Supreme Court of India, who by law was the National Law School chancellor. He also was worried how the school could retain its independence, and he was reluctant to solicit funding from foreign donors. This is why he turned down the position.

Menon told the Ford Foundation that he spent late 1986 and early 1987 recruiting top academics to his faculty. That was a matter with which Ram took issue. He had been very unhappy as he watched the faculty become regional in its representation, instead of being constituted through a nationwide or even international search for the best talent.

At first there was a national advertisement for faculty. The first batch was selected by a committee composed of Dr Menon, Mr V.R. Reddy, Dr G.S. Sharma, a national academic figure, and two other experts. The committee recommended Prof. Mitra from West Bengal; Dr K.K. Puri from Queensland, Australia, and Dr M.P. Singh from Delhi for the posts of professors. They also recommended Mr Balanchandran from Kerala as associate professor; Dr Jaigovind, originally from Karnataka but recently returned from Nigeria and Mr V.S. Mallar from Goa as senior assistant professors. The assistant professors were Mr Vijay Kumar from Tamil Nadu, Mr N.S. Gopalakrishnan from Kerala (a retired senior revenue officer and economist educated in Harvard university), and Mr Joga Rao from Andhra Pradesh.

Further additions were added in stages, but by now there was no advertisement or selection committee similar to the original one. At this stage, new faculty was more often added on the basis of acquaintanceships. Ram was now vocal about his concerns. New professors were almost entirely from Kerala or Karnataka. Ram urged the executive committee to only make appointments on a national level through advertisements.

Prof. N.L. Mitra offers a word of caution,[6]

One thing must be brought to your notice is that most of these further appointees were first put into a fixed salary because Professor Menon could not get money from any source. As such, local appointments were the only option, with fixed salaries. Even the first batch of faculty were not given dearness allowances and other benefits as announced by the Central government from time to time including house rent allowance, as well as revision of pay immediately. Excepting me, no other professors joined because of such financial uncertainty. In fact, at the end of the second academic year in 1990 it was seriously debated whether NLSIU [National Law School of India University] was a viable financial proposition and would at all survive! In fact Professor Upendra Baxi's stand for not joining as the founder-director on this ground was thought by many as perhaps the right decision.

The second dean was Prof. N.L. Mitra. He added new courses, such as financial management and law, law and economics, and others designed to introduce the student to his or her future legal specialty. A structure of integrated double degree courses in law eventually evolved.

Prof. Mitra had to retire at age 62, and there was a strong sentiment for naming Prof. Baxi as the next dean. Unfortunately, by now Prof. Baxi was 61, and the retirement age was 62. The search committee, headed by former Supreme Court Judge Venkatachalya and including Ram, proposed three names, in alphabetical order, Prof. Baxi, Prof. Mohan Gopal and Prof. Puri, although Baxi was their first choice.

Prof. Mitra was in the United States at the time for five weeks, and he returned at the end of June in 2000. On his return he received a communication from the visitor, Honorable Justice Anand—the Supreme Court Justice, the chancellor of the National Law School.[7] Enclosed was a lengthy letter from Baxi, elaborating upon the financial hardship of his relocating from the United Kingdom, the proposed term of five years, the appointment of officials to administer the National Law School when he was not there, the length of time he needed to give up his appointment at Warwick, and his proposed plans for changes in the curriculum. The visitor requested Prof. Mitra's opinion. Mitra expressed his concern over the fact that Baxi was one year short of the required retirement age, and that his intended appointment would be for five years.

Mitra learned that while he was gone some members of the Executive Council had met with Baxi during his visit to the school, not a formal meeting because the director was not present. That was unfortunate, since Prof. Mitra had proposed Prof. Baxi's name in the first place and had a plan to amend the statute in order to raise the age of retirement. Ram may not have known that. The letter from Prof. Baxi put the Visitor, Chief Justice Anand on the spot. Ram also may not have been aware of this letter.

Ram's take on the course of events left him angry. Ram has written[8] that the Executive Council considered all three names and selected Prof. Baxi, who came to the school and met with the faculty. The Visitor, Chief Justice Anand, said that it might not be possible to amend the statute in the matter of the retirement age. The crux of the problem came when Ram claimed that Prof. Mitra had sent a communication on July 24, 2000 with the following sentence: 'The Visitor instructed me to send the letter of offer of appointment to Dr Mohan Gopal [the committee's second choice] . . .'[9] Ram argues that the Visitor did not have the authority to issue this instruction. It was improper and not within his powers.

Ram was deeply offended by the action of the Visitor (Chief Justice Anand), and on August 2000, he 'informed the Executive Council . . .that they should treat me as having severed my relations with that great institution.' This was another example of Ram jumping the gun, as usual.

Prof. Mitra only remembers that Ram was a great friend of Prof. Baxi and that he had other points of conflict with Chief Justice Anand. He has not read Ram's book. Prof. Mitra emphasizes that one of Ram's greatest and most appreciated contributions at the National Law School has been his work as a teacher.

In a 1998 lecture,[10] Justice A.S. Anand said that 'the National Law School of India at Bangalore is the laboratory of an experiment, novel in several ways in higher education. It is an institution not dependent on any state or central funding for its maintenance; an institution which is academically completely free to design its course, test the product and maintain a strict quality control. It is an institution which uses multi-disciplinary knowledge to understand the intricacy of law in operation and emphasizes research skill, and applicational ability.

'If market condition has any significance, National Law School students have, broadly speaking, an assured professional career. If national focus is any relevance, the decision of the Law Ministers of the country about replicating such an institution in each of their States is an indicator of success, and if the opinion of the international teaching community and professionals is required they are the people eloquently speaking in favour of the National Law School experiment in legal education. It is perhaps the best experiment in the country in the field of legal education after the experiment in technology education in IITs and management education in IIMs.'

There are close to a million lawyers in India today, with 80,000 more graduating each year. In 2010 there were five Rhodes scholars in India. Of these, two were from the National Law School in Bangalore and one from the National Law School in Hyderabad. This is despite the fact that the National Law School class numbers 80 students, of whom perhaps 25 are reserved for backward classes. The first students were selected through a national entrance test, and students from this group won the Bar Council of India National Moot Court Competition in their very first year of legal education. The system of a national competitive examination has become the basis for a National Entrance Test. In 2008, this became the Common Law Entrance Test (CLAT), which selects candidates for all the National Law Schools in the country.

The National Law School in Bangalore surely is one of the most successful and influential new law schools established anywhere in the world during the 20th century. If you go to the websites of the National Law Schools, you will see that it has been replicated in Kolkata (Calcutta), Bhopal, Jodhpur, Hyderabad, Gandhinagar (Gujarat), Raipur, Kochi, Lucknow, Patiala, Patna, and now in Delhi. As of April 2010, the Bar Council of India recognized 900 law colleges.[11] The premier ones were the National Law School in Bangalore, the National Law School in Hyderabad and the W.B. National University of Juridical Sciences in Kolkata. In 2011, the National Law School in Bangalore was the top preference of all students in India who took the national exam (CLAT).

The National Law School model has completely changed legal education in India, upgrading it to a world-class level. For all that Ram Jethmalani's critics like to say that he does everything just for publicity, in this story, Ram is an unsung and largely forgotten hero.

26

The Mandal Report

The Mandal Commission Report lay fallow for 10 years until Prime Minister V.P. Singh decided to implement it in 1991. This caused a furore. It also caused Ram, for the first time in his life, to become an expert on the Hindu caste system and on its reflections in other religions in India. The effect on the BJP was even more profound.

Prime Minister Desai had appointed the Mandal Commission in 1978, and it submitted its report in December 1980. By that time he no longer was Prime Minister. The issue revolved around quotas. The commission proposed that 27 per cent of all positions in the central government and all educational institutions must be reserved for the 52 per cent of the population who were classified as scheduled castes, tribals, or Other Backward Classes (OBCs). This affected quotas for promotion throughout the public sector as well as all private sector activities that accepted money from the government. The commission also proposed financial, technical, and educational assistance for those members of the disadvantaged classes who needed extra assistance. All of this was quite commendable.

These recommendations were largely disregarded. The question to ask was: what changed in 1991? The change occurred when L.K. Advani and the BJP stirred up religious sectarianism in India with the claim that the Babri Masjid at Ayodhya was built on the site where the Hindu god Ram was born. This was specious, since

Ram is a mythological figure. Nevertheless, they called for the mosque to be destroyed and replaced by a temple to Ram. While most of the Muslim vote normally goes to the Congress party, the BJP now risked forfeiting the rest. Nevertheless, the BJP's Hindu political base believed that an ancient temple used to sit there, and the campaign played to their vote.

For practical purposes, until the fall of Rajiv, India had been governed by only one party, the Congress party. This incitement to build a Ram temple at Ayodhya was an effort to split the Hindu upper castes away from the Congress party, even if the BJP risked alienating the Muslim voters.[1] V.P. Singh calculated that implementation of the Mandal Report would split off the 52 per cent of the electorate who were scheduled castes or OBCs from the Congress party, thus offsetting the lost Muslim votes and shrinking the Congress party's share from 35–40 per cent to perhaps 25–30 per cent. When Parliament voted to implement the Commission's recommendations, every member sat calculating the effect on their vote bank.

Students protested violently, and there even were instances of self-immolation. Both the press and the public attacked the quotas. Having fled his home in Pakistan because of sectarian strife, Ram has an almost visceral dislike of politics based upon religion. On the other hand, his experience as a member of a minority immigrant community has always made Ram sensitive to the problems of minorities. In the end, he defended the report vigorously. Ram truly believes that the problems of India can never be solved until the backward classes reach parity with the privileged classes.

Ram wrote an impassioned article for the *Indian Express*[2] deploring the condition of 'the 500 million of us living like swine, searching in hunger for putrefied edibles in the dumps of trash discarded by the rich . . . Some of these swine are sentenced forever to degrading occupations like collecting carcasses of dead animals and carrying baskets of human excreta on their head. It is absurd to expect a feeling of human solidarity from humans whose self-esteem, self-confidence, motivation and ambition are all destroyed by social injustice.'

In 1990 and 1991, the government issued two office memoranda with instructions for implementing the long-dormant Mandal Commission Report.[3] Two petitioners immediately filed a PIL in the Supreme Court challenging the report. The case was *Indra Sawhney & Ors. vs. Union of India.*[4] The issue was one of reservation of government jobs for the OBCs. N.A. Palkhiwala, K.K. Venugopal and 10 other lawyers represented the challengers, with almost the whole bar on their side. Ram, representing the state of Bihar, was accompanied by eight younger lawyers and supported by Lataa, who worked devotedly on the brief, but he was the senior advocate to argue in defence of the Mandal Commission Report. Justice Reddy was heard to say that on one side was an array of lawyers, and on the other was Ram Jethmalani alone.

The issue was of such importance to the upper classes that one Member of Parliament who had not practised law since entering Parliament, donned his bands and went to court to fight for his class. The court actually asked Ram why they needed to hear this case after so many cases had come to court on similar issues. Ram answered that these had been decided by high caste judges. This was slick, because it was his good luck to have more than one OBC judge on this bench.

The petitions first went to a Constitution Bench, in which seven judges considered a long list of vexing issues. On August 8, 1991, Judge B.J. Reddy issued a 254-page opinion which referred the case to a nine-judge Special Bench, to 'finally settle the legal position relating to reservations.'

Judge Reddy issued the 160-page final judgement on November 16, 1992.

This was one of the first big constitutional cases in Ram's career, and the issues were of great social, political, religious, and legal importance. What is the caste system? What are castes? What are backward, or scheduled, classes? Should there be affirmative action for some of these groups? Who? For the first time in his life, Ram had to study the entire caste system. One colleague says that before he started Ram did not even know what caste he was. Whether that is true or not, Ram pored over it laboriously. He needed to know whether other religions in India had backward classes, and he also had to know how Indian society treats communities of former OBCs who have converted to Christianity, Islam, or Buddhism.

Key to the whole argument was one Article in the Indian Constitution:

Article 16 (4) of the Constitution: 'Nothing in this article shall prevent the State from making any provision for the reservation of appointments or posts in favour of any backward class of citizens which, in the opinion of the State, is not adequately represented in the services under the State.'

To interpret this article, the judges had to analyse: whether class means caste, how to define backward class, when reservations would be permitted, which reservations are permitted, whether a means test should be permitted to separate out the affluent members of backward classes, and whether poverty should be the sole criterion for defining a backward class. Finally, they had to decide whether the yardsticks used by the Mandal Commission to identify a large group of castes as a 'backward class' are constitutionally valid.

To understand the arguments in this case, we will take them one at a time, rather than the conventional way they are presented in court. Normally one side presents all its arguments, followed by the other side presenting its case. To make it easier for the non-lawyer to follow, we will present the arguments in a point-counterpoint format.

The main complaint against the Mandal Commission was: 'The first attack against the Report is that it is perpetuating the evils of caste system and accentuating caste consciousness.' In particular, N.A. Palkhiwala said that the Constitution is casteless, prohibits reservation on the basis of caste, and that reservations based on caste would be retrograde.

Palkhiwala based this argument on three Articles of the Indian Constitution:

Article 14 says: 'The State shall not deny to any person equality before the law or the equal protection of the laws within the territory of India.' It also prohibits 'discrimination on grounds of religion, race, caste, sex or place of birth'.

Article 15, says in part:

(1) The State shall not discriminate against any citizen on grounds *only* of religion, race, caste, sex, place of birth or any of them . . .

(2) No citizen shall, on grounds only of religion, race, caste, sex, place of birth or any of them, be subject to any disability, liability, restriction or condition . . .

(4) Nothing in this article or in clause (2) of Article 29 shall prevent the State from making any special provision for the advancement of any socially and educationally backward classes of citizens or for the Scheduled Castes and the Scheduled Tribes . . .

Article 16 (1): 'There shall be equality of opportunity for all citizens in matters relating to employment or appointment to any office under the State.'

Ram insisted that, 'when two persons or two communities, or two groups of citizens, by historical circumstances, are rendered unequal so far as competition in life is concerned, making a provision for them is providing equality. There is no violation of Article 14 if by some action you are making unequals equal.'

Ram called the court's attention to Article 15(4), which makes it clear that nothing prevents the state from helping certain classes of citizens to advance.

Ram submitted that the words in Article 16 (1) 'there shall be equality of opportunity' can only mean that 'the State is under a constitutional obligation to remove inequality.' He said that it is the duty of the state to create this equality, and that is explained explicitly in Article 46: 'The State shall promote with special care the educational and economic interests of the weaker sections of the people, and, in particular, of the Scheduled Castes and the Scheduled Tribes, and shall protect them from social injustice and all forms of exploitation.'

Ram further showed that the Constitution allows reserved seats for scheduled castes and tribes in the legislature.

Ram pointed out the many safeguards in the Constitution for minorities, backward and tribal areas, and those who have suffered similar discrimination.[5]

He drew a clear distinction between Article 16 (3), which allows reservations for the poor, women, or any other class, and 16 (4), which is only intended for backward classes.

The real dispute was over the yardsticks used to define 'backward classes' or 'Other Backward Classes', in the Mandal Commission Report. That report used three tests for determining a backward class: social backwardness, educational, and occupational. Using these criteria, it listed 3743 backward castes, and the office memoranda issued by the central government required reservations for all of these groups.

Ram's definition of 'backward classes' was: clusters of castes, largely a conglomeration of various Shudra castes, the lowest castes. He said the concept was better understood in southern India, and that the Madras Services Manual defined the terms quite frankly in terms of castes.

The petitioners argued that reservations should apply to all the *economically* backward.

Ram disagreed strongly, 'Poverty is not a necessary criterion of backwardness; it is in fact irrelevant. The provision for reservation is really a programme of historical compensation. It is neither a measure of economic reform nor a poverty alleviation programme.' The point is that certain communities have accumulated a deficit of power, wealth, and culture due to their caste, and that is what needs to be rectified.

According to Ram, 'backward classes' in Article 16 (4) means the 'Shudra castes which [are] located between the three upper castes (Brahmins, Kshatriyas and Vaishyas) and the out-castes (Panchamas) referred to as Scheduled Castes'.

Succinctly, Ram's argument was that the word 'class' in Article 16 (4) means 'caste'. He further argued that 'Backward classes are castes and reservations for castes are valid', and that reservations for backward classes do not represent discrimination on the grounds of caste alone. The Constitution prohibits discrimination on the basis of caste only, but it may be allowed for the combination of caste plus historical oppression. Ram characterized the other side as saying '. . . caste is a closed door. It is not a path—even if it is—it is a prohibited path under the Constitution.'

N.A. Palkhiwala's actual argument was: 'A secular, unified and caste-less society is a basic feature of the Constitution. Caste is a prohibited ground of distinction under the Constitution. It ought to be erased altogether from the Indian Society. It can never be the basis for determining backward classes.'

Ram dismissed Palkhiwala's claim that the Indian Constitution has no caste. Ram calls this a dream for the future, not an expression of present reality. He said the writers of the Constitution lived in a society of extreme inequality, and they mandated compensatory actions designed to produce equality.

Palkhiwala also criticized the Mandal Commission Report for inventing castes for non-Hindus.

Ram argued that certain groups of Christians, Muslims, and others had converted to escape their lowly status. Even so, they remained as poor as ever and as tied to the lowest jobs in society. There also is a bewildering heterogeneity of Shudra castes, depending on the region. Even Sikhs have a backward class. Ram said one reason why the word 'class' was used in the Constitution, rather than caste, was to accommodate caste-like groups among non-Hindus.

In its final decision the court held: 'Reservation under Article 16 (4) being for any class of citizens and citizen having been defined in Chapter II of the Constitution includes not only Hindus but Muslims, Christians, Sikhs, Buddhists Jains etc. the principle of identification has to be of universal application so as to extend to every community.'

The court further held that there is a value in affirmative action programmes that are established in order to redress inequality and it said only those classes who are socially and educationally backward can be identified as backward classes. It also said that 'the Constitution prohibits discrimination on grounds only of religion, race, caste, sex, descent, place of birth, or residence', but that other criteria 'such as poverty, illiteracy, demeaning occupation, malnutrition, physical and intellectual deformity', may be relevant 'to identify socially and educationally backward classes of citizens for whom reservation is intended'.

The court also endorsed means testing to exclude the wealthy from affirmative action programmes and said, 'Poverty demands affirmative action. Its eradication is a constitutional mandate.'

The court recommended that reservations remain well below 50 per cent of the total seats or posts available and only apply to initial appointments, not to promotions.

In its final judgement, the majority upheld the validity of the 1990 Office Memoranda and said the 1991 Memoranda 'requires— to uphold its validity—to be read, interpreted and understood as intending a distinction between backward and more backward classes on the basis of degrees of social backwardness and a rational and equitable distribution of the benefits of the reservations amongst them'.

The court also ruled that 'The Government of India, each of the State Governments and the Administrations of Union Territories shall, within four months from today, constitute a permanent body for entertaining, examining and recommending upon requests for inclusion and complaints of over-inclusion and under-inclusion in the lists of other backward classes of citizens.'

Furthermore, in an inspired move the court created a new concept: 'Within four months from today the Government of India shall specify the bases, applying the relevant and requisite socio-economic criteria to exclude socially advanced persons/ sections ("creamy layer") from "Other Backward Classes".' The implementation of the 1990 memorandum should exclude 'such socially advanced persons, e.g. the *creamy layer*'.

The judges commented, 'The recommendations made in the present Report after a long lull since the submission of the Report by the First Backward Classes Commission are supportive of affirmative action programmes holding the members of the historically disadvantaged groups for centuries to catch up with the standards of competition set up by a well advanced society.'

The court dismissed one powerful argument against quotas: 'Yet another argument on behalf of . . . anti-reservationists was addressed contending that if the recommendations of the Commission are implemented, it would result in the sub-standard replacing the standard and the reins of power passing from meritocracy to mediocrity; that the upshot will be . . . demoralization and discontent and that it would revitalize [the] caste system, and cleave the nation into two—forward and backward—and open up new vistas for internecine conflict and fissiparous forces, and make backwardness a vested interest. The above tortuous line of reasoning, in my view is not only illogical, inconceivable, unreasonable and unjustified but also utterly overlooks the stark grim reality of the . . . suffering from social stigma and ostracism in the present day scenario of hierarchical caste system.'

The court also mentioned that Ram opposed limiting the number of reserved positions to 50 per cent. Ram's rationale was that under Article 16 (1) or 16 (4) 'any limitation on reservation would defeat the very purpose of this Article falling under Fundamental Rights'.

The court elaborated upon its interesting concept, the so-called 'creamy layer', meaning those members of the backward classes who are above a certain income level, and highly advanced socially as well as economically and educationally. 'A further submission has been made stating that the benefits of reservation are often snatched away or eaten up by top creamy layer of socially advanced backward class who consequent upon their social development no longer suffer from the vice of social backwardness and who are in no way handicapped and who by their high professional qualifications occupy upper echelons in the public services and therefore, the children of those socially advanced section of the people, termed as "creamy layer" should be completely removed from the lists of "Backward Classes" and they should not be allowed to compete with the children of socially under-privileged people and avail the quota of reservation.'

This was an enlightened attempt to address the problem that occurs in the United States, where minority students cunningly take advantage of affirmative action even if their parents are successful graduates of Ivy League schools.

The court concluded that, in accordance with the Mandal Commission recommendations, 'the entire scheme should be reviewed after 20 years', noting that Ram had proposed an interval of 10 years.

This was a great win for Ram, and the affirmative action programme that the court sustained has been critical to the progression of members of the backward classes out of their century-old shackles, into greater educational opportunities and into jobs of which their ancestors could only dream.

Ram collected only a small fee for representing the state of Bihar, subsidizing the rest himself, as he often does when he really believes in a cause. In fairness, critics of quotas could well say that Palkhiwala was right. Affirmative action in India has led to many abuses. Some students go to great lengths to show that they come from backward classes or that they are tribals. Affirmative action surely prevents some of the students with the highest test scores from becoming the high-quality doctors, engineers, and other professionals that India needs to compete in the modern world. Regardless, it is clear that with this case Ram has taken his place in a distinguished list of lawyers who can be called social activists.

For just that reason, it may seem ironic that in Ram's next big constitutional case he appeared to take off this white hat to defend Hindutva, which many regard as the shameful basis of highly divisive sectarianism in public life. Of course, Ram would say it is not.

27

The 1990s, Hindutva, Ayodhya, and Retaliation

The word 'Hindutva' immediately inflames passions in India. Two parties, the Rashtriya Swayamsevak Sangh (RSS) and the Bharatiya Janata Party (BJP), have conjured up the term to win Hindu votes, and the term is linked inextricably to the destruction of the Babri Masjid at Ayodhya. In a landmark case, Ram had the opportunity to define it, and to define the word 'Hindu'. Even more challenging, he had to define what constitutes a religion.

To Muslims, the term 'Hindutva' has explicitly anti-Muslim, racist overtones. Some academics have called use of the word a fascist effort to produce cultural hegemony. On the other hand, for Hindus, the word embodies Indian nationalism, and it would include Hindus, Sikhs, Buddhists, and Jains. The RSS would go further and claim it encompasses anyone born in India, be it Hindus, Muslims, Christians, or Parsis, since they all grew up steeped in Hindu culture.

One man who came to embody communalism (sectarianism) was Bal Thackeray, the founder of the Shiv Sena party. Thackeray started his career as a political cartoonist, later founded a newspaper, then a local Marathi party. In his speeches he was given to hyperbole, and he had a dark history.

On June 5, 1970 Krishna Desai, a Member of the Legislative Assembly of Maharashtra (MLA) and leader of the Communist

Party of India (CPI), was murdered by unknown attackers.[1] Desai at the time was a popular leader of the textile workers in Bombay, and thousands of workers marched in his funeral procession. The Communist Party and 'Opposition leaders directly accused the Shiv Sena and the Congress state government in general, and Bal Thackeray and Vasantrao Naik in particular.'[2] Bal Thackeray reportedly boasted about the murder and threatened that more was to come.[3]

By June 8, seven suspects had been arrested. In all, 19 young members of the Shiv Sena party were charged and 16 convicted. Ram represented the suspects before the High Court of Bombay, and three were acquitted, including one main suspect. That episode is often cited as the beginning salvo of Shiv Sena party power in Bombay.[4] Ram's defence of the Shiv Sena party was met with widespread disapproval.

The B.N. Srikrishna Commission expressed a commonly held view when it blamed Thackeray for instigating the 1992–93 Mumbai riots: 'From January 8, 1993 at least, there is no doubt that the Shiv Sena and Shiv Sainiks took the lead in organising attacks on Muslims and their properties.' It describes Thackeray as the 'veteran general commanding his loyal Shiv Sainiks to retaliate by organised attacks against Muslims.'

The B.N. Srikrishna Commission's verdict was the most severe indictment ever of the Shiv Sena. The blame inevitably fell on Hindutva.

Ram has written,[5] 'It is unfortunate that Hindutva as practised by some has come to mean ill-will and hatred against those who do not subscribe to one or the other sect of Hinduism, mainly the Muslims and Christians.' In the same article Ram writes, 'The BJP must win allies by aggressively countering the false propaganda being levelled against it about communalism and obscurantism.'

The Hindutva case was decided in 1996,[6] and Ram later wrote[7] what could be called the essential statement of the issue:

> My complaint against the BJP has been that the Hindutva projected by it for its electoral purposes is a counterfeit Hindutva.

Its core has no resemblance to the real philosophy. Hindutva, properly understood, is neither the product nor the property of any political party, not even the Jana Sangh of old and the BJP of today. It was not manufactured at the Shiv Sena home in Mumbai or at the RSS offices in Delhi. Hindutva is the core of the Indian Constitution to which all citizens of India swear allegiance and complete loyalty and, as the Supreme Court has said in 1995, 'is a way of life or a state of mind and cannot be equated with or understood as religious Hindu fundamentalism'.

I will never forget the day Ram told me with a thrill in his voice that he had a case in which he needed to define whether Hinduism is a religion. Not only that, he had to *define a religion*. The task at hand was to show the Supreme Court that Hindutva is not the same as Hinduism and that Hinduism is not actually a religion.

Two related cases went to the Supreme Court on the same day, one of *Ramesh Yeshwant Prabhoo*, and the other of *Bal Thackeray v. Shri Prabhaker Kunte*. The cases were appeals from the Bombay High Court, arising from a December 1987 election. The High Court had declared Dr Prabhoo's election void, and it ruled that Thackeray was guilty of corrupt election practices.

The charge was that Ramesh Yeshwant Prabhoo, a candidate from Vile Parle constituency to the Maharashtra State Legislative Assembly, and his agent Thackeray 'appealed for votes on the ground of the returned candidate's religion and that they promoted or tended to promote feelings of enmity and hatred between different classes of the citizens of India on the grounds of religion and community'. At issue were three outrageous speeches that Thackeray had given for the candidate.

Dr Prabhoo ran as an independent candidate with support from the Shiv Sena party, because the Shiv Sena was not recognized for the Maharashtra Legislative Assembly elections. Thackeray spoke as the leader of the Shiv Sena. The court quotes from a speech that Thackeray gave in Marathiat Vile Parle in November 1987. The English translation that was furnished to the court read: 'We are fighting this election for the protection of Hinduism. Therefore, we do not care for the votes of the Muslims. This country belongs to Hindus and will remain so.'

On December 12, Thackeray spoke near a Hindu temple. Again his speech was given in Marathi, but the English translation was: 'Hinduism will triumph in this election and we must become hon'ble recipients of this victory to ward off the danger on Hinduism, elect Ramesh Prabhoo to join with Chhagan Bhujbal who is already there. You will find Hindu temples underneath if all the mosques are dug out. Anybody who stands against the Hindus should be showed or worshipped with shoes. A candidate by name Prabhoo should be led to victory in the name of religion.'

The third speech was given at an outdoor rally on December 10, and again Thackeray's speech is translated from Marathi: 'We have come with the ideology of Hinduism. Shiv Sena will implement this ideology. Though this country belongs to Hindus, Ram and Krishna are insulted. (They) valued the Muslim votes more than your votes; we do not want the Muslim votes. A snake like Shahabuddin is sitting in the Janata Party, man like Nihal Ahmed is also in Janata Party. So the residents of Vile Parle should bury this party (Janata Party).'

To start with, the speeches in Marathi had used the word 'Hindutva', but the translator, at a loss for an English word, had translated this by using 'Hinduism'—the Hindu religion—as a synonym. That was Ram's first argument—Hindutva and the Hindu religion are two entirely different things. An additional argument was that quoting examples from Hindu mythology did not constitute solicitation of votes on the basis of religion.

That being said, Ram had a steep hill to climb. He started by saying that any restrictions on constitutional guarantees of free speech are invalid, 'unless the speech is prejudicial to the maintenance of public order'. Ram next argued specifically that 'only a direct appeal for votes on the ground of "his" religion subject to its tendency to prejudice the maintenance of Public order' is within the 'limited scope of the relevant statute'.[8]

The court agreed readily with his point: 'Shri Jethmalani is right that . . . the element of prejudicial effect on public order is implicit. Such divisive tendencies promoting enmity or hatred between different classes of citizens of India tend to create public unrest and disturb public order.'

Ram went on: 'A speech in which there be a reference to religion but no direct appeal for votes on the ground of his religion does not fall within the relevant sub-section of the act. That was the key: "The public speeches in question did not amount to appeal for votes on the ground of his religion and the substance and main thrust thereof was "Hindutva" which means the Indian culture and not merely the Hindu religion.'

Ram said, 'The public speeches criticized the anti-secular stance of the Congress Party in practising discrimination against Hindus and giving undue favour to the minorities which is not an appeal for votes on the ground of Hindu religion.'

Now we come to the definition of Hindutva. The court says, 'The next contention relates to the meaning of "Hindutva" and "Hinduism" and the effect of the use of these expressions in the election speeches.' The court presented the arguments: 'Both sides referred copiously to the meaning of the word "Hindutva" and "Hinduism" with reference to several writings. Shri Jethmalani referred to them for the purpose of indicating the several meanings of these words and to emphasise that the word "Hindutva" relates to Indian culture based on the geographical division known as Hindustan, i.e., India.'

Following Ram's argument, the court quotes, 'The historical and etymological genesis of the word "Hindu" has given rise to a controversy amongst indologists; but the view generally accepted by scholars appears to be that the word "Hindu" is derived from the river Sindhu otherwise known as Indus which flows from the Punjab. "That part of the great Aryan race," says Monier Williams, "which immigrated from Central Asia, through the mountain passes into India, settled first in the districts near the river Sindhu (now called the Indus). The Persians pronounced this word Hindu and named their Aryan brethren Hindus. The Greeks, who probably gained their first ideas of India from the Persians, dropped the hard aspirate, and called the Hindus "Indoi".' Ram was on his home ground, Sindh.

The court continues to reference Ram's submission, Dr Radhakrishnan's *The Hindu View of Life*, p.12: 'That is the genesis of the word "Hindu". When we think of the Hindu religion, we find it difficult, if not impossible, to define Hindu religion or even adequately describe it. Unlike other religions in the world, the Hindu religion does not claim any one prophet; it does not worship any one God; it does not subscribe to any one dogma; it does not believe in any one philosophic concept; it does not follow any one set of religious rites or performances; in fact, it does not appear to satisfy the narrow traditional features of any religion or creed. It may broadly be described as a way of life and nothing more . . . The term "Hindu", according to Dr Radhakrishnan, had originally a territorial and not a credal significance. It implied residence in a well-defined geographical area.'

This was Ram's argument exactly.

The court moves on to the *Encyclopaedia Britannica* definition of Hinduism: 'It properly denotes the Indian civilization of approximately the last 2,000 years, which gradually evolved from Vedism, the religion of the ancient Indo-European who settled in India in the last centuries of the 2nd millennium BC. Because it integrates a large variety of heterogeneous elements, Hinduism constitutes a very complex but largely continuous whole, and since it covers the whole of life, it has religious, social, economic, literary, and artistic aspects. As a religion, Hinduism is an utterly diverse conglomerate of doctrines, cults, and way of life.... In principle, Hinduism incorporates all forms of belief and worship without necessitating the selection or elimination of any.' Again we hear Ram's point.

The court even accepts the argument that Article 25 of the Indian Constitution says that 'all persons are equally entitled to freedom of conscience and the right freely to profess, practise and propagate religion, section 2 (b) says "reference to Hindus shall be construed as including a reference to persons professing the Sikh, Jaina or Buddhist religion." On this last point, the judges made it clear that references to Hindus should include Jains or Buddhists.'

Now moving on to Hindutva: 'These Constitution Bench

decisions, after a detailed discussion, indicate that no precise meaning can be ascribed to the terms "Hindu", "Hindutva" and "Hinduism"; and no meaning in the abstract can confine it to the narrow limits of religion alone, excluding the content of Indian culture and heritage. It is also indicated that the term 'Hindutva' is related more to the way of life of the people in the sub-continent. It is difficult to appreciate how in the face of these decisions the term "Hindutva" or "Hinduism" per se, in the abstract, can be assumed to mean and be equated with narrow fundamentalist Hindu religious bigotry.'

The plaintiffs had not established that Hindutva and Hinduism are the same, which they needed to do to provide the base for their evidence.

The court summarized: 'Ordinarily, Hindutva is understood as a way of life or a state of mind and it is not to be equated with, or understood as, religious Hindu fundamentalism.' Citing quotes Ram had submitted from Maulana Wahiduddin Khan, it wrote, 'The strategy worked out to solve the minorities problem was, although differently worded, that of Hindutva or Indianization. This strategy, briefly stated, aims at developing a uniform culture by obliterating the differences between all of the cultures coexisting in the country. This was felt to be the way to communal harmony and national unity. It was thought that this would put an end once and for all to the minorities problem.'

The court agreed with Ram: 'It is, therefore, a fallacy and an error of law to proceed on the assumption that any reference to Hindutva or Hinduism in a speech makes it automatically a speech based on the Hindu religion as opposed to the other religions or that the use of words "Hindutva" or "Hinduism" per se depict an attitude hostile to all persons practising any religion other than the Hindu religion.'

The court rejected the English translation of Thackeray's third speech, finding that the translator confused the word 'Hindutva' with the word Hinduism, but it still affirmed the High Court on both of these appeals, ruling that Thackeray's speeches were corrupt practices under the statute, and voiding Prabhoo's election. Given the egregious nature of these speeches, it hardly could have done otherwise.

Ram took extraordinary pleasure in the intellectual exercise of studying Hinduism and whether it is a religion; as well as studying Hindutva and how it differs from Hinduism. This was the memorable part of the case for him. While this client still lost his elected seat, Ram points out another case decided on the very same day, involving the same issues, in which the client did preserve his seat.[9] On appeal was a High Court decision voiding the election of a Manohar Joshi. Tape recordings, shorthand records, and video cassettes documented that Bal Thackeray had said: 'The result of these elections will not only depend on the solution to the problem of food, cloth but the same will also decide whether in the state the flame of Hindutva will grow or will be extinguished. If in Maharashtra the flame of Hinduism is extinguished, then anti-national Muslims will be powerful and they will convert Hindustan into Pakistan.'

For one thing, Ram argued that the petition 'does not state the place, date and time when the said cassettes are alleged to have been played. It further does not mention the names of the persons who are alleged to have played the said cassettes.' The court added that it must be proved that display of any video cassette was with the candidate's consent.

On Hindutva, the court quoted from the Prabhoo case:

We have already indicated in the connected matters . . . Bal Thackeray v. Prabhakar K. Kunte and Ors.. . . . decided today, that the word 'Hindutva' by itself does not invariably mean Hindu religion and it is the context and the manner of its use which is material for deciding the meaning of the word 'Hindutva' in a particular text. It cannot be held that in the abstract the mere word 'Hindutva' by itself invariably must mean Hindu religion.

Since the other side had never proved that the candidate consented to playing the offending cassettes, the court rejected the cassettes as evidence.

It did not help that the candidate himself had made the inflammatory statement 'that the first Hindu State will be established in Maharashtra'. The court found the statement to be despicable, but it held that it was not an appeal for votes on the grounds of his religion, therefore, it was not a corrupt practice.

The court lingered over several technical points, but it did conclude that the High Court decision 'is contrary to law and is, therefore, set aside. The result is that no ground is made out for declaring the appellant's election to be void'. While Hindutva was not the only swing issue in this decision, its definition certainly was pertinent, and that was the definition that Ram had shepherded through the other cases that same day. Ram also remembers that he won this case for his client.

The Hindutva decisions set precedents that remain important today. Ram had successfully formulated a distinction between Hindutva and Hinduism, and he was successful in convincing the court to spell it out. Because of Ram's arguments, the court stated for the first time that Hinduism is not a religion. It also supported the BJP contention that the Hindutva of which they speak is infused with an inherent spirit of tolerance. These arguments and decisions remain profoundly controversial, but Ram has quoted them ever since.

All of these legal distinctions notwithstanding, L.K. Advani still made a fateful decision to progress through northern India towards Ayodhya in what he called a rath yatra, a pilgrimage to a holy site. He travelled in a motorcade decorated to simulate the annual Hindu temple chariot procession, and his announced goal was to build up sentiment for destroying the mosque. Although he was arrested on the way, his effort was only too successful, because in December 1992, Hindu mobs brought down the Babri Masjid at Ayodhya, sparking sectarian riots all over northern India.

True to form, when L.K. Advani and the president of the BJP were arrested for promoting the violence, Ram condemned the arrest and offered his own utopian solution, 'A scenario much to be wished for is Hindus and Muslims jointly and lovingly constructing both a mosque and temple in close proximity.'

Of course, what actually happened were riots that paralysed the country. Hindus and Muslims engaged in murder and mayhem, with trains attacked, flights almost non-existent.

We were in India during the riots. A friend told us she took a train in Mumbai that she used to take as a school girl, and it barely managed to outrun an angry mob with burning torches that was surging towards the train.

Travel was disrupted everywhere. In Hyderabad with Ram at the time, we worried about catching a flight to Bombay after we finished touring the ruins in Hampi. Because a nation-wide airline strike had suspended most flights, our only chance would be for Ram to contact Hegde, who did get us on a plane from Hyderabad to Mumbai. At a New Year's Eve party at his club, Hegde teased that he hoped we did not mind if our flight was on Aeroflot. My husband almost had a heart attack. Meanwhile, Ram danced serenely with Hedge's girlfriend, his eyes closed dreamily.

The March 12, 1993 Mumbai Bombings

In March 1993, Mumbai suffered a series of bomb blasts, which killed over 250 people and injured two or three times as many, purportedly as a retaliation for the Muslim deaths the previous year. Authorities blamed Dawood Ibrahim, then in Dubai. Ram says it was a reflex reaction, because they always blamed Dawood for everything.

One day while in London, Ram received a call from Dawood, asking him to defend him, but Dawood insisted he negotiate as preconditions for his return that he would be tried only for the blast case and, most important, that he would be allowed out on bail, rather than imprisoned while awaiting trial. Ram asked him if he was serious, and he contacted Mahesh, who consulted with the commissioner of police, A.S. Samra, his deputy M.N. Singh, and the Chief Minister, Sharad Pawar. Predictably, they refused to give any such guarantees,[10] and Prime Minister Narasimha Rao agreed with them. Ram informed Dawood that there was nothing he could do.

Ram says there was not a shred of evidence connecting Dawood to the bombings. That is why he was willing to come to India. After all, he says, 'If you cannot extradite someone; if he is beyond your jurisdiction, and he wants to come voluntarily, you should let him come. That shows that he is not guilty.' The courts and the public did not agree.

When the case reached the Supreme Court in 1996,[11] the court wrote that, on March 12, 1993, 'As Bombay set down to work, blasting of bombs, almost simultaneously, took place at important centres of commercial activities like Stock Exchange, Air India, Zaveri Bazar, Katha Bazar and many luxurious hotels.' The damage 'surpassed all imagination, as it was ultimately found that the blasts left more than 250 persons dead, 730 injured and property worth about Rs 27 crores destroyed'.

The CBI charge-sheeted '145 persons . . . under various sections of the Penal Code and the Terrorists and Disruptive Activities (Prevention) Act, [and it] framed charges against 127 persons, discharging at the same time 26. One died and two became approvers. (The total thus comes to 146).'

Of these, '(1) Abu Asim Azmi; (2) Amjad Aziz Meharbaksh; (3) Raju alias Raju Code Jain; and (4) Somnath Thapa have approached this Court having felt aggrieved at their having not been discharged. The State of Maharashtra has approached the Court seeking cancellation of bail granted to appellant Thapa.' In this case, Ram represented Thapa.

The court framed three questions of law: a) 'What are the ingredients of "criminal conspiracy" as defined in Section 120-A of the Penal Code ?' b) 'When can charge be framed ?' and c) 'What is the effect of repeal of TADA ?' Ram, lecturing like a law professor, furnished the relevant court decisions and explained the statutory definitions. 'The thrust of Shri Ram Jethmalani's argument is that to find a person guilty of conspiracy there has to be knowledge of either commission of any illegal act by a co-conspirator or taking recourse to illegal means by the co-conspirator, along with the intent to further the illegal act or facilitate the illegal means.'

Another way of saying it was: 'Shri Jethmalani, therefore, submits that mere knowledge that somebody would commit an offence would not be sufficient to establish a case of criminal conspiracy, unless there be evidence to show that all had acted in concert or had agreed together to commit the offence in question.'

On the next point, Ram instructed 'that a prima facie case can be said to have been made out before charge can be framed'. The court says, 'According to Shri Jethmalani, a prima facie case even be said to have been made out when the evidence, unless rebutted, would make the accused liable to conviction.'

Ram's client, Somnath Thapa, was an additional collector of customs, accused of knowingly abetting the smuggling by sea of arms, ammunition, and explosives for terrorists to use in India. To do so, he was accused of taking a bribe of Rs 22 lakhs. In return, he was supposed to have misled his subordinate officers into lying in wait at the wrong expected landing point. He was currently out on bail, and the state of Maharashtra sought to cancel his bail. The court analysed the evidence and found it wanting, Ram arguing that Thapa did not know that the shipment contained arms, ammunition, or explosives. The appeal was dismissed.

Meanwhile a Special Court had been set up to try the accused under TADA, first holding hearings next door to the Bombay Sessions Court, later moving to the Arthur Road Central Jail in 1994. By October 2000, 684 witnesses had been examined, and in September 2003 the case came to a close. Sentencing began in 2006.[12]

In 2006, Thapa was one of those found guilty and convicted.[13] According to Sri,[14] Thapa was given life imprisonment, but he asked the court to give him death, because he was dying of cancer. In 2008 he died of lung cancer.[15]

Sanjay Dutt

Sanjay Dutt is a popular Bollywood actor and the son of Sunil Dutt—himself a film actor and a Member of Parliament. When his involvement in the Mumbai blasts of 1993 came out, the public followed the story avidly. Sanjay 'was convicted in November 2006 for illegal possession of a 9 mm pistol and an AK-56 rifle but was acquitted of more serious charges of criminal conspiracy under the now defunct anti-terror TADA.'[16] With long-standing ties to the Dutt family and with the father a colleague in Parliament, Ram brought the first appeal to court. Of course, Sunil Dutt had once beaten Ram in a run for Parliament, but that was nearly forgotten by now.

The charge initially brought against him was that he 'knowingly and intentionally procured from accused Anees Ibrahim Kaskar . . . Manzoor Ahmed Sayed Ahmed 3 AK-56 rifles, 25 hand grenades and one 9 mm. pistol and cartridges for the purpose of committing terrorist acts'. In a confession, Dutt 'admitted receiving three AK-56 rifles on 16.1.1993 along with ammunition from the aforesaid persons adding that two days later he returned two of them but retained only one for the purpose of self-defence. The petitioner further stated that in view of the tense communal situation as a result of the incident at Ayodhya on 6.12.1992 and the serious threats given to petitioner's father Sunil Dutt, then a Member of Parliament, for his active role in steps taken to restore communal harmony and serious threats to petitioner's sisters also, all of whom were residing together, the petitioner agreed to obtain and keep one AK-56 rifle with ammunition for protection of his family without the knowledge of his father.'

In a case decided on August 18, 1994[17] by the Designated Court for Greater Bombay, the attorneys of record were Ram, Mahesh, Rani, Lataa, Sri Jaisinghani, Shanti Bhushan, and Kapil Sibal, all for a bail application. They argued that mere possession 'cannot constitute an offence under Section 5 of the TADA Act, and has to be dealt with only under the Arms Act, 1959.' Though Sanjay was granted bail at first, it would not last. Several questions of law were raised about interpretation of the TADA law, and these were referred to a Constitutional Bench of the Supreme Court.[18] From there, the case moved in and out of court. Sanjay was in jail for 16 months in 1994–5 and again for several weeks in 2007. He filed multiple appeals, none involving Ram, and on March 21, 2013 the Supreme Court sentenced him to five years.[19]

Public sentiment has run strongly in Sanjay's favour, many

believing that he really never was privy to the actual terrorist plot, and that he really did just keep a rifle for protecting his family. Besides he was a film idol.

Unfortunately, the general public still believes that the concept of Hindutva is responsible for the sectarianism behind the violence at Ayodhya and for the Mumbai blasts, making them sceptical as Ram holds aloft the ideal definition of pure Hindutva that he cherishes.

Also unfortunately, the aftermath of Ayodhya would be a polarization of Indian politics, with the BJP moving towards a stridently pro-Hindu position and leaving the Congress party as the more inclusive party. Now, pitting Hindu against Muslim, a virtual two-party system resulted. This left Ram, a liberal who is opposed to the suppression of human rights and to communalism, in an uncomfortable place, since he was increasingly dependent on the RSS and the Shiv Sena for his Parliament seat, thus also on Bal Thackeray. And the BJP was starting to slip away from him.

28

Corruption: Fighting it, Defending it

Ask anyone, and they will tell you that one of India's greatest problems is corruption. Also ask anyone, and they will tell you that Ram Jethmalani is one of India's greatest lawyers. So, when Ram takes aim at corruption, the country pays attention.

Ram has fought for years against the Gandhi dynasty and its trail of corruption, yet he defends corrupt politicians. He rails against dacoits in political power who impoverish India, but he represents stockbrokers who personify corruption. In his mind, these are not contradictions. He feels a responsibility to expose corruption to sunlight but also to make sure that every citizen, even if corrupt, has proper representation in court.

Ram has powerful allies in his latest fight against governmental corruption, most recently the famous Anna Hazare and even the volatile Subramanian Swamy, who now is united with Ram in a crusade to get black money from foreign banks to India. Long before that though, was the Vohra Committee.

On July 9, 1993, the Indian government appointed a high-profile commission chaired by the Home Secretary, N.N. Vohra, to investigate the interconnections between criminals, the mafia, politicians and bureaucrats in India. As the investigation proceeded, it also showed links to the military.

The Vohra Committee completed its report on October 5,

1993,[1] but its recommendations lay fallow. In July 1995, the murder of a political activist provided a graphic demonstration of the links between politicians and the mafia, and the press dug up the Vohra Committee recommendations, trumpeting that they never had been implemented. The public was outraged. The report finally went to Parliament in August 1995, without annexures or the list of the politicians that the report named. The names were suppressed on the grounds that their publication would hurt their reputations. Dinesh Trivedi, a Member of Parliament from West Bengal, submitted a written request for the missing portions of the report and the list to be made public. When they were not, he sued.

Ram argued the case on behalf of Trivedi, the Public Interest Legal Support and Research Centre (PILSARC) and the Consumer Education and Research Centre (CERC).[2] They sued the Union of India, the Ministry of Finance, the director of the Research and Analysis Wing (RAW), the director of the Central Bureau of Investigation (CBI), the director of the Intelligence Bureau (IB), and the special secretary to the Ministry of Home Affairs.

The court wrote,

The petitioners allege that a cursory analysis of the Report reveals the following disturbing aspects: (1) several governmental agencies have, in their written reports, indicated that they are aware of the vast local, national and international links of criminal syndicates; (2) these links are such that they amount to a parallel system of government; (3) the common citizen is unprotected and must live in constant fear of his life and property; (4) even the members of the judicial system have not escaped the embrace of the mafia; and (5) the existing criminal justice system is unable to deal with the activities of the mafia.

It is further observed that these criminal elements have developed an extensive network of contacts with bureaucrats, government functionaries at lower levels, politicians, media personalities, strategically located persons in the non-Governmental sector and members of the judiciary; some of

Ram at 18 years

Ram and Rani, 1971

(L–R) Sarah Morris, Ram, Boolchand, Rani, Ya'akov Morris

(L–R) Maya, Ya'akov Morris,
Rani, 1970

Ram with his father

(L–R) Sarla, Boolchand, Sundri,
Parvati, Ratna

Ram with Shobha, Suresh, Ratna, and Suresh's parents

At Shobha's wedding. (L–R) Durga, Ram, Ratna, Rani, Sundri's daughter Venu, Ratna's mother, and Shobha

(L–R) Durga, Shobha, Ram

At Shobha's wedding. (L–R) Suresh, Shobha, Ram

(L–R) Mahesh, Ratna, and Ram in London

Ram and Shobha, Delhi House, 1978

With Ratna

Ram and Kail, 1986

Ram with Agasthya, 1986

Ram with Amartya, 1986

Hampi, 1992. (L–R) Kanta Bhambhani, Lataa, Martin
Adelman (author's husband), Ram, and author

Ram in Michigan in the nineties

Ram and Ramakrishna Hegde, 2000

Mahesh's wedding, 2000. (L–R) Suresh's father, Janak, with Kail
on his lap, Monica, Rani, Shobha, Ram, Sri Jaisinghani,
and Sheila Jaisinghani

Shobha, Rani, and Durga

Shobha and Rani

(L–R) Janak, Shobha, Ram, Rani, and Mahesh

Top row: (L–R) Girish, Sonil, Haseena, Ali, and Sejal; bottom row:
Janak, Shobha, Ram, Rani, Mahesh, and Serena, in 2002

Sonil, Ram, and Gerish in Detroit

Ram and Suresh with two granddaughters, Anica
(on Suresh's lap) and Riana (on Ram's lap)

(L–R) Janak, Monica, Suresh, Shobha, Rani, Mahesh, Haseena, Ram, and Ratna

Ram with L.K. Advani (L)

Boolchand and Maya

Ram with Narendra Modi (L) and L.K. Advani (R)

(L–R) Sonil, Tony, and Girish

At Ram's 90th birthday party. With Shobha

At Ram's 90th birthday party. With Nusli Wadia

At Ram's 90th birthday party. With Shobhaa Dé and her husband

At Ram's 90th birthday party. With daughters-in-law Hasina (L) and Monica (R)

At Ram's 90th birthday party. With Amit Shah (L)

At Ram's 90th birthday party. (R–L)
Serena, Ram, and his grandson Amartya

At Ram's 90th birthday party. With Mohan

At Ram's 90th birthday party. With Anil Ambani

At Ram's 90th birthday party. With former
chief minister of Maharashtra, Prithviraj Chavan

At Ram's 90th birthday party. (R–L) Ram,
Sri Jaisinghani, and Nusli Wadia

these criminal syndicates have international links, sometimes with foreign intelligence agencies.

This is a shocking series of statements. It is no wonder the government tried to suppress the report or, when that failed, to diminish its impact. It is no wonder the press took up the cause, nor is it any wonder the public pushed for answers. This is an indictment of a whole country and the way it operates.

Furthermore, the petitioners 'allege that the document tabled in the Parliament is not the complete report but betrays an incomplete substitute prepared hurriedly for the purpose of meeting the demand in Parliament and suppresses vital information regarding the unholy connections between politicians, bureaucrats, criminals and anti-social elements'. They point out that the original report was 100 pages, and the redacted report that went to Parliament was only 11.5 pages.

No surprise that Trivedi was suspicious!

Ram emphasized that the Vohra Committee Report essentially addressed cases 'involving narco-terrorist elements and smuggling of arms and ammunitions into the country', which he said were 'properly and wholly within the domain of the executive power of the Union'.

The government had taken some action by appointing a so-called Nodal Agency, and this agency had held discussions with the political parties. Ram was not impressed: 'In his view, setting up a Nodal Agency would serve no purpose for it would be as prone to failure as the agencies it sought to supervise had proven themselves to be. Instead, he urged us to set up a Committee consisting of two retired Judges of the Supreme Court with sufficient experience of criminal matters, to probe into the disclosures that would be made consequent to our directions'.

In its opinion, the court considered whether the petitioners had a right to 'be informed not only of the contents of the report, but also of the details of the various reports, notes, letters and other forms of written evidence that was placed for the consideration of the Vohra Committee.' The court expressed its concern, writing that where 'it is clearly contrary to the public interest for a document to be disclosed, then it is in law immune from disclosure'.

The judges were reluctant 'to direct the disclosure of the supporting material which consists of information gathered from the Heads of the various Intelligence Agencies to the general public'. One reason was that 'not all of the information collected and recorded in intelligence reports is substantiated by hard evidence. Often on the basis of unverified suspicion names are thrown by people to save their own skins'. In short, 'quite frequently, individuals are shortlisted based purely on the investigators' hunches and surmises or on account of the past background of the suspects'.

The court then shrewdly quoted Ram against himself. As it happened, Ram's name was the only one that appeared in the public version of the report, and the court says 'Shri Jethmalani has objected to this lone disclosure by stating that when the government sought to pursue extradition proceedings against Iqbal Mirchi in London, it could not produce even "an iota of evidence" against him.'

Finally, the court refused to order further disclosures of names or annexures, but it did concede Ram's criticisms of the Nodal Agency. The court was willing to consider Ram's proposal for Special Courts, but for now, it ordered a 'high level committee be appointed by the president of India on the advice of the Prime Minister'. Frankly, Judge Ahmadi did not give them much. Ironically, this case provided fuel for the Right to Information movement in India.

Sri Jaisinghani does not see corruption in India as a solvable problem, 'In India, 99 per cent of corruption is consensual. In a system where there are more bribe givers than bribe takers, who is to blame?' He says that every service is subject to a service tax, sales tax or toll, but when the anti-corruption activists ask for these laws to be enforced, 'There will be no complainant.'

'We are thankful when they accept the bribe,' he says.

He quotes Churchill's warning when India was fighting for self-rule, 'You are giving freedom to born rascals.'

Operation West End was a clever demonstration of the Vohra

Committee's findings. A news portal, *Tehelka*, set up a sting to expose corruption in the defence establishment. Its reporters posed as representatives of a sham corporation called West End,[3] and they offered to sell a certain military device to Indian officers. Incidentally, the device was entirely fictional. On March 13, 2001, *Tehelka*, with a flourish, treated a roomful of high-powered invited guests to video footage that documented hours of conversations between their undercover reporters, members of the defence establishment, and politicians who were filmed while accepting bribes. The government's response the next year was to appoint a commission to investigate *Tehelka*!

Ram was the counsel for Shankar Sharma of First Global, a company which bankrolled *Tehelka*.[4] Sharma was thrown in jail on a trumped-up charge of violating the Foreign Exchange Act. In appearing before the Tehelka commission,[5] Ram asked that 'he be first allowed to cross-examine finance ministry official Devinder Gupta [who] had filed an affidavit alleging financial motives behind *Tehelka*'s "operation westend".' The government said it would produce Gupta at the end of the hearings.

Ram 'submitted that the conduct of the union government should fulfil three conditions: it should be in public interest, must not look arbitrary and must not be devoid of transparency'. Citing section 135 of the Indian Evidence Act, he reminded the commission that 'The order in which witnesses are produced and examined shall be regulated by the law and practice for the time being relating to civil and criminal procedure respectively, and, in the absence of any such law, by the discretion of the Court.' Thus they could not be high-handed about it.

Fourteen lawyers took the side of *Tehelka* and Shankar Sharma, including Ram, Mahesh, Rani, and Shanti Bhushan. According to *the Times of India*,[6] 'two former union law ministers—Ram Jethmalani and Shanti Bhushan—came down heavily on Tuesday on the NDA government for arresting and launching a "draconian witch-hunt" against the owner of First Global, Shankar Sharma.' According to the same article, 'Ram Jethmalani said the government has made a mockery of the Justice K. Venkataswami Commission now probing the allegations made by the Tehelka tapes'. Ram is quoted as saying, 'The government has not even allowed the accused to be present before the commission. Things that are happening today did not happen even during the emergency . . . I am ashamed to have been a part of this government once.'

The Venkataswami Committee[7] was to probe 'the government's charge that *Tehelka* and its "angel investor", First Global, owned by Shankar Sharma and Devina Mehra, had a financial motive and that the defence scam expose was so timed as to engineer a collapse in the stock market. First Global, it was alleged, benefited from it financially'.

Devinder Gupta, an under secretary in the Finance Ministry, had filed the first affidavit on behalf of the government, but the government did not want him to testify. So A.A. Shankar, additional director of income tax, led off on the stand for two days.

Outlook reports that Ram grilled him, and it quotes the *Tehelka* counsel as saying that, 'Jethmalani demolished Shankar's testimony, suggesting that the "financial motive" idea being touted by the government was a mere "smear campaign". In those two days, Shankar admitted that he had no knowledge of Gupta's affidavit and merely appended his signature on the affidavit as a witness. "Jethmalani warned him that he would be tried for perjury," says Bhushan. Newly appointed Solicitor General Kirit Rawal disagrees. "Shankar did not capitulate and withstood the cross-examination," he told *Outlook*.'

Shoma Chaudhury wrote that when Ram argued before the Venkataswami Committee, he did so 'Foot placed insolently— tactically—on a stool, hand in pocket, voice booming, teasing, suddenly exploding, in three days Ram had run a lance through the government's case and exposed its perjury. The judge was eating out of his hand, the witnesses were whimpering, and the law officers of the land were running for cover. It was a spectacle of a lifetime'.[8]

Ram tells the story that when the first witness was called, the subsequent witnesses were about to be dismissed, as was customary. Even his juniors wanted them to be dismissed, but he said, 'No. I want them to hear what will happen to the first witness.' The first witness was their boss.

Halfway through the cross-examination, the other witnesses went to the chairman en masse and refused to testify. Soon after, the government wound up the Committee.

Amidst the allegations, George Fernandes resigned as Defence Minister on March 15, but he was reinstated on October 16, 2001. *Tehelka* writes:[9] 'Jumping from one conspiracy theory to another, George Fernandes variously accused *Tehelka's* Operation West End of being: an ISI plot, an Opposition plot, a plot engineered by "Middlemen who had lost their access to the defence ministry . . .", [or] a Hinduja backed story.'

An honest man, Venkataswami resigned from his commission when he was accused of a conflict of interest for serving in another appointed capacity, the Authority for Advance Rulings, in the Income Tax Department. In fact, he resigned from both appointments.[10] Afterwards he said that the *Tehelka* tapes indeed were authentic, and that the government was trying to suppress his report. The government replaced him with Justice Phukan in January 2003. The Phukan Commission restricted its investigation to whether the *Tehelka* tapes were authentic.[11] *Tehelka* wrote, 'A week earlier, we had turned our backs on the Commission of Enquiry. In a masterful performance, Ram Jethmalani had blown craters through the government's case against First Global and *Tehelka*.'

Tehelka wrote in multiple articles: 'Early November: Over three days, eminent lawyer Ram Jethmalani cross-examines government witnesses in the Venkataswami Commission. Exposes the government's lies. Threatens to sue the government officers for perjury. The Attorney and Solicitor General of India ask for an adjournment. The case is never taken up again.'

Tehelka quotes a constitutional expert, A.G. Noorani: 'Never in the half century of the Commission of Inquiry Act, 1952, was the body ever asked to probe into the credentials of those who had made the charges. The focus was on the message, never the messenger. If this move is allowed to pass muster, the press will be effectively muzzled.'[12]

Under relentless government pressure, and after repeated raids on their premises, the *Tehelka* offices finally were forced to shut down in December 2003. The government even searched the income tax filings of their investors. Finally, two and a half years later, the CBI began to focus on the actual culprits.[13] Bangaru Laxman, the former BJP president, who was filmed accepting a bribe, was sent to jail in April 2012, but he was let out on bail in less than a year. The *Tehelka* web portal re-emerged as a weekly paper; later a magazine.

Tarun Tejpal, in a letter of thanks to everyone who helped *Tehelka*, focuses on Ram, writing, 'Ram Jethmalani—rare celebrity whose reality is greater than his image—for adopting us as a cause and freely giving of his house, heart, wallet and formidable legal arsenal.'[14]

The *Tehelka* sting may have taken place during a BJP administration, but during the many years in which the Congress party was in control, the country was rife with crony capitalism. When Rajiv Gandhi was in power, the government was a magnet for candidates interested in financial gain. Even the press pandered to maintain access to their sources. By the time the BJP came in, it had learned well at the knee of the Congress party. Interestingly, Ram fully supported a sting of a BJP administration, even though historically he has been close to the BJP. In fact, when he gets on a tear fighting corruption, Ram makes little distinction between parties. As a result, neither party feels it can completely trust him.

In 1994, a formal notice in a legal publication said, 'Jethmalani quits legal practice—Eminent lawyer and member of Rajya Sabha Ram Jethmalani has announced his retirement from the bar on his 71st birthday and said he would devote his time and energy to teaching law and his work in Parliament.'[15]

This was the first of many such announcements, but nobody really took notice. My husband said it just was a ploy to raise his fees. Even so, friends and colleagues pleaded with him to take their case, just this once. For a couple of years, a sign on the front gate of his house announced that he would take no more legal cases. After a while, the sign quietly came down.

Meanwhile, politicians under a cloud of corruption have lined up outside Ram's door.

In some cases, they have even been in the right. Against all likelihood, the respected L.K. Advani once was accused of racketeering. Like Ram, a Sindhi from Karachi, Advani started his career with the RSS, became a member of the Rajya Sabha at an early age, and won a seat in the Lok Sabha from Delhi in 1991. He later became president of the BJP and Deputy Prime Minister. His was the incitement that caused the demolition of the Babri Masjid in Ayodhya, and he has had to live with the blame.

One day in 1991, in the course of a money laundering investigation of militants in Kashmir, the police raided the Delhi home of some hawala brokers, the Jain brothers. Hawala is an informal banking system that is notoriously easy to corrupt. The CBI pursued a rather leisurely investigation of the matter, until Ram encouraged two journalists to file a PIL with the Supreme Court in 1993, in order to request a serious timetable. Once the investigation started in 1995, one brother, S.K. Jain, admitted to 29 payoffs to politicians. As it happened, the Jain brothers kept an intriguing diary of their transactions, naming many important political figures. In time, the name L.K. Advani appeared, and he immediately was charged under the Prevention of Corruption Act of 1988. In 1996, the sessions court held that there was a prima facie case against L.K. Advani, V.C. Shukla, and the four Jain brothers.

The charge against the Jain brothers was that they had conspired in 1988 and 1989 to 'receive unaccounted money and to disburse the same amongst themselves, friends, close relations and amongst different persons including the public servants and political leaders . . . Shri S.K. Jain lobbied with different public servants and government organisations in the power and steel sectors of the Government of India for the purposes of pursuing of award of various contracts to different foreign bidders with the motive of getting illegal kickbacks . . . by receiving major portion of the same from foreign countries through hawala channels.'

Advani resigned his seat in Parliament, abstained from running in the 1996 elections, and called Ram.

When Ram agreed to represent him, the press accused him of

shifting positions for his own personal benefit, because he had pushed for the PIL in the first place. How could Ram defend Advani now? Ram explained that when the initial prosecution began, Advani had not been named. The CBI decided later to prosecute Advani even though, according to Ram, he was innocent. Before he took the case,[16] Ram consulted with the Attorney General, the chairman of the Bar Council, and Fali Nariman, an ex-Attorney General, all of whom agreed that he had a right to represent Advani. Ram also invited Vajpayee to attend one of the court hearings, to squash rumours of discord between them over his representing Advani.

The Jain brothers' records had been arranged to make it appear that they had paid Rs 60 lakhs to L.K. Advani. As Judge Shamim wrote, 'The Jains individually as well as collectively were in the habit of making payments to influential political leaders and public servants of high status and accepting official favours from them.'

Senior advocates Ram, Kapil Sibal, and R.K. Anand argued, 'There is absolutely no evidence against the petitioners except the alleged diaries and the note books, the entries wherein are not even worth the paper on which the same have been recorded, as the same are inadmissible in evidence.'

Ram's most telling argument was that, to be admissible, accounts must be written in a 'book of account', but 'A book containing minutes of cash paid, only, is not properly a book of account,' and of most importance, 'A diary is not admissible in evidence under the rule admitting books which are used in the regular course of business and kept by the party as "books of account".'

Clearly, the entry had to be made in a book, but 'A bundle of sheets detachable and replaceable at a moment's pleasure can hardly be characterised as a book of account.' The charges against Advani were based on notes containing the ambiguous initials LKA, and these were written on a loose slip of paper inserted between the pages of a diary. Ram pointed out that there were no dates on the sheet, no sum of money listed and no witnesses named. Ram produced a Delhi telephone book to show the court how many people had the initials LKA.

'Jethmalani's special weapon is his rapier-sharp wit.[17] Nothing brought that in play as much as the Hawala scam case ...The judge, reflecting the public perception about tainted politicians, made a pre-emptive observation, "Mr Jethmalani, all these politicians appear to be corrupt. Do not expect any relief from me."

'Jethmalani replied without a pause: "My Lord is absolutely right. These politicians deserve no mercy. But the law is different. Consider this: if My Lord dismisses my case and I go back home and write My Lord's initials on my diary with a sum of Rs. 10 lakh written against it, would My Lord be chargesheeted for it?"

Indeed the judge ruled: 'I thus conclude that there is no evidence against the petitioners which can be converted into legal evidence.'

Ram must have cooked up that crack early one morning as he sat on his porch, thinking about the case. He just had to wait for an opening.

Ram disputes that there was any quid pro quo for his action in this case. Yes, he was interested in a future appointment as a minister, and yes, he knew Advani might well have the power to recommend him some day, but Ram denies that this was why he represented him.

Many years later when questioned by the press about whether he has sometimes 'squeezed his way' into politics by taking up politically sensitive cases such as this one, Ram countered that while others have used money to obtain political influence, he has used his brain. Then he asks, 'Which is worse?'

Moving from the respectable politician to the highly disreputable, Ram also represented Phoolan Devi,[18] a low-caste woman, an outlaw, and a famous folk legend. A temperamental and troublesome girl when she was young, her family married her off at age 16 to a much older man who lived a comfortable distance away. Soon she left him to become the consort of a man who led a gang of dacoits (bandits). The gang eventually split over a conflict between the lower caste and the higher caste members, and her lover was murdered. In one version of the story, she was kidnapped and gangraped by higher caste gangsters over a three-week period. In another version, the gangrape first was by the dacoits themselves, then by a whole village of higher caste men. Somehow she fled into the jungle afterwards, turning into the famed 'Bandit Queen', who led her own gang of low-caste bandits. This gang committed violent robberies, according to the myth, only of upper-class villagers. The day of her revenge came at Behmai village, the place where she had been gangraped. Cold-bloodedly, she ordered her own bandits to line up all the higher-caste men, and execute them.

After that, she fled to the jungle, sheltered by her many supporters. The longer she eluded capture, the more the public celebrated her as a low-caste heroine. She finally surrendered voluntarily, on favourable terms. In a symbolic gesture, she ceremoniously laid down her weapons before the goddess Durga and a portrait of Gandhi in front of an adoring crowd of thousands who had walked for miles to bear witness. She went to jail on February 12, 1983 for 55 instances'of heinous offences, e.g. dacoity and murder'.

Ram represented Phoolan in 1994 when she finally was allowed out on parole. Ram had argued 'that her right to speedy trial guaranteed under Article 21 of the Constitution has been violated and her continued custody was without any lawful authority'.

As the court wrote, 'The petitioner alleges that atrocities were committed on her and members of her family by persons belonging to the upper castes and she was also the victim of gang rape, which drove her to adopt a life of crime; this criminal past is the cause for a large number of criminal cases for offences of dacoity and murder etc. against her in the State of Uttar Pradesh.'

Ram argued that there was no justification for further prosecution 'since the petitioner has already been in custody for a total period of eleven years when according to the terms of surrender she was to undergo imprisonment for a total period of eight years only'.

Phoolan Devi never returned to jail. She even won two Parliament terms. A book was written about her life, *India's Bandit Queen: The True Story of Phoolan Devi*. That was made into a film, which she tried to keep off the air, only relenting when Channel 4 paid her enough money. Documentaries, a BBC programme, and an autobiography all romanticized her life, but nothing could save her from the revenge of rival bandits. In the end she was assassinated. Her obituary was published when she was 37.[19]

The name Harshad Mehta appears on every list of Ram's most infamous clients. Mehta was a prominent Mumbai stockbroker who was accused in 1990 of pumping up the price for the stock of a cement company until it rose astronomically. He did this by convincing buyers that a company should be valued on the basis of how much it will cost to create a similar company to replace it, not at its value at the time of original purchase.

In 1992, Mehta and his associates were accused of manipulating the Bombay Stock Exchange to cause a precipitous increase in prices. When the scheme was exposed, many banks were stuck with worthless notes. The *Times of India* columnist Sucheta Dalal exposed the scam on April 23, 1992,[20] and she co-authored a book on the subject, *The Scam: Harshad Mehta and Ketan Parekh*. The chairman of one small bank committed suicide. The stock market crashed. Mehta was charged with 72 criminal offences and 600 civil suits, which were still in court when Mehta died of a heart attack in 2002. The scandal was the subject of a movie, *Gafla*.

Mehta first approached Ram in 1993[21] to admit he had paid off Narasimha Rao, the Prime Minister, to help him out of the scandal. Ram went to Vajpayee, and both agreed the story had to be brought to light. In June 1993, Mehta, with Ram at his side, told the press he had sent a suitcase of one crore, in denominations of Rs 50, to Rao. When the press questioned whether this much money could fit in a suitcase, Ram demonstrated that it would. The press immediately accused him of a publicity stunt.

Accused of fabricating a sensational story, Ram answered as usual: if the allegation against Rao was false, why did he not sue for defamation? He also asked why Rao did not request the CBI or Parliament to investigate him in order to clear his name. To Ram, any such omission demonstrates guilt.

When the Reserve Bank of India found that brokers had diverted large amounts of money from various financial institutions, this became known as the Security Scam of 1992. To deal with it,

Parliament passed the Special Court Act of 1992. Harshad Shantilal Mehta's legal battles started in this Special Court.

The court was to consist of one or more Judges of the High Court, nominated by the Chief Justice, and it began sitting immediately. It was charged to obtain speedy recovery of the money, punish the guilty, and restore confidence in the integrity of India's financial institutions. In 1998, the Supreme Court had to adjudicate the powers of the Special Court—did it have the power to assess tax liabilities, attachable mortgaged/pledged properties, penalties and interest? As it turned out, the language of the act was fuzzy.

Mehta's case came to the Supreme Court on appeal in 2001,[22] the lawyers arguing over whether the Special Court had the authority to pardon. Ram represented Mehta. The case began because there were two separate applications before the Special Court, both asking for a grant of pardon.

The court first quoted Ram's arguments, 'While enacting the Act the provision conferring power to grant pardon was deliberately omitted and this almost conclusively shows that such power was not intended to be conferred, is the submission of Mr Jethmalani.' This means that the legislature did not intend to confer the power of pardon on the Special Court. The court continued 'we find that Mr Jethmalani is right in contending that the power to grant pardon is not an inherent power of a criminal court and is a substantive power to be specifically conferred.'

At the end nothing could convince the court to let Mehta off. 'Our conclusion, therefore, is that the Special Court established under the Act is a court of exclusive jurisdiction . . . It is a court of original criminal jurisdiction and has all the powers of such a court under the Code . . . We are of the opinion that the learned Special Court rightly rejected the application of the appellants for revocation of the order of pardon.'

Even after Mehta died, Ram represented his interests in 2003,[23] and Mahesh represented another defendant in the same case. Nariman observes with disapproval the delays that led to this case not coming to a conclusion until 10 years after its inception.[24] Ram refuted most of the charges against Mehta with ease, 'from the aforesaid five transactions, it is apparent that the investment/loan was for a short period . . . the amount is received and paid on due dates. There is no loss to MUL (Maruti Udyog Ltd) or to the UCO Bank [a commercial bank owned by the government] and the Bank has received commission for the said commercial transactions.'

Ram argued, 'Admittedly, five transactions took place between MUL and [Mehta] during the period from end of January to beginning of May, 1991. As per the first transaction, [Mehta] lent money to MUL. Loan period was for a period of 32 days and the interest rate was 12.75 per cent. MUL returned the loan amount on due date with agreed interest.'

Furthermore, 'Mehta returned the borrowed amount on due date with interest in each transaction. All the said four transactions were backed by [bank receipts] as collateral security and the [bank receipts] were backed by requisite number of units. Loan was for a short period . . .' In each instance Ram explained that Mehta's actions were neither misappropriation of money nor were they dishonest.

The court writes of Ram's defence, 'It is his submission that it is absurd to suggest that [Mehta] committed any offence or offences, but the prosecution is a piece of political revenge against [Mehta] for disclosing certain facts to the press against the political leaders [Rao]. He contends that transactions were loan transactions because in all these transactions the rate of interest and number of days for which the loan was being advanced was settled before the money and the units changed hands. This is consistent only with the transaction being a loan transaction.'

Finally, 'The learned senior counsel submitted that FIR was lodged after investigation for seven months and charge-sheet was submitted after more than one year and eight months, which itself indicates that CBI knew that there was no case to be put up before a court and the investigation was kept alive for sordid and dishonest motive.'

In short, the case was political, because the CBI had pursued this case and others in order to 'intimidate and blackmail' one witness for not supporting Mehta's June, 1993 declaration that he had paid Rs 1 crore to Prime Minister Rao. Ram's point was that if this key witness had supported Mehta's allegation, he would have been prosecuted.

You have to hand it to Ram. Mehta had been the poster boy for financial corruption in India since 1992, tried and convicted by the press over a 10-year period. The public never doubted his guilt. Still, Ram made such convincing arguments that the court bought most of them. Nevertheless, the court still confirmed Mehta's conviction.

Another corruption case that the press mined extensively was the so-called 'fodder scam'.[25] This started when Sushil Kumar Modi, the Opposition leader in the Bihar State Assembly, filed a Public Interest Litigation (PIL) in the Patna High Court against two previous Chief Ministers of the state of Bihar, Lalu Prasad Yadav and Rabri Devi, husband and wife, whose demonstrated assets greatly exceeded their known sources of income. As reported by the *New York Times*,[26] the scandal involved $285 million stolen over 20 years in one of the country's poorest regions, the eastern state of Bihar. The money came from agricultural support programmes designed to help 350 million poverty-stricken farmers.

The Times wrote, 'According to indictments in the case, politicians and senior officials in Bihar invented phantom livestock herds, then made fraudulent payments for fodder and medicine for the animals, as well as for artificial insemination equipment.'

The PIL was an appeal from a Patna High Court order to the CBI to investigate 'large-scale misappropriation of public funds to the extent of several hundred crores of rupees by indulging into fraudulent transactions and falsification of accounts in the Animal Husbandry Department . . .which has come to be known as "Fodder Scam".' The director of the CBI appealed to the Patna Court for more time to submit his report, and the Patna Court barred him from participating, because he was interfering with the investigation.

In a 1996 appeal to the Supreme Court, the Attorney General argued that there was no reason to bar the director of CBI from the case. Ram argued on behalf of Modi that the Patna High Court had concluded correctly that the director of the CBI was trying to interfere with the investigation 'to shield some powerful persons'.

The court agreed that, 'It does appear that the directions given by the Director, CBI which led to presentation of an incomplete picture of the material collected during the investigation up to that stage before the Division Bench hearing the matter gave rise to the impression in the Division Bench that the Director, CBI was withholding some material information from the High Court.'

The court held that the CBI needed to work as a team and that the director should participate in the investigation.

The fodder scam case returned to the Supreme Court in 1997, with Ram arguing for the defendants, who did not include Prasad at that time.[27]

In 2000, Prasad and his wife were charged with misappropriation of funds. They surrendered but were granted bail by the Patna High Court; this bail was extended several times. In 2001, Ram represented Prasad in a bail application before a CBI Special Court 'as replacement for Laloo Yadav's lawyer Kapil Sibal, who at the eleventh hour expressed his inability to come'.[28]

In 2003,[29] Lalu Prasad and Dr Jagannath Mishra went to the Supreme Court to appeal a 2002 decision of the Jharkhand High Court that had refused to amalgamate a group of corruption cases into one joint trial. Ram represented the appellants, but the court did not agree to the amalgamation.

Could we say that by helping Lalu, Ram contributed to saving the Indian Railways? Of course that would be a stretch, but in fact, when Lalu became Minister of Railways in 2004, he was widely regarded as having virtually saved the Indian Railways. When he came in the railways were heading towards bankruptcy, and at the end of his tenure they were showing huge profits, a turnaround for which many gave Lalu the credit; of course, there were others who believed the credit should go to his predecessor, Nitish Kumar. After Lalu left that ministry though, he faced allegations of using the position for his personal enrichment,[30] and he still was not done with the fodder scam.[31]

In 2010, Lalu Prasad appealed one element of the ongoing fodder scam case to the Supreme Court,[32] with Ram as his lawyer.

By then, Lalu had spent over 10 years in and out of court. The court wrote: 'The main question presented . . . is, namely, as to whether the State Government (of Bihar) has competence to file an appeal . . . acquitting the accused persons when the case has been investigated by the Delhi Special Police Establishment (CBI).'

Before the Supreme Court, Ram argued on technical grounds that the state should not be allowed to appeal. Indeed, the Supreme Court ruled that the state government of Bihar had no right to appeal.

Concurrently with the fodder scam cases, Lalu faced an accusation of accumulating disproportionate assets. He and his wife were charged and acquitted, and that decision was appealed to the Supreme Court. The appeal was dismissed, reviewed again by the court, and dismissed again.

Prasad's cases continue to wend its way through the courts, with Ram representing him in July 2013 before the Jharkhand High Court in an effort to change a judge, citing concerns of possible judicial bias. This request was denied. 'There were a total of 61 cases filed originally, of which 44 had been disposed of. Yadav is an accused in six cases, of which five are being heard by the court of the special judge.'[33] In October 2013, Prasad was convicted by the CBI Special Court in Ranchi.[34] Ram was not representing him.

29

Judicial Accountability

Surely everyone will agree that delayed justice is the bane of the Indian courts. Worse, any lawyer who ever practised in the lower courts can cite numerous instances of frank corruption. Nobody in India knows these problems better than Ram, and nobody has devoted more energy than he has to correct them.

This is a cause Ram has worked on for years. He writes, 'A Judge is the guardian of the small man and his bundle of rights that . . . enable him to realize the fullest material, moral and spiritual potential, and which enable him to expand to the utmost the frontiers of his body, mind and soul. No Judge must aspire for harmony with the legislature and the executive.'[1]

Ram deplores judicial elections. He tells of a judge who was paralysed from the waist down and always won his campaigns for re-election. The fifth time he ran, the manager of the opposing party came to his boss and said, 'Sir, we have found a solution to our problem.' He asked, 'What is it?' 'Sir, this time we have found a judge who is paralysed from the waist upwards.'

Ram first introduced the Ram Jethmalani Private Bill into Parliament in 1981. This would put judicial appointments to the Supreme Court and the High Courts under the purview of a commission consisting of a member of the government, the Opposition leader, the Bar, a local representative, a member of the Supreme Court Bar, law professors, and jurists. That was Ram's ideal system, but despite his efforts to introduce the bill several times, it never came to a serious vote.

As he writes,[2] 'In 1990, the then National Front Government, in a rare act of self-effacement, introduced in the Lok Sabha the Constitution 67th Amendment Bill. This bill sought to transfer the power of judicial appointments from the executive to a National Judicial Commission', which would consist of the Chief Justice of India, two Supreme Court Judges, also the Chief Judge, and two other judges of any High Court to which an appointment is to be made. The government of Prime Minister V.P. Singh ended that year, and so did the career of that bill.

Ram has long decried judicial corruption and incompetence, 'Serious allegations of misconduct were widely aired in June 1990. Justice Mr S.K. Desai, the seniormost puisne Judge of the Bombay High Court had to resign as he was transferred following an allegation that he had attempted to influence Justice Mr M.P. Konia in a case that was pending before the two of them. Some years ago, Rs 32 lakh were discovered from the house of Chief Justice Mr Veeraswamy. The CBI registered a case involving this recovery which is still pending.'[3]

'Former Chief Justice of India Mr Venkataramaiah publicly stated that out of a total of about 450 High Court Judges all over the country, as many as 90 "were out practically every evening, wining and dining either at a lawyer's house or at a foreign embassy". He said that there were charges of corruption against at least 88 High Court Judges. And several Judges had their sons and close relatives practice in all the High Courts.'

Ram gives as an example of judicial incompetence the two judges who refused to listen to a modern form of scientific evidence. Ram saw the use of DNA evidence when he was in the United States during the Emergency. In 2005 he represented the well-known Swami Premananda in a case of alleged rape. When he tried to present the DNA evidence before two Justices of the Indian Supreme Court, Justice Agarwal and Justice Sema, they refused to allow it, claiming they could not understand DNA evidence! Equally as absurd, according to Ram, was their tacit acceptance[4] that the police had a right to beat the alleged victim at the police station until she confessed that Swami Premananda had raped her.

Ram recalls writing an article asserting that judges who cannot understand DNA evidence either should resign or be impeached for 'intellectual deficiency'. He actually sent it first to the judges. When he received no response, he forwarded it to every Supreme Court judge. Again no response, so he published it in *Asian Age*. Nobody resigned, but Ram had made his point. Despite his needling, Ram says proudly that when both judges retired, they still called him personally to invite him to their retirement parties.

Well . . . there are two sides to this story. The other side was expressed by the indignant judges, who wrote, 'The facts of this case, as revealed by the prosecution, shocked the judicial conscience. It illustrates a classic example as to how the insatiable lust for sex of . . . Swami Premananda leads to the raping of 13 Ashram girls and murder of one Ravi. The Ashram which is supposed to be God's abode turned out to be devil's workshop. [Swami Premananda] to whom the inmates of the Ashram regarded as God having the divine power turned out to be a monster. It is a classic case of betrayal of fatherly and divinely trust of the inmates of the Ashram girls who were mostly orphans and destitute . . .'

'The facts of the case also illustrate a classic example as to how a game-keeper has become a poacher or a treasury guard has become a robber. From the facts as disclosed by the prosecution, some of the victim girls were brought up by [Swami Premananda] since when they were aged about 2, 3 and 6 years. They were reared to be butchered later when they attained the age.'

Ram argued that the girls had been coerced into accusing the swami of rape through harsh treatment at the police station. He also argued that it was consensual sex, not rape. The court would have none of it.

Here is Ram's version of the story,[5]

Swami Premananda, who was originally running an orphanage in Sri Lanka, migrated to South India after the ethnic riots in his native country. He founded a new ashram in Fathimanagar about 30 miles away from Trichy in Tamil Nadu.

The background of the police visit was a conspiracy of three actors to expose what they called evil happenings in the Ashram. Among these three actors, the principal one was a young man called Anand Mohan, an unemployed lothario of Trichy . . . during these visits he got involved in torrid affairs with two female inmates. One was Suresh Kumari who approached him to help with securing a false school certificate. She complained that Swamiji was the obstacle in securing it. The second woman on his agenda was a German teacher by the name of Ella. He planned to marry her and make himself a lucrative career somewhere in Europe. Ella however disappointed him. In the eyes of Anand Mohan, the swami was the villain who frustrated his ambitions. The swami told Ella that Anand Mohan is an immoral drunkard and the marriage would surely end in divorce. Anand Mohan had thus a score to settle with the swami and his institution.

The story of Arul Jyothi in this background is easy to understand.From the age of two, she was brought up in the swami's ashram in Sri Lanka. When the swami migrated to India, she followed him along with some other children of the ashram. She first lived in Trichy and after three years shifted to its present site in Fathimanagar. In July 1996 . . . she was 21 years old.

Ram recounts the prosecutor's case against the swami:

Eight years earlier she was raped in her own room where she was sleeping alongside another girl. She complained to none. After three years the swami had a second act of sex with her. Still after another year the swami called her to his room but she did not go. Thereupon in the presence of more than 200 persons in the dharmasala, the swami pulled her hair, knocked her against the wall and pricked her eyes with a stick. She alleged still a fourth act of rape five days before the arrest of the swami on November 19, 1994. She admitted that she had never told anybody about these forcible rapes. One hour before his arrest the swami told her that he will soon return and asked her to keep her mouth shut. While in police custody she discovered that she was pregnant.

On February 21 1995 she was aborted. In cross-examination the steps, stages and installments in which Arul Jyothi's story was fabricated from time to time was brought out with great clarity.

Ram's response was that a medical exam showed her to be 'used to sexual intercourse', and that

The police then got another statement from her after the medical examination. In her statement as recorded by the police she mentioned none of the acts of rape as deposed to in courts but alleged a totally different one and only one and not four. She declared that one day at 3 p.m. in the puja room she had intercourse with the swami, but this was with her consent. She gave neither the date, nor the month, nor the year of this single act of sexual intercourse.

But she admitted that at that time she was 19 years old. This act even if admitted to be true, did not make out any offence of rape. But it is obvious that police pressure was building up and they had managed at least to secure this not very helpful admission from her. It certainly damaged the image of the swami as a spiritual man but no charge of rape could be sustained on this story.

At the trial, the police got DNA evidence from the Hyderabad Forensic Laboratory to prove that the swami had fathered the foetus aborted from Arul Jyothi. Never had an expert been so demolished by cross-examination. His record was shown to be that of a miserable fake. When it was shown to him that the alleged examination of the foetus was not even done by using recognised enzymes which would identify the polymorphic sites, he threw up his hands and said that the whole experiment was done by his associate who alone can explain. The foetus was also examined by Dr Wilson Wall, an expert attached to the Home Office in London. He reported that the foetus was certainly not fathered by the swami. But a respectable scientist of international repute, who came to give evidence when no other experts were available in India, was brushed aside as being interested evidence.

Ram's British expert witness, Dr Wilson J. Wall, reviewed the techniques that the Indian laboratory used to examine the DNA evidence, pronouncing, 'When I say that the Accused has not fathered this foetus, what I mean to say is that there is not even a chance, or even an infinitesimal chance of him being the father.'[6]

After reading the court's bitter condemnation of the swami and Ram's defence, it is easy to see why emotions run so high in criminal law cases. We also see why advocates for one side of a story tend to demonize those on the other side. In this case, Ram's client 'was sentenced to two life imprisonments and denied the benefit of any remissions, which are admissible to all prisoners'.

Whether this is an example of judicial incompetence is for the reader to judge.

Ram claims the Indian judiciary began to decline in 1973 during the Emergency, when Indira Gandhi adopted the concept of a 'committed judiciary'. Ram wrote,[7] 'Mr Mohan Kumaramangalam, lawyer and politician . . . claimed that judicial appointments cannot be made without reference to the social philosophy of the judges.' This led to the idea of 'committed judges'. It was in search of this paradigm that Mrs Gandhi 'superseded Justices Shelat, Hegde and Grover and appointed Justice A.N. Ray as the Chief Justice'.

The legal commentator A.G. Noorani, wrote, 'On December 28, 1979, Justice T.P.S. Chawla of the Delhi High Court delivered a 347-page judgment quashing the prosecution of Indira Gandhi and Pranab Mukherjee for refusing to testify before the Shah Commission. In some 50 pages, Justice Chawla considered the issues of judicial review of the Emergency and the relevance of the oath of office to a Minister's accountability to law. Those pages reek of error.'[8]

Ram writes of the first attempt to impeach a Supreme Court justice: 'The people have not forgotten the notorious case of Justice V. Ramaswami. A Parliament-appointed Enquiry Committee of three judges found him guilty on various counts of corruption. However, the ruling party prevented his removal and ensured the defeat of the impeachment motion by the simple device of not voting.'[9]

On July 20,1990,[10] the Chief Justice of the Supreme Court announced in court that he would take action after the media had reported that Justice Ramaswami had made 'ostentatious expenditure' on his official residence as Chief Justice of Punjab and Haryana. 'The Chief Justice constituted a committee consisting of Justices B.C. Ray, Jagannath Shetty and M.N. Venkatachalaiah of the Supreme Court seeking their advice on the question whether the involvement of Justice V. Ramaswami in certain proceedings in relation to certain administrative decisions and certain other administrative acts and omissions as Chief Justice of Punjab and Haryana High Court would render it embarrassing for him to function as a judge of the Supreme Court of India.'

Their advice was that he did not need to desist from judicial functions while the matter was pending. 'This led to an unprecedented resolution by the Supreme Court Bar Association on February 1, 1991, calling for the impeachment of Ramaswami and calling upon the Chief Justice not to assign him any judicial work.' Ram went to Chief Justice Sabyasachi Mukherjee to make this request. To his credit, Justice Mukherjee complied, saying in a lengthy letter dated 20 July, 1990, 'I was constrained, in those circumstances, to advise Brother Ramaswami to desist from discharging judicial functions so long as the investigations continued and his name was cleared on this aspect.'[11] This prudent decision did not last long beyond Justice Mukherjee's premature death in September 1990.

At Ram's request, the Lok Sabha formed a committee under the Judges (Enquiry) Act of 1968, consisting of Supreme Court Justice P.B. Sawant, Chief Justice P.D. Desai of the Bombay High Court and Justice O. Chinnappa Reddy, a retired Supreme Court judge. Then the next day, Prime Minister Chandrashekhar's government fell and the Lok Sabha was dissolved.

As a result, Subramanian Swamy, now the Law Minister, and G. Ramaswamy, the Attorney General, ruled that the committee's mandate had lapsed. In response, Ram and several other lawyers formed the Sub-Committee on Judicial Accountability, and filed a petition with the Supreme Court to reinstate the committee.

In May 1991,[12] the court directed the Committee to resume its investigation of Judge Ramaswami.

The case returned to the Supreme Court in October.[13] Ram, Shanti Bhushan, Prashant Bhushan, the Additional Attorney General, the Solicitor General, and 32 other eminent lawyers represented the petitioners. Kapil Sibal, who had represented Ramaswami before Parliament, filed a petition in his defence. The petitioners asked, 'first, that the Union of India be directed to take immediate steps to enable the Inquiry Committee to discharge its functions under the Judges (Inquiry) Act, 1968 and, second, that during the pendency of the proceedings before the Committee the concerned Judge should be restrained from performing judicial functions and from exercising Judicial powers'.

Ram argued that in India, 'impeachment motions are *sui generis* in their nature and that they do not lapse' in contrast to the British tradition. His other argument was that 'The Speaker merely decides that the matter might bear investigation.' He went on, 'No decisions affecting the rights, interests or legitimate expectation can be said to have been taken. Sri Jethmalani sought to point out that these proceedings could not be equated with disciplinary or penal proceedings. The Speaker does not decide anything against the Judge at that stage.'

On the first point, the court said that under the Judges Act, that statement that a motion 'does not lapse upon the dissolution of the House is a binding declaration.' So the Sub-committee won.

On the second point, the court did not bar Judge Ramaswami from exercising his judicial powers during the pending investigation, because that would mean that the Supreme Court would be sitting in judgement on one of their own judges, whose power is not vested in the court. On this point, the Sub-committee lost.

The impeachment procedure has three steps in India. Steps one and two are for Parliament to appoint a judges' committee and for the committee to proceed according to judicial standards. This decision by the court allowed it to take the third step, which was to go back to Parliament for a vote.

The Parliamentary committee did find Ramaswami guilty of 11

out of 14 charges.[14] However, when it reported its recommendations to the Lok Sabha on May 11, 1993, the motion failed for lack of a majority, and a two-year effort came to a fruitless end.

Ram and the Sub-Committee were not done with Ramaswami. They filed a petition[15] before the Supreme Court to institute proceedings against Justice V. Ramaswami for criminal contempt because he had written a letter to the Enquiry Committee making 'certain sweeping allegations against certain Judges and the Judiciary'. The court expressed its unhappiness about the episode, but it declined to institute contempt proceedings.

In the 1999 elections, Ramaswami ran for the Lok Sabha and failed, so he finally he did leave the court, but not through impeachment.

Another attempt to clean up the judiciary came in 1998, when Ram, Shanti Bhushan, and four other members of the Sub-Committee on Judicial Accountability sent a petition to the Chief Justice objecting to the appointment of Justice M.M. Punchhi as Chief Justice of India, based on seven instances of alleged misconduct.

According to *Outlook*, 'The allegations against Punchhi range from passing orders on matters in which he had a personal interest to protecting a fellow judge (V. Ramaswami) accused of improprieties to accepting plots of land from former Haryana chief minister Bhajan Lal in exchange for a favourable ruling.'[16]

According to *Rediff*: 'Jethmalani has made it clear that nothing short of an inquiry by Chief Justice of India J.S. Verma into the allegations against Justice M.M. Punchhi would stop the Committee on Judicial Accountability [CJA] from pressing for an impeachment motion against the judge.[17]

'Justice Punchhi is the country's second senior-most judge, against whom the CJA has levelled serious allegations. The timing of these allegations—the judge is likely to get the country's top judicial job next January—has created a storm in the legal world, and the Supreme Court Bar Association last week suspended seven CJA members, including Jethmalani, for submitting a memorandum against the judge.

'Caught in the whirlpool of such serious questions, the Supreme Court Bar Association unanimously decided on Tuesday to suspend the lawyers who raise doubts about the judge. Though the suspended members can practise in court, they will not be able to use the SCBA library or enter the bar's chamber.'

In fact, fewer than 600 of the 3000 members of the Supreme Court Bar Association even were present to vote that day when the Bar suspended Ram and his colleagues. Ram essentially laughed it off. It was just one of many times Ram has been suspended or kicked out of an association, party or office. And the judge was appointed anyhow.

Ram kept trying to ensure that judicial appointments would meet his standards:[18] 'The Committee on Judicial Accountability (CJA) has expressed concern at the government returning the recommendation of the Supreme Court collegium for elevation of Allahabad High Court Chief Justice C.K. Prasad to the Supreme Court on the ground that it was made without proper verification.'

Two other judges came under such heavy scrutiny that they both eventually resigned. One was Justice Soumitra Sen, a judge of the High Court of Calcutta, accused of misappropriation of funds when he was a practicing lawyer. After a Committee of Inquiry gave an unfavourable report to the Rajya Sabha and that body voted in favour of removing him, the judge sent in a letter of resignation before the Lok Sabha had a chance to vote. Similarly, Justice P.D. Dinakaran of the High Court of Madras, later Chief Judge of the High Court of Karnataka, was being considered for appointment to the Supreme Court when accusations surfaced that he had 'illegally amassed wealth/assets on a large scale'.[19] A motion was introduced in the Rajya Sabha to remove him, and a Committee of Inquiry was appointed. Again, once he saw that the proceedings were not trending in his favour, Justice Dinakaran sent in a letter of resignation.

Ram was not the only one waging a war against corrupt and incompetent judges. Another was Prashant Bhushan, a lawyer and social activist, son of the eminent lawyer Shanti Bhushan. He has been active in the Centre for Public Interest Litigation, the

People's Union for Civil Liberties and the Committee on Judicial Accountability. He also has been the convener of the Working Committee of the Campaign for Judicial Accountability and Judicial Reforms. He and his father both marched in support of Anna Hazare, in his campaign against corruption. In an article published on September 5, 2009, he said in an interview with *Tehelka* that out of the last 16–17 Supreme Court Chief Justices, half were corrupt. One Justice he cited specifically was Justice S.H. Kapadia, accused of a conflict of interest. The judge had shares in a company that had a matter before him, although the judge maintained that the counsel knew that and had registered no objection. Harish Salve, a senior advocate, filed a contempt of court suit against Bhushan,[20] and Bhushan filed a lengthy affidavit repeating the assertion that half of the last 16–17 Chief Justices of the Supreme Court have been corrupt and documenting the basis for this assertion.[21]

Defending him in this case, Ram made the following interesting argument:[22]

'All contempt charges in the high courts are subject to the defence that a bone fide belief in the truth is a defence, even if this 'truth' may not be objectively true. This is because the Indian Legal Code applies this principle to all offences, and even contempt falls under the definition of an offence. While nobody seems to read it, the definition of an offence in the Indian Legal Code has certain specified instances followed by a catch-all category, for any "offence punishable by a fine or imprisonment".'

Otherwise, the argument would have to be based on the Contempt of Courts Act, 1971 as modified in 2006, which reads that 'the court may permit, in any proceeding for contempt of court, justification by truth as a valid defence if it is satisfied that it is in public interest and the request for invoking the said defence is bona fide'. Thus, the contempt laws would only allow truth as a defence, but the Indian Legal Code allows a *bona fide belief* that the statement is true, an easier matter to prove.[23]

This was clever. Instead of arguing from the laws on contempt of court as expected, Ram went back to the Indian Legal Code itself. As Ram says, this helps the judges, because they will not have to make a finding that a judge was corrupt. Bhushan could be acquitted just because he believed he was telling the truth.

In the November 10, 2010 decision, the court considered arguments challenging whether Harish Salve had the standing to bring the case, but it dismissed these objections, concluding that it would schedule a hearing. Meanwhile, the attorneys were free to file affidavits on the matter within the next eight weeks. Since the judge was still on the court, proceedings were likely to remain on hold until his retirement.

Ram explains how hard it is to get rid of an incompetent judge:[24] 'The provisions of the Contempt of Court Act 1971 make it extremely difficult to undertake a critical appraisal of the judiciary. A criminal prosecution against a Judge can be launched only with the prior permission of the President of India which is unexpected and can come only in the rarest of rare cases . . .' He goes on to say that, 'Theoretically, impeachment is available, but its procedure is too cumbersome.'

'Impeachment, a purely political remedy, must be scrapped and the powers of the federal court conferred on the National Judicial Commission. Instead of having two different commissions for appointments to the Supreme Court and High Courts, there should be one. Only the state government and the leader of the opposition in the state legislature must be consulted for High Court appointments.'[25]

Ram wryly notes one relevant court decision,[26] 'On the core issue . . . whether in the appointing process the executive was paramount, or judiciary was paramount, the Judges said that it is the executive alone, which will decide . . . I am glad that, that part of the judgement has been reversed. It had produced in a short time two kinds of judges—those who know law and those who know the law minister.'

The interminable delays in Indian court cases were a problem that Ram really wanted to address as Law Minister. 'It is a scandal that 30 million cases are pending in the subordinate courts. Prestigious law commissions have time and again reported that we need to multiply our courts five times.' A British judge, Sir

Michael Fysh, who once practiced law in India, told this author that he had argued cases in which the original plaintiff was dead, the respondent was dead, and the original judge was dead. He said that delays of 25 years between the start of a case and a final verdict were not uncommon. Nevertheless, once he became Law Minister, Ram's championship of a bill to correct this problem set the entire Bar against him.

Ram has long advocated increasing judges' salaries to decrease the incentive for corruption, and while he was in the Cabinet as Minister of Urban Affairs it happened. 'Before April, 1998, the salaries of Supreme Court and High Court judges were very low ... the Government of India promulgated the High Court and Supreme Court Judges (Conditions of Service) Amendment Ordinance 1998. Its objective was to raise the salaries and pensions of judges in the High Courts and the Supreme Court.'[27] Ram talked a great deal about how important this was when he was a minister, his passion making a big impression on this author and her husband.

Three cases, called the judges' cases,[28] dealt with judicial appointments. Before these, judges were appointed by the Union Law Minister. The first case, in 1980, concerned transfers of judges from one High Court to another. This was overruled by the Supreme Court in what is called the First Judges case.[29] In this, the court said that the recommendation of the Chief Justice of India with respect to a judicial appointment was not constitutionally binding.

That decision was appealed to a nine-member bench in *Supreme Court Advocates-on-Record Association vs. Union of India 1994 SC 268, the Second Judges* case. This case resulted in the creation of a Judicial Collegium, consisting of the Chief Justice of India and two senior-most Supreme Court judges. The problem that emerged was that the three did not necessarily agree.

The Third Judges' case was the Special Reference No. 1 of 1998, decided on October 28, 1998 by a bench of nine judges, which re-established the Judicial Collegium in a new format. The Chief Justice of India now forms a collegium of the four senior-most puisne judges of the Supreme Court in order to appoint justices of the Supreme Court or to transfer any High Court judge.

To appoint a High Court judge, the Chief Justice must consult the two senior-most judges of the Supreme Court, including any Supreme Court justice who may come from the High Court to which the appointment is to be made. So, if an appointment is to be made to the Madras High Court, the collegium consults the senior-most judge of the Supreme Court who came originally from the Madras High Court.

Unfortunately, that has led to a different set of problems. Instead of ministers showing favouritism in appointing judges, now the system has judges appointing judges, often the ones they favour, a potentially incestuous matter.

The *Indian Express* suggests that the drawbacks of the current collegium are the administrative burden, non-transparency, and a limited choice of candidates. The reporter says, 'A National Judicial Commission remains a proposal.'[30]

After Ram last introduced his bill, it was resurrected by the Constitution (98th Amendment) Bill of 2003, introduced by then Law Minister Arun Jaitley. This too lapsed.

Now 'two important bills concerning the judiciary came before the Rajya Sabha on 5 September—the Constitution (One Hundred and Twentieth Amendment) Bill, 2013, (LX of 2013) and the Judicial Appointments Commission Bill, 2013 (LXI of 2013).'[31] Ram opposed both, the first bill because it 'sanctifies the Commission by the introduction of Article 124 A in the Constitution', but it does not prescribe its composition in the Constitution. That remains open to change by any subsequent administration, potentially returning to control by the executive. Of interest, he writes, 'the Bills have been passed . . . I was the lone opponent, and I am confident that the Constitution Amendment Bill cannot pass the test of judicial scrutiny.'

30

Rani

The year Rani died, she wrote an autobiography. It is unpublished, but it will help us tell the story of Rani and her father. When Ram was elected to Parliament in 1977, he essentially moved to Delhi, to a house that Parliament provided, first a house on Janpath, next on Harishchandra Marg and now at 2 Akbar Road, opposite the Prime Minister's house. When she moved to Delhi, Rani first lived in the bungalow in Friends's Colony when she ran the 'de facto Israeli Embassy'. Over the subsequent years she stayed in other Delhi apartments, but for many years her real home was with her father.

In 1987 Rani finally moved to an apartment on Feroze Shah Road. She married when she was in her forties, in a ceremony held at Ram's house on Harishchandra Marg Lane, and she stayed in the same apartment after her divorce until she became ill.

Rani was Ram's family in Delhi. Their relationship was father–daughter, senior lawyer–junior lawyer, and something of a long-running high drama. Still, Rani and Ram depended on each other. Rani decorated Ram's house, ran the domestic establishment, hired the servants, fired the servants, and hosted their social events. In addition, Rani acted as co-counsel on many of Ram's cases, especially in the 1980s and 1990s.

Rani immersed herself in the cultural and artistic life of Delhi, the poetry readings, recitals, and art openings. She entertained the great, popular, and famous in the arts at their house, but she also supported the work of Buddhist lamas, who would visit to express their gratitude. She dressed in elegant saris, striking shawls, and precious jewellery; shopping for more at every possible opportunity but giving away clothes, jewellery, everything to her friends for special occasions or even just to make them happy.

The relationship between the father and daughter was volatile. Rani wrote that her personal life had a pattern of inappropriate relationships, but she objected strongly to her father's peccadillos too. Sometimes she made her point in the house with slammed doors, fire and brimstone. When Rani became enraged, she would move out to stay with friends or she would rent an apartment for a time. Once she moved out because of an argument about a servant. Anyhow Rani always would come back. When Ram travelled to conferences, he loved to have his glamorous daughter with him, even if he had to wait endlessly for her to finish her shopping.

None of this gives a picture of Rani in her captivating, sophisticated prime. With her long brown hair down, or piled high on her head, her tawny skin, high cheekbones, womanly shape, and tiny waist, she always turned heads. Her taste was impeccable, accessories the latest. One evening for a special event, she was dazzling in a simple necklace of round gold discs and a stiffly draped sari that looked like spun gold.

Rani could be imperious. Our first encounter in 1973 made an indelible impression. When she met us at the airport, Rani asked me for my programme. I had brought some silk from a trip to Thailand, and I proposed we go to a tailor early in the trip, so my new outfits would be ready when I left. Rani promptly asked whether we should go to her expensive tailor or her cheap tailor. Too embarrassed to ask what she meant, I humbly showed her the precious Thai silks that I had brought all the way around the world from my last trip to Asia. She looked at them and said, 'We will go to my cheap tailor.'

I also recall one evening when Rani suggested we join the family at a wedding party. I was aghast, because I had not brought a suitably elaborate wardrobe or jewellery. Assured that nobody knew me anyhow, I put on the most appropriate silk sari and the best piece of jewellery that I had. Since I have become a silversmith and I create silver jewellery with coloured gemstones, fortunately I had proudly brought a few examples of my most impressive work.

At the affair, I saw broad diamond necklaces hanging in loops from strands of three carat diamonds, diamond chandelier earrings, diamonds in the nose, the hair and on bracelets— in some cases all on one woman! I asked Rani if all these diamonds were real. She said, 'Oh yes. It would not be auspicious to wear anything that is not real. You cannot wear'—and here she lifted up the choicest pendant I had brought on the trip—'costume jewellery like this'.

There was much more to Rani than that though. Before she started in private practice, Rani taught constitutional law at the postgraduate level at Kishinchand Chellaram College. In her law practice, Rani became a senior advocate, and she worked with Ram on many cases.

Like Indira Gandhi, who was first her father's hostess and consigliere, before she became his successor, Rani once saw herself as following Ram in his career. On the other hand, Rani began to focus increasing amounts of time on defending beaten and burned wives. Once, Rani represented an aggrieved family and Ram represented the oppressive husband. After some time in practice, Rani founded the Mahila Dakshata Samiti to fight the social evils that plague women in India. Later she served on the board of Commit-2-Change, a non-profit organization started by Shobha's daughter- in-law Sejal Gehani. Ram came to believe she was marginalizing herself in the legal profession. In his view, she stereotyped herself as a female lawyer, rather than doing the muscular cases necessary for a serious career.

In her autobiography, Rani explains, 'Campaigns and advocacy for women's human rights took a lot of my time, leaving me little time for practice in the Supreme Court. Advancing the law creatively made my practice meaningful and challenging. I was not cut out to be the kind of the renowned lawyer my father is. He is the country's greatest criminal lawyer, perhaps the greatest cross examiner of all time and also a great constitutional lawyer. As a human rights lawyer I was selective of clients and chose consciously to refuse cases against those accused in dowry death cases and cases of cruelty and crimes like rape against women. My personal experiences of a woman in a patriarchal and unequal society had been a defining experience.'

In the early 1980s, Lataa Krishnamurthy came to work for Rani as her junior, but Lataa soon saw that Rani's was not the type of practice she wanted. As soon as she had an opportunity to work with Ram, Lataa gravitated towards his practice, and the lodestone of his star. Meanwhile, Rani's range of cases became narrower, and her NGOs competed with her law practice.

To give a sense of the woman that was Rani, we can share portions of her writing:[1]

Rani wrote of her mother:

My mother was named Durga—after the powerful Hindu goddess. According to Hindu mythology the goddess Durga fought many mahishasuras—demons and evil forces. So did my mother. She was only 16 [sic] when she married Ram, my father— he was 18 then. It was an arranged marriage. She adored him even after he married a second time. He never divorced my mother. She was only twenty-six at the time. I was four. She lived in denial at first, later resignation and then acceptance. She was a great survivor. I took after her in that respect.

My mother did not exercise power. Patriarchy is very deeply entrenched in Hindu society. She chose powerlessness—it was the only way to keep her marriage intact with two young daughters. My step mother resented this—she wanted to be the only wife. My mother wielded that power.

Her mother's position as the first wife influenced Rani profoundly, and she devoted her life to helping powerless women. She defended many dowry disputes, both as a lawyer and through her NGOs. She told us horrific stories of women saved from unthinkable abuses. One woman was left pinned on the floor of a hot balcony for a month. Wives were burned. Husbands and their mothers worked in collusion to pour oil on the wife, set her on fire, and bribe the police to write up a report that the wife's sari had caught fire in the kitchen. As she explained, the mother resented the wife, and both of the perpetrators hoped to entrap another wife afterwards, in order to obtain another dowry. And these cases were not confined to one social class, or one religion. She spoke of these abuses in conferences all over the world. At these conferences, she made lasting friendships.

I have always loved Singapore because of its orchid gardens, avenues of green trees and impeccably clean roads. I have been a visitor to Singapore several times for workshops and conferences in the 80s and 90s. Those were hectic, energetic and passionate days. It was as part of the Asia–Pacific Women's movement. I was at the time an Executive Member of an NGO, the Asia–Pacific Forum on Women, Law & Development with headquarters in Malaysia (now relocated to Chiang Mai in Thailand). Many warm, intimate and enduring friendships were cemented at these gatherings. Our common problems were shared and discussed. Strategies to raise awareness were devised and determined efforts were launched to make women visible, by insisting on a Human Rights Agenda to make governments accountable.

My friends were all women of unique integrity, character, imagination and courage. There were Asma Jehangir and Hina Jilani from Lahore in Pakistan who fought tyrannical regimes, and Noeleen Heyzer whose powerful vision and leadership made her the natural choice as director of UNIFEM. There were so many women who deftly guided, with deep commitment, the Beijing Declaration of Human Rights and Platform of Action. Like my friend Professor Virada Somaswasdi in Thailand, Farida Hussain from Malaysia, Savitri, Nandini and Radhika Coomaraswamy from Sri Lanka, Salma in Bangaldesh and so many others. These incredible women were my mentors and soul sisters.

Their initiatives and ceaseless zeal in ensuring human rights for women inspired me to go to West Sahara in 1996—a virtual desert where the West Saharan women had assumed leadership since their men were at war with the Moroccans who had occupied their desert land. Along with many other women we celebrated the 50th anniversary of the West Sahara government in exile.

Under the stars at night I asked these brave West Sahara women what would happen once they had driven the Moroccan armies out of West Sahara. Would they be equal or would the Islamic personal law prevail once the Revolution was successful? These were disturbing questions and there were no reassuring answers.

Mongolia was another mind-blowing experience. In 1999, I visited Ulan Bator with my Philippine colleague Jean. We were there to discuss the implementation of Human Rights under their newly enacted Constitution. Our Mongolian sisters were eager to understand concepts which were new to them having been under Russian subjugation for so long. We explained to the Russian Women Judges of the Supreme Court of Mongolia, how Public Interest Litigation in India had enlarged access to justice and human Rights. We provided them with new insights and visions of the priceless gift of democracy and the benefits of Constitutional Government.

In 1995, Rani edited a book, *Kali's Yug: Empowerment, Human Rights and Dowry Deaths*. The articles, several by Rani, offered legal innovations for improving the status of women. In her introduction, she explains that Kali originally stood for feminine energy. Kali is another name for the goddess Durga, Rani's mother.

WARLAW distributed the book at a conference in Beijing, China. 'Mr V.P. Singh [the future prime minister] had kindly consented to draw the cover picture of a spiritually and dynamic Kali. Kali is the dark and powerful goddess who challenges the social status quo. She is the Devi, a symbol heralding a dynamic social order inspired by compassion and equality for all regardless of sex. If women could make these connections that the Goddesses represented they would be catalysts for much needed changes in their lives. In 1994 I attended the Vienna Conference of Human Rights. It was a very special occasion where India ratified the Convention on

Elimination of All Forms of Discrimination against Women 1979 (CEDAW)—the magna carta of women's human rights.

'The powerful women's movements at the Convention insisted that governments hold state actors responsible for ensuring a violence-free atmosphere in the private spaces of the family where women were most exposed to violence. We succeeded in convincing world leaders that violence against women, even if not in the public domain, was a violation of the Human Rights of Women if the State did not take action against such pervasive private oppression.'

Rani wrote in another book chapter[2] that under Hindu law, property rights and succession laws are unfavourable to women. One example was her own attempt to adopt a Muslim child. This is impossible under Hindu law, and there is no secular law in India. Calling her father a male chauvinist, she says that one of her motives for studying these legal matters came from seeing the way women were treated in her community. During the Emergency she noticed dowry offences in the paper every day. A propos, she helped organize a woman's wing of the Janata Party.

Just before *Roe vs. Wade* passed in the US, Rani gave a memorable speech at the UN. Sandra Day O'Connor, Gloria Steinem, Ethyl Kennedy, and Bella Abzug were in the audience. Ethyl Kennedy invited her over afterwards. The speech began: 'Ladies, I come from a country of many Calcuttas.'

Rani found spiritual relief in the Hindu practices of Vedanta, which she discovered at the Vivekananda Institute in Bangalore. Later she become devoted to the Mother and Sri Aurobindo, and she often went on retreat to their ashram in Pondicherry. She also studied Buddhism with Tibetan monks.

Ram shares Rani's admiration for Aurobindo's great philosophical work, *Savitri*. He calls it one of the greatest pieces of poetry ever written. Ram's copy has page after page of notes and comments written in his tiny handwriting. That should not surprise anyone who has ever sat and nursed a drink on his porch on an evening with a group of local literati, only to find the conversation suddenly veer into everyone's personal concepts of karma and reincarnation.

Rani wrote about planning for her father's return from the United States after the Emergency:

> I had personally met Shri Morarji Desai to request him to permit my father to stand as a Janata Party candidate, particularly since he had been very active in raising public opinion abroad against the emergency. Mr Desai could not assure me a seat for my father since he felt that my father should not have left India. Instead he asked me whether I would stand for elections.
>
> He chided me for practicing divorce law and went on to tell me about his own marriage. He narrated that his wife, Gajraben had not been to school and was uneducated when they married. He felt that this was not a reason to divorce her, despite the incompatibility. Instead he tried to teach her and educate her as much as he could. Mr Morarji Desai reminded me a great deal of my grandfather who would preach to my father about the evils of social drinking. Like Morarji Desai my grandfather also believed in urine therapy!

As Rani tells it, anxiety over whether her father would return safely from America without being arrested gave her a near-fatal intestinal haemorrhage in 1977. That fateful evening, Ram landed, made a great speech at the airport to his adoring fans, and returned home to a big celebration. And Rani began to haemorrhage:

> There was no one at home except a servant. My father and family had left to attend a felicitation meeting for my father. I called a friend, since my condition was deteriorating. A family physician was asked by my friend to come immediately and check my condition.
>
> My family doctor was at a cocktail party—he was reluctant to come. He did so eventually. Since I was bleeding, he immediately administered an injection of Largactil. He should have sent me to a hospital. Instead, he left to resume his cocktail party which I had interrupted. After he departed, the bleeding started again; I was once again drained in a pool of blood. Fortunately, by that

time my father returned. He was shocked to see my condition. He lifted me in his arms and rushed me in a car to the Jaslok Hospital. I was immediately administered eight bottles of blood which was a life-saving and divine intervention.

And so, Rani became infected with Hepatitis C.

On March 18, 1997, her mother died, a gentle woman who had lived only for her family. It is hard to describe the woman they lost. Durga built a life for herself, and she was supremely realistic about it. She still retained her beauty to the end of her life. She became plump, and her face filled with lines, but her eyes retained their wicked flash of humour, her mouth its radiant smile. Durga had an innate intelligence, largely unrecognized by her family as is the case of so many women who missed out on a formal education. Looking at her children, one can see that she passed on her looks, her brains, and her sense of humour.

After she died, many friends and family, both of close and remote acquaintance, came to pay their respects. One story Durga herself would have appreciated. The Chief Minister of Maharashtra, Manohar Joshi, came to make a condolence call at a time when Ram had been trying to catch him to discuss an important matter. At the house the minister spoke to Ram at length about how sorry he was and how he remembered what fun they used to have at the great parties his wife gave. Realizing that the man had confused her with Ratna, Ram said nothing. Suddenly Ratna entered the room. The minister turned pale, but he recovered quickly. Turning to the other guests, he said, 'Ram would also fake his own wife's death to get me to come over.'

Rani practised law even as her health deteriorated. Her father clearly agreed with Desai about her practice. Still, Rani did what she could with her dwindling energy.

Twenty years after her blood transfusion she was diagnosed with cirrhosis at the University of Michigan. Shobha and this author, both physicians, did the research to find out what was necessary, and after months of exhortation, Shobha persuaded her to go on the list for liver transplantation. Up until then she had been patronizing purveyors of vedantic medicine and spiritual cures, even enriching one alternative medicine practitioner with a monthly retainer. This was not new. She had always been superstitious about her liver. Since childhood she had referred to a small whitehead on her cheek as a rat bite which would slowly weaken her liver. As a child, one day she got into a fight with Shobha, and Shobha hit her cheek. She screamed that she had hit her on her bite; she would become sick and weaken her liver. Her liver was weak. Maybe she was prescient.

Rani went into liver failure when she was in New York to address the UN. She had just returned from a trip to Nepal, and had contracted an infection there which probably precipitated the crisis. Nevertheless, pushing herself, she went off to New York.

In 1997, I am invited to participate in a U.N. meeting on the constitution of the proposed International Criminal Court . . . Many other women's NGOs are participating. The focus is on crimes such as the mass rape of women and children in Bosnia and Rwanda. I attend the meetings every day at the U.N. On the last of the meetings in August, 1997 it was decided that India's Independence Day would be celebrated with a concert by the great maestro & Sarod player, Pandit Ali Akbar Khan to mark the occasion and the end of the U.N. Session. I had developed a fever. I had not been looking or feeling well.

When I returned from the Concert I was cold and shivering with a shooting fever. Fortunately my sister arrived from Detroit. She is a doctor and noticed that my eyes were yellow. I also had ascites. She called my friend Vandana and together they decided to rush me, in an ambulance, to the Mt. Sinai Hospital.

Rani was deathly ill. While she was in the hospital in New York Deepak Chopra sent her Ayurvedic medicines and a masseur, and she wrote '. . . Bella Abzug, who contested as Mayor of New York, is a friend and ally in the women's movement. She visits me on a wheelchair in the hospital.'

When she was allowed to leave the hospital, Rani came back to Shobha's home in Michigan. Ram came too, and the family held an intimate celebration of his 75th birthday. Rani remembered it as festive. To us it seemed sombre, nothing like the gala affair he had in India. When we last saw Rani in Michigan, she showed all the signs of liver failure. Her skin, which used to be a lovely olive colour, had gone greyish-yellow with jaundice. Her abdomen, once so slim, was distended with fluid.

Up until recently, Rani was not ready for a transplant. Now she was too sick, and the university sent her home to die.

She stopped in London on the way home, to say her goodbyes. As they ate lunch, a friend asked her what on earth was wrong. Rani told her. The friend immediately took out her cellphone and called a friend of hers, the premier liver surgeon in London, perhaps in the world. He came over that evening:

'My friend Namita Punjabi brought Dr Nigel Heaton the noted legendary transplant surgeon of all of Europe and England to my hotel at St. James' Court. He examines my medical reports and agrees to arrange for a liver transplant at the King's College Hospital in London.'

Nobody could forget that time. Rani was in the hospital for six months while Dr Heaton's team tried to get her in shape for surgery, assuming a donor could be found. Maya came to the hospital and spent time staying in Rani's room, as did Shobha. Most of the time, Shobha and Ram stayed in a London hotel owned by the Tata family. Rani's servant girl remained at her side at the hospital. Rani lay in the hospital, holding the picture of her mother. Ram consulted his astrologer in India.

On December 19, 1997, the servant called the hotel to tell Shobha and Ram, 'They have taken away Miss Rani.'

Shobha asked what time she died. The girl said, 'No. They have taken her for surgery.'

Ram and Shobha rushed to the hospital. There had been an automobile accident right outside, and a liver suddenly had become available. Ordinarily, the British healthcare system would not allow a liver to be transplanted into a foreign national unless there was no British citizen ready and qualified to receive it; however, by a remarkable turn of fortune, this liver could not be transplanted into a British citizen. It was blood type B-positive, and most British are type-A. Miraculously, the best match would be with an Indian.

In less than a week after the operation, Rani's ascites was gone, her skin was turning back to its normal golden colour, and she was starting to heal.

Shobha accompanied Rani when she returned to India and moved into an apartment in Ram's house. As she developed new medical problems, practitioners of various stripes turned up to help. One was a paediatrician who specialized in reiki—the laying-on of hands—who proposed treating both Rani's ailments and Ram after his knee replacement, at Rs 1000 a visit. Shobha tried to get her out of the house, but she was insistent. 'That's all right, I can do treatment from outside the door.' Shobha tried to shoo her even further away, but she said, 'I can do reiki from home.' Finally Shobha asked, 'The farther away you go, does it get more expensive or less?'

Shobha returned to the United States. Rani had a reprieve for a few years, but her medical problems continued to evolve. In time she developed brittle diabetes, and her kidneys deteriorated. Despite everything, she kept up with her NGOs, continued looking after her adopted son Ali and took her trips to Pondicherry.

Finally, in 2005 Rani's doctor told her she needed a kidney transplant.

I look composed when my father visits me. Quietly I tell him the doctors' verdict. He is visibly shattered. I hasten to add that I am not inclined to undergo another surgery. On the other hand the thought of dialysis for the rest of my life is alarming. I tell him that I will bide my time before I make a final decision. When he departs he is a very sad man. There is no spring in his step. His face, which glows with the pride of his many achievements, is crestfallen. He is in deep thought. Perhaps he feels partially responsible for my physical break down.

Rani's adopted son Ali wanted to donate one of his kidneys, but he was not a related donor. Mahesh matched, but he was about to have hip surgery and was the father of a family. Rani did not want him to give up a kidney. Now she needed an unrelated donor.

My wonderful and compassionate Buddhist friend, Tsering Dolkar assured me that she would find me a Tibetan donor. We are both trustees of the Karmakaju Buddhist Foundation. His Holiness Tai Situ Rinpoche, Kachu of the Karmapa who has a monastery in Sherabling in Himachal Pradesh promised to donote his kidney, if necessary. Earlier, after my liver transplant in 1998, I had visited His Holiness the Dalai Lama in Dharamshala and, in a personal meeting with him, he had in reply to my question about the Buddhist view on organ donations stated that organ donation was an act of 'seva' and compassion which was good for one's karma and should be encouraged.

Meanwhile my family and my father in particular, were trying to tap their contacts for possible donors. My father got in touch with Dr Vijayalaxmi in Chennai, a reputed medical practitioner and social worker. She was an election campaigner for my father during various elections. Due to Dr Vijayalaxmi's tireless efforts one of her patients, Mr Murugan, who happened to be a religious person and an accomplished musician offered to donate his kidney.

Ram clearly was anguished over Rani as her condition deteriorated, but he has always been able to compartmentalize his feelings; they do not show unless you know him well. Still, his face always darkened when he talked about her medical condition, or Janak's. One year, when Shobha had life-threatening reflux, Mahesh was considering hip surgery, Janak was recovering from a serious illness, and Rani was beset with tribulations, he shared the worry that these illnesses had been visited on the children in Biblical fashion for the sins of the father. But I have only heard him say that once.

Ram has paid for these medical problems quite literally. No insurance covered Rani's medical or surgical costs. When Rani was hospitalized in New York, Ram paid. When she was in the hospital for six months in London and had a liver transplant, Ram paid. Ram paid for trips to Singapore for Rani, the family and the kidney donor, as well as the operation and the fancy for-profit hospital that printed out a fresh bill every few days, to be paid in full if she wanted to stay. When Rani transferred into an ICU in Delhi, Ram paid. As Rani approached the end, she went fearfully into the hospital at every new symptom, all at Ram's expense. Cost was never any object.

It was not just a matter of money. Ram also took responsibility for Rani's adopted son Ali when Rani was too ill to look after him, just as he used to cajole him back when Ali was a small boy and ran away from school. With all this, Rani felt she had become a burden; she had let her father down.

Rani, Shobha, Sundri, and the kidney donor travelled to Mount Elizabeth Hospital, Singapore for the kidney transplant, done on May 30, 2006. It had to be outside the country because of laws passed in India to prevent sales of organs by poor people for the benefit of the rich, laws that Rani wrote about later, arguing that they needed to be changed. Shobha had to push to be sure Rani went through with the transplant. After the transplant, an infection threatened to destroy the new kidney.

Discouraged and weary of Singapore, Rani fought a raging infection. Sick as she was, she checked herself out of the hospital to go directly to the ICU in the Apollo Hospital in Delhi, where she stayed for months, hovering between life and death. Shobha flew back to Delhi from the US, watching carefully to be sure nobody removed the infected kidney, as the doctors had threatened to do. As Rani faced death in the hospital, Ram was desperate to do something. At that time, one guru in Delhi, simply called Guru by his admirers, was very popular with all the politicians. Ram insisted that Shobha consult him.

Those days Shobha had such severe gastroesophageal reflux that she looked anorexic. Despite that and despite her inherent suspicion of any character with only one name, she visited Guru. Before she could obtain an audience with him, she had to participate in a ceremony, a darshan, which required a ritual meal. The food from his kitchen was so spicy she found it inedible with her reflux, but Maneka Gandhi, an ardent follower of Guru, sat at the same table and wagged her finger at Shobha that she must eat.

Ram saw Guru once, and Shobha saw Guru four times. She insists she is a woman of science, not superstitious at all, and when Guru informed her she had to come back, she balked. Her father was adamant that she must return and that she must bring Mahesh, who also had reflux. She did, and both of them did their best to avoid eating the food, without success. When Shobha's turn came for an audience, Guru gave her a copper pot to take home. Her instructions were to wash it repeatedly, fill it with water, put it out in the moonlight to be bathed by the rays of the moon and bring the water to Rani to drink before dawn.

Meanwhile, Rani's condition had become so alarming that Shobha was afraid to refuse the copper pot. She gave it to her servant to wash, filled it with water and dutifully brought it to the hospital, an hour and a half drive away. Rani drank the water.

What was killing Rani was a pulmonary infection with pulmonary edema. The following morning, a doctor aspirated fluid from her lungs, and she recovered.

Rani now moved into Ram's house on 2 Akbar Road. Unfortunately the kidney transplant did not save Rani for long, and she went back into kidney failure. Some time later, with inopportune timing, Ram's house began a major renovation project. The space that had served as Rani's apartment was reconfigured, and she had to move out. She was furious.

Ram once had bought a penthouse apartment in Gurgaon, a suburb of Delhi, when it looked like he would not be re-elected to the Rajya Sabha. Rani had bought an apartment in the Gurgaon building too, and she decorated both apartments. Her fantasy probably was that her father would move upstairs; she would live downstairs, and once again they would be together, just like in the old days. Rani moved out of 2 Akbar Road to Gurgaon in 2008, because, even though everyone told her not to, she had sold the Feroze Shah Road apartment in 2006. She insisted it brought her bad luck.

When Rani moved to Gurgaon, she took all of her antiques and paintings from 2 Akbar Road and decorated the apartment elegantly with her Indian paintings and sculpture. The problem was that she was too frail to ride the train, and the move left her stuck in an apartment that was two hours away by car, far from her friends, her father, her shopping, and her beloved cultural activities. Her friends remember how she waited for visits from her father, instructing her staff to cook just what he liked, preparing at great length whenever she thought she would see him.

Meanwhile the transplanted kidney failed completely. At Shobha's insistence, she went back to Singapore, returned to Gurgaon and dwindled for 18 more months, running to the hospital with each new crisis, steadily losing weight, and hope.

When Rani became unable to manage, Shobha went back to India to stay with her, to keep her apartment in order, her medicines straight and her emergency room trips to a minimum. At the last minute, Rani even went down south to Cooimbatore for an alternative treatment, but that too failed. When she returned to Delhi, it was to the ICU. She spent her last two months in Mumbai, back in Advent.

Rani died on New Year's Eve, 2011.

Shobha contributed much of the history for this chapter. When she read it over, she looked at me with tears in her eyes, and she said it should finish with, 'I have never known a sister who misses her sister so much.'

31

First Law Minister, then Minister of Urban Affairs

It was no secret that Ram wanted to be Law Minister. He denied it of course. When asked about it, his answer was, 'My clerk makes twice as much as an honest minister.'

At times the position seemed close, but now it would happen, albeit with stops and starts. The first opportunity came in 1996, when Vajpayee was sworn in as Prime Minister. Atal Bihari Vajpayee, Ram's contemporary, was an old freedom fighter who never married and who devoted his life to his country. He helped found the Jan Sangh Party, which later became the BJP, served in the Lok Sabha as a minister under Morarji Desai, and then led the Opposition. When the BJP emerged as the largest party in 1996, he was invited to form a government, but building a coalition proved to be hopeless. With L.K. Advani's support, Vajpayee took the helm, briefly.

Advani had not run because of the pending hawala case. Ram was an independent, not a member of the BJP, but it was no surprise when Advani called to tell him he would be a minister.

Ram was sworn in as Union Minister of Law, Justice and Company Affairs on May 13, 1996. Durga was proudly in attendance, so excited that she asked Rani to help her get ready.

Ram's first move after he was sworn in as Law Minister was to announce he would investigate former Prime Minister Narasimha

Rao and the incorrigible Chandraswami for corruption. Next, he told the press that Advani was innocent in the ongoing hawala case. The press called foul, since he was Advani's lawyer and he was the Law Minister. Reproved by Vajpayee, Ram offered to resign if Vajpayee thought it necessary. He did not.

Who was Narasimha Rao and why did Ram want to investigate him? Rao, too, was an old freedom fighter, an Indira Gandhi loyalist and the leader of the Congress (I) party. After Rajiv was assassinated, Rao earned praise as Prime Minister for trying to dismantle the Licence Raj, reverse the socialist policies of his predecessors, and introduce market reforms into the economy. Unfortunately, he was in office when the Babri Masjid at Ayodhya was destroyed in 1992, and that tarnished him.

Unrelated to Ayodhya, Rao faced corruption charges. In 1993 he was accused of bribing legislators in anticipation of a no-confidence vote. He and the slippery Chandraswami were charged with creating forged documentation that V.P. Singh's son had opened a large bank account for him in St Kitts. Rao and Chandraswami also faced a bribery charge in Great Britain. In 1993, Harshad Mehta announced he had paid off Rao to hush up his own scandal. After Rao stepped down as Prime Minister, the scandals continued to dog him.

Meanwhile, Vajpayee was trying to assemble a governing majority, but many of the existing political parties were communal, regional, or too small to give him the needed numbers. In short, he needed to talk with everyone, even Rao, and Ram's public attack on him did not help. The press simply smirked.

One thing that was expected of the new Cabinet headed by Atal Behari Vajpayee was that the new ministers would think twice before opening their mouths. But on Thursday, a few hours after they were sworn in, they refused to keep quiet.[1]

'The irrepressible Ram Jethmalani led all the way. The maverick law minister held forth about his plan to try former Prime Minister P.V. Narasimha Rao in the hawala and St Kitts cases—not to talk of Bofors—even without waiting for a collective party decision. Jethmalani who still heads the Pavitra Hindustan Kazhagam—an attempted political outfit— also boasted that as long as he is there there would be no move to buy over MPs to save the Vajpayee Government. In fact, the BJP is apprehensive that Jethmalani could be as disastrous for a government as a, say, Subramanian Swamy.

The irrepressible Ram Jethmalani indeed.

Falling short of a ruling coalition, Vajpayee's government fell on May 13, 1996—after 13 days. Ram's next chance to be a minister would come on March 19, 1998.

Ram returned to the Cabinet when Vajpayee became Prime Minister on March 19, 1998, not as Law Minister, but, surprisingly, as Union Minister of Urban Affairs and Development. At least this ministry provided him with a palatial bungalow—one of those designed by the famous Sir Edwin Luytens during the time of the Raj. In a compound for senior members of the government and with the prestigious address of 2 Akbar Road, it sits behind a wall on a prime corner across a traffic circle from the house of the Prime Minister. On Republic Day, regimental bands march towards the India Gate in full blast right past Ram's gate.

This sprawling old British house is surrounded by several acres of broad lawn, where Lataa now has put in flower beds and a large kitchen garden. Clients, would-be clients, and lawyers wait on lawn chairs at white metal tables, hoping to catch Ram. Overhead, a troupe of monkeys sometimes frolics in the tree tops, unless Ram's latest part-time employee, a langur (big monkey) is there to scare them off. Ram sometimes allows friends or political associates to use the grounds for weddings or anniversary parties, and more than one evening we have found lavish decorations, bright lights, throngs of guests, and multiple food stations all over the yard. One night, we saw many lakhs' worth of silken finery drenched by a torrential downpour.

The property has several out-buildings which have been repurposed repeatedly over the years. One building now is Lataa's office, and another is a guesthouse, which has hosted a colourful range of inhabitants. One day, a stranger on a train asked Ram if he had a place for him to stay. Already a Member of Parliament, Ram invited the man to sleep at his house in Delhi for a fortnight until he could get his affairs straightened out. He stayed for weeks. One day, Ram's daughter Rani, exasperated after hearing him call imperiously for his laundry, threw him out.

More recently a man who claimed to be related to a dear friend from pre-Partition days in Pakistan told Ram that his daughter had been in a serious car accident and was paralysed from the neck down. The Pakistani doctors had given up all hope of recovery, and they suggested he try treatment in India.

Of course, Ram paid for both father and daughter to be flown in from Pakistan, and he put the daughter in a top Delhi medical facility for several weeks. Meanwhile, the father parked himself at Ram's Delhi guesthouse, wined, dined, and shopped at Ram's expense. He even wanted his son to come to India. The daughter's state remained unchanged but the hospital bills were exorbitant. It was not until Shobha, as a doctor, pointed out the futility of the child's treatments and Lataa, pointing to the bills, exerted some persuasion, that the gentleman decided it was time to go back home.

That was only one of many incidents. One day, an unknown person was found to have stayed overnight, and the police were called to investigate. In the course of their investigations, the police identified some 30–40 people who were regularly sleeping in the servants' quarters, all of them on Ram's payroll.

Deepchand, Ram's long-time aide, is a legend himself, known for consistent service under the influence. Shobha says that 'after 9 p.m. the entire staff is half-drunk, not to mention Deepchand'. She insists that the more incompetent the staff in Ram's house, the higher the pay.

Ram has built an enclosed badminton court, where he plays every morning with a group of friends. They all take turns playing doubles, his partner running back and forth madly while Ram reaches to return shots with deadly accuracy. At the end of the game, his partners are sweating profusely, and Ram is grinning. His relationship with his badminton partners is so casual that at one party one of his partners lifted Ram up in his arms and carried him to the microphone to deliver his remarks.

Ram's family laughs that it is just their luck their father is so honest. They say that he must be the only one to hold the portfolio of Urban Development who only spent money of his own on his house, instead of leaving office with a fortune.

Oh, another perk came with the ministry. Ram was assigned a not very reassuring-looking security man who always took up a seat in the car next to the driver, leaving room for one fewer passenger. His very omnipresence seemed to give Ram the impulse to give him the slip. In the United States on one visit, we remember an evening when we drove to a party across town and Ram let the embassy car drive Shobha and Suresh so he could rest comfortably in our car while my husband drove.

Jayalalithaa and Subramanian Swamy

There was a reason why Ram's first ministry was not the Law Ministry. Starting even before Ram's first days as a minister, Ram, Jayalalithaa, and Subramanian Swamy had been embroiled in a long, drawn-out comic opera. To give the reader a feel for this, and for many of the subsequent controversies in Ram's ministries, we will quote liberally from the contemporaneous press, with all its salacious breathlessness, sometimes its frank error, and occasionally its helpful details.

In 1993 Subramanian Swamy had filed a petition in Madras High Court to challenge Jayalalithaa's election to her state Legislative Assembly.[2] In 1996, Swamy sued Jayalalithaa for corruption, but the court dismissed the suit because she was already under investigation. When Swamy challenged that order, the petition was dismissed.[3] Swamy continued to file petitions against Jayalalithaa for years.

In 1998, the BJP needed Jayalalithaa's party in their coalition if they wanted to stay in office. That put Jayalalithaa in the catbird seat, and she knew how to use it. A former film actress, later an exceedingly corpulent Chief Minister of Tamil Nadu,[4] she already had six criminal cases against her, against the All India Anna Dravida Munnetra Kazhagam (AIADMK) party secretary, against several of her ministers and others. These alleged improprieties in property acquisition; favouritism for one hotel; partiality in coal mine and granite quarry allotments; and they claimed she gave colour televisions to bribe village voters. There were 39 more cases too, dating back to when she was Chief Minister.

Jayalalithaa wanted M. Thambidurai[5] to be Law Minister. Ram says that she overrated the power of the Law Minister, but subsequent events showed her calculations to have been shrewd, 'On March 18, 1998, M. Thambidurai became only the second Law Minister in independent India to be sworn in despite the lack of a legal background— the first was Subramanian Swamy, who held the portfolio in Chandrashekhar's government. The very next day, Thambidurai made his agenda clear when he declared that all the cases against Tamil Nadu Chief Minister J. Jayalalithaa had been foisted by her political rivals.'

The Jayalalithaa–Swamy–Ram story had its origins in the Jain Commission in 1995, when Swamy was hostile to Jayalithaa and Ram defended her. The libel suit that arose out of this first went to trial in 1998, and, as we have seen, it ended with the case *Ram Jethmalani vs. Subramanian Swamy*, not decided until January 3, 2006. Meanwhile, Swamy turned into a political ally of Jayalalithaa. While the lawsuit festered in the background, Subramanian Swamy would surface regularly in the press with a standard litany of charges against Ram.

The newspapers enjoyed all of this.[6] 'The news broke that for the 1998 general election, the BJP would ally, in Tamil Nadu, with J. Jayalalitha's AIADMK, Subramanian Swamy's Janata Dal, and V. Gopalaswamy's MDMK among others. The turnaround was, frankly, mind-boggling. After all, what was Dr Swamy doing in Tamil Nadu? Carrying out an intense campaign for the ouster of Jayalalitha's government, alleging wholesale corruption by the lady.'

By 1998, Jayalalithaa was not only pleading with Vajpayee to not appoint Ram as Law Minister, but she also campaigned vigorously for Swamy to be in the Cabinet. Knowing that Ram had represented her before the Jain Commission, the Prime Minister asked him to call her and try to persuade her to back down. Unfortunately, as Ram admitted, 'That night I almost had a fight with her.' He reminded her about Swamy's earlier statement that his one-point programme was to destroy her. It was ridiculous, therefore, for her to push on his behalf. 'How can you insist?' he asked incredulously. When she persisted, forgetting that he was supposed to placate her and that the Prime Minister was also present, he sputtered, 'I am sorry but I have never heard such nonsense.'[7]

Once the Cabinet was appointed, Jayalalithaa redoubled her efforts to get rid of Ram, even writing to the Prime Minister to request that both Ram and Hegde, now the Commerce Minister, be removed from the Cabinet, claiming there were charge-sheets against them.

Jaswant Singh went to talk to Jayalalithaa:[8]

Sources said that Jaswant Singh did some 'plain talking'. He apparently told Jayalalithaa that the BJP would not accept her three major demands: dismissal of the Dravida Munnetra Kazhagam (DMK) Government in Tamil Nadu; the removal of Ram Jethmalani and Ramakrishna Hegde from the Union Cabinet; and action against a private television channel based in Chennai. The sources added that Jaswant Singh ruled out a place for Subramanian Swamy in the coordination committee.

In April, 1998, Jayalalithaa attacked both Ram and Hegde, and Ram got into a public mud-slinging battle with her. Jayalalithaa went so far as to demand that 'chargesheeted Union ministers should step down', meaning Ram and Hegde.[9] Alarmed, the Prime Minister warned Ram that they needed Jayalalithaa in their coalition. Again Ram offered to resign. Vajpayee agreed, but later, both thought better of it. There was good reason to believe Swamy was behind this too.

Ram went after Swamy in an article[10] that said, 'His has been a life of character assassination, malicious mendacity and sordid blackmail of any one who happens to cross his path. Nobody has been able to deflect him from his criminal course of conduct because few have the inclination to take on this vicious viper and expose him for what he really is. This diseased insect cannot be disinfected. He has to be crushed and carefully incinerated. It is not enough to throw him into the gutter. That is his natural habitat. There he will grow and flourish.'

Swamy fired back in kind, but it must be remembered that the only suit either of them ever filed against each other arose out of the Jain Commission because 'it was highly improper and unjustified on the part of Dr Subramanian Swamy to pass any remarks against the counsel Shri Jethmalani appearing on behalf of Ms Jayalalitha'. And today Ram and Swamy are great allies. Go figure.

In February 1999, Jayalalithaa's hand-picked Law Minister Thambidurai nullified the appointment of a three-judge bench that was supposed to try 46 corruption cases against her in Tamil Nadu. Thus these cases went back to the sessions court, many of whose judges she had appointed. In April, again Ram tried to resign in protest, but the Prime Minister did not accept his resignation.

The course of Ram's ministry can best be told through stories of the controversies. To understand their impact on public affairs, and on the public's perceptions of Ram, we will look at them through the eyes of the Indian citizen who picks up his newspaper in the morning and forms his opinions from what he reads.

National Judicial Commission Controversy

In July 1998, Ram came into conflict with the Prime Minister when he made a speech promoting his proposal for a National Judicial Commission. The Prime Minister called him shortly afterwards, unhappy that he had expressed a personal opinion as a Cabinet minister, especially as Minister for Urban Affairs. Ram suspected that Attorney General Soli Sorabjee had reported a misleading version of the speech to him, neglecting to mention that the proposal already was part of the BJP party manifesto. Once more Ram offered to resign, but the Prime Minister did not take him up on it.[11]

The *Indian Express* wrote: 'Urban Affairs Minister Ram Jethmalani today assured a delegation of lawyers that he would take up with the government the issue of the constitution of a national judicial commission to hear complaints against judges at all levels.[12] This meeting took place after a large demonstration by lawyers, who 'staged a march to Parliament to protest against alleged corruption in the judiciary, especially at the lower levels'.

Parliament demanded his resignation, but Ram defended his proposal, reminding them that there had been a long history of deadlocks between the senior judges who made selections under the existing process. In Parliament,[13] Ram answered sharp criticisms for his supposedly intemperate and unauthorized remarks by saying,

I was delivering a Key-Note Address at an organisation of the Lawyers of India organised by the Bar Council of India, and Sir, I have not lost my right to even impress upon my own Government that in our National Agenda to which we are publicly committed, we have placed ourselves to creating of a National Judicial Commission.

So, what I said at this Conference was what I have been pleading for in my public life even long before I became a Minister. The Minister's role is not to speak inconsistently with the Cabinet decision upon the point. The Cabinet has taken no view upon this particular matter. If and when it does, I will have to put myself in conformity with the Cabinet decision. But until then my convictions and my conscience of many years ago remains intact and I have the right under the Constitution to express my views and even impress my views upon the Government of the day.

Though the Opposition criticized him, Ram's proposal actually would have the leader of the Opposition on the Commission. This National Judicial Commission was the same proposal he had promoted for years, and the Prime Minister had evidently forgotten that his party had endorsed it. Maybe he never read it.

Central Vigilance Commission Controversy

Once he became a minister, Ram discovered how hard it was to do anything without running up against the entrenched governmental bureaucracy. This is not his cup of tea. When he wants to take a position, or to swing into action, he wants to do it, not to spend his time getting bureaucrats to sign off on it. One of his early conflicts with the bureaucrats was over appointments to a Central Vigilance Commission (CVC). In the Jain hawala case, the Supreme Court gave guidelines for establishing this new commission, which was supposed to shield appointments such as Chief of the CBI or the Enforcement Directorate from governmental meddling. Since the CVC also was charged to supervise the investigations these important bodies carried out, it would diminish the authority of the Prime Minister, who was in no hurry to appoint it. Eventually, Vajpayee appointed a Cabinet committee consisting of Ram, the Law Minister and two other ministers to oversee the drafting of an ordinance that would provide the Cabinet's view of how to choose the head of the CVC.

The government had asked the Law Commission to draft a bill in April 1998. Their draft used language straight from the court: that the CVC should consist of outstanding civil servants *and others* of 'impeccable integrity'. Though they submitted their report by August 12, it was not given to the Cabinet committee when they met on August 20.

Meanwhile the bureaucrats from the department of personnel wrote their own proposed ordinance, calling for a four-member CVC composed only of bureaucrats and civil servants, including the personnel secretary, dropping the words 'and others'. Significantly, this committee of bureaucrats would have to give permission before the CBI could investigate any high level officials or other bureaucrats, either in government or in any nationalized industry. Ram was enraged. First he held a meeting of the responsible bureaucrats at his house to call them on the carpet, but they insolently refused to defer to the Law Commission's language. Ram wrote a furious letter to Vajpayee, complaining of their insubordination, but the ordinance that issued on August 25 was the bureaucrats' version.[14]

In Parliament,[15] one Member said: 'As far as this legislation is concerned, it is all right, but some explanation is to be given by the hon. Minister. I have read in some newspapers that one of the senior members of the present Cabinet, a leading advocate of the Supreme Court has charged that this Ordinance—when they prepared the Ordinance and promulgated it—did not take into consideration the suggestions put forward by the Law Commission. It is not my comment; it has come in the papers. Shri Ram Jethmalani questioned them as to why were the suggestions of the Law Commission not taken into account?'

During the debate in Parliament, one member emphasized that the specific language used by the court was preserved in the Law Commission draft, but not in the government draft: 'Committee will consist of the Leader of the Opposition and the C.V.C. would be selected from a panel of outstanding civil servants *and others with impeccable integrity*—these words were deleted.' Another member added pointedly, 'One of the main objectives behind giving statutory basis to CVC is to get it free from administrative or other control of any Ministry or any other power or body.'

The final ordinance amounted to a complete bureaucratic takeover. Ram and Law Minister Thambidurai went together to Vajpayee's house, 'It is also learnt that Jethmalani and Thambidurai then approached the Prime Minister with their resignation letters. The Prime Minister, however, pacified them and said that the changes they wanted would be taken up for consideration when the ordinance came up for ratification by Parliament.'[16]

Business Standard[17] reported '. . . Prime Minister A.B. Vajpayee is said to be in no mood to accede to Jethmalani's demand for changes in the Central Vigilance Commission Ordinance. Instead, he is likely to go ahead with the appointment of members of the CVC through the three-member panel consisting of himself, Union home minister L.K. Advani and Leader of the Opposition Sharad Pawar during the next week.' Incidentally, if true, that would have given him even more power than he received in the bureaucrats' ordinance.

In response to a petition, the Supreme Court eventually ruled that the ordinance must use the language from the court opinion that had created the CVC. A chastized government had to quickly revise their ordinance before they sent it to Parliament. The final version reverted back to the language that Ram knew perfectly well it needed to have.

Alphons Controversy

Ram appointed a swash-buckling personal secretary:[18] 'The most controversial private secretary to a minister is K.J. Alphons, who gives the impression that he and not Ram Jethmalani is the real boss of the Urban Development ministry. The private secretary cheekily refers to the septuagenarian Jethmalani by his first name and is in the habit of sending chits and instructions to his erstwhile colleagues in the Delhi Development Authority (DDA) in the name of the minister, even when Jethmalani is out of the country.'

Alphons, known as the Demolition Man, had demolished more than 14,000 unauthorized buildings when he was the Delhi Development Authority Commissioner in the 1990s. A strong and ambitious character, Alphons took pleasure, as did Ram, in thumbing their noses at the sluggish, inefficient bureaucracy, and together they made enemies.

Delhi Development Authority Controversy

In his new position, Ram approached each issue just as he would a legal case. He examined all the underlying statutes, practices, and assumptions, looking for weakness, corruption, inefficiency, and incompetence. By nature more an advocate for change than an apologist for any existing system, Ram was a dangerous man from the point of view of comfortable government functionaries. One institution that sat squarely in his sights was the DDA.

Ram told the *Indian Express*[19] that he planned to streamline the DDA, and to 'scrutinise and revamp its panel of lawyers which deals with thousands of litigation cases every year'. Ram claimed that most of this litigation was false and had been dragging on for years; most of the lawyers on the panel had not been chosen on merit, and there was rampant collusion between lawyers and bureaucrats to prolong the cases.

He further claimed that the DDA built houses 'on a fraction of the land that it had acquired over the years'. Not only that, 'Thousands of flats were built in Dwarka with no attention to attendant civic amenities . . . many have already crumbled before they were even occupied.' On a recent visit to Dwarka, Ram 'had given the civic agencies a time bound ultimatum to provide basic amenities such as water, power and roads, so that the flats there could be made habitable'.

In the same article, 'Speaking to *Express Newsline*, the minister, who has been calling for a revamp of the 37-year-old organisation, said that the DDA has completely failed in its objective for which it was set up. "In my view, the DDA outlived its utility long time ago and it should now be either done away with, or drastically scaled down . . . its performance in the last three decades is nothing short of a national scandal," Jethmalani said.'

The commentator Prem Chand Sahajwala put it quite plainly:[20]

When under Vajpayee, he became Minister for Urban Development; he took the DDA to task for creating thousands of fictitious petitions in connivance with several lawyers so that . . . the lawyers as well as the corrupt officers of the DDA might earn lots of money from the exchequer. He would then take the [ministry] officials as well as the DDA officials to the colonies where the DDA had allotted flats to thousands of people but Jethmalani would question the dumb-stuck officials as to where is the electricity and water here? Have you provided them with these facilities?

In short, the DDA discovered to its dismay that it was up against a Ram Jethmalani instead of a normal, passive government minister. Ram would have to go; it was only a matter of time.

FERA Violation Controversy

Some of the most serious attacks against Ram came from Subramanian Swamy, who alleged that Ram had violated the Foreign Exchange Regulations Act (FERA). The papers reported: 'The Union minister for urban development is under scrutiny for spending $200,000 obtained from various sources abroad way back in 1987 without declaring this expenditure to the Indian government.'[21]

Another article[22] adds that Subramanian Swamy not only accused Ram of a FERA violation, but he also called for an official report on a trip that Ram and Hegde made to Taiwan, insinuating that it was a boondoggle.

The *Indian Express* reported,[23] 'AIADMK leader J. Jayalalitha had demanded Jethmalani's removal from the Union Cabinet accusing him of having made certain admissions under oath before a metropolitan magistrate in Mumbai with regard to receipt of substantial amounts of foreign currency abroad in possible violation of section 8(1) of FERA.'

Also, the *Indian Express*[24] reported this tidbit about Jayalalithaa, 'She is also pressing hard for the ouster of Urban Development Minister Ram Jethmalani after the recent spat between them. The initiation of an informal inquiry by the Enforcement Directorate today into the FERA violation allegations against him has heightened speculation about his possible exit from the Government.'

So Swamy and his new best friend Jayalalithaa levelled the same charges. Thinking, as they tend to, 'where there is smoke there is fire', what on earth must the public have thought about Ram?

The *Indian Express* captured the exchange, 'Today, Swamy dug out his own brand of dirt on Jethmalani in his letter to the PM. An alleged FERA violation, an alleged ban by the Bombay TADA Court on the high-profile lawyer—Swamy pointed an accusing finger at Jethmalani. He claimed that the Enforcement Directorate was awaiting the Government's political clearance to prosecute Jethmalani in the FERA case. As for the TADA Court's ban, Swamy said it was because of Jethmalani's "material interest arising out of his advocacy of the notorious gangster, Dawood Ibrahim."[25]

'Jethmalani was equally damning. He accused Swamy of having links with the LTTE, of scuttling the Bofors probe as law minister in the Chandra Shekhar Government, of being a "bosom friend" of notorious godman Chandraswami, of being "a megalomaniac" with ambitions of becoming Prime Minister of India.'

Though one writer[26] called Subramanian Swamy 'The Loonyswamy of Madurai', his attacks on Ram must have been wearying, to say the least.

The papers[27] did make Ram look shady: 'Janata Party president Subramanian Swamy's attack on Cabinet minister Ram Jethmalani may not be a mere publicity stunt after all. According to information available with *Outlook*, the Directorate of Enforcement (DOE) is currently "investigating the case" against Jethmalani and has prima facie concluded that "there does appear to be a violation of foreign exchange rules".'

'While Jethmalani has asserted that the case, which was investigated after Swamy publicly repeated these allegations in 1995, is closed, the DOE emphatically disagrees. Agency insiders say that what has made matters worse for the minister is an earlier defamation proceeding filed by him against godman Chandraswami in which he had himself admitted to using the funds abroad to finance an investigation into the Bofors case. The DOE has already moved the Bombay high court to access the original documents in the defamation case. The agency is also planning to send a team to the US to authenticate the bank transactions.'

Swamy charged that Ramnath Goenka and Chandraswami, aide Ernie Miller were among the main contributers, along with Janak and his wife, who he mistakenly identified as his daughter, 'Statements of bank accounts in possession with *Outlook* show that on July 28, 1987, $50,000 was transferred from Miller's Euro Bank Corporation account in Grand Cayman to Janak Jethmalani's account in Citibank, New York.' Note the variance from another claim that $200,000 was transferred.

During the 1993 suit, Swamy had said that Ram 'while categorically asserting that he "did not receive any money from anybody abroad", admitted that money was deposited in his son's US account "as a contribution towards the expenses for the Bofors investigation". Therein he also asserted that Chandraswami tried to persuade his son to open a secret account for the investigation, and though both he and his son declined to do so, his son "received a phone call from Ernie Miller, who introduced himself as Chandraswami's disciple and sent a contribution towards the Bofors investigation".'[28]

Another article reported, 'Asked whether the present status of examination of the allegations was similar in nature to the Preliminary Enquiry (PE) conducted by the Central Bureau of Investigation (CBI), the officials replied in the negative saying the ED inquiry was much below the level of PE.'[29]

Ram's vindication came on May 7: 'Commerce Minister Ramakrishna Hegde and Urban Development Minister Ram Jethmalani have secured a clean chit from the ruling Bharatiya Janata Party.'[30]

'The BJP . . . has asked Pramod Mahajan, the prime minister's political advisor, to brief the media every day. It was at his media conference on Thursday that Mahajan revealed there was no case against Hegde and Jethmalani. "I can say you have violated the Foreign Exchange Regulation Act, but that does not mean any agency is investigating such a case. We have not asked any agency to investigate and we don't know about any investigation," Mahajan said.'

The allegations were pure nonsense. Mahesh says, 'The FERA matter was entirely misconceived. It had to be formally looked into because Subramanian Swamy put it in the public domain. Janak was a United States citizen and received money from an untainted overseas source for a cause in the public interest, viz. unearthing corruption at the highest levels of government. After going through the motions the FERA authorities accorded a quiet burial to the case. No one including Swamy protested.'

Ram says that nobody really paid any attention to Swamy's charges. 'He is a bit of a crank, you know.'

Now Ram and Swamy are on the same side in the war against

corruption, and Ram urges, 'Don't say anything about Subramanian Swamy.' Indeed.

Still, can you imagine a minister trying to do serious work under this barrage of onslaughts? Admittedly, Ram enjoys fencing with opponents, and he has even been known to dare someone to sue him, looking forward to trouncing him. Still, even he must have found all of this a bit difficult when he really wanted to make a difference in this ministry.

Sitaram Bhandar Trust Controversy

Ram also butted heads with the bureaucrats over land allocations in south Delhi, specifically prime land owned by the Sitaram Bhandar Trust, a religious body that operates temples in Rajasthan. Ram and his government had announced a goal of building 2 million new homes a year for the poor, and he needed this 70-acre plot in order to develop a large tract in Delhi. One of Ram's most innovative proposals was a privatization scheme in which the land would be denotified, that is, given back to the owners, but this would only happen if they fulfilled certain conditions, such as building a school and a hospital, as well as establishing a fund for the poor. Opponents suggested he had been bribed to privatize the land, and they generally cast wild aspersions on his motives.

The *Indian Express*[31] said that Ram had overruled his own ministry officers when he 'ordered the Delhi Development Authority (DDA) to implement his order denotifying 68 acres of prime land in the capital belonging to the Sitaram Bhandar Trust. The order denotifying the land in Karkardooma—estimated to be worth Rs 1000 crore—had been passed by Jethmalani in June this year but was on hold since Secretary Kiran Aggarwal declined to implement it.'

Subramanian Swamy immediately leaped up to announce that Ram's decision to denotify the land was illegal, and to demand a CBI inquiry.

'Jethmalani said, however, that his order is valid and consistent with his recent decision to allow private builders to construct houses in the capital. The proceedings for acquiring the trust's land were initiated way back in 1958 but it took the DDA nine years to pass a formal acquisition order, which in any case was never implemented. The trust later went to court against the acquisition order and matter has been under litigation since the last three decades.'

The Supreme Court had directed the ministry to denotify the land, but nothing had happened until Ram found the file.

'Aggarwal and other ministry officials however challenged the minister's orders on the grounds that the issue was still under litigation (in the Delhi High Court). Other objections included: since the DDA had acquired the trust's land for building houses for poor people, it would be against public interest to allow the land for private development; since Sitaram Bhandar Trust was a religious trust, it would not be proper to allow it to engage in building activity on the land; such an order would open the floodgates as many similar demands pending with the government.'

MS Shoes Controversy

One of the highest profile controversies in Ram's ministry came when he opposed a Housing and Urban Development Corporation (HUDCO) plan to turn an existing property in south Delhi into a mixed residential–commercial complex. The highest bidder for the development contract was Pavan Sachdeva, the chairman of MS Shoes, a company that once was an actual shoe export company before it diversified as far afield as real estate. The complication was that the CBI had arrested Sachdeva in 1995,[32] accusing him, together with officials of the Securities and Exchange Board of India and several merchant bankers, of a criminal conspiracy to manipulate the stock market. Sachdeva also was accused of violating the Customs Act in 1985 when arranging with foreign investors to finance a project to build a large hotel complex in Delhi. He was fined, and the project came to a halt, leaving MS Shoes short of money to pay back existing loans.

According to Ram, the stock market conspiracy allegation never went to court, and the CBI had cleared MS Shoes of any criminal charges. Still, the stigma of corruption was attached to Sachdeva's name.

The part of the project that Ram reviewed was for mixed residential–commercial use. On this, Sachdeva had to pay about Rs 100 crores in instalments to HUDCO. He paid the first instalment, and he needed to pay the second and third instalments after he began construction. He had borrowed heavily on this prospect, but HUDCO never obtained the needed completion certificate in time for construction to start, nor were water, electricity, or sewage lines in place. Sachdeva defaulted on his second payment.[33]

MS Shoes filed suit in the High Court and did receive an extension of its payment schedule. Nevertheless, HUDCO re-tendered the bid. The case went back to court. The District Court said 'the plaintiff long back had parted with 40 per cent of the total price of the project in return of which he has got nothing till date but the cancellation of his allotment. The additional document brought on record by the plaintiff [has] a lot to speak in respect of a prima facie case being in favour of the plaintiff'.

Even before Ram began his term as minister, two Members of Parliament had asked in the Rajya Sabha on March 20, 1997 why another builder on a related project received a time extension, but MS Shoes did not. Dissatisfied with the response, 35 Members of Parliament from several parties had asked the ministry to look into the matter.[34]

Ram called for the file when he became a minister. He concluded that HUDCO was in the wrong, because it had not obtained the clearances and sanctions it was obligated to get, and that was why Sachdeva could not make timely payments. Ram's decision flew in the face of the recommendations of Ms Kiran Aggarwal, the secretary of the Ministry of Urban Affairs. Aggarwal, stinging from her dispute with Ram over a subway bid—which we will come to shortly—complained to the Prime Minister that it would be improper to talk to Sachdeva during the pendency of a court case, the amount of money involved would require approval from the Finance Ministry and Ram was showing favouritism to Sachdeva.

Subramanian Swamy promptly obtained leaked copies of the relevant papers and took them to the press, claiming that Ram had ulterior motives for his decisions both in MS Shoes and the Sitaram Bhandar Trust. Reportedly he wrote the Prime Minister,'He (Ram Jethmalani) should be dismissed and prosecuted!'[35]

'Coming down heavily on his critics, mainly Subramanian Swamy for giving only partial facts in order to malign his intentions in both the MS Shoe and the Trust cases, Jethmalani narrated the entire facts and chronology of events to justify his actions.[36]

' . . . he said HUDCO's action in cancelling the allotment to MS Shoes even after it paid a first installment of Rs 40 crore for a ready built guest house priced at Rs 100 crore, was against public interest and "unsustainable in a court of law".'

'HUDCO was at fault in cancelling the allotment and forfeiting the first installment sum of Rs 40 crore paid by MS Shoes when the latter had defaulted payment of second installment on the ground that HUDCO was not in a position to hand over possession of the plots within the stipulated time period as it did not have clearances from any of the concerned agencies,' the Union affairs minister said. He said the law ministry after perusing a court order in favour of MS Shoes had noted in the file that 'the allotment of land in favour of MS Shoes has been illegally cancelled by HUDCO'.

'He also defended his decision [on] Sitaram Bhandar Trust saying "my ministry has cleared in 1998 a file pending for 39 years and is executing in substance a decision taken by late Prime Minister Rajiv Gandhi in 1987".'

In the same article Ram also argued that the court of additional district judge gave a finding in favour of MS Shoes saying the company has succeeded 'prima facie in establishing the fact that till date Hudco is not in a position to perform its part of obligations and the completion certificate of the project has not been obtained . . .'

The *Indian Express* quoted Swamy,[37] '"Since Jethmalani is promoting the cause of rich builders and estate agents at the cost of the poor masses, he should either step down from the minister's post or be dismissed by the Prime Minister. He should also be prosecuted under the Prevention of Corruption Act by the CBI,"

Swamy added. He also alleged that Jethmalani had committed an error of commission in the MS Shoes land scam, which necessitated a detailed investigation by the CBI. Jethmalani had reportedly passed an "unprecedented order" restoring the land worth Rs 350 crore to MS Shoes Ltd, owned by Pawan Sachdeva. Calling the BJP government "a disaster", Swamy said Opposition secular forces would seek to form a government after the outcome of the forthcoming Assembly elections in four states.

Even after Ram no longer held the post of Minister of Urban Affairs, the papers continued to parrot these accusations. The Indian public read this sort of article day after day for years; it watched TV interviews that rehashed the same material, and it doubted Ram. Here is one article from 2000:

> Jethmalani himself faced serious charges of impropriety in the M.S. Shoes case, which has its origins when he was Minister for Urban Development. He clarified that there was no justification for insisting that a private citizen (the promoter of M.S. Shoes) should forfeit about Rs 40 crores on the grounds that he had failed to make a timely payment of installments due to the Housing and Urban Development Corporation (Hudco). He claimed that when these allegations against him first surfaced, he had asked the CBI to record a first information report (FIR) and investigate the matter. He undertook to waive all his privileges and immunities as a Minister if the CBI wished to expedite its inquiries.[38]

The same article continues, 'The Janata Party leader, Dr Subramanian Swamy has demanded the immediate arrest and prosecution of Jethmalani in the case, now that he is no longer a Minister.'

Subramanian Swamy continued hounding Ram in the press, but he never proved any of his allegations.

Ram even wrote to the CBI inviting them to investigate and clear his name because he knew he had no personal or business connection with either MS Shoes or Sitaram Bhandar Trust. He also wrote to the Prime Minister, but the government never took the allegations seriously enough to warrant a real investigation.

As far as the propriety of the MS Shoes decision, it has never been challenged in court.

Kiran Aggarwal Controversy and the Delhi Mass Rapid Transport System

Kumar Mahesh, a civil servant himself, says that the code for a civil servant is simple. When faced with a new idea, first consult the rules. If the action is permitted, say yes. If it does not fit the rules, look to past decisions. If it was not permitted in the past, or if it is within a grey area, say no. All of this takes time. Ram's modus operandi was to move as fast as possible, which meant that he constantly outpaced the civil servants.

There also is a chain of command among the bureaucracy. Kiran Aggarwal would not endorse an action until she received positive recommendations from two people one rung below her, Rajiv Takru and J.P. Murthy, and it required time for each of them to research each question. Meanwhile, the desires or goals of the minister had to compete with their needs to maintain seniority within the ministry.

The contract to be general consultant on Delhi's biggest construction project, the Delhi Mass Rapid Transport System, became a major source of conflict with Ms Aggarwal, who was at the same time the president of the Indian Administrative Service (IAS) Officers' Association, the ex-officio chair of the Delhi Metropolitan Railway Corporation, and the secretary of the Ministry of Urban Affairs. The contract had been given to a Japanese firm, but Ram condemned the process for not being transparent. Moreover, the criteria for technical evaluation had been kept secret, even from him, and Ram castigated Aggarwal for issuing a letter to the firm even before the Cabinet committee had passed on it. Worse, she had agreed to their demand for a Rs 440 crore fee. Ram went to the Prime Minister with his objections, and the consultants immediately lowered their rates from Rs 440 crore to Rs 208 crore, vindicating his suspicions.[39]

No doubt the bureaucrat who most incurred Ram's displeasure

was Aggarwal. In all, Ram had three areas of complaint about her: the mass transit system, the Sitaram Bhandar Trust case, and the MS Shoes case. Finally he removed all important duties from her desk and handed them to her junior, causing the bureaucrats to circle the wagons protectively around her.

The papers ate up the gossip:[40]

Jethmalani had a few weeks earlier divested secretary Aggarwal of her duties following a difference of opinion over the reallocation of prime land to a private firm in Delhi. While Jethmalani insisted on the re-allocation at the earliest, citing a court order, the secretary wanted the matter to be referred to the Law and Finance Ministry before taking a final decision as it could incur huge losses to the exchequer.

Aggarwal, who is president of the IAS Officers' Association, is acting tough. While special secretary S.S. Chattopadhya is practically handling the ministry's work, Aggarwal and two others, additional secretary Hemendra Kumar and joint secretary S. Banerjee, are on Jethmalani's hit list. On Jethmalani's birthday bash last week, all were in attendance except the three.

The press repeatedly put out a bogus story of a CBI investigation that never happened:[41]

Now, however, Aggarwal seems to be duly vindicated. The Central Bureau of Investigation has virtually endorsed the stand she took. The CBI report submitted to Vajpayee recently says that Jethmalani's order to hand over a prime piece of plot to Pavan Sachdeva—yes, of the MS Shoes Ltd, well, fame—would result in a loss of over Rs 600 million to the exchequer.

Aggarwal had opposed the move tooth and nail. For which the minister stripped her of all powers and arbitrarily delegated the same to the additional secretary

Another questionable order the CBI has indicted the minister for pertains to the acquisition of some land in Delhi belonging to the Sitaram Bhandar Trust, owned by the Birlas. Over 60 hectares was to be acquired way back in the '60s. The first installment of the compensation had been paid, but the trust sought to challenge the acquisition order in a Delhi court.

Even before the matter could be settled legally, Jethmalani stepped in, and he sought to reverse the nearly-three-decade-old acquisition order on the ground that the Delhi Development Authority no longer needed it. As could be expected, this again found Aggarwal on his back. She fought valiantly, but the minister shook her off. Now the CBI has upheld her objections and panned the minister for seeking to bestow undue benefits on the private trust.

'The Prime Minister's Office has sought to buy peace with urban affairs minister Ram Jethmalani by agreeing to transfer urban affairs secretary Kiran Aggarwal from the ministry.[42]

'Whether or not shifting Aggarwal could satisfy Jethmalani and convince him not to rake up the CVC issue would be clear only after he returns from his six-day tour of Israel when the orders for transferring Aggarwal is expected to be passed.'

This is a perfect example of absolute press misinformation. The truth is that there never was any CBI investigation of Ram. That is a fact, but you might try to imagine how Ram felt, reading this nonsense while trying to do an important job.

Ram went off on his trip to Israel. The papers reported that when he returned he found that the Prime Minister's Office had rebuffed all three of his complaints: about Aggarwal, about the bidding process on the Delhi metro and about MS Shoes. Aggarwal's fellow bureaucrats had even convinced the Prime Minister that Ram must reinstate Aggarwal, giving back her earlier responsibilities.

Ram's critics were way off the mark on their accusations in MS Shoes, the Trust, and the mass transit system. Of course, Ram had acted with magisterial disregard for the niceties of working with bureaucrats. Of course he had relied on his own judgement as a lawyer without deferring to the ministry establishment or the rest of the government. Those would be appropriate objections. Ram took bribes? No. Maybe if one of the businessmen involved had an attractive wife Ram could have been tempted to sin, but it would have been completely out of character for him to favour one disputant over another for his own financial gain. The accusations against him were an example of what Freud would have called projection—the accusers simply demonstrated what they would have done in the circumstances. Their accusations told more about them than they did about Ram.

The day after Ram returned from Israel, celebrations began for his 75th birthday. The Sindhi community gave a grand party in his honour, as they always did, but this one was even more festive. The legal community went all out with a Symposium in his honour at Symbiosis University in Pune. The family threw him a magnificent 75th birthday gala, with maybe 1000 guests. Ram delightedly kissed all the women on the lips and called them darling. The party was packed with politicians of all political parties, friends, Bollywood stars, lawyers, judges, diplomats and corporate tycoons. The media covered it extensively. And, in spite of everything, Vajpayee came, to Ram's immense satisfaction.

Aggarwal, finally, was transferred to another ministry, and Ram even invited her to his house for a farewell event. Ram, true to form, wanted them to end up friends.

Despite Ram's run-ins with the bureaucracy, he always was supportive of those he considered deserving. An IAS officer and author, Achala Moulik, was side-lined in her quest for a selection grade position, which means one based on merit. Believing in her abilities, Ram arranged for Arun Jaitley to argue her case in the Central Administrative Tribunal, which did award her the position she sought in her ministry. Mahesh Kumar comes from a backward state plagued with Naxalite activity, but Ram supported his pursuit of an MBA in 2000 and helped him to pursue an LLM from the London School of Economics. Ram also generously helped other students to obtain LLMs abroad.

Still, he could be severe, even with his own assistant, Alphons. When an important businessman came from London to see Ram, Alphons asked him to help sponsor his son's artistic work in England. For that offence, Ram issued an official letter calling it a conflict of interest. When Prime Minister Vajpayee's foster son-in-law, Rangan Bhattacharyya, called Ram on the hotline, the RAX telephone, Ram refused his call, saying, 'I don't take the call of son-in-laws on the RAX.' It took a certain amount of courage to refuse a relative of the Prime Minister.

In the middle of all the controversies, Ram can point to three major accomplishments during his tenure as Minister of Urban Affairs. The most important was the repeal of the Urban Land Ceiling Act. Another was that he 'carried out his party's manifesto of building 2 million houses', and, to do it, he supervised a new National Housing Policy. The third was that he promoted government transparency by offering any interested person the opportunity to pay Rs 10, one rupee per page, to see the ministry files under the provisions of a pending Freedom of Information Bill. He believed so strongly that such an act was essential that he instituted an open administration even before it was passed or was implemented in any other ministry. He says, 'That became a cat amongst the pigeons.'

Freedom of Information

The indomitable civil rights lawyer Prashant Bhushan wrote:

> In 1999, when Ram Jethmalani was the Minister for urban development, he passed an administrative order in his ministry that any citizen would be entitled to inspect and take photocopies of any file in his ministry. In his order, Jethmalani pointed out that the Supreme Court had in at least two Constitution bench decisions held that the citizens have the right to get information about all aspects of government functioning.[43]
>
> Though the government of India had already committed itself to enacting a right to information legislation when Jethmalani passed his order, the Cabinet Secretary, on the instructions of the Prime Minister, restrained Jethmalani from giving effect to his order. This prompted the Centre for Public Interest Litigation and Common Cause to file a writ petition in the Supreme Court

seeking effectively three reliefs: 1) that the Cabinet Secretary's restraint on Jethmalani's order be declared unconstitutional and violative of the citizens right to information; 2) that section 5 of the Official Secrets Act, which makes it an offence for a public servant to disclose any information that has come to his knowledge in his official capacity, be declared unconstitutional; 3) that the government of India be directed to frame and issue suitable administrative instructions on the lines of the Press Council's Right to Information Bill, to effectuate the citizens right to information, pending suitable legislation on the subject.

Naturally when Ram opened his ministry to everyone, it terrified the government bureaucrats who were doing an excellent business in bribes. The Prime Minister even wrote to Ram to request he hold off, the excuse being that a Freedom of Information Bill was in the process of being enacted, along with an amendment to the Official Secrets Act, but neither ever was passed under Ram's administration. The Freedom of Information Bill was introduced in Parliament in 2000; in 2002 the Supreme Court directed that the bill be implemented; in December 2002 it finally passed in Parliament, and it received presidential assent in January 2003.

Prof. V.C. Vivekanandan of the Nalsar University of Law teaches his students that Ram was actually the father of India's Freedom of Information Act. He teaches that, by opening up his ministry records to anyone who wanted to pay a nominal fee, Ram set the stage for the later legislation. That would make it one of Ram's most significant accomplishments in the Ministry of Urban Affairs.

Two Million New Houses and a New National Housing Policy

Ram introduced a National Housing Policy with aplomb, calling the two-day Housing Ministers' Conference of 1998 to develop an action plan for building 2 million houses, as required by the National Democratic Alliance manifesto. He promised to build them in the North-east, and mainly for the poor. Ram took great pride in seeing that these 2 million new housing units began to go up in his first year as a minister.

On World Habitat Day celebrations on October 5–6, 1998, Ram inaugurated a two-day seminar on Safer Cities, and also in 1998 he released a draft National Housing and Habitat policy.

The Government of India announced that, 'The 17th session of the [United Nations Centre for Human Settlements] UNCHS Habitat was held in Nairobi from 5th to 14th May'99. A delegation under the leadership of Shri Ram Jethmalani, the then Urban Development Minister participated in the deliberations and presented the view point of government of India, on the issues of implementation of Habitat Agenda and Agenda 21 relating to Urban Environment. The Indian Delegation made a very impressive presentation during the session.'[44]

The government also released Ram's statement at that conference:[45]

> The Government of India is committed to pursue the goals set in the policy framework and co-operate with other member countries to work for a better world with adequate shelter for all.
>
> In this connection, he enumerated some of the steps taken during the recent past which included adoption of the National Housing and Habitat Policy . . . The Minister listed the steps that the Government of India has adopted towards the implementation of the Habitat Agenda of the United Nations. The multi-pronged approaches to achieve the objectives included removal of legal and regulatory constraints for increasing the housing activities and the increased flow of housing finance by the Government and financial institutions.

The *Indian Express*[46] wrote, 'Describing the new government housing policy as "revolutionary", Jethmalani said government wanted the private sector to take part in the new venture in a big way . . . To fill up the deficit of 33 million houses in the country, the government had formulated the ambitious national housing project with a target of constructing two million houses every year,' he added.

'Jethmalani said, under the new policy, government would function as a facilitator for boosting housing activity in the country. Answering a question, he said Foreign Direct Investment (FDI) in housing projects had been cleared "in principle" by the Cabinet.'

The new Housing and Habitat Policy 1998[47] went to Parliament on July 7, 1998. In order to achieve the objective of constructing 2 million more housing units a year, HUDCO sanctioned the building of one lakh houses by the end of the year. Part of this programme projected a national network of building centres to train workers in low cost construction skills and to produce building materials by using agro-industrial wastes. Ambitious, and visionary.

Ram floated some fairly radical ideas in his ministry: private sector redevelopment of slums, tax breaks for the housing industry, construction loans, private 'mini-townships', reductions in DDA staff, pre-fab housing, and the replacement of much of Luytens' Delhi with multistorey residential complexes. This last would have required significant self-denial; that was where he lived and had built his prized indoor badminton court!

Ram offered targeted tax breaks as an inducement for builders to construct more houses for the poor, but these were criticized as potentially less profitable than the margins on expensive housing. However,[48] 'A key aide to Jethmalani, K.J. Alphons, said the government was only following resolutions adopted at Habitat II in Istanbul in 1996, which demanded that governments promote efficient land markets and remove all obstacles that hamper equitable access to land.'

'Jethmalani has begun with the capital city. Last Saturday, he ordered scrapped the 36-year-old monopoly of the corruption-ridden, Delhi Development Authority (DDA) to buy and develop land in the capital.' Further, 'Jethmalani's package for Delhi included the regularisation of nearly 1,600 squatter colonies, including slums and unauthorised constructions, which had mushroomed up all over Delhi and even acquired electricity and water connections through bribery.' The article also said that Ram 'has now allowed private builders to make external commercial borrowings (ECB) to develop land unacquired by DDA and is preparing to announce a new policy allowing foreign direct investment (FDI) in India's housing sector for the first time'.

The *Indian Express*[49] quoted Ram:

> My Government has promised to build two million houses this year, out of which 750,000 are in the urban sector. But the budget has not given me a single rupee. I do not want to destroy my reputation by being a minister for a year in which I have delivered nothing. To build 750,000 houses without a rupee is a magician's job.
>
> The Delhi Development Authority (DDA), for instance, has 20,000 pending cases. Everyday I receive cases in which I feel some of the DDA chaps deserve to be shot. They are so callous and cruel. I am the one who ended their illegal monopoly in housing which they were enjoying from 1961.

Government press releases[50] touted Ram's proposals:

> Conversion of Property in Delhi from Leasehold to Freehold—A proposal relating to modification in the scheme of conversion is under consideration of the Government. The present scheme covers the flats constructed by the Cooperative Group Housing Societies including Multi Storied flats on land leased by the Delhi Development Authority.
>
> Success of Housing Policy—TheGovernment's policy is to provide as additional 2 million housing units per annum.
>
> Surplus Land Acquired by Various Bodies—The power to acquire and take physical possession of the surplus land under the Urban Land (Ceiling & Regulation) Act, 1976 vests with the State Governments. As per the records available, the extent of surplus land acquired and taken over under the Urban Land (Ceiling and Regulation) Act, 1976 by the State Governments during the period from March, 1990 till date is 2,115.31 hectares approximately.

These and other similar announcements represented the ideas of Ram, the activist social reformer who wanted to make a difference and perhaps to poke a stick or two in the eye of the bureaucracy. Unfortunately, he was not in office long enough to ensure that the most original of his privatization ideas would be implemented.

Repeal of the Urban Land Ceiling Act

Many consider the passage of the Urban Land (Ceiling and Regulation) Repeal Act of 1999 to be one of Ram's greatest achievements. Its importance was that it repealed the Urban Land Ceiling Act of 1976, something that activists had been trying to do for years. Ram accomplished this by first pushing through an ordinance on January 9, 1999, then a bill that he moved in Parliament on May 8.

In its prologue, the original Urban Land Ceiling Act (ULCA) explained its purpose:

> To provide for the imposition of a ceiling on vacant land in urban agglomerations, for the acquisition of such land in excess of the ceiling limit, to regulate the construction of buildings on such land and for matters connected therewith, with a view to preventing the concentration of urban land in the hands of a few persons and speculation and profiteering therein and with a view to bringing about an equitable distribution of land in urban agglomerations to subserve the common good.

With all this high-flown rhetoric, *Times of India*[51] wrote:

> The . . . aim was to prevent a handful of well-endowed people from hoarding land and artificially controlling prices. But over the years, it led to massive corruption and the government was barely able to recover much land for public housing.
>
> In 30 years, the state government received just 2,426 flats in Mumbai from builders. Many politicians allotted these flats to their cronies and favoured ones.

Another publication[52] used even stronger language, 'Misused ULCRA has been the bane of the housing and construction industry for the last two decades. Large blocks of urban land have stayed locked up, creating an artificial scarcity. The government identified 220,674 hectares of vacant land in 8,000 sites as excess, but only about 50,046 hectares had been lawfully vested in state governments. Till November 1997, only about 19,020 hectares (nine per cent) of this had actually been taken over by the states.

'The result: large-scale speculation, taking property beyond the reach of the average Indian. Says Jethmalani: "Construction of houses in urban metros like Delhi is at a standstill and one of its main stumbling blocks is the ULCRA. It is a totally useless Act, an instrument of corruption and has failed in its prime objective." By repealing the law, Jethmalani expects to increase supply of urban land for construction, which should bring prices down.'

In short, the act hindered development on large tracts of urban land, and its main beneficiary was the government, which used it to confiscate land from private owners.

Ram decided to solve this problem himself:[53] 'Though the Bill for repealing the Act was now pending before the standing committee of Parliament, Jethmalani said "I do not want to wait for long, already half-of-the year has gone, so I am going to repeal the Act with an ordinance."'

The newspapers were pessimistic that the act could ever be repealed:[54] 'Urban Affairs Minister Ram Jethmalani has proposed the repeal of the Urban Land (Ceiling and Regulation) Act, 1976, in the belief that this would improve drastically the housing situation in the country. But, given the history of the legislation, his attempt is unlikely to succeed.'

The article went on: 'In the past decade . . . even governments with comfortable majorities in Parliament, have had to abandon their attempts to amend the law in the face of stiff resistance from various quarters. Yet, Union Urban Affairs Minister Ram Jethmalani, who introduced a bill in the last session of Parliament to repeal the Act, was sanguine about its smooth passage.'

Few would disagree that the act restricted the housing supply for the poor and middle class or that it had become a vehicle for corruption, but it had a strong constituency in the government. Ram's tactic for getting the legislation through was simple and original. He pushed the bill through under an article of the Constitution that allows the centre to legislate as long as two or more states request the legislation. In this way, the bill would become effective in the union territories first and subsequently in those states which pass an 'Adoption Resolution'. So, once Parliament enacted a bill of repeal, it took effect immediately in Delhi and in the other states that requested the bill. Maharashtra and the rest were expected to follow with their own adoption resolutions. The effect was to achieve a repeal that had eluded proponents for decades.

Another accomplishment that his associates smile about was that he broke the toilet monopoly, which probably occasioned plenty of potty jokes in the ministry, knowing Ram. One NGO, Sulabh Sauchalay, had a monopoly over public toilets across the country, and its performance was abysmal. Ram worked with Fuad Lokhandwala,[55] who came from America with the idea of building modern toilets in India funded by advertisements on the three outside walls. 'The pay-and-use toilets, with charges of only one or two rupees, were so good that Delhi's Chief Minister Sheila Dixit, who always supports good initiatives, gave him 40 more spots. Soon the fame of these toilets spread to Mumbai, prompting a visit by its mayor, municipal commissioner and senior officials. They invited Lokhandwala to build 96 such toilets in the country's commercial capital.'

Ram approved the project, but it met resistance even within his own ministry. Two fine modern demonstration toilets were built, one near the Supreme Court, and the other in the Lodi Gardens, but the same article says that vested interests have fought them ever since, 'One of them even sent hooligans to attack him and his men for not paying up. Bureaucrats created hurdles for the same reason. So far Lokhandwala has been able to construct only nine toilets on Mumbai's municipal plots. In New Delhi, NDMC's bribe-seeking officials have refused to renew his contract at many places.'

Ram also implemented another policy as part of an urban poverty alleviation programme—a tax exemption for 'Interest on loan for self occupied property up to ceiling of Rs. 75,000'.[56] The number of rupees has changed, but the exemption still remains policy.

When Ram finally left the ministry on June 14, 1999 after 15 months, he felt sad, because he had much left to accomplish.

32

Law Minister at Last

On October 13, 1999, Ram finally became the Minister of Law and Justice. In short, Law Minister.

Throughout Ram's tenure as Law Minister, the newspapers publicized every jot and tittle of controversy. Some speculated from the beginning that Ram would leave early when his Parliament term ended in March, but Vinod Pandey, his astrologer, read Ram's horoscope, predicting that Ram would continue rising steadily toward the zenith of his career. Pandey was smart enough to give Ram consistently encouraging readings, but he completely missed the end of Ram's ministry before it came.

Again, press quotations would continue the Jayalalithaa–Swamy saga, but the new feuds that were about to develop would be more ominous.

In the spring of 1999, Jayalalithaa consulted closely with Subramanian Swamy on how to bring down the Vajpayee government.[1] 'Swamy also told her that the Congress (I) might hesitate to move a no-confidence motion against the government when Parliament met on April 15. She could set the ball rolling by withdrawing support at the earliest, he indicated. In the event of a trial of strength, Subramanian Swamy told her, the government was bound to collapse.'

Still trying to get rid of the corruption suits against her, Jayalalithaa threatened to withdraw from the coalition unless the Tamil Nadu government was dismissed. In March, Ram recommended they let her go. Jayalalithaa announced that she would pull out of the coalition, and, a week later on April 15,[2] Subramanian Swamy called for a vote of no-confidence.[3] The government lost by one vote on April 17, 1999.[4] The Congress party proved unable to form a new government, leaving a shaky caretaker government in place until the fall of 1999, when new elections brought Vajpayee back into power for five years.

One commentator observed that[5] Ram was at a disadvantage as Law Minister following Thambidurai, 'Jayalalithaa's man who knew nothing about the Law or the Law Ministry.' Under Thambidurai, Soli Sorabjee, the Solicitor General, had been de facto in charge of the Law Ministry. This would not be true with a Ram Jethmalani as Law Minister. When he came in, Ram 'demarcated the turfs of law minister and the Solicitor General [sic], which was not acceptable to Soli, and as such a feud followed.' In fact, Sorabjee was the Attorney General.

All that being said, Ram had opinions to write and work to do at the Law Ministry offices in Shastri Bhawan in Delhi. He also had to notify the ministry where he was all the time, because security officials would jump to attention to escort him from his car into the airport, through the VIP lines, to the VIP lounge, to the plane and off the plane, grabbing his specially marked bags off the luggage belt for him when he arrived. Actually, that did not differ much from the treatment he received before his ministry and that he receives now, though during his ministry all this attentiveness was at its most confining.

Constitutional Amendment for Scheduled Castes and Tribes

While he was Law Minister, Ram moved to increase the term of reservation for scheduled castes and scheduled tribes by 10 more years through his sponsorship of the 84th Constitutional Amendment Bill in the Lok Sabha. This was a bill 'seeking further extension of reservations for SC/ST for a period of ten years with effect from January 26, 2000 in government jobs and elected bodies.' During the debate in Parliament, he announced that 'A three-day convention of scheduled caste and scheduled tribe (SC/ST) Members of Parliament will be held before the winter session to discuss all pending issues on reservations.'[6]

During the discussion Ram introduced his idea, 'I had been thinking that I should informally call all members who represent the scheduled castes and scheduled tribes in both the Houses, not for a four-hour discussion, but for a three-day convention when every single issue including those issues which require legislation and which do not require legislation would be discussed threadbare and we must draw out a plan.'[7]

The Parliament discussion went well, and a number of Members of Parliament came out in support. Subsequently, Constitutional Amendment 79,[8] as introduced by Ram, was passed, extending 'the reservation of seats for SC, ST and Anglo-Indians in the Lok Sabha and Legislative Assemblies for next 10 years.'[9]

The Prime Minister did not comment, but while planning the conference, Ram received a message from his office indicating that this subject was not under his jurisdiction. When they met, Ram told him, 'I am not calling this conference for my personal gain . . . I am not interested in becoming the leader of the backwards.'

The Prime Minister retorted, 'You want to become everyone's leader.'[10]

Ram then made the arch suggestion that the conference be transferred over to Maneka Gandhi, the Minister for Social Justice and Empowerment. Since she was not known at all as a friend of the backward classes, they promptly announced they would not participate. The Prime Minister relented, and Ram ended up running his conference, with considerable success. Afterwards, the backward classes did regard him, correctly, as their champion.

In many people's eyes, this bill, plus the *Indra Sawhney* case, did make Ram the Father of Social Justice in India. Surely no one has done more for them or has shown less personal prejudice towards them. It was not widely known, but for quite some time Ram had a Harijan (an untouchable) as his cook. Normally, this would be unthinkable for a higher-caste Hindu.

Appointment of the Solicitor General

During the caretaker government, Ram butted heads with Attorney General Soli Sorabjee over the appointment of the Solicitor General.[11] Sorabjee wanted his former junior, Harish Salve. Ram insisted on his former junior, Sri Jaisinghani,[12] known for his role in fighting the *Kissa Kursi Ka* case. With his usual stubbornness, Ram offered to resign if Sri was not appointed. The Prime Minister solved the problem by appointing both, naming Sri the Additional Solicitor General, an equivalent position.[13] The article quotes a note Ram wrote to Sorabjee, with a very telling sentence: 'My power is my renunciation, the ability to quit.'

Politics

When Ram's Rajya Sabha term ended in March 2000, he almost did have to quit. He considered running for the Lok Sabha, but he decided to run again for the Rajya Sabha as an independent from Maharashtra, counting on support from the Shiv Sena and the BJP. Suddenly, he found out that Jawahar Goel, the brother of Subhash Chandra of Zee TV, had filed as a candidate for the Rajya Sabha from Maharashtra. That meant seven candidates were running for six seats, splitting the vote, and necessitating an election. The backroom horse trading went on for days.[14] If Ram lost, he could only remain Law Minister for six more months after he left Parliament, but he vowed not to continue even one more day if he lost. Goel's manoeuvre looked like an attempt to get Ram out of the Law Ministry, but an attempt by whom?

Some suggested Ram buy the needed votes, but that was out of the question. A parade of would-be helpers approached him with advice. Chandraswami surfaced to offer his help. Deepak Bajaj, a local backroom man, claimed to be Ram's relative, and to be privy to important political gossip. Finance Minister Yashwant Sinha went to Subhash Chandra to persuade his brother to withdraw. Ram and Sinha contacted the local leaders of the BJP and the Shiv Sena, and they assured him of their support. Vajpayee assured Ram of his support. Advani called, saying that Chandra had told him that Goel would withdraw. Ram's cellphone never stopped ringing.

On the day of the deadline, Ram was scheduled to go to Mumbai for a ceremony Rani had arranged on the anniversary of Durga's death. Before leaving, Ram met with Sinha, Chandra, and some others who had endorsed Goel, and it was clear that they were stalling. Sinha escalated the pressure on Chandra until he finally agreed to call Goel, and ask him to withdraw. Finally Sinha called in the afternoon of March 18, just before the 3 p.m. deadline for filing.[15] Ram made sure that Goel was escorted personally to the returning officer.

On March 29, 2000, Ram re-entered the Rajya Sabha, only to become entangled with the trio of Attorney General Soli Sorabjee, Chief Justice Anand, and Arun Jaitley, Ram's successor as Law Minister. In view of what happened next, one wonders who had been behind all that pre-election manoeuvring.

Clearly, Ram wanted to stay in the Cabinet or he would not have fought so hard in the trenches to win the 2000 election. Still, he was not willing to accept the restrictions that went with being a minister or to stick to the government party line when he wanted to speak out. Ram is devoted to the truth as he sees it, but he cares little for ingratiating himself with a political party. He expects his political support to come either from politicians who have been his clients or those who fear that some day they will need to be. He will not compromise his principles for votes. He holds himself to a high standard of honesty, which he interprets to mean that he will not cater to a party, government, or even former allies, if he believes they are in the wrong. If he thinks a party compatriot is wrong, he goes after him, and if he thinks a former opponent is in the right, he joins forces with him. Even his closest friends say that his party never can take his support for granted. Above all, the pure joy he takes in being a full-throated advocate trumps everything. People say he is naïve, but he knows the stakes. After all, his son, Mahesh, says, 'In Delhi, everyone walks around carrying your horoscope.'

Now that Ram would continue to be Law Minister, he entered

into a series of confrontations that culminated in his resignation. What were the issues?[16]

The New Civil Procedure Code

In December 1999, Ram introduced a Code of Civil Procedure (Amendment) bill in the Lok Sabha,[17] intended to shorten the time between introduction of a lawsuit and a final judgement. It proposed to make the plaintiff swear that what he says is the truth, would require a summons to be delivered within 30 days, and the defendant to respond within 30 days. It also streamlined the process of issuing a summons as well as various other documents. Documents would have to be submitted in duplicate, allowing a copy to go to the other party in time for him to reply within seven days; lists of witnesses would have to be submitted within five days; and no party would be permitted more than three adjournments. It set rupee limits below which no appeals would be allowed, abolished certain second appeals, encouraged out-of-court settlements, required an expeditious decree after a judgement, and required copies of judgements to be made available in a timely fashion.[18]

Ram did not write this bill. It was the product of extensive research by the Law Commission of India. According to the 163rd Report of the Law Commission,[19] an official bill first was introduced to the Rajya Sabha in 1997.[20] The Law Commission sent out 43 questionnaires requesting feedback, and it held conferences in Delhi, Allahabad, and Hyderabad to consult with the Bar and the judiciary. Then it incorporated suggested modifications. The Bar had ample opportunity to weigh in, if it had paid attention.

The bill, drafted pursuant to Law Commission recommendations, addressed multiple sources of delay in the administration of justice, step by step, proposing a solution for each of the delays that contributed to the huge backlog in the Indian courts. The first amendment to the Code to be proposed since 1976,[21] the abuses it proposed to correct had made the Indian courts into an international laughing stock. Many lawyers made their careers and their entire income just by filing adjournments. The passage of this bill was to be one of Ram's proudest achievements.

During the discussion in Parliament, with his comprehensive knowledge of the existing law, Ram parried all objections easily. On the subject of restrictions on appeals, for example, he said, 'We are not abolishing the right of appeal. What we are abolishing is the right of second appeal in petty cases. We are only taking away one intermediate appeal. The second appeal, Sir, even otherwise, lies on point of law only, and it does not lie on issues of fact.'

He also acknowledged that government bureaucrats caused many court delays. Ram promised, as Law Minister, that the government would increase the number of judges, fill vacancies, and increase judges' salaries. The increase in salaries was to decrease the incentives for frivolous litigation or postponing cases just to ratchet up legal fees. This was a position that he had espoused for years, explaining that the common man ordinarily sees the law at its lowest level, the magistrate, and this magistrate needs to be paid enough to be incorruptible.

The Lok Sabha passed the bill on December 20, 1999, and the uproar began. On February 24, the lawyers went on strike, demanding the new bill not be implemented.[22] Police broke up the mêlée with tear gas, water cannons, and a lathi charge. Proceedings were paralysed in 10,000 courts. On February 25, Ram termed the strike 'regrettable and unfortunate as it was avoidable'.[23] He also said that 'this controversy is one which is eminently capable of being resolved by intelligent argument. The ugly consequences of the strike are there for everyone to see.' The chairman of the Bar Council of India presented a letter to the President of India, asking for him to intervene.

'Lawyers, however, say that they have been pushed to the wall by Union Law Minister Ram Jethmalani's "brash" attitude. In their view, Jethmalani, who has served as a Senior Advocate in the Supreme Court, has sought to distort issues arising from the lawyers' protests: by projecting the view that the lawyers' opposition to the amendments was motivated by pecuniary considerations.'[24] To make things worse, Ram said, 'If he were to choose between monetary benefits of advocates and the public interest, he would gladly choose the latter.'

The lawyers primarily objected to the restrictions on pleadings, examination of witnesses by court-appointed commissioners, provisions encouraging out-of-court settlements, the 30-day time frame for filing a summons, the 30-day time frame for filing a defendant's written statement, elimination of one level of appeal from the High Court and the restriction on appeals of awards less than Rs 25,000.

To add fuel to the fire, a working paper from Ram's ministry proposed amendments to the Advocates Act that 'would require advocates to subject themselves to an assessment once every five years in order to renew their professional licences'.[25] Ram defended it by saying that the proposal for lawyers to take a written test in order to renew their registration came from the Law Commission, and it had been reviewed by the Bar Council of India in 1977.[26] That paper also would allow foreign lawyers to practise in India. These last two proposals really hit practising lawyers in the stomach.

The Bar claimed that litigants would be deprived of essential rights, and that the main cause for court delays was a shortage of judges.

On March 9, the Supreme Court Bar Association expelled Ram from membership, citing '"unbecoming and hostile behaviour" towards the legal community when they agitated against amendments to Civil Procedure Code (CPC) and against the foreign lawyers.'[27] The same article reported that 'Jethmalani, who arrived here from a foreign trip this afternoon, in his terse resignation letter, said, "I hereby resign from your Association. I do not deserve you and you do not deserve me."'

The Bar Association also expelled two senior advocates who did not observe the strike; it resolved to stay on strike for 15 more days, and it demanded suspension of the police officers who had charged them with lathis.

The lawyers' anger at Ram was evidence of how effectively he had used his prestige to move the bill.

After one of the expelled lawyers filed a petition, the Supreme

Court issued contempt notices to the 20 officers of the Supreme Court Bar Association.[28] In response, more than 400 lawyers filed petitions in support of the association officers.

The question of whether lawyers have the right to strike went to court.[29] The Supreme Court ruled that 'no Bar Council can even consider giving a call for strike or a call for boycott . . . In case any Association calls for a strike or a call for boycott, the concerned State Bar Council and on their failure the Bar Council of India must immediately take disciplinary action against the Advocates [who called for a strike] . . . Further it is the duty of every Advocate to boldly ignore a call for strike or boycott.'

With all the tumult, enforcement of the amendments was suspended until 2002, but then Parliament decided to put them into effect. In July of that same year, the Tamil Nadu Bar Association 'brought a constitutional challenge' to their enforcement.[30] In a decision written by Chief Justice Kirpal in October, 2002, the Supreme Court upheld the constitutionality of the law, though it acknowledged some practical problems in implementation. It made suggestions on the alternative dispute resolution section and established a five-person committee to 'study the reforms and to make additional recommendations.'[31]

An amended version of the act passed on May 24, 2002,[32] allowing exceptions to the 30-day limitation for a summons, restoring the ability of either party to amend his pleadings up until the date of a trial, providing exceptions to the time limit on submitting defendant's statements, adding additional rules for submitting oral arguments, refining the rules for submitting cross-examination, providing an exception for the 30-day rule on pronouncing judgement, and removing the restriction to three adjournments.[33] In all, the changes were cosmetic—the substance remained intact.

Conflict with Attorney General Sorabjee

As Law Minister, Ram found himself head-to-head with Attorney General Sorabjee. The conflict probably was inevitable; Sorabjee was used to working with Ram's predecessor, whom he could dominate easily. In contrast, both Ram and Soli Sorabjee were men with strong personalities and strong opinions. Whether or not Sorabjee created some of these problems in order to replace Ram with a more congenial Law Minister must remain a subject of speculation. What we do know is that Ram set off sparks, and Sorabjee fanned the fires.

The issues included: Ram's decision in MS Shoes, the appointment of Jaisinghani as Additional Solicitor General, the slow work pace of government attorney B.P. Aggarwal, Sorabjee's advice to the government on the Telecom Regulatory Authority of India (TRAI), Sorabjee's consulting fees for advising the Hindujas, Sorabjee's appointment to the National Commission to Review the Working of the Constitution, and disagreement over a change of venue for Jayalalithaa's corruption cases.

The Hindu flatly said that the problem was: 'About the Attorney General, the Law Minister is of the view that though a constitutional appointee, the Attorney General is an official attached to the Law Ministry and the Minister is not always bound by his advice, as the latter can only advise.'[34]

MS Shoes controversy

Some claimed that MS Shoes started the conflict with Sorabjee. As Minister for Urban Development, Ram took the position 'that there was no justification for insisting that a private citizen (the promoter of MS Shoes) should forfeit about Rs 40 crores on the grounds that he had failed to make a timely payment of instalments due to the Housing and Urban Development Corporation (Hudco).'[35]

When unsavoury rumours circulated about his motives, Ram had waived all his ministerial privileges and immunities, inviting the CBI to investigate him and clear his name. Even that did not mollify his enemies, and the accusations continued into his Law Ministry.

Once Ram became Law Minister, the papers reported that

Kuldip Nayar of the Rajya Sabha had raised the issue of the MS Shoes project with the Prime Minister in a letter seeking clarifications on

> Jethmalani's alleged attempt to bail out Sachdeva's company with regard to its dispute with HUDCO. Nayar was told that the matter had been referred to the A.G. [Sorabjee]. Subsequently, Nayar sent another reminder, and on July 24 he raised the matter in the House. Apparently, the government has got a report from the CBI some months ago on the MS Shoes case. This was referred to the A.G., who sought a detailed CBI investigation into certain aspects of the case. The A.G. had also apparently stated that Jethmalani, as Law Minister, should be kept out of the HUDCO appeal in court.[36]

The key word in this report was 'apparently'. The reporter says that *'apparently* the government has got a report from the CBI'. Apparently, the reporter was wrong, because there never was a CBI investigation.

Another Aggarwal—Attorney Aggarwal

On February 10, Sorabjee wrote a letter to Law Secretary R.L. Meena complaining that government attorney B.P. Aggarwal took so long in drafting 11 appeals that the statute of limitations had lapsed. Ram's response was that Sorabjee had no business writing directly to his secretary; moreover, it had been Ram's predecessor, Thambidurai, who appointed Aggarwal—while Sorabjee was the Attorney General!

He also wrote that Aggarwal had been briefed not by his ministry but by the Commerce Ministry, headed by Murasoli Maran of the DMK. 'Your insinuation . . . is unwarranted and impertinent.' The epistolary battle escalated with Sorabjee retorting that Aggarwal was indeed briefed by the Commerce Ministry official on the advice of an official of the Law Ministry.[37]

Telecom Regulatory Authority of India

'During the tenure of the caretaker government last year, Sorabjee became the arbiter in a dispute involving cellular service licencees and then Communications Minister Jagmohan over unpaid licence fees. The licensing policy was changed into a revenue-sharing policy at Sorabjee's instance. Jethmalani holds him responsible for a Rs 4,000-crore revenue loss.'[38]

In his book, Ram quotes the first opinion Sorabjee wrote on the telecom licences. He then alleges that Sorabjee released a subsequent, changed, opinion after telecom got to him, in effect using him as their lobbyist. He further alleges that under statutory rules the proper fee for Sorabjee's two opinions should have been Rs 10,000, but the government paid him a fee of Rs 75,000 for his conferences and for the second opinion.[39]

Sorabjee insisted he received a lower amount than that, justifying it because 'the matter called for a major investment of time on his part. Under the rules, he further clarified, law officers are entitled to charge fees.'[40]

Hinduja Consultation Fee

Since Ram and the Hindujas were fellow Sindhis, there was 'a perception of him shielding those involved in the Bofors case. Jethmalani now accuses Sorabjee of a conflict of interests by advising the Hindujas in their dispute with the Power Ministry over counter-guarantees in the Andhra Pradesh project.'[41]

'The former Law Minister alleges that Sorabjee tendered advice to the London-based business family, the Hindujas, even as the Central Bureau of Investigation (CBI) was investigating them for involvement in the Bofors pay-offs scandal. He strongly disapproved of the fact that the government continued consulting Sorabjee on policy matters, such as telecom transactions, when he was charging exorbitant sums as legal fees.'[42]

Ram alleged that Sorabjee had submitted two opinions favourable to the Hindujas and unfavourable to the government.

He further claimed that Sorabjee's monthly government retainer precluded him from advising anyone else on matters affecting the government.[43]

Ram's most scathing criticism was that an investigative reporter claimed that Sorabjee had collected a legal fee of Rs 125,000 from the Hindujas.

Sorabjee responded, 'The opinion he gave the Hindujas was in connection with their proposed power project in Andhra Pradesh and this was done only after due permission was obtained from the then Law Minister, Rangarajan Kumaramangalam. It had no connection whatsoever with the Bofors case and, in fact, had a bearing on the inflow of valuable investments into the country.'[44]

After Arun Jaitley replaced Ram as Law Minister, not surprisingly, he gave Sorabjee a clean bill of approval for his consulting, 'Jaitley said there were precedents where A-Gs had been given permission to advice [sic] private parties and offered to lay such instances on the table of the House.

'This was challenged by the Opposition including Congress members and legal experts Kapil Sibal and H.R. Bharadwaj, who said the Attorney General had committed grave impropriety by giving advice to Hinduja brothers and demanded that Attorney General be summoned to the bar of the House to explain his conduct.'[45]

Ram was on tenuous ground here, because after leaving the ministry he would represent the Hindujas in court, despite the outcry that after accusing them in the Bofors investigation, now he was defending them. Ram would point out that the two situations were not equivalent. While he cast aspersions on them in the past, additional information had given him reason to believe that that they were innocent of the charges in the current lawsuit. Sorabjee's behaviour involved a direct contemporaneous conflict of interest.

The National Commission to Review the Working of the Constitution

Vajpayee appointed this Commission on February 22, 2000, with instructions to report on March 31, 2002.[46] Ram objected to Sorabjee being on the Commission, 'on the ground that no government law officer should be a member of a supposedly independent body with political functions.'[47] The Commission did include a former Attorney General, former Speaker of the Lok Sabha, and other former Members of Parliament, so Ram's criticism apparently was that Sorabjee was a current office holder in the government.[48] This objection was a bit of provocation in this fraught relationship.

Jayalalithaa, Again

In 1998, when Jayalalithaa tried to get her corruption cases transferred to more congenial courts, Sorabjee supported her demand.[49] 'Jethmalani had also accused Sorabjee of "pliancy" when the centre issued a notification transferring corruption cases against the All India Anna Dravida Munnetra Kazhagam (AIADMK) supremo, Jayalalithaa, and others, from Special Courts to regular courts during Vajpayee's previous term as Prime Minister'.[50] Again Ram offered to resign in protest. Finally the Supreme Court struck down the transfer, vindicating Ram.

Conflict with Chief Justice Anand

The other major figure with whom Ram came into conflict was the Chief Justice. One sharp disagreement occurred over the judge's role in appointing the Dean of the National Law School in Bangalore, but there was much more. Perhaps Justice Anand wanted a Law Minister who would be more deferential to the court. That would not be Ram.

Judicial Appointments

'The present leadership of the Supreme Court has a soft spot for Sorabjee as he was the architect of the strategy for defeating former Chief Justice M.M. Punchhi's idea of limiting the consultative process for judicial appointment to a handful of judges. Following Sorabjee's advice, there was a presidential review and Justice Punchhi's interpretation was discarded. A believer in judicial appointments being effected through a National Judicial Commission, Jethmalani came into conflict with Anand who wants the status quo to persist.'[51]

This referred to Chief Justice Punchhi's 1998 appointment of a nine-judge bench which recommended that a judicial collegium of five make judicial appointments.[52] Punchhi himself faced impeachment, but that never went anywhere.

Justice Anand's Wife

The confrontation between Ram and Anand became personal when a newspaper alleged that illegal payments had been made on land owned by Chief Justice Anand's wife, Mala, and his mother-in-law.

'The issue against Chief Justice Anand, head of the country's judiciary and the third highest constitutional authority after the President and vice-president, was first raised by the magazine *Kalchakra* (against which the Supreme Court had passed severe strictures in 1997) in its February 2000 issue.'[53]

'The article made allegations against not the Chief Justice himself but his wife and mother-in-law, saying they got compensation— against the rules—for land owned by them in Madhya Pradesh.'

'The issue was taken up by the Madras-based fortnightly *Frontline*, which asked how compensation could be paid for land after 20 years, when the law of limitation puts a bar of 12 years.'

Since this publication was not considered reliable, Ram paid little attention until he heard that Chief Justice Anand held him responsible for the story. 'When *Kalchakra*, a magazine run by Vineet Narayan of the Jain hawala case fame, published allegations of impropriety against Anand's wife I called on him (chief justice) at his residence,' states Jethmalani. 'He admitted to me that he believed I had encouraged this publication.'[54]

At that meeting, Ram thought he had set the issue to rest and that Justice Anand 'had apparently been satisfied with the explanation proffered. But to avoid all misapprehensions, he had requested the CJI on July 17 to send him a note on his version of the facts in the case, which could be placed on record.'[55]

The interesting question was: who set up Ram by planting the story that he was behind this news report? It could have been any of those who preferred a new Law Minister.

Appointment to the MRTP

Ram further incensed the Chief Justice when, on his authority, the Cabinet appointed retired Patna High Court Chief Justice B.M. Lal as chairman of the Monopolies and Restrictive Trade Practices (MRTP) Commission. The Chief Justice complained that by precedent he should be consulted. Ram responded that in only one instance had the Chief Justice been consulted on the appointment of a sitting judge. There was no precedent nor was there any previous instance in which the Chief Justice was consulted on the appointment of a retired judge. However, still smarting over accusations against his wife, he retaliated by refusing to administer the oath of office to B.M. Lal.

Frontline reported,

Chief Justice Anand objected to not being consulted on the appointment of the head of the MRTPC and complained to Vajpayee . . . The CJI had refused to swear in Jethmalani's nominee, Brij Mohan Lal, the recently retired Chief Justice of the Patna High Court, even though his appointment was notified by the government with the concurrence of the Prime Minister. Justice Anand pointed out that the government ought to have consulted him before selecting Lal for the post. Jethmalani argued that he was not bound to consult the CJI over this appointment, as Lal was a retired Judge and there was no precedent of prior consultation with the CJI in such cases. The instances cited by Justice Anand pertained to appointments to tribunals, which the MRTPC decidedly was not.[56]

'An angry Anand wrote to the Prime Minister, complaining

about overturning a "settled convention", and saying that the Law Minister was "discourteous and intemperate". When Vajpayee referred the letter to Jethmalani, he shot off a "Dear Chief Justice of India" letter, setting off yet another incendiary chain of exchanges.'[57]

Throughout this controversy, Ram was busy working on replacing India's antiquated Monopolies and Restrictive Trade Practices Act. He went to England to seek additional information and he brought Adrian Majumdar, former deputy director of Economics at the United Kingdom Competition and Markets Authority, in the Office of Fair Trading, to India for consultations. Majumdar is a co-author of a textbook on competition, a lecturer on the subject at King's College, and an author of several provisions of the United Kingdom Competition Act. India's new Competition Act of 2002 was written as a result of Ram's efforts. Since the Act was passed on January 13, 2003 and implemented as the Competition (Amendment) Act of 2007, the credit went to Ram's successors.

Prevention of Terrorism (POT) Bill

In the middle of all this, Ram came out against a bill that Union Home Minister L.K. Advani was promoting in Parliament. Even though Advani had been his sponsor as Law Minister, Ram could not help but remember with sympathy the many detenus he had defended when Indira Gandhi misused her preventative detention laws, and he instinctively opposed any new law that would empower the government to imprison political enemies. Unfortunately for Ram, Advani had been interested in this bill ever since the 1999 Kargil War with Pakistan.

The Law Commission wrote the Prevention of Terrorism Bill of 2000 as a replacement for the Terrorist and Disruptive Activities (Prevention) Act (TADA), which had been allowed to lapse in 1995 due to widespread abuse. Even in 2000, there still were detenus in jail under TADA. The press termed some of the provisions in the new bill draconian, and the parliamentary debate was contentious.

After a number of amendments,[58] the bill was passed on October 24 as the Prevention of Terrorism Ordinance of 2001.[59]

The papers reported that Ram was opposed to the Prevention of Terrorism Bill, 2000, and he would recommend to the Cabinet that they not go ahead with it, despite the fact that the Law Commission recommended it.

"'I am personally totally against the enactment of any special law against terrorism as it is bound to be misused by the police," Ram told PTI over the phone from Mumbai.'[60]

The National Human Rights Commission opposed the bill too, but after the 2001 Jaish-e-Mohammed terrorist attack on Parliament, Advani would redouble his efforts to pass it. Ironically, when the bill came back to the Rajya Sabha in 2002, Ram defended it. It was too late to help him hold Advani's support for his position as Law Minister, but the September 11 attack in America caused Ram to reconsider the bill. As the papers said, 'Jethmalani's support to the Bill, therefore, was intriguing.'[61]

Intriguing indeed, because Ram paid heavily for criticizing the bill when he was the Law Minister, 'Actually, Jethmalani's position was weakened after he riled his mentor Home Minister L.K. Advani with his opposition to the new TADA bill. Yet, Advani did try a compromise by proposing Jethmalani be shifted to another department. But Vajpayee stood his ground.'[62]

Srikrishna Commission of Inquiry

The Samajwadi Party, Congress party and others petitioned the Supreme Court to implement the Srikrishna Commission Report on the 1992–93 Mumbai riots. The report blamed Bal Thackeray for inciting the riots with his inflammatory editorials, but Thackeray's party, the Shiv Sena, threatened they would burn down Mumbai if he were arrested. Since the Prime Minister was anxious to keep the Shiv Sena in his coalition, he was pleased when Ram informed him that the statute of limitations was up for Thackeray's arrest. At the Prime Minister's request, Ram thereupon went off to meet

Thackeray. At the same time, the Chief Justice was delivering a loud tirade in court about Ram's assurances, claiming they were inconsistent with the government affidavit. Some observers believed that the rant, utterly uncalled for, must have been planned in advance. Significantly, Sorabjee was present and silent.[63]

According to one reporter, 'The event that led directly to his ouster was the hearing in the Supreme Court of a public interest petition[64] seeking directions to the Maharashtra state government to initiate prosecution in line with the recommendations of the Srikrishna Commission of Inquiry. This hearing, he pleads, was unconnected to the legal and political position he had taken on the prosecution of Shiv Sena chieftain Bal Thackeray in a case connected to the 1993 communal violence in Mumbai.'

'Though strictly speaking a distinct issue, the Supreme Court perhaps was justified in observing that the recent public statements of the Sena partisans in the Union Cabinet were contrary to the spirit of the affidavit filed in the Srikrishna matter.'[65]

The *Indian Express* reported,[66] 'On Friday, a three-judge bench of the Supreme Court, while hearing a batch of petitions on the implementation of the report of the Srikrishna Commission which probed the Mumbai riots, had disapproved of the statement of central ministers on the Maharashtra government's decision to prosecute Thackeray.

"Is there something called collective responsibility or not?" the bench, headed by Chief Justice A.S. Anand, asked and wondered "whether this concept is not known to this government".'

The same evening, Jethmalani hit out at the Chief Justice saying he should have realized that he was making comments about a minister 'who knows his law as well as anyone else'.

In another report, 'One charge against Mr Jethmalani is that he was voicing an opinion in favour of Mr Bal Thackeray which he should not air when the matter is before court.' The reporter wrote that Ram had the right to say 'that Mr Thackeray's arrest and prosecution can be ordered only after the limitation period is condoned by court, the Minister is simply voicing his argument.'[67]

The Matter of Bal Thackeray

In July, Bal Thackeray was released from arrest because the statute of limitations had elapsed since he was charged with promoting communal enmity. The Maharashtra state government vowed to appeal this ruling.

One report said,

> Jethmalani, who was elected to the Rajya Sabha with Shiv Sena support, had come out openly against the decision of Maharashtra's Congress–NCP government to prosecute Thackeray for his allegedly inflammatory editorial in the Shiv Sena mouthpiece *Saamna* against minorities during the 1993 Mumbai riots. He had said the state government had no powers to arrest Thackeray for an offence as old as seven years and that the Centre could issue directions to the state against such a move.[68]

Ram was not the only one of this opinion.

> Others such as Minister for Information Technology Pramod Mahajan and Minister for Information and Broadcasting Arun Jaitley shared Jethmalani's view that the case against Thackeray, in connection with inflammatory writings by him in 1993 in the Sena's organ, *Saamna*, is barred by the statute of limitations.[69]

Resignation

Justice Anand castigated Ram in court on July 21. The press immediately flocked to interview Ram, and his responses were incendiary. Meanwhile, Sorabjee and Arun Jaitley reported to Vajpayee 'that the government and the judiciary were on a collision course and some action had to be taken, or they "would have to face the music".'[70]

On July 22, Ram was driving to the Mumbai airport, bound for Pune to address a group of law students, when his mobile phone rang. It was Jaswant Singh, the Minister for External Affairs. The call came, as narrated by Prem Sahajwala,[71] from 'senior minister Jaswant Singh. Imagine Jethmalani resting comfortably on his seat in the car and responding to the call and Jaswant Singh telling him that I am sorry to inform you . . .

'And Jethmalani completes the sentence—that the Prime Minister wants me to resign as Law Minister . . .

'Jaswant Singh shyly says yes.'

According to Ram,[72] in his telephone call Singh said, 'It is my very painful duty to inform you that the PM wants you to resign; of course, this does not affect our friendship.'

Ram said, 'Tell the PM that he will get my response from the nearest fax machine that I can get. Jaswant, do tell the PM that I am on my way to Pune and my resignation will be with him before sunset.'

When he reached Pune, Ram wrote out his resignation and faxed it to the Prime Minister at 6 p.m. Then he called to inform his secretary, and proceeded to work on his speech for the Symbiosis Law College on Law Day, the next day. That same Sunday, his resignation went to President K.R. Narayanan.

Prem Sahajwala describes what happened at the law school: 'The audience in the auditorium of the hall is happily listening to an announcement that the Law Minister had just arrived in the college and would be soon here on the stage to address them. And lo! Jethmalani is here on the stage. He starts his speech, as the audience doesn't stop the unending session of clapping and clapping. But Jethmalani begins the speech by saying that before I start my speech I would like to inform you that I am no longer the Law Minister for whom you have been waiting for hours!'

According to Gera, Ram finished his speech, turned off his cellphone and went out with friends in his customary hearty way. Ram says he remembers nothing of that evening. He was too dazed. He told nobody what happened, but when the press found out, it was all over him like a blanket.

The *Indian Express* reported, '"The Prime Minister had to make a choice between a pliant attorney general and a no-nonsense law minister. He has made his choice," Jethmalani told reporters the moment he showed up at the Law Day 2000 function organised by the Symbiosis Society on Sunday morning.'[73]

Ram had threatened to resign numerous times, but each time a conversation with Vajpayee resolved the matter. This time Vajpayee sent a messenger to call him, and Ram found it humiliating. Later he claimed he was ready to resign before he set out for Pune, but this was not the way he expected his ministry to end.

'The funny thing is,' says Mahesh Jethmalani, 'Vajpayee actually liked him.'

'"My former Law Minister just cannot keep quiet," the Prime Minister quipped and said despite his repeated advice, Jethmalani went on expressing views even on issues that did not really concern his ministry.'[74]

On Monday morning, Arun Jaitley called Ram to tell him he had been appointed Law Minister. On Tuesday Ram invited Jaitley to his house and asked him about his meeting with the Prime Minister. Jaitley denied that they had discussed Ram at that meeting, and Ram offered him any help he might need in his new position. No suspicions had entered his mind yet.

Official Secrets Act

Once he realized that his previous friends and colleagues were shunning him, Ram became consumed with the desire to explain his point of view in a statement to the Rajya Sabha.

While he was going over his speech with Mahesh and some close friends late on the night of July 24, Rani called. Sorabjee had asked her over and requested her to call Ram. On the phone, Sorabjee talked with Ram about their longtime friendship, and he was almost in tears over Ram's harsh words about him to the press. Ram was on the verge of comforting him until Mahesh brought him up short. Thus prompted, Ram asked for his apology in writing. It arrived, but without the tears or the protestations of friendship.[75]

When Ram presented his written speech to the chairman of the Rajya Sabha, he appended documents in annexures marked 'secret and confidential', but the chairman refused any appended documents whose release might require clearance. Ram never gave the speech.

'An infuriated Jethmalani revealed a mass of documents that showed the extent of power rivalry in the legal administration. Ironically, this prompted attacks on him in Parliament for violating the Official Secrets Act, an expedient diversion from the issues at stake.'[76]

One commentator[77] said that the government might prefer to let Ram be, even for

> . . . violation of the Official Secrets Act, with the former law and justice minister releasing copies of confidential official correspondence to the newsweekly *India Today*. The letters were uploaded on the magazine's web site on Saturday morning.
>
> A cross-section of senior advocates, who insisted on anonymity, said that by going public with the documents, Jethmalani had thrown the gauntlet to the government while simultaneously targeting the Chief Justice.
>
> Jethmalani has openly violated the Official Secrets Act, 1923, and broken the oath of office and secrecy he took when assuming charge as a minister of the Union. 'The oath clearly says a minister will not divulge any official communication even after demitting office,' a senior advocate pointed out.

The Speech to Parliament

'"A minister's resignation is not a private matter between the Prime Minister and the Minister and the whole nation is entitled to know what has been going on." Ram Jethmalani, former Union Law Minister, began his unread statement to the Rajya Sabha with these ominous words. Thwarted from placing his woes before the House to which he belongs, he chose to release his statement to the media on July 27.'[78]

Still, as the article points out, the government might not have wanted to take on Ram. '"Despite that, Jethmalani remains one of

India's best lawyers. At the bar, we often say that from number 1 to 10 is Jethmalani, then come the rest like Soli Sorabjee and Fali Nariman. Thus, if the government actually makes a case against him, it will be fighting a very tough opponent," said one advocate.'

On April 10, Ram had his say before the Rajya Sabha:

I am here only to defend myself against some observations that have been made. The Prime Minister's action in asking me to resign is both legal and constitutional. He has complained that I have not learnt the lesson of silence. It is too late to change myself. Truth must be loudly trumpeted from housetops. It is my proud claim that I have lived by this teaching. My view on the judiciary and the executive relationship seems to be, unfortunately, different from that held by the government. All my life I have fought for independence and glory of the judiciary, I will not surrender my executive privilege to please a judge. It has been said that I am guilty of breaching the Officials Secret Act, and that I have committed theft. I recognize that in the heat of the debate such words are often used. I know that the honourable members have really no intention of insulting me.

No document is confidential, and every citizen, individually, and the public, collectively, has the right to know the contents of the document. A document cannot be made confidential either by agreement or by stamping it as 'secret'. The copies of documents used by me have been in my personal possession since 20 July 2000. If any member of my personal staff is harassed in any manner, it will be an act both dirty and mean, and will evoke an appropriate response from me. My right to explain my resignation is also a reflection of the people's right to know. My actions have been consistent with the stiffest standards of public probity and ethics.

The law relating to the use of so-called confidential documents by Members of Parliament is so well laid down. My quoting from a secret or confidential document, or placing a copy thereof on the Table of the House, does not amount to committing any offence under the Official Secrets Act. Whenever one quotes a so-called secret document, he should be able to authenticate it. I have done that.

One point is about the announcement of a committee of enquiry against me. The Government can go on wasting public time and energy. I cannot object to it.[79]

On August 1, 2000, Ram again addressed the Rajya Sabha. Some of his points were:

'Making or keeping copies of one's own correspondence is theft will shock the dumbest Law Student.'

'A document cannot be made confidential either by agreement or by stamping it as secret and putting it in some safe or locker.'

'The law about use of documents by a Member is to be found in any standard textbook and it was laid down as follows as far back as 1965.'

Accomplishments

The passage of the Code of Civil Procedure (Amendment) Act of 1999 has to be tallied up among Ram's significant achievements. Though implementation was suspended until the lawyers calmed down, and though subsequent amended versions of the bill were enacted during the tenure of his successor, Ram was the one who shepherded it through in the first place. In his mind though, this was just the first step in a fundamental reorganization of the judiciary. That is why the judiciary had to get rid of him.

As an administrator Mr Jethmalani was moving ahead like a bulldozer with a brain. In our judicial system, the process is very just but the people fail to get expedient justice. Mr Jethmalani had a scheme to reorganise the judiciary to deliver speedier justice. He had a plan to recruit better talent as judges and his moves inspired public confidence that he was going to act. His regret after resignation is that he could not complete the mission of judicial reorganisation. The country should realise that the justice machinery has to be reorganised immediately to deliver

speedier justice. If Mr Jethmalani is a wizard of law, he was a
tough administrator too.[80]

Talking to the press after his resignation, or what he called his
'sacking', he 'also threw a calculated barb against bureaucrats
obstructing the repeal of 1,300 redundant laws. His remark
that "every law contains a source of power and affluence for
bureaucrats" drew guffaws when he admitted that his best efforts
had succeeded.'[81]

In the same article, Ram said that he had sworn to reform the
legal system in two years.

One of Ram's innovations was consistent with his lifelong quest
to reform the judiciary. He put up a box in his office and invited
applicants for judgeships to submit their applications, with an
appended list of cases they had argued and copies of their income
tax submissions for the last three years. The concept was to identify
lawyers with significant legal experience and professional success
who were qualified to be High Court judges.

While Ram was Law Minister, on February 22, 2000, the
Ministry of Law, Justice and Company Affairs resolved to
constitute a National Commission to review the working of the
Constitution.[82] Accordingly, Prime Minister Vajpayee appointed
the commission the next day, under the chairmanship of Justice
Venkatachaliah, charging it with the responsibility of reviewing the
Constitution to identify those provisions that needed improvement.
The final report was not adopted until March, 2002, when it was
submitted to Ram's successor, Arun Jaitley. Meanwhile, it released
several consultation papers. One recommendation was to institute
reservations for women members of state and central legislative
assemblies.

Based on these recommendations, Ram piloted the Women's
Reservation Bill or the Constitution (108th Amendment) Bill,
which would reserve one-third of all seats in Parliament and state
assemblies for women. The newspapers reported that opposition
to the bill was so fierce in 1999 that the documents were snatched
out of his hands,[83] but by 2010 a variation of Ram's bill was again

under consideration. By March, 2013, the bill finally had passed the Lok Sabha, and it was pending in the Rajya Sabha.[84]

One distinct accomplishment that Ram could chalk up was the 10-year extension in the reservations for scheduled castes. Those who worked with him in this effort truly consider him one of the outstanding exponents of social justice in India.[85]

The Competition Act of 2002 deserves a place in Ram's ledger of accomplishments. While not formally passed until after he left office, Ram did all the groundwork to create the bill. The previous MRTPC Act had dated from 1969, and it was hopelessly out of date. The new law brought India into the twenty-first century.

Another accomplishment was Ram's implementation of the recommendations of the Commission on Review of Administrative Laws. The Commission's 1998 report identified 1,300 statutes that were outdated, but so far only 200 had been repealed.[86] Examples were the Excise (Malt Liquors) Act, 1890, and the Excise (Spirits) Act, 1863, according to which a citizen can drink only with a permit, or the Boiler Act, which, in the absence of boilers to regulate, was used to regulate anything that looked like a boiler. There also was the Godown Act, passed to regulate godowns (dockside warehouses) during the British Raj. More pernicious were the Societies Registration Act (1860), IPC (1860), Carriers Act (1865), Evidence Act (1872), Indian Trusts Act (1882), Transfer of Property Act (1882), and Bankers Books Evidence Act (1891). These acts were kept on the books by governmental bureaucrats paid to administer them, but Ram commanded enough respect in Parliament for it to comply fully with his requests to revoke the many antique pieces of legislation that he had identified. Ram remembers issuing lists of 10–40 obsolete laws for elimination each week, and he estimates that 500 or more were revoked during his tenure.

Ram is also proud of having a hand in appointing three good judges during his law ministry—Judge Dhananjaya Chandrachud, the son of the former Chief Justice of India, appointed as Chief Justice of the Allahabad High Court; Justice Sharad A. Bobde, appointed Additional Judge of the Bombay High Court; and Judge Ajay M. Khanvilkar of the Bombay High Court. Another contribution to judicial probity was designed to give judges more benefits—Ram was the first to grant permission for high court judges to fly first class. In Ram's estimation, to the extent that a judge saw his job as high status, he would not want to compromise the position by misbehaviour. He believes that the changes he instituted 'made it possible for honest judges not only to exist, but to flourish'.

All that being said, Ram says that the Ministry of Urban Affairs was one in which a minister actually could accomplish something, but that as Law Minister, 'All you do is write opinions favourable to the government without charge.'

The truth is that Ram enjoyed the attention and perks of his ministership, but he felt uncomfortable with many of the restrictions on his daily movement. Security people and staff cramped his style. If he wanted to get away, he had to elude two wives, Rani, and his security detail. Once he managed to elude his security man so well that he was caught in a downpour and had to walk back to his car. When he caught a ride with a passing couple, they were shocked to realize they were driving the Law Minister. He chafed at all official constraints, whether on his movements or his speech. He says, 'Diplomacy is the art of artfully lying.' While a 'little white lie' about an evening entertainment might not bother him, he finds pressure to misrepresent his position on a public or a legal issue to be absolutely unacceptable, despite any exhortations of his party or government. In fact, the more they exhort, the more hard-headed he gets.

Aftermath

The ultimate beneficiary of this battle was the man who succeeded Ram as Law Minister, Arun Jaitley. One wonders if Sorabjee and Anand were helping him achieve this position all along.

That was the view that Ram espoused in his book *Big Egos, Small Men*. While it may have embarrassed his family, the book was Ram's way of venting his resentments and explaining his positions. Not surprisingly, the book included many annexures.

33

Kashmir, Politics, and Terrorism

In 2002, Kashmir enjoyed free and transparent elections, and Ram received much of the credit. Moreover, this paved the way for the democratic elections of 2004, in which the turbulent state of Kashmir voted just as every other state in India did, according to the will of its people. Ram can take the credit for that too. How was this possible?

In Ram's life, no sooner does one phase end, than another begins. He has an endless talent for reinventing himself. When his career as Law Minister came to a close, he was devastated, but he still had more political races to run. He still planned to stay in Parliament, and, never one to think small, he even talked about running for President. More immediately though, at age 78, Ram needed a big project, and the India–Pakistan Kashmir dispute was perfect. As an Indian from what is now Pakistan who speaks Urdu and who sincerely admires the best in Muslim culture, he was a natural go-between.

The Kashmir Conflict

Ever since the Partition, Kashmir has been a tinderbox. Kashmir only joined India because Maharaja Hari Singh Dogra was Hindu, even though a majority of the population was Muslim. His choice was unacceptable to Pakistan, and the subsequent history has been one of Pakistan trying to bring Kashmir back into the Muslim fold.

Just a word of explanation, use of the word Kashmir in this sentence is a convenient, though somewhat inaccurate, way of referring to three geographic regions—Jammu, Kashmir, and Ladakh—as one.

War first broke out after Partition when Pakistani fighters, many dressed as tribals, crossed the Kashmiri border. This was the First Indo-Pakistani War, 1947–48. Pursuant to a January 5, 1949 United Nations resolution, Sheikh Abdullah, the former Prime Minister of Jammu and Kashmir, negotiated a ceasefire with Nehru in 1949, agreeing to a plebiscite—which never happened—and creating a ceasefire line eventually known as the Line of Control. Article 370 of the Indian Constitution was enacted on October 17, 1949, giving Jammu and Kashmir a special status and internal autonomy. It limited Indian jurisdiction in Kashmir to the three areas specified in the Instrument of Accession of 1947: defence, foreign affairs, and communications, but that was not enough to satisfy dissidents. Significantly, Article 370 specified that the status of Jammu and Kashmir could not be changed without the concurrence of the 'Constituent Assembly of the State of Jammu and Kashmir.'

In 1954, Kashmir's accession by India was formally ratified, although proponents of a plebiscite continued to agitate. The problem was that the United Nations resolution of 1949 said the plebiscite would be held only after the conditions of a previous UN Resolution of August 13, 1948 were fulfilled. This said that for a ceasefire and truce to be implemented, Pakistan would have to withdraw its troops from Jammu and Kashmir, after which India would have to withdraw its troops.[1] These conditions were forgotten later by Pakistan and the separatists, who kept harping on a plebiscite. In any case there could be no plebiscite once a portion of Kashmir came under Chinese control.

In 1962, China bit off a chunk of Kashmir to build a road in the Himalayas. In 1965, thousands of Pakistani troops flowed across the Line of Control, starting the Indo-Pakistani War of 1965, the Second Kashmir War. With thousands of casualties, the war now involved the air force, and it saw some of the worst tank warfare since the end of World War II. It ended with the Tashkent Declaration, signed in January 1966.

Lal Bahadur Shastri signed on behalf of India. Ram believes
that treaty should have solved the Kashmir issue, because the
parties agreed 'not to have recourse to force and to settle their
disputes through peaceful means,' and second, that they both would
'discourage any propaganda directed against the other country.'
Unfortunately, Shastri, the only non-Nehru family Prime Minister
up to then, died immediately, spawning conspiracy theories. Perhaps
his own Congress party killed him. Perhaps the Nehru family
wanted to write him out of history. It was a pity; Ram calls Shastri
the most authentic Gandhian of them all.

In 1971, a border war began in East Pakistan, and it convulsed
the nation, creating millions of refugees and thousands of casualties.
The war spread to Kashmir, Rajasthan, and over to Karachi,[2] ending
with the creation of Bangladesh. In July 1972, Prime Minister Indira
Gandhi of India and President Zulfiqar Ali Bhutto of Pakistan signed
the Simla Agreement, which said that any final settlement of the
Kashmir dispute would be decided bilaterally.[3] It also said that 'the
line of control resulting from the cease-fire of December 17, 1971
shall be respected by both sides.' Indian history has not been kind
to that agreement though, because Bhutto slickly made a late-night,
unwritten and unfulfilled, private guarantee to Mrs Gandhi. His
proposed bargain was that he would honour her demand to convert
the Line of Control into an international border in exchange for
his demands to get Indian soldiers out of large portions of Pakistan
and to bring thousands of Pakistani soldiers home from India. That
agreement did not survive the fall of Bhutto's government.

In November 1974, representatives of Prime Minister Indira
Gandhi and of Sheikh Abdullah signed the Kashmir Accord, which
maintained that Jammu and Kashmir would continue to be 'a
constituent unit of the Union of India', which shall 'continue to
be governed by Article 370 of the Constitution of India.' Both the
Kashmiri Opposition parties and Pakistan condemned this.

The Soviets invaded Afghanistan in 1979, and that war ended
in 1989. The Russians went home, but many militants, as well as
munitions, moved to Kashmir. Conversely, thousands of Kashmiris
went to Pakistan for military training. It also was in 1989 that

Al Qaeda emerged, soon to spread into Kashmir.

Admittedly not an unbiased source, the Hindu American Foundation reported, 'Pakistan's military and Inter-Services Intelligence Agency (ISI) planned and orchestrated an Islamist insurgency in India's state of Jammu and Kashmir starting in 1989. According to former Pakistani Ambassador to the US, Husain Haqqani, the objectives of Pakistan's support for the insurgency were two-fold: (1) destabilize India through asymmetric warfare by fomenting violence in Jammu and Kashmir through militant groups, and (2) spread global jihad.'

'Supporting jihad in Kashmir became an instrument of official Pakistani state policy and the ISI organized and centrally controlled the insurgency, while dictating the operations and targets of the militants groups. A separate Kashmir cell was created within the ISI responsible for recruiting, training, and arming militants.'

'Kashmiri terrorists also have ties with Al-Qaeda and militant groups operating in the Pakistan-Afghanistan border areas, which continue to be the center of Islamist terror networks, fundamentalism, drug trafficking, illicit trade in small arms, and international terrorism.'[4]

According to another article, 'While Pakistan's claim that it is only providing moral and diplomatic support for an indigenous freedom struggle in Kashmir Valley, may be true to some extent, it is equally true that Pakistan is arming and training foreign militants as well as indigenous militants. In November 1995, a BBC documentary programme showed evidence of camps in Azad Kashmir and Pakistan, supported by the Jamaat-i-Islami (political wing of the Hizb), where fighters were trained and openly professed their intention of fighting in Kashmir.'[5]

A 2010 article[6] essentially confirms this story, 'Former military ruler Pervez Musharraf has admitted that Pakistan had trained underground militant groups to fight in Kashmir, the first such admission by a top leader of the country.'

Violent insurgencies washed over Kashmir throughout the 1990s, during which almost the entire Pandit community—the indigenous Hindus—left Kashmir. In February 1994, both houses of Parliament in Delhi unanimously resolved that Jammu and Kashmir are an integral part of India and that Pakistan must vacate their part of the state, called the POK—Pakistan occupied Kashmir.[7] The upshot of the resolution is that the Line of Control can never be finalized as a border until the POK is returned, which is not going to happen.

India and Pakistan both tested nuclear bombs in 1998 and, frightened, they signed the Lahore Declaration on February 21, 1999 in order to head off a nuclear race between them. This also included a joint commitment to resolve the Kashmir dispute, but in May 1999 war broke out in the Kargil region of Kashmir, halting implementation of the treaty. First Pakistani troops, then Indian militants, moved across the Line of Control, and the world feared a nuclear war.

Not surprisingly, there were thousands of deaths as combatants fought at incredibly high altitudes, in some cases up to 22,000 feet. Situated in a valley in the Karakoram Range, the Siachen Glacier is 76 kilometres long and two to eight kilometres wide. Blizzards can reach speeds of 300 kilometres per hour, leaving six to seven metres of snow. The temperature drops routinely to -40 degrees centigrade, and the wind chill factor makes it far worse.[8] Some call this glacier the Third Pole.

By July 2001, Indian troops had regained the upper hand, but when General Musharraf of Pakistan went to Agra for a two-day summit with Prime Minister Vajpayee, negotiations broke down completely.

The December 13, 2001 Attack on Parliament

In 2001, a near-catastrophe drew Ram into the heart of the Kashmiri conflict. The Delhi High Court describes 'a macabre incident that took place close to the noon time on 13th December, 2001 in which five heavily armed persons practically stormed the Parliament House complex and inflicted heavy casualties on the security men on duty. This unprecedented event bewildered the entire nation and sent shock waves across the globe.'[9] The High

Court observed, 'The fire power was awesome enough to engage a battalion and had the attack succeeded, the entire building with all inside would have perished.'

Five militants were killed on the spot, and a 17-day manhunt produced four more accused co-conspirators. One of them, Professor S.A.R. Gilani, became Ram's client at the request of the High Court. The Supreme Court gave the details: 'Five heavily armed persons entered the Parliament House complex in a white Ambassador Car . . . heavily armed with automatic assault rifles, pistols, hand and rifle grenades, electronic detonators, spare ammunition, explosives in the form of improvised explosive devices viz., tiffin bombs and a sophisticated bomb in a container in the boot of the car made with enormous quantity of ammonium nitrate.'

Fortunately, the Vice-President's motorcade was parked in the driveway, partially impeding access to the building, and forcing the terrorists to jump out of their cars. They 'quickly started laying wires and detonators.' Security forces reacted immediately, and 'In the gun battle that lasted for 30 minutes or so, these five terrorists who tried to gain entry into the Parliament when it was in session, were killed. Nine persons including eight security personnel and one gardener succumbed,' the Supreme Court said. Sixteen others were injured.

The plotters were said to be the leaders of the banned militant organization known as 'Jaish-e-Mohammed'. This is an organization widely believed to be an arm of Pakistan. The trial before the Special Court of the Delhi High Court lasted six months; it involved 330 documents, with 80 witnesses for the prosecution and 10 for Professor S.A.R. Gilani alone. Mohammad Afzal, Shaukat Hussain Guru, and S.A.R. Gilani were convicted under the Prevention of Terrorism Act (POTA), and they received life and death sentences and fines. This may not appear to make sense, but the life sentences and the death sentences related to different charges. Navjot Sandhu (Afsan Guru) was acquitted of all charges except one, and she was sentenced to five years plus a fine. (The court uses the given names of the suspects along with their aliases.)

The Division Bench of the High Court of Delhi confirmed the

death sentences for Mohammad Afzal and Shaukat Hussain Guru, but it acquitted S.A.R. Gilani and Navjot Sandhu (Afsan Guru).

The court gives their interrelationships: 'It may be mentioned that the accused Mohd. Afzal and Shaukat Hussain Guru are related, being cousins. The 4th accused Navjot Sandhu (Afsan Guru) is the wife of Shaukat Hussain. The third accused S.A.R. Gilani is a teacher in Arabic in Delhi University. It is he who officiated [at] the marriage ceremony of Shaukat Hussain Guru and Navjot Sandhu who at the time of marriage converted herself to Islam.'

The case against Professor Gilani relied heavily on cellphone records, because, as the Supreme Court said, 'there was a call from Shaukat's number to the cellphone number 9810081228 (subsequently discovered to be that of S.A.R. Gilani) and there was a call from Gilani's number to Shaukat's number 10 minutes later. Moreover, it was ascertained that Gilani's number was in constant touch with the other two accused, namely, Shaukat and Afzal. It transpired that Afzal's cellphone bearing the number 9811489429 was reactivated on 7.12.2001 and the first call was from Gilani's number.'

Telephone taps of three suspects revealed that Gilani had received three calls from Srinagar in the Kashmiri language: one from his brother, one from Shaukat, and one from Shaukat's wife. The court's Hindi translation implied that they had discussed the attack on Parliament. Gilani was arrested on December 15, 2001. He led the authorities to the house of Shaukat, who led them to the other suspects. The key question became whether the translation was accurate.

One argument, as the Supreme Court said, was,

Shri Jethmalani contended that Afzal in the course of his interview with the TV and other media representatives, a day prior to recording of a confession before the DCP, while confessing to the crime, absolved Gilani of his complicity in the conspiracy. A cassette (Ext.DW4/A) was produced as the evidence of his talk. DW-4, a reporter of Aaj Tak TV channel was examined. It shows that Afzal was pressurized to implicate Gilani in the confessional statement, according to the learned counsel.

Professor Gilani's colleagues organized a group called Delhi University Teachers in Defence of S.A.R. Gilani. Their statement[10] began:

> The Delhi University Teachers in Defence of S.A.R. Gilani has been deeply concerned about the denial of justice to a fellow teacher, S.A.R. Gilani, an accused in the case concerning the attack on the Parliament on December 13, 2001. Shockingly, Gilani was convicted by the Special Court, designated under the Prevention of Terrorism Act (POTA), and given the death penalty only on the basis of a telephonic conversation in Kashmiri with his brother, lasting two minutes and sixteen seconds. However, the defence argued that both the procedure and the content of the translation from Kashmiri to English were seriously flawed.[11]

The letter goes on:

> In an amazing violation of journalistic ethics, one TV channel repeatedly telecast a "recreation" of the attack on the Parliament based only on the version of the prosecution in an attempt to prejudice public opinion. Unfortunately, the Supreme Court allowed the telecasting of a film that pronounced Gilani guilty even before judgement was delivered. It is a matter of great concern for us that the same film is being telecast again now when the judgement of the High Court is due.
>
> To add to the trial by the media, several fundamentalist organizations have openly threatened violence against lawyers who have dared to defend Gilani. Not even a lawyer as eminent as Mr Ram Jethmalani was spared when he decided to defend Gilani in the High Court. Jethmalani's office was vandalized in Mumbai by the Shiv Sena.
>
> S.A.R. Gilani is personally known to many of us. He is a popular teacher and a serious scholar. Many of us remember

his engaging discussions with students and friends. We also remember him as a person always willing to give time to help others.

The public believed that Gilani was guilty and that Ram was wrong to defend him. There were many protests. The Shiv Sena did attack the offices of Mahesh and Ram in Mumbai when they found out that Ram was going to defend Professor Gilani. Mahesh needed security for his offices and home during and after this case. Gilani was assaulted and in 2005 he was shot, in an unsuccessful assassination attempt. Many of Ram's political colleagues in Delhi disapproved of Ram's advocacy in this case, but it did prove helpful later in his dealings with Syed Ali Shah Geelani in Kashmir. Beyond that, it consolidated Ram's credentials with Muslims, who could never accuse Ram of sectarianism after this.

In the end, the Supreme Court upheld Mohammed Afzal's death sentence, but it reduced Shaukat's sentence to 10 years plus fines. It also upheld the acquittals of Professor Gilani and of Sandhu, Shaukat's wife.

The Supreme Court explained Gilani's acquittal:

There is no evidence to the effect that Gilani was maintaining personal or telephonic contacts with any of the deceased terrorists. There is no evidence of any participative acts in connection with or in pursuance of the conspiracy. He was not connected with the procurement of hideouts, chemicals and other incriminating articles used by the terrorists. Speaking from the point of view of probabilities and natural course of conduct there is no apparent reason why Gilani would have been asked to join conspiracy. It is not the case of the prosecution that he tendered any advice or gave important tips/information relevant to the proposed attack on Parliament. None of the circumstances would lead to an inference beyond reasonable doubt of Gilani's involvement in the conspiracy. There is only the evidence of . . . the landlord of Shaukat, that he had seen the deceased terrorists and Gilani visiting the house of Shaukat two or three days prior to 13th December.

We are, therefore, left with only one piece of evidence against accused S.A.R. Gilani being the record of telephone calls between him and accused Mohd. Afzal and Shaukat. This circumstance, in our opinion, does not even remotely, far less definitely and unerringly point towards the guilt of accused S.A.R. Gilani. We, therefore, conclude that the prosecution has failed to bring on record evidence which cumulatively forms a chain.

The judges quote the High Court's characterization of the telephone evidence:

Indeed the voice was so inaudible that we could not make head or tail of the conversation. We tried our best to pick up the phonetical sounds where there was a dispute as to what words were used, but were unable to do so. Testimony of PW 48 reveals that he could not analyse the talk as it was highly inaudible. PW 48 is a phonetic expert. If he could not comprehend the conversation in a clearly audible tone, the probability of ordinary layman picking up the phonetic sounds differently cannot be ruled out. The prosecution witness, PW 71, Rashid, who prepared a transcript of the tape is fifth class pass and it was not his profession to prepare transcript of taped conversation. The possibility of his being in error cannot be ruled out. Benefit of doubt must go to the defence.

After exhausting all possible appeals, Afzal went to the gallows on February 8, 2013. Protests erupted all over Kashmir and Pakistan.[12]

A lawyer who heard Ram's arguments in court recounts a dramatic story: 'Legend had it that when approached by Nandita Haksar, a famous human rights activist to defend Gilani, Mr Jethmalani had asked to meet Gilani's wife. When Mrs Gilani arrived at Mr Jethmalani's office, it was rumoured that he asked her, "Can you put your hand on the Quran and swear that your husband is innocent?" Apparently without any hesitation she did. And that was enough for Mr Jethmalani to stand against the clamour of his party and a nation hungry for blood to defend Gilani. Standing spellbound in court, I will never forget how he carried the entire court, which remained in pin drop silence for two-and-a-half hours every day for 40 days. He argued the law and facts of the case with such finesse that at the end of 40 days there wasn't a person in that court room who didn't believe in his heart and mind that Gilani was innocent.'[13]

Arundhati Roy wrote a vehement defence of Gilani[14]:

> Consider the Mobile phone call records: Stared at for long enough, a lot of the "hard evidence" produced by the Special Cell begins to look dubious . . . The call records that were produced to show that Shaukat, Afzal, Geelani and Mohammad (one of the dead militants) had all been in touch with each other very close to the time of the attack were uncertified computer printouts, not even copies of primary documents. They were outputs of the billing system stored as text files that could have been easily doctored and at any time. For example, the call records that were produced show that two calls had been made at exactly the same time from the same SIM card, but from separate handsets with separate IMEI numbers. This means that either the SIM card had been cloned or the call records were doctored.

Roy also writes that the Mohammad Afzal conviction was based on a coerced confession, but he was too poor to get the help that Professor Gilani could. She then claims, 'On December 21, 2001, when the Government of India launched its war effort against Pakistan it said it had "incontrovertible evidence" of Pakistan's involvement. Afzal's confession was the only "proof" of Pakistan's involvement that the government had! . . . Think about it. On the basis of this illegal confession extracted under torture, hundreds of thousands of soldiers were moved to the Pakistan border at huge cost to the public exchequer, and the subcontinent devolved into a game of nuclear brinkmanship in which the whole world was held hostage.'[15]

The Kashmir Committee

In 2000, the Jammu and Kashmir Assembly passed a resolution calling for restoring their pre-1953 status, but the resolution was rejected out of hand by the Delhi Union Cabinet.[16] Ram found this frustrating, because the Assembly had shown itself open to talks about autonomy, and it was not advocating secession. He told Advani that this was an opportunity, but Advani was adamant, even though former Prime Minister Rao had said that if they only asked for autonomy 'the sky is the limit'. He just insisted they leave four areas of responsibility for India: defence, currency, foreign affairs, and communications. L.K. Advani told the press that there would be no talks with Pakistan unless it agreed to stop abetting cross-border terrorism.

Musharraf and Vajpayee did meet in 2001, but the talks produced little of substance, reportedly because of Advani's 'hawkish tendencies'. In April 2001, New Delhi appointed K.C. Pant as its first official interlocutor on Kashmir, but the Hurriyat refused to meet him. Pant was able to meet the separatist leader Shabir Shah and former Jammu and Kashmir Chief Minister Mir Qasim, but that was all.

In 2002, Ram approached the Kashmiri law student whom he had sponsored at the National Law School of Bangalore, and asked him to arrange a meeting with a group of Kashmiri separatists, the Hurriyat. In June, Ram met with some 45 men, all armed to the teeth, in a room. First he asked each one to speak his mind for five minutes. After that he requested permission to speak. He spoke in Urdu, a language which he has rarely used since childhood, for over 45 minutes. One could have heard a pin drop. He pleaded with them not to boycott the coming elections, and finally, they promised to end their opposition. Some even promised to run for election. They all embraced him, one by one. Ram remembers scratchy beards and the distinct odour of men who could use a bath. The meeting was a great success. Notably, they asked Ram if he knew other like-minded senior Indian figures willing to form a committee to continue the dialogue.[17]

That was how the Ram Jethmalani Kashmir Committee began in August of 2002 as an unofficial, private effort.[18] Ram was the chairman; other members were Vinod Grover, a retired Indian Foreign Service officer; eminent lawyers Ashok Bhan, Fali Nariman, and Shanti Bhushan; Jawaid Laiq from Amnesty International; Dileep Padgaonkar, editor of the *Times of India* and M.J. Akbar, editor of *Asian Age*.

Searching for official interlocutors, the government had appointed Pant, and once briefly Arun Jaitley, to be a 'point man for negotiating what has been termed as "devolution of powers" to Jammu and Kashmir,' but there had been no result.[19] Now it was the turn of a non-governmental effort.

In August, Ram announced that the Kashmir Committee would begin a three-day tour of Jammu and Kashmir to talk with the All Parties Hurriyat Conference (APHC). One meeting was with Jammu and Kashmir Democratic Freedom Party chief Shabir Shah, lawyers, intellectuals, and journalists.[20] The Kashmiris requested a promise that the government would stop custodial killings and release key political prisoners such as Syed Ali Shah Geelani and Yasin Malik. They also asked for the Disturbed Area Act and Armed Forces Special Powers Act to be withdrawn.[21] The meeting went well, but activists criticized it. Journalists reported that it ran into a setback as soon as Ram emphasized the government's intention to proceed with the state Assembly elections that were scheduled for September and October.

By August 18, the Hurriyat had softened its position on the elections, and Chief Minister Farooq Abdullah muted his opposition to talks with the Kashmir Committee. He even offered to step down from his position if that would facilitate Hurriyat participation in the elections.[22]

By now Ram was convinced that the polls should be postponed, but, believing that the Hurriyat's refusal to participate was dictated by Pakistan, the Election Commission would not budge.

The Hindu reported that the Hurriyat and Shabir Shah had insisted that India must recognize Kashmir as a problem, any solution must involve Pakistan, and the purpose of the elections must be to elect representatives who could negotiate a solution to the Kashmir problem with the government.[23]

In the ensuing days, Ram urged the government to postpone the elections, but they stood pat. Ashok Bhan, the convener of the Kashmir Committee, invited Shabir Shah and Abdul Gani Bhat for further talks.[24] After their first round of talks, and in anticipation of a second round in Delhi, the APHC announced they were 'ready for a constructive and meaningful dialogue with the Govt. of India without any pre-conditions and for the permanent resolution of the issue.' The reason they gave was that Prime Minister Vajpayee had made an encouraging speech at the Red Fort on August 15. Referencing past mistakes in Jammu and Kashmir, he 'rekindled an otherwise dwindling hope in Kashmir.'

Significantly, the APHC said, 'We are not against the principle of elections. We are ready to participate in an election if it can pave the way for a permanent settlement of the issue.'

By August 30, after a second round of talks, the Kashmir Committee and the Democratic Freedom Party released a joint statement saying, 'It was agreed yet again that violence as a principle or as a strategy has no role in the resolution of any problem anywhere in the world including the Kashmir problem.'

They also announced that 'the DFP led by Mr Shabir Shah has in principle agreed to participate in the elections.' They required certain confidence-building measures though, to include 'release of those persons who have been illegally/unfairly jailed, honourable and dignified return of migrants, greater accountability of the Special Operations Group and other anti-insurgency groups, speedy trial of those jailed for petty offences, constitution of a commission to probe into custodial killings and disappearance of persons, facilitation of an intra-Kashmir dialogue.'

The APHC and the Kashmir Committee also released a joint statement which eschewed violence, emphasized that 'all those who had been forced to migrate from the state should return and be fully rehabilitated, with full protection of their rights, [and] called on the governments of India and Pakistan to make all efforts at the earliest opportunity to create conditions for reducing tensions on the Indo-Pak border.' The Kashmir Committee itself 'indicated its readiness to meet the KC [Kashmir Committee] of Pakistan at a mutually convenient time and place.' We will come back to the Kashmir Committee of Pakistan.

Then 'just on the day that leaders [of APHC] were persuaded to come to Delhi, the government insolently and unwisely shut its doors on them . . . The Home Minister [Advani] told Shanti Bhusan that he would not talk to them because they were in touch with Pakistan. In reality, they were, and they made no secret of it. When they offered to participate in the dialogue with Indian leaders, they were doing it with the concurrence of Pakistan. That made the talks all the more significant and eminently desirable.'[25]

Ram says the government wilfully disregarded all the concessions the Kashmiris made to the Kashmir Committee. Furthermore, the Prime Minister's speech at the Red Fort was statesmanlike, but it was not followed up by action. In February 2003, a member of the Rajya Sabha asked the government what actions it planned. Their response was to appoint N.N. Vohra to conduct more talks.

After their third round of meetings, two in Kashmir and one in Delhi, the Kashmir Committee and the APHC released another joint statement in which they again agreed to abjure violence, 'rise above traditional positions', 'abandon extreme stands', and 'be firmly committed to democracy, protection of human rights, respect for ethnic, religious and linguistic pluralism'.

This was when Shabir Ahmed Shah[26] told *Sindhisshaan* magazine that 'Some elements in the central government as well as the state government are actively trying to sabotage the efforts of the Kashmir Committee led by Mr Ram Jethmalani. Former Law Minister Mr Jethmalani is like my elder brother and I have very high regards for him.'

He said several figures had spoken against the committee, 'and also the Deputy Prime Minister L.K. Advani has said that government won't talk, after initially having praised the efforts of the Kashmir Committee in the Parliament . . .' He referred to the Kashmir Committee as 'a bridge between India and Pakistan, and between India (Government of India) and Kashmir (Kashmiri people).'

In the same interview, he said, 'The talks cannot fail between me and the Kashmir Committee. The Kashmir Committee does not represent the government of India but the people of India.' Most poignantly, 'The Kashmir Committee members have understood our views and agreed with us that the Kashmir issue should be resolved only through talks. And for such talks to begin a congenial atmosphere needs to be created. Those prisoners who are rotting in jails for twelve–twelve years without any cases or crimes proved against them should be released; in fact I myself have spent over 23 years of my life in prisons in detention. The Amnesty International has given me titles "Prisoner of Conscience" and "Nelson Mandela of Kashmir".'

The *Times of India* reported, 'In a toughening of stand, Deputy Prime Minister L.K. Advani today virtually ruled out any talks with the Hurriyat or the imposition of governor's rule or postponement of the Assembly elections in Jammu and Kashmir, asserting that the Centre would now talk only with elected representatives from the state. The statement given in an interview with a private television channel practically reverses a proposal to hold talks with the Hurriyat which has declined to participate in the coming elections.'

Advani had accused the Hurriyat of following the dictates of Pakistan, saying that Pakistani President Pervez Musharraf's August 14 address, in which he denounced the elections as 'farcical', gave a clear message to the Kashmiris not to participate.

Yet another problem held back the Hurriyat—the discouraging effect of Hurriyat leader Abdul Ghani Lone's assassination.

Ram had encouraged the Law Minister of Jammu and Kashmir, Abdul Ghani Lone, who was also the leader of the APHC, to take a more liberal stance and to participate in the upcoming elections. On May 21, 2002, after a speech in Dubai in which he proposed talks between the Hurriyat and the Indian government, unidentified gunmen assassinated him near Srinagar. Both Pakistan-based Lashkar-e-Tayiba and local Kashmiri militants claimed responsibility.[27] Then on September 11, militants assassinated his brother, Mushtaq Ahmad Lone, the Indian Minister for Law and Parliamentary Affairs.

Ram went to Kashmir to pay a condolence call to his family. In retrospect, his contacts with the Lone brothers caused him trouble. As a report said, 'Union Minister of State for External Affairs and National Conference President Omar Abdullah today said that his party had "decided to have no further contact or association" with Mr Ram Jethmalani's Kashmir Committee for it was a "Congress political committee". In a statement here, Mr Abdullah said the "secret meeting" of Mr Sajjad Lone of the Peoples' Conference and Mr Saifuddin Soz of the Congress at the residence of Mr Jethmalani in the presence of other committee members had only gone to prove the misgivings of Dr Farooq Abdullah about the objective of the committee.'[28]

The papers reported that Ram's Kashmir Committee could not convince the Hurriyat to participate in the elections once they began to attach strings and preconditions. The Kashmiris complained that the corrupt ministers Congress had imposed on Kashmir took their money. Ram responded that Kashmir should elect their own local leaders, challenging them to fight for free elections with equal rights for Muslims and Hindus, and with observers to monitor them. Ram told them that in a democracy there can be no secession; the best way is to hold elections.

The October 30, 2002 elections in Kashmir ended the reign of the National Conference (NC), and the Abdullah family. 'What made these elections different from those previously held in the State was that nearly all political parties, independent candidates, non-governmental groups, human rights activists, media (both domestic and foreign) and most importantly, the international community, appreciated the credibility of the elections and the results that followed it.

'Observers termed the verdict as an anti-NC mandate of the people who clearly wanted a change in the State. The elections are also a victory of the ballot over the bullet as the participation in all the phases was around 40–45 percent.'[29]

'Indian political analyst Mahesh Rangarajan described the election outcome as "a political earthquake", commenting that "this is the best chance for some measure of normalcy".'[30]

Looking back on the elections, the Chief Minister 'Mufti Muhammad Sayeed Thursday said the 2002 assembly elections were the turning point in the political history of the Jammu and Kashmir. "These elections not only restored peoples' faith in the democratic institutions but the government formed after these polls had also changed political discourse in the State".

"'After getting power, we released all political prisoners and disbanded the notorious Special Task Force (STF) to restore confidence among the masses," he said. "The PDP-led coalition gave a new direction to governance and addressed diverse issues effectively with the result that successive Prime Ministers could come here and reach out to the people and understand their problems."'[31]

The BJP-led central government could not help but note that the elections ousted their allies, the National Conference. That may explain some of their discontent with Ram's Kashmir Committee. It did, however, give the lie to any allegations that the elections were 'farcical'.

One report maintained,[32]

The 2002 polls were important for several reasons. New Delhi sought to ensure that an election was held in which the entire spectrum of Kashmiri political opinion was reflected. A free and fair election with large-scale participation may bolster the Indian claim that the democratic process had worked and that Kashmir is a willing and integral part of India. It also may blunt both domestic and international criticism of India's handling of the security situation in the state as well as weaken Pakistani claims to the territory. A large voter turnout was not anticipated after militant separatist groups threatened violence against any and all participants in the elections, both candidates and voters alike.

We vividly remember sitting with Rani in her Delhi apartment that night, surrounded by her exquisite glass and silver, as Ram appeared on one TV programme after another, and it became clear that all the TV hosts gave Ram and his Kashmir Committee the credit for the dramatic success of these elections. We also remember that the last interviewer apologized for keeping Ram away so late from his evening Scotch.

By December 2002, members of the Hurriyat Conference were criticizing the talks with the Kashmir Committee, calling for trilateral talks with India and Pakistan 'in some friendly country under the supervision of United Nations, as the Hurriyat constitution provided . . . in case the UN resolutions on Kashmir could not be implemented.'[33]

The Hurriyat itself then split, with Syed Ali Shah Geelani leading the rejectionist faction. The timing was unfortunate, because the Kashmir Committee had just hammered out an agreement with the Hurriyat proclaiming: 'Terrorism and violence are taboo. A lasting and honourable peaceful resolution must and can be found. The resolution must be acceptable to all political elements and regions of the State. Extremist positions held by all for the last five decades have to be and will be abandoned. Kashmiri Pandits will be rehabilitated with honour and rights of equality.'

By February 2003, the papers reported that the government was actively seeking to replace Ram's Kashmir Committee.[34] 'It is common knowledge that it was none other than the Deputy Prime Minister L.K. Advani himself who had given "green signal" to Jethmalani to set-up a private citizen's group consisting of eminent Indian intellectuals to seek and break ice with the separatist bandwagon in Kashmir, more than ever, the hard to pin down, All Party Hurriyat Conference. . . .

'Nevertheless, Kashmir Committee failed in its primary objective to rope in APHC, something which did not go [down] well with New Delhi. Furthermore, in the post-election scenario, the position of New Delhi on Kashmir has enhanced radically, and such any future negotiations with APHC and company would take place largely on the "terms and conditions" laid down by the Home Ministry.'

While all this was going on in 2003, lightning struck Ram twice. First, Janak developed a mass in his brain. It turned out that it was not cancer, but Janak's illness, partial recovery, and rehabilitation were a terrifying experience for the whole family. Ram did everything he could to give his beloved son the best care possible.

Second, on September 22, 2003, the *Tribune* of Chandigarh announced: 'Mrs Ratna Jethmalani, wife of former Law Minister and eminent criminal lawyer Ram Jethmalani, died in Mumbai early this morning. She was 79. Mrs Ratna, who was admitted to Breach Candy Hospital after she fell and sustained injuries in the hip sometime back, went into coma a few days ago. Her husband was at her side when the end came at 0630 hours in the hospital. Mr Ram Jethmalani had postponed his birthday celebrations last week owing to her hospitalisation.'

Ratna's death saddened Ram as few things ever have. The fresh garland of marigolds on her picture today is a reminder that the bond between them was deep and long-standing. Losing her reminded him of his own mortality. Ram, however, is a survivor. After all, he concentrates on his work, and he saw Kashmir as his most important work during that time.

Nevertheless, after only six months, Ram announced that he was suspending the activities of his Kashmir Committee in order to give N.N. Vohra a free reign to work towards peace.[35] Even so, the Hurriyat leaders brushed Vohra off just as they had Pant, insisting they would not talk to any functionary from New Delhi lower than the Prime Minister. In 2008, N.N. Vohra would be appointed the Governor of Jammu and Kashmir.

Ram was not done with Kashmir, nor is he yet. From 2003 through 2004, Ram met multiple times with Pakistani parliamentarians and opinion leaders either in India or Pakistan. In May 2003, Ram's Kashmir Committee met with a group of Pakistani parliamentarians who visited India for the Pakistan–India People's Forum for Peace and Democracy (PIPFD). Sherry Rehman gives an overview of this period of optimism and enthusiasm.

Ambassador Sherry Rehman, a Sindhi, and later Pakistan's Ambassador to the US from 2011 to 2013, delivered a paper at a Delhi conference,[36] saying, 'Mr Bhandara and I were on the first parliamentary delegation to India, in May 2003, against the advice of our Foreign Office and the Indian one, but to our delight and amazement we found that we met a fair amount of notables and officials and of course parliamentarians; we encountered a tidal wave, a tsunami of welcoming arms and people and institutions, we did not have enough time to meet people, and since that visit we have been back about seven or eight times either institutionally or personally. So far, 120 Indian parliamentarians have visited Pakistan, and 80 Pakistani parliamentarians have been to India.'

Ambassador Rehman observed, 'For the process to work on an institutional level, the human element must be operational in terms of basic confidence-restoration measures.' The human element was Ram's speciality.

In May 2003, the *Economic Times* wrote,[37] 'Happy over their week-long trip to India, Pakistani lawmakers have made it clear that . . . "They (militant leaders) will have no other chance than to accept a cease-fire if the talks between India and Pakistan make some headway and there is increased contact between people of the two countries," the leader of 12-member Pakistani MPs Ishaq Khan Khakwani told reporters last night.

'To a question whether they would be conveying the feelings of Indian political leaders to their prime minister, Mr Khakwani said, "We will not only submit a detailed report to the government but also apprise it (sic) of the fruitful conversation with the leaders of the political parties and intelligentsia."

'Asked about their experience in the country, he said, "It has been wonderful and I hope that a parliamentarian delegation will also come from India to Pakistan. The more we have people-to-people contact, the more we will be able to thrash out our differences and work for peace."'

While in India they met the Kashmir Committee. The *Economic Times* report quoted Khakwani as saying, 'The talks were fruitful and we were unanimous on the view that we should try to iron out differences between the two countries and contribute for peace.' He also said he would request the Pakistani government to set up an 'official' Kashmir Committee as soon as possible so the two committees 'could meet and contribute towards peace.'

In August 2003, Ram wrote that 'In December, an unofficial group of Pakistani Parliamentarians crossed into India . . . Sherry Rehman was one of them. She is a Member of the National Assembly of Pakistan and former editor of the *Herald*. On her return to Pakistan, she wrote that the original referendum promised to Kashmir by the UN "looks like it is ready to die a natural death".'[38]

Next, Ram visited Pakistan. In August 2003, 'Even as India today rejected Pakistan President Pervez Musharraf's proposal for a ceasefire along the Line of Control (LoC), the Rashtriya Janta Dal President, Mr Laloo Prasad Yadav, Mr Ram Jethmalani, Chairman on Kashmir Committee, Mr Saleem Sherwani, a former Foreign Minister and other members of Parliament, returned to India after attending a two-day South Asian Media Association Convention.'[39]

In August 2003, Pakistan's *Daily Times* reported from Lahore,[40] 'Mr Jethmalani told *Daily Times* in an exclusive interview, during his recent visit to Pakistan with a delegation of Indian parliamentarians and journalists to attend a peace conference and a reception hosted for him by human rights activist Asma Jehangir, it was Pakistan and Pakistanis that complicated the Kashmir issue.'

Ram's Indian delegation consisted of parliamentarians, media personnel, and experts. In Islamabad, at the August 10–11, 2003 meeting of the South Asia Free Media Association (SAFMA), Ram addressed an audience in which President Musharraf was sitting. Looking right at him, he said, 'Mr President, don't insist on a settlement of the Kashmir problem before India and Pakistan become friends. Let India and Pakistan become friends first.'[41] With their Pakistani colleagues, the delegation released a statement recommending a series of confidence-building and conflict resolution proposals.[42]

After their four-day stay in Pakistan, 'touched by the love and affection they had received, the Indian delegates said people of both countries would force their respective governments to undertake a direct dialogue on the Kashmir issue. General Musharraf already had softened his stand, and Ram expressed the hope that 'the

Kashmir dispute could be resolved amicably'. Uncharacteristically, he refused to give any details on the proposed dialogue, in order to not complicate the issue.

That encounter was why Musharraf, frustrated over his meeting with Vajpayee, chose to send his own four-point proposal through an intermediary, M.P. Bhandara, to Ram in 2003. Ram read the points, suggested some inconsequential changes, and sent word back that if Musharraf approved, he would publish the points as his own proposals to Pakistan. The result was that, with Musharraf's concurrence, Ram published Musharraf's four-point statement of principles for solving the Kashmir conflict, somewhat modified, as the working paper of the Kashmir Committee. The points were National Conference (NC) autonomy, self-rule, mediation and negotiation, including arbitration. These were similar to the four-stage plan Musharraf himself released in June of 2003.[43]

'Indian Kashmir Committee Chairman Ram Jethmalani said on Wednesday he had noticed in his meetings with Pakistani leaders that Islamabad's stance on Kashmir was more flexible than before . . . Asked about his meeting with President General Pervez Musharraf, Mr Jethmalani said the meeting was confidential, but he had been given a message by Gen. Musharraf for Indian Prime Minister Atal Behari Vajpayee which he would pass on. Mr Jethmalani said Gen Musharraf is a committed and mature politician who acted reasonably. "I have a lot of respect for him," he added.'[44]

Ram came back from that South Asia Free Media Association meeting convinced that peace was at hand, but soon after came a dire Pakistani threat: 'Lashkar-e-Taiba, a Pakistani terror group, likes to threaten to blow up India's dams. Last year a Pakistani extremist, Abdur Rehman Makki, told a rally that if India were to "block Pakistan's waters, we will let loose a river of blood".'[45]

Ram wrote in December 2003, 'Between October 31 and November 3, 2003, a dozen of our Pakistani friends arrived in Delhi and settled down to a free and frank diagnosis and the search of an effective prescription. Our guests included prestigious politicians, poets, journalists, generals and diplomats, men of religion and captains of industry. For four days at a stretch, they talked with candour, conferred with wisdom and endeavored to discover a statesmanlike solution.'[46]

According to Ram, Mr M.P. Bhandara led one of the delegations of Pakistani parliamentarians, and after he returned to Pakistan he wrote an article for the *Asian Age* in which he suggested a roadmap for the negotiations to succeed. He also presented a paper with similar proposals at a conference, titled 'What makes the peace process irreversible?'[47] The Kashmir Committee believed these views carried great weight.

Attempts to solve the Kashmir question continued on many fronts. An August 2003 report showed that Ram was involved in Track II—meaning private, person-to-person—discussions as early as July 2003. Ram said, 'at the Centre for Strategic and International Studies in Washington that "If he is (Musharraf) replaced, things in Pakistan will deteriorate, with great implications for the security of the world and of India."'[48] Ram and members of the Kashmir Committee also met privately in Delhi with the US ambassador to India, Robert Blackwell, during the same period.

Another early attempt at a Track-II approach which Ram endorsed was the US-based Kashmir Study Group, established in 1996 by Farookh Kathwari, an American from Srinagar. Ram travelled to the United States to meet with them in November 2011, and Kathwari met Ram in India to discuss his proposals. This group put forward reasonable ideas, and it had the distinct advantage that it was not pushing any separatist agenda. It had the support of the American state department, and until Musharraf left, it enjoyed a direct line to him, echoing many of his own ideas that he put in a February 2005 proposal based on self-governance and demilitarization.

In 2004, 'On January 22, leaders of the All Parties Hurriyat Conference (APHC) . . .were in Delhi for what has been termed a "historic" dialogue with the Central government on the issue of Jammu and Kashmir. The leaders met the Deputy Prime Minister, L.K. Advani, and also had an unscheduled meeting with the Prime Minister, A.B. Vajpayee. The APHC leaders announced after the meeting that they had held "amicable, free, frank, fair and fruitful" discussions. The meeting created both optimistic and pessimistic speculations about some of the important issues with regard to a long-term resolution of the Kashmir dispute.'[49] The joint statement they released said that the government would quickly review the cases of Kashmiri detenus, and it projected a continuation of the dialogue in March. Ram was widely believed to have paved the way for these talks.

Ambassador Rehman wrote in November 2004,[50] that she was 'one of the parliamentarians who recently crossed over the Wagah border for a five-day yatra of New Delhi on the invitation of the Pakistan–India Peace Forum.' Highly critical of the BJP government, she wrote, 'Strikingly, the highest level of optimism came not from the mainstream media or the security establishment, but from opposition politicians and from key members of civil society.' That trip may have been part of the Friendship March from Karachi to Delhi that the Pakistan–India People's Forum for Democracy announced would be held from June 11 to October 2, 2004.[51]

So many groups were working on the Kashmir problem at the same time or at overlapping times that it is difficult to discuss these efforts in an orderly way. Some of these, and some of Ram's efforts, have been called Track II diplomacy—unofficial attempts at conflict resolution. An example was the Pugwash International meeting in Kathmandu from December 11–14, 2004. This is an organization of 'great thinkers' founded by Bertrand Russell, and it has received a Nobel Prize for its work against nuclear arms.

A description of the conference is revealing.[52]

It has been an important milestone in Track Two diplomatic discourses in the context of India and Pakistan on Kashmir . . . The tone, tenor and broad-based participation and the reconciliatory attitude from all across the board reflected the positive change that has characterized Indo-Pak relations in 2004. This was a broad-based conference gathering a large number of participants from India and Pakistan including from both sides of the LoC in Jammu & Kashmir. The participants included prominent people drawn from academic, diplomatic, military,

political and business backgrounds . . . Significantly, no Kashmiri
separatist leader was prevented from attending this conference.[53]

Significantly and *prevented* are the operational words. Exactly
because there was no support from key separatists, this effort
confined itself to pondering non-controversial issues. They
recommended improvements in bus services, border crossings, trade
contacts, water resources, and environmental projects, all highly
commendable, but of little interest to the insurgents. In contrast,
Ram's approach was bottom-up. He established relationships with
grass-roots politicians and dissidents on the ground in Kashmir,
especially with Syed Ali Shah Geelani. This conference mainly
involved participants from India, Pakistan, and overseas. Of course,
it did kindly refrain from preventing the locals from coming.

Between the time that Ram's first Kashmir Committee wound
down its activities and the time it reconstituted itself as the second
Kashmir Committee after the 2010 Kashmir riots, multiple official
contacts and Track II activities were taking place.

The 2002 elections had primed the way for the 2004 elections:
'The 2004 parliamentary elections in Jammu and Kashmir
reaffirmed trends already in evidence since the 2002 assembly
elections in the state. Despite the continued threat of militancy
and the politics of separatism running a course parallel to electoral
politics, the improved showing of the People's Democratic Party in
the Kashmir Valley and the resurgence of the Congress in Jammu
establishes two things. First, that issues relating to a Kashmiri
identity have now found a space in the electoral agenda beyond an
exclusive, separatist platform and, second, the politics of division
in Jammu, either of religion, caste or tribe, as encouraged by the
BJP and the National Conference, has been firmly rejected.'[54]

Another report said of the 2004 election, 'By bringing an end
to dominance by a single party and ushering in coalition politics, it
had democratized the electoral space . . . the assembly election of
2002 was an important milestone . . . for it succeeded not merely in
increasing the credibility of the electoral process, but also in giving
a sense of satisfaction to the people for their role in the making and

unmaking of their government.'[55] Also, the militants calmed down.

When the 2004 election swept out the BJP and brought in the Congress party, it increased the distance between the government and Ram's work in Kashmir, but the pace of talks, conferences, and study groups on Kashmir picked up markedly. The reasons are hard to determine. Certainly the players had changed. Also, the atmosphere in Kashmir had improved since the elections of 2002.

One high-level effort was the Composite Dialogue Process between India and Pakistan, conceived of in 1997 and finally starting in April, 2003. It revived again in June 2004 after Vajpayee's January visit to Musharraf in Pakistan and a September meeting between Prime Minister Manmohan Singh and President Musharraf during the UN General Assembly. This was an attempt to solve eight outstanding technical issues involving Kashmir. Some of its accomplishments included formalizing the ceasefire along the Line of Control, resumption of India–Pakistan bus, truck and train links, improved air and maritime cooperation between the countries and with Srinagar, a joint judicial commission and improved communications between think-tanks. Joint terrorism initiatives and bilateral trade relations also were under active discussion, but the wind went out of the sails after the attacks in Delhi in November, 2008.[56]

At the same time, a 'back channel' was established between 'National Security Adviser J.N. Dixit on the one side and President Musharraf's aide Tariq Aziz on the other. Following Mr Dixit's demise in 2005 his position was taken over by Special Envoy Satinder Lambah who held around 15 rounds of negotiations with his counterpart between 2005 and 2007.'[57]

By early 2007, the back-channel talks on Kashmir had become 'so advanced that we'd come to semicolons,' Kasuri recalled.[58] A senior Indian official who was involved agreed. 'It was huge—I think it would have changed the basic nature of the problem,' he told me. 'You would have then had the freedom to remake Indo-Pakistani relations.' Aziz and Lambah were negotiating the details for a visit to Pakistan by the Indian Prime Minister during which, they hoped, the principles underlying the Kashmir agreement would be announced and talks aimed at implementation would be inaugurated.

'Neither government, however, had done much to prepare its public for a breakthrough. In the spring of 2007, a military aide in Musharraf's office contacted a senior civilian official to ask how politicians, the media, and the public might react. "We think we're close to a deal," Musharraf's aide said, as this official recalled it. "Do you think we can sell it?" . . . Regrettably, the time did not look ripe.'

The moment passed. Musharraf lost power in 2008, and so did any understanding he had negotiated.

The government continued to seek solutions, always between officially sanctioned groups, not with the Hurriyat.

In 2006, Prime Minister Manmohan Singh started a new initiative—Roundtable Conference and Working Groups. However, the recommendations of the five Working Groups: On Cross-LoC Relations, Center-State relations, Human Rights and Economic Development—are yet to be implemented.

Yet another Round Table was held in May 2006, this time in Srinagar, which was well attended by all standards. Mirwaiz Umar Farooq subsequently denounced the process and pointed out that it could only be successful if it was part of a broader dialogue with the Hurriyat as well as with people across the border, including the government of Pakistan. This was the time when General Musharraf in Pakistan was actively looking for a Kashmir settlement and was telling the moderate Hurriyat to continuously raise the necessity of involving Islamabad in the talks on Kashmir. Separatist leaders like Yasin Malik and Shabir Shah also chose to boycott the second roundtable talks.[59]

In 2010, the government appointed journalist Dileep Padgaonkar, academician Radha Kumar, and former Central Information Commissioner M.M. Ansari as a team to prepare a roadmap to resolve the Kashmir issue, however they fell into such disagreement among themselves that Ram says they ended up barely speaking to each other. According to one report, 'The separatists refused to meet the team. Their only achievement was entering house of Moulvi Abbas Ansari, where he offered them tea.'[60] According to another, 'During their one-year-long interlocution barring meeting senior Hurriyat leader Abbas Ansari they failed to engage any significant separatist leader. Even Ansari later accused them of gate crashing.'[61]

> Their appointment was followed December last by an initiative of non-Congress and non-BJP political parties at New Delhi to form 'Committee for Promotion of Dialogue with Jammu and Kashmir' which is primarily seen as Left's parallel initiative to the appointment of interlocutors . . . It launched a 'campaign for peace and justice in Kashmir', besides the panel had also demanded number of confidence building measures including revocation of AFSPA and Public Safety Act (PSA) and release of political detenus.
>
> The main opposition, BJP too joined the race and constituted its parliamentary study group on Kashmir. The five member BJP team headed by former party president Rajnath Singh is touring Jammu and Srinagar to meet people of different shades of opinion 'to gauge their aspirations'.[62]

The Heidelberg papers, published by the Department of Political Science of the South Asia Institute at the University of Heidelberg, write, 'Before the Islamabad Summit in January 2004, there have been more than thirty-five occasions, in which the Heads of State in India and Pakistan have met[63] [and] at least twelve rounds of talks between 1989 and 1998 before the Lahore and Agra Summits . . . All these attempts invariably broke down, due to the failure of both governments to reach an understanding on Kashmir.'

What the renewed official contacts and conferences did accomplish was to re-establish bus and trade links with Kashmir and to constitute a Joint Judicial Committee of judges from both countries in 2008 to investigate the problem of prisoners in India, Kashmir, and Pakistan. Over 500 prisoners were released between 2003 and 2009 in response to a major Kashmiri complaint.

Also, according to the Heidelberg papers, 'During the period from 2004–2007, General Musharraf put forward various proposals for resolving the Kashmir imbroglio. In November 2003 in an interview with the BBC Radio Urdu Service, Musharraf re-introduced his "four-step" approach to Kashmir, one he had tentatively put across during the Agra talks which offered to eliminate all options unacceptable to India, Pakistan and the people of Kashmir and then evolve a consensual solution.'

These four steps were: 1) Official talks were to commence, 2) All involved should acknowledge the centrality of the Jammu and Kashmir dispute, 3) Any proposal unacceptable to India, Pakistan or Kashmiris would be taken off the table, and 4) The best solution acceptable to India, Pakistan, and the Kashmiris will be taken.

'It is believed that the Musharraf's "four-step" proposal was discussed amongst the officials of both countries during the course of Composite Dialogue Process. In September 24, 2004, General Musharraf and Indian Prime Minister, Dr Manmohan Singh met in New York and signed a joint statement indicating that they would start looking into various options on Kashmir and take the peace process forward,' the Heidelberg papers said.

On December 5, 2006, Musharraf offered a new iteration of his four-point formula, emphasizing improved trade and transportation across the Line of Control, self governance, demilitarization, and joint management of Jammu and Kashmir. The truth was that even if Musharraf and Singh had agreed on any four-point formula, Singh remained restricted by the February 1994 Parliament resolution, which set the precondition that Pakistan first must vacate POK (Pakistan Occupied Kashmir).

The Heidelberg papers describe meetings between the commerce secretaries of India and Pakistan, meetings on the Composite Dialogue, meetings between the ministries of tourism and culture, and five sets of home/interior secretary level talks between India and Pakistan, covering trade, economic issues, terrorism, and drug traffic, all between 2004 and 2008, and all suspended in July 2006 after the Mumbai train bombings. After that they resumed, only to stop after the November 26, 2008 attacks on the Taj Mahal Palace and Oberoi hotels, and other sites in Mumbai.

The papers conclude that the dialogue did not resolve any of the major issues, because of the 'unreasonable positions' of the parties and 'mutual distrust of one another'.

The problems in Kashmir went far beyond communication and trade relationships. They went straight to a lack of governance by the Chief Minister, the brutal police who ran Kashmir as a police state, and the periodic shakedowns of anyone under suspicion. There also were events such as a 2007 bombing of the Samjhauta Express (the friendship train) from Delhi to Lahore in which 68 were killed, a 2009 attack on Hurriyat leader Fazl Haq Qureshi in Srinagar, and a 2010 gun battle in the Punjab Hotel at Lal Chowk in Srinagar.

Another disaster—riots in Kashmir—finally stimulated Ram to restart the Kashmir Committee. In an interview on June 4, 2011,[64] Ram said he had revived the Kashmir Committee after the 2010 riots in which a dozen, perhaps several dozen, young people were killed, '"For more than one reason, we left the mission half way. We did this mainly because allegations were leveled that we were obstructing the dialogue process in Kashmir, launched by the NDA government. It was none else but the then NDA government which impeded our role . . ." Jethmalani said the four-point proposal of former Pakistan president Pervez Musharraf with slight modifications can provide the basis for the settlement of Kashmir issue.'

These riots, the worst in years, started as protests against India, but then broadened: 'Indian-administered Kashmir witnessed widespread violence Monday that killed 18 people and left 80 wounded, some critically. Pro-independence mobs defied a round-the-clock curfew to stage protests against India and against a Florida pastor's now-canceled plans to burn the Quran, leading to fierce clashes with Indian security forces.'[65]

'Tens of thousands of Kashmiris staged angry street

demonstrations today after government forces killed four people and injured 31 during the latest unrest against Indian rule in the disputed Himalayan region . . . Two months of violent clashes with security forces have left at least 55 people dead in Indian-controlled Kashmir—mostly protesters who have been shot.'[66]

Indians insist that violence in Kashmir is instigated by militants from across the border, and that the level of violence is a function of Pakistan's government, the actions of the Pakistani ISI and army and the jihadists. None of this can be solved by well-meaning international conferences.

Ram's Kashmir Committee was re-energized when Asma Jahangir, a friend of Rani's and a preeminent Pakistani human rights activist, was elected chairman of the Supreme Court Bar Association of Pakistan in November 2010. This was propitious, because Ram was elected chairman of the Supreme Court Bar Association of India at the same time. At Ram's invitation in March 2011, Asma led a 130-lawyer delegation of the Pakistan Supreme Court Bar to New Delhi and Jaipur for a four-day visit.[67] Ram went all out to entertain them royally, and he assured them that the people of India were dying to have peace and friendship with the people of Pakistan. Ram was at his most eloquent, and his speech moved the audience to tears.

'In the friendly atmosphere of Jaipur, every resolution was unanimous,' as Asma reported when she returned to Pakistan after the meeting. Ram wrote of the key points on which they achieved unanimous agreement:

'1.   The two governments shall forthwith denounce war as an instrument of national policy and enter into a "no war" treaty, which shall be registered with the United Nations. The obligation shall be absolute without any loopholes or escape routes.

'2.   All disputes shall be solved by negotiation or agreed mediation.

'3.   The unsettled ones shall be settled by decision of agreed judicial tribunal and, failing that, by reference to the

  International Court of Justice if the dispute is of justiciable character and in other cases by arbitration of agreed arbitrators or by the international arbitration tribunal in existence.

'4. A permanent advisory body of the two Bar Associations shall be created with equal representatives of the two associations to educate public opinion and bring democratic pressure to bear on both governments to act on and enforce these resolutions as early as possible.'[68]

After the Pakistani delegation returned home, the Chief Justice of Pakistan, Iftikhar Muhammad Chaudhari, invited Ram to bring a delegation of Indian lawyers to Islamabad to discuss the development of the Indian judiciary with their Pakistani counterparts. Most likely, this actually was an invitation from Prime Minister Zardari, extended through the Chief Justice. In April 2011, Ram brought Rajiv Dhavan, a lawyer teaching at Oxford; Shoma Chaudhury, a journalist for *Tehelka*; and M.M. Krishnamani, later the President of the Supreme Court Bar, to Karachi and Islamabad. There they felt an overwhelming outpouring of love and hospitality, and scores of Pakistani friends told them of the wonderful reports they had received about the meetings in Delhi and Jaipur.[69]

On this visit, Chief Justice Chaudhari invited Ram to meet Pakistan's President Asif Ali Zardari, the former husband of Benazir Bhutto, and, like Ram, a Sindhi from Karachi. Ram sat with him in informal conversation until 1 a.m. It would have been fascinating to be a fly on the wall as the two Sindhis talked—in English though, because others were present who did not speak Sindhi. Newspaper reports of the delegation's visit were quite favourable.[70]

In August 2012, 'Senior BJP leader, leading legal luminary, Rajya Sabha MP from Rajasthan and former Union Law Minister Ram Jethmalani has revived his Kashmir Committee (KC). He revived it after his meeting with Pakistan President Asif Ali Zardari in Pakistan last month. Jethmalani claims that he had fruitful discussions with Zardari and it was his discussion with him which motivated him to revive the KC. He made these claims on August

4 in Srinagar during his interaction with those seeking separation from India.'[71]

Ram invited Madhu Kishwar to be the convener of the reconstituted committee. A friend of Rani's, Madhu publishes a magazine called *Manushi*. She wrote that though Ram's Kashmir Committee went dormant after the successes of its first year, the anti-government demonstrations in 2010 caused Ram to revive it in April 2011, 'after intensive dialogues with leading actors of Pakistani civil society organizations, and senior judges, politicians as well as the President and Prime Minister of Pakistan. They all communicated to him the need to create a platform that would garner all the forces desiring peaceful and democratic resolution of the Kashmir problem and enduring peace between India and Pakistan.'[72]

Madhu wrote, 'Three of the present members of the Kashmir Committee, former Law Minister Shanti Bhushan, former Ambassador V.K. Grover and eminent editor and journalist M.J. Akbar were members of Kashmir Committee I as well. A significant addition to KC II is Waheed Ur Rehman, a journalist from Pulwama district of Kashmir.' M.J. Akbar and Dileep Padgaonkar had resigned from the Kashmir Committee in 2004, after Ram's announcement that he would run in the elections against Vajpayee; they said that gave the committee political overtones.

Madhu further wrote that in June 2011 the second Kashmir Committee met in Kashmir with separatists, politicians, professionals, academics, and businessmen. In July they met with Kashmiri Pandits who had been scared away from their ancestral homes by Muslim militants. The next meeting was in Ladakh.

The separatists told them they wanted to return to their pre-1953 status, in which the central government only had control of defence, finance, foreign affairs, currency, and security. The Kashmir Committee insisted that there were other functions India could not give up: 1) the jurisdiction of the Supreme Court, 2) the Election Commission and 3) the jurisdiction of the Comptroller and Auditor General of India.

The renewed Committee garnered favourable reviews:

Unlike Kashmir interlocutors, who failed to bring separatists, human rights activists and civil society groups on board during their year-long exercise, Ram Jethmalani's Kashmir Committee in past three days has created a flutter in Kashmir by entering into dialogue with all.

First, Jethmalani had an extensive meeting with Syed Ali Shah Geelani, the chairman of hardline faction of Hurriyat Conference. Jethmalani said he would take up the issue of Geelani's continuous house arrest in the Supreme Court. . . . After Geelani, Jethmalani had detailed meeting with Hurriyat moderate faction chairman Mirwaiz Umar Farooq. Mirwaiz had refused to give audience to Kashmir interlocutors. He also met senior separatist leader Shabir Ahmad Shah. On Sunday he heard human rights activists, lawyers and traders.[73]

The key was Geelani. Though he still advocates a plebiscite, he says Ram is a fair man, is independent, and will recommend the right ideas to the central government. Gradually, Geelani is becoming slightly less pro-Pakistan, but he remains a man of principle. In Kashmir, that might just mean that you only take money from one side.

Throughout the discussions, Ram emphasized the formula he had negotiated with Musharraf. The third meeting was on a Sunday at the house of Shabir Shah, with delegates from the Hindu, Muslim, and Sikh communities. Shah was pleased to hear that Ram had visited Pakistan with positive results. Next they met the chairman of the National Front, Nayeem Khan, at his office, where they heard an extensive list of grievances against the state government, the police, the judiciary, and the legal community in Kashmir.

In their meetings, several members of the Jammu Kashmir Liberation Front (JKLF) complained that the many killings and detentions they had suffered were incompatible with serious talks. The committee also met key leaders at their homes or offices: the People's Democratic Party (PDP) President Mehbooba Mufti, Maulana Abbas Ansari, Sajad Lone, Congress President

Professor Saifuddin Soz, and Yasmin Raja, the leader of the Muslim Khawateen Marakaz. Finally, they met with a 12-member group from the Kashmir Press Association, business associations, families of activists, and youth groups.

Not everyone was a fan of the committee's activities. Masood Hussain of the *Economic Times* wrote in August 2012, 'Since 2002, Ram Jethmalani has been active on Kashmir front. But he has maintained an impeccable record—his very visit creates a controversy. Last summer he set people fuming everywhere between Srinagar and Delhi when he compared the situation in Kashmir with that of Nazi Germany'[74]

Hussain says the leaders of the National Conference (NC) have recently boycotted talks with Ram and the Kashmir Committee and that 'Its activities led to a series of fruitless talks between Prime Minister Vajpayee, Home Minister L.K. Advani and moderate separatists.'

As far as all that is concerned, we must remember that every commentator has an agenda, and in Kashmir we need to ask whether the writer is in favour of or opposed to any peaceful settlement leaving Kashmir part of India.

Another snipe by a habitual critic was, 'The National Conference (NC) party has asked the Omar Abdullah government not to allow Kashmir Committee (KC) chairman and noted Supreme Court lawyer Ram Jethmalani to enter the state "to vitiate the peaceful atmosphere and derail the peace process. The government should not allow people like Ram Jethmalani to enter the state during summers because they come here to misguide and hoodwink the people, and also derail the process of peace in Jammu & Kashmir," an NC spokesperson said.'[75]

The *Times of India* wrote that hard-line leaders who met with the Kashmir Committee never changed their positions to any significant extent, despite the warm fuzzy feelings that Ram expressed to the press.[76] Ram ran up against multiple factions, multiple opinions, and no common agenda. All the separatists have their own agendas, and it is not unusual for them to take money both from the Pakistani side and the Indian side.

Today the conflict is largely centred in the Kashmir Valley, which comprises only a fraction of Indian-controlled Jammu and Kashmir. A majority in Jammu and Ladakh are Hindu today, and they want to remain within India. Only Srinagar would have a pro-Pakistan majority. While a plebiscite may seem to be the obvious solution, any plebiscite supervised by the UN will only be allowed under the Indian flag after Pakistan has completely withdrawn. These are difficult conditions for achieving a breakthrough.

Despite the dearth of support from the government of India, Ram remains undaunted.

The *Greater Kashmir* reported on February 5, 2012,[77]

To seek a peaceful resolution of Kashmir issue, track II diplomacy has been reactivated with Kashmir Committee head and former Union Law Minister, Ram Jethmalani taking lead role this time, a vernacular news agency KNS reported on Saturday. Quoting sources it said Jethmalani motivated Hurriyat Conference (G) chairman, Syed Ali Shah Geelani, to meet number of former diplomats, army officers and politicians at his Akbar Road residence in New Delhi on Friday evening . . . Among others Kamal Sibal, Shanti Bhushan and N.N. Jha were also present in the meeting. 'It is for the first time since 2010 that track II diplomats have become active on Kashmir . . .' sources added.

In fact, on February 3, 2012, Ram held a reception for Geelani at his Delhi home, inviting over 25 Kashmiris and Indian policy-makers to talk with him in order to find out if he had softened his position. A Facebook posting by one Zafar Chaudhary[78] marvelled at how unusual it was to see Geelani introduced to prominent Indian figures in such a public way. As he described the interaction though, the best that could be said was that Geelani was willing to show up and talk, but he remained adamant that there must be a referendum on self-determination. There was no evidence that he had changed his views.

In *Conscience of a Maverick*, Ram reprinted five articles on the subject, four originally published from September 2002 to August 2003, and one in 1997. This was not all he wrote, either. Reporters comment that Ram and the Kashmir Committee released too many statements; negotiations should remain behind closed doors. But the Kashmiris talked *to* Ram. The Indian and Pakistani governments talked *about* the Kashmiris. High-level conferences convened *to make plans for* Kashmir. Prime Ministers appointed official representatives *to hold official meetings about* Kashmir. Think tanks *studied* Kashmir, and they wrote reports. But Ram went to Kashmir, spoke to the Kashmiris in their own language, in their own houses, and drank tea with them. He made condolence calls, joined them in the iftar meal during Ramadan, and he hugged them in friendship. One wonders how much all these officials would have accomplished without Ram's courtship of the most intransigent among the Hurriyat.

A reporter for *Caravan*[79] dismisses official emissaries Pant, Jaitley, and Vohra as ineffective. He also dismisses the 'use of Indian civil society actors in back-channel and official—but not publicly declared—interlocutors such as former RAW Chief A.S. Dulat, then PMO man and India's National Security Advisor R.K. Mishra,' and, he says, 'the "musical chairs" policy of changing interlocutors needs to be done away with and the dialogue process needs to be institutionalised by appointing a robust parliamentary peace panel for a period of at least ten years.'

In 2012, the *Times of India* reported:

> Unlike Kashmir interlocutors, who failed to bring separatists, human rights activists and civil society groups on board during their year-long exercise, Ram Jethmalani's Kashmir Committee in past three days has created a flutter in Kashmir by entering into dialogue with all.
>
> First, Jethmalani had an extensive meeting with Syed Ali Shah Geelani, the chairman of hardline faction of Hurriyat Conference. Jethmalani said he would take up the issue of Geelani's continuous house arrest in the Supreme Court.
>
> After Geelani, Jethmalani had detailed meeting with Hurriyat

moderate faction chairman Mirwaiz Umar Farooq. Mirwaiz had refused to give audience to Kashmir interlocutors. He also met senior separatist leader Shabir Ahmad Shah. On Sunday he heard human rights activists, lawyers and traders. 'If any person comes in his individual capacity we have no issues in talking to him,' said Shakeel Kalander, president, Chamber of Commerce and Industries. 'We are not averse to have interaction with civil society and different groups from India,' he said.[80]

The reality is that many of the players sincerely like Ram, and they trust him. They know he does not represent the government officially, but they would rather talk to him than to any of the official governmental interlocutors. M.J. Akbar describes Ram as a good facilitator, with the caveat that, to be successful, any such efforts require 'the trust as well as the commitment'. He feels that the government of India has not been receptive to Ram's efforts for the past 10 years and that the Kashmir Committee's most important role was to help abate the anger of the 1990s. Now he says it is up to the Kashmiri youth, especially young women, to compare the prospect of life in Pakistan with life in India. The young are the ones who ultimately will decide.

That is all true, but atmosphere is important. If India rejects them, dissidents will opt for Pakistan. The aura of caring and genuine goodwill that Ram—when he is on top of his game—is able to establish with such facility encourages them to opt for India.

In 2013, the Jammu and Kashmir People's Democratic Party released a working paper that offered a self-rule framework for Kashmir.[81] This party, founded by former Union Home Minister Mufti Mohammed Sayeed, advocates self-rule, not autonomy; during a meeting in Delhi with Hurriyat leaders, Ram urged the government to accept it. He also said that it is a great document, which should be the basis of government negotiations. Despite that, the government has not responded so far.

In 2011, several of Geelani's men were charged with running an illegal hawala scheme, and at Geelani's personal request, Ram is representing one of them in court right now. Geelani is no doubt pleased. Ram has called Geelani Kashmir's 'biggest aspirant for peace,' and 'my elder brother'. When Ram and Geelani call a press conference, observers note that they say diametrically opposite things, but Geelani holds Ram's hand the whole time. Geelani is the Hurriyat Conference chairman, and he is known as the hard-liner who has the largest following in Kashmir. Who could have a better chance to make progress in negotiations with him than Ram Jethmalani?

34

Cases after the Law Ministry

After Ram left the Law Ministry, his practice flourished. He argued 70 published cases in the Supreme Court between 2001 and 2012 alone, and he topped every list of the highest-paid lawyers in India. *India Today*[1] claims that at age 89, he made two to four times as much per appearance as any other lawyer among the top 10 in India. Still, the vast majority of his cases are pro bono. One of his former juniors says that if anyone walks into his office and, instead of calling him Mr Jethmalani, says 'Hello Ram,' 'there is no possibility of a fee'.

We have to marvel at the fact that a lawyer his age could remain at the summit of his profession in a country of 1.2 billion litigious people, all crowding to be heard. Grandparents remember him from their youth, their grandchildren pack the classroom when he lectures, and everyone pushes into his courtroom when he argues a case. Now we will reveal his secret, as a bonus for those who have read this far and for young lawyers everywhere who have asked: he works hard, thinks deeply, has a mordant wit, and he probably knows the law better than anyone else alive.

Still, Ram has considered retirement. In 2005 the latest notice appeared on Ram's gate announcing, 'I will no longer take up any more legal cases. People are welcome for other reasons.' Just as another such notice did before, it went softly away.

Ram's practice ranges from election law to constitutional law, criminal, civil rights, terrorism, smuggling, preventative detention, family law, malpractice, contracts, almost every branch of law, but he really shines when it comes to the rules of evidence.

Can Parliament expel a crook?

In 2007, an interesting constitutional question came before a bench of five judges of the Supreme Court: whether or not Parliament has the authority to expel its own members. On December 12, 2005, a TV programme showed 10 MPs of the Lok Sabha and one from the Rajya Sabha accepting money for raising certain issues in Parliament or for taking certain positions in Parliament. This led to extensive publicity.

A parliamentary inquiry concluded that the House could impose punishments and these could include withdrawal, suspension or expulsion from the House. Parliament resolved to expel the accused members, but they claimed that they could only be expelled for breach of privileges and thus the matter would have to be dealt with by the Privileges Committee.

Citing Article 105, Ram and another lawyer, Mr Lekhi, represented the expelled members in the subsequent court case,[2] arguing that all the powers and privileges of the British House of Commons had not been inherited by the Parliament under the Constitution of India, and the power of expulsion is one of those powers that was not inherited.

As legal commentator Milan Dalal explains, they also argued[3] that 'there was a "denial of principles of natural justice in the [Parliamentary] inquiry proceedings." The commentary continues, 'The petitioners' final two arguments involved the scope of judicial review. They argued that the Supreme Court "is the final arbiter on the constitutional issues and the existence of judicial power" and "that the constitutional and legal protection accorded to the citizens would become illusory if it were left to the organ in question to determine the legality of its own action".'

As described in *The Hindu*,[4] the government testified that the Parliament was not subject to judicial review.

The Hindu also quotes Ram as adding other arguments that the expelled members 'state that proper opportunity was not given to them to defend themselves; they were denied the opportunity of defending themselves through legal counsel or to give opportunity to explain; the request for supply of the material, in particular the un-edited versions of videography for testing the veracity of such evidence was turned down and doctored or morphed video-clippings were admitted into evidence, the entire procedure being unduly hurried.' This was based on the rules of evidence—vintage Ram.

In the same vein, *The Hindu* quotes Ram as claiming that 'The decision of expulsion . . . violated all sense of proportionality, fairness, legality, equality, justice or good conscience, and it being bad in law also because, as a consequence, the petitioners have suffered irreparable loss inasmuch as their image and prestige had been lowered in the eyes of the electorate.'

In its verdict, according to Dalal,[5] 'the court ruled the power of expulsion did not conflict with any other constitutional provisions . . . Based on this analysis, the majority stated it was unable to find any reasons why Parliament "should be denied the claim to the power of expulsion arising out of remedial power of contempt".'

Dalal summarizes:

Recent decisions in the Coelho [a case discussed in his paper] and Raja Ram Pal cases show the court is more willing to undertake judicial review by permitting examination of both Parliament's legislative and non-legislative roles. Such action has allowed the court to tackle issues ranging from invalidating laws that have nothing to do with land reform, to stemming political corruption . . . Given the seminal nature of these Indian Supreme Court decisions, however, the cases are likely to have a lasting impact on not only Indian constitutional law, but also the way Parliament crafts laws and constitutional amendments in the future.

At least the expelled members of Parliament had the satisfaction of knowing that they had the best possible legal representation, and it gives the lie to those whose criticism is that Ram should not defend criminals because he always wins. This may be largely true, but not always.

Ram's reputation attracts clients from the highest echelons of Indian politics and society, not necessarily criminal cases, some simply over business or personal matters, and some have gone on to become life-long friends. Any look at some of his most famous clients would start with Nusli Wadia, the Birla family, and the Ambanis.

Nusli Wadia

We first met Nusli Wadia one day outside Ram's apartment, and my husband was so impressed with how knowledgable he was that he impulsively invited him upstairs to continue the conversation. When Wadia left, Ratna asked us, 'Do you know who that was? It is Mohammad Ali Jinnah's grandson.'

My husband gasped, suddenly remembering the pictures of Jinnah that we had just seen in Hyderabad. He said immediately that Wadia looked just like Jinnah, but healthy, not ill with consumption.

Surprisingly, even though his grandfather was the founder of Pakistan, Wadia is a Parsi. To be accurate, his grandfather was a 'Shi'ite Muslim who married a Parsi . . . whose daughter Dina married a Parsi of part-Irish descent'.[6]

Ram met Nusli Wadia through Ramnath Goenka. *Outlook*[7] describes Wadia as 'The grandson of Jinnah, the godson of J.R.D. Tata, the chairman of Bombay Dyeing & Manufacturing Co. Ltd. The heir apparent to the Tata empire, the prodigal manager, the controversial CEO.' With all that, Nusli Wadia has been like one of Ram's own sons.

The article recounts that in the 1980s Wadia feuded with the Ambanis, and later came into conflict with a former friend, Rajan Pillai, over the chairmanship of Britannia Industries.[8]

In 1993, a group of Congress Members of Parliament requested a probe of Wadia, for a scattershot set of allegations about, as *Outlook* reported, 'links with the underworld, his role as a Pakistani spy and a clandestine link with Aneeta Ayub, a Pakistani starlet then based in Mumbai. They also claimed that Nusli had visited Dubai soon after the Mumbai bomb blasts to meet Dawood. These too were proved false.'

With Wadia and Ambani at odds in 1986, the *Indian Express* ran a series of articles by Arun Shourie and S. Gurumurthy that accused Dhirubhai Ambani of customs violations, the use of tax havens, questionable loans, and even of smuggling a whole factory into India.[9]

In 1987, the director of the Enforcement Directorate, Bhure Lal, an associate of Finance Minister V.P. Singh, announced that a US detective agency, Fairfax, would investigate tax violations by rich industrialists.[10]

One article accused Nusli Wadia of being instrumental in the decision to hire Fairfax to investigate the business affairs of Reliance, Ambani's company. 'When the Fairfax investigation fell afoul of Rajiv, the CBI raided the *Indian Express*[11] guest house in Delhi' where they purportedly found what Vir Sanghvi described as 'two sloppily forged letters allegedly written by the head of the American detective agency (Fairfax) investigating Reliance and addressed to Bhure Lal. In the letters, the agency referred to its investigations into the bank accounts of the Bachchan brothers and Sonia Gandhi's family in Italy. In retrospect, the letters looked like obvious forgeries—even at the time, many journalists, including myself, wrote that they were forgeries—but they had a dramatic effect when they were handed to Rajiv.[12]

'Here, at last, was confirmation of what the Ambanis had long been suggesting: V.P. Singh and Ramnath Goenka were not targeting Dhirubhai Ambani alone. The real target was Rajiv Gandhi . . . Everybody knows what followed. Rajiv became suspicious of Goenka. The press baron responded by attacking Rajiv.'

Just before the Bofors scandal broke, Michael Hershman, the head of Fairfax, said in an interview that V.P. Singh had been removed as Finance Minister just as a key witness was about to reveal kickbacks. With the Gandhi administration under suspicion, Rajiv appointed a commission consisting of Justices M.P. Thakker and S. Natarajan to investigate Fairfax and V.P. Singh.[13]

During this investigation, Wadia checked into a Delhi hotel one fine evening, and a clerk entered his name in as an Indian citizen, not realizing that he was a British citizen. Some claimed that Pillai put out the story; others that Ambani did. Charged with a FERA violation, Wadia was served deportation orders in 1989, but Ram, representing him before the Commission, argued it was harassment. At first denied a visa to enter India, Wadia obtained a stay from the Bombay High Court until he became an Indian citizen.

On August 1, 1989, another bombshell dropped when Bombay detectives arrested both a general manager of Reliance and 'Prince Babaria', a popular band leader, for a conspiracy to kill Wadia. The Bombay High Court verdict describes a convoluted plot with payoffs to multiple players, which moved forward until the designated hitman finally chickened out.[14]

With his health failing, the patriarch Dhirubhai Ambani asked Ram to set up a meeting with Wadia, which went off peaceably at Mahesh's house. Still, when Ambani died in July 2002, Wadia was not at his funeral.[15]

To this day, Wadia's business, Bombay Dyeing, remains a client of Ram's, and Wadia remains one of Ram's closest friends.

Birla

The Birla family is one of the richest in India. They were the only Indian family to make the Forbes list of billionaires in 1987, 'with a net worth close to $2 billion'. The Ambani family did not reach the list until 1994, but their reported net worth approached $7 billion in 2005.[16] The Birla fortune started with a nineteenth-century Bombay trading house, which moved to Calcutta and became an empire comprising petrochemicals, textiles, automobiles, and telecommunication.[17] Mahatma Gandhi was assassinated while he was living in the Birla mansion. Now this mansion is the National Gandhi Museum.

In a stunning development, when she died in July 2004, Madhav Prasad Birla's widow left her entire estate—worth Rs 2500 crore, about half a billion dollars—to her accountant.[18] This completely cut out her family. There were no children, but battle lines formed anyhow.

The couple had made a joint will in 1982. The husband, Madhav Prasad Birla, died in 1990. In April 1999, at age 71, the widow, Priyamvada Devi Birla, executed a new will, leaving her whole estate to one executor, her accountant, Rajendra Singh Lodha.

The Birla family challenged the legality of the will; then in 2004 it challenged the probate in the Calcutta High Court. The Calcutta High Court dismissed the opposition, and it appointed the grandson as the executor.

All of them appealed to the Supreme Court. Ram represented Krishna Kumar Birla, one of the cousins, representing the family, which wanted the estate to go to charity. Arun Jaitley represented the grandson, and he argued that his rights should not have been dismissed when he was named the executor.

The big question was why Shrimati Birla left everything to Lodha. Lodha, an accountant, had been the director and a trusted associate of Birla Enterprises since the days of her husband. Shrimati Birla came to rely on her accountant for all things financial in her life, trusting him more than her family. Some said he paid far more attention to her than her family did.

As the court put it, 'After the death of late Madhav Prasad Birla in or about July, 1990 the deceased who has had no formal education relied and continued to rely on the petitioner and reposed and continued to repose complete trust and confidence in the petitioner in the matters pertaining to all her financial affairs by reason whereof, the petitioner was at all material times, privy to all information concerning the personal and financial affairs of the deceased. The deceased also sought and obtained advice from the petitioner with regard to her assets, savings and investments.' Gossips had other theories.

Lodha won that round. The Supreme Court let him probate the 1999 will, named him the sole beneficiary of the estate, and dismissed all the other appeals with costs. It is not easy to break a well-written will.

While alive, both husband and wife transferred money to five trusts, the beneficiaries of which were three charitable institutions. In 2004, Ram represented the family, which accused Lodha of a criminal conspiracy to mislead Shrimati. Birla into signing over the trusts to him. The Chief Judicial Magistrate in Alipur ruled it a prima facie case of criminal activity.

In December 2004, Ram again represented the Birla family when Lodha appealed to the Calcutta High Court.[19] In his press interviews Ram said that Lodha had converted an estate 'earmarked for charity for 20 years, into personal property in three days.' In July, the Calcutta High Court dismissed Lodha's appeal.[20] In February, 2006, the Supreme Court dismissed petitions seeking to quash the criminal case against Lodha.[21]

Meanwhile, Lodha died in 2008.[22] That year Mahesh represented the family, arguing that Lodha had forged the will.[23] In 2010, the family went to court claiming the trusts were irrevocable trusts. The court appointed a team of three independent administrators, headed by a former Justice of the Supreme Court, to oversee the estate.

By 2012,[24] the heirs continued after the Lodhas, now represented by Lodha's son, in the Calcutta High Court. They claimed the widow was vulnerable because she had impaired mental function due to age and medical problems. In August 2012, the Calcutta High Court ruled that independent administrators should control her assets, not the Lodhas.

Posthumously, 'Eight years later, after millions spent in legal battles, a disciplinary committee of the regulator, Institute of Chartered Accountants of India (ICAI), has held Harsh Vardhan Lodha, 45, legal heir of R.S. Lodha, guilty of professional misconduct.' This was because 'The Companies Act, 1956, prohibits acceptance of audit by a director of a company or shareholder of the company under audit.'[25]

Ambanis

The Ambani case[26]—a fraternal battle within the richest family in India—fascinated the public. A report in 2002 said, 'Reliance manufactures a full 3% of India's Gross Domestic Product. It is responsible for 5% of India's exports. It contributes 10% of the indirect tax revenues of the Government of India. It commands 15% of the weightage on the Sensex. It makes 30% of the total profits of all private companies in India put together.'[27]

The father, Dhirubhai Ambani, had built Reliance Industries Ltd. (RIL) into a vast empire of oil and gas exploration, oil refining, petrochemicals, textiles, yarn, polyester and communications.[28] After Dhirubhai died in 2002, a feud started between the older son, Mukesh—said to be worth $21.5 billion[29]—and the younger son, Anil, worth only $5.2 billion.[30] At that time Mukesh reportedly was the richest man in India and Anil the eleventh richest. The 27-floor billion-dollar 'house' with three helipads that Mukesh built is just down the street from Shobha's Mumbai apartment on Altamount Road.

In 2005, the mother mediated a dispute that developed between them after their father died, and the family announced 'an amicable settlement is arrived at in respect of all disputes between the Ambani Brothers. It was stated that Mukesh Ambani will take over the responsibility for RIL and IPCL, and Anil Ambani will take over the responsibility for Reliance Infocomm Ltd, Reliance Energy Ltd, and Reliance Capital Ltd.'

The peace did not last. Given the size and complexity of their interests, conflict was inevitable. And the government became involved. 'In the year 1999, the Government of India announced a New Exploration and Licensing Policy . . . This policy provided that various petroleum blocks could be awarded for exploration, development and production of petroleum and gas to private entities.'

Under this 1999 policy, Reliance Industries Ltd won a major tender for gas exploration.

The court wrote, 'It is the policy of the Government that Petroleum Resources which may exist in the territorial waters, the continental shelf and the exclusive economic zone of India be discovered and exploited with utmost expedition in the overall interest of India and in accordance with good International

Petroleum Industry Practice.' In effect, this meant that all natural assets that are below the ground, such as oil, belong to the government.

Ram and Mahesh represented Anil and Reliance Natural Resources Ltd (RNRL). Under the Memorandum of Understanding their mother had mediated, Anil was to receive 'a specified entitlement of oil and gas at the price at which RIL [Mukesh] had agreed to supply gas' to the power company.[31]

The problem was that the gas price which they had negotiated was $2.34/mmBtu, and the government had set a ceiling of $4.20 in 2007. Mukesh claimed it was government policy that he must sell at the higher price, and Anil insisted that he was entitled to buy at the lower price they had agreed upon. Mukesh claimed that the government's gas pricing policy trumped their private agreement. As it was a 'production securing contract' between Mukesh and the government, he could not deal with the gas as his own. If his contract were detrimental to the national interest, the court would deem it an unenforceable contract. The case went first to the Division Bench of the Bombay High Court, next to the Supreme Court.

After 26 days of argument, the Supreme Court ruled to 'direct the parties to renegotiate as to the suitable arrangements for supply of gas . . . Such renegotiations shall be within the framework of governmental policy and approvals regarding price, quantity and tenure for supply of gas. The renegotiations shall commence within eight weeks from today at the initiative of RIL and shall be completed within a period of six weeks from the day of commencement of negotiations.'

Two judges found in favour of Anil (RNRL) on one issue and in favour of Mukesh (RIL) on all the others. The third found in favour of RIL on all issues. In sum, Ram's client Anil lost. Government intervention on the side of RIL had predetermined the verdict.

At the age of 86, Ram stood all day long in court for 26 days, arguing this case. The judges offered him the opportunity to sit, in deference to his age, but he would not consider addressing the court while seated. He has never disclosed his fee, but since *India*

Today[32] claims that Ram is by far the highest-paid lawyer in India and that he routinely charges Rs 10–20 lakh[33] per appearance, we can be sure it was more than that. Various newspapers have speculated about what multiple of that sum he must have charged per day in the Reliance case, some guessing as high as $200,000 or more per day.

Incidentally, a paper from Harvard[33] reports incomes for top Indian lawyers, with Abhishek Manu Singhvi at Rs 50 crore in 2010–11, Shanti Bhushan at Rs 18 crore in 2011, and Ram at Rs 8.4 crore ($1.7 million) in 2011, so that would put Ram's yearly income third, assuming that these reports are accurate.

Anyhow, Ram emphasizes that 90 per cent of his cases are pro bono.

35

Minorities

Mother Teresa's organization was Ram's client, and its headquarters are in Ram's constituency. Ram did not represent her as a lawyer, but he did collect money from his rich clients for her. Once he told us about an impertinent conversation with her about her mission. Ram told her that while she might obtain personal satisfaction from washing the feet of the poor, she could do a lot more for them by working toward laws that would give them greater rights.

Lataa Krishnamurthi has often participated in Ram's work for minority rights. The granddaughter of lawyers, Lataa studied law in her hometown of Pondicherry, received a master's degree from Madras University and then worked for the Bar Council of India as a Research Officer. After that she joined the Supreme Court Legal Aid Panel. She became Ram's junior associate in 1988. Since 2010 she has been a partner in his practice, working on a wide range of cases.

Christians

One case Ram and Lataa were involved with concerned the rights of the lowest caste citizens in India. Low-caste Hindus are protected under the Constitution, but when they try to escape their lower caste (Dalit) status by becoming Christian, they suffer the same discrimination as they did when they were Hindu Dalits, however, they do not have the same protections. This is the argument Ram made for the All-India Christian Federation:

'There are about 20 million Dalit Christians who are on record in India. A petition from the All-India Christian Federation (AICF) has been filed with the Supreme Court of India seeking reservations for all Dalits irrespective of their religious faith. Responding to this plea, a Bench comprising Chief Justice K.G. Balakrishnan and Justice B.S. Chauhan issued a notice to the Ministry of Social Justice and Ministry of Minority Affairs seeking their responses to the petition on January 6, 2010.'[1] Ironically, Judge Balakrishnan came from a family which had become Christian several generations before, and he had converted back to Hinduism. On this case, the court stalled by appointing a study committee, which has not yet reported back.

The Dalai Lama and the Karmapa

True to form, Ram stepped into an international controversy between China and India, involving competing Tibetan leaders in India and the thorny matter of China's refusal to acknowledge Sikkim as part of India. It all started with a strange dilemma—two different leaders disagreed over naming the true successor to the 16th Karmapa, the third highest position in the Tibetan Buddhist hierarchy. The traditional procedure for choosing a new Karmapa is for Tibetan teachers, called rinpoches, to use mysterious signs and symbols in order to recognize a small child who must be the reincarnation of the last Karmapa. They then give the child suitable religious training. In this case, two rival Tibetan religious leaders made two different choices. One child, Orgyen Trinley Dorje, was chosen by Tai Situ Rinpoche in 1992, and he was recognized as such by the Dalai Lama. In the same year, Shamar Rinpoche identified another child, Trinley Thaye Dorje. Both contenders now live in India.

Trinley Thaye Dorje left China as a child in 1994, went to Delhi to study, and now lives in Kalimpong, India. Since he was the first to arrive, his sponsor, Shamar Rinpoche, calls him the

Indian Karmapa, and Tai Situ's protégé, Orgyen Trinley Dorje, the Chinese Karmapa.

Based on the endorsement of the Dalai Lama, both Ram and George Fernandes supported Orgyen Trinley Dorje when he arrived in India from China.[2] His home is in Dharamsala, close to the Dalai Lama.

The circumstances under which Orgen Trinley Dorje left were murky. The western press reported that in 1999 the 14-year old 'Chinese Karmapa' walked across the Himalayas in eight days to escape Chinese repression. The Indian press calculated he could not have walked nearly 1450 kilometres, through eight feet of snow, over a 17,000-foot pass in eight days. His supporters countered that many Tibetans have done just that. The competing version of this story was that the Chinese staged this escape so the young Karmapa would go to Sikkim, bring back a mysterious Black Crown from a monastery there to China, and become a national hero. Realizing that was impossible, he went to the Dalai Lama in Dharamsala, who welcomed him warmly.[3] There is another version of the story, in which the Chinese secretly replaced the original Orgyen Trinley Dorje with a smarter and older student just before he left China.

'When Orgyen Trinley Dorje, 17th Karmapa of the Karma Kagyu sect of Tibetan Buddhism, finally left his monastery and entered Nepal, waiting to receive him was Tai Situ Rimpoche, one of the 16th Karmapa's four regents.'[4]

The prize in this rivalry was control of the 250-year-old Rumtek monastery in Sikkim, the seat of the Kagyupa sect of Tibetan Buddhism and the location of the famed Black Hat. With reputed assets of a billion dollars, it is one of the richest monasteries in the world.[5]

Asia Times wrote in 2003 about a legal case, not one of Ram's, that some claim shows which Karmapa is legitimate, although it is really just a real estate dispute.[6] 'An Indian court in Sikkim ruled that the assets of Rumtek belong to the Karmapa Charitable Trust . . . [claimed by] another claimant to the Karmapa throne, Karmapa Thaye Dorje, whom they say has the right to take over the monastery.' On appeal, 'In July 2004, the Supreme Court gave control of the Rumtek monastery to the Karmapa Charitable Trust, controlled by Trinley Thaye Dorje.' In other words, the monastery was awarded to the competing Karmapa, not Orgyen Trinley Dorje, sponsored by Ram's client, Tai Situ.[7] Of some interest, this author originally read this case, in English, on an Indian site. Now that has been taken down, and the case is only accessible on a Chinese site, in Chinese.

Lataa argued another case brought by the same Lama Shree Narayan Singh who brought the last one.

If one legal tussle was not enough, another has just commenced. On December 19, the Delhi High Court[8] issued a summons to the Dalai Lama and the Indian government claiming as illegal the declaration of Urgyen Trinley as the 17th Karmapa and calling for his expulsion from India. The case, filed by Lama S.N. Singh, alleges that the Dalai Lama was wrong in backing the recognition of Urgyen Trinley as the 17th Karmapa, and claims that his birth date in 1985 is wrong, saying that medical records indicate that he is much older. In addition, it claims the Chinese game plan is to annex Buddhist regions of the Himalaya, and that the easiest way for the Chinese to establish a base in Sikkim is to install their own Karmapa candidate, and China's man is Urgyen Trinley.

Lama S.N. Singh's petition was rejected by the court, which said, 'I am of the considered opinion that this court has no jurisdiction to intervene in the present matter as the same is a matter of policy as it is not against any statute or the Constitution.' The court also wrote that it 'is also barred by limitation,' since the case originated in 1992. Apart from the legal battles, the practical fact is that the Dalai Lama gave his support to Orgyen Trinley Dorje, and the majority of the Tibetan people follow the lead of the Dalai Lama.

Opponents of Orgyen Trinley Dorje sought to have Tai Situ banned from entering India for conspiring to 'dismember' Sikkim from India, but Ram remained a steadfast supporter. 'Ram Jethmalani, lawyer, now Union law minister, has known Tai Situ for a "half-decade" and been a loyal friend. In 1994, when Tai

Situ was banned from India and faced a CBI case, Jethmalani's juniors provided him legal help. Jethmalani also wrote to then home minister Rajesh Pilot.' Calling Tai Situ 'a high-ranking, learned monk against whom there was no clear case,' Ram said the government had no business barring him from re-entering India.

'On December 2, 1996, Jethmalani wrote to then foreign minister I.K. Gujral describing the ban on Tai Situ as "irrational and anti-national . . . Someone tells me he is suspected of Chinese connections and others tell me his Dalai Lama connection is not acceptable. The truth of the matter is nobody knows."'[9] In 1998, as Urban Affairs Minister, Jethmalani wrote to the Home Ministry objecting to the ban on Tai Situ, and in August, the Union Home Secretary lifted the ban.

This was despite a letter the persistent Lama S.N. Singh wrote to Prime Minister Vajpayee in 1998 urging 'the continuance of prohibitory ban imposed on Tai Situ Rinpoche of Sherabling, Himachal Pradesh.' He also said, 'We are aware that Tai Situ has been Mr Jethmalani's client since 1993.'[10]

In 2003 Ram invited a stellar gathering to his house for a prayer meeting at which the Dalai Lama was to be the guest of honour. The Dalai Lama accepted, but he was warned off by a highly placed figure in the government who claimed there would be a danger to his security if he visited the Jethmalani house:[11]

A prayer meeting arranged by noted criminal lawyer and MP Ram Jethmalani for 'hope, peace and goodwill in 2003' gave way to anger as he claimed that the supreme spiritual leader of Tibet, the Dalai Lama, had been 'prevented' from attending the same. Though one of the top spiritual leaders of Tibet, Tai Situ Rinpoche attended the meeting along with ambassadors of some countries, Jethmalani could not come to terms with the disappointment caused to his invitees by the absence of the Dalai Lama at the function.

Even though Ram was unhappy about losing the opportunity to entertain the Dalai Lama, he proceeded with his prepared speech:

'Yes we ended year 2002 and ushered in its numerical successor 2003. But it is only an imaginary line we have crossed, a dividing line that exists only in man's artificial memory. In fact we float in a continuum, an eternal one, with no beginning or end. All the baggage of the past clings to us, however much we want to discard it. Decline of true Religion, jettisoning of constitutional values, threat of terrorism and the spectre of Armageddon, make our efforts at looking and acting cheerful, artificial and unconvincing. To relieve this mood of despondency my friends and I decided to secure even for a short time the benign presence of His Holiness the Dalai Lama. He is a repository of religious wisdom, a store house of charity and compassion, a fountain of robust optimism and good cheer—not to forget his puckish sense of humour.

'I am grateful that he so graciously agreed to meet us and share with us some noble truths and perhaps point to some new path out of the current mess. This has been frustrated by some bureaucrat or Minister, whom I have yet to identify, by telling him that his visit to the Jethmalani home involves threat to his security.' Ram then went on to his point: 'As we enter the new year the civilized world has one supreme concern; how to win the war against terrorism?'

'I wonder if I am right in believing that we cannot win this war without enlisting the active cooperation of powerful allies from within the world of Islam itself particularly its spiritual leaders who will speak loud and clear that Islam is not about Jihad or martyrdom or false illusions of God rewarding murderers with haunting Houris . . . It is my view that we must take powerful lanterns, and identify the intrepid ones who are willing to reinterpret the ancient religious texts to create space for modernity, pluralism and democracy. Specifically to defeat terrorism in Kashmir, we have to win the hearts of Kashmiri Muslims.'

Defying the accusations that he was a Chinese plant, Ram also entertained the Karmapa Orgyen Trinley Dorje in his Delhi home. This fell on the same day in 2005 on which the Shiv Sena attacked his Mumbai office over the Professor Gilani case. Ram intended this obvious sign of support to quiet the question about the Karmapa—whether he really escaped 'clandestinely after giving a slip to the Chinese as claimed by him or was it a choreographed escape organized by the Chinese intelligence to create a split among the followers of His Holiness the Dalai Lama, undermine his authority and project the Karmapa as the interim head of the Tibetan Buddhists after the death of His Holiness till the Dalai Lama's successor is chosen by the Chinese Communist Party by stage-managing the identification of the child who is his incarnation.'[12]

In view of Ram's deep suspicion of Chinese intentions on the Indian border, it may seem curious that Ram consistently supported Tai Situ and his protégé Karmapa despite the claim that they are Chinese agents. The key was the Dalai Lama's endorsement. It also would not have displeased Ram when many asserted that 'The Karmapa's escape to India was the single most humiliating incident for China's Tibet policy in decades.' [13]

In January 2011, the Indian government raided the monastery in Dharamsala, suspecting the Karmapa of holding a large sum of foreign currency, possibly obtained by money laundering. Of some relevance, when Shobha, my husband and I visited this Karmapa, we saw an obviously rich young couple from Hong Kong—dressed as if they were about to attend a fancy ball—sitting with a photographer, a large golden Buddha on a platter and a number of large gift boxes for the Karmapa. It would not take too many donors like them to fill up his coffers. Ram and Lataa did defend the Karmapa successfully against the charges of possessing foreign currency, explaining that he had yet to learn how to report his donations properly. Surely, when we met him, he gave the impression of being inexperienced. All he could say about Ram was, 'He is very old.' Shobha and Suresh had a longer interview with him later that year.

Ram and Lataa also took another case, of a Tibetan boy identified by Tai Situ in Chishul, near Lhasa, the capital of Tibet. This child was brought to Sikkim at age four as a reincarnation of Jamgon Kongtryl Rinpoche, the abbot of a retreat centre near Kalimpong who had recently died. The boy was adopted by a Sikkimese lady, but she made an error in filling out his passport, which gave the government an excuse to deport him and to send out a notice that he was a threat to national security.[14] The legal appeals continue.

Other Minorities

India has plenty of lawyers, but people from the farthest reaches of the country still call Ram. In a case decided in 2010,[15] he defended Kunga Nima Lepcha, the Chief Minister of Sikkim, after four members of an Opposition party asked the CBI to investigate him for alleged corruption in awarding state contracts.

The state of Sikkim, located in the northeastern corner of India, did not become a state of India until 1975, and, as we have seen, China is still not reconciled to the accession. India had not yet enforced its income tax in Sikkim when this case went to court. The petitioners claimed that when he ran for office in 2004, Lepcha deliberately understated his family income. They further claimed he had misappropriated assets since his election. The Supreme Court ruled that it was not proper for it to request such an investigation; if it handed down a court order for an investigation, that would prejudice the outcome. It admonished the petitioners either to go directly to the CBI or to the High Court of Sikkim.

A group of aggrieved employees[16] called Ram from Nagaland, which is as far away from Delhi, in terms of distance and culture, as one can go without leaving India. In the far Northeast, the state of Nagaland was formed by the State of Nagaland Act of 1962, which transferred part of the state of Assam to a new state of Nagaland. The population has strong ties to Assam to the north and to Burma, now Myanmar, to the south.

Ram represented the Nagaland Senior Government Employees Welfare Association in a dispute over pensions for civil servants. He 'submitted that retirement by way of superannuation in respect of government employees is permissible only on the basis of age and not on the basis of length of service.'

Ram 'vehemently contended that even if it be assumed that the alternative method of retirement by way of length of service is permissible in law,' the 2nd Amendment Act, 2009, which requires government employees to retire after 35 years of service violates Article 14 of the Constitution and is 'arbitrary, unreasonable and unconstitutional'. That was all he could say. The appeal was dismissed.

On a personal level, Ram has for years been a charitable patron of Dr Samant, a professor in the eastern state of Orissa—now called Odisha—who runs two outstanding institutions. One is KISS (Kalinga Institute of Social Sciences), which hires tribal children in the Naxalite areas to give them jobs and a future. Naxalites are Maoists. The other is KITS (Kalinga Institute of Technological Sciences), which provides these children with a college-level education and undertakes technical projects that subsize KISS. Ram often attends functions there, and he contributes money for some of their projects.

Dr Binayak Sen

In March 2011, in a major civil rights case, Ram took an appeal for Dr Binayak Sen to the Supreme Court. The court wrote: 'Sen, Vice President of People's Union of Civil Liberties, was convicted for sedition and sentenced to life imprisonment along with Naxal ideologue Narayan Sanyal and Kolkata businessman Piyush Guha for colluding with Naxals to establish a network to fight the state.'[17]

Ram's defence of Dr Sen caught the attention of civil liberties experts around the world. 'Jethmalani, who had argued the bail plea in the High Court, had dubbed the charges against Sen as politically motivated and had said, "The whole case is nothing but political persecution."

'Sen's conviction and sentence had led to outrage in many quarters, including international bodies of Human Rights.

'In the petition prepared by senior advocate Ram Jethmalani it has been submitted that Sen has already spent two years in jail after his arrest and he should be allowed to come out on bail during the pendency of appeal in the High Court.'[18]

The history was: 'In May 2007, Dr Sen was detained for allegedly supporting the outlawed Naxalites, thereby violating the provisions of the Chhattisgarh Special Public Security Act 2005 (CSPSA) and the Unlawful Activities (Prevention) Act 1967.'[19] Chhattisgarh is a state in central India.

'On 24 December, 2010, the Additional Sessions and District Court Judge B.P. Varma, Raipur, found Binayak Sen, Naxal ideologue Narayan Sanyal and Kolkata businessman Piyush Guha, guilty of sedition for helping Maoists in their fight against the state.'[20]

'The Maoists have been leading an armed movement to capture political power in 13 states in India over four decades, and claim to be fighting for the poor, dispossessed and marginalized. Dr Sen ran mobile clinics in the interior of Chhattisgarh, one of the states most affected by the Maoist insurgency. In 2005, he led a 15-member team that published a report criticizing the Salwa Judum, which Human Rights Watch calls "a state-supported vigilante group aimed at eliminating Naxalites".'[21]

In a letter written in 2011, a group of 40 Nobel laureates appealed for the overturn of his life sentence, calling Dr Sen 'an exceptional, courageous, and selfless colleague, dedicated to helping those in India who are least able to help themselves.'

His defence was, 'Earlier, I had helped establish a hospital for mine workers in the area. As a logical outcome of my work, I was involved with human rights work, and was the general secretary of the state unit of the Peoples' Union for Civil Liberties. In this capacity I was instrumental in documenting and exposing deaths due to hunger and malnutrition, and to the displacement of over 600 tribal villages by the state-sponsored militia called Salwa Judum.'[22]

In a February 2011 case in Chhattisgarh,[23] the Chhattisgarh government accused Dr Binayak Sen of sedition, because Dr Sen had visited Naxalites in jail multiple times and Maoist materials had been found in his possession. Ram said, 'I have never seen such oppression from the State government. This literature, what they call sedition is available in the market.' He argued that mere possession of these materials was not sedition. Ram said, 'Not a single document was produced to show that Dr Sen either preached or propagated Maoist ideology.'

Dr Sen's defenders included Ram, Lataa, and four other lawyers. An eight-member delegation of the European Union attended the proceedings to give him their support.[24] Nevertheless, bail was denied.

In 2012 though, 'The Supreme Court on Friday granted bail to Dr Binayak Sen, observing that no case of sedition was made out against the rights activist, who was convicted and sentenced to life imprisonment by a trial court in Chhattisgarh. A Bench of Justices H.S. Bedi and C.K. Prasad, after hearing senior counsel Ram Jethmalani for the petitioner and senior counsel U.U. Lalit for the State, granted bail to Dr Sen.'[25]

Human rights activists have lauded this case as a major victory, even though Dr Sen still faces the charge of supporting Maoists. At least he does so, as Ram points out, as a free man.

36

Big Business, Black Money, and the 2G Spectrum

Ram's version of the classic quote is: 'All power corrupts—and the fear of losing power corrupts absolutely.'

For years the press has beaten the drums about all the Indian black money stashed in private European accounts, and that has given Ram a new crusade—or perhaps a new battle in an old crusade. The Bofors scandal may have been the opening salvo, but the long-running theme has been the Jethmalani family battle against corruption in general, and the Nehru–Gandhi family corruption in particular.

Ram has a number of powerful allies in this latest fight against corruption—the now famous Anna Hazare, and the always surprising Subramanian Swamy.

In *India Today*,[1] Ram wrote: 'India is a rich country but large sections of the nation have been condemned to misery and almost non-human existence by the powerful dacoits who have over the years stolen enormous wealth belonging to the nation. An estimate of the booty is about $1,500 billion.'

Ram continued: 'The November 1991 issue of *Schweizer Illustrierte*, the most popular magazine of Switzerland, carried an exposé of 14 politicians from developing nations who had stashed their bribes in Swiss banks. It alleged that Rajiv Gandhi was one of them, and put his figure at 2.5 billion Swiss francs. *Schweizer*

Illustrierte is not some rag; it sells some 210,000 copies.'

Using his time-honoured test of whether or not an allegation is true, Ram threw down the gauntlet: 'The Gandhi family has neither denied the allegations, nor taken legal action against the Swiss magazine or Indian politicians like Subramanian Swamy, who has charged that illicit monies are being recycled through the stock market.'

His coup de grace was, 'In the pending litigation in the Supreme Court, the Indian Government has admitted that it has received a list of names from Berlin but is refusing to disclose them on a false pretext. The Government is controlled by the thieves themselves and the stolen property can only be recovered by demolishing this Government and sending some of its leaders to jail.'

The pending litigation he refers to is the PIL which Ram filed with the Supreme Court.

Ram often quotes the following:[2] 'The USSR KGB maintains contact with the son of the Premier Minister, Rajiv Gandhi (of India) . . . R. Gandhi expresses deep gratitude for the benefits accruing to the Prime Minister's family from the commercial dealings of the firm he controls in cooperation with the Soviet Foreign trade organisations. R. Gandhi reports confidentially that a substantial portion of the funds obtained through this channel are used to support the party of R. Gandhi.'[3]

In short, Ram is aiming directly at a Prime Minister. It is no wonder that the following headline appeared on January 9, 2013: 'RamJet voted "most badass lawyer" on US site, ahead of Gandhi, Ambedkar, and Jinnah.'[4] 'Silicon Valley-based Q&A site *Quora*, which is popular in the California tech community that includes many Indians, non-resident or otherwise, has voted Ram Jethmalani as the world's "most badass lawyer".'

'Jethmalani, whose name was suggested by physicist and University of Mumbai MSc student Niranjan Sankaran, leads the poll on the site with 158 votes as of going to press. His closest competitor is Gandhi, with 36 votes.' Ram has grandchildren older than these techies who admire him in California.

Black money has long been the scourge of India. The 2010

Global Financial Integrity report[5] says:

> From 1948 through 2008 India lost a total of $213 billion in illicit financial flows (or illegal capital flight). These illicit financial flows were generally the product of: corruption, bribery and kickbacks, criminal activities, and efforts to shelter wealth from a country's tax authorities. The present value of India's total illicit financial flows (IFFs) is at least $462 billion.
>
> Total capital flight represents approximately 16.6 percent of India's GDP as of year-end 2008; illicit financial flows out of India grew at a rate of 11.5 percent per year while in real terms they grew by 6.4 percent per year, India lost $16 billion per year from 2002–2006.

In a paper[6] written for a BJP task force, the economist Shri Gurumurthy wrote that the Swiss authorities never recognized currency violations or tax evasion as offences, so if there was no criminal offence under Swiss law, information on offshore accounts could not be divulged. Now a breakthrough agreement between the United States and Switzerland has caused the Swiss banks to recognize tax evasion in any country as an offence in Switzerland.

Gurumurthy cites the Global Financial Integrity estimates of illegal Indian money held abroad—about 50 per cent of the Indian GDP at the end of 2008. He claims that almost three-quarters of India's underground economy is out of the country and that more than two-thirds of this money went abroad after 1990.

Gurumurthy names three major sources for the Indian black money in European banks: the Hasan Ali hawala case, payoffs to Ottavio Quattrocchi in the Bofors case, and money belonging to the Gandhi family. We will come back to the Hasan Ali case. He says the Gandhi and Quattrocchi families have been closely connected; they have stayed at each other's houses numerous times and that Quattrocchi and Sonia have met 21 times since Rajiv's death.

The Income Tax Appellate Tribunal (ITAT) asserts, 'On September 3, 1986, Bofors remitted a sum of $7.34 million to a

Swiss bank account of AE Services. From this account, an amount of $7.12 million was transferred to an account in the name of M/s Colbar Investment Limited, Panama . . . It found that Quattrocchi and his wife Maria controlled the accounts of Colbar Investments and Wetelsen Overseas. The appellate order says $7,123,900 was transferred to account of Colbar Investment, while another $7.943 million was transferred from the account of Wetelsen Overseas. Investigations revealed that Chadha and Quattrocchi transferred the funds received from Bofors frequently from one account to another and from one jurisdiction to another.'[7]

Gurumurthy writes that the CBI froze Quattrocchi's account 20 years ago and he left India in 1993 during the Narasimha Rao Congress government. In 2004, the CBI allowed him to withdraw the money, presumably under pressure from Sonia Gandhi. In 2011, an income-tax tribunal ruled that kickbacks of Rs 41.2 crore went to the late Win Chadha and to Quattrocchi in the Bofors deal, and that both were liable for back taxes. This was one day before a Delhi court hearing at which the CBI had planned to drop charges against Quattrocchi.

A photocopy of an October 31, 2011 Swiss Bank Corporation release on one website shows an entry of Rs 198,356 crore deposited in the name of Rajiv Gandhi,[8] first among 10 major Indian account holders. The next closest was Harshad Mehta, at Rs 135,121 crore. We know we must be sceptical of photocopies, but it certainly looks convincing.

In a *Sunday Guardian* article,[9] Ram cross-examined the government about why it stonewalled while it claimed it was working to repatriate all the black money in foreign banks:

1. While demanding information from the countries or the banks in which this money is suspected to be stashed, have you told them that you are investigating the serious offence of money laundering and the monies stashed away are the proceeds of criminal activities and are not the proceeds of any legitimate trading activity?

2. Is it true that after the German government received the

names of these dacoits by bribing an employee of the Liechtenstein bank, the German government announced that they will share this information with every friendly government which is interested, without any cost or condition?

3. Did the German government supply us with names of these grand criminals without insisting on any condition of confidentiality?

4. Are you prepared to make public the document under which you claim the condition of confidentially was imposed by the Germans?

5. Is it not true that against the notorious Hassan Ali and his Calcutta accomplices, you have only slapped a demand of tax amounting to about Rs 71,000 cr, based upon the amount lying to his credit in one account only?

6. Is it not true that he has four accounts and not one and you have never asked the German government or any other government that these are the products of crime and are not cases of mere tax evasion?

7. Is it not true that the Swiss were prepared to give full information and that they informed us in early 2007 that if you are investigating money laundering, we will give you all the information required?

8. Is it correct that for nearly four years you have not responded to this request?

9. Is it true that you have approached the Bombay court and obtained Letters Rogatory on the footing that Hassan Ali and his accomplices have made this illicit money out of arms sales, particularly in transactions with Adnan Khassogi, a notorious arms dealer?

10. Is it true that you have been deliberately using the double taxation avoidance treaty when it does not apply?

11. Is it true that you have not ratified the United Nations Convention against corruption though you signed it nearly five years ago? What is the reason?

12. Is it true that even Switzerland has signed and ratified it?

13. Is it true that you are not ratifying it because it means the confiscation of the money involved, whereas you are busy evolving a scheme of amnesty to enable these dacoits to enjoy their ill-gotten wealth on payment of even less than what the Income Tax Act Law would bring to us?
14. Now that you have admitted that you have received names and that you are busy collecting taxes from them, why don't you tell the people of India who they are?
15. Lastly, have you read the statement presented by Matthias Bachmann of the Permanent Mission of Switzerland to the United Nations, New York on 20 October 2010, which makes it clear that the Swiss are willing to give the information but you are not willing to receive it?

Ram writes of the government: 'Its silence to this day is ominous.'

Ram has written:

Let's also look at the case of the U.N. Convention against Corruption which the Indian Government signed in the year 2005. The government has been boasting that it has demonstrated its commitment to fight corruption by ratifying this charter on 9 May 2011, seven years after signing it. One does not need to wonder at the sudden desire to ratify the Charter. It is well known that this was done because of pressure by the anti-corruption wave led by Anna Hazare and Baba Ramdev, which was gathering overwhelming momentum.[10]

He analyses the treaty the government is hiding behind: 'As a criminal lawyer of long standing and with some facility in dealing with circumstantial evidence, my reading of the Protocol to amend the Double Taxation Avoidance Agreement, signed by India and Switzerland in August 2011, leads me . . . to the following conclusions . . .'

Starting from there, Ram sequentially demolishes each of the government's claims.

He also explains:[11] 'The Germans, by paying an employee of a Liechtenstein bank, have managed to get the names of thousands of German tax evaders and money launderers. The Germans have offered friendly Governments, including India, the names of these tax evaders. A spokesman for the German finance ministry, Thorstein Albig, indicated in March 2008, that they would give the information free. This official offer from the Germans reached India with further details, primarily because Indians were the largest number in the list of offenders, and their deposits of illicit wealth were over $1,500 billion. It is impossible to believe that the Germans have insisted that these names should be kept secret from the Indian nation. Surely the Germans wanted them to be punished, and not protected by the secrecy that the Government of India uses to protect a gallery of rogues.'

Ram writes in the same article that the Swiss ambassador denied in 2011 that he had received any requests from the Indian government for information about money deposited illegally in Swiss banks. In contrast, the American government had pressured Swiss bank UBS for information about American accounts, 'Portions of the money have been recovered, and UBS has committed to pay a fine of $780 million to settle the claim that it has defrauded US Internal Revenue Service.'

Ram writes that the United States, United Kingdom, and France all prosecuted their own citizens if they were on the list.

On April 22, 2009, the *Deccan Herald*[12] reported:

Former Union law minister Ram Jethmalani on Tuesday filed a public interest litigation (PIL) in the Supreme Court seeking its directive to the Centre to bring back over Rs 70 lakh crore ($1.4 trillion) of illegal money allegedly stashed away in foreign banks between 2002 and 2006.

Union Home Minister P. Chidambaram, when he held the finance portfolio, had publicly acknowledged the black money. Leader of Opposition L.K. Advani had also allegedly admitted that he was aware of all these facts, said the petitioners who have formed a forum called Citizen India. The government failed to enforce the law to bring back the money because influential politicians were involved in the racket, said Jethmalani.

At the time that Ram filed the PIL, he described it to us with enthusiasm, but commentators were totally dismissive, giving the PIL little chance to get anywhere.

The court on July 4 wrote that Citizen India's stated objective was 'to bring about changes and betterment in the quality of governance, and functioning of all public institutions.'

The actual PIL[13] filed with the Supreme Court listed 14 lawyers for the petitioners, 10 for the government, and 23 representing the Securities and Exchange Board of India (SEBI). The lead lawyer was Anil Divan, and the second listed was Lataa Krishnamurthi. The court scheduled the case for hearing on July 5, 2011, and it requested a compliance report by August 15, 2011.

The Hindu[14] wrote that the PIL was not connected to the BJP or to any political party. It was filed in the name of Ram Jethmalani, and of 'former Punjab director-general of police K.P.S. Gill, former Lok Sabha secretary-general Subhash Kashyap, artist Gopal Sharman and academic B.B. Dutta', on April 22 'before a bench consisting of Chief Justice K.G. Balakrishnan, Justices P. Sathasivam and Mukandakam Sharma.'

Even so, the government charged that the PIL was politically motivated, in part because Mahesh was running for Parliament on the BJP ticket at the time that the petition was filed.

The *Indian Express*[15] wrote on May 5, 2009: 'The UPA Government on Monday was caught off guard on the issue of black money stashed in foreign banks when the apex court asked why no action had been taken so far under the five-year-old Money Laundering Act as sought by petitioners like senior advocate Ram Jethmalani.'

Anil Divan objected to the attempt to link the petitioners to the BJP. 'They are independent Indian citizens and have no contact with the BJP or any other political party but are distinguished citizens in their own field.'

Twelve trusts, owned by 26 Indians and Non-Resident Indians, were in Swiss, German, and Liechtenstein banks. Ram said the Indian government had framed its request for the names of these illegal Indian account holders as a search for income tax evaders, since it knew that the Swiss government would not honour such a request because of the Double Taxation Treaty.

As Ram writes:[16] 'Examination of the events of August 2010 show that on the 30th of that month . . . the government entered into the Amending Protocol between the Swiss Confederation and the Republic of India for the Avoidance of Double Taxation with respect to taxes on income.' He goes on to explain, though, that the controversy about concealed funds has nothing to do with double taxation.

On January 27, 2011,[17] the Supreme Court demanded the government submit an action report containing more names than the 26 they already had provided. The court asked, 'Is it from arms dealing . . . drug peddling? These are very serious issues.'

Before we go any further, we must consider one more player— Hasan Ali. Gurumurthy summarizes[18] Hasan Ali as a horse breeder from Pune, and a small time crook. He became involved in the hawala business, then with Adnan Khashoggi (of Bofors fame), with a Kolkata businessman, Tapuria, as a front. In 2007, an income tax authority raid revealed three secret Swiss bank accounts in his name containing $8.6 billion.

The Enforcement Directorate waited two years before issuing a notice to show cause, allowing him time to withdraw $6 billion. The Swiss authorities did freeze some of the Khashoggi money, calling it 'funds from weapons sale'. The rest could have been frozen, but it was not. Hasan Ali was arrested on January 2, 2007, holding three passports, and he promptly entered a hospital complaining about his heart. The crime inspector checked him out and spirited him back to Pune.

Hasan Ali absconded in 2008, surrendered, and was allowed out on bail. The Swiss authorities never cooperated with India to recoup his unpaid income taxes. So, which politician was Hasan Ali fronting for, and did the money come from defence deals? In the middle of this, Mahesh found a strange scoop.

'In his sensational revelation Shri Mahesh Jethmalani said that that the Crime Branch of Mumbai Police in Mumbai has a video recording of the secret meeting between Hasan Ali, who was absconding in the Enforcement Case of $8 billion against him, the then Chief Minister of Maharashtra Vilasrao Deshmukh and the Political Advisor to the Congress Party President Shri Ahmed Patel, and Shri Ghafoor Ahmed Khan, who was later appointed as the Police Commissioner of Mumbai at Hotel Centaur [now known as Tulip] in Mumbai on 8.11.2008.' As the article shows, Ali was sitting in a meeting in which Deshmukh and Patel (Sonia Gandhi's political secretary) were deciding to appoint Hasan Gafoor as Mumbai's police commissioner.[19]

Ram's PIL went to the Supreme Court on July 4, 2011. The court wrote:[20] 'The worries of this Court relate not merely to the quantum of monies said to have been secreted away in foreign banks, but also the manner in which they may have been taken away from the country, and with the nature of activities that may have engendered the accumulation of such monies.' Specifically, 'such monies may be transferred to groups and individuals who may use them for unlawful activities that are extremely dangerous to the nation, including actions against the State.'

The court continued,

The Petitioners contend: (i) that the sheer volume of such monies points to grave weaknesses in the governance of the nation, because they indicate a significant lack of control over unlawful activities through which such monies are generated, evasion of taxes, and use of unlawful means of transfer of funds; (ii) that these funds are then laundered and brought back into India, to be used in both legal and illegal activities; (iii) that the use of various unlawful modes of transfer of funds across borders gives support to such unlawful networks of international finance; and (iv) that in as much as such unlawful networks are widely acknowledged to also effectuate transfer of funds across borders in aid of various crimes committed against persons and the State, including but not limited to activities that may be classifiable as terrorist, extremist, or unlawful narcotic trade, the prevailing situation also has very serious connotations for the security and integrity of India . . .

The Petitioners also further contend that a significant part of such large unaccounted monies include the monies of powerful persons in India, including leaders of many political parties . . . Further, the Petitioners also contend that the efforts to prosecute the individuals, and other entities who have secreted such monies in foreign banks, have been weak or non- existent.

The court then cited Hasan Ali Khan, served for back taxes of Rs 40,000 crores, and his front man, Tapuria, served with a notice for Rs 20,580 crore. Despite dealings of $1.6 billion in 2001–05, and $8.4 billion in Swiss banks, there had been no serious investigation, interrogation, or public information provided about the case.

Of interest, Hasan Ali's money was in Switzerland's UBS. In 2007 the Reserve Bank of India had stopped UBS Security India Private Limited from expanding in India through a takeover of Standard Chartered Mutual Funds. In 2008 it reversed its stance, raising the suspicion of governmental pressure.

The Supreme Court said, 'We must express our serious reservations about the responses of the Union of India. In the first instance, during the earlier phases of hearing before us, the attempts were clearly evasive, confused, or originating in the denial mode.' However, 'it was submitted to us that the Union of India has recently formed a High Level Committee, under the aegis of the Department of Revenue in the Ministry of Finance, which is the nodal agency responsible for all economic offences.'

This Special Investigation Team (SIT) was to be headed by two former Supreme Court judges, and it 'shall be charged with the responsibilities and duties of investigation, initiation of proceedings, and prosecution . . . of: (a) all issues relating to the matters concerning and arising from unaccounted monies of Hassan Ali Khan and the Tapurias; (b) all other investigations already commenced and are pending, or awaiting to be initiated, with respect to any other known instances of the stashing of unaccounted monies in foreign bank accounts by Indians or other entities operating in India; and (c) all other matters with respect to unaccounted monies being stashed in foreign banks by Indians or other entities operating in India that may arise in the course of such investigations and proceedings.'

The SIT was ordered to provide a comprehensive action plan for addressing these abuses, with periodic reports back to the court, and the government was ordered to cooperate.

On disclosure of documents, the court said:

Apparently, as alleged by the Petitioners, a former employee of a bank or banks in Liechtenstein secured the names of some 1400 bank account holders, along with the particulars of such accounts, and offered the information to various entities. The same was secured by the Federal Republic of Germany . . . which in turn, apart from initiating tax proceedings against some 600 individuals, also offered the information regarding nationals and citizens of other countries to such countries. It is the contention of the Petitioners that even though the Union of India was informed about the presence of the names of a large number of Indian citizens in the list of names revealed by the former bank employee, the Union of India never made a serious attempt to secure such information and proceed to investigate such individuals.

The response of the Union of India may be summed up briefly: (i) that they secured the names of individuals with bank accounts in banks in Liechtenstein, and other details with respect to such bank accounts, pursuant to an agreement of India with Germany for avoidance of double taxation and prevention of fiscal evasion; (ii) that the said agreement proscribes the Union of India from disclosing such names, and other documents and information with respect to such bank accounts, to the Petitioners, even in the context of these ongoing proceedings before this court; (iii) that the disclosure of such names, and other documents and information, secured from Germany, would jeopardize the relations of India with a foreign state; (iv) that the disclosure of such names, and other documents and information, would violate the right to privacy of those individuals who may have only deposited monies in a lawful manner; (v) that disclosure of names, and other documents and information can be made with respect to those individuals with regard to whom investigations are completed, and proceedings initiated; and (vi) that contrary to assertions by the Petitioners, it was Germany which had asked the Union of India to seek the information under double taxation agreement, and that this was in response to an earlier request by Union of India for the said information.

In light of the above we order that:

(i) The Union of India shall forthwith disclose to the Petitioners all those documents and information which they have secured from Germany, in connection with the matters discussed above, subject to the conditions specified in (ii) below;

(ii) That the Union of India is exempted from revealing the names of those individuals who have accounts in banks of Liechtenstein, and revealed to it by Germany, with respect of whom investigations/enquiries are still in progress and no information or evidence of wrongdoing is yet available;

(iii) That the names of those individuals with bank accounts in Liechtenstein, as revealed by Germany, with respect of whom investigations have been concluded, either partially or wholly, and show cause notices issued and proceedings initiated may be disclosed;

(iv) That the Special Investigation Team, constituted pursuant to the orders of today by this Court, shall take over the matter of investigation of the individuals whose names have been disclosed by Germany as having accounts in banks in Liechtenstein, and expeditiously conduct the same.'

Ram wrote:[21] 'On 4 July 2011, the Supreme Court passed its judgement in the *Ram Jethmalani and Others vs. Union of India and Others* case. It is popularly known as the *Black Money* Case . . . The Supreme Court order records the reluctance and disinclination of the government to take stringent action in the *Hasan Ali* case. The government is seen in an utterly pathetic light, with its culpability slowly but surely getting exposed, indulging in (and I quote the words of the Court), evasion, confusion and denial, slow investigation and lack of seriousness, inadequate and unsatisfactory replies to the Court on critical issues, such as, granting licence to UBS, whose antecedents were suspect.'

In September, the government asked[22] 'to modify the order dated 4th July, 2011 and to delete the directions relating to the Special Investigation Team.'

As the Supreme Court observed, 'Before the Application could be moved by the learned Attorney General, Mr Anil B. Divan, learned Senior Advocate appearing for the Writ Petitioners, took a preliminary objection that the interlocutory application was not maintainable . . . in effect, in the guise of an application for modification, the Respondents/Applicants were wanting either a re-hearing and/or review of the order passed on 4th July, 2011.'

The first opinion was written by Justice Altamas Kabir: 'The objections raised by Mr Anil B. Divan and supported by Mr Shekhar Naphade, regarding the maintainability of I.A. No.8 of 2011, are, therefore, rejected and the said application may therefore be proceeded with for hearing.'

The second opinion was by Justice Surinder Singh Nijjar: 'I would not be able to concur with the view taken by my Learned Brother. My Learned Brother has rejected the preliminary objections raised by Mr Anil Divan and Mr Shekhar Naphade, appearing for the writ petitioners and directed the application to proceed for hearing. In my opinion, the application is not maintainable for a number of reasons.'

Finally: 'Since we have differed in our views regarding the maintainability of I.A. No.8 of 2011 filed in W.P. No.176 of 2009, let the matter be placed before Hon'ble the Chief Justice of India, for reference to a third Judge. Altamas Kabir.'

And so it sat until May 2014, when, as we will see, the court finally directed the government to reveal the names of 26 Indians with account in Liechtenstein Bank.

'Shanti Bhushan in 1968 proposed the first Jan Lokpal Bill —a bill to appoint an anti-corruption ombudsman—which was passed in the Lok Sabha in 1969, but before it could be passed by the Rajya Sabha, the Lok Sabha was dissolved and the Bill lapsed. Lokpal Bills were introduced eight times[23] from 1971 to 2008, but were never passed.' Anna Hazare, a social activist, announced he would go on a fast from April 5, 2011, to move the bill. On June 4, Baba Ramdev started an indefinite fast to recover 'black money stashed in foreign banks by Indian politicians, businessmen and bureaucrats, and [to declare] it a national asset.' He also demanded a strong Lokpal Bill and advocated measures to eradicate corruption, poverty, and crime.

Baba Ramdev is a sanyasi. Normally that would mean he renounces all worldly possessions, wears saffron robes, and takes a vow of poverty. Ramdev, however, is a yoga guru featured on TV; teaches across the world and has a huge celebrity following at his ashram. His admiring followers credit him for promoting a resurgence of ayurvedic medicine and popularizing pranayama yoga worldwide.[24]

On June 4, Baba Ramdev held a major public event, which the Delhi police attacked brutally, spawning a case that Ram took to the Supreme Court.[25] The court spun a riveting tale:

On 27th February, 2011, an Anti-Corruption Rally was held at Ramlila Maidan, New Delhi where more than one lakh persons are said to have participated. The persons present at the rally included Baba Ramdev, Acharya Balakrishna, Ram Jethmalani, Anna Hazare and many others.

Continuing with his agitation for the return of black money to the country, Baba Ramdev wrote a letter to the Prime Minister on 4th May, 2011 stating his intention to go on a fast to protest against the Government's inaction in that regard. The Government made attempts to negotiate with Baba Ramdev and to tackle the problem on the terms, as may be commonly arrived at between the Government and Baba Ramdev. This process started with effect from 19th May, 2011 when the Prime Minister wrote a letter to Baba Ramdev asking him to renounce his fast. The Finance Minister also wrote a letter to Baba Ramdev informing him about the progress in the matter.

On 27th May, 2011, the DCP (Central District), on receiving the media reports about Baba Ramdev's intention to organize a fast unto death at the Yoga Training Camp, made further enquiries from Acharya Virendra Vikram requiring him to clarify the actual purpose for such [a] huge gathering. His response to this . . . was that there would be no other programme at all, except residential yoga camp. However, the Special Branch, Delhi Police also issued a special report indicating that Baba Ramdev intended to hold indefinite hunger strike along with 30,000-35,000 supporters and that the organizers were further claiming that the gathering would exceed one lakh.

. . . the crowd at the Ramlila Maidan swelled to more than fifty thousand. No yoga training was held for the entire day.

Keeping in view the fact that Jantar Mantar could not accommodate such a large crowd, the permission dated 24/26th May, 2011 granted for holding the dharna was withdrawn by the authorities.

At about 11.30 p.m., a team of Police, led by the Joint Commissioner of Police, met Baba Ramdev and informed him that the permission to hold the camp had been withdrawn and that he would be detained. At about 12.30 a.m., a large number of CRPF, Delhi Police force and Rapid Action Force personnel, totaling approximately to 5000 (as stated in the notes of the Amicus. However, from the record it appears to be 1200), reached the Ramlila Maidan. At this time, the protestors were peacefully sleeping. Thereafter, at about 1.10 a.m., the Police reached the dais/platform to take Baba Ramdev out, which action was resisted by his supporters. At 1.25 a.m., Baba Ramdev jumped into the crowd from the stage and disappeared amongst his supporters. He, thereafter, climbed on the shoulders of one of his supporters, exhorting women to form a barricade around him. A scuffle between the security forces and the supporters of Baba Ramdev took place and eight rounds of teargas shells were fired. By 2.10 a.m., almost all the supporters had been driven out of the Ramlila Maidan.

. . . it is the submission of respondent No.4 that it is ironic that persons fasting against failure of the Central Government to tackle the issue of corruption and black money have been portrayed as threats to law and order. Citizens have a fundamental right to assembly and peaceful protest which cannot be taken away by an arbitrary executive or legislative action.

. . . the argument advanced by Mr Ram Jethmalani, Senior Advocate, is that, in the earlier meetings, both at the Ramlila Maidan and Jantar Mantar, no untoward incident had occurred, which could, by any standard, cause an apprehension in the mind of the Police that there could occur an incident, communal or otherwise, leading to public disorder, in any way. The revocation of permissions as well as the brutality with which the gathering at the Ramlila Maidan was dispersed is impermissible and, in any case, contrary to law. The Ground belongs to the Municipal Corporation of Delhi and the permission had duly been granted by the said Corporation for the entire relevant period. This permission had never been revoked by the Corporation and as such the Police had no power to evict the public from the premises of Ramlila Maidan. The Police had also granted a 'No Objection Certificate' (NOC) for holding the meeting and the withdrawal of the NOC is without any basis and justification.

Ram argued that the public was 'entitled to a clear and sufficient notice before the Police could use force' there, and that:

It is contended that Police itself was an unlawful assembly. It had attacked the sleeping persons, after midnight, by trespassing into the property, which had been leased to the respondent-Trust. The use of tear gas, lathi charge, brick-batting and chasing the people out of the Ramlila Maidan were unjustifiable and brutal acts on the part of the Police. It was completely disproportionate not only to the exercise of the rights to freedom of speech and expression and peaceful gathering, but also to the requirement for the execution of a lawful order. The restriction imposed, being unreasonable, its disproportionate execution renders the action of the Police unlawful. This brutality of the State resulted in injuries to a large number of persons and even in death of one of the victims. There has also been loss and damage to the property.'

The police response was that they had only given permission for 4000–5000 people to gather for a yoga camp. To complicate things, 'Ramlila Maidan is surrounded by communally hyper-sensitive localities,' code words for Muslim areas. Finally the police claimed that Baba Ramdev, by exhorting his followers to form a cordon around him, created the melee, which turned into a stampede.

The court points out that the crowd was well below the capacity of the site, security had been stepped up, and the crowd was completely peaceful until the police awakened them suddenly. Only then did they become agitated, frightened, and confused. Significantly, 'The threat of going on a hunger strike extended by Baba Ramdev to personify his stand on the issues raised, cannot be termed as unconstitutional or barred under any law. It is a form of protest which has been accepted, both historically and legally in our constitutional jurisprudence.'

The court concluded: 'From the facts and circumstances that emerge from the record before this Court, it is evident that it was not a case of emergency. The police have failed to establish that a situation had arisen where there was imminent need to intervene, . . . but from the material placed before the Court, I am unable to hold that the order passed by the competent authority and execution thereof are mala fide in law or in fact or is an abdication of power and functions by the Police.'

Nevertheless, 'I have held that [Baba Ramdev] is guilty of contributory negligence. The Trust and its representatives ought to have discharged their legal and moral duty and should have fully cooperated in the effective implementation of a lawful order passed by the competitive[sic] authority'

The court ordered the state government and the Commissioner of Police to investigate the circumstances, to discipline the police 'who have indulged in brick-batting, have [sic] resorted to lathi charge and excessive use of tear gas shells' or other impermissible methods, as well as those police who did not aid the injured. The police were also required to register criminal cases against those police or members of the crowd who destroyed property. Persons who died or were injured were to receive just compensation.

While the court's rhetoric was grander than its verdict, this was a significant civil rights case, and the verdict could have been worse.

Ram says that the government has filed additional vindictive corruption cases against Ramdev in retaliation for his call for transparency in the disposition of black money. Ram has not been his lawyer in these cases, but he defends him strongly in the press. When asked whether it sullies his reputation to associate with such a man, Ram reminds the press that none of these charges has been proved. Beyond that, he says that sometimes in life one must select the least corrupt people as allies, 'If I take the assistance of a small thief to fight big dacoits, I am prepared to do it.'

Anna Hazare started another fast on June 8, 2011, and another in August 2011, this one in front of 50,000 people. His demand was for a strong Lokpal Bill that would create an independent body to investigate corruption cases. The government countered with threats to arrest him. Hazare led a march to the Prime Minister's house, and a Lokpal Bill finally did go to Parliament, one that Ram says has been completely watered down. In February 2013, 14 amendments still were under consideration.[26]

Ram charges[27] that:

The UPA Government is trying to use every trick of the trade to provide escape routes for black money looters. Take, for example, the complex strategy being adopted to change the colour of money from black to white, with a unique Fair and Lovely amnesty recipe. The press reported in 2011 that the Central Board of Direct Taxes (CBDT) was 'seriously considering' recommending to the government a scheme on the lines of the Voluntary Disclosure of Income Scheme (VDIS) announced in 1996 to bring back black money stashed in tax havens abroad for productive use in India. It is reported that the source of the money will not have to be disclosed, but criminal action will be taken if the money (or the assets) pertain to proceeds of crime.

Ram has nothing good to say about these amnesty plans. He wrote later:[28]

On 21 May 2012, Finance Minister Pranab Mukerjee tabled a 'White Paper on Black Money' in the Lok Sabha. It is an amazing document that seems to conceal rather than reveal information. Mr Mukherjee gives absolutely no information to the public regarding the legal sword of Damocles hanging over his government's head, in the form of the Supreme Court judgement announced in July 2011, in the Public Interest Litigation that I filed in the Supreme Court in 2009.

He claims that the paper used outdated figures and,

Interestingly, the Paper officially discloses a figure regarding Indian accounts held with Swiss banks, at around only US $213 billion (as against $88 billion projected by the International Monetary Fund, and $213.2 billion by GFI), down 60% between 2006 and 2010. A reasonable conclusion that can be drawn is that black money holders, in anticipation of international and national public pressure (not governmental) are transferring their money around to other safe havens, the safest, it is said, being India. The last two years have seen several enabling statutes and mechanisms to stealthily repatriate the ill-gotten wealth back to India.

Ram held Finance Minister Pranab Mukherjee responsible for the black money cover-up, threatening to run against him for President of India until the name of Purno Sangma emerged as a challenger, apparently with more support than Ram had. Ram represented Sangma in a petition to the Supreme Court, in an attempt to disqualify Mukherjee. He alleged that on the day he filed as a candidate Mukherjee was occupying an office of profit as chairman of the Indian Statistical Institute of Kolkata, which would make his filing illegal. 'Team Mukherjee has said this is factually incorrect as Mr Mukherjee quit this position even before he resigned as Finance Minister last week.'[29]

The Supreme Court dismissed the Sangma petition by a verdict of three to two for Mukherjee, [30] even though one of the judges had been appointed by Mukherjee. Traditionally, he would have recused himself, but he did not.

In the midst of battling corruption at all levels, we see Ram suddenly defend a corrupt industrialist in a massive scandal that normally he would deplore. 'After initially offering to become the special public prosecutor in the 2G scam case, maverick BJP MP and eminent lawyer Ram Jethmalani appeared for Unitech boss Sanjay Chandra before the Delhi High Court on Friday.'[31]

The term 2G is short for second generation wireless telephone technology. This technology is digital, allows digital encryption of telephone signals, is faster than analogue and allows the transmission of digital messages. In a country like India, it has made telephone services available to hundreds of millions who never had telephone lines at all. India is a rapidly growing mobile phone market that is second only to China in size. The 2G Spectrum Case[32] was over secret deals to grant licences for cellphones to use portions of the electromagnetic spectrum as this new technology came in.

It all started with a shockingly brazen call for applications:

On 10 January 2008, at 2.45 p.m., an announcement was posted on the DoT website stating that letters of intent (LOIS) for issuance of licences bundled with spectrum would be given to applicants between 3.30 p.m. and 4.30 p.m. The announcement added that application fees running into thousands of crores of rupees would have to be paid immediately by demand draft, along with supporting documentation.[33]

This was the highly touted Department of Telecommunications first come, first served offer. Obviously, only those who were tipped off in advance could apply. Further charges of manipulation surfaced because the government had sold the 2G licences in 2008 at the 2001 price. Many of the 122 companies that bought the licences had little or no experience in the field, and many quickly resold the licences at a huge profit. The Comptroller and Auditor General of India (CAG) estimated that the government might have lost as much as Rs 176,645 crore (approximately $31.97 billion). Other estimates ranged from a zero loss[34] to the Telecom Regulatory Authority of India's claim that the government would gain between Rs 3000 crore and Rs 7000 crore.[35]

This scam was number two on a *Time* magazine list[36] of 'Top 10 Abuses of Power.' *Time* wrote of 'allegations that led to Raja resigning late last year, he presided over the underpricing of bandwidth to mobile companies—apparently in return for bribes—which some estimate may have cost the Indian government around $7 billion. That figure makes it hands down the largest episode of graft in Indian history, and played a part in the withering defeats Raja's party sustained in local elections in early May.' This referred to former Telecom Minister A. Raja, a former Member of Parliament from the Dravida Munnetra Kazhagam Party.

Sanjay Chandra was the chairman of Uninor, a joint venture between the Indian real-estate company Unitech and the Norwegian company Telenor; he was also the managing director of Unitech. In November 2010, 'The CBI Special Court charged Chandra of cheating, forgery, criminal conspiracy and corruption, under the Indian Penal Code and Prevention of Corruption Act. Chandra had moved the Delhi High Court last week for quashing these charges, framed in October last year.'[37] This was when Raja was accused of preferentially allotting airwaves in 2008.

In May 2011, Ram represented Sanjay Chandra before the Delhi High Court, submitting 'that he has been unfairly roped in as an accused on unsubstantiated allegation of conspiracy. There is no evidence of meeting of mind between the petitioner Sanjay Chandra and either of the co-accused persons. Unitech Group of Companies were innocent applicants for UAS Licences and the petitioner had nothing to do with the decision of the public servants to change the policy of first come first serve or to change the cut off date.'

Ram said that 'the petitioner ought to have been released on bail by taking a bond with or without sureties for his appearance during trial.'

The court denied bail:[38] 'taking into account the gravity of the accusation against the petitioners a reasonable possibility of their interfering with the process of justice by tampering with the evidence, I do not deem it appropriate to release the petitioners on bail at this stage when the further investigation in the matter is going on and the trial is yet to begin.'

The Supreme Court wrote in November,[39] 'The cutoff date of 25.09.2007 was decided by accused public servants of DoT primarily to allow consideration of Unitech group applications for UAS licences.' On whether or not the company qualified to apply, 'The Unitech Group Companies were in business of realty and even the objects of companies were not changed to "telecom" and registered as required before applying. The companies were ineligible to get the licences till the grant of UAS licences.'

'Shri Ram Jethmalani, learned senior counsel appearing for the appellant Sanjay Chandra, would urge that the impugned Judgment has not appreciated the basic rule laid down by this Court that grant of bail is the rule and its denial is the exception.'

Ram argued that Chandra had cooperated with the investigation throughout, was not arrested during the investigation, that there was no threat of him tampering with witnesses and 'further contends that it was only after the appellants appeared in the Court in pursuance of summons issued, they were made to apply for bail, and, thereafter, denied bail and sent to custody.'

The court said:

He would state that the High Court has ignored even the CBI Manual before issuing these directions, which provided for bail to be granted to the accused, except in the event of there being commission of heinous crime . . . Shri Jethmalani submitted that there is not even a prima facie case against the accused and would make references to the charge sheet and the statement of several witnesses. He would emphatically submit that none of the ingredients of the offences charged with were stated in the charge sheet. He would further contend that even if, there is a prima facie case, the rule is still bail, and not jail, as per the dicta of this Court in several cases.

Shri Jethmalani would submit that as the presumption of innocence is the privilege of every accused, there is also a presumption that the appellants would not tamper with the witnesses if they are enlarged on bail, especially in the facts of the case, where the appellants have cooperated with the investigation. In recapitulating his submissions, the learned senior counsel contended that there are two principles for the grant of bail—firstly, if there is no prima facie case, and secondly, even if there is a prima facie case, if there is no reasonable apprehension of tampering with the witnesses or evidence or absconding from the trial, the accused are entitled to grant of bail pending trial.

Ram also made his case in the press: '"The allegation that Unitech group companies were ineligible for the licenses as their object clause did not mention telecom as one of their area of business is absurd and foolish," noted criminal lawyer Ram Jethmalani, appearing for Chandra of Unitech Wireless.'[40]

The report went on, 'Responding to allegations of special prosecutor U.U. Lalit that Unitech was "ineligible" for the UAS licence,' Jethmalani said that Unitech started as a real estate company and later 'changed the object clause,' but 'this did not amount to cheating'.

In November, the Supreme Court, in accordance with Ram's arguments,[41] granted Chandra bail after seven months in jail in the 2G Spectrum case. This decision actually created a new precedent. In it, the court laid down liberal principles of bail that, while not new, represented a significant change from the immediate past. Bail law had been broadened during the Emergency, but later it was narrowed in an atmosphere dominated by fear of terrorists. This had rendered a number of subsequent court judgements per incuriam, meaning that they lacked a due regard for the existing law that prescribed requirements for bail. The Sanjay Chandra case, in the opinion of some lawyers, may have restored the earlier bail law to such an extent that now almost anyone can get bail.

The question of legitimacy of the licences granted in the telecom case went back to the Supreme Court in February 2012 on a PIL filed by Subramanian Swamy, now the president of the Janata Party. The *Times of India* reported, 'In a major development having implications for the corporate sector, the Supreme Court on Thursday cancelled the 122 2G spectrum licences granted by former telecom minister A. Raja on the ground that they were issued in a "totally arbitrary and unconstitutional" manner.'[42]

In March 2013, *The Hindu*[43] alleged that senior government officials had coordinated their testimony on the 2G affair before both a Joint Parliamentary Committee and a Public Accounts Committee set up to investigate it. The coordination allegedly was intended to protect Prime Minister Manmohan Singh.

In the wake of the 2G Spectrum case, Ram represented Kanimozhi Karunanidhi, a member of the Rajya Sabha from Tamil Nadu and daughter of a former Chief Minister of that state, whom the media loudly accused of crony capitalism. The CBI had arrested her for involvement in the 2G Spectrum scam in 2011, alleging that she had a 20 per cent interest in a TV station, and she had influenced former telecom minister A. Raja to route a large sum of money to it. She was refused bail both in the lower court and the Delhi High Court, where Ram represented her. In November 2011,[44] on her fifth attempt to get out on bail, the Delhi High Court took a cue from a recent Supreme Court decision and granted her bail, although Ram was no longer her lawyer in this trial.

On the law, Ram was crystal clear. A TV interviewer [45] pointed out that the High Court had refused bail because of the 'gravity of the offense'. Ram explained that is not legally relevant as a criterion for withholding bail.

Ram explained that while there is always a theoretical possibility that someone who is out on bail may tamper with the evidence, 'it must be a reasonable possibility. But the prediction of a reasonable possibility has to be based upon your previous conduct. Have you at any stage interfered with it? Have you at any stage run away from police investigation? Have you made yourself scarce, have you refused to attend a hearing in court?'

The interviewer then argued that since she was such an important person, she would be more apt to influence witnesses, to which Ram responded, 'It is not the law of the country that merely because a person is an influential person, they should be denied bail.'

The interviewer went on to read the bribery charges against her. Ram answered, 'Where have you found that? It has never happened in the history of our courts, that in bribery offences, bail has been ultimately denied.'

Meanwhile, while Kanimozhi continued to fight the charges against her, she was elected to the Rajya Sabha from Tamil Nadu, with Congress support, in June 2013.

Kanimozhi is not the only politician who has sought Ram's help to get out of jail on the great monopoly board of Indian politics. Several other names appear routinely whenever the press lists Ram's most dubious clients. For that reason, we will look briefly at three more cases.

One was Amit Jogi, the son of former Chief Minister of Chhattisgarh Ajit Jogi, the prime accused in the murder of the National Congress Party Treasurer, Ram Avatar Jaggi. Jaggi was shot in front of a police station in Raipur on June 4, 2003; the central investigative agency arrested Amit Jogi in 2005 and charged him with plotting the murder of Jaggi. Twenty-eight people were arrested in connection with an alleged conspiracy, the charge-sheet giving the motive as robbery. The prosecution claimed it was politically motivated because Jaggi was perceived as a threat to the ruling Congress party that was headed by Ajit Jogi, Amit's father.

Amit's father was in precarious health. In April 2004, Ajit was critically injured in an auto accident, which left him paralysed and in a wheelchair. On November 24, 2005, he suffered a massive heart attack, and on December 3, 2005 Amit first appealed to the Supreme Court for bail in order to attend to his father. That application was dismissed. The Chhattisgarh High Court granted Amit bail on April 30, but Jaggi's family appealed to the Supreme Court, which again denied bail on May 3, 2006.[46] Ram's sole appearance for Jogi was in conjunction with a bail application, but that was enough to earn Amit a place in any list of supposed unsavoury clients associated with his name.

Perhaps Ram was not wrong. On May 31, 2007, a Special Court convicted 24 people, of whom 19 received life sentences and nine received five years' rigorous imprisonment. Jogi was acquitted for lack of evidence. The CBI immediately announced its intention to appeal.

Another notorious client was Y.S. Jaganmohan Reddy, the son of the late Chief Minister of Andhra Pradesh, the president of the YSR Congress party, and a Member of Parliament from Andhra Pradesh. A popular politician, he was campaigning in the by-elections on May 27, 2012 when the CBI arrested him for allegedly accumulating disproportionate assets—more than Rs 3000 crore—from political favours.[47] The YSR Congress insisted he had been politically victimized, and they petitioned the court in a challenge to his arrest. In June 2012, Ram represented Reddy before the Andhra Pradesh High Court, saying that 'CBI had adopted a partisan and vindictive approach towards Jagan, and there was nothing to suggest that he had been non-cooperative with CBI, or he was tampering with the evidence. Jagan was being harassed by the CBI at the behest of its political bosses.'[48]

In an appeal to the Supreme Court on August 9, 2012, Ram argued[49] that the Andhra High Court and the CBI court judge had disregarded established principles of bail, but he still was denied bail. On his third appeal, Jagan was released on bail from the Chanchalguda Central Jail on September 24, 2013, to wild acclaim from his constituency.

Yet another jailed politician who turned to Ram is B.S. Yeddyurappa. On August 28, 2011, the Karnataka High Court posted the hearing of a petition by the former Chief Minister, B.S.

Yeddyurappa, challenging his indictment on an alleged illegal grant of a mining lease. Yeddyurappa had been charged with corruption for two reasons. One was for allegedly manipulating land allotments in Bangalore for the benefit of his sons and the other for taking kickbacks from companies for mining licences. Representing Yeddyurappa on the matter of the mining licence, Ram denied that he was the one who granted the mining lease in question, saying it had been granted in 2007 by a previous Chief Minister.[50] On October 17, 2011, the *Times of India* reported[51] that Ram flew in from New Delhi to argue his case in the Karnataka High Court. There he quashed the complaint, but the record does not show that he represented him further.

In December 2012,[52] after multiple bail applications—in which Ram was not involved—he finally got out on bail, returning to his adoring public.[53]

The press continually harps on a list of what it considers shameful politicians who have been associated with Ram's legal practice. Notwithstanding the fact that even corrupt politicians are entitled to have a lawyer, actually, in the instances we have just looked at, Ram just presented arguments for bail. These normally entail giving assurances to the court that his clients were not flight risks and had shown no predisposition to tamper with witnesses in a future trial. He did not necessarily claim they were innocent of any charges. That is a different legal issue. Now they literally are free to defend themselves.

Now in a real switch, in 2005, Ram represented an entity that he characterized as a victim of Standard Chartered Bank's criminally negligent practices. Shortly afterwards he turned around and represented the same bank in the case *Standard Chartered Bank vs. Andhra Bank Financial Services*, May 5, 2006. Of course law professors explain that this is not uncommon. When a defendant sees how good the lawyer is on behalf of the other side, they may well hire him for their own defence in their next case.

The more interesting case of the two was in 2005. The Supreme Court wrote,[54] 'The question that arises for consideration is whether a company or a corporate body could be prosecuted for offences for which the sentence of imprisonment is a mandatory punishment.'

In this case a record number of more than 80 lawyers were named as counsels, a testament to the importance of this case as well as to the money involved. It arose[55] out of an alleged FERA (Foreign Exchange Regulation Act) violation in 1991–92, because of which the bank had already returned the disputed money to India.

'Once the amount remitted out of the country was repatriated, the bank claimed, the proceedings were illegal as the purpose was to prevent economic losses to the country. In 1993–94, the ED issued show-cause notices against the bank and its employees alleging contravention of the provisions of FERA.'

Standard Chartered Bank had challenged notices issued to them under FERA in 1994 by the Bombay High Court. This appeal said that the penalty under FERA is imprisonment, and the bank's lawyers maintained that 'in a case where the offence is punishable with a mandatory sentence of imprisonment, the company cannot be prosecuted as the sentence of imprisonment cannot be enforced against the company,' that is, a corporation cannot go to prison.

Remember that Ram was not on Standard Chartered Bank's side in this case, and he went for as much as he could get. If a corporation could not be put in jail, at least it could be fined.

'Senior counsel Shri Jethmalani contended that if a corporate body is found guilty of the offence committed, the court, though bound to impose the sentence prescribed under law, has the discretion to impose the sentence of imprisonment or fine as in the case of a company or corporate body the sentence of imprisonment cannot be imposed on it and as the law never compels to do anything which is impossible, the court has to follow the alternative and impose the sentence of fine,' the court said.

Ram also argued 'that Section 11 of IPC defines the word "person" to include a company.'

The court worried that, as long as it had the option either of imposing imprisonment or a fine, it might prosecute the bank for a minor offence, but in a larger offence, where imprisonment is mandatory, the bank could escape prosecution.[56]

Standard Chartered Bank argued that since the Indian

Parliament knew a corporation could not be jailed, 'the legislative intention was *not* to prosecute the companies or corporate bodies . . . when the sentence prescribed cannot be imposed, the very prosecution itself is futile and meaningless.'

They also argued that the court did not have the discretionary power to choose only one punishment, for instance only to award a fine. On behalf of the respondents, Ram argued that the company was criminally liable, and the court can impose a fine alone in order to be sure the offence will not go unpunished.

In a split verdict, three to two, the court went with Ram's argument, holding: 'As the company cannot be sentenced to imprisonment, the court cannot impose that punishment, but when imprisonment and fine is the prescribed punishment the court can impose the punishment of fine which could be enforced against the company.'

One legal analyst[57] calls this a landmark case. 'The Standard Chartered Case adds a new chapter to the evolution of law as to criminal liability of a corporate body in India, starting from the non-liability of corporations for crimes committed, to the non-liability due to the physical impossibility of imposing the punishment and the dilemma in cases where the punishment meted out is both imprisonment and fine. The judgment is important for it sheds light upon the statutory construction of criminal statutes, departing from the traditional principle of strict interpretation and establishing the applicability of the principle of purposive interpretation.'

Both the press and the public accuse Ram of fighting publicly against corruption, then—in more than one whiplash-inducing switch—accepting large sums of money for defending crooks. Yet, like Robin Hood, the folk hero who took money from the rich to give to the poor, Ram collects large sums from rich miscreants to offset the cases that he does pro bono. Still, Ram has other motives, besides his disgust for the conditions in an Indian prison. While his actions may seem paradoxical, Ram has an almost visceral hatred of corruption, but his anger is just as great over abusive governmental prosecutions or detentions. He has seen too much of both, and he is not prepared to stomach either one without a protest.

37

Hits and Misses

Ram has garnered many honours and he has tilted at many windmills.

The World Peace Through Law Centre elected Ram vice-president in 1973, later electing him honorary president of the Australia and Asia Section. In 1977, at a meeting in the Philippines, World Peace Through Law awarded him their prestigious Human Rights Award for his fight against authoritarianism during the Emergency.

During this time the Marcos family ruled the Philippines. Ram delivered a stirring acceptance speech that was broadcast to a large crowd by a loudspeaker. In it he boomed out, 'Democracies must show their flag in countries which deny democracy.' Midway through his speech, his microphone was cut off. That evening a charming and gracious Imelda Marcos met Ram at the reception. Ram introduced himself, but Imelda waved off the introduction, saying, 'Oh, you do not have to introduce yourself. What do you think I am doing here?'

Ram said, 'Yes. You blacked out my speech this morning.' Imelda smiled her lovely smile and answered, 'Oh, that was against the speech, not against you.'

In 1997, the World Freedom Coalition presented Ram with the International Valiant for Freedom Award, an honour that has also been bestowed upon the Dalai Lama and other notables.

Ram was a recipient of the prestigious 2006 Gusi Peace Prize for Social Justice and Humanitarian Law. The Gusi Peace Prize International is given by a charitable organization based in Manila, Philippines, and that is where it holds its annual award ceremonies. It was established to recognize individuals or groups across the world who have distinguished themselves as outstanding exemplars of society or who have contributed towards peace and respect for human life and dignity.

The International Council of Jurists, which is jointly sponsored by the All India Bar Association and the Indian Council of Jurists, awarded Ram their International Council of Jurists Award in December, 2008.

Ram has long been active in international Sindhi organizations, and Sindhi websites fairly burst with pride over his accomplishments. In October 1989, Ram and Dial Gidwani inaugurated the Indian Institute of Sindhology, Ram later serving as its president. Ram and his friends Bhagwan and Dial Gidwani established the American Institute of Sindhulogy in Chicago on August 6, 2000. This institute has helped make the Indus Valley civilization a popular subject of study all over America. It has awarded several research grants, and through some of these, the Japanese have produced some excellent scholarly literature on the Mohenjodaro civilization.

The Global Sindhi Council was created 'on the auspicious occasion' of Ram's 83rd birthday, September 14, 2006, naming Ram Jethmalani and L.K. Advani among their most eminent leaders. Ram served as its president in 2011.

As a guest speaker at the Sindhi Association of North America Annual Meeting in Houston, 2010, Ram was introduced as 'the most prominent Sindhi from India'. His speech there may contain the most accurate and brief summary to date of his view of Islam: 'I am not a religious person because so much blood has been shed in the name of religion that navies of the entire world can easily swim in it. Mohammad . . . was the greatest prophet of all times because he assigned more strength to the ink of a pen as compared to the sword. Consequently, Muslim cities became centres of scholarship and Muslims pulled Europe out from the Dark Ages. However, when Muslims became book burners and destroyers of civilisations they were enslaved.'[1]

Ram spoke at the Sindhi Sammelan in Florida in 1999 and again in Chicago in 2000. There he urged the members to read *Return of the Aryans* by Bhagwan S. Gidwani, saying, 'It is also a history of human thought, more particularly of the variegated strands of Hindu thought and the metaphysical search of the Hindu mind. The Vedas and the Upanishads were the glorious, though late, products of the amazingly inquisitive Aryan mind that had not been ensnared by dogma or commitment to any small god.'[2]

Ram is the chief patron of the Global Sindhi Council, a past officer of the World Sindhi Congress and a past officer of the Sindhi Association of North America. He was a speaker at the 24th International Conference on Sindh held by the World Sindhi Congress in London on October 13, 2012. It actually would be hard to find a Sindhi organization anywhere which Ram has not addressed, and he has been an officer or at least an honorary officer of many. More than once we have found him in Washington lobbying to obtain American support for aggrieved Sindhis in Pakistan, not the least of whose complaints is over water, the lifeblood of their agriculture. The World Sindhi Organization routinely gives Ram a grand party every September in Mumbai on the occasion of his birthday.

In 2005, petitioners challenged the mention of Sindh in the Indian national anthem,[3] claiming the possibility of an international outcry over this mention since the state today is in Pakistan. Appearing for the All India Sindhi Council, Ram led the intervenors in defence of his homeland before the Supreme Court.[4] 'Is the petitioner the person who typifies the interest of 100 crore population of India,' the noted lawyer asked. Ram answered his own question by saying that so far nobody had ever opposed the word Sindh in the national anthem when it was sung 'day in and day out across India.'

Ram then proudly reminded the court that 'when the world was taking pride in the fact that the first civilisation was started in Rome, it was discovered later that the Indus Valley Civilisation was the oldest.'

He said that 'The word "Indus" was derived from "Sindhu", the river on the banks of which the world's oldest civilisation thrived . . . The petitioner does not know this golden chapter of Hindustan and wants to destroy it by seeking deletion of the word "Sindh" from the national anthem,' he argued.

Writing in its opinion, 'The case against the threat to delete Sindh from India's National Anthem was valiantly and passionately argued by Mr Ram B. Jethmalani before the Supreme Court of India,' the Supreme Court dismissed the petition. Sindh remains in the national anthem.

As a result, the Bharatiya Sindhi Global Alliance asked Ram to be its 'Chief Patron and lead the community.'[5] This was another 'hit' for Ram.

There were also some 'misses.' In April 2004 Ram dropped a thunderbolt. He announced his intention to run against Vajpayee for the Lok Sabha in Lucknow. Some called him a gross opportunist devoid of all principle. Even his family objected. Still, despite a recent surgery on his knee, he was determined to fight. Even Nusli Wadia begged him not to run, and not to leave the BJP. But he did both.

Mahesh did what he could. Along with other BJP leaders who represented Ram, he even put his head together with Jaswant Singh, representing Vajpayee, to formulate the words Vajpayee would use in a public announcement designed to bury the hatchet. Vajpayee dutifully issued an appeal to Ram through the media, asking him in essence: Why are you fighting an old friend? We have spent so many years together, why should we be seen to be fighting? This kind of conflict is not necessary. He even called Ram a national treasure. Although Ram had already filed his nomination form in Lucknow, he said he would let it be known that he was withdrawing because he had to be with Janak, who was critically ill in London. He authorized Mahesh and Sri to send the withdrawal form to Lucknow; then he went urgently to London, leaving his signed withdrawal form with Mahesh.

It turns out that the withdrawal form needed a signed cover letter. Mahesh told the messenger to file the withdrawal form, with a letter signed by Sri for Ram, with Ram and Mahesh's consent. Then Ram had a change of heart, saying that people were pressuring him to run. Someone had even staged a hunger strike. He thereupon announced to the press that he would indeed stand for election. He also told the press that someone in his office had forged his signature on the cover letter: 'Somebody in my office has jumped the gun.' All this meant that something had to be done urgently about the letter and withdrawal form that had already been sent.

As it happened, when the messenger arrived with the letter and the withdrawal form, he simply handed it over in the office, not to the returning officer himself. This was because the returning officer, who was also the magistrate, had been suspended the day before for not maintaining public order when Congress gave out free saris to local women and caused a near-riot. The newly appointed returning officer was not to come in until the next day. For that reason, technically, they had not complied with the election rules, which said the letter and form had to be given to the returning officer himself. Mahesh instructed the messenger to retrieve the letter and form, using a ruse that the letter lacked a Hindi signature, which they needed to affix, and that they needed to hand the letter and form directly to the returning officer. Then they tore the papers up. And that is how Ram managed to run.

The house was full of astrologers and fortune tellers. That was when they told him to put rings on each finger, each stone selected for its property of bringing good luck. They conducted pujas and predicted victory. The astrologers were paid well and their predictions were rosy. We remember sitting on the back porch while Ram, confident at first, tried to collect the political support he needed.

Initially, Ram announced he would only proceed if all the Opposition parties united behind him, but by the time he announced this, they had not. His support supposedly came from the Congress party, the left and a few minority parties. When asked whether the Congress was providing any financing or giving any speeches, Ram said that they supported him, but it was their policy not to canvas against a sitting Prime Minister. Still, he remained encouraged because every time he drove into Lucknow from the airport, supporters cheered him all the way in. Lataa was one of the few of his stalwarts to actually go to Lucknow to work on the campaign. True to form, Ram asked Vajpayee 10 questions a day. Ram put many of his old hobby horses on the platform, such as transparency, and requested Vajpayee to send the Gujarat riot cases outside of the state.

Part of his platform came from *Tehelka*'s Operation West End sting. He snorted that Prime Minister Vajpayee described the sting as a 'wake-up call to the nation' then set up a Commission of Inquiry to investigate *Tehelka*. He asked if Vajpayee could be trusted with the nuclear button.

When the election results came in, Ram had received just enough votes to not be required to forfeit the filing fee for his candidacy.

Ram remained out of the BJP from 2004 until 2010, when the papers report that he wrote 'a letter to BJP President Nitin Gadkari expressing his desire to join the party and represent it in Rajya Sabha . . . Jethmalani's letter, copies of which were sent to senior BJP leaders including L.K. Advani earlier this week, states that he is keen on entering the Upper House of Parliament from Madhya Pradesh, where the party is in power.'⁶ And that is what he did.

The honeymoon with the BJP lasted until his expulsion from the party in 2013.

And life marched on. 'To speak only of Mr Jethmalani as a lawyer would be an injustice to this colourful personality and his famed weakness for the fairer sex. It isn't out of place to say that legend has it that, recently . . . Mr Jethmalani requested the judge to adjourn the matter as he was not feeling too well. The judge, it is said, readily obliged and asked Mr Jethmalani how old he was. Mr Jethmalani is said to have replied: "My lord, different parts of my body feel different ages—my heart is definitely 17."'⁷

Ram calls himself 'a sinner with a clean conscience.' Indeed, much of his lifestyle is an open book, much of it known, for better or for worse, by the whole country. The parts the public does not know about would be the yoga, the regular push-ups, and the treadmill he uses daily in Pune. He also chants a mantra which, once it has been chanted 500,000 times, is supposed to give freedom from the cycle of life. He once told me that if he loses a night of sleep he can make up for it by the simple expedient of standing on his head. Now he no longer does it. People also may not know of his daily 8 a.m. badminton game before breakfast when he is in Delhi or Mumbai. They might guess, though, if they saw him walking purposefully through the airport every few days, at age 90.

In fact, while everyone knows that Ram loves his scotch in the evening, few know that he has become a strict vegetarian. He eats only breakfast, picks at lunch and dinner and fasts on Tuesdays. Before dinner, when not beset by lawyers clamouring for his time, he likes to start at 8 p.m. with a glass of scotch or brandy with warm water. Then he can be tempted by a bit of pizza and some ice cream for dessert. His favourite venue when he goes out to dinner is a neighbourhood pizzeria.

Ram professes complete indifference to food, which is ironic. His Delhi kitchen staff cooks up pots of food; Ram picks at a few snacks, and everyone else in the house eats the rest, putting away as much as possible for their relatives. Despite Ram's neutrality about food, his daughters and wives have always loved to go to the latest restaurants and five-star hotels for dinner, dressed to the nines, and Ram escorts them just to make them happy. They do get a kick out of walking in with him, because typically, a hush falls over the restaurant, diners put down their silverware, and all eyes follow him to his table. The waiters rush over to make sure he is comfortable, and to shake his hand. When the time comes to order, he will whisper to the nearest woman, 'Order whatever you want, darling. I'll just eat a little of it.'

We once watched him chat up a stout, homely waitress, teasing her and calling her darling, until she was all giggly. She clearly was ready to follow him anywhere. He has been called irresistibly charming.

Ram's election as president of the Supreme Court Bar Association in 2010 was a definite 'hit'. A Harvard Law School[8] article estimates that in 2011, 1,273,289 lawyers across India were enrolled in State Bar Councils. In 2013, the Supreme Court Bar Association listed

6806 active members, plus some 3500 non-resident and temporary members. In other words, the article estimates that senior advocates represent less than 1 per cent of the lawyers in India, which has only some 'thousand senior advocates, including some four hundred designated by the Supreme Court.'[9] On the next page, the authors estimate 'the number of pre-eminent seniors,' the ones they call Grand Advocates, 'at the Supreme Court today is something on the order of 40 to 50,' and they believe that adding the number of lawyers with a comparable status at the High Courts would give 'at most a hundred that make up what one observer refers to as the "giants and legends of the litigation system".' This places Ram at the top of a rarified stratum of the Bar.

Still, 2010 was the same year that Ram took the notorious Jessica Lal murder case—a definite 'miss'. It would be fair to say that, of all the criminals Ram has defended, Manu Sharma has a special place among the most reviled. Even Ram's family opposed his taking the case. His son Mahesh says it was among 'three of his most perfidious moments,' the other two being his defence of Sanjay Chandra in the 2G Spectrum case and his defence of the Hindujas.

Ram contends that he could not refuse when the father, Vinod Sharma, a wealthy member of Parliament representing Haryana for the Congress party, came to him in tears, begging him to defend his son. Yet this is the same father who was accused of bribing witnesses before the lower court, an offence for which some claim he forfeited the moral right to Ram's services. Others say that it is no surprise the father came crying—they all did, but the ones who wielded political influence caught Ram's ear. Not necessarily true, but that is what critics assume.

In March 2002, Ram went to the Delhi High Court, which initially granted bail. When the case came back for an extension of bail,[10] the court quaintly told the following story:

It was unfateful day of 29th of April 1999. Around 300 to 400 people had attended that party. After 1.00 a.m. or so 70–80 people remained while other had left. It was 2.00 a.m. in the night when Malini Ramani and deceased Jessica Lal and complainant

Shyan Munshi and a waiter were present Along with 5–6 more persons in the restaurant when the petitioner-accused along with his friends came there and asked the waiter to serve him the drink.[sic] At first instance the waiter did not oblige him. When accused insisted for being served with the drink deceased Jessica Lal and Malini Ramani intervened and told him that the party was over and no liquor was left. It was at that point of time that the petitioner-accused is alleged to have threatened that he would have to adopt his own methods to get the drink. The deceased Jessica Lal again tried to persuade that there was no reason to feel angry. It is alleged that this infuriated the petitioner who took out the Pistol from his pants and fired one shot in the ceiling and the other shot aiming at Jessica Lal which he hit at her fore-head on the left side. As a result she fell down and was removed to Aslok Hospital with the help of Jatinder Raj and Madan Waiter.

The police arrived immediately and seized the pistol, Manu Sharma's arms licence, a photograph, a diary, and a cassette. The court continued, 'The interim bail of the petitioner was granted mainly on account of the non-availability of a crucial witness who was a Nepali boy and was employed as a servant in Amandeep Gill's house for long.'

The court ruled that it was inappropriate to prolong the bail, and it requested the missing witness be located immediately.

On February 21, 2006, the Additional Sessions Judge in Delhi acquitted Manu Sharma after several witnesses changed their stories. *Tehelka* produced evidence that at least one witness was bribed to turn hostile.[11] Later the witnesses faced charges for perjury. The public virtually foamed at the mouth over the acquittal.

The case came back on December 18, 2006. Ram argued that the evidence did not prove Manu Sharma was even present at the time of the shooting, nobody who knew him saw him enter the café, and witnesses who did not know him at all had been coerced by the police to testify against him. He also argued that the room was too crowded for witnesses to see what happened, the key witness was not in a place where she could see the shooting and she was drunk anyhow; another witness was planted, an incriminating cartridge was planted in the car in which it was found and there was good evidence that two different firearms had been fired. Still, the Delhi High Court held Sharma guilty[12] and sentenced him to rigorous imprisonment for life, calling the key witness in the last trial a liar.

In 2008, the case came back on appeal.[13] The court stuck to facts that were essentially the same as those recited in the last trial:

'Shortly stated, the case of the prosecution was that on April 29–30, 1999, a party was organized at "Tamarind Café" inside Qutub Colonnade. It was a private party where certain persons were invited and liquor was served. Jessica Lal (since deceased) and one Shyan Munshi were in charge of the bar. It was the allegation of the prosecution that appellant Sidhartha Vashisht (Manu Sharma) along with his friends came there and asked for liquor. Jessica Lal and Shyan Munshi did not oblige him by providing liquor since the bar was closed. According to the prosecution, the appellant got enraged on refusal to serve liquor, took out his .22 pistol and fired two 3 rounds, first into the ceiling and the second at Jessica Lal. Jessica Lal fell down as a result of the shot which proved fatal and she died. According to the assertion of the prosecution, several persons witnessed the incident. Beena Ramani, who was present, stopped the appellant and questioned him as to why he had shot Jessica Lal. She also demanded weapon from the accused but the accused did not hand over pistol and fled away.'

The court initiated further proceedings on its own accord on December 20, 2006, to ascertain whether 32 of the witnesses had committed perjury when they had unexpectedly turned hostile to the prosecution's case.[14] Of interest, the court concluded in May 2013 that there was a conclusive case only against two witnesses, and they had committed perjury because of intimidation. The court thereupon proposed a witness protection programme for them.

In 2010, one last appeal[15] was dismissed, and the life sentence was left unchanged. Ram complained that his client was tried and convicted by the media, which had prejudiced the case in court.

Why were the press and the public so furious with Ram? It was because they assumed that when he takes a case, his client, guilty or innocent, always will get off. Since many eyewitnesses saw this crime, and since the alleged shooter was viewed as a rich, self-indulgent playboy, the public was outraged at the very idea of him walking away a free man. Nevertheless, he did not, despite Ram's best efforts to discredit the evidence.

Mahesh says that one problem was that the law allowed the witnesses who identified Sharma in the first place to reverse their testimony. He proposes a change in the law that would require witnesses to sign statements, with a 48-hour window allowed in which they can change the statement. This would be to counter any objection that the police had coerced the original statement.

The next case has major political significance because it was part of an attempt to incriminate a future candidate for Prime Minister. Amit Shah, the former Home Minister of Gujarat, is a member of the BJP, and he is known to be close to Narendra Modi. Modi, then Chief Minister of Gujarat, is blamed by Muslims for delaying the governmental response to the 2002 riots in Gujarat, and in 2014 he was elected Prime Minister. Ram is convinced that Modi responded in an appropriate time-frame, and he has written numerous articles in support of him. Now these legal cases were another route for the Congress party to attack their competition. They wanted to create an excuse to send Modi to jail, and that manoeuvre was up to Ram and Mahesh to counter.

In a 2010 bail application[16] filed on behalf of Amit Shah, the Gujarat High Court quotes Ram:

> The case relates to conspiracy with regard to Sohrabuddin fake encounter by the Gujarat Police as well as the Andhra Pradesh Police. He submitted that as it is stated in the brief facts of the case in the charge sheet itself, the investigation revealed that during the year 2004, the criminal gang of Sohrabuddin had become very active in the areas of Rajsamand, Nathdwara, Sukher and Udaipur districts of Rajasthan.
>
> Sr. Counsel Mr Ram Jethmalani submitted that this is the background in which the alleged conspiracy is said to have taken place between the Gujarat and Rajasthan police to eliminate

Sohrabuddin, which led to filing of the present case . . . accused is the ex-Home Minister of the State (A-16) arraigned for the alleged conspiracy which is not borne out from any material and evidence. Learned Sr. Counsel Mr Ram Jethmalani strenuously submitted that it is no less than a figment of imagination and fiction story created and concocted by the respondent-CBI for ultimate political motive.

Sohrabuddin and his wife were killed while they were being transported by the Andhra Pradesh Police. The accusation was that it was a 'fake encounter', an encounter staged to cover up a police assassination. The court said, '. . . the main offence alleged against the applicant is kidnapping and killing of Sohrabuddin and his wife. The CBI has not alleged any overt act or presence of the applicant even remotely, and to implicate the accused [Amit Shah] he has been alleged to have been involved in conspiracy with the other co-accused based upon inadmissible hearsay, unreliable and concocted evidence of the witnesses . . .

'. . . the Government itself has accepted that it was a fake encounter and reported before the Court. However, the investigation came to be transferred to the CBI for the reason that the Gujarat Police was not able to identify the seven personnel of the police force of Andhra Pradesh State' who accompanied Sohrabuddin and his wife.

Ram outlined a byzantine conspiracy between witnesses, the police and a group of builders who owed large sums of money on bank loans, all of whom had motives to do away with the Sohrabuddins. He claimed blame was being shifted deliberately to Amit Shah, the Home Minister of Gujarat, and, tacitly, from him to Narendra Modi. He said the CBI investigation was dishonest, 'resulting in a mockery of justice'. From there he went on to explain that the court had to consider the nature and character of the evidence. The court wrote, 'He submitted that the court has to consider whether, on the basis of such evidence, the present applicant could be denied bail and in fact it would be a case for acquittal.'

Ram lectured the court on the rules of evidence. The court wrote about Ram's argument:

> . . . that there is no direct evidence and the conspiracy with regard to killing of Sohrabuddin and his wife has therefore to be considered on the basis of circumstantial evidence as there is no other evidence. He emphasised and submitted that there has to be an evidence of such nature which can be said to be cogent and convincing for suggesting an inference about the involvement of the accused in the conspiracy.
>
> Learned Sr. Counsel Mr Ram Jethmalani emphasised that in fact the State Government has accepted before the Hon'ble Apex Court about the fake encounter and therefore the Court may consider when the evidence against the accused is so concocted, unreliable and even the genuineness of such audio-video recording can be doubted whether it can be said to be a sufficient evidence suggesting the involvement of the accused in the conspiracy. He emphasised and submitted that as suggested by the theory of the prosecution CBI with regard to extortion or conspiracy for extortion leading to the killing of Sohrabuddin, there is no case, there is no evidence and in fact there has to be some semblance of evidence or instance where the applicant can be said to have been indulging in such activity. CBI has not been able to throw any light or collect any evidence even when the charge sheet is filed. Learned Sr. Counsel Mr Ram Jethmalani therefore submitted that it is nothing but a political victimisation merely because he was the Home Minister of an opposition party ruling the State which has led to such fabricated stories.

That was Ram's most important point: this was a political manoeuvre, not a serious criminal case. The court allowed his client, Amit Shah, to go out on bail.

Narmada Bai, the 55-year-old illiterate mother of one Tulsiram Prajapati, brought a related case.[17] She claimed her son was killed in a 'fake encounter', to keep him from being a material witness in the Sohrabuddin case.[18] The mother begged for a CBI investigation and for compensation.

Sohrabuddin and his gang were wanted for murder. While he was hiding from the police, a man working as a police informer had lured Sohrabuddin and his wife into taking a bus trip. That was when the police supposedly pursued the bus; creating an encounter, and killing Sohrabuddin and his wife.

Geeta Johri, Inspector General of Police, was in charge of the investigation. According to the court, 'Rubabbuddin Sheikh [wrote a letter] to the Chief Justice of India about the killing of his brother Sohrabuddin Sheikh in a fake encounter . . .' Rubabbuddin Sheikh's letter asked the CBI to look into the involvement of Tulsiram Prajapati, 'a close associate of Sohrabuddin, who was allegedly used to locate and abduct Sohrabuddin and his wife Kausarbi, and was thus a material witness against the police personnel.' Now they had to question Tulsiram.

While Narmada's son Tulsiram was in jail during an investigation for other criminal cases, he sent out two letters requesting extra security, because he believed there was a conspiracy to kill him. One was a 'letter to the Chairman, National Human Rights Commission (in short "NHRC") alleging that there was conspiracy among the police officials of Gujarat, Rajasthan, Maharashtra, etc. to do away with him in a fake encounter by cooking up a false story of running away from custody.'

He wrote that 'the Gujarat Crime Branch and Anti Terrorist Squad (in short "ATS") were very notorious for staging fake encounters.' He knew he was about to be interrogated by Geeta Johri, as she had investigated the Sohrabuddin case.

Narmada said, as the court wrote, 'her son was being escorted by Udaipur (Rajasthan) Police from Ahmedabad to Udaipur in a train. When the train was passing through Himatnagar—Shymlaji Stretch, the deceased sought permission to go to the toilet. The policemen escorted him to the toilet where two of his accomplices disguised as passengers attacked the policemen by throwing chilli powder in their eyes. When the policemen called for the other members of the escort party, the goons fired at them and jumped off the moving train. In response, the police opened fire but the accused fled in the cover of darkness after shooting back at the police . . .'

Indeed, the police report said that while fleeing from the police Tulsiram had fired at them; they fired back in self-defence, and thus he had been killed 'in an encounter'.

The police denied that Tulsiram was the material witness they wanted to talk to; they said it was the police informer. Ram again represented Amit Shah, who had been arrested but released on bail after three months. Ram contended that the police were already investigating, and the 'conduct of the CBI does not inspire any confidence' because they named Tulsiram as the third person in the Sohrabuddin case even before they completed their investigation.

The court cited numerous discrepancies in investigations by both the police and the CBI, but it ruled that the police records should be given to the CBI so they could complete the investigation. Any question of compensation would have to come later. Amit Shah, Ram's client, was not implicated.

These cases had a significance that went far beyond the misdeeds of gangsters and corrupt police. Ram also defended Narendra Modi against irresponsible attacks by the press:

> Former minister Amit Shah's lawyer, Ram Jethmalani, on Thursday said in court that the CBI's real target behind its arrest of Shah in the Sheikh fake encounter case was Gujarat chief minister Narendra Modi . . . Jethmalani said that the probe agency's motive behind Shah's arrest was political. 'The aim of the CBI was to get to the chief minister of the state (Modi), and Shah was the last step of the ladder to reach him,' he alleged.[19]

The Hindu gives Ram's explanation:

> Jethmalani said, 'The Centre had hatched a conspiracy with CBI to target Chief Minister Narendra Modi and his government and the first among them was Amit Shah.'
>
> Criticising the CBI for foisting a case on Amit Shah 'without a piece of evidence' to support its case, he said: 'The Central government was targeting Mr Modi due to political reasons and

Amit Shah was only a medium through which it could achieve it.'[20]

Mahesh represented Shah when he filed a writ in April 2013,[21] 'owing to the filing of fresh FIR . . . by the Central Bureau of Investigation (CBI) . . . arraying him as an accused in view of the directions given by this Court to the Police Authorities of the Gujarat State to handover the case relating to the death of Tulsiram Prajapati.'

The court did not allow fresh charges against Amit Shah, concluding that 'the second FIR . . . filed by the CBI is contrary to the directions issued in judgment and order dated 08.04.2011 by this Court . . . and accordingly the same is quashed.'

What was behind the hostility against Modi? According to *Gujarat Riots: The True Story*,[22] the events in Gujarat started in 2002 when 58 Hindus were burned alive by a mob of Muslims who boarded a railroad car compartment, locked it and set it on fire. They claimed later that the fire was an accident. Hindu mobs in Gujarat then attacked and murdered Muslims. The number is in dispute—Hindus say 790 Muslims and 254 Hindus were killed, with a total of 223 people missing. Muslims say, 'Over a thousand lives, possibly many more, were lost over the next few weeks. Over 100,000 Muslims were pushed into the state's ramshackle refugee camps, where basic amenities were minimal and living conditions abysmal.'[23]

Modi was the Chief Minister of Gujarat, and he was accused of deliberately moving slowly before he imposed a curfew or called in the police, in order to allow time for the Hindus to retaliate. His answer was that 'Police Authorities have fired more than 3900 rounds, they have used more than 6500 rounds of tear gas and arrested more than 2800 people. One should also take a note of the fact that 90 people have been killed in police firing which shows that police showed no lenient approach towards elements spreading violence, arson and looting.'

Because Ram and Mahesh defended Modi, they were labelled anti-Muslim. An unknown person even made threats against

Haseena and her children, and police were posted outside their home for two months afterwards.

Ram has written repeatedly that no evidence has been produced to tie Narendra Modi to the Sohrabuddin killings. In April 2012, a Special Investigation Team (SIT) absolved Modi of any involvement in the Gulbarg massacre, arguably the worst episode of the riots. The SIT report on the riots 'has given Modi a clean chit and exonerated him of all charges.'[24]

The same article went on:

On the meeting held on February 27, 2002 . . .

Modi told the SIT that it was his constitutional duty to review the situation and ensure the safety, security and development of the people of Gujarat. He said that at the meeting, he told officials that law and order be maintained at all cost and had also appealed to people to maintain harmony. He told the SIT that he had asked the concerned officials to keep in touch with local army authorities and had held a series of such law and order review meetings thereafter and addressed the press also.

On what he had done to check the riots . . .

Modi told the probe team that he had issued press statements appealing to people to maintain harmony and that his appeal for peace and communal harmony was aired on Doordarshan [the public service broadcaster] as well. He further said that he had requested the Union home minister and the defense minister to expedite the deployment of the army.

. . . Modi further said that perhaps for the first time in the country, a committee was constituted under the chairmanship of the governor to review rehabilitation efforts.

This high-level committee included leader of the opposition, members from the chamber of commerce, members from prominent NGOs etc.

That committee absolved Modi completely.

Ram defended a former BJP legislator from Gujarat, Kalubhai Maliwad, who too was implicated in the Gujarat riots, and the press went after him again. 'Ram Jethmalani had earlier represented Centre for Peace and Justice, an NGO that had filed an application to hand over the investigation of the Gujarat riots in a separate matter although connected with the larger issue of Gujarat riots.'[25]

Kamini Jaiswal, the opposing attorney, accused Ram of inconsistency, 'By the courts records, one can see that Mr Jethmalani had represented the victims earlier. Now, he is representing the accused in this matter. Isn't this conflict of interest?'

Ram denied the accusation of impropriety, saying that on behalf of the NGO he simply had asked for a change of venue, 'If the public has no confidence in the courts, the trial must be moved.'

Notwithstanding all his work for Modi, in May 2013, the Press Trust of India reported, 'Rebel BJP MP Ram Jethmalani, who had been critical of the BJP leadership and had revolted against then party chief Nitin Gadkari, was on Tuesday expelled from the primary membership of the party for six years on charges of "breach of discipline".' This occurred several weeks after the press claimed 'he had barged into a parliamentary party meeting and questioned his continued suspension'.

Intertwined with all this was Ram's relations with L.K. Advani. Ram is proud of defending Advani in the Jain hawala case, and their friendship harks back to their background, both Sindhis from Pakistan. On Raksha Bandhan, when sisters tie a traditional bracelet on their brothers' wrists, Ram became a 'rakhee brother' of Advani's wife, just as he is with his own sisters. After he received the notice of expulsion from the party in November 2012, Ram wrote to Advani's wife to say he would no longer see Advani, since Advani was part of the vote to expel him. Ram also publicly called Advani senile. The media simply laughed, since Advani is younger. Ram changed the characterization to politically ambitious.

That was based on Ram's suspicion that Advani wanted to run for Prime Minister instead of Modi. Be that as it may, with prodding from Mahesh, both Advani and Modi came to Ram's festive 90th birthday party in Delhi on September 15, 2013. All the newspapers ran the picture of the three of them sitting in a row, with Ram in the middle, the reporters laughing that the two rivals insisted that Ram sit between them, but on the day after the party, Advani formally endorsed Modi as the BJP candidate.

Why did the BJP bother to expel a famous senior member? For six years? At 89? Why did the press devote so much ink to it? These are interesting questions. The answers lie in Ram's sui generis status as a celebrity. What actually happened was that the party formally summoned him to their meeting, so he showed up. There he dared them to expel him since nothing in the party charter says it is illegal to speak out against the leadership. When they did, he threatened to serve the BJP with a 'show cause notice', a preliminary to suing them, claiming that the order to expel him must be set aside, since the party has no jurisdiction and no basis for their action.

Ram has told the press it was a matter of his personal honour. Of course while he certainly might enjoy getting the better of the BJP leadership, he definitely wanted nothing to interfere with Modi's campaign for Prime Minister. The BJP on their part needed his wholehearted support of Modi. While some preliminary legal skirmishing began before the election, both sides still might eventually consider any further public conflict unproductive. At his age, Ram has denied any personal ambitions under a Modi government, but we can speculate about what he might want.

Throughout the years leading up to the election of 2014, Ram told the media that his last remaining political aspiration was to get rid of India's current corrupt leadership and to replace it with an honest government. Still, in private conversations, he says his larger objective is to see the major democracies of the world—the United States, Israel, India, and Japan—unite to promote the ideals of democracy for all. He tells his family and his intimates that this is his final goal.

38

Ram's Man Modi

This was only one part of an effort to which Ram devoted over two years of his life to one effort—the election of Narendra Modi to the office of Prime Minister of India. He fought, wrote, made speeches, and argued on his behalf against bitter critics. He was expelled from the BJP for attacking signs of corruption within the party, but, as the elections approached, Ram's articles in the *Sunday Guardian* continued to be a drumbeat of support for Modi.

In May 2014, Narendra Modi won the Indian elections, achieving the first non-Congress party parliamentary majority in Indian history. With 272 seats necessary for a majority in the Lok Sabha, the BJP won 283 seats. With its allied parties in the National Democratic Alliance, it won control of 336 seats, the biggest election victory since 1984. This, of course, was when Rajiv Gandhi won in a sympathy vote after the assassination of his mother, Prime Minister Indira Gandhi. In 2014, however, Rajiv's son, Rahul Gandhi, took the Congress party down to a low of 44 seats. This meant that the Congress party and its allies garnered some 23 per cent of the vote, with the BJP and its allies at about 38 per cent.

Despite this overwhelming success, a Modi win had been far from a forgone conclusion. Modi had been bedeviled by accusations that threatened to swamp any future candidacy. The United States even refused in 2005 to grant Modi a visa, citing a law that refused entry for violation of religious freedom.

Ram did not have a long-standing personal relationship with Modi. He actually only met him for the second time in December 2012, when the George Washington University Law School India Project travelled to Gujarat. There Ram met them and arranged a personal interview with Modi, but he had long been writing about the 2002 confrontation.

Ram published some of his best arguments in a February 16, 2013 article in the *Sunday Guardian*, 'Let the Truth Be Known about Modi.' He begins his summary with:

> Let me inform the people of a few instances of deliberate disinformation against Modi, which gained huge currency during the last 10 years, backed by the malicious hate campaign, which the SIT investigation has proved to be completely false.
>
> The country was made to believe that Modi sat complacent and inert while the riots were searing Gujarat. The evidence indicates otherwise. Immediately after the Godhra train burning, on the evening of 27 February 2002, the Gujarat Chief Minister summoned an emergency meeting of top ranking officials of the government, took steps to deploy the Rapid Action Force (RAF), State Reserve Police, local police at sensitive points. Since the army at Ahmedabad Cantonment had been called at the border in view of the attack on Parliament earlier, the Chief Minister requested the then Defence Minister telephonically on 28 February 2002 to immediately deploy army battalions to tackle the situation, which were deployed immediately.

The next allegation he lays to rest was that there had been a pogrom:

> Undisputed statistics presented to the SIT show that in the first six days of the riots, 61 Hindus and 40 Muslims were killed in police firing. The death of any person in police firing is tragic. But does a police firing death toll with 60% casualties being Hindu indicate a pogrom by the state government against Muslims?

Another charge was that the government did not investigate cases of rape, to which Ram says, 'Evidence before the SIT establishes that this was pure fiction, that all rape complaints were being investigated and some convictions had already taken place.'

Another canard Ram skewered was that 'the riots were a conspiracy supported by the Gujarat government. The Justice Banerjee Committee report claiming the Godhra train burning to be an accident was held illegal by the High Court of Gujarat. The SIT also rejected the accident theory, and found on reinvestigation that the Godhra carnage was indeed a conspiracy to burn and bake the unwary passengers and the riots were a reaction. This fact is now judicially established in the trial of Godhra incident by the sessions judge appointed by the then Chief Justice of Gujarat High Court as directed by the Supreme Court.'

With these points, along with a powerful description of how Modi's enemies had crafted a tissue of lies, Ram fully rebutted any allegations stemming from 2002, the only real material that the Congress party had against Modi.

When Ram appeared in court to represent a former BJP legislator from Gujarat, Kalubhai Maliwad, who too, was implicated in the Gujarat riots, the press went after him. 'Ram Jethmalani had earlier represented Centre for Peace and Justice, an NGO that had filed an application to hand over the investigation of the Gujarat riots in a separate matter although connected with the larger issue of Gujarat riots.'[1]

Kamini Jaiswal, the opposing attorney, accused Ram of inconsistency.

Another article[2] alleged that Ram had struck a deal for the BJP to support him for the Raj Sabha, when 'he took his lawyer's brief to defend one of the Gujarat riot accused, BJP leader Kalubhai Maliwad, during the period when the Supreme Court-appointed Special Investigation Team (SIT) had issued summons to Narendra Modi for questioning in the riot cases . . . The intention was clear—Jethmalani was appearing to question the grounds for summoning Modi. And this, he forcefully did inside the courtroom. He questioned the legality of the court's order directing a probe into the involvement of Modi and 62 others even without hearing them.' In that article, the reporter was close to the truth.

Tehelka[3] gave the sequence. On March 26, 2008, the Supreme Court ordered the state of Gujarat to set up an SIT to probe the riot cases. On April 27, 2009, the court ordered the SIT to look into the roles played by Modi and 63 others. On June 5, 2009, the Gujarat High Court rejected a petition by Maliwad, one of the 63, to stop the SIT inquiry. On July 30, 2009, the state of Gujarat appealed to the Supreme Court, saying that it would exceed its jurisdiction to investigate Modi. Modi was summoned in March 2010, and four days later, Kalubhai Maliwad, represented by Ram, filed an application to the Supreme Court to recall its order of April 2009. *Tehelka* clearly viewed Maliwad as a 'proxy for Modi'.

The Hindu reported[4] on March 24 that Modi had announced he was ready to appear before the SIT and 'his lawyer, Mahesh Jethmalani, confirmed to *The Hindu* on Tuesday both the existence of the summons and the fact that the Gujarat Chief Minister had sent in his reply the day before.' While Ram was the senior member of Modi's legal team, Mahesh took several of the important cases. On March 27, Modi appeared and was questioned for over five hours. CNN-IBN[5] reported that the SIT 'has concluded in its 541-page closure report that Gujarat Chief Minister Narendra Modi took all possible steps to control the 2002 post-Godhra riots and questioned the motive behind filing a complaint against him by a riot victim four years after the communal violence.'

Ram made his views of Modi quite clear to the press, through television interviews and in the *Sunday Guardian*. Mahesh served as a very effective and articulate official spokesman for the BJP during the run-up to the election. Mahesh was then replaced by M.J. Akbar, editor of the *Sunday Guardian*, who had the added advantage of being a Muslim. From its launch in January 2010, Ram's articles in the *Sunday Guardian* bruited allegations of corruption against the Congress party, and from 2011 they consistently pushed Modi for Prime Minister.

A count of articles that Ram wrote for the *Sunday Guardian* shows that 17 were exposures of the Nehru–Gandhi dynasty, and its latest scion, Rahul. Thirteen attacked corruption, black money, and the defects of the Lokpal Bill. Thirty promoted Modi, debunked any link of Hindutva with communalism, and disputed any link between the Congress party and secularism. Ram's first article written explicitly in support of Modi was 'The Rise and Rise of Tomorrow's Prime Minister Narendra Modi,' published on November 6, 2011.

Many articles went straight to the allegations against Modi, and demolished them. On November 13, 2011, his headline was, 'Gujarat Minorities Have Made Peace with Modi'. On December 25, 2011, it was, 'UPA, Media Have a Brazen Mission to Demonize Modi'. On October 27, 2012, Ram asserted, 'Attempts to Malign Modi Have Failed'. On February 16, 2013, he insisted, 'Let the Truth Be Known about Modi', and on November 30, 2013, he asked, 'Who Is Afraid of Narendra Modi?' Ram's critiques and refutation of the allegations against Modi were devastating, providing all the arguments that any supporter would need to defend him.

Ram's victory lap article[6] went on to give the current status of his black money case, a case that undergirded the whole Modi campaign. He wrote:

Narendra Modi is aware of my five years of legal battle in the Supreme Court to have a Special Investigation Team supervised by two ex-judges of the Supreme Court to carry out the task of recovering our stolen money. The Manmohan Singh government, under orders of Sonia Gandhi and her son managed to frustrate the Supreme Court judgement of July 2011 constituting an SIT for this purpose. This corrupt action was rejected as vexatious by the new three-judge bench of the Supreme Court headed by Justice Dattu on 26 March 2014. But what is most shameful is that even as election results were coming in on 16 May, Additional Solicitor General Siddharth Luthra moved the Supreme Court for relief in the shape of stay of the constitution of the SIT, which P. Chidambaram badly wants. The Hon'ble Judges summarily rejected the frivolous and dishonest request.

In fact, the Supreme Court[7] had broken the impasse created by the previous split two-man panel. Ram had finally won. The court had then constituted an SIT consisting of retired Supreme Court judges M.B. Shah and Arijit Pasayat. The court 'further directed the Centre to make public by sharing with petitioner, senior advocate Ram Jethmalani, all details regarding 26 account holders in Liechtenstein Bank in Germany who were investigated in the case' since 'the information relating to these 26 individuals had been received from the German Tax department in 2009. Of the 26, investigation against 18 individuals is over and prosecution has been launched.' Ram even wrote that he went to Germany in this connection.

In his May 18 article, Ram reminds readers that 'I have repeatedly stated in public and to the press that Sonia and her family are the chief beneficiaries of the plunder of US $1,500 billion, equivalent to Rs 90 lakh crore.' This is one last reminder of the juicy material he had handed to Modi to exploit.

Putting this in context, for years Ram has pounded on the subjects of corruption by the Congress party, by Sonia Gandhi, by the Gandhi–Nehru family; of money that mysteriously went to Italian associates of the Gandhi family; black money hidden in Swiss and other foreign banks by the Gandhis; and widespread government corruption. Modi could not find a better campaign issue than this, and Ram has been the feistiest and loudest voice in it. All this he presented to Modi, gift-wrapped.

Campaigning for Modi, Ram always drew an audience. On March 14, he convened a meeting of 10,000 lawyers, assembled in the Talkatora Stadium in Delhi, the crowd so huge that half of them stood outside the 6000-seat arena. In front of the multitude was a sign: 'Lawyers for Modi and Modi for Lawyers'. A picture of Modi appeared on the right, and a picture of Ram on the left. Ram had brought this to pass by sending a communication to bar councils all over India. In fact, lawyers came from all over India to what was called an All India Lawyers Meeting. Speakers included Vaiko, the leader of the MDMK; Aishwarya Bhati, the secretary of the Supreme Court Bar Association; Rajiv Khosla, the newly elected president of the Delhi High Court Bar Association; and Pinky Anand, now the Additional Solicitor General in the Supreme Court, who had been pressured not to attend. The featured speakers were Ram, and finally, Modi, who delivered a stem-winder. From start to finish, this was a Ram Jethmalani show, demonstrating to Modi that he could command a crowd of that size, demonstrating to the assembled lawyers the depth of support that Modi had in the legal community despite some efforts by Modi's competitors to suppress it, within and without the BJP.

One of Ram's speeches on YouTube[8] is a must-see—his keynote speech on October 3, 2013 at New Delhi's Thyagaraj Stadium, given to 7000 students at the conclusion of the Manthan, a convocation of 20,000 college students from 700 colleges in India. Although Ram was positioned as the lead-in to a speech by Narendra Modi, the candidate for Prime Minister, Ram took the back seat to nobody. He walked up the podium and introduced himself as 90 years old, but someone who works a longer day than any of the students in the audience do; the audience clapped wildly. When he began to talk, his stature, which has shrunken over the years, seemed to grow taller, his bushy white eyebrows knit in intensity, and his voice rose in a basso crescendo. He talked about his distrust of mixing religion with political affairs, about the past greatness of Islam, about the right of women to have parity in political assemblies, and about the disgraceful corruption that is impoverishing India. He made an impassioned plea to the young students in the audience to educate themselves, so they will be prepared to take back the country, and then he began to set up Modi's speech.

Ram started out by saying that he had no personal political ambitions, even though, parenthetically, he would be better qualified to be Prime Minister than many. At that, the audience rose to its feet, clapped, whistled, and cheered until he had to wave the students down. He emphasized that he had one man, and one man only, in mind for that position, clearly looking at Modi. It was a bravo performance.

In interviews, Ram has been asked if he wanted to be Prime Minister, and his answer has been, 'How can I aspire to be Prime

Minister when they are prepared to offer it to Rahul Gandhi. I have not fallen that low. I am not in such a class.'

He also says, 'Rajiv Gandhi was nothing but a pilot. If a person from a slum becomes a pilot, that's an achievement, but if a person from a family like Nehru's becomes a pilot, it means that he must have been a duffer, but nobody writes that truth.' This only enhanced Rahul's image as a laughing stock, an image that he himself cemented on TV during the campaign.

Notwithstanding all his work for Modi, in May 2013, Ram was expelled from the BJP.

While some preliminary legal skirmishing began before the election, the case was deferred until after the election.

Friends and family wondered why Ram bothered to engage in a public dispute with the BJP just before the election. It was counterproductive, they worried. Then again, one might ask if it could have had the beneficial effect of providing a public demonstration that the BJP had rejected a tainted leader, Gadkari, thus showing that the BJP was fully committed to the battle against corruption? After all, Ram was expelled for a breach of party discipline, not for his opposition to Gadkari. The publicity would have to help Modi.

The expulsion and the resultant public wrangling between L.K. Advani and Ram certainly created more public interest than one might expect from a confrontation between two old political war-horses.

After all, this wrangling had occurred because Advani expressed an interest in running for Prime Minister instead of Modi. This raises the question of why Ram did favour Modi over Advani. Let there be no mistake. It would have been in Ram's power to attack Modi so powerfully that his future candidacy would have been crippled. It would have been an option for Ram to back away from defending Modi or any associates of his whose convictions could have segued into a legal case against Modi. It might even have been comfortable for Ram to support an old associate, Advani. Nevertheless, Ram felt deeply that Modi was the man India needed, and that he was the one man who could lead India from a path of corruption to a path of business, investments, jobs, and development.

Against many expectations and with considerable prodding by Mahesh, both Advani and Modi came to Ram's 90th birthday party in Delhi on September 15, 2013. There was much snickering in the press that Advani and Modi greeted each other with visible coldness, the story repeated over and over, generally incorrectly. The truth was that Mahesh, who had engineered their joint appearances at the party, felt that their meeting was perfectly cordial, and on the day after the party Advani formally endorsed Modi as the BJP candidate. Probably the publicity just helped Modi.

At his age, Ram denies any personal ambition. Following the election, Mahesh went off on vacation, and Ram went shortly afterwards. Still, Ram has made clear what he expects from a Modi Prime Ministership. He summarizes his demands in his May 18 *Sunday Guardian* article: 'Narendra Modi is completely aware of the test through fire that awaits him. He has so many priorities to attend to—reducing prices, creating jobs, revving up the economy, development, finding ways of uprooting the deep tendrils of corruption under a Modi government.' Then he makes a plea to Modi to heal the communal rifts that marred the pre-election politics. But Ram looked forward to other things, and for them, we can look to some of the things that the national and international press anticipated.

On May 16, 2014, Daijuworld.com reported from Islamabad that 'Prime Minister Nawaz Sharif Friday congratulated BJP leader Narendra Modi for winning the Indian election and invited him to visit Pakistan.' This followed an unconfirmed report that one of Modi's first actions after the election was to send a friendly note to Pakistan.

Immediately following the election, the United States sent Modi an invitation to visit, apparently forgetting their previous ban. While Modi's immediate reaction was not reported to be enthusiastic, certainly Ram—with his predilections—will expect the relationship to warm up.

On March 17, 2014, Palash Ghosh wrote an article titled, 'India

2014 Elections: Narendra Modi, Israel's Best Friend in South Asia' in the *International Business Times*. In it, he reports that in the past 13 years, while Modi was Chief Minister of Gujarat, Israel has invested heavily in Gujarat, and officials from Gujarat and Israel have visited back and forth developing economic relationships as well as carrying out joint projects in industrial research and development, solar power, water recycling, and desalination plants. This cooperation has extended to pharmaceuticals, infrastructure, and huge investments from Israel for the construction of semiconductor fabrication plants.

As Chief Minister of Gujarat, Modi has already visited Israel once, and he has spoken of making history by being the first Indian Prime Minister to visit Israel.

Interestingly, the last time India expanded its ties with Israel was under the BJP government of 1999–2004, a government in which Ram was a minister.

On May 18, 2014, the *Economic Times* headlined, 'Narendra Modi Keen to Deepen Ties with Israel: Benjamin Netanyahu.' Netanyahu had called Modi to discuss Modi's expressed desire to further develop ties between India and Israel.

The same day, Gordon Chang wrote an article in *Forbes*, titled 'China: Biggest Loser in India's "Modislide" Election.' In it he points out that the biggest loser in the election was not Rahul Gandhi, but China, writing: 'Gandhi is not the biggest loser overall, however. That honor belongs to Beijing, because it's certain that in the coming years direct foreign investment will head to India instead of China.' In fact, under Modi's leadership, Gujarat already had been called the China of India, since Modi had created a real free-market economy that supported new infrastructure, the inflow of new business, and the creation of new jobs.

Chang writes that 'China's economy, the motor of its rise, is sputtering and on the edge of an historic failure. At the same time, Beijing is intensifying its discriminatory investigations of multinationals.' As he says, 'In a deteriorating economy, Beijing's blame-the-outlanders policy may be good politics, but it is very bad economics, especially in the long run.' He anticipates that as

China is becoming more unfriendly to outsiders, India is poised to become more welcoming. This certainly would be music to Ram's ears, as he still has not forgiven China for its as-yet-unpunished inroads into Indian border territory.

Ram has said and written many times that if you do not change the water in a swimming pool it becomes a swamp. It seems that India has listened.

39

Public Intellectual

Ram is both brilliant and disconcerting. He will join forces with someone to pursue a cause even if he has fought against him in the past. He will defend a political party on one issue, later charge it with malfeasance on another. He starts grand enterprises that make even his supporters wonder, then he ups the ante. People with less vision never know when to take him seriously.

Sometimes he appears not to take himself seriously. Before beginning a speech to a group of jurists in London he said, 'This morning I expected an odour of sanctity, but instead I get an odour of mothballs.'

With all that, Ram is a loner. Before beginning a case, or a political quest, he consults with himself first, often for weeks at a time. Some of his plans represent pure theory and logic. More often they are the result of pure gut feeling. Friends say that he acts first and uses his intellect later to make his actions appear logical. Finally, he uses his personal charm to bring others along with him.

Ram, Mahesh, and Rani have opposed the Nehru–Gandhi family since the Emergency. Mahesh calls it a fight between the feudal forces of a dynastic cult and constitutional liberties. He claims the Congress system is bereft of ideology, and it is personality-based, not programme-based. Ram's greatest political successes have come when he has exposed its corruption and misuse of power. His speech during the Rajya Sabha[1] debate over the Lokpal and Lokayukta Bill of 2011 had garnered 21,736 hits on YouTube by September 20,

2013. It went viral as an example of India's Parliament in action, everyone on their feet shouting, all at the same time.

According to Mahesh, Ram's drive to expose the black money in foreign banks shrewdly hijacked the BJP platform. Perhaps, but it has been all of a piece with his ongoing battle to expose the Nehru–Gandhi family, one that he has waged throughout his entire career.

The Congress party has benefited from crony capitalism, and it exerts a powerful influence on the press, much of which self-censored during its rule for fear of losing its direct line to the government. In response, in January 2010, at the age of 87, Ram started his own newspaper. Although members of the Bar traditionally have been Ram's most influential constituency, *The Guardian* provided him with a bully pulpit from which he can preach to the rest of India.

The Writer and Newspaperman

Ram wrote articles for the *Indian Express* for years since the time of the Emergency. Later he wrote for *Asian Age*, for the *Journal of the Bar Council of India* and for many other publications across the land. At Ram's urging, Mahesh and a colleague once began a journal, *Lex et Juris*, when Mahesh started his practice in the 1980s, but that was short-lived.

With the bulk of the Indian media biased towards the government, Ram came to the conclusion that it was time for a completely new newspaper. This idea gave birth to the *Sunday Guardian*, a perfect vehicle for Ram to disseminate his commentary weekly, free of restrictions by a nervous mainstream media, and for him to publish regular columns supporting his candidate of choice in a national election. He used personal finances in the beginning, but later he obtained funding from outside supporters. Ram is the chairman; the editor-in-chief is M.J. Akbar, an eminent journalist who started the *Telegraph* and is also a former editor of *Asian Age*. With a rapidly increasing circulation, the paper not only has a Muslim editor, but it also has writers and columnists from all religions and all political persuasions, consistent with Ram's philosophy of pluralism. It is published in Delhi, Mumbai, and Chandigarh, and it is distributed free of charge to Members of Parliament as well as to other major political organizations. Soon it will come out in Pune, and eventually in a large city in the south.

Ram writes, but it would not be accurate to call him a journalist. He makes no pretence of being objective; he is the quintessential advocate, and he advocates for a wide range of ideas that he believes are important to the future of India. Americans would describe him as a public intellectual. As Akbar says, given India's widespread corruption, Ram will never lack for material.

Politics and a Run for President

Before he started his own newspaper, Ram started his own political parties, all for the same reasons that he writes—to jump-start a solution of India's multitude of problems. When in April 1987 he formed a party, he named it Bharat Mukti Morcha—a movement for the salvation of India. The name itself revealed Ram's dream. Virtually a one-man party, it did not save India, and Ram had to disband it rather than continue spending his own money on it.

In 1995 he started the Pavitra Hindustan Kazhagam Party. He calls it an act of rebellion because he 'could not reconcile himself to any existing political party and he wanted to present his manifesto of what good government should be.' One wag said that when Ram had finished all the political parties he started his own. The word 'pavitra' means 'pure'. Hindustan is the traditional word for India. 'Kazhagam' is a Tamil word suggested by Lataa's father, signifying a party of the south as well as the north. Ram claims that he never expected the party to win an election; it was simply a vehicle for advocacy. The party platform was: transparent government, economic liberalization, attention to overpopulation, and implementation of the Mandal Commission reservations for other backward classes.

Encouraged by enthusiastic crowds at party rallies, Ram invested his own money and the money his clients contributed, spending large sums on party workers and attracting a wide variety of hangers-on. Despite his high hopes, the party did not win a single seat in the 1996 election, and Ram had to accept the reality that it would have to close up shop. The nine candidates they ran had such poor showings that they had to forfeit their security deposits. One, Anil Gote, spent lavishly on himself during the campaign, and was arrested in 2003[2] for his role in passing counterfeit government stamp papers in a multi-crore scam that sucked in police officers from the Mumbai police commissioner down. 'At one time, the whole Bombay police force was in jail,' one commentator laughed. It seems the politicians and police were more moved by pecuniary motives than Ram's high-minded objectives.

The experience of this political party has been cited as an example of Ram's naivete, which it could well have been, but other factors were in play. When Ram is in, he is all in. He truly does not care about the money. He has no interest in being an accountant, poring over expense reports. Whatever it costs to make his point, he is prepared to pay.

Ram also takes a certain delight in gambling. He has been known to visit a casino in London more than once, always putting his money on number five in Russian roulette, and always going for high stakes. In card games he was known to play for Rs 50 a point, reading a book at the same time or even dozing off, but apparently following the action, because he always would wake up in time to play exactly the right card. He has also been known to visit the horse races, not often, but probably enough to explain why Janak became interested in owning horses. If Ram bets on a losing horse, he takes the consequences in fine fettle, laughing and joking about it.

In 1992, Ram made the quixotic decision to run for President, even though he knew the Congress party planned to run the then Vice-President, Shankar Dayal Sharma. He says his purpose was to promulgate his own concept of the office of President. He wrote that the existing President was a figurehead, but that 'Surely the President was not designed to be a glorious notary public.' In the same article,[3] he wrote that 'The next President must be one with endowments that ensure that Indian democracy is safe in his hands. The next President must, therefore, be one who can honestly claim that he protested against the corrupt system and refused to be its beneficiary.'

Ram promised in his campaign speeches to 'provide the glue that rebinds the nation together. I will bring justice to the scheduled castes and tribes and all the weaker sections who have been exploited in the past and continue to be exploited by our new rulers.'

His announcement came with no support from any political party, and it distressed both friends and family. The only sign that anyone took him seriously was that he was assigned two security guards, who obligingly followed him everywhere. The BJP basically disregarded him, backing an independent tribal candidate from the Northeast, G.G. Swell. Ram did receive 100 signatures from legislators on his nomination forms, but he finally bowed to pressure. He withdrew after Vajpayee wrote him a letter, telling him he had made his point.

Ram claims that he knew all along that he could not get elected on party votes, putting the lie to those who snickered that he just did not get it. Of the four candidates on the ballot in 1992, Sharma received 675, 864 votes, G.G. Swell received 345, 485, and Ram received 2704.[4] At least he did not have to forfeit his filing fee.

In India, as in any other country, votes go to loyal members of their party who are canny, who will engage in the required political manoeuvring, and who will sacrifice convictions when necessary. That is not Ram. He ran to express his beliefs. Would he have liked to become President? Yes. Did he think he would? Probably not. He wanted an excuse to write and speak about his own ideas.

Some time later, in 1999, Ram wrote a lengthy article, later republished in *Conscience of a Maverick*,[5] in which he spelled out the 'role of the President under the Constitution of India' in precise legal detail. In this article he shows that even where the President appears to have been given meaningful powers, Article 53 of the Constitution effectively limits them by requiring consultation with relevant bodies, such as the Council of Ministers.

One case established the sole right of the President to act without consultation, *the State of Maharashtra vs. A.R. Antulay*—yes, the Antulay whom Ram fought in court for all those years—which said that if the question of a sanction of a Prime Minister or member of the Cabinet comes up, the President 'will have to perform that function without seeking the advice of the Cabinet, i.e. in his sole discretion.' That surely is a limited area of power.

Ram's main point, as expressed in this article, is: 'Whatever be the President's legal powers, his real power rests on his moral stature and the public esteem he enjoys.'

Given his political history, some have called Ram a political flirt, saying he flitted from the BJP to the RSS, to the Shiv Sena, to parties of his own creation, and even to the Congress party when it suited him. Ram smiles. 'If you call me a political flirt, flirting is one of my great strengths,' he says.

It is true that Ram's political support has come from all over the map. Flirting? Maybe, but more likely it is pragmatism. Here is the summary of his political campaigns: Ram first approached the Congress party for a ticket to run for Parliament. He ran for the Lok Sabha in 1971 as an Independent, with support from the Bharatiya Jan Sangh and the Shiv Sena parties. He was elected to the Lok Sabha from the Janata Party in 1977 and in 1980. When he lost his campaign for re-election in 1984 he ran on the BJP ticket. In 1988, he was elected to the Rajya Sabha from the BJP. In 1994 he was re-elected to the Rajya Sabha as an Independent backed by the Shiv Sena and the BJP, pointedly not as Shiv Sena. From March 19, 1998 to July 23, 2000 he was a minister in a BJP government. He was re-elected to the Rajya Sabha in 2000 as an Independent, supported by the Shiv Sena and the BJP.

Ram ran against Vajpayee in 2004 as an Independent, which was the last time he contested for the Lok Sabha.

In April 2006, it was the Congress party that nominated Ram to the Rajya Sabha for a three-and-a-half-year term, recommended by Lalu Prasad, as a 'distinguished national personality'. This completed the term of Vidya Niwas Misra, a poet from Uttar Pradesh who died mid-term.

In July 2010, Ram was appointed to the Rajya Sabha from Rajasthan from the BJP with a term that lasts until 2016. Now he is out of the BJP, at least at the time of writing. My husband recently asked Mahesh who will sponsor his father's run for Parliament in 2016.

On Non-violence

Ram the intellectual has made many celebrated speeches. In a June 7, 2012 address[6] to the Bhartiya Vidya Bhavan Institute of Indian Culture on the 'Relevance of Non-violence and Teachings from Ancient Civilizations,' he gives a sweeping historical overview of Middle Eastern and sub-continental religions, reminding the audience that Gandhi was a follower of the Jain religion, which teaches absolute non-violence. He also says that Gandhi was influenced by Jesus' Sermon on the Mount, and that Jesus was inspired by the Buddhist missionaries Ashoka sent from India, some of whom even met the Essenes in Jerusalem. He draws the thread of connection by quoting the Dead Sea scrolls, suggesting the Essenes learned their 'sexual chastity, non-violence and 'love the enemy' morality from Ashoka's Buddhist missionaries, and that they could have imparted these ideas to Jesus.

Ram reminds the audience that the Bhagavad Gita did not propound non-violence. Saying that 'Gandhi dismissed the entire Gita as an allegorical fiction,' he adds that Gandhi's great contribution was to recognize that 'An appeal to British conscience and character was the only solution . . .' Ram believes that Gandhi succeeded because the British were 'exhausted by a horrendous war,' and in London 'a brand of honourable Labour Party statesmen [came into power] who were ashamed of the moral incongruity of fighting the Nazi and fascists in Europe but retaining their unwanted Colonial rule over Indians. The last conclusive action that won freedom for us was not a non-violent one but the Naval Mutiny in Bombay.'

Ram describes Gandhi's view of non-violence as 'an ideal, saintly one, [whose] appeal for the masses lay rather in its passive and negative character. This vitality-sapping character of ahimsa [non-violence] was not conspicuous, because of the overwhelming numbers of Indians who made it a practical success in India but only against the civilized British.' In contrast, Ram believes that 'There are enemies who need to be destroyed before they destroy us.' In particular, 'Never turn your other cheek to a vicious aggressor.'

In conclusion, Ram says,

> The solution is not non-violence by India or a few states. Complete universal disarmament is a mirage. Even if that happens, humans will still fight with sticks and stones true to their genetic structure of hunting animals . . . We must build our bodily strength and not allow ourselves to be sapped by the debilitating thoughts and deeds which have led to the conquest of the civilized world by barbarians possessed of superior vitality and will to subjugate and enslave the comfort-loving weaklings. We shall not imitate them though and become aggressive predators like some of our ancestors.

It is not surprising that Ram changed his stand on terrorism after the violence of 9/11 in the United States. He had stood for all possible rights and protections for detenus under the Terrorist and Disruptive Activities Act of 1987, but when the law was amended after September 11, 2001, Ram agreed that some new restrictions on protection for terrorists were warranted.

On Islam

Ram has a unique relationship with Islam. As a Hindu refugee from Pakistan, he says that much of the evil in the world is perpetrated by fanatics and barbarians in the name of religion. He is especially concerned about the radical adherents of Islam. Yet, the Sindh where he grew up enjoyed a harmonious synthesis between Hinduism, Islam, and the Sufi religion, and Ram has always been vocal in his appreciation of the great Muslim poets and sages.

Ram has defended minorities throughout his life. He also is

fearless in addressing them. Speaking to 200 Muslims at a Rotary Club, Ram once said, 'I would not be happy to have only one God. I am happy that I have 1000 gods.'

Ram has earned the admiration of Aligarh Muslim University students for opposing a Parliament attempt to cut off the grants they receive as a minority university, which designation allows 50 per cent of the seats to be reserved for Muslims. A group of students took the matter to the Allahabad Court, and Ram made a personal donation towards their activities. In gratitude for his position in Parliament, Ram received two invitations from Aligarh, one to address the university and the other to address the Aligarh Movement in Cleveland, Ohio, where he was proud to be their first non-Muslim speaker.

When he spoke at Aligarh University in July 2013, the *Muslim Mirror News* reported that Ram

> . . . said he was sure that the Supreme Court would overturn the Division Bench judgement of Allahabad High Court, which stripped AMU of its minority status.
>
> He said he had moved a private member's bill in Parliament in 1980 for the restoration of AMU's minority character and when the 1981 AMU Amendment Bill was being debated in the Parliament, he had given some suggestions, but they all went unheeded.
>
> Jethmalani said there was 'no doubt that the AMU is a minority institution'. The granting of the legal status of a university in 1920 had in no way diluted its main character, that it was established by Muslims and for Muslims of India, he added.[7]

His address[8] in Cleveland, Ohio lauded the accomplishments of Muslim scholars through the ages, but warned that Muslims must return to their intellectual roots, focusing on education above all else. The speech begins with comments about the founder of the university, Sayyid Ahmed Khan:

I was born in 1923 and Sir Sayyid Ahmed Khan had finished his glorious tenure of eighty years on this Planet a quarter of a century before. I became a qualified lawyer in 1941 and it is, as far as my memory goes, at or about that time that as a student of Indian History, I had valuable and refreshing information about the venerable and enviable life of one of the great Indians our country had produced in the previous century. He lived between 1817 and 1898.

Most of you are perhaps more familiar with the details of his life than I have ever been. Therefore, I will not regale you with those, however interesting their recall to memory is even today.

I will refer to only a few prominent ones which in my opinion greatly influenced his thinking and course of action. This sensitive young man could not have failed to be influenced by what was happening to one Islamic country after the other. European powers were grabbing them, subjugating them and exploiting them as was the wont of colonial powers of the time . . .

Sir Sayyid Ahmed Khan doubtless shared fully the feeling of humiliation of all thinking Muslims. They were seized with the fact that something terribly tragic was happening in Islamic history. The suicide bombers of modern times show at least to some Muslims that the community is pitted against hopeless odds. The Muslim experience inside India was equally depressing. Though there was a titular Mughal ruler in Delhi, he was a king without troops and without subjects. The real ruler was the East India Company which propagated the fiction that it was ruling on behalf of the Mughal kings. Everybody knew that he had neither power nor riches. The Muslim nobility and professional elite— the Sharif, would drown their sorrows by privately sneering at Britain's presence. Some turned to sycophantic poetry and others nostalgically recalled the by-gone days of phenomenal Muslim glory . . .

As one eminent historian has recorded, 'A new element had come to be introduced into the social situation of the Indian Muslims; it was the well known Pan-Islamic Movement initiated and organized by Jamal-ud-din Al-Afghani (1839–97). The declared objective of this Movement was the union of all Islamic states under a single Caliphate and a strong Muslim empire which should be able to liberate all Muslims from western cultural and political domination and resist western economic intervention and exploitation. Jamal-ud-din Al-Afghani visited India and went round a number of places meeting a good many leaders of the Indo-Muslim society.' It is in this background that one must now look at the events of 1857 when Sir Sayyid Ahmed Khan was just 40 years old, events which have come to be retrospectively described as India's "first war of independence".'

Ram describes those events, followed by Khan's role in establishing Aligarh University, and then he segues into his own philosophy:

I must hasten to explain my own personal attitude to religion. Marx told us that religion is the opiate of the people. I think he was wrong. Opium suggests something which numbs you, makes you sluggish and often puts you to sleep. Far from being an opium, it is an aphrodisiac for horror, a Benzedrine for Bestiality. All the fleets of the world could easily swim in the spacious comforts of the ocean of innocent blood which has been spilt in the name of religion. The crusades, the inquisitions, the ignorance of the dark ages, terrorism and war are huge items on the debit side of its balance sheet. I concede that religion has brought some hope to the frustrated and forlorn and some comfort to those suffering from intensity of pain and cruelty. Religion has been at best a Placebo. I believe that kindness is all that this sad world needs. I have therefore a one line religion: 'we must live a life governed by reason but inspired by love'.

Let me now turn to the legacy of Sir Sayyid Ahmed Khan and share with you what I believe were the chief components of his priceless legacy:

First: Religion and its teachings are not inconsistent with science and its view of the universe. He . . . used the mildest terminology that in its peculiar domain science will prevail over the belief systems of religion. He did not accept the fatalistic Hindu belief that the stars alone determine our destiny as well as the Moslem belief in Kismet. His attitude to religion was that of a rational sceptic . . .

Second: He was clearly of the view that Moslems must revert to the old rationalist interpretation of the Holy Quran of the Mutazila School and turn their back on any inconsistent teaching . . .

Third: Indian Muslims must no longer look out of India and waste their energy on recovering their Arab, Turkish or Persian roots but strive to be the most beautiful flower in India's bouquet of numerous religions, races and tribes.

. . . The Prophet of Islam established his unique superiority over other god men by being the only one to preach that 'those who walked in search of knowledge walked in the way of God; that the ink of the scholar was more valuable than the blood of a martyr; fight against those who fight you but do not commit aggression.'

Muslims were at the zenith of their glory when they seriously heeded his sublime message. Islam civilized the west and rescued it from the darkness of the middle ages. Arabic literature had presented the best of Greek Philosophy. For three centuries Christianity saw Islam advance, saw it capture the Christian people and lands one after another, dominate Christian trade and commerce. Christians even suffered the humiliation of being called infidels. Unfortunately they [Muslims] jettisoned the message; their decline started, ending in the enslavement of virtually the entire Muslim world. In 1150 Caliph Mustanjid at Baghdad ordered and burned all the philosophic works of Avicenna, 44 years later Emir Abn Yusuf Yaqub-al Mansur, then at Seville ordered the burning of all works by Averroes; he forbade his subjects to study philosophy and urged them to throw into the fire all books of philosophy wherever found. Ibn Habib was put to death for studying philosophy. Contrast the great Sadi and Gazali and you will understand the tragedy that was overtaking Islam.

Ram describes the rise of Wahhabi Islam and goes on,

How does one account for suicide squads, each member convinced of immediate entry into paradise and the company of enchanting Huris? A deadly combination of opium called Religion and Hashish can alone accomplish this. I have not investigated nor have I been informed by any one what awaits the female suicide bomber in Paradise! If you also believe in God, for his sake do not believe he is running a brothel. Martyrdom is the only way in which one can become famous without any ability or character.

Ram concluded:

Education is not imparted only by the teachers. It is also the duty of the intelligentsia. Those who are proud of the Aligarh movement must show the courage to warn all their compatriots that a society that produces suicide murderers in quantity is essentially committing suicide. Iran and Saudi Arabia are funding the entire world's terror infrastructure. They cannot overlook the certainty that one day the terror that they spread will end up in their own backyard. Just look at what is happening to Pakistan. The people of Pakistan are my kith and kin. I grieve in their misfortunes and wish them a better future. But they too must abandon the way of terror and war. They too have to emerge from the darkness of superstition . . .

Get rid of Fear, cultivate Courage.

Fear Believes—Courage doubts.

Fear falls on earth and prays—Courage stands erect and thinks.

Fear retreats—Courage advances.

Fear is barbarism—Courage is Civilization.

Fear believes in witchcraft, devils and ghosts—Courage is robust science.

The Iconoclast

Ram loves to shock. When asked his views of God, he may answer that his God is 'a bumbling fool and a sadist. I'm not even sure he exists, but like a good lawyer, I give him the benefit of doubt.' When asked about the many times he has switched sides on an issue, he said, 'You must love the gods, but never more once the greater gods arrive.'[9]

This author wonders whether this public scepticism tells the whole story. Ram is too interested in the works of great thinkers of all religions, in mysticism, astrology, and numerology to be as totally atheistic as he sounds.

Speech in Support of the Indo–US Nuclear Agreement

Ram delivered a powerful speech in Parliament on the Indo–US nuclear agreement[10] saying, 'The deal is the greatest post-Independence achievement of India in the field of foreign relations and the biggest feather in the cap of the Congress government.'

He reminded his audience that in May 1998 India exploded their 'second nuclear bomb, 24 years after the first. Without losing much time Pakistan responded by its own explosion.' Facing international opprobrium, expressed through sanctions and penalties, 'An unnamed nuclear official complained to one of the national dailies that since 1975, the developed countries have stopped giving us vital technology, thus affecting our nuclear power generation which at the moment is pitiably low at 1,700 megawatts. At this very time, China deepened our frustration by conducting its 44th nuclear weapon test on June 7, 1996.'

Ram says Indian energy requirements have grown. He continues:

Thanks to Manmohan Singh and his deft handling of the US government that the latter not only agreed to condone our 1998 impudence, but to do something significantly more. The Americans would actively help us to shop for and purchase nuclear fuel from the Suppliers Group without being obliged to sign the Non-Proliferation Treaty.

India sorely needs at least 50,000 megawatts of electric energy to keep its industries running and to compete with the rest of the world in the somewhat difficult regime of globalization and WTO regulations.

Let us now dispose of the major arguments designed to kill the deal. First, does the deal interfere with India's sovereignty?

Ram says no and adds:

Every contract, treaty or covenant freely entered into imposes obligations not to act in defiance of the terms agreed upon. This is exertion of sovereignty and not its denial or dilution.

Does the deal impose any ceiling on our deterrent capacity? The answer is 'no' . . . India is not preparing for nuclear aggression against anyone nor is it at the moment threatened with nuclear aggression . . .

It is true that the Agreement can be terminated by one year's notice creating a right to reimbursement for investments made, but this is true of all international treaties.

The critics are raising the bogey of international inspection of our nuclear arsenal. India has nothing to hide. In any event, the critics should make a candid public confession that our uranium-enrichment plants, our plutonium reprocessing plants or our planned plutonium producing fast-breeder reactors remain on the military list, and all are beyond the supervision and regulation by the IAEA.

The most conclusive evidence in favour of the deal is that all our known enemies are against it.

In Summary

For years Ram has told the media that his last remaining political aspiration was to get rid of India's corrupt leadership and to replace it with an honest government. Still, in private conversation, he says his larger objective is to see the major democracies of the world—

the United States, Israel, India, and Japan—unite to promote the ideals of democracy for all. He tells his family and friends that this is his final goal.

One of Ram's greatest admirers is his brother-in-law Mohan Shahani. He says he can describe Ram in just a few words: he is the most generous person he has ever known (even to his enemies); he has an extraordinary sense of humour (he suffers fools gladly); he has tremendous energy and a phenomenal amount of courage. He has no pride—when he stays with his sister Maya in Mumbai he does not even trouble her for a cup of tea. Money means nothing to him. This author might comment that the only financial planning anyone can remember him interested in was with an attractive financial planner. Mohan says he uses his legal acumen to win political battles and his political strength to win legal cases. And he is absolutely dedicated to his law students.

We might add that he is a lover, and he is a formidable opponent. He thrives in the public eye, and he is the patriarch of his entire extended family. For his 90th birthday parties—both in Mumbai and Delhi—his family, friends, colleagues from the Bar, the judiciary, and top industrialists showed up in large numbers. So did many Sindhis, Bollywood stars, the glitterati, his tennis partners, major figures of Parliament and the government, clients, the media, and the cultural elite—all coming to show their love, many to give homage, some just hoping to be photographed in Ram's presence. The television coverage went on for days, but as a matter of routine the evening news frequently interviews either Ram or Mahesh about the important events of the day.

My husband says that above all, Ram is a teacher.

Ram tells interviewers, 'Today I'm living in the departure lounge, waiting for my delayed flight to leave.'

At 90, Ram has many more flights of fancy to make, and we may expect to look up one day and see him soaring overhead, flying straight for the sun.

Acknowledgements

This author is indebted to many people for furnishing material, reading portions of this book, making helpful comments, and doing their best to keep me from error. First among all is Shobha Gehani, who inspired me to write the book, worked with me all along, housed and fed me in her Mumbai apartment, gave me invaluable inside history, read the whole text numerous times, furnished corrections and admonishments, and put up with my compulsiveness when I was stymied by delays. Lataa Krishnamurthy has given me hours of her time, made invaluable suggestions to improve more than one difficult case discussion, and taken responsibility for making sure that I received materials, photos, cases, or whatever else I required. P.R. Mala, a lawyer in Ram's office, located obscure cases and helped make many arrangements for me with the greatest of patience.

Many members of the Jethmalani family have been most generous with their time, and I hesitate to try to name them individually for fear that I will leave some out. In particular though, Mahesh Jethmalani helped me numerous times by clarifying the arcane field of Indian politics, putting some of his father's cases in perspective and telling a few tales out of school. Mohan Shahani also deserves special mention, because of the many hours he spent with me, spinning tales of Indian history, family history, and of Ram's early days. Nevertheless, all errors that may remain in the book must be considered my responsibility. I am very grateful for Nalini Gera's biography of Ram, and I am proud to follow in her footsteps. I owe the historian Benny Morris special thanks for making a chapter of his father Ya'akov Morris's unpublished autobiography freely available to me, and also for his graciousness in reading and commenting on my Israel chapter. Similarly I am indebted to Ram for providing me with the unpublished autobiography of Rani Jethmalani, portions of which I have been able to quote.

I owe Shobhaa Dé my immense gratitude for sponsoring this book and making all the necessary arrangements for its publication. Similarly, I owe many thanks to my editors, Milee Ashwarya and Paloma Dutta, for all their efforts to shepherd this book through its gestation while Milee actually her own bouncing baby girl.

Among many others who have helped greatly, I must include Sri Jaisinghani, for reviewing important legal write-ups and for furnishing wonderful anecdotes, as well as M.J. Akbar and Ambassador Vinod Grover, who both gave me invaluable perspective in their areas of expertise. Mahesh Kumar gave me invaluable insights into the world of the Indian bureaucracy, and helped me move the process of assembling materials. Arun Shourie supplied the 10 questions-a-day articles from the *Indian Express* after all of us had scoured our libraries for them fruitlessly. When I had nearly given up on locating it, Judge Randall Rader went to his court librarian and obtained the entire transcript of the Fraser Committee testimony within an hour.

Oddly, some of the material for this book came to me through what seems to be more than just luck. Right while I was writing the chapter on the National Law School, my husband told me that Professor N.L. Mitra was visiting Washington and they were scheduled to have dinner together. After that, I was fortunate to be able to interview him, and he was kind enough both to read an early draft and to contribute supplementary material to the chapter. Mr Shrikumar Poddar happened to be staying in Ann Arbor, very near my home in Michigan, just when I needed information about Ram's activities in the United States during the Emergency, and he provided useful background. While we were in Israel, Ambassador

Mark Sofer was kind enough to give me a telephone interview on the strength of a chance contact through a chauffeur of the American Embassy in Tel Aviv.

In addition, my learned friend David Waldshan has earned my thanks for patiently listening to a draft of the entire book as I read it to him and made corrections. Paul Natinsky, the editor of Detroit Medical News, was kind enough to go through the first few chapters to help me with style rules. In Delhi, Mr Fali Nariman gave me copies of his books and gave me several fine quotes.

Of inestimable importance, my husband Professor Martin Adelman encouraged me throughout this project, even when I almost was too busy to talk. He also has given me invaluable support by explaining confusing points of law and by teaching me over the course of more than 50 years how lawyers think. Ram himself has given me many hours of his time to provide the history that he alone knows and to explain complicated cases, even while his time is constantly claimed by lawyers clamouring after him. As you have read, he still is always busy. At 90.

Notes

1. The Exile

1   'Democracy in India', *American Bar Association Journal*, February, 1977, Volume 63, p. 243.
2   Malhotra, Inder, *Indira Gandhi* (London: Coronet Books, 1989), p. 91.
3   Ibid., p. 134.
4   *ADM Jabalpur v. S.S. Shukla* on April 28, 1976, 1976 AIR 1207, 1976 SCR 172.

2. Sindh

1   Jethmalani, Ram, *Maverick Unchanged, Unrepentant* (New Delhi: Rupa Publications, 2014), p. 255.

3. The First Important Relationships

1   Hasan Mansoor, 'Ali Ahmed Brohi Passes Away Aged 83', *Daily Times*, Pakistan, January 12, 2003, www.dailytimes.com.pk/default. asp?page=story_1-12-2003_p7_45.
2   Rani Jethmalani, from her unpublished autobiography.

4. Early Career

1   Gera, Nalini, *Ram Jethmalani: The Authorized Biography* (New Delhi: Penguin, 2002), p. 23.

5. Partition

1 'The Forgotten Volunteers: Indian Army WWII Part 1/5' BBC, www.youtube.com/watch?v=6TU1dQK-j-4&list=PLFC09D542C311D647&index=1.

2 Metcalf, Barbara D. and Thomas R. Metcalf, *A Concise History of Modern India*, Second Edition (Cambridge: Cambridge, 2006), pp. 204–210.

3 Fazila, Vazira and Yacoobali Zamindar, *The Long Partition and the Making of Modern South Asia* (New York: Columbia, 2007), p. 49.

4 Ibid., p. 48.

5 Mohan Shahani, personal communication.

6. Bombay

1 Khuhro, Hamida, *Mohammed Ayub Khuhro: A Life of Courage in Politics* (Lahore–Rawalpindi–Karachi: Ferozsons Ltd, 1998), p. 23.

2 Gera, Nalini, *Ram Jethmalani: The Authorized Biography* (New Delhi: Penguin, 2002), p. 74.

7. Early Practice in Bombay

1 *The Mumbai Protector: A Magazine for the Mumbai Police* Vol. 1 (2), 2009.

2 Gera, Nalini, *Ram Jethmalani*, Ibid., pp. 52, 54.

8. Refugee Cases

1 Jethmalani, Ram, 'In Memoriam: Khatu Cooper', Bombay Bar Association, April 1, 2004, www.bombaybar.com/in_memoriam/khatu_cooper.php.

2 *Sanwaldas Gobindram vs. State of Bombay and Anr.* on 17 November, 1952, AIR 1953 Bom 415 (1953) 55 BOMLR 478 ILR 1953 BOM 836.

3 *Ram Bhagwandas vs. Municipal Corporation of the City*, on December 2, 1955, AIR 1956 Bom 364.

4 Yadiv, Yogandra, 'Devanagiri Script and Mahatma Gandhi', *The Gandhi–King Community*, July 29, 2012, http://gandhiking.ning.com/profiles/blogs/devanagari-script-and-mahatma-gandhi-1.

5   Constituent Assembly of India, Vol. VII, Constituent Assembly Debate on December 8, 1948, *Indian Kanoon.*

6   Dwivedi, Sharada and Rahul Mehrotra, *Bombay: The Cities Within* (Bombay: Eminence Private Designs Ltd, 1995), pp. 268–71.

9. Smugglers and Lovers

1   Mehrotra, Rahul and Sharada Dwivedi, *The Bombay High Court: The Story of the Building – 1878–2003* (Bombay: Eminence Designs, 2004) provided the details, although I have toured the building too.

2   *Laxmipat Choraria v. State of Maharashtra, 1964* on January 17, 1964 (1965) 67 BOMLR 618.

3   Sethi, Aarti, *The Death of Mr. Love, The Honourable Murder: The Trial of Kawas Maneckshaw Nanavati* (Sarai Reader, 2005), www.sarai.net/publications/readers/05-bare-acts/03_aarti.pdf.

4   *Achanak.*

5   Sri Jaisinghani, personal communication.

6   Galanter, Marc and Nick Robinson, 'India's Grand Advocates: A Legal Elite Flourishing in the Era of Globalization', HLS Programme on the Legal Profession Research Paper Series No. 2013–5, November 2013, pp. 18–19, Harvard Law School Programme on the Legal Profession.

7   Sri Jaisinghani, personal communication.

10. The 1960s and China

1   Singh, Swaran, 'Panchsheel, Three Agreements and Five Principles', http://ignca.nic.in/ks_41062.htm.

2   Malhotra, Inder, *Indira Gandhi: A Personal and Political Biography* (London: Coronet Books, 1989), p. 77.

3   Jethmalani, Ram, *Maverick Unchanged, Unrepentant* (New Delhi: Rupa Publications, 2014), p. 54.

4   Jethmalani, Ram, *Conscience of a Maverick* (New Delhi: UBSPD, 2007), p. 152.

11. The Bar and the Bar Council

1   Galanter, Marc, and Nick Robinson, 'India's Grand Advocates: A Legal Elite Flourishing in the Era of Globalization', HLS Programme on the Legal Profession Research Paper Series No. 2013–5, November 2013, pp. 2–6, Harvard Law School Programme on the Legal Profession.

2 Keswani, Bhagwan, personal communication.
3 Nariman, Fali S., *Before Memory Fades: An Autobiography* (New Delhi: Hay House, 2010) p. 85.
4 Galanter, Marc, and Nick Robinson, 'India's Grand Advocates: A Legal Elite Flourishing in the Era of Globalization', HLS Programme on the Legal Profession Research Paper Series No. 2013–5, November 2013, p. 15, Harvard Law School Programme on the Legal Profession.
5 Jaisinghani, Sri, personal communication.
6 Chaudhury, Shoma, 'The Angry Young Man', *Tehelka*, June 25, 2005. http://archive.tehelka.com/story_main12.asp?filename=hub062505the_angry.asp.
7 Gera, Nalini, *Ram Jethmalani: The Authorized Biography* (New Delhi: Penguin, 2002), p. 76.

12. Israel

1 Jethmalani, Ram, *Conscience of a Maverick* (New Delhi: UBSPD, 2007), p. 24.
2 Kumaraswamy, P.R., *India's Israel Policy* (New York: Columbia University Press, 2010), p. 20.
3 Indiandiaspora.nic.in/diasporapdf/chapter9.
4 Manasseh, Rachel, *Baghdadian Jews of Bombay: Their Life and Achievements* (Great Neck: Midrash Ben Ish Hai, 2013), p. 128.
5 Ya'akov Morris, unpublished autobiography, courtesy of Benny Morris.
6 Kumaraswamy, P.R., *India's Israel Policy* (New York: Columbia University Press, 2010) p. 129.
7 Rachel Manasseh, *Baghdadian Jews of Bombay: Their Life and Achievements* (Great Neck: Midrash Ben Ish Hai, 2013) uses the name Indo-Israel Friendship League on pp. 208 and 221.
8 The author of *Train to Pakistan*.
9 Jethmalani, Ram, *Conscience of a Maverick* (New Delhi: UBSPD, 2007), p. 139.
10 Dubek, Ephraim, personal communication.
11 Jerusalem Summit, *Right Web*, May 1, 2013, http://rightweb.irc-online.org/profile/Jerusalem_Summit.
12 Sofer, Mark, personal communication.
13 Prime Minister Harper sponsored the 'World Conference on Anti-Semitism' in Ottawa Canada in November 2010.

13. 1970s

1   *Bhanudas Krishna Gawde vs. Paranajape & Ors.* On September 1, 1975, 1976 CriLJ 534.

2   Jethmalani, Ram, 'The Chairman's Page: Darkness Descends', *Journal of the Bar Council of India*, February 1973, p. 5.

3   Kumar, Maj. Gen. Nilendra, *Nani Palkhivala: A Role Model* (Universal Law Publishing, 2009) http://books.google.com/books p. 5.

4   Jethmalani, Ram, 'Palkhivala and Supreme Court Judges', *Conscience of a Maverick* (New Delhi: UBSPD, 2007), pp. 49ff.

14. The Emergency and Its Aftermath

1   Dhar, P.N., *Indira Gandhi, the Emergency and Indian Democracy* (New Delhi: Oxford University Press, 2000) p. 158.

2   Malhotra, Inder, *Indira Gandhi: A Personal and Political Biography* (London: Coronet Books, 1989) pp. 130–41.

3   Article 356 of the Indian Constitution allows the central government to impose direct federal rule on a state under certain specified circumstances.

4   Jethmalani, Ram, *Maverick Unchanged, Unrepentant* (New Delhi: Rupa Publications, 2014), pp. 60, 23.

5   *ADM Jabalpur vs. S.S. Shukla* on April 28, 1976, 1976 AIR 1207, 1976 SCR 172.

6   The habeas corpus case, kvtrust.blogspot, March 27, 2006, http://kvtrust.blogspot.com/2006_03_01_archive.html.

7   D'Souza, Jos. Peter, 'ADM Jabalpur vs Shivakant Shukla: When the Supreme Court Struck Down the Habeas Corpus', *PUCL Bulletin*, June 2001.

8   D'Souza, Jos. Peter, 'ADM Jabalpur vs. Shivakant Shukla: When the Supreme Court Struck Down the Habeas Corpus', *PUCL Bulletin*, June 2001.

9   This phrase was added as a correction in a personal communication from Ram Jethmalani.

10 Nariman, Fali S., 'Remembering Chief Justice Y. V Chandrachud', *Indian Express*, July 19, 2008. www.indianexpress.com/news/remembering-chief-justice-y.v.-chandrachud/337610/.

11 'Judge Bhagwati Pleads Guilty for ADM Jabalpur Case', *Law Resource India*, September 16, 2011, http://indialawyers.wordpress.com/2011/09/16/justice-bhagwati-pleads-guilty-for-adm-jabalpur-case/.

12 Jhangiani, Mukesh, 'TAG Archive', United News of India, May 12, 2004, mukeshjhangiani.worpress.com.
13 Justices Aftab Alam and Asok Kumar Ganguly.

15. America

1 Jethmalani, Ram, 'Return of the Renegade', Chairman's Page, *Journal of the Bar Council of India* Vol. 6 (3 and 4), 1977, p. vi.
2 Ibid., p. x.
3 'A Lawyer under Fire', *American Bar Association Journal*, September 1976, Vol. 62, p. 1181.
4 Pappu, Shyamla, 'Rebuttal from India', *American Bar Association Journal*, February 1977, Vol. 63, p. 243.
5 Poddar, Shrikumar, personal communication.
6 218. Telegram 347 from the Embassy in India to the Department of State, January 8, 1976, 1105Z. Source: National Archives, RG 59, Central Foreign Policy Files. Unclassified; Priority.
7 220. Telegram 863 from the Embassy in India to the Department of State, January 17, 1976. Ibid.
8 223. Telegram 28315 from the Department of State to the Embassy in India, February 5, 1976, 1656Z. Ibid.
9 Source: National Archives, RG 59, Central Foreign Policy Files. Secret; Nodis. It was drafted by Kux and approved on November 11 in S. The meeting took place in the Secretary's suite at the Waldorf Astoria Hotel. Kissinger was in New York to attend the UN General Assembly.
10 Hearings before the Subcommittee on International Organizations of the Committee on International Relations, House of Representatives, Ninety-fourth Congress. June 23, 28, 29; September 16 and 23, 1976.
11 Kux, Dennis, *India and the United States: Estranged Democracies* (Washington: National Defence University Press, 1992), p. 345, http://books.google.com/books/about/India_and_the_United_States. html?id=zcylFXH9_z8C.
12 India. p. 1, www.ipu.org/parline-e/reports/arc/INDIA_1977_E.PDF.

17. Member of Parliament

1 Gera, Nalini, *Ram Jethmalani: The Authorized Biography* (New Delhi: Penguin, 2002), p. 128.
2 Keswani, Bhagwan, personal communication.

3   Gera, Nalini, *Ram Jethmalani: The Authorized Biography* (New Delhi: Penguin, 2002), p. 132.

4   Malhotra, Inder *Indira Gandhi: A Personal and Political Biography* (London: Coronet Books, 1989) p. 202.

5   Kumar, Virendra, and S.P. Agrawal, 'Committees and Commissions in India', in *Shah Commission of Inquiry 1977*, Vol. 15, Part 1 (Concept Publishing Co., 1993) p. 179ff, http://books.google.ca/books?id=4gb 2Ry4JLGYC&source=gbs_navlinks_s.

6   Malhotra, Inder, *Indira Gandhi: A Personal and Political Biography* (London: Coronet Books, 1989) p. 203.

7   'Shah Commission Report on Emergency Excesses: Lost And Regained', *Indian Herald*, June 26, 1975.

8   Malhotra, Inder, *Indira Gandhi: A Personal and Political Biography* (London: Coronet Books, 1989) p. 206.

9   Gera, Nalini, *Ram Jethmalani: The Authorized Biography* (New Delhi: Penguin, 2002), p. 204.

10   Jethmalani, Ram, 'Indira Was Both Loved and Hated', *Sunday Guardian*, May 15, 2013, www.sunday-guardian.com/analysis/indira-was-both-loved-and-hated.

11   Lok Sabha Debates, pp. 450–86, http://books.google.com/books?id=g VE3AAAAIAAJ&p=PT62&lp=PT62&dq.

12   Malhotra, Inder, *Indira Gandhi: A Personal and Political Biography* (London: Coronet Books, 1989) pp. 212–13.

13   In *Re the Special Courts Bill 1978 vs. Date of Judgement 01/12/1978* on December 1, 1978.

14   Malhotra, Inder, *Indira Gandhi: A Personal and Political Biography* (London: Coronet Books, 1989) p. 213.

15   *State Through Delhi . . . vs. Sanjay Gandhi* on May 5, 1978: 1978 AIR 961, 1978 SCR (3) 950.

16   Gera, Nalini, *Ram Jethmalani: The Authorized Biography* (New Delhi: Penguin, 2002) p. 196.

17   *State Through Delhi vs. Sanjay Gandhi*, May 5, 1978, 1978 AIR 961, 1978 SCR (3) 950.

18   Gera, Nalini, *Ram Jethmalani: The Authorized Biography* (New Delhi: Penguin, 2002), pp. 198–200.

19   *Maneka Sanjay Gandhi & Anr. vs. Rani Jethmalani*, on November 23,1978. 1979 AIR 468. 1979 SCR (2) 378.

20   *Maneka Gandhi vs. Indira Gandhi and Anr.* on August14, 1984. AIR 1985 Delhi 114, 1984 (7) DRJ 238.

21   Jaisinghani, Sri, personal communication.

22 VC *Shukla vs. State (Delhi Admin)* on April 11, 1980. 1980 AIR 1382, 1980 SCR (3) 500.

18. Early 1980s

1   Celebs Bio Haji Mastan; Scribd.com August 18, 2011.
2   Gera, Nalini, *Ram Jethmalani: The Authorized Biography* (New Delhi: Penguin, 2002), p. 84.
3   *Union of India & Others vs. Haji Mastan Mirza* on February 23, 1984, 1984 AIR 681, 1984 SCR (3) 1.
4   'One Dead One Caught', *Hindustan Times* archives Mumbai, October 22, 2006, www.hindustantimes.com/News-Feed/NM18/One-dead-one-caught.
5   Mahesh Jethmalani, personal communication.
6   *A.K. Roy etc. vs. Union of India and Anr.* on 28 December, 1981, 1982 AIR 710, 1982 SCR (2) 272.
7   Boray, Sameer, et al., 'A Look into the Past: AK Roy v. Union of India', September 9, 2011, http://letstalkaboutthelaw.wordpress.com/2011/09/28/a-look-into-the-past-ak-roy-v-union-of-india/.
8   *R.S. Nayak vs. A.R. Antulay* on February 16, 1984, 1984 AIR 684, 1984 SCR (2) 1985.
9   *R.S. Nayak vs A.R. Antulay & Anr.* on 17 April, 1986, 1986 AIR 2045, 1986 SCR (2) 621.
10 *Abdul Rehman Antulay etc. & Ors. vs. R.S. Nayak etc.*, December 1991, AIR 1992 SC 1701, 1992 (2) BLJR 1319, 1992 CriLJ 2717.
11 *Abdul Rehman Antulay etc. & Ors. vs. R.S. Nayak Etc.*, Dec. 1991, Sri L.N. Misra, former Union Minister for Railways.
12 Malhotra, Inder, *Indira Gandhi: A Personal and Political Biography* (London: Coronet Books, 1989), p. 226.
13 *State of UP vs. Dr. Sanjay Singh* on 27 January, 1994, 1994 SCC Supl (2) 707.

20. Sikhs and the Punjab

1   *Ram Jethmalani etc. vs. Union of India etc.* on June 19, 1984, 1984 SCR (3) 926, 1984 SCC (3) 696.
2   *Ram Jethmalani & Ors vs. Union of India (UOI)* on June 20, 1984, 1984 (2) SCALE 214, (1985) 1 SCC 116.
3   *Ram Jethmalani & Ors. vs. Union of India (UOI)* on June 25, 1984, (1984) 3 SCC 571.

4   Mitta, Manoj, and H.S. Phoolka, *When a Tree Shook Delhi* (New Delhi: Roli Books, 2007). This is the basis for the history in this section.
5   Badal, Harsimrat Kaur, 'Badal Testimony in Lok Sabha on 29 April, 2010', *IndianKanoon*.
6   Jethmalani, Ram, 'Why I Defend the Accused', *Sunday Guardian*, June 8, 2013.
7   Jethmalani, Ram, 'Defence of the Despised', in *Conscience of a Maverick* (New Delhi: UBSPD, 2007), pp. 120ff.
8   *Kehar Singh & Ors vs. State (Delhi Admin.)* on August 3, 1988, 1988 AIR 1883, 1988 SCR Supl. (2) 24.
9   *Simranjit Singh Mann, Son of S vs. State of Punjab & Ors* on March 27, 1995 1995 CriLJ 3264.
10   Jaisinghani, Sri, personal communication.

21. Late 1980s

1   Rani Jethmalani, unpublished autobiography.
2   *Sharad Birdhi Chand Sarda vs. State of Maharashtra* on 17 July, 1984 AIR 1984 SC 1622.
3   *Abdul Latif Abdul Wahab Sheikh vs. B.K. Jha & Anr.* on February 9, 1987 AIR 725 1987 SCR (2) 203.
4   Gera, Nalini, *Ram Jethmalani: The Authorized Biography*. (New Delhi: Penguin, 2002), pp. 338–343.
5   Aggarwal, S.K., *Investigative Journalism in India* (New Delhi: Mittal Publications, 1990) p. 9, http://books.google.com/books.
6   Gera, Nalini, *Ram Jethmalani: The Authorized Biography* (New Delhi: Penguin, 2002), pp. 338–343.
7   *Ram Jethmalani vs. The Director*, on November 25, 1986.
8   *Delhi High Court Director, Central Bureau . . . vs. Ram Jethmalani* on 16 March, 1988 35 (1988) DLT 34, 1988 (15) DRJ 19.
9   Curtis, Polly, 'House of Lords Suspends Three from Parliament in Expenses Clampdown', *Guardian*, October 18, 2010, http://www.theguardian.com/politics/2010/oct/18/house-of-lords-mps-expenses.
10   Jethmalani, Ram, http://parliamentofindia.nic.in/lsdeb/ls12/ses2/0405089809.htm.
11   'Chandraswami Acquitted in St. Kitts Case', *Times of India*, October 26, 2004, http://articles.timesofindia.indiatimes.com/2004.
12   'Chandraswami to Pay Rs 9 Crore as Penalty: SC', *Indian Express*, June 15, 2011, http://www.indianexpress.com/news/chandraswami-to-pay-rs-9-crore-as-penalty-sc/804078/.

13 A crore is 10 million rupees, or $21,400, depending on the exchange rate.

14 Langa, Mahesh, 'Controversial Godman: Can Asaram Come Clean on the Sexual Allegations?', *Hindustan Times*, August 29, 2013, http://www.hindustantimes.com/India-news/Ahmedabad/Controversial-godman-Can-Asaram-Bapu-purge-himself-off-his-latest-scandal/Article1-1114370.aspx.

15 'In Search of Devi . . . Mallika Sarabhai Performance', *Osho World*, April, 2000, http://www.oshoworld.com/events/2000/Devi_Mallika.asp.

22. Defending Politicians

1 *Dronamraju Satyanarayana vs. N.T. Rama Rao* on January 2, 1988, AIR 1988 AP 62.

2 *Gadakhyashwantrao Kankarrao vs. Balasahib Vikhe Patil* on November 19, 1993, 1994 AIR 678 1994 SCC (1) 682.

23. Bofors

1 Bhushan, Prashant, *Bofors: The Selling of a Nation* (New Delhi: Vision Books, 1990) is the prime source for the history in this chapter.

2 Ray, Shantanu Guha,'Death of a Scandal', *Tehelka*, October 17, 2009, Issue 41, Vol. 6, http://tehelka.com/death-of-a-scandal/.

3 Jethmalani, Ram, *Maverick Unchanged, Unrepentant* (New Delhi: Rupa Publications, 2014), p. 70.

4 Ibid., p. 70.

5 Bhushan, Prashant, *Bofors: The Selling of a Nation* (New Delhi: Vision Books, 1990), p. 33.

6 Jethmalani, Ram, 'Letter to Rajiv Gandhi', *Indian Express*, June 18, 1987.

7 Shourie, Arun, first person account, accessed in July, 2013, in Archives, indiarightsonline; the same story appears in: Gera, Nalini, *Ram Jethmalani: The Authorized Biography* (New Delhi: Penguin, 2002), pp. 247–8.

8 Mahesh Jethmalani, personal communication.

9 To avoid confusion, we will use only a single spelling of Quattrocchi, even though the questions sometimes used variant spellings.

10 Jethmalani, Ram, *Maverick Unchanged, Unrepentant* (New Delhi: Rupa Publications, 2014), p. 71.

11 '1989: Scandal in India Columbia Journalism School', http://centennial. journalism.columbia.edu/1989-scandal-in-india/.

12 Gera, Nalini, *Ram Jethmalani: The Authorized Biography* (New Delhi: Penguin, 2002), p. 239.

13 Mahesh Jethmalani, personal communication.

14 Gera, Nalini, *Ram Jethmalani: The Authorized Biography* (New Delhi: Penguin, 2002), p. 254.

15 Bhushan, Prashant, *Bofors: The Selling of a Nation* (New Delhi: Vision Books, 1990) p. 210.

16 Herbaugh, Sharon, 'Journalists, Opposition Politicians, Protest Defamation Bill', September 5, 1988, AP NewsArchive, http://www. apnewsarchive.com/1988/Journalists-Opposition-Politicians-Protest-Defamation-Bill/.

17 Jethmalani, Ram, 'Evasive Denials Proved Bofors Guilt', *Sunday Guardian*, July 16, 2013.

18 Ray, Shantanu Guha, 'Death of a Scandal', *Tehelka*, October 17, 2009, http://archive.tehelka.com/story_main43. asp?filename=Ne171009death_of.asp.

19 *Srichand P. Hinduja vs. State through CBI* along with . . . on 31 May, 2005, 121 (2005) DLT 1, 2005 (82), DRJ 494.

24. The End of Rajiv Gandhi

1 Metcalf, Barbara D. and Thomas R. Metcalf, *A Concise History of Modern India* (Cambridge: Cambridge, 2001), p. 260.

2 Jethmalani, Ram, *Maverick Unchanged, Unrepentant* (New Delhi: Rupa Publications, 2014), p. 177.

3 Ibid., p. 181.

4 Ragothaman, K., *Conspiracy to Kill Rajiv Gandhi* (New Delhi: Manas, 2013), p. 28.

5 An excellent play-by-play account of the assassination is at www. sinhaya.com/Rajiv.html.

6 *State of Tamil Nadu through . . . vs. Nalini and 25 Others* on 11 May, 1999.

7 Kaarthikenyan, D.R. and Raju, Radha Vinod, *The Rajiv Gandhi Assassination* (New Delhi: Sterling Publishers, 2008), p. 205, http:// books.google.com/books?id=7MqfCkBGdQ8C&printsec=frontcover &source=gbs_atb#v=onepage&q=Jethmalani&f=false.

8 Kasli, Shelly, 'Great Game India—The Final Battle Is Only for the Bravest', March 7, 2013, http://greatgameindia.wordpress.

com/2013/03/07/subramanian-swamy-the-mossad-stooge-the-assassination-of-rajiv-gandhi/.

9   Gandhi, Thirumurugan, 'A Doubt Does Arise Regarding Chandraswami's Complicity and Involvement', September 21, 2013, http://www.theweekendleader.com/Causes/795/Plea-for-justice.html.

10 *Ram Jethmalani vs. Subramaniam Swamy* on December 21, 2001, 96 (2002) DLT 284, 2002 (62) DRJ 188.

11 *Ram Jethmalani vs. Subramaniam Swamy* on January 3, 2006, AIR 2006 Delhi 300 126 (2006) DLT 535.

12 Transcripts, Parliament of India, http://parliamentofindia.nic.in/lsdeb/ls12/ses2/0405089808.htm, accessed 10/4/2013.

13 *Ram Jethmalani vs. Subramaniam Swamy* on January 3, 2006, AIR 2006 Delhi 300 126 (2006) DLT 535.

14 Gopalakrishnan, Karthika, 'Madras HC Stays Execution of Rajiv's Killers', *Times of India*, August 30, 2011, http://articles.timesofindia.indiatimes.com/2011-08-30/india/29944974_1_mercy-pleas-mercy-petition-santhan.

15 Dhamija, DrAshok, 'Delay in Deciding Mercy Petitions on Death Penalty', *Tilak Marg*, Febuary 24, 2013, www.tilakmarg.com/tag/supreme-court.

16 'Rajiv Gandhi Assassination: Madras HC Stays Execution of 3 killers', *Indian Express*, August 31, 2011, http://www.indianexpress.com/news/rajiv-gandhi-assassination-madras-hc-stays-execution-of-3-killers/839197/.

17 'Ram Jethmalani Meets Rajiv Gandhi Case Convicts in Jail', *Times of India*, November 13, 2011, http://timesofindia.indiatimes.com/india/Ram-Jethmalani-meets-Rajiv-Gandhi-case-convicts-in-jail/articleshow/10709871.cms.

18 *L.K. Venkat vs. Union of India & Ors.* on May 1, 2012.

19 'Delay No Ground for Mercy in Terror Cases', *The Hindu*, April 12, 2013, http://www.thehindu.com/news/national/delay-no-ground-for-mercy-in-terror-cases/article4609566.ece.

20 'Stay Executions Until Bhullar Case Verdict', *The Hindu*, February 19, 2013, http://www.thehindu.com/todays-paper/tp-national/stay-executions-until-bhullar-case-verdict/article4429792.ece.

21 *Shatrughan Chauhan & Anr vs. Union of India & Ors*, on January 21, 2014, Writ Petition (Criminal) No. 55 of 2013.

22 'SC Agrees to Reconsider Bhullar's Plea for Life', *Times of India*, January25, 2014, http://articles.timesofindia.indiatimes.com/2014-01-25/india/46600729_1_mercy-plea-devenderpal-singh-bhullar-mercy-

petitions.

23 Mahapatra, Dhananjay, 'UPA Gov't Unwilling to Let Rajiv Gandhi Killers Escape Noose', *Times of India*, January 30, 2014, http://timesofindia.indiatimes.com/india/UPA-govt-unwilling-to-let-Rajiv-Gandhi-killers-escape-noose/articleshow/29570120.cms.

25. The National Law School

1 Nariman, Fali S., Lecture in Pune Symposium on Ram's 75th birthday, September 14, 1998, quoting Drucker–Schumpeter conversation in Drucker, Peter and Nakaichi, Isao, *Drucker on Asia* (New York: Routledge, 2011), pp. 109–110.

2 Gera, Nalini, *Ram Jethmalani: The Authorized Biography* (New Delhi: Penguin, 2002), p. 139.

3 Prof. N.L. Mitra, personal communication.

4 Karnataka Act 22 of 1986.

5 Krishna, Jayanth K., 'Professor Kingsfield Goes to Delhi: American Academics, the Ford Foundation, and the Development of Legal Education in India', *American Journal of Legal History*, October, 2004.

6 Prof. N.L. Mitra, personal communication.

7 Jethmalani, Ram, *Big Egos, Small Men* (New Delhi: Har-Anand, 2000), p. 44.

8 Ibid., pp. 42–46.

9 Ibid., p. 45.

10 Anand, A.S.H.L., Sarin Memorial Lecture in the City of Roses, 1998, ebc-india.com.

11 Harvard Law School Programme on the Legal Profession, The Indian Legal Profession, 2011, http://www.law.harvard.edu/programs/plp/pdf/Indian_Legal_Profession.pdf.

26. The Mandal Report

1 Mahesh Jethmalani, personal communication.

2 *Indian Express*, August 10, 1990, quoted in Gera, Nalini, *Ram Jethmalani: The Authorized Biography* (New Delhi: Penguin, 2002) pp. 278–279.

3 August 13, 1990 and September 25, 1991, discussed in legal case below.

4 *Indra Sawhney & Ors. vs. Union of India* on November 16, 1992, AIR 1993 SC 477, 1992 Supp 2 SCR 454.

5 Articles 340 and 338.

27. The 1990s, Hindutva, Ayodhya, and Retaliation

1   Dey, J., 'Crime Diary: The First Murder in Mumbai's Mill District was that of an MLA', *Midday*, January 24, 2010, http://www.mid-day.com/news/2010/jan/240110-mla-murder-mills.htm.

2   Dhawale, Ashok, 'The Shiv Sena: Semi-Fascism in Action', *The Marxist*, Vol. 16 No. 2, April–June 2000, http://www.cpim.org/marxist/200002_marxist_sena_dhawle.htm.

3   Giri, Saroj, 'Bal Thackeray, or Why the Communists did Nothing', *Sanhati*, November 22, 2012, http://sanhati.com/excerpted/5823/.

4   Prakash, Gyan, *Mumbai Fables* (Princeton University Press, 2010), pp. 204–205, accessed July 2013, http://books.google.com/books?id=TeRWxaJLoDUC&p=PA204#v=onepage&q&f=false.

5   Jethmalani, Ram, *Maverick Unchanged, Unrepentant* (New Delhi: Rupa Publications, 2014), pp. 111,117.

6   *Dr Ramesh Yeshwant Prabhoo vs. Shri Prabhakar Kashinath Kunte*, (1996) 1 SCC 130 [11/12/1995.

7   Jethmalani, Ram, *Maverick Unchanged, Unrepentant* (New Delhi: Rupa Publications, 2014), p. 108.

8   Sub-section 3A of the Representation of People Act of 1951.

9   *Manohar Joshi vs. Nitin Bhaurao Patil* on 11 December, 1995, AIR 796 1996 SSC (1) 169.

10 'Pawar Confirms Dawood's Offer', *Times of India*, November 15, 2005, http://articles.timesofindia.indiatimes.com/2005-11-15/mumbai/27850702_1_dawood-sharad-pawar-indian-govt.

11 *State of Maharashtra etc. vs. Somnath Thapa, etc.* on 12 April, 1996, AIR 1744, 1996 SCC (4) 659.

12 '1993 Mumbai blasts—A Peep into History', *Midday*, March 21, 2013, http://www.mid-day.com/news/2013/mar/210313-1993-mumbai-blasts-a-peep-into-history-sanjay-dutt-babri-masjid-news-national-mumbai.htm.

13 '93 Blasts Case: Somnath Thapa Found Guilty', *Hindustan Times*, November 28, 2006, http://www.hindustantimes.com/News-Feed/NM20/93-blasts-case-Somnath-Thapa-found-guilty/Article1-178518.aspx.

14 Sri Jaisinghani, personal communication.

15 '93 Blasts Convict Ex-Customs Officer Dies', *Times of India*, April 11, 2008, http://articles.timesofindia.indiatimes.com/2008-04-11/india/27756105_1_blasts-tada-court-customs-collector-somnath-thapa.

16 'Sanjay Dutt Case', *Indian* Express, May 10, 2013.

17 *Sanjay Dutt vs. State through CBI, Bombay* on August 18, 1994, JT1994(5)SC225a, 1994(3)SCALE790, (1994)5SCC402, [1994] Supp2SCR729, 1994(2)UJ474 (SC).

18 *Sanjay Dutt vs. State through CBI, Bombay* on 9 September, 1994, 1994 (2) ALT Cri 573, 1995 CriLJ 477.

19 Ghosh, Shamik, 'Sanjay Dutt Convicted in 1993 Blasts Case, Gets 5 Years in Jail', NDTV, March 21, 2013, http://www.ndtv.com/article/india/sanjay-dutt-convicted-in-1993-bombay-blasts-case-gets-5-years-in-jail-345095.

28. Corruption: Fighting it, Defending it

1 Vohra Committee Report, 1993, reproduced on *Sanjeet Sabhalok* blog, December 26, 2010, accessed 10/4/2013, http://networkedblogs.com/cfegj.

2 *Shri Dinesh Trivedi, M.P. & Ors vs. Union of India & Ors.*, on 20 March,1997.

3 Teipal,Tarun, 'The Tehelka Exposé', *Tehelka*, www.taruntejpal.com/The Tehelkal.

4 'Government Shielding Official: Jethmalani', *Times of India*, February 21, 2002, http://articles.timesofindia.indiatimes.com/2002-02-21/india/27119344_1_shankar-sharma-jethmalani-affidavit.

5 'Jethmalani for Cross-Examining Official', *Times of India*, April 18, 2002, http://articles.timesofindia.indiatimes.com/2002-04-18/india/27107898_1_jethmalani-gupta-venkataswami.

6 'Govt Rapped for Sharma Witch-Hunt against Tehelka Alleged', *Times of India*, February 6, 2002, http://articles.timesofindia.indiatimes.com/2002-02-06/india/27133109_1_tehelka-tapes-justice-k-venkataswami-commission-shankar-sharma.

7 Krishnan,Murali,'Justice Denied', *Outlook*, December 9, 2002, http://www.outlookindia.com/article.aspx?218269.

8 Chaudhury, Shoma, 'The Angry Young Man', *Tehelka*, June 25, 2005, http://archive.tehelka.com/story_main12.asp?filename=hub062505the_angry.asp.

9 'Government Harassment of *Tehelka*: Broad Points', *Tehelka*, http://archive.tehelka.com/channels/Investigation/bangaru/GOVERNMENT.htm.

10 Nariman, Fali S., *The State of the Nation* (New Delhi: Hay House, 2013), p 283

11 Chaudhury, Shoma,'The Making of a Paper', *Tehelka*, http://archive.

tehelka.com/story_main.asp?filename=te013004our.asp&id=4.

12 'Government Harassment of *Tehelka*: Broad Points', *Tehelka*, http:// archive.tehelka.com/channels/Investigation/bangaru/GOVERNMENT. htm.

13 Dhavan, Rajeev, 'The *Tehelka* Commission', *The Hindu*, October 15, 2004, www.hindu.com/2004/10/15/stories.

14 Tejpal, Tarun J, *The Best of Tehelka* (Buffalo Books, 2003), p. 374.

15 http://listserv.indianetwork.org/cgi/wa.cgi?A2=INDIA-D;5e9358d.9409C, 19 September, 1994.

16 *L.K. Advani vs. Central Bureau of Investigation, Delhi High Court*, on April 1, 1997, IIIAD Delhi 53 1997 CriLJ 2559, 1997 (4) Crimes 1.

17 Mahapatra, Dhananjay, 'India's Top 10 Lawyers', *Times of India*, January 9, 2010.

18 *Phoolan Devi vs. State of MP & Ors* on November 27, 1996.

19 This story of Phoolan Devi is based largely on her obituary, 'Phoolan Devi', July 26, 2001, in *The Telegraph*, http://www.telegraph.co.uk/ news/obituaries/1335253/Phoolan-Devi.html.

20 Dalal, Sucheta, 'Harshad Mehta and Ketan Parekh Scam', first published in *Times of India*, April 23, 1992, accessed at *Flame*, 2011, http://flame. org.in/knowledgecenter/scam.aspx.

21 Gera, Nalini, *Ram Jethmalani: The Authorized Biography* (New Delhi: Penguin, 2002), p. 258.

22 *Harshad S. Mehta & Ors vs. the State of Maharashtra* on 6 September, 2001.

23 *Ram Narain Poply, Pramod Kumar . . . vs. Central Bureau of Investigation*, 14 January, 2003, AIR 2003 SC 2748 2003 CriLJ 4801, JT 2003 (1) SC 184.

24 Nariman, Fali S., *The State of the Nation* (New Delhi: Hay House, 2013), p. 302.

25 *Union of India & Ors vs. Sushil Kumar Modi & Ors* on November 5, 1996.

26 Burns, John, '"Fodder Scam" Could Bring Down a Shaky Government', *New York Times*, July 2, 1997, http://www.nytimes.com/1997/07/02/ world/fodder-scam-could-bring-down-a-shaky-indian-government. html.

27 *Union of India & Ors vs. Sushil Kumar Modi & Ors* [1997] INSC 68 (January 24, 1997), *Advocate Khoj Law Library*, http://www. advocatekhoj.com/library/judgments/index.php?go=1997/january/68. php.

28 Soroor Ahmed, 'Laloo Prasad Yadav Surrendered Before CBI Special Court', November 26, 2001, rediff.com, http://www.rediff.com/news/2001/nov/26laloo1.htm.

29 *Lalu Prasad Yadav vs. State through CBI (A.H.D.)*, Ranchi, Jharkhand, August 26, 2003, AIR 2003SC 3838.

30 'BJP Accuses Lalu of Corruption; Asks PM to Drop Him',*Oneindia News*, August 12, 2008, http://news.oneindia.in/2008/08/12/bjp-accuses-lalu-of-corruption-asks-pm-to-drop-him.

31 'Charges framed against Lalu, Mishra in fodder scam', *Times of India*, March 1, 2012, http://articles.timesofindia.indiatimes.com/2012-03-01/india/31113067_1_fraudulent-withdrawal-fodder-scam-cbi-court.

32 *Lalu Prasad Yadav & Anr. vs. State of Bihar & Anr.* on April 1, 2010.

33 Majumdar, Ushinor, 'Fodder Soup Heating Up for Lalu', July 1, 2013, *Tehelka.com,* http://www.tehelka.com/lalus-fodder-scam-petitions-dismissed-by-hc/.

34 Yadav, Anumeha, 'Lalu Prasad, Mishra, among 45 Convicted in Fodder Scam Case', October 1, 2012, *The Hindu*, http://www.thehindu.com/news/national/lalu-prasad-mishra-among-45-convicted-in-fodder-scam-case/article5184894.ece.

29. Judicial Accountability

1   Jethmalani, Ram, *Conscience of a Maverick* (New Delhi: UBSPD, 2007), p. 97.

2   Ibid., p. 101.

3   Ibid., p. 107.

4   *Kamalanantha and Ors vs. State of Tamil Nadu* on 5 April, 2005.

5   Jethmalani, Ram, 'Our Men in Black', *Justice for Premananda*, June 15, 2005, http://www.justice-for-premananda.org/en/legal/jethmalani/,accessed at the *Deccan Herald*, June 15, 2005, originally in *Asian Age*, 2005.

6   'The DNA Tests Affair', *Justice for Premananda*, http://www.justice-for-premananda.org/en/legal/dna/.

7   Jethmalani, Ram, *Conscience of a Maverick* (New Delhi: UBSPD, 2007), p. 104.

8   Noorani, A.G., 'Dark Days', *Frontline*, Vol. 28, Issue 07, March 26–April 6, 2011.

9   Jethmalani, Ram, 'Too High a Horse', *Tehelka*, August 22, 2009.

10 'First Impeachment of Judge Case: Justice V. Ramaswami', Gyan

Central, October 12, 2012, http://www.gyancentral.com/forum/law-preparation/legal-aptitude-preparation/7055-first-impeachment-judge-case-justice-v-ramaswami.html.

11 Nariman, Fali S., *The State of the Nation* (New Delhi: Hay House, 2013), p 363 ff.

12 *Sub-committee on Judicial Accountability vs. Union of India & Ors* on 8 May, 1991, AIR 1598, 1991 SCR (2) 741.

13 *Sub-committee on Judicial Accountability Etc. Etc. v. Union of India* on 29 October, 1991, 1992 AIR 320,1991 SCR Supl. (2) 1.

14 Sawant Committee Report, indiancorruptjudges.com.

15 *Sub-Committee on Judicial Accountability v. Justice V. Ramaswami*, 1994 1995 SCC (1) 5,1994 SCALE (4) 634.

16 Kang, Bhavdeep, 'Grand Jury at Large', *outlookindia.com*, January 5, 1998.

17 'Jethmalani Firm on Impeachment Motion against SC Judge', *Rediff.com*, October 6, 1997, http://www.rediff.com/news/oct/06sc.htm.

18 Venkatesan, J., 'Promotions Should be Transparent: Judicial Accountability Panel', *The Hindu*, December 20, 2009, http://www.thehindu.com/news/national/article67521.ece.

19 Nariman, Fali S., *The State of the Nation* (New Delhi: Hay House, 2013), p. 367–371.

20 *Amicus Curiae vs. Prashant Bhusan & Anr.* on 10 November, 2010.

21 Bhushan, Prashant, 'My Honest and Bonafide Perception', *Outlook*, December 9, 2009, http://www.outlookindia.com/article.aspx?263230.

22 Ram Jethmalani, personal communication.

23 Mahendra, 'A Case of Contempt', September 21, 2007, http://skeptic.skepticgeek.com/2007/09/21/a-case-of-contempt/.

24 Jethmalani, Ram, *Conscience of a Maverick* (New Delhi: UBSPD, 2007), p. 106 ff.

25 Jethmalani, Ram, *Maverick Unchanged, Unrepentant* (New Delhi: Rupa Publications, 2014), p 125.

26 Jethmalani, Ram, *Conscience of a Maverick* (New Delhi: UBSPD, 2007), p 101.

27 Acts and Rules governing the service conditions of Supreme Court judges, Ministry of Law and Justice (As modified upto 1.4.2009) *mha.nic.in/pdfs/TheHCJudgesAct1954*.

28 Datar, Arvind P., 'Judicial Appointments—The Indian Perspective By a Senior Advocate', Madras High Court, www.law.cam.ac.uk/faculty-resources/10000862.doc.

29 *S.P. Gupta vs. Union of India& Ors.* on December 30, 1981, AIR 1982

SC 149 1981 Supp (1) SCC 87 1982 (2) SCR 365.
30 Rajagopal, Krishnadas, 'The Collegium Controversy', *Indian Express*, August 24, 2011, http://m.indianexpress.com/news/the-collegium-controversy/836029/.
31 Jethmalani, Ram, 'Two Bills that Threaten Democracy', *Sunday Guardian*, September 9, 2013.

30. Rani

1 Rani Jethmalani's unpublished autobiography is the source of the quotes from Rani.
2 Gavito, Alexandra Sanchez, *A Woman's Wheel of Life* (New Delhi: Viva Books, 2004), pp. 123–127.

31. First Law Minister, then Minister of Urban Affairs

1 'All the Prime Minister's Men', *Outlook*, May 29, 1996, http://www.outlookindia.com/article.aspx?201430.
2 *Dr Subramanian Swamy vs. J. Jayalalitha and Ors* on November 15, 1993 1994 1 MLJ 314.
3 *Dr Subramanian Swamy vs. J. Jayalalitha* on August 20, 1996, 1997 CriLJ 2481 (1994) IMLJ 314.
4 Subramanian, T.S.,'No Respite', *Frontline,* Vol. 14, No. 25, December 13–26, 1997.
5 Panneerselvan, A.S., 'Unsettling the Bench', *Outlook*, March 22, 1999.
6 Panicker, Prem,'The Man People Love to Hate', *Rediff*, March 17, 1998, www.Rediff.com/news/1998/mar/17sswamy.
7 Gera, Nalini, *Ram Jethmalani: The Authorized Biography* (New Delhi: Penguin, 2002), p. 169.
8 Subramanian, T.S.,'Dealing with Jayalalitha', *Frontline,* Vol. 15, No. 10, May 9–22, 1998.
9 'AIADMK Ministers Flay Hegde, Jethmalani's Comments on Jayalalitha, Coalition Shaky', *Rediff*, April 17, 1998, http://www.rediff.com/news/1998/apr/17vkr.htm.
10 Jerath, Arati R., 'Enfant terrible in their element', *Indian Express*, April 19, 1998.
11 Gera, Nalini, *Ram Jethmalani: The Authorized Biography* (New Delhi: Penguin, 2002), p. 172.
12 'National Judicial Panel Soon, Says Jethmalani', *Indian Express*, August 4, 1998, Expressindia.indianexpress.com/news/ie/daily.

13 XII Lok Sabha Debates, Session II (Monsoon) Monday, July 20, 1998.
14 Gera, Nalini, *Ram Jethmalani: The Authorized Biography* (New Delhi: Penguin, 2002), p. 176.
15 Lok Sabha Debates on the Statutory Resolution and Government Bill on 15 March, 1998.
16 Mahalingam, Sudha,'Vigilance Commission', *Frontline*, Vol. 15, No. 19, September 12–25, 1998.
17 Sinha, Bharti, 'PMO to Transfer Urban Affairs Secy', *Business Standard*, September 10, 1998.
18 'Inside Track', *Indian Express*, May 31,1998, http://expressindia. indianexpress.com/news/ie/daily/19980531/15150784.html.
19 Sinha, Sanjiv, 'DDA outlived its utility long time ago, says Ram Jethmalani', *Indian Express*, November 7, 1998.
20 Sahajwala, Prem Chand,'Ram Jethmalani, An Interesting Personality', sulekha.com 2007, http://creative.sulekha.com/ram-jethmalani-an-interesting-personality_233914_blog.
21 Joshi, Charu Lata and Srikanth, B.R., 'Jethmalani Nails Jethmalani', Outlookindia.com, May 18, 1998.
22 'PM should allow ED probe into Jethmalani's FERA violation, says Swamy', *Rediff .com*, 22 April, 1998, http://www.rediff.com/news/1998/apr/22swamy.htm.
23 'ED studying charges against Jethmalani', *Indian Express*, May 4, 1998, http://expressindia.indianexpress.com/ie/daily/19980504/12450134. html.
24 Jerath, Arati, 'To Expand Cabinet or Not, is BJP's Dilemma', *Indian Express*, May 4, 1998.
25 Jerath, Arati, 'EnfantTerrible in Their Element', *Indian Express*, April 19, 1998.
26 Kantha, Sachi,'Sri Subramanian Swamy, the Loonyswami of Madurai', *Ilankai Tamil Sangam*, August 14, 2012, http://www.sangam. org/2012/08/Subramanian_Loonyswamy.php.
27 Joshi, Charu Lata and Srikanth B.R., 'Jethmalani Nails Jethmalani', Outlookindia.com, May 18, 1998.
28 Ibid.
29 'ED studying charges against Jethmalani', *Indian Express*, May 4, 1998, http://expressindia.indianexpress.com/news/ie/ daily/19980504/12450134.html.
30 Ramachandran, Rajesh,'BJP clears Hegde, Jethmalani', Rediff.com, May 7, 1998, http://www.rediff.com/news/1998/may/07raj.htm.
31 Sinha, Sanjiv, 'Jethmalani Prevails, Denotifies Prime Delhi Land', *Indian*

Express, October 8, 1998.

32 Bavadam, Lyla, 'The MS Shoes Affair', *Frontline*, Vol. 17, Issue 16, August 5–18, 2000.

33 Gera, Nalini, *Ram Jethmalani: The Authorized Biography* (New Delhi: Penguin, 2002), p. 304.

34 Jethmalani, Ram, *Big Egos, Small Men* (New Delhi: Har-Anand, 2000), p. 85–87.

35 'He (Ram Jethmalani) should be dismissed and prosecuted!', *Indian Express*, August 30, 1998, http://www.indianexpress.com/ Storyold/48932/.

36 'Ram Jethmalani Defends Stand on Land Allotment', *Business Standard*, September 7, 1998, http://www.business-standard.com/article/specials/ ram-jethmalani-defends-stand-on-land-allotment-198090701034_1. html.

37 'He (Ram Jethmalani) should be dismissed and prosecuted!', *Indian Express*, August 30, 1998, http://www.indianexpress.com/ Storyold/48932/.

38 Venkatesan, V.,'The Jethmalani Revolt', *Frontline*, Vol. 17, Issue 16, August 5–18, 2000, http://www.frontline.in/static/html/ fl1716/17160200.htm.

39 Gera, Nalini, *Ram Jethmalani: The Authorized Biography* (New Delhi: Penguin, 2002), pp. 301–302.

40 Bhushan, Ranjit, 'But, Barkis Isn't Willing', *Outlook* , September 8, 1998, http://www.outlookindia.com/article.aspx?206231.

41 Kapoor,Virendra, 'Cooked!' Rediff.com, February 6, 1999, http://www. rediff.com/news/1999/feb/06buzz.htm.

42 Sinha, Bharti, 'PMO to Transfer Urban Affairs Secy', *Business Standard*, September 10, 1998, www.business-standard.com/article/specials/pr on April 17, 2013.

43 Bhushan, Prashant, 'The Freedom of Information Bill 2002, National Campaign Committee for the People's Right to Information', http://www.freedominfo.org/2002/12/freedom-of-information-law-approved-in-indi.

44 Performance of Programmes/Schemes—Urban Employment and Poverty Alleviation, p. 6, http://mhupa.gov.in/pdf/performance/2002-2003/6. pdf.

45 'Jethmalani Reiterates India's Commitment to Shelter for All', Government of India Press Information Bureau, May 6, 1999, http:// pib.nic.in/archieve/lreleng/l0599/r060599.html.

46 'UCLA will be repealed soon, says Jethmalani', *Indian Express*,

October 8, 1998, http://expressindia.indianexpress.com/ie/daily/19981008/28150694.html.

47 Ministry of Urban Development Annual Report, 1998–1999, www.urbanindia.nic.in/quickaccess/ann_report/1998–1999.

48 Raj, Dev, 'Development-India: State Monopoly on Housing Scrapped', Inter Press Service, ipsnews.net/1998/06 report.

49 Sarin, Ritu, 'I have complete evidence of the conspiracy against me', *Indian Express* September 6, 1998, expressindia.indianexpress.com.

50 Latest Press Information Bureau Releases (Government of India) headlines pib.nic.in/archieve/ireleng/10399.

51 Bharucha, Nauzer K., 'Urban land ceiling act remains a controversial issue', *Times of India*, July 17, 2012, http://articles.timesofindia.indiatimes.com/2012-07-17/mumbai/32713069_1_errant-builders-ulcra-urban-land-ceiling-act.

52 Mukherjee, Arindam, 'High-Rise Solutions', outlookindia.com, May 25, 1998.

53 'UCLA Will Be Repealed Soon, Says Jethmalani', *Indian Express*, October 8, 1998, http://expressindia.indianexpress.com/ie/daily/19981008/28150694.html.

54 Mahalingam, Sudha, 'The False Ceiling', *Frontline*, August 1–14, 1998.

55 Kulkarni, Sudheendra, 'Public Toilets and Patriotism', *Indian Express*, March 21, 2010, http://www.indianexpress.com/news/public-toilets-and-patriotism/593496/0.

56 Performance Of Programmes/Schemes—Urban Employment & Poverty Alleviation, p. 8, http://mhupa.gov.in/pdf/performance/2002-2003/6.pdf.

32. Law Minister, Finally

1 Venkatesan, V., 'The Countdown to Collapse', *Frontline*, Vol. 16 (9), April 24–May 7, 1999.

2 Muralidharan, Sukumar, 'The End of an Ordeal', *Frontline*, Vol. 16 (9), April 24–May 7,1999, http://www.frontline.in/static/html/fl1609/16090040.htm.

3 'BJP's One-vote Defeat in 1999 Was Narrowest in History', *Times of India*, July 20, 2008, http://articles.timesofindia.indiatimes.com/2008-07-22/india/27945828_1_pramod-mahajan-vajpayee-orissa-chief-minister.

4 'Vajpayee Loses Confidence Vote by 1 Vote', Rediff.com, April 17, 1999, http://www.rediff.com/news/1999/apr/17vote.htm.

5   Sahajwala, Prem, 'Ram Jethmalani, an Interesting Personality', Sulekha.
    com, 2007, http://creative.sulekha.com/ram-jethmalani-an-interesting-
    personality_233914_blog.

6   '3-Day MPs Convention to Discuss Reservations Threadbare', Rediff.
    com, October 27, 1999, www.rediff.com/news/1999/oct/27reser.htm.

7   Lok Sabha Debates, 'Regarding Discussion on the Constitution . . . on
    27 October, 1999', www.indiankanoon.org/doc/445721/.

8   Ram's proposed 84th Amendment would become the 79th Constitutional
    Amendment, but that is a technicality.

9   Important Articles and Amendments of the Indian Constitution for
    CLAT 2013, September 14, 2012, www.gyancentral.com/forum/
    law-preparation/legal-aptitude-preparation/6505-important-articles-
    amendments-indian-constitution-clat-2013-a.html.

10 Gera, Nalini, *Ram Jethmalani: The Authorized Biography* (New Delhi:
    Penguin, 2002), p. 314.

11 Gupta, Harish, 'Solicitor-General's Appointment Courts Major
    Controversy', *Indian Express*, July 6, 1999, http://expressindia.
    indianexpress.com/news/ie/daily/19990706/ige06046.html.

12 'Jethmalani Pressed Jaisinghani's Case for Solicitor-General', *Statesman*,
    July 6, 1999, www.accessmylibrary.com/article-1G1-55092185/
    jethmalani-pressed-jaisinghani-case.html.

13 Mitra, Sumit, 'The Wrath of Ram', *India Today*, August 7, 2000, http://
    indiatoday.intoday.in/story/ram-jethmalani-blames-his-dismissal-as-
    law-minister-on-attorney-general-soli-sorabjee/1/244478.html.

14 Gera, Nalini, *Ram Jethmalani: The Authorized Biography* (New Delhi:
    Penguin, 2002), pp. 183–91.

15 Ibid., pp. 183–91.

16 Mitra, Sumit, 'The Wrath of Ram', *India Today*, August 7, 2000, http://
    indiatoday.intoday.in/story/ram-jethmalani-blames-his-dismissal-as-
    law-minister-on-attorney-general-soli-sorabjee/1/244478.html.

17 Lok Sabha Debates, 'Discussion on the Code of Civil Procedure
    (Amendment) . . . on 20 December, 1999', www.indiankanoon.org/
    doc/401632/.

18 The Code of Civil Procedure (Amendment) Act of 1999—Indian
    Railway, www.indianrailways.gov.in/railwayboard/view_section.jsp?l
    ang=0&id=0,1,304,366,533,1044,1050.

19 Law Commission of India, 'One Hundred Sixty Third Report on
    The Code of Civil (Amendment) Bill, 1997,' November 1998, http://
    lawcommissionofindia.nic.in/101-169/Report163.pdf.

20 Lok Sabha Debates, 'Discussion on the Code of Civil Procedure

(Amendment) . . . on 20 December, 1999', www.indiankanoon.org/doc/401632/.

21 The Code of Civil Procedure 1908, www.wipo.int/wipolex/en/text.jsp?file_id=201630.

22 'Lawyers' Strike Paralyses Courts, Jethmalani for Dialogue', *Indian Express*, February 24, 2000, http://expressindia.indianexpress.com/news/ie/daily/20000225/ina25023.html.

23 'Lawyers' Strike Regrettable: Jethmalani', *The Hindu*, February 25, 2000, www.hindu.com/2000/02/25/stories/02250001.htm.

24 Venkatesan, V., 'Lawyers against an Act', *Frontline*, Vol. 17 (5), March 4–17, 2000, www.frontline.in/static/html/fl1705/17050310.htm.

25 Ibid.

26 'Judicial Reforms a Priority', *Tribune*, March 29, 2000, www.tribuneindia.com/2000/20000330/nation.htm#5.

27 'Striking Lawyers Expel Jethmalani from their Association', *Indian Express*, March 9, 2000, http://expressindia.indianexpress.com/news/ie/daily/20000310/ina10016.html.

28 Venkataraman, R., 'Bar and Bench on Collision Course', *Telegraph*, March 16, 2000, www.telegraphindia.com/1000317/front_pa.htm.

29 *Ex-Capt. Harish Uppal vs. Union of India & Anr* on 17 December, 2002.

30 *Salem Advocate Bar Association vs. Union of India (UOI)* on 25 October, 2002 AIR 2003 SC 189, 2002 (6) ALT 1SC, 2003 (3) AWC 2238 SC.

31 Chodesh, Hiram, *Mediating the Uniform Civil Code*, p. 13, http://today.law.utah.edu/wp-content/uploads/2010/06/Mediating-the-Indian-Uniform-Civil-Code-8-26-09.pdf.

32 The Code of Civil Procedure (Amendment) Act 2002, *Gazette of India*, May 24, 2002, http://unpan1.un.org/intradoc/groups/public/documents/apcity/unpan006185.pdf.

33 'What are the Latest Amendments in Civil Procedure Code 1908?', February 23, 2013, http://kehkelenge.wordpress.com/tag/salem-advocate-bar-association-v-union-of-india/.

34 'The Jethmalani Controversy', *The Hindu*, October 10, 2000, http://hindu.com/2000/10/10/stories/13100643.htm.

35 Bavadam, Lyla, 'The M.S. Shoes Affair', *Frontline*, April 6, 1995, www.frontline.in/navigation/?type=static&page=flonnet&rdurl=fl1716/17160230.htm.

36 Ibid.

37 Venkatesan, V., 'The Jethmalani Revolt', *Frontline*, Vol. 17 (16), August 5–18, 2000.

38 Mitra, Sumit, 'The Wrath of Ram', *India Today*, August 7, 2000, http://

indiatoday.intoday.in/story/ram-jethmalani-blames-his-dismissal-as-law-minister-on-attorney-general-soli-sorabjee/1/244478.html.

39 Jethmalani, Ram, *Big Egos, Small Men* (New Delhi: Har-Anand, 2000), p. 71.

40 Venkatesan, V., 'The Jethmalani Revolt', *Frontline*, Vol. 17 (16), August 5–18, 2000.

41 Mitra, Sumit, 'The Wrath of Ram', *India Today*, August 7, 2000, http://indiatoday.intoday.in/story/ram-jethmalani-blames-his-dismissal-as-law-minister-on-attorney-general-soli-sorabjee/1/244478.html.

42 Venkatesan, V., 'The Jethmalani Revolt', *Frontline*, Vol. 17 (16), August 5–18, 2000.

43 Jethmalani, Ram, *Big Egos, Small Men* (New Delhi: Har-Anand, 2000), p. 121.

44 Venkatesan, V., 'The Jethmalani Revolt', *Frontline*, Vol. 17 (16), August 5–18, 2000.

45 'PM Rejects Jethmalani Claim, Orders Inquiry into Info Leak', *Indian Express*, July 28, 2000, http://expressindia.indianexpress.com/news/ie/daily/20000729/ina29035.html.

46 Ministry of Law, Justice and Company Affairs, Department of Legal Affairs, http://lawmin.nic.in/ncrwc/ncrwcreport.htm.

47 Mitra, Sumit, 'The Wrath of Ram', *India Today*, August 7, 2000, http://indiatoday.intoday.in/story/ram-jethmalani-blames-his-dismissal-as-law-minister-on-attorney-general-soli-sorabjee/1/244478.html.

48 'National Commission to Review the Working of the Constitution (2001)', *India Prospect*, 2013, http://indiaprospect.org/Blog/?p=15.

49 Jethmalani, Ram, *Big Egos, Small Men*. (New Delhi: Har-Anand, 2000), p. 108.

50 Venkatesan, V., 'The Jethmalani Revolt', *Frontline*, Vol. 17 (16), August 5–18, 2000.

51 Mitra, Sumit, 'The Wrath of Ram', *India Today*, August 7, 2000, http://indiatoday.intoday.in/story/ram-jethmalani-blames-his-dismissal-as-law-minister-on-attorney-general-soli-sorabjee/1/244478.html.

52 Rudolph, Lloyd, and Susanne Hoeber Rudolph, *The Success of India's Democracy* (Cambridge: Cambridge University Press, 2001), p. 140, http://books.google.com/.

53 Diwanji, Amberish K., 'Government May Prefer to Let Jethmalani Be', Rediff.com, July 29, 2000.

54 Mitra, Sumit, 'The Wrath of Ram', *India Today*, August 7, 2000, http://indiatoday.intoday.in/story/ram-jethmalani-blames-his-dismissal-as-law-minister-on-attorney-general-soli-sorabjee/1/244478.html

55 Venkatesan, V., 'The Jethmalani Revolt', *Frontline*, Vol. 17 (16), August 5–18, 2000.

56 Ibid.

57 Mitra, Sumit, 'The Wrath of Ram', *India Today*, August 7, 2000, http://indiatoday.intoday.in/story/ram-jethmalani-blames-his-dismissal-as-law-minister-on-attorney-general-soli-sorabjee/1/244478.html.

58 Venkatesan, V., 'A Terror of a Bill', *Frontline*, Vol. 17 (16), August 5–18, 2000, www.frontline.in/navigation/?type=static&page=flonnet&rdurl=fl1716/17160240.htm.

59 The Prevention of Terrorism Ordinance of 2001, www.satp.org/satporgtp/countries/india/document/actandordinances/POTO.htm.

60 'Law Minister Opposes POT Bill', *Tribune*, July 16, 2000, www.tribuneindia.com/2000/20000717/nation.htm#4.

61 Venkatesan, V., 'POTA Prospects', *Frontline*, Vol. 19 (7), March 30–April 12, 2002, www.frontline.in/navigation/?type=static&page=flonnet&rdurl=fl1907/19070220.htm.

62 Mitra, Sumit, 'The Wrath of Ram', *India Today*, August 7, 2000, http://indiatoday.intoday.in/story/ram-jethmalani-blames-his-dismissal-as-law-minister-on-attorney-general-soli-sorabjee/1/244478.html.

63 Gera, Nalini, *Ram Jethmalani: The Authorized Biography* (New Delhi: Penguin, 2002), p. 324.

64 Venkatesan, V., 'The Jethmalani Revolt', *Frontline*, Vol. 17 (16), August 5–18, 2000.

65 Mitra, Sumit, 'The Wrath of Ram', *India Today*, August 7, 2000, http://indiatoday.intoday.in/story/ram-jethmalani-blames-his-dismissal-as-law-minister-on-attorney-general-soli-sorabjee/1/244478.html.

66 Shekhar, Chandra, 'President Accepts Ram Jethmalani's Resignation', *Indian Express*, July 24, 2000.

67 'The Jethmalani Controversy', *The Hindu*, October 10, 2002, http://hindu.com/2000/10/10/stories/13100643.htm.

68 Shekhar, Chandra, 'President Accepts Ram Jethmalani's Resignation', *Indian Express*, July 24, 2000.

69 Venkatesan, V., 'The Jethmalani Revolt', *Frontline*, Vol. 17 (16), August 5–18, 2000.

70 Gera, Nalini, *Ram Jethmalani: The Authorized Biography* (New Delhi: Penguin, 2002), p. 325.

71 Sahajwala, Prem Chand, 'Ram Jethmalani, an Interesting Personality', Sulekha.com, 2007, http://creative.sulekha.com/ram-jethmalani-an-interesting-personality_233914_blog.

72 Jethmalani, Ram, *Big Egos, Small Men* (New Delhi: Har-Anand, 2000), p. 8.

73 'Jethmalani Blames Soli for His Exit from Cabinet, AG Rebuts Charge', *Indian Express*, July 23, 2000, http://expressindia.indianexpress.com/news/ie/daily/20000724/ina24032.html.

74 'PM Rejects Jethmalani Claim, Orders Inquiry into Info Leak', *Indian Express*, July 28, 2000, http://expressindia.indianexpress.com/news/ie/daily/20000729/ina29035.html.

75 Gera, Nalini, *Ram Jethmalani: The Authorized Biography* (New Delhi: Penguin, 2002), p. 329.

76 Mitra, Sumit, 'The Wrath of Ram', *India Today*, August 7, 2000, http://indiatoday.intoday.in/story/ram-jethmalani-blames-his-dismissal-as-law-minister-on-attorney-general-soli-sorabjee/1/244478.html.

77 Diwanji, Amberish K., 'Government May Prefer to Let Jethmalani Be', Rediff.com, July 29, 2000.

78 Venkatesan, V., 'The Jethmalani Revolt', *Frontline*, Vol. 17 (16), August 5–18, 2000.

79 Gera, Nalini, *Ram Jethmalani: The Authorized Biography* (New Delhi: Penguin, 2002), pp. 330–31.

80 Haridas, N., 'The Jethmalani Controversy', *The Hindu*, October 10, 2000.

81 'Jethmalani Blames Soli for His Exit from Cabinet, AG Rebuts Charge', *Indian Express*, July 23, 2000, http://expressindia.indianexpress.com/news/ie/daily/20000724/ina24032.html.

82 Report of the National Commission to Review the Working of the Constitution, http://lawmin.nic.in/ncrwc/finalreport/v1ch1.htm.

83 Dhawan, Himanshi, 'Women's Reservation Bill to Come Up in Parliament Today', *Times of India*, February 25, 2010, http://articles.timesofindia.indiatimes.com/2010-02-25.

84 'Lok Sabha Speaker Meira Kumar Calls for Women's Empowerment', *Times of India*, March 9, 2013, http://articles.timesofindia.indiatimes.com/2013-03-09/india/37581570_1_international-women-s-day-women-s-reservation-bill-speaker-meira-kumar.

85 Kumar Mahesh, personal communication.

86 Vij-Aurora, Bhavna, 'Inheritance of Laws', *Outlook*, February 19, 2007, http://m.outlookindia.com/story.aspx?sid=4&aid=233926

33. Kashmir, Politics, and Terrorism

1 'Resolution Adopted by the United Nations Commission for India and Pakistan on 13 August 1948', www.mtholyoke.edu/acad/intrel/uncom1.htm.

2 'Indo-Pakistani War of 1971', GlobalSecurity.org, www.globalsecurity. org/military/world/war/indo-pak_1971.htm.

3 *Kashmir: Nuclear Flashpoint* is the source for the Kashmir timeline; quotes in this chapter, unless otherwise indicated, www.kashmirlibrary. org/kashmir_timeline/kashmir_chapters/bloodshed.shtml.

4 The Indian State of Jammu & Kashmir Policy Brief: 2011–12, www. hafsite.org/human-rights-issues/indian-state-jammu-kashmir-policy-brief-2011-2012.

5 *Kashmir: Nuclear Flashpoint*, 'Bloodshed So Far', www.kashmirlibrary. org/kashmir_timeline/kashmir_chapters/bloodshed.shtml.

6 'Yes, We Trained Militant Groups against India: Musharraf', NDTV, October 5, 2010, www.ndtv.com/article/india/yes-we-trained-militant-groups-against-india-musharraf-57135.

7 Parliament Resolution on Jammu and Kashmir, adopted February 22, 1994, www.satp.org/satporgtp/countries/india/document/papers/ parliament_resolution_on_Jammu_and_Kashmir.htm.

8 Padder, Sajad, 'The Composite Dialogue between India and Pakistan: Structure, Process and Agency', *Heidelberg papers in South Asian and Comparative Politics*, February 2012, http://archiv.ub.uni-heidelberg. de/volltextserver/13143/1/Heidelberg_Papers_65_Padder.pdf.

9 *State (NCT of Delhi) vs. Navjot Sandhu @ Afsan Guru*, on 4 August, 2005.

10 Statement to the press, Delhi University Teachers in Defence of S.A.R. Gilani, September 19, 2003, www.sacw.net/new/ indefenceofJilani092003.html.

11 'Open Letter to India's Prime Minister, Re: The Attack on Parliament and Its Implication', September 13, 2003, www.sacw.net/new/ indefenceofJilani092003.html.

12 Naqvi, Muneeza Mohammed, 'Afzal Guru Executed: India Hangs Man for 2001 Parliament Attack, Protests Erupt In Kashmir', *Huffington Post*, September 2, 2013, www.huffingtonpost.com/2013/02/09/ mohammed-afzal-guru-executed-india-parliament_n_2652291.html.

13 Rao, Nandita, 'Legal Legend', currentnews, June 6, 2013, http:// currentnews.in/2011/12/05/legal-legend/.

14 Roy, Arundhati, 'And His Life Should Become Extinct: The Very Strange Story of the Attack on the Indian Parliament', *Outlook*, October 30, 2006, www.outlookindia.com/article.aspx?232979.

15 Ibid.

16 'Cabinet Rejects J&K Autonomy Resolution'; 'Decision Unfortunate: NC', *Tribune*, both articles July 4, 2000, www.tribuneindia.

com/2000/20000705/main1.htm.

17 Ram Jethmalani, personal communication.

18 Ram Jethmalani, personal communication.

19 'Dialogue with Understanding', *Greater Kashmir*, July 20, 2002.

20 Joshi, Arun, 'Jethmalani Starts J&K Visit Today', *Hindustan Times*, August 15, 2002.

21 Bukhari, Shujaat, 'Shabir Shah Meets Kashmir Panel', *J&K News*, August 16, 2002.

22 Pandit, M. Saleem, 'Hurriyat Softens, Poll Options Open', *Sunday Times*, August 18, 2002.

23 Dubey, Muchkund, 'Kashmir Policy II', *The Hindu*, August 22, 2002.

24 'Kashmir Panel Calls APHC, PFP for Talks', *Pioneer News Service*, August 23, 2002.

25 Jethmalani, Ram, *Conscience of a Maverick* (New Delhi: UBSPD, 2007), pp. 302ff.

26 Vaswani, Mahesh, memo to Ram Jethmalani, private correspondence, August 2002.

27 Peer, Basharat, 'J&K Minister Mushtaq Ahmed Lone Shot Dead by Militants', Rediff.com, September 11, 2002, www.rediff.com/election/2002/sep/11jk.htm.

28 'NC Snaps Contacts with Kashmir Panel', *Tribune*, October 7, 2002, www.tribuneindia.com/2002/20021008/j&k.htm#2.

29 Imam, S.H., 'Jammu and Kashmir Assembly Elections 2002: Ending National Conference's Reign', *J&K Insights*, October 30, 2002, www.jammu-kashmir.com/insights/insight20021030.html.

30 Jayasekera, Deepal, 'Kashmir Election Results in Defeat for Ruling Party', *World Socialist Web Site*, October 22, 2002, www.wsws.org/en/articles/2002/10/kash-o22.html.

31 '2002 Election Was Turning Point: Mufti', *Greater Kashmir*, June 8, 2012, www.greaterkashmir.com/news/2012/Jun/8/2002-election-was-turning-point-mufti-72.asp.

32 Kronstadt, K. Alan, 'CRS Report for Congress, Elections in Kashmir', December 5, 2002, http://fpc.state.gov/documents/organization/19700.pdf.

33 'Hurriyat Divided on Talks with Kashmir Committee', *Times of India*, December 29, 2002, http://articles.timesofindia.indiatimes.com/2002-12-29/india/27292857_1_kashmir-committee-hurriyat-union-minister-ram-jethmalani.

34 Watt, Romeet K, 'Who Would Be New Delhi's Interlocutor?', *Kashmir Telegraph*, February 2003.

35 'Kashmir Committee Makes Way for Vohra', *Times of India*, February 23, 2003, http://articles.timesofindia.indiatimes.com/keyword/kashmir-committee.

36 Kumar, Radha, Anjali Puri, and Saurabh Naithani, 'What Makes A Peace Process Irreversible', Conference Report 2005, p. 78 ff, www.delhipolicygroup.com/pdf/What_makes_a_Peace_Process_Irreversible.pdf.

37 'Pak MPs: Militants Will Have to Accept Ceasefire', *Economic Times*, May 17, 2003, http://articles.economictimes.indiatimes.com/2003-05-17/news/27519213_1_india-and-pakistan-cease-fire-kashmir-committee.

38 Jethmalani, Ram, *Conscience of a Maverick* (New Delhi: UBSPD, 2007), p. 286.

39 Walia, Varinder, and Pawan Kumar, 'Indian MPs Return from Pakistan: Claim Pak Has Softened Stand on Kashmir', *Tribune*, August 13, 2003.

40 Gillani, Waqar, 'Misinterpretations Complicated Kashmir: Jethmalani', *Daily Times*, August 18, 2003, www.dailytimes.com.pk/default. asp?page=story_18-8-2003_p7_22.

41 Personal communication.

42 'Pakistani-India Parliamentarians, Journalists and Experts Conference on Confidence-building and Conflict-resolution', Islamabad, Pakistan, *Times of India*, August 12, 2003, www.satp.org/satporgtp/countries/pakistan/document/papers/india_pak_mp.htm.

43 Jethmalani, Ram, *Conscience of a Maverick* (New Delhi: UBSPD, 2007), pp. 309–10.

44 Naseer, Khawaja, 'Pakistan More Flexible: Jethmalani', *Daily Times*, August 14, 2003, www.dailytimes.com.pk/default. asp?page=story_14-8-2003_p7_11.

45 'Unquenchable Thirst', *The Economist*, November 19, 2011, www.economist.com/node/21538687.

46 Jethmalani, Ram, *Conscience of a Maverick* (New Delhi: UBSPD, 2007), p. 234.

47 Kumar, Radha, Anjali Puri, and Saurabh Naithani, 'What Makes A Peace Process Irreversible', Conference Report 2005, p. 86, www.delhipolicygroup.com/pdf/What_makes_a_Peace_Process_Irreversible.pdf.

48 Akhlaque, Qudssia, 'Ram Jethmalani: The Maverick Politician', *Dawn*, August 11, 2003, http://archives.dawn.com/2003/08/11/nat6.htm.

49 Kumar, Satish, and Joseph Kuba, 'Government: All-Party Hurriyat Conference (APHC) Dialogue', *Foundation for National Security*

Research, January 2004, http://demo.aadico.com/fnsr/government-all-parties-hurriyat-conference-APHC-dialogue.php.

50 Rehman, Sherry, 'Making History, Article on Pak–India Relations, India Visit', November 28, 2004, http://sherryrehman.com/?p=772.

51 Pandey, Sandeep, 'Karachi-to-Delhi Friendship March', June–October 2004, December 15, 2003, www.sacw.net/peace/karachiDelhiMarch2004.html.

52 Parthasarathy, G., 'Track II and Back Channel Diplomacy in India–Pakistan Relations', December 24, 2010, http://indiandiplomacy.blogspot.com/2010/12/track-2-and-back-channel-diplomacy-in.html.

53 Baba, Noor Ahmed, 'Pugwash Conference on Kashmir: Some Reflections', *Institute of Peace and Conflict Studies*, January 20, 2005, www.ipcs.org/article/indo-pak/pugwash-conference-on-kashmir-some-reflections-1620.html.

54 Chawdhary, Rekha, and V. Nagendra Rao, 'Jammu and Kashmir: Electoral Politics in a Separatist Context', *Economic and Political Weekly*, December 18, 2004, www.epw.in/special-articles/jammu-and-kashmir-electoral-politics-separatist-context.html.

55 Ibid.

56 Padder, Sajad, 'The Composite Dialogue between India and Pakistan: Structure, Process and Agency', *Heidelberg papers in South Asian and Comparative Politics*, February 2012, http://archiv.ub.uni-heidelberg.de/volltextserver/13143/1/Heidelberg_Papers_65_Padder.pdf.

57 Parthasarathy, G., 'Track II and Back Channel Diplomacy in India–Pakistan Relations', December 24, 2010, http://indiandiplomacy.blogspot.com/2010/12/track-2-and-back-channel-diplomacy-in.html.

58 Coll, Steve, 'The Back Channel', *New America Foundation*, March 2, 2009, http://newamerica.net/node/9454.

59 Banerjie, Indranil, 'Kashmir, A History of Failed Interlocutors', *Vivekananda International Foundation*, January 8, 2011, www.vifindia.org/article/2011/march/24/Kashmir%E2%80%93A-History-of-failed-Interlocutors.

60 'Of History, Talks and Negotiations', *Daily Rising Kashmir*, June 6, 2013 (accessed September 20, 2013), www.risingkashmir.in/news/on-history-talks-negotiations-48647.aspx.

61 Ganai, Naseer, 'To Take Peace Initiative Forward, Jethmalani Holds Crucial Talks on Kashmir', *India Today*, August 7, 2012, http://indiatoday.intoday.in/story/ram-jethmalani-holds-crucial-talks-in-jammu-and-kashmir/1/212172.html.

62 Muddasir Ali, 'Ram Jethmalani to Launch Reanimated Kashmir

Committee', *Greater Kashmir*, April 18, 2010.

63 Padder, Sajad, 'The Composite Dialogue between India and Pakistan: Structure, Process and Agency', *Heidelberg papers in South Asian and Comparative Politics*, February 2012, http://archiv.ub.uni-heidelberg. de/volltextserver/13143/1/Heidelberg_Papers_65_Padder.pdf.

64 Maqbool, Umer, 'NDA Incapacitated Our Earlier Initiative: Gen Musharraf's 4-Point Formula Can Provide Basis for Settlement: Jethmalani', *Greater Kashmir*, June 4, 2011, www.greaterkashmir.com/news/2011/jun/5/-nda-incapacitated-our-earlier-initiative--36.asp.

65 Ahmad, Mukhtar, '18 Dead Amid Kashmir Protests against India, U.S.', *CNN World*, September 13, 2010, www.cnn.com/2010/WORLD/asiapcf/09/13/india.kashmir.violence/index.html.

66 'Kashmir Protests Erupt into Violence after Government Troops Kill Four', *Guardian*, August 13, 2010, www.guardian.co.uk/world/2010/aug/13/kashmir-protests-killed-ramadan.

67 Jethmalani, Ram, 'Our Peace Mission to Pak is Greeted with Love', *Sunday Guardian*, April 2011, www.sunday-guardian.com/analysis/our-peace-mission-to-pak-is-greeted-with-love.

68 Jethmalani, Ram, *Maverick Unchanged, Unrepentant* (New Delhi: Rupa Publications, 2014), p. 28.

69 Jethmalani, Ram, 'Our Peace Mission to Pak is Greeted with Love', *Sunday Guardian*, April 2011, www.sunday-guardian.com/analysis/our-peace-mission-to-pak-is-greeted-with-love.

70 'Don't Blame Pakistan for Non-state Actors: Zardari', *Hindustan Times*, May 10, 2011, www.hindustantimes.com/India-news/NewDelhi/Don-t-blame-Pakistan-for-non-state-actors-Zardari/Article1-695636.aspx.

71 Om, Prof. Hari, 'Will KC Also Go to Jammu to Listen to Her Woes?', *Greater Jammu*, August 11, 2012, www.greaterjammu.com/2012/20120812.

72 Kishwar, Madhu Purnima, 'A Citizen Initiative for Exploring a Consensual Solution to the Kashmir Problem', *Manushi*, 2013, http://manushi.in/articles.php?articleId=1579.

73 Ganai, Naseer, 'To Take Peace Initiative Forward, Jethmalani Holds Crucial Talks on Kashmir', *India Today*, August 7, 2012, http://indiatoday.intoday.in/story/ram-jethmalani-holds-crucial-talks-in-jammu-and-kashmir/1/212172.html.

74 Hussain, Masood, 'Ram Jethmalani's Committee Keeps Date with Controversies in Kashmir', *Economic Times*, August 9, 2012, http://articles.economictimes.indiatimes.com/2012-08-09/news/33118755_1_kashmir-committee-ram-jethmalani-kashmir-issue.

75 ul-Hassan, Ishfaq, 'Ram Jethmalani Visit Triggers Storm in Kashmir', *DNA*, June 7, 2011, www.dnaindia.com/india/1552445/report-ram-jethmalani-visit-triggers-storm-in-kashmir.

76 Pandit, M. Saleem, 'Jethmalani Talks Kashmir, Geelani Talks about Weather', *Times of India*, August 9, 2012, http://articles.timesofindia.indiatimes.com/2012-08-09/india/33117698_1_ram-jethmalani-kashmir-issue-kashmir-committee.

77 'Track II Diplomacy on Kashmir Reactivated', *Greater Kashmir*, February 5, 2012, www.greaterkashmir.com/news/2012/Feb/5/track-ii-diplomacy-on-kashmir-reactivated-37.asp.

78 Chaudhary, Zafar, 'An Evening with Geelani and Jethmalani', February 9, 2012, www.facebook.com/syedaligeelani/posts/385577764791966.

79 Ahmad, Wajahat, 'Kashmir: In Search of a Peace Process', *Caravan*, November 1, 2010, http://caravanmagazine.in/perspectives/kashmir-search-peace-process.

80 Ganai, Naseer, 'To Take Peace Initiative Forward Jethmalani Holds Crucial Talks on Kashmir', *India Today*, August 7, 2012, http://indiatoday.intoday.in/story/ram-jethmalani-holds-crucial-talks-in-jammu-and-kashmir/1/212172.html.

81 'Self-rule framework', *Jammu and Kashmir People's Democratic Party*, 2013, http://jkpdp.org/self-rule/self-rule-framework/.

34. Cases after the Law Ministry

1 Singh, Gyanant, 'Meet India's Supermen in Black', *India Today*, October 21, 2012, http://indiatoday.intoday.in/story/meet-india-supermen-in-black/1/225634.html.

2 Raja Ram Pal vs. the Honourable Speaker, Lok Sabha & Ors on 10 January, 2007 JT2007(2)SC1

3 Dalal, Milan, 'India's New Constitutionalism: Two Cases that Have Reshaped Indian Law', Law Digital Commons, 2008.

4 Venkatesan, J., 'Parliament Cannot Sack Members: Jethmalani', *The Hindu*, September 2006.

5 Dalal, Milan, 'India's New Constitutionalism: Two Cases that Have Reshaped Indian Law, 2008.

6 'Jinnah's Progeny—Punishment for Hypocrisy—Jinnah Must be Rolling in His Grave', *Friday Times*, Pakistan, November 17, 2000, http://ghatok-dalal.tripod.com/jinnah.html.

7 Ghosh, Shekhar, 'CEO of Controversy', *Outlook*, October 20, 1997, www.outlookindia.com/article.aspx?204439.

8   '10 Corporate Battles to Remember', *Mint*, May 9, 2010, www.livemint. com/Companies/fmsQP3Oc7x5PMyTvJgoQzO/10-corporate-battles-to-remember.html.

9   Thakurta, Paranjoy Guha, 'The Two Faces of Dhirubhai Ambani', 2003, www.india-seminar.com/2003/521/521%20paranjoy%20guha%20 thakurta.htm.

10   Krishna, Ananth V., *India Since Independence: Making Sense of Indian Politics* (Pearson Education India, 2011), pp. 298–300, http://books. google.com/books?id=8v7Vr2iQUHkC&dq=India+Since+Independen ce:+Making+Sense+Of+Indian+Politics,+by+Ananth+V.+Krishna&sou rce=gbs_navlinks_s.

11   Ghosh, Shekhar, 'CEO of Controversy', *Outlook*, October 20, 1997, www.outlookindia.com/article.aspx?204439.

12   Sanghvi, Vir, 'Nusli Wadia', March, 2011, http://virsanghvi.com/People-Detail.aspx?Key=11.

13   Mehta, Ved, *Rajiv Gandhi and Rama's Kingdom* (Yale University Press, September 1996), p. 126, http://books.google.com/books?id=XvAWA CuBTVgC&dq=Mehta,+Ved++Rajiv+Gandhi+and+Rama%E2%80% 99s+Kingdom&source=gbs_navlinks_s.

14   *The State of Maharashtra vs. Kriti V. Ambani and Another* on 6 October, 1990, 1991 (1) BomCR 32, 1992 CriLJ 1647.

15   Gera, Nalini, *Ram Jethmalani: The Authorized Biography* (New Delhi: Penguin, 2002), p. 359.

16   Karmali, Naazneen, 'India's Richest', *Forbes*, August 13, 2007, www. forbes.com/2007/08/05/india-billies-richest-oped-cx_nka_0813billies. html.

17   Birla Institute of Management Technology, http://bimtech.wordpress. com/founders/birla-family/.

18   *Krishna Kumar Birla vs. Rajendra Singh Lodha and Others* on March 31, 2008.

19   'Birla–Lodha Legal War Turns Acrimonious', *Economic Times*, December 15, 2004, http://articles.economictimes.indiatimes. com/2004-12-15/news/27394762_1_mp-birla-sk-daga-sn-prasad.

20   'Kolkata HC Quashed Lodha Appeal', *Moneycontrol.com*, July 2, 2005, www.moneycontrol.com/news/current-affairs/kolkata-hc-quashes-lodha-appeal_171772.html.

21   'SC Asks Lodha to Face Trial in Criminal Case', *Times of India*, February 4, 2006, http://articles.timesofindia.indiatimes.com/2006-02-04/india-business/27821694_1_criminal-proceedings-criminal-case-mp-birla-group-assets.

22 'Protect Priyamvada Birla's Assets: HC to Administrators', *Indian Express*, August 24, 2012, http://archive.indianexpress.com/news/protect-priyamvada-birlas-assets-hc-to-administrators/992275/.

23 *Krishna Kumar Birla vs. Rajendra Singh Lodha* (2008) 4 SCC 300 [31/03/2008]

24 'Rahman, Shafi Battle for Billions', *India Today*, February 25, 2012, http://indiatoday.intoday.in/story/battle-for-m.p.-birla-fortune-icai-indicts-lodhas/1/175181.html.

25 Ibid.

26 *Reliance Natural Resources Ltd vs. Reliance Industries Ltd* on May 7, 2010.

27 Shenoy, T.V.R., 'A Superman named Ambani', Rediff.com, July 8, 2002, www.rediff.com/news/2002/jul/08flip.htm.

28 Reliance Industries Ltd website www.ril.com/html/aboutus/aboutus.html.

29 'Mukesh Ambani', *Forbes*, March 2013, www.forbes.com/profile/mukesh-ambani/.

30 'Anil Ambani', *Forbes*, March 2013, www.forbes.com/profile/anil-ambani/.

31 Niranjan, V., 'The Supreme Court's Judgement in the Reliance Dispute, Part I', *IndiaCorpLaw*, May 7, 2010, http://indiacorplaw.blogspot.com/2010/05/supreme-courts-judgment-in-reliance.html.

32 Singh, Gyanant, 'Meet India's Supermen in Black', *India Today*, October 21, 2012, http://indiatoday.intoday.in/story/meet-india-supermen-in-black/1/225634.html.

33 That would have been $16,200–32,400 in November 2013.

34 Galanter, Marc, and Nick Robinson, 'India's Grand Advocates: A Legal Elite Flourishing in the Era of Globalization', HLS Programme on the Legal Profession Research Paper Series No. 2013–5, November 2013, p. 11, *Harvard Law School Programme on the Legal Profession*.

35. Minorities

1 'Feeling Betrayed: Dalit Christians Fighting with Christianity against Discrimination', *News Bharati*, October 9, 2012, www.newsbharati.com/Encyc/2012/10/9/Feeling-Betrayed-Dalit-Christians-fighting-with-Christianity-against-discrimination.aspx.

2 Jerath, Arati R., 'Fernandes Lobbying for Karmapa—Tibetan Guru', *Indian Express*, January 18, 2000, http://expressindia.indianexpress.com/news/ie/daily/20000118/ifr18046.html.

3   'Buddha's Not Smiling: Uncovering Corruption at the Heart of Tibetan Buddhism Today', *American Buddha*, www.american-buddha.com/cult. buddhanosmiling.13.htm.

4   'Mystery Monk—Tai Situ Can Cut Deals with Beijing and Have an Entry Ban Lifted in Delhi', *Enlightened Heart*, February 7, 2000, www. karmapa.org.nz/news/74/67/Mystery-Monk---Tai-Situ-can-cut-deals-with-Beijing-and-have-an-entry-ban-lifted-in-Delhi/.

5   Chhetri G., 'Twist in the Tale', *Sunday*, December 13–29, 1998, accessed on Lama Shree Narayan Singh, website http://lamashree.org/hhkarmapa_titt.htm.

6   Gearing, Julian, 'The Tale of Two Karmapas', *Asia Times*, December 24, 2003, www.atimes.com/atimes/China/EL24Ad02.html.

7   *Tshurphu Labrang vs. Karmapa Charitable Trust & Ors*, on 5 July 2004.

8   *Shree Narayan Singh vs. Union of India & Ors* on 31 March, 1997, decided on October 20, 2009.

9   Chakravarty, Sayantan, 'Mystery Monk', *India Today*, February 7, 2000.

10 Lama, Karma Gampu, and Dugo Bhutia, 'Memorandum to Vajpayee', *Lama Shree Narayan Singh*, July 31, 1998, http://lamashree.org/legal_04_pmmdugo.html.

11 'Dalai Lama "Prevented" from Attending Function: Jethmalani', *Phayul.com*, January 5, 2003, www.phayul.com/news/article.aspx?id=3553&t=1&c=1.

12 Raman, B., 'The Controversy over Karmapa', *Hill Post*, February 5, 2011, http://hillpost.in/2011/02/the-controversy-over-karmapa/26058/.

13 Tharoor, Ishaan, 'Why India Is Investigating a Reincarnated Tibetan Lama', *Time*, February 3, 2011, www.time.com/time/world/article/0,8599,2046124,00.html.

14 *Miss Kunzang Lhamu Chungyapla vs. Union of India* W.P. © No. 4021 of 2010.

15 *Kunga Nima Lepcha & Ors vs. State Of Sikkim & Ors* on March 25, 2010.

16 *Welfare Association & Amp; Ors vs. The State Of Nagaland & Amp; Ors* on July 6, 2010.

17 'Supreme Court to Hear Binayak's Bail Plea', NDTV, March 11, 2011, www.ndtv.com/article/india/supreme-court-to-hear-binayak-s-bail-plea-90890.

18 'Supreme Court to Hear Binayak Sen's Bail Plea on March 11', *The Hindu*, March 5, 2011, www.thehindu.com/news/national/supreme-

court-to-hear-binayak-sens-bail-plea-on-march-11/article1512109.ece.

19 'Five High-profile Sedition Cases in India', Rediff.com, September 13, 2012, www.rediff.com/news/slide-show/slide-show-1-five-high-profile-sedition-cases-in-india/20120913.htm#3.

20 Ibid.

21 Vyawahare, Malavika, 'A Conversation With: Human Rights Activist Binayak Sen', *New York Times*, December 10, 2012, http://india.blogs.nytimes.com/2012/12/10/a-conversation-with-human-rights-activist-dr-binayak-sen/.

22 Ibid.

23 *Dr Binayak Sen 2 Pijush . . . vs. State of Chhattisgarh* on February 10, 2011.

24 'HC Allows EU Team to Attend Binayak Sen Case Proceedings', *Indian Express*, January 24, 2011, www.indianexpress.com/news/hc-allows-eu-team-to-attend-binayak-sen-case-proceedings/741682/.

25 Venkatesan, J., 'Binayak Sen Gets Bail in Supreme Court', *The Hindu*, April 15, 2011, www.thehindu.com/news/national/article1698939.ece?homepage=true.

36. Big Business, Black Money, and the 2G Spectrum Scam

1 Jethmalani, Ram, 'Dacoits Have Looted India', *India Today*, December 17, 2010, http://indiatoday.intoday.in/story/dacoits+have+looted+india/1/123602.html.

2 Albats, Yevgenia, *The State within a State: The KGB and Its Hold on Russia—Past, Present, and Future, Historical Documents of the KGB* (Farrar, Straus and Giroux Paperbacks, 1994) p. 223, excerpted from book on Amazon.com, accessed September 2013.

3 Kalyanaraman, Dr, 'Indian Blackmoney Abroad Report (IBAR) by Four Renowned Experts, BJP Task Force Report on Black Money, February 27, 2011, http://barmaidtoemperess.wordpress.com/2011/page/24/.

4 Ganz, Kian, 'RamJet Voted "Most Badass Lawyer" on US site, ahead of Gandhi, Ambedkar, Jinnah', *Legally India*, January 9, 2013, www.legallyindia.com/Fun-and-games/ramjet-voted-most-badass-lawyer-ahead-of-gandhi-ambedkar-jinnah.

5 Kar, Dev, 'The Drivers and Dynamics of Illicit Financial Flows from India: 1948–2008, A November 2010 Report', *Global Financial Integrity*, http://india.gfintegrity.org/.

6 Gurumurthy, Shri, et al., 'Indian Black Money Abroad: In Secret Banks and Tax Havens, Second Report of the Task Force on the Steps

to be Taken by India, Bharatiya Janata Party, http://www.scribd. com/doc/112664078/indian-black-money-abroad-a-report-by-shri-gurumurthy-chartered-accountant-chennai-shri-ajit-doval-former.

7   Mehrishi, Ashish, 'Quattrocchi, Chadha Were Paid Commission in Bofors Deal', *India Today*, January 3, 2011, http://indiatoday.intoday. in/story/quattrocchi-chadha-bofors-gun-deal-case/1/125410.html.

8   Swiss Documents-Rajiv Gandhi-1,98,000 crore, A/C Details *Ramani's blog*, December 27, 2011, http://ramanan50.wordpress. com/2011/12/27/swiss-bank-reveal-indian-names-signed-documents-with-details/.

9   Jethmalani, Ram, 'Black Money, State Collusion and National Fraud', *Sunday Guardian,* May 16, 2013.

10 Jethmalani, Ram, *Maverick Unchanged, Unrepentant* (New Delhi: Rupa Publications, 2014), p. 197.

11 Ibid., p 217.

12 'Jethmalani Files PIL over Black Money', *Deccan Herald*, April 22, 2009, http://archive.deccanherald.com/Content/Apr222009/ national20090422131668.asp.

13 Item No. 63(PH), Court No. 9 Section PIL, Supreme Court of India Record of Proceedings, Writ Petition (Civil) No(S). 176 of 2009, http:// supremecourtofindia.nic.in/outtoday/wc17609.pdf.

14 Venkatesan, J., 'Jethmalani: PIL on Black Money not Politically Motivated', *Delhi Compass*, May 5, 2009, http://blogs.thehindu.com/ delhi/?p=20774.

15 'SC Asks Centre to File Response on Black Money PIL', *The Indian Express*, May 5, 2009, www.indianexpress.com/news/sc-asks-centre-to-file-response-on-black-money-pil/454627.

16 Jethmalani, Ram, *Maverick Unchanged, Unrepentant* (New Delhi: Rupa Publications, 2014), p. 199.

17 'Black Money Case: Do Black Money Sources Include Drugs, Asks Court', NDTV, January 27, 2011, www.ndtv.com/article/india/black-money-case-do-black-money-sources-include-drugs-asks-court-81786.

18 Gurumurthy, Shri, et al., 'Indian Black Money Abroad: In Secret Banks and Tax Havens, Second Report of the Task Force on the Steps to Be Taken by India, Bharatiya Janata Party, http://www.scribd. com/doc/112664078/indian-black-money-abroad-a-report-by-shri-gurumurthy-chartered-accountant-chennai-shri-ajit-doval-former

19 Gurumurthy, Shri, et al., Ibid., p. 58.

20 *Ram Jethmalani vs. Union of India* (2011) 8 SCC [4/7/2011].

21 Jethmalani, Ram, *Maverick Unchanged, Unrepentant* (New Delhi: Rupa

Publications, 2014), p. 203.

22 *Ram Jethmalani vs. Union of India* (2011) 9 SCC [23/9/2011].

23 Jethmalani, Ram, *Maverick Unchanged, Unrepentant* (New Delhi: Rupa Publications, 2014), p. 164.

24 'Journey of Ramdev from Ramkrishna Yadav to Baba Ramdev', *News Track India*, August 11, 2012, www.newstrackindia.com/newsdetails/2012/8/11/296-Journey-of-Ramdev-from-Ramkrishna-Yadav-to-Baba-Ramdev.html.

25 In Re: *Ramlila Maidan Incident Dt.4/5.06.2011 vs. Home Secretary, Union of India and Ors* on February 23, 2012.

26 'Govt Clears 14 Major Changes to Lokpal Bill', *The Indian Express*, February 1, 2013, www.indianexpress.com/news/govt-clears-14-major-changes-to-lokpal-bill/1067697/.

27 Jethmalani, Ram, *Maverick Unchanged, Unrepentant* (New Delhi: Rupa Publications, 2014), p. 195.

28 Jethmalani, Ram, *Maverick Unchanged, Unrepentant* (New Delhi: Rupa Publications, 2014), p. 208.

29 Ghosh, Shamik, and Abhinav Bhatt, 'President Polls: Team Sangma Challenges Pranab Mukherjee's Nomination', NDTV, July 2012, www.ndtv.com/article/india/president-polls-team-sangma-challenges-pranab-mukherjee-s-nomination-238561.

30 Anand, Utkarsh, 'In Split Verdict SC Dismisses Sangma Plea against Pranab', *Indian Express*, December 6, 2012, www.indianexpress.com/news/in-split-verdict-sc-dismisses-sangma-plea-against-pranab/1040985.

31 '2G Scam: Ram Jethmalani Appears for Unitech Boss Sanjay Chandra', *Times of India*, April 30, 2011, http://articles.timesofindia.indiatimes.com/2011-04-30/india/29490398_1_sanjay-chandra-unitech-group-companies-surendra-pipara.

32 *Sanjay Chandra vs. Central Bureau of Investigation*, (2012) 1 SCC.

33 Ramanan50, '2G Spectrum Scam—Full Story, Origin, Growth (?) and Modus Operandi', *Ramani's Blog*, December 25, 2010, http://ramanan50.wordpress.com/2010/12/25/2g-spectrum-scam-full-storyorigingrowth-and-modus-operandi/.

34 'No Loss to Govt from 2G Spectrum Allocation: Sibal', *The Hindu Business Line*, January 8, 2011, www.thehindubusinessline.com/todays-paper/article2325809.ece?ref=archive.

35 Mahapatra, Dhananjay, '2G Loss? Govt Gained over Rs 3,000cr: Trai', *Times of India*, September 7, 2011, http://articles.timesofindia.indiatimes.com/2011-09-07/india/30122800_1_spectrum-trai-2g.

36 Tharoor, Ishaan, 'Top 10 Abuses of Power—India's Telecoms Scandal', *Time*, May 17, 2011, www.time.com/time/specials/packages/article/0,28804,2071839_2071844_2071866,00.html.

37 '2G Case: HC Notice to CBI on Unitech's MD Sanjay Chandra's Plea against Plea Framing', *Economic Times*, January 10, 2012, http://articles.economictimes.indiatimes.com/2012-01-10/news/30611809_1_money-trail-kiran-khaitan-spectrum-allocation-case.

38 *Sanjay Chandra vs. CBI* on 23 May, 2011.

39 *Sanjay Chandra vs. CBI* on 23 November, 2011.

40 '2G Scam: Unitech Did not Manipulate Records to Become Eligible', *DNA*, April 29, 2011, www.dnaindia.com/india/1537620/report-2g-scam-unitech-did-not-manipulate-records-to-become-eligible.

41 *Sanjay Chandra vs. CBI* on 23 November, 2011.

42 '2G Scam: SC Scraps 122 Licences Granted under Raja's Tenure, Trial Court to Decide on Chidambaram's Role', *Times of India*, February 2, 2012, http://articles.timesofindia.indiatimes.com/2012-02-02/india/31016262_1_spectrum-licences-2g-spectrum-allotment-case.

43 Singh, Shalini, 'Officials Colluded on 'Agreed Approach' to Testify before JPC and PAC on 2G Scam', *The Hindu*, March 13, 2013, www.thehindu.com/news/national/officials-colluded-on-agreed-approach-to-testify-before-jpc-and-pac-on-2g-scam/article4502721.ece.

44 'Kanimozhi Granted Bail by Delhi High Court in 2G Case', *Times of India*, November 28, 2011, http://articles.timesofindia.indiatimes.com/2011-11-28/india/30449976_1_asif-balwa-rajiv-b-agarwal-sharad-kumar.

45 'Kanimozhi's Lawyer, Jethmalani, on Why She Deserves Bail, NDTV, January 13, 2011, www.ndtv.com/article/india/kanimozhi-s-lawyer-ram-jethmalani-on-why-she-deserves-bail-111957.

46 *Amit Jogi vs. State of Chhattisgarh and Anr.* on 3 May, 2006, citations: 2006 CriLJ 3349.

47 'All Eyes on Jaganmohan Reddy Once Again as He Walks Out of Jail', *Times of India*, September 24, 2013, http://articles.timesofindia.indiatimes.com/2013-09-24/india/42360303_1_ysr-congress-congress-working-committee-ys-jaganmohan-reddy.

48 'CBI Is Vindictive towards Jagan Mohan Reddy, Says Ram Jethmalani,' *Post*, June 28, 2012, http://post.jagran.com/CBI-is-vindictive-towards-Jagan-Mohan-Reddy-says-Ram-Jethmalani-1340819684#sthash.XcA1WnBw.dpuf.

49 'SC Dismisses Jagan's Plea against His Arrest in DA Case', *Economic Times*, August 9, 2012, http://articles.economictimes.indiatimes.

com/2012-08-09/news/33118837_1_jaganmohan-reddy-assets-case-jagan-reddy.

50 'Hegde Has Been Misled: Ram Jethmalani', CNN-IBN, August 28, 2011, http://ibnlive.in.com/news/hegde-has-been-misled-ram-jethmalani/178740-60-115.html.

51 Kumar, N.D. Shiva, 'Netas Hire Star Lawyers to Escape Jail', *Times of India*, October 17, 2011, http://articles.timesofindia. indiatimes.com/2011-10-17/bangalore/30288979_1_top-lawyers-court-proceedings-sirajin-basha.

52 Criminal petition No. 5416/2012 and 5417/2012, High Court of Karnataka in Bangalore on July 26, 2012.

53 'Mining Scam: BS Yeddyurappa, Aides Granted Bail', *DNA*, December 11, 2012, www.dnaindia.com/india/1775974/report-mining-scam-bs-yeddyurappa-aides-granted-bail.

54 *Standard Chartered Bank & Ors etc. vs. Directorate of Enforcement and Ors etc.* (May 5, 2005), AIR2005SC2622 http://jajharkhand.in/judg/sc/pdf/CRIMINAL%20LAW/CRIMINAL%20PROCEDURE

55 Singh, Sanjay, 'SC Seeks Govt's Views on ED Move against StanChart', *Economic Times*, September 25, 2007, http://articles.economictimes. indiatimes.com/2007-09-25/news/28396823_1_fera-banks-for-such-violations-stanchart.

56 Joshi, Lorandos, 'Corporate Criminal Liability in India', Lorandos Joshi website, www.lorandoslaw.com/Publications/Corporate-Criminal-Liability-India.shtml.

57 Kumar, Shashank P., 'Standard Chartered Bank Case: A Jurisprudential Analysis', *Social Science Research Network*, July 20, 2006, http:// papers.ssrn.com/sol3/papers.cfm?abstract_id=1348425.

37. Hits and Misses

1 Sindhi Association of North America, www.sanalist.org/sana/newsite/annual_conventions_2010.html.

2 Jethmalani, Ram, 'Return of the Aryans—An Odyssey', Sindhudesh. com, www.sindhudesh.com/old_website/history_rota.html.

3 'SC Reserves Verdict on Anthem, Jethmalani Bats for "Sindh"', *Outlook*, April 27, 2005, http://news.outlookindia.com/items. aspx?artid=294972.

4 *Sanjeev Bhatnagar vs. Union of India & Ors* [2005] Insc 339 (13 May 2005).

5 Gidwani, Dial V., 'Bharatia Sindhi Global Alliance', Sindhudesh.com,

May 16, 2005, www.sindhudesh.com/old_website/thesindhi_bsga.html.

6   'Ram Jethmalani Wants to Join BJP', *DNA*, June 3, 2010, www.dnaindia.com/india/1391570/report-ram-jethmalani-wants-to-join-bjp.

7   Rao, Nandita, 'Legal Legend', *Current News*, June 6, 2013, http://currentnews.in/2011/12/05/legal-legend/.

8   Galanter, Marc, and Nick Robinson, 'India's Grand Advocates: A Legal Elite Flourishing in the Era of Globalization', HLS Programme on the Legal Profession Research Paper Series No. 2013–5, November 2013, p. 5, Harvard Law School Programme on the Legal Profession.

9   Ibid., p. 4.

10 *Sidharth Vashisht @ Manu Sharma vs. State* on 20 March, 2002, IVAD Delhi 477, 2002 (3) Crimes 370.

11 'Tehelka Reveals the Truth behind the Jessica Lall Murder Investigation Cover-ups in a 60 minute Star News Expose', *Case Ke Kaatil* aired at 9 p.m., September 26, 2006, http://archive.tehelka.com/story_main19.asp?filename=Ne093006JESSICA.asp.

12 *State vs. Sidharth Vashisht & Ors* on 18 December, 2006.

13 *Sidharth Vashisht @ Manu Sharma vs. the State* (Nct of Delhi) on 12 May, 2008.

14 *State (Gnct of Delhi) vs. Sidharth Vashisht @ Manu Sharma & . . .* on 22 May, 2013.

15 *Sidharth Vashisht @ Manu Sharma vs. State* (Nct Of Delhi) on 19 April, 2010.

16 *Amitbhai vs. Central* on 29 October, 2010.

17 *Narmada Bai vs. State of Gujarat & Ors* on 8 April, 2011.

18 *Rubabbuddin Sheikh vs. State of Gujarat & amp; Ors*, on 12 January, 2010 2 SCC 200.

19 'CBI Is After Narendra Modi, Says Ram Jethmalani', *DNA*, September 17, 2010, www.dnaindia.com/india/1439084/report-cbi-is-after-narendra-modi-says-ram-jethmalani.

20 Venkatesan, J., 'CBI Falsely Implicated Amit Shah in Sohrabuddin Case, Jethmalani Tells SC', *The Hindu*, March 10, 2011, www.thehindu.com/news/national/other-states/cbi-falsely-implicated-amit-shah-in-sohrabuddin-case-jethmalani-tells-sc/article1523816.ece.

21 *Amitbhai Anilchandra Shah vs. CBI & Anr.* on 8 April, 2013.

22 *Gujarat Riots: The True Story, 2007*; the site offers free excerpts from forthcoming book http://www.gujaratriots.com/.

23 Varshney, Ashutosh, 'Contemporary Conflicts—Understanding Gujarat Violence', *Social Science Research Council*, March 26, 2004, http://conconflicts.ssrc.org/archives/gujarat/varshney/.

24 Gagdekar, Roxy, 'Narendra Modi as Encountered in SIT Report', *DNA*, May 10, 2012, www.dnaindia.com/india/1686943/interview-narendra-modi-as-encountered-in-sit-report.

25 'Conflict of Interest—Ram Jethmalani and Kamini Jaiswal Spat', *Bar & Bench*, April 30, 2011, accessed September 2013, http://barandbench.com/content/conflict-interest-ram-jethmalani-and-kamini-jaiswal-spat#.UdxXP2fD9dg.

38. Ram's Man Modi

1 'Conflict of interest—Ram Jethmalani and Kamini Jaiswal Spat', *Bar & Bench*, April 30, 2011, accessed September, 2013, http://barandbench.com/content/conflict-interest-ram-jethmalani-and-kamini-jaiswal-spat#.UdxXP2fD9dg.

2 Joshi, Poornima, 'The Wandering Ram Jethmalani', *India Today*, June 13, 2010.

3 Chakrabarti, Samrat, 'Modi's Waterloo?', *Tehelka*, March 27, 2010.

4 'Modi Responds to SIT Summons', *The Hindu*, March 24, 2010.

5 'How SIT Report on Gujarat Riots Exonerates Modi: The Highlights', CNN-IBN, May 11, 2012.

6 Jethmalani, Ram, 'Modi: Exalted Planet in Our Horoscope', *Sunday Guardian*, May 18, 2014.

7 'Supreme Court Reconstitutes SIT to Expedite Probe into Black Money Case', *Indian Express*, May 1, 2014, http://indianexpress.com/article/india/india-others/black-money-case-supreme-court-reconstitutes-sit-to-monitor-probe/.

8 YouTube, http://m.youtube.com/watch?v=-yiFuHGQpw0&desktop_uri=%2Fwatch%3Fv%3D-yiFuHGQpw0, accessed October 15, 2013.

39. Public Intellectual

1 'Jethmalani's Black Money Remarks Create Flutter in Rajya Sabha.mp4', YouTube, 2011, accessed on September 20, 2013.

2 'SJP's Anna Gote Arrested for Stamp Paper Scam', *Economic Times*, July 1, 2003, http://articles.economictimes.indiatimes.com/2003-07-01/news/27519316_1_stamp-papers-abdul-karim-telgi-india-security-press.

3 Jethmalani, Ram, 'Making of the President', *Indian Express*, December 6, 1997, http://expressindia.indianexpress.com/ie/daily/19970612/16350533.html.

4   'Presidential Election from 1952 to 1997: Brief Notes', http://eci.nic. in/eci_main/miscellaneous_statistics/PresdElec/BriefNotes.pdf.

5   Jethmalani, Ram, *Conscience of a Maverick* (New Delhi: UBSPD, 2007), pp. 205–17.

6   Jethmalani, Ram, 'Relevance of Non-violence and Teachings from Ancient Civilizations,' an address to the Bhartiya Vidya Bhavan Institute of Indian Culture, June 7, 2012, New York, reprinted in Jethmalani, Ram, *Maverick Unchanged, Unrepentant* (New Delhi: Rupa Publications, 2014), p. 266.

7   'Jethmalani to Support AMU for Minority Status', *Muslim Mirror*, July 5, 2013, http://muslimmirror.com/eng/jethmalani-to-support-amu-for-minority-status/.

8   'Address to the Aligarh Movement in the New Millennium and Education of Minorities in India', July 28, 2007, Cleveland, Ohio.

9   Chaudhury, Shoma, 'The Angry Young Man', *Tehelka*, June 25, 2005, http://archive.tehelka.com/story_main12.asp?filename=hub062505the_angry.asp.

10 Jethmalani, Ram, 'Indo-U.S. Nuke Deal', *Deccan Chronicle*, August 15, 2007, http://archivenews.blogspot.com/2007/08/us-has-offered-india-great-deal.html.

Bibliography

Bhushan, Prashant, *Bofors: The Selling of a Nation* (New Delhi: Vision Books, 1990).

Dhar, P.N., *Indira Gandhi, the 'Emergency', and Indian Democracy* (New Delhi: Oxford University Press, 2000).

Dwivedi, Sharada, and Rahul Mehrotra, *Bombay: The Cities Within* (Bombay: Eminence Private Designs Ltd 1995).

Fazila, Vazira, and Yacoobali Zamindar, *The Long Partition, and the Making of Modern South Asia* (New York: Columbia, 2007).

Gavito, Alexandra Sanchez, *A Woman's Wheel of Life* (New Delhi: Viva Books Private Ltd, 2004).

Gera, Nalini, *Ram Jethmalani: The Authorized Biography* (New Delhi: Penguin, 2002).

Hewitt, Vernon, *Political Mobilisation and Democracy in India: States of Emergency* (London: Routledge, 2009).

Jethmalani, Ram, *Big Egos, Small Men* (New Delhi: Har-Anand, 2000).

Jethmalani, Ram, *Conscience of a Maverick* (New Delhi: UBSPD, 2007).

Jethmalani, Ram, *Maverick Unchanged, Unrepentant* (New Delhi: Rupa Publications, 2014).

Jethmalani, Rani, *Autobiography*. Unpublished

Khuhro, Hamida, *Mohammed Ayub Khuhro, A Life of Courage in Politics* (Lahore-Rawalpindi-Karachi: Ferozsons Ltd, 1998).

Kumaraswamy, P.R., *India's Israel Policy* (New York: Columbia University Press, 2010).

Malhotra, Inder, *Indira Gandhi: A Personal and Political Biography* (London: Coronet Books, 1989).

Manasseh, Rachel, *Baghdadian Jews of Bombay: Their Life and Achievements* (Great Neck: Midrash Ben Ish Hai, 2013).

Mehrotra, Rahul, and Sharada Dwivedi, *The Bombay High Court—The Story of the Building 1878–2003* (Bombay: Eminence Designs, 2004).

Metcalf, Barbara D., and Thomas R. Metcalf, *A Concise History of Modern India* (Cambridge: Cambridge, 2001).

Mitta, Manoj, and H.S. Phoolka, *When a Tree Shook Delhi* (New Delhi: Roli Books, 2007).

Mukherji, Nirmalangshu, *December 13: Terror over Democracy* (New Delhi: Promilla, 2005).

Nariman, Fali S., *Before Memory Fades* (New Delhi: Hay House, 2010).

Nariman, Fali. S., *The State of the Nation* (New Delhi: Hay House, 2013).

Ragothaman, K., *Conspiracy to Kill Rajiv Gandhi* (New Delhi: Manas, 2013).

Singh, Khushwant, *Train to Pakistan* (New Delhi: Roli Books, 2006).

Index